Understanding Unjust Enrichment

This book is a collection of articles based on Understanding Unjust Enrichment, a symposium held at the University of Western Ontario in January 2003. The articles, written from the perspective of English, Australian, Canadian, German and Jewish law, deal with numerous theoretical and practical issues that surround restitution and unjust enrichment. The articles outline recent developments across the Commonwealth, explain the unjust enrichment principle and its component parts, and address discrete issues such as tracing, choice of law, disgorgement damages for breach of contract, and the use of unjust enrichment in the cohabitation context.

Understanding Unjust Enrichment

Edited by

JASON W. NEYERS, MITCHELL McINNES and
STEPHEN G.A. PITEL

• HART •
PUBLISHING

OXFORD AND PORTLAND OREGON
2004

Published in North America (US and Canada) by
Hart Publishing
c/o International Specialized Book Services
5804 NE Hassalo Street
Portland, Oregon
97213-3644
USA

Hart Publishing is a specialist legal publisher based in Oxford, England. To order further copies of this book or to request a list of other publications please write to:

Hart Publishing, Salters Boatyard, Folly Bridge, Abingdon Rd, Oxford, OX1 4LB Telephone: +44 (0)1865 245533 Fax: +44 (0) 1865 794882
email: mail@hartpub.co.uk
WEBSITE: http//:www.hartpub.co.uk

British Library Cataloguing in Publication Data
Data Available

ISBN 1-84113-423-6 (hardback)

Typeset by Olympus Infotech Pvt. Ltd., India, in Sabon 10/12 pt.
Printed and bound in Great Britain by
TJ International Ltd, Padstow, Cornwall

Foreword

Unjust enrichment is now firmly established as a central feature of private law obligations in the common law world. Yet the precise meaning and scope of the unjust enrichment principle remain elusive. The debate is complex and multi-faceted, and one of its most remarkable features is the significant collaboration between bench, bar and legal academics. Borrowing heavily from the creative work of academic lawyers who identified unjust enrichment as a unifying legal principle, modern courts in Canada and many other common law jurisdictions have used the concept to escape the apparent confines of older and more rigid legal categories. Lawyers and judges, striving to do justice in particular cases, find unjust enrichment to be a powerful and flexible tool. But in the eyes of other scholars, these bold and adventurous moves give rise to questions of consistency, predictability and doctrinal integrity. As the courts struggle with the practical problem of elaborating and applying coherent doctrine, legal scholars debate the nature of unjust enrichment and its theoretical underpinnings. Some urge the courts on, while others are more skeptical of the exercise and urge restraint. The result has been an extraordinarily rich and stimulating debate about the very nature of private law obligations.

This fine collection of articles by many of the world's leading unjust enrichment scholars—first presented at a symposium at the Faculty of Law, University of Western Ontario in January 2003—makes an important contribution to this vitally important area of private law. This book offers a rich array of practical and theoretical perspectives on unjust enrichment. One finds magisterial command of the legal doctrine, mingled with penetrating and insightful examination of the theory and philosophy of unjust enrichment.

I congratulate Jason Neyers for his superb organizational effort in mounting the symposium. I also congratulate Jason, Mitchell McInnes and Stephen Pitel for their editorial effort in producing this volume. Finally, I would like to commend the many fine scholars who have written these articles. All who aspire to understand unjust enrichment will appreciate their effort.

The Honourable Robert J. Sharpe
Justice of the Court of Appeal for Ontario
June 2003

Contents

Contributors

Kit Barker, MA, BCL, Senior Lecturer in Law, University of Southampton.

Peter Benson, AB, MSc, LLB, LLM, Professor of Law, University of Toronto.

Jeffrey B. Berryman, LLB, MJur, LLM, Professor of Law, University of Windsor.

Michael Bryan, PhD, MA, BCL, Professor of Law, University of Melbourne.

Andrew Burrows, BCL, MA, LLM, QC, Norton Rose Professor of Commercial Law and Fellow of St Hugh's College, University of Oxford.

Robert Chambers, BEd, LLB, DPhil, Associate Professor of Law, University of Alberta.

Gerald H.L. Fridman, MA, BCL, LLM, QC, FRSC, Emeritus Professor of Law, University of Western Ontario.

Peter Jaffey, BA, LLM, Professor of Law, Brunel University.

Dennis Klimchuk, BA, MA, PhD, Associate Professor of Philosophy and Law, University of Western Ontario.

Thomas Krebs, LLB, BCL, DPhil, University Lecturer in Commercial Law and Fellow of Brasenose College, University of Oxford.

John D. McCamus, BA, MA, LLB, LLM, Professor of Law, Osgoode Hall Law School of York University.

Mitchell McInnes, BA, LLB, LLM, PhD, Associate Professor of Law, University of Western Ontario.

Jason W. Neyers, BA, LLB, MSt, Assistant Professor of Law, University of Western Ontario.

Stephen G.A. Pitel, BA, LLB, LLM, PhD, Assistant Professor of Law, University of Western Ontario.

Stephen Waddams, BA, MA, PhD, LLB, LLM, SJD, FRSC, Goodman/Schipper Professor of Law, University of Toronto.

Ernest J. Weinrib, BA, PhD, LLB, FRSC, University Professor and Cecil A Wright Professor of Law, University of Toronto.

1

Understanding Unjust Enrichment: An Introduction

JASON W. NEYERS

I. INTRODUCTION

ONE MIGHT ARGUE that the legal community is not in need of another book on unjust enrichment. Are we not overwhelmed by the current volume of material, both academic and judicial? Has not enough been said on this topic? In other words: Why more? Why now?

Despite these first impressions, however, there are three reasons why this is a fitting time for a re-examination of unjust enrichment. The first reason is that in the increased volume of material, one can begin to see the formation of analytical 'camps': the broad, the narrow and the sceptical (to borrow the definitions of Steve Hedley).[1] With this comes the danger, not yet realized, that the camps will at some point cease to be mutually referential and will instead focus on elucidating their visions of the law without addressing the thoughts and ideas of those not sharing the same intellectual framework. With this fragmentation, however, also comes an opportunity, if the lines of communication are kept open, for an improved and more coherent doctrine. Thus, the legal community is in need of fora in which thesis and antithesis can become synthesis.

The second reason for re-examination stems from the growing divergence not only in the doctrinal positions held by the leading unjust enrichment scholars but also among the leading commonwealth jurisdictions. English courts have largely followed and applied the Birksian model, which focuses on a search for unjust factors or reasons for restitution.[2] Canadian courts,

[1] S Hedley, 'Unjust Enrichment: A Middle Course?' (2002) 2 *Oxford University Commonwealth Law Journal* 181, 182–83.

[2] The English test for when an enrichment is unjust requires proof of: (1) an enrichment to the defendant, (2) which is gained at the plaintiff's expense, (3) as a result of an unjust factor; see P Birks, *An Introduction to the Law of Restitution* (Oxford, Clarendon Press, 1989). For a judicial application, see *Banque Financière de la Cité v Parc (Battersea) Ltd* [1999] 1 AC 221 (HL).

however, have borrowed from the Quebec civil law[3] and adopted a model that, at least in theory, ignores unjust factors and instead allows recovery whenever there is no juristic reason for the enrichment.[4] Australia, always less enamoured with the holus-bolus application of unjust enrichment,[5] has started to diverge more noticeably from the English law by reshaping its doctrine through the equitable language of conscience.[6] If the principle against unjust enrichment is to remain mutually understandable, an effort will have to be made by all to seriously consider insights from other jurisdictions.

The third reason for re-examination is the increasing complexity of the recent scholarship, which attempts to explain and integrate the most difficult areas of the private law (such as tracing, constructive trusts, accessory liability, and subrogation) into the principle against unjust enrichment.[7] As attention gets focused on extending the reach of the principle to new areas, less attention is focused on refining and questioning the principle itself (whatever its jurisdictional form). Moreover, this natural tendency to 'stand on the shoulders of giants' means that basic questions—such as 'what is an enrichment?' or 'what are legitimate expectations?'—are often forgotten in the enthusiasm to extend unjust enrichment to new legal frontiers. Thus, the legal community is in need of scholarship that occasionally goes 'back to the basics' of a particular legal doctrine.

The articles collected in this book were all presented, in one form or another, at the Understanding Unjust Enrichment symposium held at the University of Western Ontario on January 25, 2003. They were chosen in order to respond to these three reasons for re-examination and to thereby further our understanding of unjust enrichment. Thus, the articles in this book represent the major camps of analytical thought in the law of restitution, bring together authors from across the Commonwealth, and focus on the basic doctrinal questions outlined above. They are organized into five groupings that roughly correspond to the order of their presentation at the symposium. The first reviews developments in different commonwealth jurisdictions. The second examines the nature and scope of unjust

[3] See *Cie Immobilière Viger v Lauréat Giguère Inc* [1977] 2 SCR 67 (SCC), now codified in CCQ arts. 1491–92. For a short explanation of why this might have occurred see L Smith, 'The Mystery of "Juristic Reason"' (2002) 12 *Supreme Court Law Review* 211, 215–19.

[4] The Canadian test for when an enrichment is unjust requires proof of: (1) an enrichment, (2) a corresponding deprivation, and (3) an absence of any juristic reason for the enrichment; see *Pettkus v Becker* [1980] 2 SCR 834; (1980) 117 DLR (3d) 257 (SCC). I say 'in theory' since some Canadian courts, while using the language of 'lack of juristic reason,' still search for unjust factors: see Smith (n 3).

[5] See eg, SJ Stoljar, *The Law of Quasi-Contracts* (Sydney, Law Book Co, 1964); J Dietrich, *Restitution: A New Perspective* (Leichhardt, NSW, Federation Press, 1998); IM Jackman, *The Varieties of Restitution* (Leichhardt, NSW, Federation Press, 1998).

[6] See *Roxborough v Rothmans of Pall Mall Australia* (2002) 76 ALJR 203 (HCA) and the insightful comment by RB Grantham, 'Restitutionary recovery *Ex Æquo et Bono*' [2002] *Singapore Journal of Legal Studies* 388.

[7] This is discussed in more detail in McInnes, below (n 16).

enrichment from a theoretical perspective. The third examines the concept of enrichment from both a common law perspective and the perspective of other legal traditions. The fourth addresses emerging topics in unjust enrichment. Finally, the fifth scrutinizes the use of unjust enrichment in the family setting.

II. UNJUST ENRICHMENT ACROSS THE COMMONWEALTH

In the first article, Andrew Burrows examines recent developments in the English law of restitution, focusing on mistake, change of position and proprietary restitution.[8] In relation to the law of mistake, Burrows argues that the current English position is both satisfactory and straightforward and is to be preferred to a civilian system of looking for a lack of juristic reason for a payment. Likewise, he finds the current English thinking on change of position to be equally sound and applauds its expansive position, which limits the use of estoppel and allows for both causal detriment (as opposed to true detrimental reliance) and anticipatory (as well as subsequent) reliance. He is not as enthusiastic, however, about the current English position on proprietary restitution, which holds that there is a true division between the law of property and the law of unjust enrichment. Burrows contends that this unnecessary dichotomy will do injustice in some cases—by obstructing the operation of the change of position defence in 'property' cases—and not allow full justice in others—by removing the ability of judges to give proprietary relief in 'unjust enrichment' cases. Towards the end of his article, he suggests that the next decade is likely to see 'significant judicial developments' recognizing partial failure of consideration as an unjust factor, amalgamating the various rules on tracing, absorbing knowing receipt, refining the principle from *Attorney-General v Blake*[9] and creating a choice of law rule for unjust enrichment.

In contrast to the shorter-term perspective taken by Burrows, Gerald Fridman examines the common law and equitable antecedents that have become united into the modern law of unjust enrichment.[10] From this historical survey, Fridman attempts to answer the question of what makes an enrichment 'unjust' in Canadian law. In the end, he concludes that the only way to answer that question is through an analysis of the precedents and their case-by-case extension, rather than through the broad generalizations or resorts to general notions of morality and policy that seem so popular with Canadian appellate courts.

[8] A Burrows, 'The English Law of Restitution: A Ten-Year Review' ch 2.
[9] [2001] 1 AC 268 (HL).
[10] GHL Fridman, 'Unjust Enrichment (Dis)Contented' ch 3.

In his article, Michael Bryan examines the current state of the principle against unjust enrichment in Australia and its relationship with the conscience-based doctrines favoured by many Australian commentators.[11] After examining the history and reception of unjust enrichment into Australian law, he concludes that much of the academic attack mounted by English commentators on unconscionability is misplaced, especially in relation to the doctrines surrounding relief from unconscionable bargains. Although Bryan finds the arguments against unconscionability overdone, he maintains that Australian law is not well-served by its increasing tendency to ignore unjust enrichment. Instead, he finds that the principle is indeed helpful since it can guide judges in properly deciding which defences and remedies should be available in situations traditionally conceptualised as solely the province of equity.

III. THE THEORY OF UNJUST ENRICHMENT

What is meant by the principle against unjust enrichment? This is the question that Kit Barker seeks to answer in his contribution to the collection.[12] His conclusion is that it is best understood as an inclusive legal principle that encompasses all lower-level legal rules and causes of action that allow for gain-based awards in private law. As such, he argues that it is wrong to attempt to separate disgorgement from autonomous unjust enrichment, since they share enough 'family resemblances' to both be included under the unjust enrichment principle. Barker also argues that since this principle includes so many diverse legal rules, attempts to explain it solely as a manifestation of corrective justice are largely mistaken. Rather, the case law has shown that the courts have sometimes employed deterrence, fairness, public policy and localized distributive justice to reach palatable solutions in difficult cases.

Taking Barker's arguments one step further, and against the current tide of theoretical literature,[13] Dennis Klimchuk contends that a claim in autonomous unjust enrichment is not an instance of Aristotelian corrective justice at all.[14] This position is based on the fact that the paradigmatic claim of unjust enrichment—ie that of a mistaken payor for restitution—does not display the 'doing and suffering of the same harm' that is indicative of the other areas of the law, such as tort, which are said to be based in

[11] M Bryan, 'Unjust Enrichment and Unconscionability In Australia: A False Dichotomy?' ch 4.
[12] K Barker, 'Understanding the Unjust Enrichment Principle in Private Law: A Study of the Concept and Its Reasons' ch 5.
[13] See eg, E Weinrib, *The Idea of Private Law* (Cambridge, Harvard University Press, 1995); L Smith, 'Restitution: The Heart of Corrective Justice' (2001) 79 *Texas Law Review* 2115; M McInnes, 'The Measure of Restitution' (2002) 52 *University of Toronto Law Journal* 163.
[14] D Klimchuk, 'Unjust Enrichment and Corrective Justice' ch 6.

corrective justice. Instead, relying on §1 of the *Restatement of Restitution*, Klimchuk argues that an unjust enrichment claim is really an instance of localized distributive justice: localized in the dual sense that it is limited to the parties to the transaction and based only on the reason for impugning the transfer between them (eg the mistake).

In his article, Peter Jaffey argues that two theories of unjust enrichment are evident in the law and legal literature, one weak and one strong.[15] The weak theory is that there are claims to restitution recognized by the common law that arise from the receipt of a benefit. The strong theory asserts that all such claims are based on the principle against unjust enrichment. Jaffey argues against the leap many scholars have made from the (trite) weak theory to acceptance of the strong theory. Instead he offers alternative justifications why the law forces benefits to be returned—justifications that are grounded in the basic legal concepts of property and ownership, contract and agreement, wrong and punishment. In the end, his article questions whether anything is to be gained by continuing to use the amorphous concept of unjust enrichment in either its weak or strong sense.

IV. THE NATURE OF ENRICHMENT

Narrowing the focus slightly, the articles in the third grouping seek to determine when a defendant can be said to be enriched. Mitchell McInnes' answer, which he bases on an integration of commonwealth judicial decisions and academic analysis, is rooted in the concept of freedom of choice.[16] He argues that a defendant is legally enriched to the extent that he or she assumed financial responsibility for the benefit. Deploying this simple yet fundamental premise, McInnes offers resolutions to many of the thorny enrichment issues surrounding the receipt of pure services; claims of subjective devaluation and overvaluation; and situations of free acceptance, incontrovertible benefit and specific restitution. Using the concept of free choice, he also explains how both the defence of change of position and reasons for restitution integrate with the concept of enrichment. Thus, McInnes' article provides analytical rigour to a question that has previously been largely addressed through judicial intuition.

In his contribution, Ernest Weinrib adds to the growing body of comparative restitution literature by outlining the intellectual history of the Jewish law's response to the problem of unrequested benefits.[17] Beyond its fascinating descriptive treatment, the article also demonstrates how the common law and Jewish law can reach vastly different conclusions on recovery,

[15] P Jaffey, 'Two Theories of Unjust Enrichment' ch 7.
[16] M McInnes, 'Enrichment Revisited' ch 8.
[17] E Weinrib, 'Planting Another's Field: Unrequested Improvements Under Jewish Law' ch 9.

while still sharing a similar concern for the autonomy of the individual and deploying similar conceptual devices. Many thanks are due to Weinrib for bringing to our attention the concepts and sources of a legal tradition that would otherwise be inaccessible to the vast majority of those engaged in understanding unjust enrichment.

In a similar vein, Thomas Krebs' article approaches enrichment from a comparative perspective.[18] In it he elucidates the way that German law categorises and responds to claims based on one party's supply of an unrequested benefit. Relying on the German experience, he argues that English law should be wary of moving to the pure 'lack of legal ground' approach seemingly typified by the Jewish law and the Canadian formulation of unjust enrichment, since even the German law still searches for 'positive reasons for restitution'—although often in a way that is obscure to the common lawyer. Krebs also notes that if a legal system is to ensure that there is not too much restitution, it will have to find ways to limit claims. In a system that looks to positive reasons for restitution, this limiting can be done by both the 'unjust factors' and the concept of enrichment. Unfortunately, in a system that merely requires a lack of a legal ground this limiting can only be done by massaging, perhaps artificially, the concept of enrichment. In the end, Krebs questions whether this might not be too much strain for that concept.

V. EMERGING TOPICS

Picking up on Burrows' predictions of likely 'growth areas,' the articles in the fourth grouping deal with emerging topics in the law of restitution. Thus, in his article Robert Chambers discusses the sources and nature of claims based on tracing.[19] He argues that they are not exclusive to the law of property nor are they excluded from the law of unjust enrichment, contrary to what the House of Lords has said recently in *Foskett v McKeown*.[20] He then argues that a claim based on tracing value from one asset to another can be created by consent, by statute, by wrongdoing, or by unjust enrichment. The claims which are created by unjust enrichment may be personal claims to the value of that enrichment (possibly secured by a lien) or property claims to the enrichment itself. As a result, Chambers suggests that there are fundamental differences between personal and proprietary unjust enrichment claims, differences which must be taken into account as this area of law develops.

[18] T Krebs, 'Unrequested Benefits in German Law' ch 10.
[19] R Chambers, 'Tracing and Unjust Enrichment' ch 11.
[20] [2001] 1 AC 102 (HL).

Next, Peter Benson investigates whether the awarding of disgorgement damages for breach of contract is consistent with the fundamental principles of private law.[21] Using these principles, he argues that as a general proposition gain-based damages should not be available for breaches of ordinary contracts—ie contracts whose subject matter is neither unique nor specified—even if they are deliberate. Where the subject matter of the contract is unique, however, he concludes that gain-based damages should be available since the logic that allows disgorgement damages for violations of property rights applies equally to these breaches of contract. Thus, Benson finds that the emerging judicial consensus[22] suggesting the limited availability of contractual gain-based damages is consistent with the dictates of corrective justice.

To close this grouping, Stephen Pitel explains how disagreements over the scope and nature of unjust enrichment make characterization difficult for the purpose of the conflict of laws.[23] To overcome these difficulties, he argues that the best view of the current English position is that there is a cause of action in unjust enrichment that does not perfectly quadrate with the remedy of restitution. Using this understanding of the law, Pitel goes on to deal with the difficult conflicts cases where there might be said to be an overlap with a contractual, proprietary, or wrongs-based claim. Given the inevitability of further globalization, cross-border unjust enrichment claims are only likely to increase. Consequently, the points made should be useful for those concerned with the interplay between restitution and private international law.

VI. UNJUST ENRICHMENT IN THE FAMILY

The final grouping starts with John McCamus' examination of the uniquely Canadian jurisprudence regulating the distribution of assets on the breakdown of spousal and quasi-spousal relationships.[24] He finds that the courts' use of the concept of 'reasonable expectations' as the touchstone of liability in these cases is artificial, and instead argues that recovery is based on the frustration of the (quasi-spousal) joint venture between the parties. Given this relationship, McCamus argues that the default measure of recovery—ie the one that would have been agreed on had the parties turned their minds

[21] P Benson, 'Disgorgement for Breach of Contract and Corrective Justice: An Analysis in Outline' ch 12.
[22] As evidenced by *Blake* (n 9), *Bank of America Canada v Clarica Trust Co* 2002 SCC 43; (2002) 211 DLR (4th) 385 (SCC) and *Adras Building Material v Harlow & Jones* 42(1) PD 221 (SC Israel) translated in (1995) 3 *Restitution Law Review* 235.
[23] SGA Pitel, 'The Characterisation of Unjust Enrichment in the Conflict of Laws' ch 13.
[24] JD McCamus, 'Restitution on Dissolution of Marital and Other Intimate Relationships: Constructive Trust or Quantum Meruit?' ch 14.

to the question of remedy—should be the equal division of the surviving assets produced by their joint efforts. If this is the true basis of recovery, he notes that a quantum meruit claim for the value received should not generally be available. But, he cautions, that this does not mean, as has generally been assumed, that the constructive trust is the only appropriate remedy. Instead, Canadian courts should be open to the possibility of ordering personal remedies for the surviving value, such as an account of profits, especially in circumstances involving third party creditors.

Moving forward from the cohabition cases, Jeff Berryman examines the ability of parents to recover the contributions that they have made toward their children's university education.[25] Employing the Canadian doctrine, which he finds superior to the English model on the basis of its flexibility, Berryman contends that an arguable case can be made in favour of the parents since their 'legitimate expectation' to some recompense limits the purely gratuitous nature of this inter-generational wealth transfer. Relying on recent case law, legislation and scholarship, Berryman notes that these 'legitimate expectations' are strongest in those cultural communities that retain a vibrant tradition of filial piety, but he notes that they are also present in other Canadian communities albeit in somewhat weaker form. From this investigation, Berryman concludes that it would be a mistake for the Canadian law to abandon its use of legitimate expectations, as has been advocated by McCamus and others.[26] Rather, it should seek to better understand and integrate this useful concept so that the law of unjust enrichment can continue to adapt to changing societal circumstances.

In the final article, Stephen Waddams seeks to show how the basic concepts of the private law—contract, wrongdoing, property, unjust enrichment, and public policy—are intertwined when the courts answer difficult conceptual problems, such as those regulating restitution in the family context.[27] While others might see this interdependence as betraying a 'well-meaning sloppiness of thought,'[28] Waddams instead argues that we should accept that a complicated phenomenon like the law will sometimes require a complicated analysis—one that uses many, if not all, the basic legal concepts in a mutually supportive way. He makes clear, however, that this conclusion does not deny unjust enrichment its place as an independent and important legal concept. Instead, it indicates that unjust enrichment has now become a basic legal conception that can be deployed, with others, to answer the taxing questions put forward by the law.

[25] JB Berryman, 'Legitimating "Legitimate Expectations": A Case Study on Filial Responsibility; Can Parents Recover for Supporting Their Children at University?' ch 15.
[26] See McCamus (n 24) and M McInnes, 'Unjust Enrichment—Restitution—Absence of Juristic Reason' (2000) 79 Canadian Bar Review 459, 467–68.
[27] S Waddams, 'The Relation of Unjust Enrichment to Other Legal Concepts' ch 16.
[28] To borrow the phrase from *Holt v Markham* [1923] 1 KB 504 (CA) 573.

VII. CONCLUSION

Both the symposium and this book benefited from generous support and assistance. The symposium was sponsored by three leading law firms from London, Ontario: Harrison Pensa LLP, Lerners LLP and Siskinds. In addition, faculty staff displayed characteristic efficiency and cheerfulness in handling many aspects of the symposium's organization, and Dean Ian Holloway was steadfast in his support for the event. In preparing this book, the editors are grateful for grants from the Foundation for Legal Research (based in Vancouver, British Columbia) and the Law Foundation of Ontario, which enabled us to have the assistance of three talented law students, Cheryl Dusten, Jonathan Moncrieff and Linda Smits.

In conclusion, I and my co-editors hope that you will enjoy and benefit from these articles as much as we enjoyed hearing them presented and benefited from the discussion at the symposium. We are confident that they will be useful to anyone interested in understanding unjust enrichment.

2

The English Law of Restitution: A Ten-Year Review

ANDREW BURROWS

I. INTRODUCTION: A DECADE OF DEVELOPMENT

IN THIS PAPER I would like to examine where we have got to with the English law of restitution. More particularly, I want to consider developments over the last ten years. These are the years subsequent to the acceptance by the House of Lords in *Lipkin Gorman v Karpnale Ltd*[1] that we have an English law of restitution based on the principle against unjust enrichment. The catalyst for my looking back over the last decade has been the preparation of the second edition of my book, *The Law of Restitution*.[2] The first edition stated the law as at the end of September 1992; a time when, following on *Lipkin Gorman*, *Woolwich Equitable Building Society v Inland Revenue Commissioners*[3] had just been decided, establishing that a citizen has a right to restitution of payments demanded ultra vires by a public authority.

The story of the last decade has been one of unparalleled development and clarification of the law of restitution by the courts, combined with an explosion of academic writing. Indeed, many of the legal decisions have been expressly guided and assisted by academic opinion. If one wanted an example of the law being not merely what the courts have held but also the opinion of jurists, the English law of restitution over the last ten years provides that example. No practitioner worth his or her salt would think of coming before the Court of Appeal or House of Lords in a case about the law of restitution without being acquainted with the views of the academics, most notably Jones who, since the fourth edition in 1993, has been solely responsible for *Goff and Jones*,[4] and Birks.

[1] [1991] 2 AC 548.
[2] A Burrows, *The Law of Restitution*, 2nd edn (London, Butterworths, 2002).
[3] [1993] AC 70.
[4] Lord Goff and G Jones, *The Law of Restitution*, 6th edn (London, Sweet & Maxwell, 2002).

Let me start by giving you an immediate snap-shot of the last decade. As regards significant decisions of the House of Lords we have had, for example, *Westdeutsche Landesbank Girozentrale v Islington London BC*[5] on restitution of money paid under void contracts; *Kleinwort Benson Ltd v Glasgow City Council*[6] on the jurisdiction of the English courts to hear restitutionary claims; *Stocznia Gdanska SA v Latvia Shipping Co*[7] on total failure of consideration; *Banque Financière de la Cité v Parc (Battersea) Ltd*[8] on non-contractual subrogation; *Kleinwort Benson Ltd v Lincoln CC*[9] on restitution of payments made by mistake of law; *Foskett v McKeown*[10] on tracing and on the problematic relationship between property law and the law of restitution; *Attorney-General v Blake*[11] on restitution for breach of contract; and *Royal Bank of Scotland plc v Etridge (No 2)*[12] on rescission of a contract for undue influence. There have also been influential judgments of the Privy Council in, for example, *Attorney-General of Hong Kong v Reid*[13] on proprietary restitution in respect of bribes and *Dextra Bank and Trust Co Ltd v Bank of Jamaica*[14] on change of position. Add, to all these, important decisions of the Court of Appeal such as *Bishopsgate Investment Management v Homan*[15] on tracing, *Kleinwort Benson v Birmingham CC*[16] on passing on, and *Scottish Equitable plc v Derby*[17] on estoppel and change of position, and numerous decisions at first instance, and one can see that the English law of restitution over the last ten years has finally, albeit belatedly, come of age. It is as if the English law of restitution over the last decade has been making up for lost time.

Turning to when the first edition of my book was published, it seems astonishing now that there were only two texts on the English law of restitution (Goff and Jones, *The Law of Restitution*[18] and Birks, *An Introduction to the Law of Restitution*[19]) and a few collections of essays.[20] The position is now very different. In addition to my own book, Goff and

[5] [1996] AC 669.
[6] [1999] 1 AC 153.
[7] [1998] 1 WLR 574.
[8] [1999] 1 AC 221.
[9] [1999] 2 AC 349.
[10] [2001] 1 AC 102.
[11] [2001] 1 AC 268.
[12] [2002] 2 AC 773.
[13] [1994] 1 AC 324.
[14] [2002] 1 All ER (Comm) 193.
[15] [1995] Ch 211.
[16] [1996] 3 WLR 1139.
[17] [2001] 3 All ER 818.
[18] R Goff and G Jones, *The Law of Restitution*, 3rd edn (London, Sweet & Maxwell, 1986).
[19] P Birks, *An Introduction to the Law of Restitution* rev edn, (Oxford, Clarendon Press, 1989).
[20] P D Finn (ed), *Essays on Restitution* (Sydney, The Law Book Company Limited, 1990); J Beatson, *The Use and Abuse of Unjust Enrichment* (Oxford, Clarendon Press, 1991); A Burrows (ed), *Essays on the Law of Restitution* (Oxford, Clarendon Press, 1991).

Jones and Birks we have one other 'practitioner work' (*The Law of Restitution*, edited by Hedley and Halliwell[21]), three other textbooks (Tettenborn, The *Law of Restitution in England and Ireland*;[22] Virgo, *The Principles of the Law of Restitution*;[23] and McMeel, *The Modern Law of Restitution*[24]) as well as texts in Australia[25] and New Zealand.[26] In addition to several case-books,[27] and numerous collections of essays,[28] the last decade has also seen the publication of a series of important monographs on particular aspects of the English law of restitution. These have included, for example, Mitchell's *The Law of Subrogation*;[29] Smith's *The Law of Tracing*;[30] Chambers' *Resulting Trusts*;[31] and Panagopoulos' *Restitution in Private International Law*.[32] Books have also been written by, for example, Jaffey[33] and Hedley[34] challenging the orthodox approach to the law of restitution. Hundreds of articles on the law of restitution have been published in recent years and the subject has had its own dedicated law journal, the *Restitution Law Review*, since 1993. There is a very helpful restitution web-site run by Hedley from Cambridge[35] and a thriving internet discussion forum organised by Smith from Canada. In sharp contrast to its earlier

[21] S Hedley and M Halliwell (eds), *The Law of Restitution* (London, Butterworths LexisNexis, 2002). There is also a succinct and important chapter headed 'Unjust Enrichment' by P Birks and C Mitchell in P Birks (ed), *English Private Law* (Oxford, Oxford University Press, 2000) ch 15.

[22] A Tettenborn, *The Law of Restitution in England and Ireland*, 3rd edn (London, Cavendish Publishing Limited, 2002).

[23] G Virgo, *The Principles of the Law of Restitution* (Oxford, Oxford University Press, 1999).

[24] G McMeel, *The Modern Law of Restitution* (London, Blackstone Press Limited, 2000).

[25] K Mason and JW Carter, *Restitution Law in Australia* (Sydney, Butterworths, 1995). This text is reviewed at length by several commentators at [1997] *Restitution Law Review* 229.

[26] RB Grantham and CEF Rickett, *Enrichment and Restitution in New Zealand* (Oxford, Hart Publishing, 2000). The first text in Canada was PD Maddaugh and JD McCamus, *The Law of Restitution* (Aurora, Canada Law Book Inc, 1990).

[27] Eg, G McMeel, *Casebook on Restitution* (London, Blackstone, 1996); A Burrows and E McKendrick, *Cases and Materials on the Law of Restitution* (Oxford, Oxford University Press, 1997); RB Grantham and CEF Rickett, *Restitution: Commentary and Materials* (Wellington, Brookers, 2001).

[28] Eg, P Birks (ed), *Laundering and Tracing* (Oxford, Clarendon Press, 1995); F Rose (ed), *Restitution and the Conflict of Laws* (Oxford, Mansfield Press, 1995); WR Cornish and others (eds), *Restitution: Past, Present and Future* (Oxford, Hart Publishing, 1998); F Rose (ed), *Restitution and Banking Law* (Oxford, Mansfield Press, 1998); P Birks and F Rose (eds), *Lessons of the Swaps Litigation* (London, Mansfield Press, 2000); F Rose (ed), *Restitution and Insolvency* (Oxford, Mansfield Press, 2000); P Birks and F Rose (eds), *Restitution and Equity* (Oxford, Mansfield Press, 2000); P Birks, *The Foundations of Unjust Enrichment: Six Centennial Lectures* (Wellington, Victoria University Press, 2002).

[29] C Mitchell, *The Law of Subrogation* (Oxford, Clarendon Press, 1994).

[30] L Smith, *The Law of Tracing* (Oxford, Clarendon Press, 1997).

[31] R Chambers, *Resulting Trusts* (Oxford, Clarendon Press, 1997).

[32] G Panagopoulos, *Restitution in Private International Law* (Oxford, Hart Publishing, 2000).

[33] P Jaffey, *The Nature and Scope of Restitution* (Oxford, Hart Publishing, 2000).

[34] S Hedley, *Restitution: Its Division and Ordering* (London, Sweet & Maxwell, 2001); S Hedley, *A Critical Introduction to Restitution* (London, Butterworths, 2001).

[35] www.law.cam.ac.uk/restitution

neglect, the law of restitution can claim to have been the most debated subject in English private law over the last ten years.[36]

It will be apparent from this overview of judicial and academic developments that if I were to look in any detail at all of them I would need several articles rather than just one. What I therefore propose to do in the heart of this article is to focus in some detail on just three areas. Each is of central importance both theoretically and in practice, and in each there have been recent leading cases and continuing controversies reflected in the academic literature. In each I hope to give a clear view not only of what the law now is but also an impression of how secure that present position is.

The three areas I have chosen are: first, mistaken payments (no doubt the most common example of where restitution is sought); second, change of position (which is plainly the most important restitutionary defence); and third, proprietary restitution (raising the most difficult and, as yet unresolved, problems in the law of restitution). The three can be linked in our minds by imagining that C has made a mistaken payment to D and wants to know: first, whether it has a personal restitutionary claim to recover the value of the mistaken payment; second, whether D's spending of money on the faith of that mistaken payment affords D a defence; and third, if D has become insolvent, whether C has a proprietary restitutionary claim that will give C priority over D's unsecured creditors.

In the final part of the article, I want to refer briefly to five areas where views expressed by judges or academics in the last decade suggest that we are likely to see significant judicial developments in the next decade.

II. MISTAKEN PAYMENTS

The law on mistaken payments is, as I understand it, now easy to state and apply. Assuming that one is talking about personal, rather than proprietary, restitution, a claimant is prima facie (ie subject to defences) entitled to restitution of a non-contractual payment made by mistake if it can show that it would not have made that payment but for the mistake. The mistake may have been one of fact or, as held in the leading case of *Kleinwort Benson Ltd v Lincoln CC*,[37] one of law.

In *Kleinwort Benson* the claimant bank had made payments to defendant councils under interest rate swap transactions that had been fully executed by both parties (ie the swaps were 'closed'). Then it was decided by

[36] The experience in the United States has been very different. Until a recent mini-revival led, for example, by Professor Andrew Kull of Boston University, the subject had virtually disappeared as a separate law school course (albeit sometimes taught as part of a remedies course) and rarely featured in law journals. See J Langbein, 'The Later History of Restitution' in Cornish (above n 28) 57, 60–62.

[37] Above (n 9).

the House of Lords in *Hazell v Hammersmith and Fulham Borough Council*[38] that interest rate swap agreements were void as being outside the powers of local authorities. Kleinwort Benson had made net payments to the local authorities of £811,208. The local authorities were willing to pay back £388,114 which had been paid to them within six years of the date of the issue of the writ. But they were not willing to pay back £423,094 that had been paid prior to that date, arguing that a claim for such repayment was statute-barred. The claimant bank sought restitution of the £423,094 on the basis that it had paid under a mistake of law and that, therefore, under s 32(1) of the Limitation Act 1980 the six-year limitation period did not start to run until the claimant discovered, or could with reasonable diligence have discovered, the mistake. Further, the claimant argued that the mistake of law was not discoverable until the decision of the House of Lords in *Hazell*.

A majority of the House of Lords in *Kleinwort Benson* (Lords Goff, Hoffmann and Hope; Lords Browne-Wilkinson and Lloyd dissenting) held that there should be restitution of the money paid because it was paid under a mistake of law. The rule denying restitution for mistakes of law was abrogated, and the claim was not time-barred because s 32 of the Limitation Act 1980 applied.

The difficult question raised by the case was not so much whether the court should depart from the mistake of law rule—even the defendants conceded that the rule was unacceptable—but was rather how one should deal with changes in the law. This was in issue because the defendants argued that prior to the House of Lords' decision in *Hazell*, the settled view of the law was that interest rate swap transactions were valid.

The majority Law Lords said, in effect, that a mistake of law triggered restitution of payments made even if the mistake of law was a consequence of a change in the law by a judicial overruling of an earlier decision or by a judicial departure from a settled view. Judicial changes in the law were retrospective, and it logically followed that, at the time they made the payments, the payors were mistaken as to the law. It is also important to note that the majority effectively assimilated the law of restitution on mistakes of law with that on mistakes of fact by approving a 'but for' test of causation for both.

Lords Browne-Wilkinson and Lloyd dissented because, while agreeing with the majority that the mistake of law bar should be removed, they considered that there should be no restitution where there was a change in the law or a departure from the settled view of the law. In their view, in these situations, the payor could not be said to have been mistaken. They painted an alarmist picture of never-ending restitution claims if the majority's view

[38] [1992] 2 AC 1.

were accepted. However, with respect, this picture was flawed, because in most situations standard restitutionary defences of res judicata and compromise, as well as change of position, would operate to rule out restitution in respect of money paid on the basis of subsequently overruled old law.

Academic views on the merits of *Kleinwort Benson* can be roughly grouped into three. First, there are those, most notably Birks,[39] who consider that the decision is wrong because, where the law has been changed judicially and the payor has paid on the basis of the old law, he is not relevantly mistaken. Mistakes grounding restitution must be ones where the payor pays on the basis of data that can be verified as true or false at the time the payment is made. 'Mistakes' of law that are only revealed as such by a subsequent decision do not therefore ground restitution. The best that the payor can say is that it made a misprediction as to what the law would turn out to be. The reason why the difference between mistakes and mispredictions is so crucial is that, in relation to mispredictions, one is exercising an element of choice or judgment which is significantly different from the impairment of will necessary to ground restitution. In Birks' words:

> There is ... [a] crucial difference between decisions which are made on data which are false at the time they are made and decisions which are made on data which cannot be falsified at the time, but which are falsified later. The crucial difference consists in the fact that in the latter case there is no impairment of the decision.[40]

Second, there are those who argue that the majority was correct to award restitution but incorrect to regard the basis of the restitution as being mistake. The bank was not relevantly mistaken but was still entitled to restitution because it had paid under a contract that was void. There was therefore no legal ground for the payment. This is the view taken by a number of commentators from civilian jurisdictions, for example Meier and Zimmermann.[41] They point out that, in contrast to the common law's approach to the law of restitution which requires a claimant to establish a positive reason (an 'unjust factor') justifying restitution of a payment, be it, for example, mistake or failure of consideration or duress, the civilian approach is to award restitution unless there is a legal ground—or, as it is sometimes alternatively put, a juristic reason—for the payment. A valid contract or gift is a legal ground for a payment. But where a contract is void there is no such legal ground and restitution should follow automatically without having to establish that the payor was mistaken.

[39] P Birks, 'Mistakes of Law' [2000] *CLP* 205.
[40] *Ibid*, 224.
[41] S Meier and R Zimmermann, 'Judicial Development of the Law, *Error Iuris*, and the Law of Unjustified Enrichment—A View from Germany' (1999) 115 *LQR* 556.

Third, there are those like me who consider that the majority in *Kleinwort Benson* was correct both on the decision and on the reasoning. The bank was prima facie entitled to restitution because it made a mistake of law that caused the payment. It would not have paid had it known that the contract was void. Contrary to Birks' view, it seems to me to be false to equate questions of 'common law' to mispredictions. Certainly mispredictions should not ground restitution unless there has been a failure of consideration, because a misprediction as such indicates that the payor has taken the risk of being wrong. But the line between mistakes and mispredictions does not turn on whether data can be verified as true or false at the time the payment is made. Rather the line is between a false belief as to the present state of affairs (where we are in the realm of mistake) and a false belief as to a future state of affairs (where we are in the realm of misprediction). Just as the verification of facts may be complex and indeed, at the time, impossible (eg, because scientific techniques, like DNA testing, have not yet been developed), so too the verification of the law may be complex and indeed, at the time, impossible. But, as Lord Hope most clearly emphasised,[42] this does not mean that a person who pays on the basis of what are later proved to be incorrect facts, or is later proved to be incorrect law, has not made a mistake of fact or law respectively. Rather he or she did make a mistake of fact or law even though the proof of that mistake was only possible subsequently. His or her will has been impaired—wrong data has been fed into the decision-making—even though we can only see this subsequently and not at the time of the payment.

As regards the 'no legal ground' civilian approach, the traditional English approach of looking positively for 'unjust factors' that justify restitution is not only simpler and more transparently just, but also avoids reaching what appear to be incorrect answers in a number of situations. For example, had Kleinwort Benson known that the contract was void, so that it was indisputably making no mistake, it should surely not have been entitled to restitution. Yet on the civilian view—unless one introduces a further rule[43]—restitution follows automatically from a void contract even if the contract is fully executed and the payor is not mistaken. In addition, the civilian approach would seem to require a separate body of law to deal with mistaken gifts, yet my own view—although I am aware that a number of other commentators do not agree with this—is that if I make a gift, which I would not have made but for a mistake of fact or law, I should be, and am, entitled to restitution. So a double payment to a charity, forgetting one has made the first payment, or a gift to a charity, not realising that it pursues aims that one deplores, should and does prima facie trigger restitution—provided, of course, one can prove a

[42] *Kleinwort Benson* (n 9) 411.
[43] See Bürgerliches Gesetzbuch (BGB) § 814 (the German Civil Code).

mistake rather than a mere change of mind. I am also unclear how the 'no legal ground' approach deals with the conferral of a benefit while voluntarily pursuing one's self-interest. For example, for my own purposes I cut down trees on my own land which improves the view from my neighbour's land, thereby enhancing its value by £10,000. Am I entitled to restitution of £10,000 from my neighbour? The common law answer is straightforwardly 'no' because there is no unjust factor. I freely chose to cut down the trees. There was no mistake or duress or failure of consideration. But on the civilian model, as there is no valid contract or gift, it would seem to follow that prima facie there should be restitution in that situation.

It has been put to me that the English law on mistake is flawed because it has failed to clarify the extent to which doubt and suspicion are compatible with a claim for mistake. But, although there has been relatively little discussion of this by the English judges—the most important exception being Lord Hope's speech in *Kleinwort Benson*[44]—I do not accept that English law is flawed in this regard. The clearest way of approaching this issue of doubt and suspicion is to accept that a person can be mistaken while taking some risk that the facts or law may be different than he or she believes them to be. McKendrick[45] suggests that this can simply be resolved by the 'but for' causation test: would the claimant have paid had he or she known the truth. This seems to me to go too far. If one allows restitution whenever the claimant (who had doubts as to the facts or law) would not have paid had it known the truth, this would allow restitution despite a very high degree of doubt by the payor. Virgo goes to the opposite extreme and would rule out restitution whenever the payor was aware that there was a possibility that he or she was mistaken.[46] It is submitted that the best approach, in principle and policy, is to take a mid-position by applying a balance of probabilities test. If the payor pays, believing that the facts (or law) are *probably* what they in truth are, he or she cannot recover: his or her belief precludes restitution for mistake either on the grounds that he or she was not mistaken or that he or she took the risk of the mistake.

So while one cannot say that all matters relating to personal restitution for mistake have been resolved in English law, it does seem to me that the decision and reasoning in *Kleinwort Benson* has resolved most of them, and, more importantly, has resolved them in a way which, in contrast to the civilian approach to unjust enrichment, is both satisfactory and straightforward.

[44] Above (n 9) 410.
[45] E McKendrick, 'Mistake of Law—Time for a Change?' in W Swadling (ed), *The Limits of Restitutionary Claims: A Comparative Analysis* (London, The United Kingdom National Committee of Comparative Law, 1997) 212, 232–33.
[46] Virgo (above n 23) 161.

III. CHANGE OF POSITION

An important trend of the last ten years has been the increased focus both in the courts and in academic writings on defences to restitution, especially change of position. This was entirely predictable. Once the courts expanded the range of the unjust factors by, for example, expanding the types of mistake that trigger restitution, it was clear that the burden of controlling the scope of the law of restitution would fall to the defences. Put another way, while one used to rely on blunt and arbitrary 'control' mechanisms (for example, the old 'supposed' liability test for mistakes of fact and the refusal of restitution for mistakes of law) to give security of receipt to defendants and to ensure that there was not 'too much restitution,' one now has highly-tuned and focused defences to achieve this. Of these the most important is the defence of change of position, which, at its heart, is concerned with the defendant's good faith loss of the advantage received (ie disenrichment). This was first accepted as a defence to restitution by the House of Lords in *Lipkin Gorman*[47]. There the relevant change of position was paying out winnings to a thief on the assumption that the money he was using to bet with was untainted and was hence the gaming club's to keep, whereas in fact it had been stolen from the claimant solicitors. Although the amount of stolen money staked was much higher, the overall enrichment received by the defendant club from the stolen money was about £151,000. It was this sum that was awarded in restitution. As is expressly recognised in Lord Goff's speech, the House of Lords took a rough-and-ready, rather than a strictly logical, approach to the acute factual difficulties in applying change of position to winnings paid out on bets, since on a strict approach winnings on a bet relate to, and cancel out only, the receipt of that particular bet and not other losing bets.

The last ten years have seen the courts slowly but surely clarifying and refining the content of the change of position defence. The two most important cases have been *Scottish Equitable plc v Derby*[48] and *Dextra Bank & Trust Ltd v Bank of Jamaica*.[49]

In *Scottish Equitable*, the defendant had a pension policy with the claimant, Scottish Equitable. In 1989 he had exercised an option to take an early retirement benefit under that policy so that he was paid £36,588 and then £4,655 per annum. At this time, this left about £50,000 to be paid under the pension. Five years later, on his sixty-fifth birthday, he was told by Scottish Equitable that his pension was worth £201,938. Scottish Equitable had mistakenly forgotten about his earlier exercise of the option. In truth, his pension was worth £29,486. The defendant queried the matter

[47] Above (n 1).
[48] Above (n 17).
[49] Above (n 14).

but the higher figure was confirmed to be correct, orally and in writing, and Scottish Equitable went ahead and paid him the £201,938, which was an overpayment of £172,500. The defendant, who was held to be naïve but honest, spent £9,600 on modest improvements in his lifestyle, spent £41,700 in reducing his mortgage, and invested £121,100 in a pension which would pay him annually £11,000 more than he would otherwise have been paid. A year later, Scottish Equitable realised its mistake and sought to recover the overpayment, less the £9,600 which it conceded fell within the change of position defence. The Court of Appeal, upholding Harrison J, held that its claim to £162,900 should succeed. The £41,700 that the defendant used to reduce the mortgage did not constitute a change of position because that was a debt that he had had to pay anyway. So he was no worse off by having paid it. Further, the £121,000 paid into the pension could be unwound without difficulty, leaving the defendant with the same pension entitlement he would have had if he had not been overpaid.

Three important points emerge from the Court of Appeal's reasoning. First, change of position is not a general hardship defence. One is concerned with disenrichment, not a general change in the defendant's circumstances. As Robert Walker LJ said, 'The fact that the recipient may have suffered some misfortune (such as a breakdown in his health, or the loss of his job) is not a defence unless the misfortune is causally linked (at least on a 'but for' test) with the mistaken payment.'[50]

Second, the Court of Appeal accepted that it is not essential for the change of position defence that the defendant has suffered a loss by *relying* on the benefit being his.[51] While the payee must show that it would be pecuniarily worse off if now required to make restitution than if the benefit had not been received in the first place—ie causal detriment is required—detrimental reliance is not a requirement. While both a 'causal detriment' and 'detrimental reliance' requirement would produce the same result on most facts, the difference is brought out where the loss of the benefit is a consequence of a third party's action or a natural event—for example, where money mistakenly paid to the defendant is stolen or destroyed by fire. If one insisted on detrimental *reliance*, those situations would not constitute a change of position because there has been no reliance by the defendant which causes the loss. In contrast, they would constitute a change of position if causal detriment is sufficient. The 'causal detriment' view of the defence is preferable because it more widely protects innocent defendants, and the Court of Appeal's reasoning here is therefore to be welcomed. For example, it would surely be grotesque that a defendant who is paid £100,000 by the mistake of his or her bank, which is immediately stolen

[50] *Scottish Equitable* (n 17) para 31.
[51] *Ibid*, paras 31–32.

(ie he or she would not otherwise have lost £100,000) was (strictly) liable to make restitution of £100,000.

Third, and the main point at issue in *Scottish Equitable*, was whether the defendant could invoke the defence of estoppel so as to rule out entirely the restitutionary claim against him. The defendant's argument was that, as the defendant had indisputably detrimentally relied, at least to the extent of £9,600, on the claimant's representation that the money was owing, an estoppel against the claimant was established and it was irrelevant that the defendant had not changed his position to the full extent of the payment. Applying the leading case of *Avon County Council v Howlett*,[52] estoppel is traditionally regarded as a rule of evidence and as an all-or-nothing, not a pro tanto, defence. But the Court of Appeal decided that, even if there was no other way around *Avon*, its unconscionability exception here applied: ie it would be unconscionable for the defendant to have a total defence when the payment received was far greater than the change of position. But it is hard to see why that so-called exception will not always apply wherever the change of position is less than the payment received. In other words, the reasoning in *Scottish Equitable* implicitly shows that estoppel is an inappropriate defence in this context and has been undermined by the defence of change of position. It would be clearer and neater to recognise this explicitly, and to jettison estoppel as a standard restitutionary defence, rather than pretending that it exists but is subject to an unconscionability exception.

This is not to suggest that estoppel should disappear in the many other areas of law in which it applies. Rather the argument is that in the law of restitution, in contrast to those other areas, the injustice that estoppel seeks to prevent is entirely, and more appropriately, achieved by another defence, namely change of position.

In *Scottish Equitable* there was another argument for why estoppel should wither in the light of the acceptance of the change of position defence, described by Robert Walker LJ as the 'novel and ingenious argument [of junior counsel].'[53] According to this argument, if the payor limits its restitutionary claim by deducting the payee's change of position—or if one applies a change of position defence alongside estoppel—the payee cannot then establish the *detrimental* reliance needed for estoppel. That is, if the payee's change of position has been deducted, the payee cannot establish that it will be any worse off if it is now required to make restitution than if the payment had not been made in the first place. The argument, as Robert Walker LJ put it, is that 'the defence of change of position pre-empts and disables the defence of estoppel

[52] [1983] 1 WLR 605.
[53] Above (n 17) para 45.

by negativing detriment.'[54] While Robert Walker LJ preferred to rest his decision on other grounds, he regarded this argument as 'convincing.'[55]

Not surprisingly this novel argument has been the subject of considerable academic debate. Indeed, if the argument is correct, it may be thought to have implications for the law on estoppel generally, not just in the context of restitution. But the difficulty in applying the argument more widely is that generally estoppel seeks to protect expectations, so that it is not enough merely to ensure that the claimant's detriment is compensated. It has been pointed out to me that a similar argument has been expressly rejected in the context of an estoppel not to enforce one's rights, on the reasoning that one cannot 'buy out' an estoppel in this way.[56] In contrast, the reason why the argument seems 'convincing' in the context of restitution is precisely because the injustice with which one is concerned in that context is causal detriment, not expectation-protection. In the context of restitution, estoppel essentially duplicates in a more limited way what change of position seeks to achieve. It is therefore an unnecessary and unwarranted defence.

Two other important points on change of position emerge from the decision of the Privy Council in *Dextra Bank*. The claimant, Dextra, drew a cheque for $2,999,000 on its bankers in favour of the defendant, the Bank of Jamaica (BOJ). Dextra drew the cheque on the assumption that it would constitute a loan to BOJ under a secured loan agreement with BOJ. However, that loan agreement was never concluded. The cheque had been arranged on BOJ's behalf by agents whom BOJ reimbursed in advance of receiving the cheque. The Privy Council held that Dextra was not entitled to restitution of the money as money paid by mistake of fact because Dextra had paid the money on the basis of a misprediction (that a loan agreement would be entered into) and not a mistake. In any event, BOJ had the defence of change of position by virtue of their reimbursement of their agents.

Two main issues in relation to BOJ's change of position arose. The first was whether the change counted because it was prior to, rather than subsequent to, the receipt of the payment. The Privy Council was clear that a change of position can be anticipatory. In the words of Lords Goff and Bingham:

> Here what is in issue is the justice or injustice of enforcing a restitutionary claim in respect of a benefit conferred. In that context, it is difficult to see what relevant distinction can be drawn between (1) a case in which the defendant expends on some extraordinary expenditure all or part of a sum of money

[54] *Ibid*.
[55] *Ibid*, para 47.
[56] *Roche v Church*, The Times, 23 December 1992. I am grateful to Paul McMahon, a DPhil student at New College, Oxford, for this point. It is unaffected by the overruling of the line of authority of which *Roche v Church* formed part in *Roebuck v Mungovin* [1994] 2 AC 224 (HL).

> which he has received from the plaintiff, and (2) one in which the defendant incurs such expenditure in the expectation that he will receive the sum of money from the plaintiff, which he does in fact receive. Since ex hypothesi the defendant will in fact have received the expected payment, there is no question of the defendant using the defence of change of position to enforce, directly or indirectly, a claim to that money. It is surely no abuse of language to say, in the second case as in the first, that the defendant has incurred the expenditure in reliance on the plaintiff's payment or, as is sometimes said, on the faith of the payment.[57]

The second issue was whether the fault or negligence of the defendant in reimbursing its agents in advance ruled out change of position. The Privy Council took the view that the defendant's fault, short of bad faith,[58] was irrelevant. The fear otherwise was that the defence of change of position would become too uncertain and difficult to apply. However, this fear could perhaps be overcome by an alternative approach under which the defendant's fault does rule out change of position provided the defendant is clearly more at fault than the claimant.

In conclusion, it is of interest to note that, with the exception of rejecting the view that it is a general hardship defence, where differing views of the scope of change of position have been considered, the English courts have consistently opted for a wider rather than a narrower interpretation of the change of position defence: that is, for an interpretation that means that change of position is more likely, rather than less likely, to apply as a defence. Anticipatory as well as subsequent change of position counts, causal detriment applies rather than detrimental reliance, and bad faith rather than mere fault rules out the defence. This wide interpretation is to be welcomed as ensuring that change of position acts as a vibrant counterbalance to the expansion of the grounds for restitution.

IV. PROPRIETARY RESTITUTION

Proprietary restitution is the most complex area within the law of restitution. Over the last few years there has been important judicial and academic consideration of what the law in this area is and what it should be. Unfortunately, in this area it seems to me that the English courts have started to travel in the wrong direction.

It is important first to clarify what we mean by proprietary restitution. Most restitution is personal, in the sense that the remedy given by the

[57] *Dextra* (above n 14) 204.

[58] In *Niru Battery Manufacturing Co v Milestone Trading Ltd* [2002] 2 All ER (Comm) 705, Moore-Bick J, at para 135, thought that bad faith extended beyond subjective dishonesty and 'is capable of embracing a failure to act in a commercially acceptable way and sharp practice of a kind that falls short of outright dishonesty as well as dishonesty itself.'

courts (eg an award of money had and received, a quantum meruit or an account of profits) responds to a benefit having been received by the defendant irrespective of whether the defendant still retains particular property. Personal restitution is therefore not dependent on the existence of particular property and it does not afford priority on the defendant's insolvency. In contrast, proprietary restitution—achieved through remedies such as an equitable lien, a trust imposed after tracing, rescission revesting goods or land, or the conferment of secured rights by non-contractual subrogation—does afford priority on the defendant's insolvency and it is dependent on the defendant's retention of particular property.

The central question that we need to answer is when proprietary restitution, rather than the usual personal restitution, is, or should be, awarded to reverse unjust enrichment. One can now articulate two main views on this issue. The first, championed most notably by Virgo in *The Principles of the Law of Restitution*, is that proprietary restitution can never be awarded to reverse unjust enrichment.[59] In Virgo's view, unjust enrichment has no role to play in explaining, for example, equitable proprietary remedies imposed after tracing or the conferment of secured rights through non-contractual subrogation. Just as someone whose bicycle has been stolen retains title to the bicycle and can recover it or its value from whoever has it without reference to the law of unjust enrichment, so too equitable proprietary remedies after tracing are concerned with the vindication of the claimant's proprietary rights. Unjust enrichment is not in play, and, logically, just as change of position is not a defence to a claim for delivery up or damages for conversion, so too it is not a defence to equitable proprietary remedies imposed after tracing. At a higher level of generality, the Virgo view sees unjust enrichment as purely being part of the law of obligations and as having no role within the law of property.

The counter-view, put forward by, for example, Birks[60] and Chambers,[61] is that the Virgo view is too simplistic and narrow. Proprietary rights *are* sometimes created to reverse unjust enrichment. The difficulty is not so much whether proprietary restitution exists to reverse unjust enrichment but rather in articulating a coherent theory as to when this is so. On this view, equitable proprietary remedies after tracing, for example, are significantly different from the recovery of one's stolen bicycle. They are significantly different precisely because a new proprietary right is created in the substitute traced asset that did not previously exist. The best explanation of

[59] Virgo (n 23) 11–17, 592–97.

[60] P Birks, 'Property, Unjust Enrichment and Tracing' (2001) 54 *CLP* 231. See also P Birks, 'Restitution of Unjust Enrichment' in A Burrows and E Peel (eds), *Commercial Remedies: Current Issues and Problems* (Oxford, Oxford University Press, 2003) 131, 153–69.

[61] Chambers (above n 31); R Chambers, 'Constructive Trusts in Canada' (1999) 37 *Alberta Law Review* 173.

that new proprietary right is that it is created to reverse the defendant's unjust enrichment at the claimant's expense. Like any other restitution reversing unjust enrichment, that proprietary restitution is subject to a defence of change of position.

I essentially agree with Birks and Chambers. Unfortunately the House of Lords in *Foskett v McKeown*,[62] while not mentioning Virgo's work, has strongly endorsed his approach. A remedy imposed after tracing is, according to their Lordships, purely a matter of property law and is not concerned with reversing the defendant's unjust enrichment. In *Foskett*, a fraudulent trustee had taken money from a trust fund held by him for the claimants, mixed it with his own money in bank accounts, and used it to pay premiums on an insurance policy on his life. When he later committed suicide, the defendants (his children) were paid £1 million under the insurance policy. The claimants argued that they were entitled to a share of the £1 million proportionate to the premiums that, in breach of trust, had been paid using the trust money. Their claim succeeded before the House of Lords by a three to two majority.

Lord Millett, giving the leading speech, said, 'The transmission of a claimant's property rights from one asset to its traceable proceeds is part of our law of property, not of the law of unjust enrichment … The claimant succeeds if at all by virtue of his own title, not to reverse unjust enrichment …'[63] He later continued:

> As I have already pointed out, the purchasers seek to vindicate their property rights, not to reverse unjust enrichment … A plaintiff who brings an action in unjust enrichment must show that the defendant has been enriched at the plaintiff's expense, for he cannot have been unjustly enriched if he has not been enriched at all. But the plaintiff is not concerned to show that the defendant is in receipt of property belonging beneficially to the plaintiff or its traceable proceeds. The fact that the beneficial ownership of the property has passed to the defendant provides no defence; indeed, it is usually the very fact which founds the claim … Furthermore, a claim in unjust enrichment is subject to a change of position defence, which usually operates by reducing or extinguishing the element of enrichment. An action like the present is subject to the bona fide purchaser for value defence, which operates to clear the defendant's title.[64]

Further, Lord Browne-Wilkinson said:

> The contrary view appears to be based primarily on the ground that to give the purchasers a rateable share of the policy moneys is not to reverse an unjust

[62] Above (n 10).
[63] *Ibid*, 127.
[64] *Ibid*, 129.

> enrichment but to give the purchasers a wholly unwarranted windfall ... But this windfall is enjoyed because of the rights which the purchasers enjoy under the law of property. A man under whose land oil is discovered enjoys a very valuable windfall but no-one suggests that he, as owner of the property, is not entitled to the windfall which goes with his property by right. We are not dealing with a claim in unjust enrichment.[65]

Finally, in Lord Hoffmann's words, 'This [claim] is not based upon unjust enrichment except in the most trivial sense of that expression. It is ... a vindication of proprietary right.'[66]

It is also most disappointing that, in the latest edition of Goff and Jones, Jones has accepted this reasoning without discussing the merits of the counter-view[67] and despite the fact that, in all previous editions, Goff and Jones have adhered to the view that proprietary rights may be created to reverse unjust enrichment.

I am not suggesting that the actual decision in *Foskett* was wrong. What I am saying, first, is that it could have been satisfactorily reached applying an unjust enrichment analysis. Second, the Lords have unfortunately embraced the fiction that tracing involves the continuation of pre-existing proprietary rights from one asset to a substitute asset, whereas in reality a new proprietary right is created in the substitute asset that requires justification. Third, and most important in practice, change of position has been rejected by their Lordships in respect of proprietary remedies after tracing, whereas, in principle and policy, it should be a defence. Had the defendants on the facts of *Foskett* changed their position, they should have had a defence. And if we replay the facts of the seminal case on equitable tracing, *Re Diplock*,[68] surely what was wanted was a proprietary claim by the next-of-kin against the charities, subject to the charities' change of position defence. Yet their Lordships seem now to have it in mind, although they did not discuss *Re Diplock*, that the in rem claim belonged solely within the law of property and was not susceptible to a change of position defence. In short, incorrect results will be reached by failing to apply an unjust enrichment analysis to the proprietary claim.

A further aspect of the Birks and Chambers approach to proprietary restitution is their attempted articulation of a coherent theory as to *when* the cause of action of unjust enrichment triggers proprietary restitution, as well as the more usual personal restitution. According to their view, wherever an unjust enrichment at the claimant's expense triggers personal restitution, so too it should trigger proprietary restitution provided two additional conditions are satisfied. These conditions are: (i) the enrichment

[65] *Ibid*, 110.
[66] *Ibid*, 115.
[67] Goff and Jones (above n 4) ch 2.
[68] [1948] Ch 465.

subtracted from the claimant exists, if necessary by applying tracing rules, in an asset to which the proprietary right can attach; and (ii) the injustice arose at the moment of the defendant's receipt, rather than subsequently, so that there was never a period of time when the defendant was entitled to the enrichment. Applying this approach, mistake, duress and undue influence, for example, should and do all trigger proprietary restitution, whether through a trust or a power to revest title by rescission. On the other hand, failure of consideration, which concerns a subsequent injustice, does not and should not trigger proprietary restitution.[69] So, according to Birks and Chambers, *Re Goldcorp*[70] and *Westdeutsche Landesbank*[71] were correct in denying proprietary restitution through a resulting or constructive trust precisely because the injustice was subsequent only: the ground for restitution was failure of consideration.

I essentially agree with Birks and Chambers' theory, although I do think it helps to add that, as a matter of policy, a good reason why one would not want to allow proprietary restitution for a subsequent failure of consideration is because, at least normally, this is the classic situation where we would say that the payor has taken the risk of the payee's insolvency. Allowing proprietary restitution would therefore unacceptably undermine our law of insolvency. So if a debtor fails to repay a loan to a creditor, the creditor is not, and should not be, entitled to proprietary restitution for failure of consideration even if the debtor retains the loaned money or its traceable substitute. The creditor is an unsecured creditor and has taken the risk of the debtor's insolvency. To allow the creditor proprietary restitution would eliminate the distinction between secured and unsecured creditors.

Central to this debate about when, if at all, unjust enrichment should trigger proprietary restitution is the decision of Goulding J in *Chase Manhattan Bank NA v Israel-British Bank (London) Ltd*.[72] On 3 July 1974 by a clerical error the claimant, a New York bank, mistakenly made two payments, instead of one, of some $2 million to another New York bank, for the account of the defendant, an English bank. On 5 July 1974 the defendant knew, or should have known, of the mistake. Shortly afterwards, the defendant became insolvent. The claimant sought a declaration that the defendant became a trustee of the second $2 million payment on receipt of it on 3 July 1974. Goulding J granted that declaration. This meant that the claimant would have priority if, which did not fall to be decided by Goulding J, the claimant could show that the defendant retained the mistaken payment's traceable substitute. In reaching this decision, Goulding J thought

[69] Unless the payment was 'ring-fenced' so that the defendant was not free to use it, as in *Barclays Bank Ltd v Quistclose Investments Ltd* [1970] AC 567.
[70] [1995] 1 AC 74.
[71] Above (n 5).
[72] [1981] Ch 105.

that English law was in line with that in the United States, and he cited with approval a leading American case, *Re Berry*,[73] in which a trust of a mistaken payment had been imposed. It is also significant that Goulding J regarded the defendant's knowledge of the mistake as irrelevant.[74]

While this decision is controversial,[75] it can be justified. On the Birks and Chambers view, mistake vitiates rather than qualifies consent, so that there was never a time when the defendant was entitled to the enrichment. Moreover, the mistake meant that the claimant had not taken the risk of the defendant's insolvency. That *Chase Manhattan* was correctly decided is further supported if one extends one's examination of proprietary restitution for mistaken payments beyond trusts.[76] For example, rescission of a contract, revesting title to property in the claimant,[77] can be granted for misrepresentation[78] and formal gifts have been rescinded because of mistake.[79] Analogously, an equitable lien can be imposed for the mistaken improvement of land.[80] Perhaps most importantly, subrogation giving priority as against a subsequent lender, albeit not against all creditors, was granted by the House of Lords in *Banque Financière*[81] in which the claimant had mistakenly made a loan which benefited the subsequent lender.

Unfortunately, the House of Lords in *Westdeutsche Landesbank*[82] cast doubt on *Chase Manhattan*. In denying proprietary restitution through a resulting or constructive trust in respect of a void interest rate swap transaction, Lord Browne-Wilkinson, giving the leading speech of the majority, said that he thought the reasoning in *Chase Manhattan* was incorrect. For a trust to have arisen the conscience of the payee had to have been affected. That would only have been so once the payee knew of the payor's mistake. So while the decision might have been correct—because the payee

[73] 147 F 208 (2d Cir 1906). Several other cases in the United States have taken a similar approach. *Contra* is *Re Dow Corning Corp* 192 BR 428 (Bankr ED Mich 1996). For an excellent general discussion of the position in the United States, see A Kull, 'Restitution in Bankruptcy: Reclamation and Constructive Trust' (1998) 72 *American Bankruptcy Law Journal* 265.

[74] *Chase Manhattan* (n 72) 114.

[75] See, eg, A Tettenborn, 'Remedies for the Recovery of Money Paid by Mistake' [1980] *CLJ* 272.

[76] Within the realm of trusts, one can also regard some examples of resulting trusts imposed where an express trust has initially failed as illustrating proprietary restitution for mistake (usually of law): eg, *Morice v Bishop of Durham* (1805) 9 Ves 399 (express trust for objects of benevolence and liberality held to be void and resulting trust imposed); *Air Jamaica Ltd v Charlton* [1999] 1 WLR 1399 (pension scheme void for perpetuity and resulting trust imposed).

[77] See also rectification of a document or the land register, for mistake, where the wrong area of land has been conveyed.

[78] *Car and Universal Finance Ltd v Caldwell* [1965] 1 QB 525.

[79] *Lady Hood of Avalon v Mackinnon* [1909] 1 Ch 476.

[80] *Cooper v Phibbs* (1867) LR 2 HL 149.

[81] Above (n 8).

[82] Above (n 5).

bank knew of the payor's mistake two days after the payment and before the payee's insolvency—Goulding J's reasoning imposing a trust from the date of receipt was not. But, with respect, this emphasis on a trust only being imposed where the defendant's conscience is affected cannot be correct. It was presented as if it were an underpinning principle of all trusts. Yet an express trustee is surely a trustee from the moment property is transferred into his or her name irrespective of the trustee's own knowledge. If an aunt puts shares in the name of her niece and the niece knows nothing of what she has done, there is a resulting trust irrespective of when the niece acquires the requisite knowledge. Moreover, applying the conscience test to decide whether there should be proprietary restitution lacks justification in terms of principle or policy. If one is concerned to protect the defendant's unsecured, or even secured, creditors—which seemed to be Lord Browne-Wilkinson's primary objection to imposing a trust to effect restitution—one will not necessarily do so by insisting that the defendant knows of the mistake or other unjust factor. Applying that test, unsecured and secured creditors may or may not be able to share in a mistaken payment, depending on whether the defendant knew or did not know of the mistake before the insolvency. The law on proprietary restitution would also be rendered unacceptably uncertain, and out of line with personal restitution, if it were dependent on the claimant always establishing, perhaps at a particular moment in time, the defendant's state of mind.

Accordingly, although it appears to be the predominant view among English practitioners that, in the light of *Westdeutsche Landesbank*, *Chase Manhattan* is 'dead in the water,' I think it would be a retrograde step for that decision to be overruled.

V. FUTURE DEVELOPMENTS?

In this final part of the article I want to refer briefly to five areas where views expressed by judges or academics in the last decade suggest that we are likely to see significant judicial developments in England in the next decade—although this may be thought to be wishful thinking on my behalf!

First, it can surely only be a short time before English law finally accepts overtly that money can be recovered for a partial as well as a total failure of consideration. The arguments in principle for this move are well-rehearsed and I will not repeat them here. Certainly where money is passing both ways—so that there is no difficulty of apportionment—there is no reason to confine restitution to where no part of the counter-performance has been rendered, which is what the insistence on total failure requires. But even where money is being paid for services or goods, partial failure should trigger restitution, because the courts are perfectly capable of assessing the payee's counter-claim for the value of the services or goods rendered. In a number of cases in the twentieth century, the courts have taken an artificial construction of what constitutes total failure—eg in *Rowland v Divall*,[83] *Rover International Ltd v Cannon Films Sales Ltd (No 3)*[84] and *DO Ferguson & Associates v Sohl*[85]—or have adopted the unhelpful idea of there being a ground for restitution of absence of consideration,[86] or have automatically regarded money paid under a void contract as constituting a total failure,[87] all of which have served to disguise the fact that restitution was in reality being grounded on a partial failure of consideration. Indeed, in two cases in the last decade Lord Goff referred to the criticisms of the total failure requirement and expressly indicated that this restriction should be removed. In *Goss v Chilcott*,[88] restitution of money loaned by the claimant to the defendants was awarded despite the fact that two repayments of interest had been made. The Privy Council considered that there had been a total failure of consideration, but Lord Goff went on to say that 'even if part of the capital sum had been repaid, the law would not hesitate to hold that the balance of the loan outstanding would be recoverable on the ground of failure of consideration, for at least in those cases in which apportionment can be carried out without difficulty, the law will allow partial recovery on this ground.'[89] And in *Westdeutsche Landesbank* Lord Goff said:

> There has long been a desire among restitution lawyers to escape from the unfortunate effects of the so-called rule that money is only recoverable at common law on the ground of failure of consideration where the failure is total, by reformulating the rule upon a more principled basis; and signs that this will in due course be done are appearing in judgments throughout the common law world, as appropriate cases arise for decision.[90]

Second, it can again surely only be a short time before there is a fusion of common law and equitable tracing rules so as to enable equity's more generous rules to be applied in a common law claim. Our understanding of tracing has been considerably advanced over the last decade through the work of Smith and Birks.[91] They have emphasised that there is a difference between tracing and claiming. The rules of tracing tell us whether replacement property counts in law as a substitute for the claimant's original property, and

[83] [1923] 2 KB 500.
[84] [1989] 1 WLR 912.
[85] (1992) 62 BLR 95.
[86] *Westdeutsche Landesbank Girozentrale v Islington London BC* [1994] 4 All ER 890 (Hobhouse J).
[87] *Guinness Mahon & Co Ltd v Kensington and Chelsea Royal London BC* [1999] QB 215.
[88] [1996] AC 788.
[89] *Ibid*, 798.
[90] *Westdeutsche Landesbank* (above n 5) 682. The decision in *Goss* (above n 88) was handed down the day after that in *Westdeutsche Landesbank*.
[91] L Smith (above n 30); P Birks, 'Mixing and Tracing: Property and Restitution' (1992) 45 *CLP* 69.

its importance in the law of restitution therefore goes to whether the defendant's receipt or retention of property was *at the expense of the claimant*. The tracing rules do not in themselves determine whether the claimant has a valid restitutionary claim against the defendant. Other elements (the 'unjust factor,' the defendant's enrichment, and the non-applicability of defences) must also be satisfied. Once one accepts that the tracing rules go to whether an enrichment was at the claimant's expense, and deal with whether property stands as a substitute for other property, it is obvious that there can be no rational reason for having different tracing rules at common law and in equity. This approach to tracing is not only widely accepted by commentators but has also been strongly supported in obiter dicta of Lords Steyn and Millett in *Foskett*.[92]

Third, it seems likely that the area of the law traditionally referred to as 'knowing receipt' will properly be absorbed into the mainstream of the law of restitution, by recognising that liability rests on the cause of action of unjust enrichment. Like other analogous examples of that cause of action, such as mistake, liability should be strict, subject to defences, most importantly change of position and bona fide purchase. This of course is not the present law. As laid down by the Court of Appeal in *BCCI (Overseas) Ltd v Akindele*[93] the test for liability is rather one of whether it is unconscionable for the recipient to retain the benefit of the receipt. But unconscionability in this area, as in so many others, is vague and malleable, and merely serves to obscure what the courts are really doing. Building on the earlier work of Birks,[94] the case for strict liability subject to defences has been powerfully put by Lord Nicholls, writing extra-judicially.[95] Again the details of the argument are well-known and well-rehearsed and will not be repeated here. Some of us had hoped that the House of Lords would be able to make the decisive step in *Twinsectra Ltd v Yardley*[96] but unfortunately knowing receipt was not in issue on the appeal to the Lords. All we were therefore left with is the helpful obiter dicta of Lord Millett. He said of 'knowing receipt:'

> There is no basis for requiring actual knowledge of the breach of trust, let alone dishonesty, as a condition of liability. Constructive notice is sufficient, and may not even be necessary. There is powerful academic support for the proposition that the liability of the recipient is the same as in other cases of restitution, that is to say strict but subject to a change of position defence.[97]

Fourth, it seems inevitable that there will be a steady trickle of cases in the next few years working out the parameters of the House of Lords'

[92] Above (n 10).
[93] [2001] Ch 437.
[94] Eg P Birks, 'Misdirected Funds: Restitution from the Recipient' [1989] *LMCLQ* 296.
[95] 'Knowing Receipt: The Need for a New Landmark' in Cornish (above n 28) 230–45.
[96] [2002] 2 AC 164.
[97] *Ibid*, para 105.

decision in *Attorney-General v Blake*,[98] which for the first time recognised that an account of profits—or, as some of us still prefer to call the remedy, 'restitutionary damages'—can be awarded for breach of contract. Their Lordships made it clear that this should be an exceptional remedy to be awarded only when all other remedies for breach of contract are inadequate. But 'inadequacy' is an open-ended concept and it remains unclear just how exceptional the remedy is to be. We have already had one case, *Esso Petroleum Co Ltd v Niad*,[99] in which at first instance Sir Andrew Morritt V-C applied *Blake* to a breach of a commercial contract. In others such a remedy has been refused.[100] Although their Lordships in *Blake* regarded the question of whether the breach of contract was cynical and deliberate as not in itself decisive, it seems likely that this will be the determining factor for awarding an account of profits, along with the difficulty in assessing compensatory damages. That we are likely to have litigation in this sphere was recognised by the Lordships themselves. As Lord Steyn said, 'Exceptions to the general principle that there is no remedy for disgorgement of profits against a contract breaker are best hammered out on the anvil of concrete cases.'[101]

Fifth, the appropriate choice of law rule for claims in the law of restitution remains an open matter. If we confine ourselves to where unjust enrichment is the cause of action, and put to one side restitution for wrongs, there is support in the English courts, most recently in *Kuwait Oil Tanker Co v Al Bader*,[102] for the application of Rule 200 in Dicey and Morris.[103] As a default rule, this states that the proper law of the obligation to make restitution is the law of the country where the enrichment occurred. But most commentators who have discussed this disagree with Dicey and Morris' rule, and even the commentary within Dicey and Morris is lukewarm in its support of it.[104] Panagopoulos has succinctly summarised the arguments against the place of enrichment as follows:

> It is arbitrary; it gives a deceptively simple *locus*, yet it is often difficult to determine; it may not necessarily be connected with either of the parties, or events; and, finally, but most importantly, it can be manipulated by *mala fides* parties, who might ensure that they are 'enriched' in jurisdictions with rules that will suit their aims.[105]

[98] Above (n 11).
[99] 22 November 2001, unreported.
[100] *WWF World Wide Fund for Nature v World Wrestling Federation Entertainment Inc* [2002] FSR 32; affd without considering this point, [2002] FSR 33 (CA). See also *AB Corporation v CD Company, The Sine Nomine* [2002] 1 Lloyd's Rep 805.
[101] *Blake* (above n 11) 291.
[102] [2000] 2 All ER (Comm) 271.
[103] L Collins (ed), *Dicey and Morris on The Conflict of Laws*, 13th edn (London, Sweet & Maxwell, 2000).
[104] *Ibid*, paras 34–030, 34–036.
[105] Panagopoulos (above n 32) 166. See also A Briggs, *The Conflict of Laws* (Oxford, Oxford University Press, 2002) 198.

However, there is less unanimity among commentators as to what the correct choice of law rule or rules should be. What is clear is that choice of law in relation to the law of restitution raises a number of difficult issues, several of which await authoritative resolution by the courts, so that continuing litigation is inevitable.

VI. CONCLUSION

The last decade has been an eventful one for the English law of restitution. In this article I have sought to provide some flavour of the developments by: first, giving a snapshot of the most important cases and academic writings; second, concentrating in greater detail on three central areas—mistaken payments, change of position and proprietary restitution; and third, looking at five areas where judicial or academic views in the last decade suggest that there will be significant movements in the near future. No doubt the pace of development will slow down the further one advances from the path-breaking decision in *Lipkin Gorman*. But the pace of development in the last decade has been truly remarkable. As Dannemann has powerfully expressed it, 'Preceded and helped by scholarly work, English courts have unfrozen the law of restitution and have, particularly over the last ten years, achieved a rapid development which might have taken a century in other areas of the law.'[106]

[106] G Dannemann, 'Unjust Enrichment by Transfer: Some Comparative Remarks' (2001) *Texas Law Review* 1837, 1843.

3

Unjust Enrichment (Dis)Contented

G.H.L. FRIDMAN

THE LAW IS not antipathetic to enrichment. Indeed our society, which is both engendered and protected by the law, favours it, provided it is 'just.' What then is 'unjust' enrichment? The idea that some enrichments can be unjust and therefore unworthy of recognition and protection is one that goes back at least as far as the assize of *novel disseisin* if not before. Such unjust enrichments, however, do not seem to be what Borins JA referred to when, in *Campbell v Campbell*, he spoke of 'the venerable equitable principle of unjust enrichment.'[1] What he and other judges and academic writers mean by 'unjust enrichment' is its employment in the context of the modern, if not indeed only recently invented, law of restitution. To some restitution is founded upon, and serves to remedy, unjust enrichment.[2] There are those, however who deny that the concept of 'unjust enrichment' has a role to play.[3] For them the expression is meaningless, barmecidal, a chimera. Indeed it is open to question whether the concept of unjust enrichment is indeed a 'venerable equitable principle.'

Despite the antiquity of the case law which forms the basis of the modern law of restitution, the idea that 'unjust enrichment' was the explanation of, and unifying principle of those cases emerged only in the twentieth century. In Canada this occurred in *Deglman v Guaranty Trust Co of Canada*;[4] in England in *Lipkin Gorman (a firm) v Karpnale Ltd*;[5] in Australia in

[1] (1999) 173 DLR (4th) 270 (CA) 277.
[2] See eg, P Birks, *An Introduction to the Law of Restitution* (Oxford, Oxford University Press, 1985) 17; A Burrows, *The Law of Restitution* (London, Butterworths, 1993) 1; G Virgo, *The Principles of the Law of Restitution* (Oxford, Oxford University Press, 1999) 6. For an earlier opinion, see A Coleman, 'The Concept of Unjust Enrichment in English Law' (1979) 10 *Cambrian Law Review* 8. But has Professor Birks changed his mind? See Virgo (above n 2) 7, fn 22.
[3] See eg, S Hedley, *Restitution: Its Division and Ordering* (London, Sweet & Maxwell, 2001) chs 7–8; J Dietrich, *Restitution: A New Perspective* (Leichhardt, NSW, Federation Press, 1998). See also the references in the judgment of Gummow J in *Roxborough v Rothmans of Pall Mall* (2001) 76 ALJR 203 (HCA) 218, fn 82.
[4] [1954] SCR 725, [1954] 3 DLR 785 (SCC).
[5] [1991] 2 AC 248 (HL). See also *Woolwich Equitable Building Society v IRC (No 2)* [1993] AC 70 (HL) 196–97 where Lord Browne-Wilkinson stated that in English law there is a general

Pavey & Matthews Pty Ltd v Paul.[6] Once this happened it was inevitable that the search for the elucidation of this expression would lead to the emergence of a rift between those who favour a stricter approach to legal concepts and those who are content to leave such concepts as open and flexible as possible. One group would prefer to explain and expound restitution not on the basis of 'unjust enrichment' but by reference to specific, established instances of recovery. The other regards that as too limiting and antagonistic to the development of the law. It is another example of the age-old conflict between certainty and flexibility.

In *Peel (Regional Municipality) v Canada*[7] McLachlin J drew attention to this when she referred to various 'tensions' manifest in the evolving state of the law of restitution. One set of such tensions was the difference between what she termed the traditional 'category' approach and a second so-called 'principled' approach. The distinction between the two is obvious. In the event she concluded,[8] in what might be referred to as a typically Canadian solution, that the court must choose a middle path which acknowledges the importance of proceeding on general principles but seeks to reconcile the principles with the established categories of recovery. Despite these brave words, my personal view is that it is far from clear whether there is, or indeed can ever be, a general principle or set of principles regulating restitutionary recovery, and, in particular whether consideration of such recovery in terms of 'unjust enrichment' serves any valid, useful purpose. Discussion of this, I suggest, raises the spectre, long banished from respectable legal society, of 'quasi-contract,' as well as the age-old dichotomy and conflict between common law and equity.[9]

What I once referred to as 'the quasi-contractual aspects of unjust enrichment'[10] comprise various categories recognised by the common law as justifying recovery of money. The first of these was where the one seeking to recover never had any intention of enriching the defendant but unwittingly did so by reason of a mistake or compulsion. The second was where the one seeking recovery originally intended to enrich the other party but that intention was foiled or rendered nugatory by reason of a subsequent failure of consideration or the illegality of the contract in performance of which the payment was made. In the third category came situations where

rule giving a plaintiff a right of recovery from a defendant who has been unjustly enriched at the plaintiff's expense. See also, the cases cited by Virgo (above n 2) 7, fn 20.

[6] (1987) 162 CLR 221 (HCA).
[7] [1992] 3 SCR 762, (1992) 98 DLR (4th) 140 (SCC) 151–52 (herein cited to the DLR).
[8] *Ibid*, 153.
[9] The fusion of which has recently been advocated by A Burrows, *Hochelaga Lectures 2001—Fusing Common Law and Equity: Remedies, Restitution and Reform* (Hong Kong, Sweet & Maxwell, 2002).
[10] GHL Fridman, 'The Quasi-Contractual Aspects of Unjust Enrichment' (1956) 34 *Canadian Bar Review* 393.

payment was made to a third party, thereby benefiting the defendant, though without a request for such payment from the latter, in order for the claimant to regain his or her own goods from that third party or because the claimant and defendant were under a common liability to the one to whom payment was made. The fourth category included situations where the party seeking recovery conferred a benefit on the defendant, at the latter's request, although there was no valid, enforceable contractual obligation to do so on the party who conferred such benefit.

All these different reasons for permitting recovery were once supported doctrinally by the assertion that in every such instance there was an implied contract between the parties by virtue of which the defendant was obliged to reimburse, repay or recompense the claimant.[11] Of course such contract was not real; it was 'simulated' or, to employ a modern phrase, it was 'virtual.' In describing these situations, treatise writers invoked, improperly and metaphorically, the Roman concept of quasi-contract. These were therefore obligations arising '*quasi ex contractu*,' in contrast with those which arose *ex contractu* or *ex delicto*. Of course they were nothing of the sort. However explaining these instances in this way enabled writers, and the courts, to avoid having to fall back on some vague idea of what Lord Sumner called 'justice between man and man,'[12] which invited courts to indulge in what Lord Justice Scrutton later called 'well-meaning sloppiness of thought.'[13] In other words, nobody, at least until very recent times, considered that the underlying principle that united these various situations and provided them with a legal doctrinal provenance was the notion of 'unjust enrichment.' Indeed as recently as 1977, a quarter of a century after the decision in *Deglman*, Lord Diplock said that 'no general doctrine of unjust enrichment [is] recognised in English law.'[14] In stating this he was echoing the language of Lord Greene MR who said in 1939:

> Our law did advance in certain respects some ways towards recognizing a doctrine of unjust enrichment, but the process was stopped short, leaving certain anomalies embedded in the law.[15]

Those 'anomalies,' which today are not conceived of as such, owed nothing to any idea of unjust enrichment. Nor, ultimately, did they owe their existence to the ideas given utterance to in the famous judgment of Lord Mansfield in *Moses v Macferlan*.[16] Lord Mansfield regarded the action of

[11] They form 'the precedents which make up the legal matrix of restitution law': K Mason and J Carter, *Restitution Law in Australia* (North Ryde, NSW, Butterworths, 1995) 73.
[12] *Baylis v Bishop of London* [1913] 1 Ch 127 (CA) 140.
[13] *Holt v Markham* [1923] 1 KB 504 (CA) 573.
[14] In *Orakpo v Manson Investments Ltd* [1977] 3 All ER 1 (HL) 7.
[15] In *Re Cleadon Trust* [1939] Ch 286 (CA) 307.
[16] (1760) 2 Burr 1005, (1760) 97 ER 676 (CA), a case recently given new prominence by Gummow J of the High Court of Australia in *Roxborough v Rothmans* (n 3) 218–22.

indebitatus assumpsit, through which what became known as common law quasi-contractual claims were asserted, as an equitable action. Despite his attempts, however, it never became the equivalent of a bill in equity.[17] In other words the action from which, historically though not doctrinally, the modern law of restitution is descended cannot be considered to be part of the technical law of equity. Yet it seemed to be derived from or based upon the same underlying principles that, from early times, brought about the evolution of what ultimately became the strict law of equity. Even Baron Parke in the leading case on recovery of money paid under a mistake, *Kelly v Solari*,[18] spoke of it being 'against conscience' for the defendant to retain the money. However it would be hard to consider Baron Parke, described by Chief Baron Pollock as 'the greatest legal pedant that I believe ever existed,'[19] as a judge who was prepared to cast precedent to the winds and decide cases by the invocation of some broad, general non-technical equitable notion such as conscience or unjust benefit or enrichment. Not the Baron Parke, who said, in *Mirehouse v Rennell*: 'Our common law system consists in the applying to new combinations of circumstances those rules of law which we derive from legal principles and judicial precedents.'[20]

The common law courts, in effect, abandoned Lord Mansfield's approach. The later decisions rested recovery upon the fiction of an implied promise (which Holdsworth[21] preferred because, inter alia, it provided an element of a relationship between the parties that was wanting in a test such as natural justice, *aequum et bonum* or 'unjust benefit'). Thus, the possibly incipient idea of unjust benefit or unjust enrichment contained in the judgments of Lord Mansfield never bore fruit in the subsequent common law developments. In short, therefore, it is difficult, if not impossible to find any support for a 'venerable equitable principle of unjust enrichment' in the common law instances of what we now look upon as exemplars of restitutionary recovery.

Perhaps, then, it is from the line of cases dealing with a trustee's making of a profit or personal gain from his position as trustee, which began in *Keech v Sandford*[22] at the beginning of the eighteenth century, that the idea of unjust enrichment seeped into the law. As that case revealed, no wrongful act, in the sense of a fraudulent, careless or intentional misuse of position or office, need have been committed by the trustee to give rise to the liability to disgorge (unlike the conduct of the defendant in *Attorney-General v Blake*,[23] the decision in which has apparently sent shudders down

[17] W Holdsworth, *A History of English Law* (London, Methuen & Co, 1903) vol 12, 543.
[18] (1841) 9 M & W 54, 152 ER 25 (Ex D).
[19] Quoted in Holdsworth (above n 17) 153, fn 5.
[20] (1833) 1 Cl & Fin 546, 6 ER 1015 (HL) 1022.
[21] Above (n 17) 545.
[22] (1726) Sel Cas T King 6, 25 ER 223 (Ch).
[23] [2001] 1 AC 268 (HL).

some academic or practising lawyers' spines).[24] It was not the existence of any mens rea on the part of the trustee that triggered recovery by the cestui que trust. It was the plain fact of enrichment of the trustee at the expense of the cestui que trust. Here is the germ of the whole doctrine of unjust enrichment: the subconscious *fons et origo* of the enunciation of the doctrine by the Supreme Court of Canada in *Pettkus v Becker*,[25] which antedated by several years the very similar statement of the doctrine by Professor Birks.[26]

Central to this idea of unjust enrichment is the absence of any wrongdoing in any of the traditional common law senses, namely acting with the intention of causing harm or loss, acting intentionally knowing that the consequence of such action would be the causing of harm or loss to another, and acting negligently so as to cause harm or loss in breach of some duty to take care. Innocence of any such conduct would not excuse or legitimize the making of a gain at the expense of another. However, before any conclusion as to liability to disgorge such gain could be made it was essential to establish that, in the circumstances, the making of such gain was 'unjust.' It is clear from what has just been said that the meaning of 'unjust' was not to be elucidated by inquiring as to the intentions, motives or foresight of the party making the gain. 'Unjust' was to be construed as meaning whatever connotation a court would give to the word. This, however, created a problem. Was the enrichment in issue 'unjust' according to some legal, moral or social reasoning or principles? Or was it 'unjust' only because, in the circumstances, a court decided that conduct of the sort involved *should* be considered to be 'unjust,' despite the prior belief and understanding that there was nothing inherently reprehensible about the retention of the enrichment by the party enriched?

In *Keech*, the Lord Chancellor's decision was designed to protect an infant cestui que trust, even though the trustee had not set out to defraud or deprive the infant of the benefit of the lease. The aim of the court was to lay down a rule that would ensure that beneficiaries under a trust could not be cheated by something done, albeit in good faith, by a trustee, whose office was supposed to be exercised purely and simply for the benefit and advantage of the cestui que trust. By so doing the court was enforcing the underlying policy, indeed rationale, for any intervention by the Court of Chancery. In the common law situations, such as recovery of money paid under mistake or compulsion, the court was giving effect to a different policy, the refusal to uphold and maintain intact transactions that were inherently unreasonable and unfair and savoured, if not of fraud, at any rate of sharp practice.

[24] G Jones, *Hochelaga Lectures 2000—Unresolved Problems in the Law of Restitution* (Hong Kong, Sweet & Maxwell, 2001) 28–49. See also P Shieh, 'Brief Thoughts on *Attorney-General v Blake*—A Practitioner's View' in Jones (n 24) 69 and B Ho, 'The Significance of *Attorney-General v Blake* for Legal Scholarship' in Jones (n 24) 75.
[25] [1980] SCR 834, (1980) 117 DLR (3d) 257 (SCC).
[26] Birks (above n 2) 16–22.

Despite the fact that courts of equity and courts of common law operated on different principles and in different ways, there is no great difference between the approach favoured by courts of equity towards trustees benefiting themselves—later extended to cover defendants who were not express but 'constructive' trustees—and payors of money to or for the benefit of the defendant when such payment was not justified by contract, statute or otherwise. In both common law and equity, protection of the innocent of whom advantage was taken was the driving force behind the granting of a remedy, but these specific instances of liability were based upon settled principles rather than generalities. It is no misconception to assert that in this respect nothing has changed.

Prior to the judgment of Lord Greene in *Re Cleadon Trust*[27] the common law situations were not generally referred to as cases of unjust enrichment. The credit, or blame as the case may be, for the invocation of this expression to describe what went on in these cases must be attributed to Lord Wright in the *Fibrosa* case.[28] His Lordship used this term to collate those instances in which one person benefited at the expense of another in circumstances which rendered it, in Baron Parke's emotive phrase, 'against conscience' for such benefit to be kept. Notwithstanding Lord Wright's embrace of the expression, in England and Australia 'quasi-contract,' a term that bore no hint of the idea of unjust enrichment, rooted as it was in the historical common law categories of recovery, remained the expression of choice to denote this area of the law. JHC Morris lectured (to me and many others) on quasi-contract in Oxford in the 1940s; Winfield produced his little book, *The Law of Quasi-contracts*[29] in 1952 (a title also used by Munkman[30]); Stoljar employed the same title in Australia for his book in 1964.[31]

By way of contrast, however, the Supreme Court of Canada, as early as 1952, embraced and adopted Lord Wright's concept of unjust enrichment as a ground for recovery in *Deglman*,[32] which provided the start for a striking development of this branch of the law long before the highest courts in England and Australia were prepared to acknowledge what had been happening to the old common law categories of quasi-contractual recovery. Indeed the speed with which Canadian courts seized on the opening provided by the Supreme Court in the succeeding years—ably demonstrated, at least up to 1964, by Professor Angus—was remarkable.[33] Since then the scope of recovery has been considerably broadened, to an extent not

[27] Above (n 15).
[28] *Fibrosa Spolka Akcyjna v Fairbairn Lawson Combe Barbour Ltd* [1943] AC 32 (HL) 61.
[29] P Winfield, *The Law of Quasi-contracts* (London, Sweet & Maxwell, 1952).
[30] JH Munkman, *The Law of Quasi-contracts* (London, Pitman, 1950).
[31] SJ Stoljar, *The Law of Quasi-contracts* (Sydney, Law Book Co, 1964).
[32] Above (n 4).
[33] W Angus, 'Restitution in Canada since the Deglman Case' (1964) 42 *Canadian Bar Review* 529.

entirely accepted in England, although Australian judges appear to be more on the Canadian wavelength in this regard. Perhaps the aspect of this part of the law that has been taken to greatest lengths in Canada concerns cases in which a spouse or non-spousal partner seeks compensation for domestic, or similar services performed for the other spouse or partner. The House of Lords required something akin to a contract or some kind of agreement to such effect before relief would be granted.[34] Canadian courts require only that the services be given and resulted in a 'benefit,' in the economic sense, to the one who owned the property whereon, or in respect of which, the services were rendered.[35] In light of what is said above about *Keech* it is worthy of note that in these, and other cases which do not involve claims between spouses or men and women cohabiting without being married, the Supreme Court of Canada has embraced the idea that, where a restitutionary claim has been made out, an appropriate remedy is not only the payment of money, as is usually ordered in restitution cases, but the imposition on the defendant of a constructive trust, the remedy available in the decisions which stem from *Keech*. The adoption of an equitable remedy suggests that the origins of an instance of restitutionary recovery, whether in common law or equity, is of no consequence. In situations when relief is justified, it can take the form of common law 'damages,' as repayment has been termed in some cases, or an equitable 'constructive trust,' giving proprietary rights or interests in land.

Whatever was in the past the basis for the determination of a claim, relief will now be determined by the application of the three-fold test enunciated by Dickson J in *Rathwell v Rathwell*[36] and ensconced in Canadian law by the subsequent decisions in *Pettkus*[37] and *Sorochan v Sorochan*.[38] That test involves: (1) an enrichment; (2) a corresponding deprivation; and (3) the absence of any juristic reason for the enrichment. While the nature of 'enrichment' is obviously pertinent to the meaning and scope of 'unjust enrichment,' it is what is 'unjust' that is the element that involves the greatest difficulty for anyone attempting to analyse the meaning of and give content to 'unjust enrichment.'

In this regard the third aspect of the Canadian test of recovery, absence of a juristic reason for the enrichment, may provide a means to explain when an enrichment is 'unjust.' However there is no clear definition, if indeed any is possible, of what is a 'juristic reason' for an enrichment, although there are decisions which have held certain situations to amount, or not to amount, to such a reason. The phrase 'absence of juristic reasons'

[34] *Gissing v Gissing* [1971] AC 886 (HL).
[35] See below (nn 36–38).
[36] [1978] 2 SCR 436, 83 DLR (3d) 289 (SCC).
[37] Above (n 25).
[38] [1986] 2 SCR 38, 29 DLR (4th) 1 (SCC).

employed by Dickson CJ has been discussed and criticised, with some justification, by Professor Lionel Smith.[39] Indeed, it can be suggested, 'absence of a juristic reason,' like 'unjust enrichment,' is an indefinable notion. Both phrases or expressions seem to be examples of what Professor Julius Stone called 'a category of meaningless reference.'[40]

The more positive, optimistic response of McLachlin J in *Peel*[41] was referred to earlier. Subsequently, in *Peter v Beblow*[42] the same judge, speaking for herself and four other members of the court, held that the absence of a juristic reason for an enrichment properly raised for consideration, as it was put by the Ontario Court of Appeal in *Garland v Consumers' Gas Co*,[43] moral and policy questions. Hence the test of the absence of a juristic reason for enrichment is 'flexible.' The factors to be considered may vary with the situation before the court. Thus the relevant factors will be different in a case involving claims between different levels of government from those in a family case.[44] However, said McLachlin J, in every case, 'the fundamental concern is the legitimate expectation of the parties.'[45] However, she made clear that a subsidiary question is also whether public policy supported the enrichment.

In the context of a claim for 'spousal services' provided by a non-spouse it was argued that public policy did support the enrichment because the woman by cohabiting with the man had assumed a common law or equitable obligation to provide such services. Furthermore, it was argued that provision of such services should not be regarded as giving rise to legal claims nor, in a marital or quasi-marital relationship, to equitable claims. These arguments were rejected on two grounds. First, domestic services were no longer distinguishable economically from other contributions, such as payment towards a mortgage. Second, there were decisions of the courts along such lines.[46]

This case appears to recognise, therefore, that an enrichment will be unjust if there is no juristic reason for it: and that the determination of the existence or non-existence of a juristic reason for an enrichment depends upon factors that are so flexible, varied, and differing from case to case, that it may not be possible to do more than refer, as McLachlin J did in *Peel*, to 'injustice' and what is 'fair and just.'[47] *Ignotum per ignotius*.[48]

[39] L Smith, 'The Mystery of "Juristic Reason"' (2000) 12 *Supreme Court Law Review* 211.
[40] J Stone, *Legal System and Lawyers' Reasoning* (Stanford, Stanford University Press, 1964) 241–46, 339–41.
[41] Above (n 7).
[42] [1993] 1 SCR 980, (1993) 101 DLR (4th) 621 (SCC) 644–45 (herein cited to the DLR).
[43] (2002) 57 OR (3d) 127 (CA) 149.
[44] *Ibid*, 164–69 (Borins JA).
[45] *Peter* (above n 42) 645.
[46] *Ibid*, 646–48.
[47] Also quoted in *Garland* (above n 43) 150.
[48] An explanation that is more obscure than the thing to be explained.

Or, to put it another way, given the references to morality and policy in these judgments, we seem to be in the realm of 'palm-tree' justice, despite McLachlin J's criticism in *Peter* of the 'tendency on the part of some to view the action for unjust enrichment as a device for doing whatever may seem fair between the parties.'[49] In the rush to do substantive justice, she continued, 'the principles are sometimes forgotten.' By which, as the context suggests, she was referring to moral or policy questions. But underlying her remarks, in that case and in the earlier decision in *Peel*, it is not too imaginative, I suggest, to hear an echo of the original natural law principle, a moral rule, as stated by Pomponius, '*Jure naturae aequum est neminem cum alterius detrimento et injuria fieri locupletiorem*,'[50] that is to say that it is equitable according to nature that no one enrich themselves unjustly to the detriment of another.

There is a pronounced tendency on the part of the Supreme Court of Canada to state that legal issues can be settled by the application of 'policy.' Such comments were made in the cases concerned with whether a sexual assault by an employee was committed in the course of that employee's employment.[51] It is noteworthy that when the House of Lords had to deal with the same legal issue it was pointedly said that the question was to be resolved by reference to principle, ie the precedents, not by some vague, general notion of 'policy.'[52] It may be thought that as far as unjust enrichment is concerned there is more scope for the invocation of policy to decide questions given that the law of restitution is still in the process of evolution, whereas 'course of employment' for the purposes of vicarious tort liability is something that has been thrashed out in detail by a multitude of cases from which clear principles can be deduced. Frankly, I do not see the difference. If it is unsafe to rely on 'policy' in one area, it is equally unsafe to do so in another. However that is to assume that the court in question wishes to achieve certainty and clarity rather than the sort of flexibility that will permit it to do virtually whatever it likes on whatever so-called 'policy' grounds it chooses to discover or, perhaps, invent.

There is some similarity between the modern evolution of the tort of negligence and that of the *soi-disant* action for unjust enrichment. The former began with the decision in *Donoghue v Stevenson*,[53] just as the latter, as previously noted, began at various times in Canada, England and Australia. Following *Donoghue v Stevenson* two schools of thought emerged. Some considered that the decision created a general principle of liability for negligence capable of being applied, virtually limitlessly, to new situations. Others held the view that the case simply added a new category of liability

[49] Above (n 42) 643.
[50] Pomp. *Digest* 23, 3, 6.2.
[51] *Bazley v Curry* [1999] 2 SCR 534, (1999) 174 DLR (4th) 45 (SCC).
[52] *Lister v Hesley Hall Ltd* [2001] 2 All ER 769 (HL).
[53] [1932] AC 562 (HL).

for negligence to those already recognised by the law of torts. This dichotomy, which I and others heard about in the lectures of Theodore Tyler of Balliol long, long ago, is now defunct as a result of more recent developments in the law of negligence. However, decades after *Donoghue v Stevenson* there remains uncertainty about the true test for the existence of a duty of care and, in consequence, for the scope of liability for negligent behaviour. In this regard, I suggest, as I believe have others, that there is a parallel between the tort of negligence and restitution for unjust enrichment.

The categories of restitution, like those of negligence, may never be closed.[54] But that does not mean that every claim for restitution, any more than every allegation that the tort of negligence has been committed, will be granted or admitted by the courts. However, just as the rationale for a finding that the tort of negligence has been committed depends on whether the defendant owed the plaintiff a duty of care—and the test of such a duty continues to create problems for courts and to result in differences between the Supreme Court of Canada, the House of Lords and the High Court of Australia—so the test for restitution remains a matter of dispute between those self-same courts, even though they all employ the expression 'unjust enrichment' in their search for a governing principle.

What I would propose is that an 'unjust enrichment' for this purpose may be derived from two sources. The first, as McLachlin CJ suggested in the *Peel* case, embraces all those categories contained in precedents, stretching back hundred of years, according to which recovery, reimbursement or restitution is permitted on a variety of different grounds. The second source is not, as McLachlin CJ suggested, some general principle or principles. Instead the second source comprehends cases and situations where a court recognises a new category of recovery, reimbursement or restitution, by extension of, or analogy with an existing category.[55]

Such recognition was attempted, unsuccessfully, in *Peel*[56] in respect of the payment of money by one level of government which then tried to recover it from another level of government on the ground that the latter was properly responsible for the payments in issue. In the event it was held that this was neither a true case, nor an analogous instance of payment of money under compulsion. Restitution was denied. On the other hand in *Roxborough v Rothmans of Pall Mall Australia*[57] a new ground was recognised. The appellants' claim for recovery of money paid as part of the price

[54] *James More & Sons Ltd v University of Ottawa* (1974) 49 DLR (3d) 666 (Ont HCJ) 676 (Morden J).

[55] The astute reader may see in this statement more than a hint of Dworkin's theory of judicial action that treats what judges do as akin to various writers following on chapters written by several writers before and continuing the story along the lines of, and faithful to, the chapters composed by the preceding writers; see R Dworkin, *Law's Empire* (Cambridge, Massachusetts, Belknap Press, 1986).

[56] Above (n 7).

[57] Above (n 3).

for tobacco under invalid tax legislation was successful. This was on the ground that, while there was no total failure of consideration, a partial failure would justify recovery where the consideration that failed was severable. Here the High Court of Australia was applying a settled instance of recovery to slightly different circumstances. But, as Gummow J explained, this was not because of the application of any notion of 'unjust enrichment' but because of the existence of precedents from which it was possible to derive a new example of restitutionary recovery. As he said, citing an American writer, 'the rules of restitution developed much like the rules of equity. Restitution arose to avoid unjust results in specific cases—as a series of innovations to fill gaps in the rest of the law.'[58]

Unlike McLachlin J, whose views have been referred to earlier, Gummow J was not enthusiastic about invoking a doctrine of 'unjust enrichment' to explain the basis for the law's intervention in this, or any other case where restitution is granted. Nor is any enthusiasm for unjust enrichment to be found in the Australian case of *Cauvin v Philip Morris*[59] when a representative tobacco consumer attempted to recover the very tax money that was recovered by the tobacco company in *Roxborough*. And in a recent New Zealand case, *Bomac Laboratories Ltd v F Hoffman-LaRoche Ltd*,[60] the action was allowed to proceed not, it would seem, on the basis of there being in New Zealand a discrete cause of action for unjust enrichment but on the ground that the claim in issue fell within one of the traditionally recognised categories.

Such decisions and language, I would suggest, point to the difference between the Canadian and other approaches to this vexed area of the law. The Canadian Supreme Court is an activist court, not only in relation to constitutional, criminal or public law issues, but also, which I regard as equally as telling and a cause for concern among lawyers, in relation to matters of private, civil law. That approach to the determination of cases not only encourages 'judicial legislation,' it can also lead to uncertainty. In relation to restitution, the Supreme Court's views on 'unjust enrichment' may permit lower courts considerable flexibility and leeway in how they deal with litigation in this branch of the law—which without doubt will be commendable to some. Others, however, will be more apprehensive about what can happen when the classical structure of the older law is discarded in favour of notions that have an obvious, but superficial, appeal in these days when, it might appear, the plaintiff, like the customer, is always right.

[58] *Ibid*, 218.
[59] [2002] NSWSC 736.
[60] (2002) 7 NZBLC 103 (HC).

4

Unjust Enrichment and Unconscionability in Australia: A False Dichotomy?

MICHAEL BRYAN*

I. INTRODUCTION

THE PRINCIPAL AIM of this article is to describe and evaluate the model of unjust enrichment applied by Australian courts today. That model differs in important respects from the structure adopted by other countries, including Canada. The differences will be explained in the next section of the article, which provides a sketch of the history of the High Court's recognition of unjust enrichment and an assessment of the role of the concept in contemporary Australian law. But the real purpose of the article is to examine more closely what both Australian writers and external commentators take to be the most characteristic feature of its private law, namely the extensive application of equitable principles, and specifically 'conscience-based' doctrines, to award relief which in other systems would be granted, if at all, on other grounds. The issue is central to an understanding of the law of unjust enrichment in Australia since the existence of a vital conscience-derived equity is generally considered to be one of the reasons why the unjust enrichment principle is invoked less frequently than in other common law countries.

Speaking very generally, most Australian commentators have applauded the focus of Australian law on the avoidance of unconscionable conduct, which has been said to reflect Australia's progressive democratic spirit.[1] In contrast, outside observers, particularly English restitution scholars, have criticised this reliance on conscience-based equity on the ground that it

* I am grateful for the research assistance of Louise Close and Rosemary Parsons. Responsibility for errors is solely mine.

[1] J Getzler, 'Patterns of Fusion' in P Birks (ed), *The Classification of Obligations* (Oxford, Clarendon Press, 1997) 162.

confers a wide, loosely structured discretion on courts with a consequent loss in predictive value.

The following passage written by Justice Paul Finn captures both the suspicion entertained by Australian lawyers of the unjust enrichment concept and the concomitant preference for conscience-based doctrines:

> My concern, though, is with the allure of the [unjust enrichment] concept itself and how it may contrive legal analyses. First, to the extent that it directs attention to outcomes and to the character to be attributed to them, it is capable of concealing rather than revealing why the law would want to attribute responsibility to one party to provide satisfaction to the other. This is particularly so where, as is so often the case, it is conduct in a relationship or dealing—an expectation created and relied upon; a mistake not corrected etc—which provides the focus of legal attention and which generates the issue of legal policy for which resolution is required. This, I suspect, provides the reason why 'unconscionable conduct' and not 'unjust enrichment' (a possible effect of that conduct) has achieved the currency it has in Australian law.[2]

Contrast the views of Professor Jack Beatson and Mr Graham Virgo in their recent case note on the decision of the High Court of Australia in *Roxborough v Rothmans of Pall Mall Australia*:[3]

> While some of the uncertainty of 'unconscionability' stems from subtle differences in the approaches of different members of the High Court in particular cases, much of it is undoubtedly due to the nature of the concept, encompassing as it does both procedural and substantive impropriety, and operating in contexts ranging from fiduciary relationships to transactions normally seen as purely commercial. Overall it is more difficult to identify when a defendant has acted unconscionably than it is to determine whether a defendant has been unjustly enriched. This is because the use of the word 'unjust' is not a cipher for a general investigation into injustice. It is a concept which can be defined with some degree of precision, and by reference to cases, albeit with the assistance of academic commentary.[4]

This passage succinctly restates the view held by many restitution writers that the concept of unjust enrichment, as expounded in case law and academic writing, is more precise and predictable in its application than unconscionability, presumably even after taking into account judicial and

[2] P Finn, 'Equitable Doctrine and Discretion in Remedies' in W Cornish and others (eds), *Restitution Past, Present and Future: Essays in Honour of Gareth Jones* (Oxford, Hart, 1998) 252.

[3] (2002) 76 ALJR 203 (HCA).

[4] J Beatson and G Virgo, 'Contract, Unjust Enrichment and Unconscionability' (2002) 118 *LQR* 352, 354.

academic exegesis of the latter concept.[5] Disagreement about the merits of a broadly based doctrine of unconscionability as a ground for setting aside contracts and gifts has been overtaken by a more wide ranging debate about 'discretionary remedialism' and the desirability of permitting courts to select a remedy solely on the basis of its appropriateness to the case in hand.[6]

This article is not a contribution to the debate on discretionary remedialism, even if some of its arguments will be relevant to positions adopted in that debate. One aspect of the conduct of the debate is, however, pertinent to my analysis of unconscionability. Arguments about the merits of discretionary remedialism suffer from a tendency on the part of participants to evaluate the private law of other countries on the basis of assumptions drawn from their own jurisdiction. This is a regrettable feature of recent equity and restitution scholarship. It has resulted in serious misconceptions as to the organization and application of private law in different jurisdictions, as well as, in some cases, injecting a disagreeably chauvinistic note into scholarly inquiry. Perhaps for this reason—and in spite of greater differences in legal structure and methods of adjudication—comparison of the law of restitution between common law and civil law jurisdictions is currently proving more fruitful than comparison between common law jurisdictions.

This article pursues a more limited inquiry into the relationship between the concept of unjust enrichment and unconscionability doctrines in Australian law. The next section describes the reception of unjust enrichment in Australia, noting that it was from the outset characterised as a common law and not an equitable concept. There follows an examination of the equitable and statutory proscriptions of unconscionable conduct, together with an assessment of the significance in Australian law of the principle that equity will prevent the unconscionable enforcement of, or insistence upon, legal rights. The article next considers the argument that many of these conscience-based doctrines should properly be classified under the rubric of unjust enrichment and explores some of the consequences of accepting this argument. The final section draws some conclusions from this exercise.

[5] P Birks, *Restitution—The Future* (Annandale, NSW, Federation Press, 1992) 59–60; P Birks and F Rose, 'Editorial' (1993) *Restitution Law Review* 1; P Birks, 'Equity Conscience and Unjust Enrichment' (1999) 23 *Melbourne University Law Review* 1. In contrast, Australian criticisms of unconscionability are directed not at the equitable concept but at legislation such as the Contracts Review Act 1980 (NSW) which permit unjust or unconscionable contracts to be reopened: see McHugh J, 'The Growth of Legislation and Litigation' (1995) 69 *Australian Law Journal* 37, 43; A Duggan, 'Unconscientious Dealing' in P Parkinson (ed), *The Principles of Equity* (Sydney, Lawbook Co, 2003) 164–65 (*Principles of Equity*).

[6] See Finn (above n 2); P Birks, 'Rights, Wrongs and Remedies' (2000) 20 *OJLS* 1; S Evans, 'Defending Discretionary Remedialism' (2001) 23 *Sydney Law Review* 463.

For the benefit of those readers who like to turn to the last page of a novel before (or instead of) reading the rest, the conclusions are stated at the outset. They are as follows:

1. Criticism of the unconscionable dealings doctrine on the ground of conceptual uncertainty is largely misplaced. The concepts employed are no more indeterminate than concepts applied elsewhere in private law, and there is no evidence that application of the doctrine to commercial transactions has resulted in parties incurring higher transactions costs in consequence.
2. The High Court of Australia has placed excessive reliance on the principle that equity will prevent the unconscionable enforcement of legal rights, both as a rationalisation of existing doctrine and as a catalyst for developing new doctrine. Failure on the part of the High Court to recognise the essentially conclusory operation of the principle has resulted in some dubious doctrinal innovation.
3. Some, though by no means all, applications of the unconscientious dealings doctrine, as well as some applications of the family of doctrines rationalised on the basis of 'unconscionable enforcement of legal rights,' reverse unjust enrichment. More specifically, Australian law has been slow to recognise the role of rescission in reversing unjust enrichment. The implications of a restitutionary classification for the defences to equitable claims, and for equitable remedies, have been ignored by most Australian courts and writers, and important issues of corrective justice have been concealed by the sometimes obfuscatory language of equitable discretion.

These arguments go against the grain of a great deal of equity and restitution writing. They will be unpalatable to external critics of Australian unconscionability who on this analysis have exaggerated the instability of the concept. They will also be unacceptable to Australian judges and writers, for whom the 'large idea' of unconscionability is often contrasted to the 'small idea' of unjust enrichment. In truth, the antithesis is false. Restitutionary applications of unconscionability doctrines should be seen for what they are, namely emanations of the unjust enrichment principle, with all the consequences—including a better informed understanding of 'defendant sided' unjust enrichment—that flow from the classification.

II. THE RECOGNITION OF THE UNJUST ENRICHMENT PRINCIPLE IN AUSTRALIA

In Australia, as in other common law countries, the legal phenomenon of restitution was well known to the law long before it was rationalised on the basis of unjust enrichment. Australian law followed English law in grounding restitution on an implied contract to repay money or to pay for the performance of a service. Landmarks such as the *Restatement of Restitution* were occasionally noticed, not unsympathetically,[7] but the recognition of unjust enrichment in Australia had to await the High Court's decision in *Pavey v Matthews & Paul.*[8] Even then the reception of the principle was limited.

In *Pavey* the plaintiffs were builders who had orally agreed with the defendant to build an extension to her home. The defendant agreed to pay reasonable remuneration for the work, calculated by reference to prevailing rates of payment in the building industry. Upon completion of the work the defendant paid the plaintiff $36,000. The plaintiff claimed, however, that the reasonable value for the work done was $62,945 and sued for the balance owed on a 'quantum meruit' claim. The oral contract was unenforceable by reason of the *Builders Licensing Act 1971* (NSW) which provided that 'a building contract is not enforceable against the other party to the contract unless the contract is in writing and signed by each of the parties or his agent in that behalf and sufficiently describes the building work the subject of the contract.' A majority of the High Court, Brennan J dissenting, held that notwithstanding the statutory bar on enforcement of the oral contract, the plaintiff was entitled to a quantum meruit for the reasonable value of the building work performed.

In an important passage, with which Mason and Wilson JJ substantially agreed, Deane J stated that:

> Unjust enrichment ... constitutes a unifying legal concept which explains why the law recognises, in a variety of distinct categories of case, an obligation on the part of a defendant to make fair and just restitution for a benefit derived at the expense of a plaintiff.[9]

This dictum has provided a significant impetus for the development of the law of restitution in Australia. It has recently been cited in support of the award of interest on judgments awarding restitution in cases not covered by statutory schemes of repayment with interest.[10] It also underlies the High Court's holding in *Roxborough v Rothmans* that failures of consideration are not to be confined to failures of contractual reciprocation, though a stronger precedent for that development exists elsewhere in the High Court's jurisprudence.[11] But the recognition of unjust enrichment in *Pavey* was qualified in a number of important respects.

[7] *Mason v New South Wales* (1959) 102 CLR 108 (HCA) 146 (Windeyer J). For a full account, see K Mason and JW Carter, *Restitution Law in Australia* (North Ryde, NSW, Butterworths, 1995) ch 1.
[8] (1987) 162 CLR 221 (HCA).
[9] *Ibid*, 256–61 (Deane J), *ibid* 227 (Mason and Wilson JJ).
[10] *Heydon v NRMA Ltd (No 2)* (2001) 53 NSWLR 600 (CA), 603 (Mason P).
[11] *Muschinski v Dodds* (1985) 160 CLR 583 (HCA) 618–20 (Deane J).

First, the High Court did not identify unjust enrichment as a cause of action. It may have been recognised by the High Court as an organising principle but, as Mason and Carter remark, a 'pleading that asserts in the abstract that P was unjustly enriched at D's expense will usually be struck out.'[12] Even if it is no longer necessary to use the language of quasi-contract and quantum meruit, pleadings have in fact displayed considerable fidelity to the old causes of action. Maitland's truism that the forms of action rule us from their graves cannot be overlooked in any account of the Australian law of restitution, and Australian courts do not invariably march boldly through the clanking ghosts.[13]

Secondly, Deane J's reference to 'fair and just' restitution should not be read as an equation of unjust enrichment with broad conceptions of fairness, justice or conscience. One of several respects in which *Pavey* is a 'difficult' case is in its analysis of the ground upon which restitution was ordered.[14] Later Australian cases, faithful to the terminology of Deane J's judgement, have recognised 'acceptance' (or 'free acceptance') as the basis for the award of the quantum meruit.[15] Academic analysis prefers to rationalise the outcome in *Pavey* on the ground of a failure of consideration, the 'symmetrical' treatment of money and service claims justifying the extension of this ground from the former to the latter.[16] The source of this confusion can be attributed to failure on the part of the majority judges to identify precisely the basis of the recovery. But if the judgements left any lingering suspicion that 'fair and just' restitution provided a mandate for recovery based on generalised notions of justice and fairness, these were dispelled by the High Court's later decision in *David Securities Pty Ltd v Commonwealth Bank of Australia*.[17] This is a significant decision in the Australian law of restitution for two reasons. First, the High Court abolished the bar on recovery of payments made under a mistake of law.[18] Secondly, the High Court emphasised that an award of restitution depends on proof of an established ground of restitution, such as mistake, duress

[12] Mason and Carter (above n 7) [2904].

[13] FW Maitland, *The Forms of Action at Common Law* (Cambridge, The University Press, 1936).

[14] Another is the analysis by the majority judges of the legislative policy of the Builders' Licensing Act 1971 (NSW). See G Jones 'Restitution: Unjust Enrichment as a Unifying Concept in Australia?' (1988–89) *Journal of Contract Law* 1.

[15] *Brenner v First Artists' Management Pty Ltd* [1993] 2 VR 221 (SC); *Angelopolous v Sabatino* (1995) 65 SASR 1 (Full Court); *Andrew Shelton & Co Pty Ltd v Alpha Healthcare Ltd* [2002] VSC 248 (SC).

[16] A Burrows, 'Free Acceptance and the Law of Restitution' (1988) 104 *LQR* 576; P Birks, 'In Defence of Free Acceptance' in A Burrows (ed), *Essays on the Law of Restitution* (Oxford, Clarendon Press, 1992) ch 5.

[17] (1992) 175 CLR 353 (HCA).

[18] Relying inter alia on *Hydro Electric Commission of Nepean v Ontario Hydro* [1982] 1 SCR 347; (1982) 132 DLR (3d) 193 (SCC) 201–15 (Dickson J dissenting); *Air Canada v British Columbia* [1989] 1 SCR 1161; (1989) 59 DLR (4th) 161 (SCC).

or failure of consideration. It is 'not legitimate to determine whether an enrichment is unjust by reference to some subjective evaluation of what is fair or unconscionable.'[19] For all the rhetoric of conscience that pervades Australian judgments on restitution, the actual decisions since *David Securities* have been reached with reference to a recognised ground of restitution. While extensions of existing grounds will occasionally be entertained (as in the recent High Court decision of *Roxborough v Rothmans*[20] where restitution for failure of non-contractual consideration was recognised) the absence of any established ground will be fatal to a claim.

Despite some benevolent endorsement of Canadian constructive trust decisions in obiter dicta,[21] Australian law has never seriously considered, still less adopted, the Canadian framework for deciding restitutionary claims laid down by Dickson J in *Pettkus v Becker*.[22] No restitution case in Australia has been analysed in terms of the trinity of enrichment, a corresponding deprivation and the absence of any juristic reason for the enrichment.[23] A comparison of the merits of the Australian and Canadian analytical frameworks is not one of the aims of this article. But a brief comment on the evolution of the unjust enrichment principle in the two countries is in order. Whereas the criteria proposed by Dickson J were initially designed to govern the imposition of the constructive trust, treating unjust enrichment for this purpose as essentially an equitable concept, the early High Court decisions in Australia were decided in the context of common law claims for money had and received and reasonable remuneration for the performance of services. Canadian law has extended and applied Dickson J's equitable framework to common law claims. By contrast, any corresponding extension of the common law principles into the arena of equitable doctrine remains highly controversial in Australia.

This brings me to my final observation on the judgment of Deane J in *Pavey*. In spite of its intuitive appeal, the notion of unjust enrichment as a 'unifying legal concept' has proved to be extraordinarily elusive. What categories of case can be united under this rubric? Are the categories subsumed by the concept or do they retain their separate identities? And can unification constitute anything more than juridical stamp collecting in the absence of any recognition of unjust enrichment as a cause of action?[24] One matter is, however, absolutely clear. The organising category does not

[19] *David Securities* (above n 17) 378.
[20] Above (n 3).
[21] *Baumgartner v Baumgartner* (1987) 164 CLR 137 (HCA) 153 (Toohey J); *Bryson v Bryant* (1992) 29 NSWLR 188 (CA) 222–23 (Kirby J dissenting).
[22] [1980] 2 SCR 834; (1980) 117 DLR (3d) 257 (SCC) 273–74.
[23] For a negative assessment of the Canadian position from an Australian perspective, see WMC Gummow, 'Unjust Enrichment, Restitution and Proprietary Remedies' in P Finn (ed), *Essays on Restitution* (Perth, Law Book Company, 1990) 47.
[24] Ernest Rutherford: 'all science is either physics or stamp collecting'; from JB Birks, *Rutherford at Manchester* (London, Heywood, 1962) 108.

include most equitable doctrine. The evidence for the exclusion of equity from any systematisation of unjust enrichment is not hard to find. For example, the rationale for accounting for gains obtained through a breach of fiduciary duty has been held not to be, at least exclusively, the reversal of unjust enrichment.[25] Many restitution writers believe that the disgorgement of gains is, as a category of obligation, distinct from restitution, so the exclusion may be justifiable.[26] But if the *sole* reason for its exclusion is because accounting for gains is an equitable response to wrongdoing, and therefore falls outside the scope of the unjust enrichment principle, this essentially jurisdictional consideration will preclude full consideration of the policy choices when it becomes necessary for Australian law to decide, for example, whether an account of profits should be available as a remedy for breach of contract.[27]

Another area of equity which has not so far been brought within the scope of the unifying principle of unjust enrichment is that of rescission of a contract on equitable grounds such as undue influence, mistake, misrepresentation, breach of fiduciary obligation and, relevantly for present purposes, unconscionable conduct. Rescission is of course available at common law as well as in equity. This article will, however, focus on rescission in equity for two reasons. First, equity gives effect to the rescission of contracts on a number of grounds, including the various 'conscience-based' grounds, not recognised at common law. Secondly, the principal remedies for effecting restitution of property transferred under rescinded contracts are equitable.[28] Resulting or constructive trusts, or the making of equitable adjustments for the taking of accounts, can all be used for this purpose.[29] Even if rescission is conceptualised as the act of the party setting aside a transaction,[30] a judicial order will usually be needed to restore property to its pre-contractual titleholder.

As the next section will demonstrate, Australian law enjoys a rich case law on the rescission of unconscionable contracts. But the numerous judicial and academic analyses of that case law have never located it within the law of unjust enrichment. Exactly why the restitutionary aspects of unconscionability have been ignored will be explored later in this article.

[25] *Warman v Dwyer* (1995) 182 CLR 544 (HCA) 561 ('this is not to say that the liability of a fiduciary to account should be governed by the doctrine of unjust enrichment, though that doctrine may well have a useful part to play'). See also the introduction by Justice WMC Gummow to IM Jackman, *The Varieties of Restitution* (Leichhardt, NSW, Federation Press, 1998). Compare the analysis of the account of profits awarded for infringement of intellectual property whose rationale was stated to be the prevention of unjust enrichment: *Dart Industries Inc v Decor Corp Pty Ltd* (1993) 179 CLR 101 (HCA) 111, 114, 123.

[26] L Smith, 'The Province of the Law of Restitution' (1992) 71 *Canadian Bar Review* 672; J Edelman, *Gain-Based Damages: Contract, Tort, Equity and Intellectual Property* (Oxford, Hart, 2002).

[27] *Attorney-General v Blake* [2001] 1 AC 268 (HL).

[28] Common law remedies in conversion and for money had and received may also be available.

[29] *Alati v Kruger* (1955) 94 CLR 216 (HCA) 223–24 (Dixon CJ).

[30] J O'Sullivan, 'Rescission as a Self-Help Remedy: A Critical Analysis' (2000) 59 *CLJ* 509.

Any balanced account of the law of unjust enrichment in Australia (and particularly one written by an author who accepts the intellectual coherence of unjust enrichment more fully than most Australian writers) must record a sea change in judicial attitudes to restitution in the fifteen years since *Pavey* was decided. Deane J's beneficent unifying principle has, in the opinion of some judges and writers, become a doctrinal straitjacket.[31] Doctrine which can be organised and explained perfectly clearly in terms of other private law categories will become distorted, so the argument runs, if it is forced onto the procrustean bed of unjust enrichment. In a passage which may well prove to be as influential for the future direction of the law of restitution in Australia as Deane J's 'unifying concept,' Gummow J in *Roxborough v Rothmans* warned against an excessively programmatic application of the unjust enrichment principle:

> Considerations such as these, together with practical experience, suggest caution in judicial acceptance of any all-embracing theory of restitutionary rights and remedies founded upon a notion of 'unjust enrichment'. To the lawyer whose mind has been moulded by civilian influences, the theory may come first, and the source of the theory may be the writing of jurists not the decisions of judges. However, that is not the way in which a system based on case law develops; over time, general principle is derived from judicial decisions upon particular instances, not the other way around ... unless, as this Court indicated in *David Securities Pty Ltd v Commonwealth Bank of Australia,* unjust enrichment is seen as a concept rather than a definitive legal principle, substance and dynamism may be restricted by dogma. In turn, the dogma will tend to generate new fictions in order to retain support for its theses. It may also distort well-settled principle in other fields, including those respecting equitable doctrines and remedies, so that they answer the newly mandated order of things. Then various theories will compete, each to deny the others. There is support in Australasian legal scholarship for considerable scepticism respecting any all-embracing theory in this field, with the treatment of the disparate as no more than species of the newly discovered genus.[32]

This is a none too thinly veiled attack, not so much on the unjust enrichment principle as on overriding taxonomies of private law such as that adumbrated by Professor Peter Birks, who identifies unjust enrichment as one in a series of events to which restitution is a response. The paradox of *Roxborough v Rothmans* is that a decision which displays such marked hostility to the 'imperium of restitution'[33] actually extends the principle of unjust

[31] Jackman (n 25) and J Dietrich, *Restitution: A New Perspective* (Leichhardt, NSW, Federation Press, 1998) expound models of the law of restitution in which the role of unjust enrichment is relatively limited. In this respect they follow an Australian tradition initiated by SJ Stoljar, *The Law of Quasi-Contract*, 2nd edn (Sydney, The Law Book Co, 1989).
[32] *Roxborough v Rothmans* (above n 3) [72], [74] (footnotes omitted).
[33] *Ibid*, [173] (Kirby J dissenting).

enrichment to permit restitution on the ground of failure of consideration of payments made under valid, fully executed contracts—a novelty in terms of the previous authorities on failure of consideration.

Exactly why judicial estimation of the value of the unjust enrichment principle is so low, at least in the High Court,[34] can only be guessed at. That court's priority in *Pavey* had been to eliminate the fiction that restitution for money had and received rested on an implied contract to repay. By the time *Roxborough v Rothmans* was decided the primacy accorded to abolishing fictions had given way to a judicial preoccupation with preserving the settled territory of the older private law categories of tort, contract and trust. As Professor Birks has observed, these categories fulfil different functions and cannot be lined up together along a doctrinal continuum.[35] Nevertheless, the judgments of Gummow J and Kirby J, dissenting, reflect a genuine apprehension that restitution could destabilise settled private law doctrine.

But it would be regrettable if fears of restitutionary overreach were to preclude any reassessment of the function and scope of private law doctrine, particularly as an inquiry would reveal that very few doctrines have as their objectives the reversal of unjust enrichment. In an Australian context, it would be particularly unfortunate if equity (to which Gummow J makes explicit reference in the passage cited) were to be excluded from such an inquiry. At the risk of making conscience 'answer the newly mandated order of things' it is appropriate to examine equitable relief from unconscionable transactions with a view to determining whether (and if so, how) it reverses unjust enrichment.

III. UNCONSCIONABILITY IN AUSTRALIA

A preliminary difficulty in discussing the role of unconscionability in Australian law is that the word is often used as a shorthand expression for one or more of a number of conceptually discrete equitable doctrines which have as their objective the prevention of legally disapproved conduct.[36] For present purposes a critical distinction exists between:

1. the equitable principles granting relief from transactions procured by unconscionable conduct, which nowadays have to

[34] In lower courts the picture is not as bleak. A search of Austlii (http://www.austlii.edu.au on 07/04/03) found 86 cases in State Supreme Courts and the Federal Court containing some discussion, often brief, of the unjust enrichment principle in 2001 and 2002.

[35] P Birks, 'Definition and Division: A Meditation on Institutes 3.12' in P Birks (ed) *The Classification of Obligations* (Oxford, Clarendon Press, 1997) ch 1.

[36] 'These doctrines are commonly and barbarously described, though not in this work, by a word which has not yet found its way into the dictionaries, namely "unconscionability".' JD Heydon and PL Loughlan, *Cases and Materials on Equity and Trusts*, 6th edn (Sydney, Butterworths, 2002) [14.10] 3.

be read in conjunction with expansively drafted statutory prohibitions of such conduct, and

2. a family of equitable doctrines having as their objective the prevention of the unconscionable enforcement of legal rights. It is not a closely-knit family, nor is it introverted. New members will be made welcome. Doctrines which have been rationalised on the basis of this principle include the principles governing equitable relief against penalties[37] and forfeiture,[38] unilateral mistake,[39] estoppel[40] and a wife's 'equity' to have a guarantee of her husband's indebtedness set aside for failure on the part of the lender to explain to her the nature and effect of the guarantee.[41]

General statements can be found to the effect that all equitable doctrine, including liability for breach of fiduciary obligation, is premised on the prevention of unconscionable conduct.[42] But to treat conscience as being synonymous with equity obviously renders both concepts meaningless.

Many restitution lawyers subscribe to the view that unconscionability is a less precise term than unjust enrichment, after due allowance has been made for judicial and academic commentary expounding these concepts.[43] Is the view justified? Opinions on this question are in practice so strongly held that it is unlikely that any argument presented in this article will persuade readers already predisposed to one side or the other of the debate. Any balanced response ought, however, to distinguish between the various conscience-based doctrines and not treat 'unconscionability' as one indigestible whole.

A. Unconscionable Dealings

The principles governing the setting aside of unconscionable dealings are well established in Australian law.[44] They have been developed and refined by the High Court of Australia in a series of decisions over the past fifty years, of which the best known are *Blomley v Ryan*[45] and *Commercial*

[37] *O'Dea v Allstates Leasing System (WA) Pty Ltd* (1983) 152 CLR 359 (HCA); *AMEV-UDC Finance Ltd v Austin* (1986) 162 CLR 170 (HCA).
[38] *Legione v Hateley* (1983) 152 CLR 406 (HCA); *Stern v McArthur* (1988) 165 CLR 489 (HCA).
[39] *Taylor v Johnson* (1983) 151 CLR 422 (HCA).
[40] *Walton's Stores (Interstate) Ltd v Maher* (1988) 164 CLR 387 (HCA); *Commonwealth v Verwayen* (1990) 170 CLR 394 (HCA); *Giumelli v Giumelli* (1999) 196 CLR 101 (HCA).
[41] *Garcia v National Australia Bank Ltd* (1998) 194 CLR 395 (HCA) (*Garcia*).
[42] See Beatson and Virgo (above n 4) 354, noting that unconscionability operates 'in contexts ranging from fiduciary relationships to transactions normally seen as commercial.'
[43] See authority cited, above (above n 4–5).
[44] For an excellent short account, see Duggan (above n 5) ch 5.
[45] (1956) 99 CLR 362 (HCA).

Bank of Australia v Amadio.[46] The principles can be traced back to equity's jurisdiction to relieve against catching bargains,[47] but the High Court's proscription of unconscionable conduct has been elevated to a level of general principle never systematically attempted in the English Chancery authorities. The elaboration of principle has rationalised both the authorities on the rescission of unconscionable contracts as well as case law on the refusal of specific performance on the grounds of the defendant's unconscionable behaviour.[48] The resulting unconscionable dealings doctrine governs equitable *transactions*, not simply *contracts*, so that a gift procured by unconscionable conduct is liable to be rescinded in equity.[49]

The grounds upon which a transaction will be set aside as being unconscionable are, in outline, as follows:

1. the plaintiff must be under some special disability or disadvantage, and
2. the defendant must either have actual knowledge of the disability or disadvantage, or must be aware of the possibility that a disadvantage exists.[50]

Upon proof of these grounds by the plaintiff a transaction will be set aside unless the defendant can show that the transaction was fair and reasonable, for example by proving that the plaintiff had received adequate consideration[51] or had the benefit of legal advice which nullified the effect of the plaintiff's disadvantage in entering into the transaction.[52]

Criticism of these equitable principles has been primarily directed to the supposed indeterminacy of the term 'special disadvantage or disability.' Critics point to the fact that all the modern High Court authorities on this doctrine are characterised by strong dissenting judgments.[53] The recent High Court decision in *Bridgewater v Leahy*[54] has provided ammunition for conscience-sceptics.

In *Bridgewater v Leahy* the defendant had for many years assisted his father and uncle in running a number of grazing properties. The uncle was

[46] (1983) 151 CLR 447 (HCA).

[47] *Earl of Aylesford v Morris* (1873) LR 8 Ch App 484 (CA); *O'Rorke v Bolingbroke* (1877) 2 App Cas 814 (HL).

[48] *Cooke v Clayworth* (1811) 18 Ves 12, 4 ER 222; *Wiltshire v Marshall* (1866) 14 LT 396.

[49] *Wilton v Farnworth* (1948) 76 CLR 646 (HCA); *Louth v Diprose* (1992) 175 CLR 621 (HCA).

[50] *Amadio* (above n 46) 467–68 (Mason J).

[51] Not necessarily decisive: *Blomley v Ryan* (n 45) 405 (Fullager J).

[52] *Bester v Perpetual Trustee Co Ltd* [1970] 3 NSWR 30 (SC).

[53] *Blomley v Ryan* (above n 45) (Kitto J dissenting); *Amadio* (above n 46) (Dawson J dissenting); *Louth v Diprose* (n 49) (Toohey J dissenting); *Bridgewater v Leahy* (1998) 194 CLR (HCA) 457 (Gleeson CJ and Callinan J dissenting).

[54] Above (n 53). Beatson and Virgo (above n 4) 354 describe the decision as the 'high water mark of what can be seen as a process of discretionary "practical justice".'

elderly and, in the last year of his life, in poor health. In his final years he executed a will and transferred properties to the defendant, both transactions being expressly intended to confer a considerable financial benefit on the defendant. The will, executed in 1985, left his residuary estate to his four daughters (none of whose families had taken any interest in farming) as well as conferring an option on the defendant to buy his interest in a number of grazing properties for $200,000. The interest was then valued at $694,922. In 1988 the defendant offered to buy the greater part of these properties for $150,000. The offer was accepted by the uncle. The defendant and his wife contracted to buy the properties for their market value of $696,811 but, by the operation of a deed of forgiveness executed on the same date as the contract, the actual price paid was reduced to $150,000. Following the uncle's death nine months later, the defendant exercised the option in the will to buy for $200,000 the remaining interests in the properties excluded from the earlier contract for sale. The uncle's widow and daughters applied to have the will set aside for undue influence, and in addition to have the deed of forgiveness set aside for undue influence or as an unconscionable dealing.[55]

The High Court upheld a finding that the defendant had exercised no undue influence over his uncle in respect of either the will or the deed of forgiveness. However, a majority, Gleeson CJ and Callinan J dissenting, ordered the deed of forgiveness to be set aside on the ground that it had been procured by unconscionable conduct. The majority judgment laid stress on the uncle's age, ill health and heavy dependence on the defendant in managing his grazing properties. While the defendant's initiative in offering to buy the properties at substantial undervalue was a relevant factor in establishing the exploitation of his uncle's position of disadvantage, the judgment also made clear that the passive acceptance of a benefit could constitute an unconscionable dealing quite as much as active procurement.[56] The dissenting judgment, on the other hand, considered that the facts of previous decisions on unconscionable dealings were 'a long way removed from the facts of the present case,' and that the evidence fell well short of establishing that the uncle suffered from any kind of special disadvantage.[57]

A condition such as old age,[58] drunkenness[59] or inability to understand English[60] cannot, without more, be classified as a special disadvantage. If the law were otherwise, serious obstacles would be placed in the way of individuals with these characteristics from entering into everyday contracts.

[55] An application for family provision under the Succession Act 1981 (Qld) Part 4 was struck out for want of prosecution: *Bridgewater v Leahy* (above n 53) 480–88.
[56] Citing *Hart v O'Connor* [1985] AC 1000 (PC) 1024 (Lord Brightman).
[57] *Bridgewater v Leahy* (above n 53) 472.
[58] Contrast *Bridgewater v Leahy* with *Wilby v St George Bank* (2001) SASR 404 (Full Court) where a loan entered into by an eighty-four year old man, described as 'fit for his age' was upheld.
[59] *Blomley v Ryan* (above n 45).
[60] *Amadio* (above n 46).

All such conditions are examined by courts in the context of the specific transaction being impugned and of the impact of the alleged condition on entry into the transaction. Most successful applications to have a transaction set aside for unconscionable conduct include an element of misrepresentation, material non-disclosure (as in *Amadio*) or at least the creation of a situation in which the disadvantaged person is incapable of assessing alternative courses of action rationally (as, on the majority's interpretation of the facts, was the case in *Bridgewater v Leahy*). The contextual analysis of specific disadvantage, combined with the divisions of judicial opinions which occur in the evaluation of the context (or 'factual matrix' to adopt the term much favoured by Mason CJ), naturally invite criticisms of the doctrine on the grounds of indeterminacy and poor predictive value. But contextual inquiries are unavoidable even in jurisdictions where the doctrine of unconscionable transactions is confined to discrete categories such as 'catching bargains,' poverty or ignorance,[61] or to overreaching and oppressive conduct.[62] In all these categories complex factual inquiries will also be required in order to assess the impact of personal circumstances upon entry into an improvident transaction. Uncertainty in the application of the unconscionable dealing doctrine derives from the nature of *any* doctrine which proscribes exploitative conduct, whether that doctrine is narrowly or widely drawn, and not because the concept of special disadvantage is particularly unstable.

More serious threats to transactional security are posed by the risk of an ill-judged relaxation of the requirement that the defendant must have knowledge of the plaintiff's special disadvantage. Knowledge, for this purpose, must mean *actual* knowledge.[63] Only by imposing liability on the basis of actual knowledge of disadvantage will the doctrine's basis in victimisation be maintained, and the costs of entering into significant transactions such as land sales and bank guarantees be kept to an acceptably low level.[64] The Australian law of unconscionable dealings has not entirely avoided flirtations with the concept of constructive notice,[65] though recent authority has acknowledged that:

> If the law is to stigmatise one party's conduct as unconscionable, it must make credible demands of that party. [I]t cannot stray too far from actual knowledge

[61] *Fry v Lane* (1888) 40 Ch D 312 (CA); *Cresswell v Potter* [1978] 1 WLR 255 (Ch).
[62] *Multiservice Bookbinding Ltd v Marden* [1979] Ch 84; *Alec Lobb (Garages) Ltd v Total Oil (GB) Ltd* [1983] 1 WLR 87 (CA).
[63] Which can include wilful shutting of eyes to the existence of a special disadvantage, or actually knowing facts which would indicate to a reasonable person that a special disadvantage exists. Students of the jurisprudence of *Barnes v Addy* (1874) LR 9 Ch App 422 will be familiar with these refinements of actual knowledge.
[64] This is an important theme of Professor Anthony Duggan's writings on unconscionable dealings: A Duggan 'Is Equity Efficient?' (1997) 113 *LQR* 601, 632–35; Duggan (above n 44) 146–48.
[65] *Akins v National Australia Bank Ltd* (1994) 34 NSWLR 155 (CA).

> before it leaves itself open to the criticism of pursuing a policy of protecting the mistaken or disadvantaged under the guise of proscribing what is essentially innocent behaviour.[66]

Fears that a broadly defined doctrine of unconscientious dealings will subvert the core private law values of transactional security and predictability of outcome will be groundless as long as, first, the objective of equitable intervention is recognised as the prevention of victimisation, and, secondly, that the requirement of actual knowledge of a special disadvantage is strictly insisted upon.

The equitable doctrine of unconscientious dealings is supplemented by a variety of statutory proscriptions of unconscionable conduct, enacted by the Commonwealth and State legislatures. Space precludes detailed analysis of the provisions or of their judicial interpretation. The provision most relevant to the present discussion is s51AA(1) of the Trade Practices Act 1974 (Cth):

> A corporation must not, in trade or commerce, engage in conduct that is unconscionable within the meaning of the unwritten law from time to time of the States and Territories.

The High Court of Australia considered the meaning of this somewhat opaque section in the recent decision of *Australian Competition and Consumer Commission v CG Berbatis Holdings Ltd.*[67] A landlord of a shop in a shopping centre consented to the renewal of a lease to the tenant on condition that the latter withdrew all outstanding legal proceedings against him. A majority of the High Court, Kirby J dissenting, held that the landlord's insistence on the inclusion of this term in the lease did not constitute unconscionable conduct within s51AA(1). The majority rejected an argument, which had found favour with the trial judge, that the tenant's weak bargaining position amounted to a 'situational disadvantage.'

Both parties to the appeal agreed that s51AA(1) was to be construed in conformity with the equitable doctrine of unconscionable dealings. The agreement on this issue meant that the High Court was not called upon to decide whether the statutory definition of unconscionability was broader than its equitable equivalent, for example by including conduct amounting to an unconscionable enforcement of a legal right. Lower courts will have to make the best they can of some conflicting obiter dicta on this question. Gleeson CJ and Callinan J were of the opinion that the unconscionable dealings doctrine 'mark out the area of discourse involved' in construing s51AA(1).[68] Gummow and Hayne JJ considered that it was unnecessary to

[66] *Micarone v Perpetual Trustees Australia Ltd* (1999) 75 SASR 1 (Full Court) 115 (Debelle and Wicks JJ).
[67] [2003] HCA 18.
[68] *Ibid*, [7] (Gleeson CJ), [167] (Callinan J).

resolve the matter,[69] while Kirby J, dissenting, advocated a 'broad and beneficial' interpretation of the provision which would have extended its reach well beyond the *Amadio* doctrine.[70] Whether the statutory unconscionability of s51AA(1) will relieve against exploitative conduct not involving any element of 'special disadvantage' therefore remains an open question in Australian law, though the auspices do not look favourable for the recognition of 'broad brush' unconscionability.[71]

B. Unconscionable Enforcement of Legal Rights

The equitable and statutory principles governing the setting aside of unconscionable bargains are distinguishable from a second role that 'conscience' plays in Australian law, that of preventing the unconscionable enforcement of legal rights. The prevention of the unconscionable enforcement of, or insistence upon, legal rights is not of course a freestanding principle which, without more, justifies rescission of a contract or refusal of specific performance. We have previously noticed that it is the rationale of intervention for a number of discrete equitable doctrines, including relief against penalties and forfeiture, estoppel and unilateral mistake where the mistake was known to the other party.[72]

It is a matter of opinion whether the identification of this basis for relief has in fact assisted the rational development or exposition of equitable doctrine. In its favour, a respectable case can be made for saying that a few doctrinal anomalies have been ironed out by recourse to the principle.[73] But anomalies can be eliminated without appeal to conscience, and the principle itself suffers from being essentially conclusory. Doctrines explained in terms of the enforcement of legal rights do not necessarily

[69] *Ibid* [46].
[70] *Ibid* [65], [76].
[71] Another unresolved question is whether other 'unconscionability' provisions in the Trade Practices Act 1974 (Cth), specifically s51AB and s51AC, relieve against substantive unconscionability. Federal Court decisions, taking into account factors set out in these provisions, have held that they are not limited to remedying procedural unconscionability: *Dai v Telstra Corporation Ltd* (2000) 171 ALR 348 (Full Federal Court); *Australian Competition and Consumer Commission v Simply No-Knead (Franchising) Pty Ltd* (2001) 178 ALR 304 (FC) (Sundberg J).
[72] See text above (n 37–41).
[73] For example, in permitting relief from a vendor's forfeiture of an interest acquired by the purchaser under a contract for the sale of land where the vendor has made a late payment and time was of the essence of the contract: *Legione* (above n 38). Compare the stricter approach to permitting relief from forfeiture taken by the Privy Council decision of *Union Eagle Ltd v Golden Achievements Ltd* [1997] AC 514 (PC), and see now *Romanos v Pentagold Investments Pty Ltd* [2003] HCA 58; *Tanwar Enterprises Pty Ltd v Cauchi* [2003] HCA 57. On the other hand, suggestions that the penalties doctrine should apply to sums payable otherwise than on a breach of contract, on the ground that enforcement of the sum at law will sometimes be 'unconscionable,' have not so far been taken up: *AMEV-UDC v Austin* (1986) 162 CLR 170 (HCA) 198–99 (Deane J).

relieve against victimisation, though some, such as taking advantage of a mistake made by the other party to a contract, involve the same kind of exploitation of a position of special disadvantage found in an unconscionable dealing. But in other applications, including relief from a penalty and a wife's 'equity' to have a guarantee set aside, appeal to the principle is no more than a rationalisation of the decision to grant equitable relief. It was the conclusory nature of unconscionability to which Lord Nicholls objected in *Royal Brunei Airlines Sdn Bhd v Tan* when his Lordship indicated a preference for imposing equitable liability for assisting in a breach of fiduciary duty on the basis of dishonesty and not unconscionability:

> Unconscionable is a word of immediate appeal to an equity lawyer. Equity is rooted historically in the concept of the Lord Chancellor, as the keeper of the Royal Conscience, concerning himself with conduct which was contrary to good conscience. It must be recognised, however, that unconscionable is not a word in everyday use by non-lawyers. If it is to be used in this context, and if it is to be the touchstone for liability as an accessory, it is essential to be clear on what, *in this context*, unconscionable means. If unconscionable means no more than dishonesty, then dishonesty is the preferable label.[74]

Positing liability on the basis of preventing the unconscionable enforcement of legal rights can, as Lord Nicholls observes, not only conceal the true ground upon which liability is being imposed. It can also, by its very ambiguity as to whether transactional processes or outcomes are the ground of intervention, obscure analysis of the policies relevant to the application of an equitable doctrine.[75]

There is no need to emphasise the drawbacks of the 'unconscionable insistence on legal rights' principle. For the most part it has supplied no more than a moralistic flourish to equity judgments. Moreover, as the next section of the article will show, many applications of the principle are in no sense restitutionary. For example, the Australian law of estoppel has been premised on the unconscionable insistence on legal rights, or more accurately, on the unconscionable reliance upon the absence of a legal contract.[76] The High Court has pioneered what is generally taken to be a new head of reliance-based obligation. Dr Andrew Robertson's researches have shown, however, that in practice the language of conscience has camouflaged a surprisingly large number of cases in which courts have awarded an expectation measure of relief.[77]

[74] [1995] 2 AC 378 (PC) 392.
[75] The case law on relief from forfeiture affords a good illustration of the shifting meanings of unconscionability. See *Stern* (above n 38); NY Chin, 'Relieving against Forfeiture: Windfalls and Conscience' (1995) 25 *University of Western Australia Law Review* 110.
[76] *Thompson v Palmer* (1933) 49 CLR 507 (HCA) 547 (Dixon J); *Waltons* (above n 40).
[77] A Robertson, 'Satisfying the Minimum Equity: Equitable Estoppel Remedies after *Verwayen*' (1996) 20 *Melbourne University Law Review* 805.

Equity lawyers sometimes concede the point that the prevention of the unconscionable enforcement of legal rights is to some extent an exercise in 'ex post facto' rationalisation.[78] But in a more positive vein, they proceed to draw the critic's attention to a number of careful analyses of unconscionability which have succeeded in isolating the policies pursued by the application of conscience-based doctrines.[79] More assertively still, they argue that the conclusory flaws of unconscionability are shared with, indeed surpassed by, the beguiling circularity of the unjust enrichment principle. This is the gravamen of Justice Finn's complaint, cited at the beginning of this article. In his view, the unjust enrichment principle 'is capable of concealing rather than revealing why the law would want to attribute a responsibility to one party to provide satisfaction to the other.'[80]

There is no doubt that a mechanical 'slot machine' application of the unjust enrichment principle (unjust factor + enrichment + at the expense of the plaintiff – defences = restitution) can lead to grotesque results, especially when the formula is applied in a commercial context against a background of established assumptions as to the division of responsibility for transaction failure.[81] Any law of unjust enrichment which permits restitution for mistake without regard to any responsibility for avoiding the occurrence of the mistake, or for failure of consideration without a careful analysis of the commercial expectations of both payer and payee at the time the payment was made, would clearly be defective.[82] But there is in fact little evidence that the law of restitution is being applied formulaically as 'slot machine' unjust enrichment. The grounds of restitution and the defences to restitutionary claims, taken together, in most cases flexibly balance the values of corrective justice and transactional security in areas such as banking law and insolvency law without undermining either the specific legislative regimes which apply to these areas or the policies which those regimes promote.[83] Moreover, they generally do so without impairing the analytical coherence of the unjust enrichment principle itself.[84]

[78] *Garcia* (above n 41).
[79] See eg, P Parkinson, 'The Conscience of Equity' in *Principles of Equity* (above n 5) ch 2.
[80] Finn (above n 2) 252.
[81] The criticism of the House of Lords decision *Banque Financiere de la Cite v Parc (Battersea) Ltd* [1999] 1 AC 22 (HL) that it imposed a 'slot machine' unjust enrichment approach on a complex commercial property transaction is, in my view, well founded: M Bridge, 'Failed Contracts, Subrogation and Unjust Enrichment' [1998] *Journal of Business Law* 323.
[82] A possible criticism of the majority judgements in *Roxborough v Rothmans* (above n 3) is that they failed to examine any assumptions as to whether the risk of constitutional invalidation of the Business Franchise Licences (Tobacco) Act (NSW) was carried by the wholesaler or by the retailer.
[83] See eg, the essays in F Rose (ed), *Restitution and Banking Law*, (Oxford, Mansfield Press, 1998) and F Rose (ed), *Restitution and Insolvency* (Oxford, Mansfield Press, 2000).
[84] An Australian exception is *State Bank of New South Wales v Swiss Bank Corporation* (1995) 39 NSWLR 350 (CA) where the exercise of allocating responsibility for loss of money due to fraud on the plaintiff bank was undertaken without reference to any identified ground of restitution.

In contrast to most restitution lawyers, for whom the grounds of restitution are finite, resembling the 'numerus clausus' of civilian property law, the principle of preventing the unconscionable enforcement of legal rights is for equity lawyers open-ended, in the sense of not being confined to predetermined categories. The principle has been recently invoked in *Garcia v National Australia Bank Ltd* [85] to justify the recognition of a wife's 'equity' to have a guarantee set aside where she does not understand its nature and effect, and where the lender has not taken adequate steps to explain the terms of the guarantee to her. The 'equity' is not new, being an application of the older High Court authority of *Yerkey v Jones*,[86] but it had not previously been explained in terms of the unconscionable enforcement by a lender of its rights under the guarantee. The reaffirmation in *Garcia* of the existence of the equity, which has not been recognised in any other common law jurisdiction, is controversial. Supporters may, along with Professor Duggan, argue that the equity recognises the strategic role of the bank as 'gatekeeper,' being well placed to prevent a husband from pressuring a wife into giving her consent to acting as a surety.[87] Opponents will take sides with the dissenting opinion of Kirby J in *Garcia* that a gender and status-specific equity is anomalous and paternalistic in contemporary society.[88] This is not the place to evaluate these competing arguments. But the simple assertion that the bank has unconscionably enforced its legal rights cannot by itself settle the argument, particularly (as the High Court made clear) the lender need not have engaged in any reprehensible conduct attracting the application of the unconscionable dealings doctrine.[89] Reliance on the 'conscience' mantra does not help a court to make the difficult policy choices involved in evaluating imbalances of intra-family economic power against the need to preserve the availability of commercial lines of credit for family borrowing.

To summarise this section, any critique of the role of conscience in Australian equity must distinguish between the unconscientious dealings doctrine and the cluster of doctrines founded on the principle of unconscionable enforcement of legal rights. The former is as stable as any doctrine having as its aim the prevention of exploitation and victimisation can hope to be. The latter principle is essentially a conclusory formula which has been used to

85 Above (n 41).
86 (1939) 63 CLR 649 (HCA). The antecedents of the 'equity' are dubious. It was derived by Dixon J in *Yerkey v Jones* from the obscure Privy Council opinion delivered in *Turnbull v Duvall* [1902] AC 429 (PC), which in turn was subsequently disapproved in *Barclays Bank plc v O'Brien* [1994] 1 AC 180 (HL) 191–95.
87 A Duggan, 'Undue Influence' in *Principles of Equity* (above n 5) 422–24, applying MJ Trebilcock and SB Elliot, 'The Scope and Limits of Legal Paternalism: Altruism and Coercion in Family Financial Arrangements' in P Benson (ed) *The Theory of Contract Law* (Cambridge, Cambridge University Press, 2001) 45, 52–53.
88 *Garcia* (above n 41) 422–29. In *State Bank of New South Wales v Hibbert* [2000] NSWSC 628 it was held that the equity does not apply to a guarantee entered into by a 'de facto' spouse.
89 The majority judgments in *Garcia* held that the wife's equity was not to be construed as an application of the unconscientious dealings principle: *Garcia* (above n 41) 408.

mask the policies for applying or extending equitable principle. Being more open-ended than the grounds of restitution it is as least as likely as those grounds to conceal the reasons for ascribing legal responsibility.

IV. UNCONSCIONABILITY WITHIN THE LAW OF RESTITUTION

The first part of this article illustrated how unjust enrichment and unconscionability are usually presented as antithetical ideas. Advocates of unjust enrichment emphasise the conceptual clarity of the concept and, with growing confidence, its predictive value. In contrast, equity scholars stress the flexibility of conscience-based doctrines, their basis in community standards and their sensitivity to vulnerability and power imbalances in relationships. Features common to both legal ideas—for example their complementary roles in promoting corrective justice—are rarely noticed.

Are the conscience-based doctrines applications of the unjust enrichment principle? The question is not new and has been examined in some depth in the restitution literature.[90] But it has not been asked in an Australian context. Moreover, since the recognition of unjust enrichment in Australia coincided with the High Court's reawakened interest in equitable doctrine, Australian private law ought to shed some light on the problematic relationship between the two sources of obligation.

An obvious but important preliminary point is that not all equitable intervention on conscience-based grounds is directed at the reversal of unjust enrichment. To argue otherwise would amount to a wholly unjustifiable claim to 'restitutionary imperialism.' Conscience is not a synonym for unjust enrichment. Although the 'minimum equity'[91] necessary to give effect to an estoppel could conceivably involve the reversal of unjust enrichment, relief in estoppel does not in practice further this aim.[92] Similarly, unjust enrichment plays no part in the invalidation of a penalty clause unless the return of money paid under the clause is sought. Other doctrines have subsidiary restitutionary applications. Relief from forfeiture is not restitutionary if the only consequence is that continued performance is permitted under a contract which would otherwise have been terminated.[93] On the other hand, the restoration of money or other property consequent upon the grant of equitable relief from forfeiture constitutes the reversal of unjust enrichment, the ground of restitution being failure of consideration.[94]

[90] M Chen-Wishart, 'Unjust Factors and the Restitutionary Response' (2000) 20 *OJLS* 557.
[91] *Crabb v Arun District Council* [1976] Ch 179 (CA) 198 (Scarman LJ); *Verwayen* (above n 40) 413 (Mason CJ).
[92] Robertson (above n 77) 808.
[93] *Stern* (above n 38). It could arguably be classified as 'anticipatory unjust enrichment'. Compare the analysis of the forfeiture principles arising on wrongful death in Mason and Carter (above 7) ch 19.
[94] *Stockloser v Johnson* [1954] 1 QB 476 (CA) 488–89 (Denning LJ). The payments will not be 'forfeited' under an instalment contract for the sale of land since they already belong to

But many equitable conscience-based doctrines have, at least as one of their aims, the reversal of unjust enrichment. They include some applications of the unconscionable dealings doctrine, the setting aside of guarantees on the basis of a wife's 'equity to rescind' and rescission for mistake. Why are these doctrines not analysed as applications of the unjust enrichment principle?

The leading text, Keith Mason and JW Carter's *Restitution Law in Australia*, devotes one paragraph to relief from contracts affected by unconscionable conduct,[95] which is said to be 'a relatively narrow category'. Another paragraph properly cautions against treating unconscionability as a general basis for unjust enrichment so that both terms are reduced to little more than synonyms for fairness.[96] The impression left on the reader is that the authors recognise that restitution can be ordered of benefits transferred under unconscionable contracts where the basis in conscience is clearly defined. Nevertheless, extreme care should be exercised in invoking the unconscientious dealings doctrine as a ground of restitution if a return to the discredited notion of unjust enrichment as subjective fairness and justice is to be avoided. This is a legitimate fear, though it may be overstated in view of the High Court's insistence that unjust enrichment be referable to established grounds of restitution and not to considerations of fairness. It ought to be possible to examine the restitutionary aspects of the unconscionable dealings doctrine, as well as of specific doctrines founded on the unconscionable enforcement of legal rights principle, without incurring the criticism that to do so is to reduce the unjust enrichment principle to the level of unstructured subjective justice.

Dr John Glover has provided another 'take' on the exclusion of conscience-based doctrines from the law of restitution, by emphasising the distinction between strict restitutionary liability and the basis of equitable liability in fault:

> The independent restitutionary right imposes strict liability. Equitable liability, by contrast, is almost entirely based in fault. Restitution is not interested in the quality of the defendant's conduct. If property was mistakenly transferred, it must be restored. When consideration for a payment fails entirely, nothing the payee does or does not do affects the payer's claim. Innocence and fault are equally irrelevant to independent restitutionary claims. On the other hand, equitable liabilities are based in fault with very few exceptions.[97]

the vendor. Nonetheless, such payments attract the application of the principles governing equitable relief: *McDonald v Dennys Lascelles Ltd* (1993) 48 CLR 457 (HCA).

[95] Mason and Carter (above n 7) [1314].

[96] See *ibid* [235] criticising the dictum of Connolly J in *Kratzmann Holdings Pty Ltd v The University of Queensland* [1982] Qd R 682 (Full Court) 685 to the effect that whatever 'may be involved in the concept of unjust enrichment, it may at least be said that it poses the question whether it is unconscionable.'

[97] J Glover, 'Equity and Restitution' in *Principles of Equity* (above n 5) 103.

The distinction drawn here between equitable and restitutionary liability would be intuitively accepted by many equity lawyers, for whom Lord Ellesmere's description of the office of the Chancellor as being to 'correct men's consciences for frauds, breaches of trust, wrongs and oppressions' retains its validity as a statement of the fundamental objectives of the equity jurisdiction.[98] But the presence or absence of fault is only, at best, a very approximate basis for distinguishing equitable liability from restitutionary claims. The liability of the honest fiduciary to account for gains made in breach of duty but without fault (save in the conclusory sense noticed above) is well established in equity.[99] Moreover, it does not follow from the proposition that a recipient will be strictly liable in unjust enrichment that liability will not be imposed where fault or wrongdoing have in fact caused the enrichment. Duress and actual undue influence are grounds of restitution which are typically based on reprehensible behaviour. In some areas of restitution, absence of fault is a precondition to relief. For example, a quantum meruit will only be awarded for work done under an anticipated contract which does not materialise if the claimant's own behaviour is not the reason for the failure to conclude the contract.[100]

A third reason for excluding these doctrines from the purview of unjust enrichment is that the defendants in most of the reported decisions have not been enriched by their exploitative conduct or (in the case of the wife's equity to have a guarantee set aside) by their failure to take reasonable steps to explain the nature and effect of a guarantee. Rescission in these cases is usually executory, taking effect before the wrongdoer can derive a material benefit from her equitable wrongdoing. Even when the defendant has succeeded in obtaining a benefit from unconscionable conduct that enrichment, it is argued, is no more than an accidental feature of the claim.[101]

The validity of this argument depends on an assessment of the circumstances, if any, in which rescission operates as a restitutionary remedy. This is currently one of the most controversial questions in the law of restitution. That rescission can effect restitution is made clear by Millett LJ in *Portman Building Society v Hamlyn Taylor and Neck*:

> The obligation to make restitution must flow from the ineffectiveness of the transaction under which the money was paid and not from a mistake or misrepresentation which induced it... If the payer exercises his right of rescission

[98] *Earl of Oxford's Case* (1615) 21 ER 485, 1 Ch Rep 1, 7.

[99] *Keech v Sandford* (1726) Sel Cas T King 61, 25 ER 223; *Boardman v Phipps* [1967] 2 AC 46 (HL).

[100] Compare *Sabemo Pty Ltd v North Sydney Municipal Council* [1977] 2 NSWLR 880 (SC) with *Construction Design and Management Ltd v New Brunswick Housing Corp* (1973) 36 DLR (3d) 458 (NBCA).

[101] Glover (above n 97) 106–7.

in time and before the recipient deals with the money in accordance with his instructions, the obligation may follow.[102]

The significance of this passage lies both in its recognition that rescission can effectuate restitution, and in the conditional nature of that recognition signalled by the final words. Restitution *may* follow from the exercise of rescission, but rescission cannot be classified as a restitutionary remedy in the same way that the action for money had and received, for example, can. One obvious reason for rejecting a wholly restitutionary analysis of rescission is that the effect of an order of rescission may not be to reverse unjust enrichment but to reconstitute a contract on new terms.[103]

Leaving aside such cases, the literature on restitution can, broadly speaking, be divided into two schools of thought on the restitutionary applications of rescission. One school, adopting what might be termed a 'strong' unjust enrichment analysis, characterises rescission of wholly executory contracts as being restitutionary since the defendant is, by the exercise of rescission, required to restore to the plaintiff a chose in action, being the right to sue the plaintiff under the rescinded contract.[104] The analysis presupposes that the right of action constitutes an enrichment. For all its logical appeal no judicial decision has so far recognised this 'strong' restitutionary version of rescission. A second, 'weaker' version holds that rescission is restitutionary where the parties are returned to their pre-contractual position under a partly or wholly executed contract.[105] A judicial order compelling the wrongdoer to hold property acquired under the voidable transaction on constructive trust for the plaintiff and, if necessary, requiring the plaintiff to effect counter-restitution will be the equitable mechanism for reversing unjust enrichment. The dictum of Millett LJ is consistent with this weaker version.

Applying this version, it is not hard to find examples of the restitution of a benefit procured by unconscionable conduct following the exercise of rescission. Many are concealed by the invocation of resonant equitable maxims, such as 'doing practical justice between the parties.' On close inspection these turn out to be formulas for effecting restitution and counter-restitution. Decisions in which a defendant obtained a quantifiable benefit through an unconscionable dealing include some of the classic cases of this area of equity. One is *Wilton v Farnworth*,[106] in which

[102] [1998] 4 All ER 202 (CA) 208.
[103] *Solle v Butcher* [1950] 1 KB 671 (CA); *Grist v Bailey* [1967] Ch 532. The disapproval of these cases in *Great Peace Shipping Ltd v Tsavlivis Salvage (International) Ltd* ('*The Great Peace*') [2002] 4 All ER 689 (CA) should not be taken as a rejection of equity's jurisdiction to 'reform' a contract by rescission.
[104] N Nahan, 'Rescission: A Case for Rejecting the Classical Model?' (1997) *University of Western Australia Law Review* 66, 72–73.
[105] A Burrows, *The Law of Restitution*, 2nd edn (London, Butterworths 2002) 56–60.
[106] Above (n 49).

a deaf, dull-witted and poorly educated miner was induced to execute a deed of gift of a large inheritance to his stepson. Another is *Louth v Diprose*[107] in which a solicitor was persuaded by a woman with whom he had become infatuated to buy a house for her. In the latter case the High Court confirmed an order of the trial judge imposing a constructive trust over the house for the plaintiff without adverting to the opinion of the Court of Appeal that pecuniary restitution would have been more appropriate.[108] Since any appreciation in the value of property acquired by unconscionable conduct ought to inhere in the victim who has been deprived of that property the argument for awarding proprietary restitution in this case seems strong. Another clear example is *Bridgewater v Leahy*[109] where the nephew was enriched by his uncle's execution of the deed of forgiveness which enabled him to acquire grazing properties at substantial undervalue. In none of these cases could the defendants be heard to deny that they had been enriched. The 'reprehensible seeking out' of a benefit has always been held to constitute an enrichment.[110]

Where a guarantee has been unconscionably procured, as in the *Amadio* case or by applying the wife's 'equity' to have a guarantee set aside for lack of understanding and explanation, the lender will usually have been enriched by the taking of security over the surety's interest in the home. This will constitute an enrichment either because it is a bargained-for benefit or, again, because the lender has reprehensibly sought out the benefit.

The detailed working out of the restitutionary consequences of an order of rescission can be complex. The complexity is in part attributable to competing models of proprietary restitution which are applied to explain the consequences of rescission.[111] Dr Worthington, invoking High Court authority[112] on the application of equitable priority rules, has convincingly argued that prior to the exercise of equitable rescission a plaintiff has a mere equity to have the unconscionable transaction set aside. After exercise the defendant will, subject to the application of defences such as 'laches' or the acquisition of an interest in the property by a good faith purchaser, hold the property acquired under the contract upon constructive trust for the plaintiff.[113]

Most Australian equity lawyers would not, I suspect, be disposed to disagree with this (or some similar) analysis of the proprietary consequences of equitable rescission although they might remain unpersuaded that it needs to be expressed in the terminology of unjust enrichment. Restitution can

[107] Above (n 49).
[108] (1990) 54 SASR 438, 450 (King J); 453–54 (Full Court).
[109] Above (n 53).
[110] Burrows (above n 105) 24–25; Chen-Wishart (above n 90) 569.
[111] S Worthington, 'The Proprietary Consequences of Restitution' [2002] *Restitution Law Review* 28.
[112] *Latec Investments Ltd v Hotel Terrigal Pty Ltd (in liq)* (1965) 113 CLR 265 (HCA).
[113] *Greater Pacific Union Pty Ltd (in liq) v Australian National Industries Ltd* (1996) 39 NSWLR 143 (CA), 153 (McLelland AJA); *FAI General Insurance Co Ltd v Ocean Mutual*

certainly be effected in equity without recourse to the unjust enrichment principle. But an examination of the consequences of rescission in terms of that principle sheds light on the availability and scope of restitutionary defences and remedies, which have remained largely invisible through repetition of such time-honoured formulas as equity does 'what is practically just between the parties' or 'a plaintiff who comes to equity must do equity'.[114]

A. Defences

The defence of change of position will not be available to a party who has been enriched by her own unconscionable dealing. A basic requirement of the defence is that the recipient must have changed her position in good faith.[115] This cannot 'ex hypothesi' be satisfied where the recipient has procured the benefit by her own unconscionable conduct. But the defence ought in principle to be available to a later recipient who takes by way of gift and who therefore cannot claim to be a good faith purchaser.

A more difficult question is whether the defence can bar restitution where the benefit has been received as a result of an unconscionable enforcement of a contractual right in circumstances in which the recipient has acted in good faith, albeit (in equity's conclusory terms) inequitably. Suppose that a wife guarantees her husband's indebtedness, being a 'volunteer' (in the sense of having no interest of her own in the transaction). Suppose, further, that she has not received a sufficient explanation of the nature and effect of the guarantee, perhaps, because of an accidental breakdown in the lending bank's otherwise adequate procedures for ensuring that proper advice is given. The wife is later required under the guarantee to repay a loan to the bank, her husband having failed to make repayment. The money is applied to the discharge of her husband's indebtedness. Upon the wife's exercise of her equity to have the guarantee set aside[116] prior to a claim to restitution of the money paid, can the bank argue that it has in good faith changed its position? Even if it is accepted that the bank has incurred a detriment in applying the money to the repayment of a loan it has made,[117] it is unlikely

Protection and Indemnity Association (1997) 41 NSWLR 559 (Comm. D) 564 (Giles CJ). There is an argument for classifying the trust as resulting, see Worthington (above n 111) 38.

[114] *Erlanger v New Sombrero Phosphate Co* (1878) 3 App Cas 1218 (HL) 1278–79 (Lord Blackburn); *Alati v Kruger* (1955) 94 CLR 216 (HCA).

[115] *David* (above n 17) 384–86; *Lipkin Gorman v Karpnale Ltd* [1991] 2 AC 548 (HL).

[116] See text, above (n 83–86).

[117] The reduction of an overdraft or repayment of a loan is not necessarily beneficial to a commercial lender: *Australia and New Zealand Banking Group Ltd v Westpac Banking Corp* (1988) 164 CLR 662 (HCA) 681. Moreover, the bank might argue that it has incurred a detriment in making the loan to the husband in the honest belief that the guarantee was valid. Compare the change of position pleaded in *David* (above n 17) 384–86.

that a court would permit the defence to defeat the wife's claim to restitution. The recognition by the High Court of the wife's equity is premised on the assumption that, notwithstanding changes in the role of women in society, many wives still place considerable trust and confidence in their husbands in financial matters.[118] Accepting the accuracy of this assumption for present purposes, to permit a lender to assert the defence of change of position undermines the very policy that the High Court is promoting.[119] The recipient's interest in security of receipt, which is the function of the change of position defence to protect, should in this situation be subordinate to ensuring that lenders provide an adequate explanation to wives of the guarantees they are signing to secure repayment of loans to their husbands.

But even if a *defendant* cannot invoke the defence of change of position to defeat a claim to rescission of an unconscionable contract, a *plaintiff* should be entitled to the benefit of the defence where the process of restoring both parties to their pre-contractual position would otherwise ignore expenditure incurred in reliance on the validity of the contract.[120] This is already recognised in the allowance equity makes for the innocent party's improvements to property received under a voidable contract when they are permanent and increase the value of the property.[121] Moreover, a plaintiff under a voidable contract who, at the defendant's request, pays money received from the defendant to a third party is not required to make restitution of that money.[122] There is no good reason why the defence should not be extended to a plaintiff's unrequested payment to a third party provided that the plaintiff had made the payment in good faith upon the faith of the validity of the receipt from the defendant, and that the money was not spent on ordinary living expenses.[123] Suppose that in *Bridgewater v Leahy* the frugal uncle had applied some of the purchase money paid by his nephew for the grazing properties towards a wholly unexpected holiday for his wife and children. The uncle had received the payment under a contract which he believed at the time of his expenditure to be valid, even though it was later set aside as being unconscionable. The payment should be excluded from the process of restoring both parties to their pre-contractual position, on the ground that a plaintiff's interest in security of receipt ranks ahead of the interest of the wrongdoer in obtaining counter-restitution.

The other specifically restitutionary defence to rescission is that the plaintiff is unable to make counter-restitution to the defendant. Rescission will

[118] *Garcia* (above n 41) 404.
[119] Chen-Wishart (above n 90) 562.
[120] M Chen-Wishart, 'In Defence of Unjust Factors: A Study of Rescission for Duress, Fraud and Exploitation' (2000) *Oxford University Comparative Law Forum* 2, 11; Worthington (above n 111) 55–59.
[121] *Cooper v Phibbs* (1867) LR 2 HL 149 (HL); *Brown v Smitt* (1924) 34 CLR 1609 (HCA).
[122] *Spence v Crawford* [1939] 3 All ER 271 (HL), 282–83 (Lord Thankerton).
[123] See eg, Worthington (above n 111) 5–7 (denial of the defence to the defendant where the change of position does not affect the value of the underlying asset).

not be ordered where 'restitutio in integrum' is impossible.[124] Some restitution writers consider that the availability of personal restitution where the parties cannot be restored to their pre-contractual position has rendered this defence somewhat theoretical.[125] Its incidence may, however, be higher than is generally realised. Although modern examples of a refusal of rescission on the ground of complete impossibility of effecting 'restitutio in integrum' are hard to find, the principle of 'counter-restitution impossible' also comes into play whenever equitable relief is denied on the ground that a plaintiff coming to equity is unable (or unwilling) to do equity. This equitable bar to relief can be applied when a loan which is clearly disadvantageous to the borrower has been procured by the unconscionable conduct of the lender. In cases not covered by credit legislation[126] rescission will be dependent upon repayment of capital and payment of interest by the borrower. A recent example of the denial of restitution on the ground of failure to 'do equity' is *Wilby v St George Bank*[127] where an octogenarian borrower had borrowed money from the bank on the security of his house in order to discharge an earlier loan he and his son had made to another financial institution. After the loan had been applied for this purpose the borrower applied to have the mortgage set aside on the ground that the bank had acted unconscionably in taking the security. One of the grounds upon which the court refused relief was that the borrower had not repaid, and was not offering to repay, the principal sum lent by the bank.

But leaving aside the 'doing equity' cases, counter-restitution is more often seen as a precondition to obtaining restitution of benefits conferred under the rescinded contract. A plaintiff who wants to set aside a contract vitiated by unconscionable conduct, or for some other equitable wrongdoing, must restore property received from the defendant under the transaction. If necessary, she must also compensate the defendant for any deterioration of the property since its receipt.[128] Where services have been performed counter-restitution can be awarded through the medium of the award of an allowance for the services.[129]

The generality of the term 'equitable relief on terms' hides many examples of counter-restitution. An interesting example of concealed counter-restitution is the order made in *Bridgewater v Leahy*, discussed

[124] *Clarke v Dickson* (1858) El Bl & El 148, 120 ER 463 (KB); *AH McDonald & Co Pty Ltd* (1931) 45 CLR 506 (HCA).
[125] See eg, the discussion by P Birks, 'Overview: Defences' in P Birks (ed), *Laundering and Tracing* (Oxford, Oxford University Press, 1995), 336–41.
[126] The Consumer Credit Code, enacted in every State on the basis of the 'template legislation' of the Consumer Credit (Queensland) Act 1994 (Qld).
[127] Above (n 56). See also *Maguire v Makaronis* (1997) 188 CLR 449 (HCA) (a decision on rescission for breach of fiduciary duty). S Moriarty, 'Fiduciary Discretion' (1998) 114 *LQR* 9, 12–13.
[128] *Alati v Kruger* (n 29) 223–24.
[129] *O'Sullivan v Management Agency & Music Ltd* [1985] QB 428 (CA).

earlier in this article. The deed of forgiveness was set aside[130] and the case remitted to the Supreme Court to determine what allowance should be made in favour of the nephew on the assumption that the grazing properties had been sold to him at their full market value (ie $696,811 and not the $150,000 that he had actually paid after the execution of the deed of forgiveness). The allowance was intended to reflect the uncle's wish to benefit his nephew, evidenced by his will, as well as by the option conferred on him to buy the properties.

The majority judgement's technique of 'doing equity' reflects two distinct approaches to reversing unjust enrichment. The first is causative. Since the nephew would in any event have received most of the properties upon exercise of the option under his uncle's will, albeit for a higher price than that provided for under the deed of forgiveness, the nephew's enrichment was not wholly caused by his unconscientious receipt of the properties under the deed. The unconscionable conduct simply accelerated the receipt of most of the properties on more favourable financial terms than those contained in the uncle's will. The purpose of returning the case to the Supreme Court was to determine, more precisely than the High Court was able to do on the materials available, *how much* of the nephew's enrichment was caused by the unconscionable dealing. Any allowance to the nephew would reflect the value of the properties he would have received under the validly executed will.

An alternative, and more convincing, justification of the order is that it effected counter-restitution to the nephew who had assisted his uncle over many years in managing the properties. The allowance which the Supreme Court was required to determine, on remission from the High Court, was restitution for the significant contribution he had made to the success of the farms during his uncle's declining years. This approach assumes that the uncle's wish to benefit his nephew under the will was attributable to a desire to compensate him for his labours in managing the properties. The assumption is not unreasonable on the facts as found by the majority judgment.

B. Remedies

An unconscionable dealing is a ground for setting aside a transaction but not an independent cause of action entitling a plaintiff to damages.[131] In Professor Birks' taxonomy it is not a wrong, but a 'non-wrong'.[132]

[130] The majority would have set aside the consequential transfers to the nephew but for the fact that third parties, as well as the nephew, had interests in the properties: *Bridgewater v Leahy* (n 53) 493.

[131] *Mulcahy v Hydro-Electric Commission* (1998) 8 FCR 170. Statutory unconscionability under the Trade Practices Act 1974 (Cth), on the other hand, is a 'wrong' since it can give rise to compensatory damages under ss 82, 87.

[132] P Birks, 'Equity in the Modern Law: An Exercise in Taxonomy' (1996) 26 *University of Western Australia Law Review* 1, 40–42.

A question canvassed in some recent restitution scholarship is whether pecuniary restitution ought to be available if the restoration of property is impossible, or has been barred by the application of an equitable defence. The arguments for recognising pecuniary restitution are strong. The denial of rescission where a good faith purchaser has acquired rights in the subject matter of the transaction leaves the victim of unconscionable conduct uncompensated and undermines the policy of deterring exploitation. Monetary adjustments can be made, but only as part of the machinery of proprietary restitution. Sale, or dissipation of the plaintiff's property by the wrongdoer, will leave the plaintiff without remedy.[133] Personal restitution for benefits conferred under a void contract is in principle available on the ground of failure of consideration.[134] Why should it also not be available for benefits conferred under a voidable contract?

Australian law is familiar with the technique of awarding equitable compensation as a measure of personal restitution where proprietary rescission has been barred.[135] But the authorities have been mostly confined to instances of fiduciary wrongdoing, and it is unclear whether awards are available where other kinds of equitable wrongdoing have been committed.[136] The case for allowing awards of personal restitution seems overwhelming (whether or not we choose to label the remedy equitable compensation) since the law would otherwise be condoning unconscionable conduct when 'restitutio in integrum' is impossible or other bars to rescission apply.[137] The recent decision of Bryson J in *Hartigan v International Society of Krishna Consciousness Incorporated*[138] provides support for the proposition that orders of personal restitution, where rescission is barred, are not confined to cases of breaches of fiduciary obligation. The plaintiff applied to have a deed of gift of a farm to the defendant organisation set aside on the ground that it had been procured by undue influence. The property had been sold for $83,000 to discharge obligations owed by the defendant to Westpac Bank under a commercial bill facility. Bryson J held that the defendant had not overcome the burden of showing that, as the plaintiff's spiritual adviser, the organisation had not exercised undue influence over the plaintiff. The sale of the farm to a good faith purchaser in order to discharge the defendant's indebtedness prevented the plaintiff from recovering the property. She was held instead to be entitled to an order of personal restitution. The references in the decision to 'equitable relief' and

[133] *White v Garden* (1851) 10 CB 919; 138 ER 364 (CP).
[134] *Westdeutsche Landesbank Girozentrale v Islington LBC* [1996] AC 669 (HL).
[135] *McKenzie v McDonald* [1927] VLR 134 (SC).
[136] The South Australian Full Court would have ordered equitable compensation in *Diprose v Louth* (1990) 54 SASR 450 (Full Court). The relief ordered was not a ground of appeal to the High Court, which confirmed the trial judge's order imposing a constructive trust over the defendant's house for the benefit of the plaintiff; see *Louth v Diprose* (n 49) 638–39.
[137] Chen-Wishart (above n 120) 15.
[138] [2002] NSWSC 810 (Bryson J).

to the well known principle that 'the court has power to mould the relief to the circumstances of the particular case' mask the reality that personal restitution has been awarded, in lieu of a proprietary order consequent upon rescission, in order to reverse unjust enrichment.[139]

But the circumstances in which personal restitution will be available as an alternative to rescission need to be carefully defined. This is because the equitable considerations barring proprietary rescission may in some cases be equally applicable to defeat the pecuniary remedy. For example, a claim to rescind barred by 'laches' should not be revived under the guise of a claim for personal restitution.[140] Similarly, affirmation should defeat both remedies since it constitutes a denial of the ground of restitution. On the other hand, acquisition by a good faith purchaser of an interest in the subject matter of the unconscionable transaction should not preclude the making of an order of personal restitution against the original unconscientious recipient of the property. Indeed, it is in this very situation that a personal order will be most valuable. In other situations it is unclear whether personal restitution should be ordered. What about the victim of unconscionable conduct who receives a benefit under the transaction but who refuses, in equitable parlance, to 'do equity'?[141] One solution, consistent with existing equitable principle, is to refuse relief on the ground that restitution is conditional upon the willingness and ability of the party seeking restitution to make counter-restitution. An alternative, more civilian, approach would be to allow a set-off against the plaintiff's personal order of the value of any benefit received under the transaction, so that the plaintiff receives the difference between the enrichments received by both parties.[142] The plaintiff should be entitled to argue for a reduction in the value of any benefit received where she has changed her position since receipt, for example where money received from the defendant as part of an unconscionable transaction has been paid to a third party at the defendant's direction. If this is allowed the amount payable by way of counter-restitution will be reduced by her change of position.

V. CONCLUSION

Unconscionability in Australia needs saving from its friends quite as much as from its enemies. Every legal system provides relief against exploitation.

[139] *Ibid*, [98].
[140] In *Hartigan* (above n 138), the plaintiff was denied interest on the personal restitution order by reason of her delay.
[141] See eg, *Wilby v St George Bank* (above n 58).
[142] Chen-Wishart (above n 120) 10–11, discussing German 'saldotheorie.' Note the reservation that in cases of fraud, duress and immorality a plaintiff is only required to account for the value surviving.

The unconscionable dealings doctrine, as it has been developed in Australia, is no more indeterminate or unpredictable in its application than other grounds of equitable relief, such as undue influence or breach of fiduciary obligation. These grounds have their own penumbra of uncertainty. It is true that inquiries into unconscionable conduct are context-specific, and often of limited value as legal precedent, but the same could be said, for example, of inquiries into whether a relationship (not being one of presumed influence) is one of undue influence, or whether a demand for extra payment for performing a subsisting contract constitutes economic duress as opposed to a legitimate contract renegotiation. Doctrines focusing on imbalances of economic power are inevitably context-specific. Provided that relief is imposed on the basis of actual, and not constructive, notice of a special disadvantage, the equitable doctrine as stable as any other doctrine that relieves against exploitation. Moreover, the transaction costs incurred in ensuring compliance with its standards will be reasonable.

Similarly, statutory relief against unconscionable conduct is not objectionable provided that discretion under the legislation is exercised along the same lines as the equitable doctrine. To apply a doctrine of substantive unconscionability without an understanding of market economics is a recipe for both legal and economic incoherence, but it is too early to say whether Australian courts will develop a full-blown doctrine of substantive unconscionability. Certainly the High Court in *Berbatis*[143] evinced little enthusiasm for the notion. The indications are that the courts will not go down that path. A greater cause for concern is the reliance placed upon the prevention of unconscionable enforcement of legal rights as a conclusory technique to justify equitable intervention. Even in this context, however, unconscionability needs to be saved from other objections advanced by restitution writers to conscience-based doctrine which are misconceived. One example is the criticism of the adoption of the 'special equity' of *Garcia* on the ground that it 'would make it easier to undermine transactions with banks, with the consequence that banks will be less likely to lend money on the security of the matrimonial home or the wife's guarantee.'[144] There is no evidence that the equity in *Garcia* has made the slightest difference to bank lending to spouses on the strength of a wife's guarantee.[145] The criticism, being empirical, can only be substantiated or refuted by empirical inquiry—a kind of inquiry which most restitution writers are not predisposed to pursue.

The 'friends' of conscience-based equity have, for their part, succeeded in excluding the unconscionable dealings doctrine, together with some

[143] Above (n 67).

[144] G Virgo, *The Principles of the Law of Restitution* (Oxford, Oxford University Press,1999) 277–78.

[145] Banking practice provides for separate advice for wives, for the reasons stated in Duggan (above n 87) 423.

restitutionary applications of the 'unconscionable insistence upon legal rights' principle, from any analysis in terms of unjust enrichment. This article has suggested that the stated reasons for this exclusion—for example that unconscionability doctrines are 'fault based' whereas restitution for unjust enrichment is strict—are either specious, or else are based on exaggerated fears that recognition of unconscionable conduct as a ground of restitution might result in a false equation of 'injustice' with 'unconscionable conduct'.

The principal, but unarticulated, reason why relief from unconscionable transactions has not been identified as being part of the law of unjust enrichment in Australia is that equitable rescission has not been theorised as a remedy whose function, in effecting 'restitutio in integrum,' can be the reversal of unjust enrichment. There is now a significant body of scholarly work devoted to examining the role of rescission as a response to unjust enrichment.[146] None of the literature discusses the specifically Australian principles governing the setting aside of unconscionable transactions, though the writings offer useful insights into methods of restoring wealth procured by exploitation. The insights are relevant to an analysis of the defences to claims, as well as to the development of personal restitution as an alternative to rescission. Until the role of rescission in reversing unjust enrichment is recognised by Australian lawyers, restitution of benefits conferred under unconscionable transactions will continue to be a neglected and under-theorised topic, and Australian judges and writers will continue, erroneously, to view unjust enrichment as having nothing to do with the principles governing relief from unconscionable transactions.

[146] See especially, the analyses by Chen-Wishart (above n 90) and (above n 119); Nahan (above n 104); O'Sullivan (above n 30); Worthington (above n 111).

5

Understanding the Unjust Enrichment Principle in Private Law: A Study of the Concept and its Reasons

KIT BARKER*

> *Plato, in the Cratylus, had Socrates ask of Cratylus: 'What is the force of names and what is the use of them?' To this Cratylus replied: 'The use of names, Socrates, as I should imagine, is to inform: the simple truth is that he who knows names knows also the things which are expressed by them.* (R Summers, 'The New Analytical Jurists' (2000))

I. INTRODUCTION

THE NATURE, UTILITY and scope of unjust enrichment as a legal concept has long been the subject of heated debate. Given the volume and eminence of the thinking directed at the topic, it is with some hesitation that one embarks upon it. The ground is sensitive and jealously guarded by different jurisdictional traditions, common law and civilian. Moreover, few steps can be taken without treading on the toes of one or more other, better established fields of law or ways of thinking. This is part of the topic's danger, but also, of course, part of its attraction. Recklessly insensitive as we are to our vulnerabilities, it is always the flame that attracts us most.

It is therefore with some trepidation that I tackle this topic. My aspiration is that the perspective which this article brings to bear may help to expose the nature of disagreements about the nature of the unjust enrichment principle more clearly and, by eradicating some of the more common

* I am hugely indebted to A Halpin for his good-natured, yet piercing insights into an earlier draft of this article. All defects remain entirely my own.

sources of confusion, move the law forward with a better understanding of its own shape and aims. The perspective is theoretical in orientation and this in turn may cause some unease amongst practitioners. I am acutely aware throughout the process of Burrows' recent warning against work in this still unstable field which might attract the stigma of 'impractical scholarship,'[1] and of the duty which academics owe to the broader legal community to contribute purposefully to it. Our thinking must not become so abstracted from the practice of the law that its sense of meaning and relevance is lost.

Despite these reservations, it is a key premise of almost everything which follows that the divide between theory and coherent practice is to a large extent illusory;[2] indeed that proper practice and proper legal analysis depend at root on a clear vision of the law's foundational aims. Modes of analysis and legal reasoning which do not respect and reflect these aims—which fail to expound and clarify *reasons*—place the proverbial cart before the horse. They purport to tell us what the law should *look like* and how it should *behave*, without reference to the logically prior (and governing) question of what it is *for*. The latter inquiry is of course itself partly contingent, since our perception of the purpose of a thing is always dictated in some measure by the way it looks to us; and if our minds have already shaped or organised it in a particular way, we are likely to divine its functions accordingly. Nonetheless, the reflexive connection between what one might call analytical thinking or taxonomy on the one hand (the process of organising legal rules) and foundational thinking (divining their purposes) on the other has hitherto been under-utilised in understanding unjust enrichment.[3] This is entirely understandable, because in most jurisdictions the subject is still young. Equally, important moves have recently been made to increase the subject's theoretical maturity and to connect new intuitions to features of the emerging law.[4] It is this more 'concrete' use of theory

[1] A Burrows, 'Restitution: Where do We Go From Here?' in A Burrows, *Understanding the Law of Obligations* (Oxford, Hart Publishing, 1998) 119. See also the article which inspired these fears: H Edwards, 'The Growing Disjunction between Legal Education and the Legal Profession' (1992) 91 *Michigan Law Review* 34.

[2] For a comprehensive analysis of the relationship between law and practice, see A Halpin, *Reasoning with Law* (Oxford, Hart Publishing, 2001) ch 2.

[3] K Barker, 'Unjust Enrichment: Containing the Beast' (1995) 15 *OJLS* 457.

[4] See, eg, E Weinrib, 'The Gains and Losses of Corrective Justice' (1994) *Duke Law Journal* 277; E Weinrib, *The Idea of Private Law* (London, Harvard University Press, 1995) 140–42; E Weinrib, 'Restitutionary Damages as Corrective Justice' (2000) 1 *Theoretical Inquiries in Law* 1; J Gordley, 'The Purposes of Awarding Restitutionary Damages: A Reply to Prof Weinrib' (2000) 1 *Theoretical Inquiries in Law* 39; N McBride and P McGrath, 'The Nature of Restitution' (1995) 15 *OJLS* 33; H Dagan, *Unjust Enrichment* (Cambridge, Cambridge University Press, 1997); H Dagan, 'The Distributive Foundation of Corrective Justice' (1999) 98 *Michigan Law Review* 138; L Smith, 'Restitution: The Heart of Corrective Justice' (2001) 79 *Texas Law Review* 2115; M Gergen, 'What Renders Enrichment Unjust?' (2001) 79 *Texas Law Review* 1927; S Smith, 'Justifying the Law of Unjust Enrichment' (2001) 79 *Texas Law Review* 2177.

which to my mind holds greatest hope for the future and which ought simultaneously to allay some of Burrows' fears.

The purpose of this article is to explore what is meant by a principle against unjust enrichment in private law, and to build upon the connections and distinctions between principles, rules and reasons in such a way as to better explain the body of law which falls under it. The position taken is that, whilst meanings are culturally contingent and differ as between jurisdictions, the idea of unjust enrichment is best understood in the common law as both a coherent classificatory category (principle of interpretation) and as a normative legal principle, mediating at a higher level the reasons expressed in a broad variety of more detailed and more 'dispositive' legal rules governing the actionability of gains in private law. These rules can all be 'categorised' within unjust enrichment law because they all address the common question of when one party may sue another for gains the other has made. Moreover, whilst there are some obvious and important analytical differences between them, the rules share what Wittgenstein[5] might have referred to as 'family resemblances' in their foundational objectives (reasons). Some of these reasons are deontological (they refer to intrinsic moral values) and some—more rarely—utilitarian, but collectively they relate together to form a series of significant normative connections between the various types of unjust enrichment case.

The general tenor of the proposed thinking is that a full understanding of unjust enrichment entails two key steps. Firstly, we must surrender the essentialist view that every case referred to under that name has to share a single feature or set of features with all other cases bearing the same name. The rejection of essentialism was an important part of Wittgenstein's philosophy and enables us to accommodate difference within our legal structures. This is vital to the meaningful survival of 'unjust enrichment' as a category, because it spans such a diverse range of cases. Secondly, when it comes to identifying the reasons which underpin the principle, we may have to assume a more pluralist stance than that which has recently been taken by some writers, such as Weinrib,[6] for whom private law in general and unjust enrichment law in particular are underpinned exclusively by the values of corrective justice. Much has been done to show that that form of justice does indeed explain a good deal of the relevant law. But the unitary analysis ultimately fails. What Englard[7] has concluded to be true of tort law—that it in fact represents a complimentary mix of different and sometimes conflicting reasons—is also true of the law of unjust enrichment. The breadth of the subject matter which the field spans makes this almost

[5] Below, Part III.
[6] Weinrib (above n 4).
[7] I Englard, *The Philosophy of Tort Law* (Cambridge, Dartmouth, 1993). The conclusion is expressed briefly in ch 17.

inevitable, and whilst corrective justice should indeed be taken as the primary foundation of most unjust enrichment rules, it does not offer a full account of their internal workings.

Part Two sets the scene by providing a brief history of the debate about unjust enrichment as a concept, identifying the main roles which it has been thought to play and the various criticisms made of it in these roles. Part Three looks outward to some more general aspects of legal theory to explain why the prescription against unjust enrichment is to be characterised as a principle at all (what this means) and to provide the bare bones of a strategy for the individuation of private laws (a theory of taxonomy). Key to this part is Wittgenstein's theory of family resemblance and the rejection of overly essentialist approaches to legal classification. Acceptance of this theory explains why it is possible for a *good* categorisation of law based around unjust gain to tolerate apparent differences between its rules, without loss of coherence. Part Four examines the relationship between the unjust enrichment principle and its reasons, substituting a pluralist vision of its foundations for Weinrib's unitary one. Finally, Part Five assesses the practical implications of the conclusions we have drawn. The most important of these is that cases of 'autonomous' ('subtractive') unjust enrichment and cases of 'unjust enrichment by wrongdoing' belong in the same legal category. This is because, although they display a number of significant differences, the rules they describe both address the same basic question and they share important normative connections. This calls into question the recent thesis of a number of distinguished writers,[8] that cases in which restitution ('disgorgement') is made for wrongs have nothing to do with unjust enrichment at all and should consequently be excluded from its ambit.

II. A BRIEF HISTORY OF DEBATE: IDENTIFYING ROLES FOR UNJUST ENRICHMENT

Most jurisdictions, common law, civilian and mixed, now make reference in some way to a principle against unjust enrichment within their systems of private law, though it is expressed in different ways and construed as covering different ground.[9] The exact scope of the principle turns on

[8] Most significantly, Birks. See P Birks, 'Misnomer' ch 1 in W Cornish and others (eds), *Restitution—Past Present and Future* (Oxford, Hart Publishing, 1998); P Birks, 'The Law of Unjust Enrichment: A Millennial Resolution' (1999) *Singapore Journal of Legal Studies* 318; P Birks, 'Unjust Enrichment and Wrongful Enrichment' (2001) 79 *Texas Law Review* 1767. The effect of these contributions is to draw a 'bright line' between the two areas. See also L Smith, 'The Province of the Law of Restitution' (1992) *Canadian Bar Review* 672; D Laycock, 'The Scope and Significance of Restitution' (1989) 67 *Texas Law Review* 1277.

[9] For a particularly useful comparative summary, see B Dickson, 'Unjust Enrichment Claims: A Comparative Overview' (1995) 54 *CLJ* 100.

factors particular to the jurisdiction in question, including the broader ecology of its legal system, and one must therefore be aware, in detailing the debate, of the impact of cultural and historical factors in shaping understandings of what unjust enrichment means. Some controversies are clearly attributable to these cultural differences. That raised in Canada, for example, as to whether we should talk of *unjust* or *unjustified* enrichment stems from the influence of civilian thinking, mediated via Quebec law, upon judicial pioneers of the principle in the Supreme Court of Canada.[10] The use of the principle to effect redistribution of property on the break-up of quasi-matrimonial relationships[11] also looks strange to English lawyers and tends to be thought of as a purely pragmatic way of doing what ought to be done under a different name. Similarly, Lionel Smith has recently suggested that the only reason why the concept of unjust enrichment in Germany includes cases of restitution (or, as he would say 'disgorgement') for civil wrongs is because there is no provision for gain-based damages in the BGB.[12] All these observations contain particular truths and illustrate the more general one that the precise way in which any legal principle is understood is determined by the context and history of the culture in which it has evolved.[13]

If we nonetheless abstract as much as we can from cultural and historical influences, a common debate has emerged about the nature of unjust enrichment as an idea. Different jurists have understood it in very different ways. It has thus variously been described as an extrinsic moral standard incapable of concrete application,[14] an 'aspiration and a standard for judgement,'[15] an 'idea' underlying a variety of different parts of the law but with no claim to its own taxonomic territory,[16] an organising tool[17]

[10] Dickson J, progenitor of the principle in *Rathwell v Rathwell* [1978] 2 SCR 436; (1978) 83 DLR (3d) 289 (SCC), was clearly influenced by sitting in the earlier case of *Cie Immobiliere Viger Ltee v Laureat Giguere Inc* [1977] 2 SCR 67 (SCC). For one proponent of the 'unjustified enrichment' view, see R Samek, 'Unjust Enrichment, Quasi-Contract and Restitution' (1969) 47 *Canadian Bar Review* 1, 17. The same debate has found more recent resonance in English law in discussions as to whether 'absence of consideration' is a ground of recovery: P Birks, 'No Consideration: Restitution After Void Contracts' (1993) *University of Western Australia Law Review* 195.

[11] Eg, *Atlas Cabinets v National Trust* (1990) 68 DLR (4th) 161 (BCCA) 171 (Lambert JA); *Griffith v Anderson* (1993) 48 RFL (3d) 390 (BCCA); *Forrest v Price* (1992) 48 ETR 72 (BCSC); *Harrison v Kalinocha* (1994) 112 DLR (4th) 43 (BCCA).

[12] L Smith (above n 4) 2147, fn 135.

[13] For further illustration of this point, see M McInnes, 'The Canadian Principle of Unjust Enrichment: Comparative Insights into the Law of Restitution' (1999) 37 *Alberta Law Review* 1; Dagan (above n 4).

[14] E Abbot, 'Keener on Quasi-Contracts' (1896) 10 *Harvard Law Review* 209, 247.

[15] J Dawson, *Unjust Enrichment: A Comparative Analysis* (Boston, Little, Brown, 1951) 5.

[16] P Atiyah, *The Rise and Fall of Freedom of Contract* (Oxford, Oxford University Press, 1979) 768.

[17] A Burrows, *The Law of Restitution*, 2nd edn (London, Butterworths, 2002) 1. See also *Rod Milner Motors Ltd v Attorney General* [1999] 2 NZLR 568, 576.

or classificatory label[18] for existing legal decisions, a 'principle of justice,'[19] a generalised articulation of the common sense and policy considerations lying behind sets of legal rules,[20] a 'unifying principle,'[21] a 'legal concept' with both empirical content and predictive power,[22] a legal doctrine,[23] a cause of action[24] and a basis of liability.[25]

From this descriptive soup, four possible roles for the concept can be strained: a classificatory unit, an extrinsic norm, a legal principle and a cause of action. McCamus identified some of these for us in 1993[26] and they coincide with the intuitions expressed by Raz[27] about the way in which principles can more generally be used in law.

Firstly, the concept might operate as a *classificatory unit*, like contract or tort. In this role, it has no normative force, any more than a generic label such as 'cats' or 'dogs' does. It simply groups cases which are perceived by their observer to have more or less homogeneous characteristics. It is then an instrument of observation, organisation and understanding, but lacks any form of prescriptive power. In Raz's terms, it is a way of *interpreting* legal rules in order to accord them coherence.[28] This is one possible function for the principle in England which is identified by Burrows, though not, it seems, the primary one.[29]

A frequent criticism aimed at the concept in this role is that it is misleading, because it groups cases which are too heterogeneous. Hedley voices

[18] *Muschinski v Dodds* (1985) 160 CLR 583, 617 (Deane J). See also Lord Hobhouse in *Attorney General v Blake* [2001] 1 AC 268, 296–97, describing the principle as a 'heading' under which a variety of distinct restitutionary rights are grouped.
[19] R Goff and G Jones, *The Law of Restitution*, 6th edn (London, Sweet and Maxwell, 2002) 14.
[20] J McCamus, 'Unjust Enrichment: Its Role and Limits' in D Waters (ed), *Equity, Fiduciaries and Trusts* (Toronto, Carswell, 1993) 129, 144.
[21] *Pavey & Matthews v Paul* (1987) 162 CLR 221, 256 (Deane J); *Peel (Regional Municipality) v Canada* [1992] 3 SCR 762, 787; (1992) 98 DLR (4th) 140 (SCC) 154 (McLachlin J); C Allen, 'Fraud, Quasi-Contract and False Pretences' (1938) 54 *LQR* 201, 205.
[22] Samek (above n 10).
[23] *White v Central Trust Co* (1984) 7 DLR (4th) 236 (NBCA) 246 (La Forest JA); *Peel* (n 21) 786; 153 (McLachlin J).
[24] *Lac Minerals Ltd v International Corona Resources Ltd* [1989] 2 SCR 574, 669; (1989) 61 DLR (4th) 14 (SCC) 45 (La Forest J); *Peel* (above n 21) 788; 154 (McLachlin J). See also Smith (above n 8) 673.
[25] G Klippert, 'The Juridical Nature of Unjust Enrichment' (1980) *University of Toronto Law Journal* 356; G Klippert, *Unjust Enrichment* (Toronto, Butterworths, 1983).
[26] McCamus (above n 20).
[27] J Raz, 'Legal Principles and the Limits of Law' (1972) 81 *Yale Law Journal* 823, especially 839–42.
[28] *Ibid*, 840.
[29] Burrows (n 17) 1: '..its essential role is as an organising tool for existing legal decisions.' Note, however, that the principle is regarded as having a normative aspect (it 'is and must be, morally justifiable') and a degree of prescriptive legal force, such that it can be used to effect changes in the law (Burrows (above n 1) 102–8). The cumulative effect of this is that the author in fact sees the principle as sitting in the third role, below.

this concern with particular force.[30] We return to it later, but at this juncture it is important to note that the extent to which differences between cases are construed as material for classificatory purposes is a matter of judgment, contingent upon the purposes of the inquirer. A visitor to a library may legitimately choose to group books by their year of publication, if his or her interest is in publication patterns, rather than the profiles of particular authors. He or she may detect a connection and describe a category ('books of 1967') which other visitors do not. Provided that a coherent justification can be supplied for his or her classification method, there are no logical limits to the interpretative perspectives that he or she may bring to bear. The fact that, on this occasion, the visitor ends up with a pile of books by different authors in no sense detracts from the coherence of his or her collection, because it is based on a coherent line of inquiry. Homogeneity and heterogeneity are thus relative, and the idea of homogeneity can tolerate difference as well as similarity, provided only that differences are immaterial in terms of the classificatory method chosen. This in turn means that where Hedley sees a miscellany, others may legitimately derive a set, provided only that they can supply a rational explanation for their interpretative scheme. Such an explanation is set out further in Part Three, below. Unjust enrichment rules answer a common question about the actionability of gains in private law, and although they differ in material respects, the differences do not undermine their categorisation. Nor should they be allowed to obscure important, normative resemblances between the various rules, which flow from their underlying reasons.

A second view is that the principle expresses an *extrinsic norm*: one who is unjustly enriched at the expense of another *ought*, for reasons either moral or other, to yield up his or her enrichment in such a way as to make good the injustice. The normative aspect of the principle in this role means that it can act as a legislative or judicial reason for *changing* existing legal rules, or *making new ones*.[31] But its extrinsic nature denudes it of legal force. It is a principle, but not a principle of law. Abbot took this view in his criticism of Keener's approach to unjust enrichment at the end of the nineteenth century.[32] He claimed that the principle must be extrinsic to be

[30] S Hedley, 'Ten Questions For Unjust Enrichment Theorists' (1997) 3 *Web Journal of Current Legal Issues* Question 1. Hedley makes a further, separate criticism of the principle as category, on the basis that its proponents tend to restrict its scope for policy reasons (see Question 3). Strictly speaking, this criticism relates to the scope accorded to the principle, rather than to its function in judicial reasoning, but it also seems inevitable that some considerations of a policy nature will enter into exercises of legal taxonomy. Atiyah's distinct criticism of the principle as category (above n 16) appears to stem from its potential to upset the way he understands other categories, especially contract law.

[31] These are the second and fourth functions identified for principles by Raz (above n 27).

[32] Abbot (above n 14). See also P Birks, rev edn, *An Introduction to the Law of Restitution* (Oxford, Clarendon, 1989) 23: '... it may be that the principle can never be more than a moral aspiration.'

meaningful and that this, somewhat ironically, made it redundant. Learned Hand questioned this suggestion in the *Harvard Law Review* in the following year[33] and the reason he was right to do so is because a norm can still operate as a resource for legal thinking, even where it lacks binding force. The law is (thankfully) never immune to the influence of normative ideas, which can always assist in our assessments as to whether it is right or wrong.

Aside from the false accusation of redundancy, two other doubts have been expressed about the principle in this second role. In 1997, Hedley made the point that if unjust enrichment was indeed an extrinsic standard, no ethical basis for it had ever been identified.[34] With respect, this does not seem to have been quite true, as we shall see in Part Four. Theorists have been making connections between restitution and foundational, ethical ideas for quite some time. These ideas, admittedly dormant at the time Hedley was writing, have recently been re-awakened and vigorously refreshed by writers such as Weinrib and Lionel Smith.[35] The other, more serious concern, expressed by Birks, is that references to extrinsic standards are undesirable because they are likely to subvert judicial discipline and introduce uncertainty into the law.[36] This is a far weightier point and almost certainly explains why both common law courts and the team recently attempting a third draft of the American *Restatement of Restitution* have tended to reject any purely extrinsic interpretation of the unjust enrichment principle. They have shown themselves deeply and consistently mindful of the need to respect legal precedent.[37]

The third role identified for unjust enrichment is as a *legal principle*. In this guise, the concept has both *normative force* and (vitally) *legal status*: it states that one *must not in law* unjustly enrich oneself at the expense of another. The normative aspect means, again, that it can operate as a *reason* for changing existing legal rules—it makes the principle *dynamic*. Its legal status affords it greater weight and legitimacy in judicial argument than if it simply embodied extrinsic values, and it thereby meets Birks' main concern. Nonetheless, the concept has only limited, dispositive power. It does not

[33] L Hand, 'Restitution or Unjust Enrichment' (1897) 11 *Harvard Law Review* 249.

[34] Hedley (above n 30) Question 2: 'If there is an ethical principle against unjust enrichment, why have ethical theorists not heard of it?' He has recently repeated this point in *A Critical Introduction to Restitution* (London, Butterworths, 2001) 15: '..if unjust enrichment is really a moral notion at all, it is one which is extraordinarily hard to pin down.'

[35] Below, Part IV.

[36] Birks (above n 32) 18–19. Similar fears appear to have inspired suggestions that the field might better be referred to under the title of 'reversible' (Birks, at 19) or 'restorable' enrichment (RB Grantham and CEF Rickett, *Enrichment and Restitution in New Zealand* (Oxford, Hart Publishing, 2000) 18–19).

[37] *Lac Minerals* (above n 24) 670; 45 (La Forest J); *Peel* (above n 21) 788; 154 (McLachlin J); *Lipkin Gorman (a firm) v Karpnale Ltd* [1991] 2 AC 548, 578 (Lord Goff); *Restatement of the Law of Restitution and Unjust Enrichment*, 3rd discussion draft (Philadelphia, American Law Institute, 2000) comment (b) to s 1.

itself dispose of particular cases, but mediates a set of lower-level concepts and rules. What is meant by 'injustice,' for example, depends upon the category of case concerned and it is only by looking to the relevant category that the required elements of liability may be precisely determined. It is possible that this is the way Birks himself understood matters in his immensely important *Introduction to the Law of Restitution* in 1986,[38] and McCamus comes close to expressing the same view when he describes the principle as a general articulation of the various normative considerations lying behind sets of legal rules.[39] The idea that the principle is a higher-level mediator of lower-level ideas means that it looks 'downward toward the cases,' not upward to a starry firmament of subjective, moral considerations. In *Kleinwort Benson Ltd v Lincoln City Council*[40] both Lords Goff and Hope referred to unjust enrichment in terms of legal principle, and harnessed its apparent, normative force to abrogate the mistake of law rule in English law, which suggests that at least some of our most highly respected judges understand it in this way. Similar allusions to the concept as a principle with both explanatory power and the capacity to prompt new liability rules appear in a number of the Canadian cases.[41]

The final role for the concept is as a *legal cause of action*. By this, I think it is generally[42] meant that the concept can of itself be *legally dispositive*.

[38] Birks (above n 32) 16–17, 22. Birks here describes unjust enrichment as the generic conception of all events ('the composite event') triggering the legal response of restitution. There is, however, some doubt as to whether his account casts the principle in this third role, stemming from his assertion that the principle has no normative, dynamic aspect to it (see 23). Reflection on this passage in the *Introduction* seems to indicate, however, that the claim that the concept of unjust enrichment lacked normative power was made primarily in order to avoid characterising it as purely extrinsic (moral) and hence subjective ('the principle threatens to undo the effort taken to make [the concept of] "unjust" look downwards to the cases.') In fact, however, there is no reason why the principle should not be regarded as both intrinsic (reflected in existing cases) *and* moral (expressing moral reasons contained in those cases). Either Birks did not consider this possibility (which seems unlikely), or it may be that it is what he had in mind all along, so that he did indeed conceive of the principle in this third role. Note that the recent changes in the *scope* which Birks affords to the unjust enrichment principle (above n 8) do not affect his basic understanding of its *nature*.

[39] McCamus (above n 20).

[40] [1999] 2 AC 349, 373 (Lord Goff), 405–6 (Lord Hope). See also Lord Goff in *Lipkin Gorman* (above n 37) 578: 'I accept that the solicitors' claim in the present case is founded upon the unjust enrichment of the club, and can only succeed if, in accordance with the principles of the law of restitution, the club was indeed unjustly enriched at the expense of the solicitors ... The recovery of money in restitution is not, as a general rule, a matter of discretion for the court. A claim to recover money at common law is made as a matter of right; and even though the underlying principle of recovery is the principle of unjust enrichment, nevertheless, where recovery is denied, it is denied on the basis of legal principle.'

[41] Eg, *White* (above n 23) 246 (La Forest JA); *Peel* (above n 21) 788; 154–55 (McLachlin J).

[42] Not always. See eg, Smith (above n 8). Although the author describes unjust enrichment as 'an independent cause of action,' he clearly does not envisage it being used dispositively in the sense referred to in the text. For him the concept is purely 'conclusory' (at 675), by which it seems to be meant that it lacks any normative power. This view is then close to that questioningly attributed to Birks (see the analysis in n 38 above) and suffers from all the associated disadvantages.

Its direct application generates liability, without further reference to lower-level concepts. In this guise, it looks more like what Dworkin might refer to as a rule,[43] because of its high degree of prescriptive force. The occurrence of a particular 'event' (unjust enrichment) describes the set of conditions (the 'protasis' of the rule) under which the relevant consequence (the 'apodosis') automatically applies. Of the various restitution scholars, Klippert probably came closest to this interpretation in the 1980s.[44] He drew an analogy with the way in which a negligence principle developed into a 'basis of liability' in the wake of *Donoghue v Stevenson*.[45] Actually, the analogy does not really work, because modern cases[46] are clear that Lord Atkin's neighbour principle was never intended (and indeed for many years it was never interpreted) as an unmediated liability rule. The concept of 'proximity' in negligence is a higher-level concept which mediates a broad and often complex set of lower-level concepts, which vary as between different categories of case, in response to different types of context and policy concern. The concept is thus not conclusively dispositive of anything, though it has obvious normative weight. It sits in the third role, not the fourth. Nonetheless, as a matter of historical fact, it may at one stage have been used dispositively[47] and the same is also true of unjust enrichment in some of the earlier Canadian cases.[48] This may be attributable in part again to the influence of civilian thinking, because in civil systems, principles are generally given direct application in disposing of cases rather than acting as mediators for lower-order concepts and precedents. Being fair to Klippert, his key concern in characterising unjust enrichment as a 'basis of liability' was that it should not be locked statically into existing categories of recovery, but should have the capacity to generate new liabilities.[49] That aim is consistent with a principle of the third type, as we have said, and it may be that that characterisation is closer to his view. It is a little difficult to tell.

The criticisms made of unjust enrichment in its fourth potential role are predictable. Common law lawyers fear that it will be dangerously over-expansive and accordingly deploy a host of colourful metaphors to ward us off. The principle is thus stigmatised as a 'Trojan horse' with dangerous

[43] See further below, Part III.
[44] Klippert (above n 25).
[45] [1932] AC 562.
[46] *Caparo Industries plc v Dickman (and others)* [1990] 2 AC 605.
[47] Even this is doubtful, but the nearest English courts have come to using the principle directly to found liability is probably *Junior Books Ltd v Veitchi Co Ltd* [1983] 1 AC 520, often described as the 'high watermark' of the law of negligence.
[48] Eg, *Rathwell* (above n 10) (Dickson J); *Pettkus v Becker* [1980] 2 SCR 834; (1980) 117 DLR (3d) 257 (SCC). For a classic example of this unmediated type of use in Quebec, see *Cie Immobiliere Ltee* (above n 10).
[49] Klippert 1980 (above n 25) 386–87.

forces pregnant in its belly;[50] a 'siren song'[51] luring us to a watery grave; 'sand on the beach ... liable to get everywhere;'[52] and a 'placebo to ... heal any nagging pain.'[53] These fears echo those which attended the 'neighbour principle' in the days in the late 1980s when it was thought that negligence law was expanding too far and too fast in its protection of economic interests. It is unwise to ignore them, though in truth whether the law goes through an expansionist phase or not depends more on judicial attitudes than it does on the concepts which are in play. No concept can be immunised against—or indeed necessarily demands—radical judicial use, though the way in which it is framed may, of course, send oblique signals to its users about the need for radicalism or caution.

The doubts of restitution scholars about the concept in the fourth role are replicated elsewhere in legal theory. Raz has observed, for example, that it is rare for courts, in any field of private law, to use principles as the sole basis for decision in a particular case. It is considered preferable, he says, for reasons of both certainty and predictability, to use them as a basis for changing existing rules, or making new ones: ie, in the third role, not the fourth.

> ... [S]ince the law should strive to balance certainty and reliability against flexibility, it is on the whole wise legal policy to use rules as much as possible for regulating human behaviour because they are more certain than principles and lend themselves more easily to uniform and predictable application. It is on the whole advisable to limit the use of principles to govern the creation and application of rules in order to ensure adequate flexibility in changing them and to prevent some of their unforeseen and undesirable effects.[54]

The debate about the nature of the unjust enrichment principle can thus be crudely summarised in terms of the above four functional options. It is not easily settled because the question of role is culturally contingent and perceptions of function are also affected by differing perceptions of scope. In Canada, there is evidence of it having been used in the first, third and fourth roles. In England, where it is younger, attitudes more cautious and the civilian influence less apparent, the evidence is that it is settling into the first and third roles: as a principle around which the interpretation of legal

[50] R Samek, 'The Synthetic Approach to Unjustifiable Enrichment' (1977) *University of Toronto Law Journal* 335, 345. The hostility is not actually the author's on this occasion, but represents his perception of the way judges and others have interpreted the principle. In fact, he favours it, albeit as part of a 'synthetic approach' in which it provides a legal point of view rather than commanding exclusive jurisdiction over any particular legal territory.
[51] *Re Byfield* [1982] Ch 267, 276 (Goulding J).
[52] S Hedley, 'Unjust Enrichment' [1995] 54 *CLJ* 578, 599.
[53] G Fridman, 'Restitution Revindicated, or, the Wonderful World of Prof Samek' (1979) *University of Toronto Law Journal* 160, 165.
[54] Raz (above n 27) 842.

material takes place and as a normative legal proposition which is used as a basis for changing existing, lower-level rules or creating new ones across a broad variety of cases. It is unlikely that the fourth role will prevail in the common law, for the reasons which Raz describes. The third type of use is more attractive and viable, because it strikes a useful compromise between stability and development in legal reasoning. It implements what Stanton, writing about similar challenges facing development of the law of negligence, might describe as a principled form of incrementalism, or what McLachlin J (as she then was) would dub a 'middle path.'[55] And if unjust enrichment can indeed legitimately be used in this way as a normative concept for developing sets of legal rules (third role), it makes sense that it can also be used as a basis for interpreting and classifying them (first role). Indeed, the interpretative and developmental functions of the unjust enrichment principle go hand in hand.

III. THEORY: A CLOSER LOOK AT PRINCIPLES, RULES AND CATEGORIES

The suggestion above has been that the unjust enrichment concept may best be regarded as a legal principle with normative weight, which mediates the moral and policy reasons underlying a variety of distinct, legal rules across a broad class of cases. The various rules which it mediates all address the question of when and how gains are actionable in private law and constitute a coherent family group or category. On this basis, we should understand the principle in terms of the first and third roles identified.

For the analysis to stand firm, more must be done to explain, firstly, the characterisation of the prescription against unjust enrichment as a '*principle*' and, secondly, the way in which it can legitimately come to provide the basis for a distinct '*category*' of law.

A. Principles and Rules: Unjust Enrichment as a Legal Principle

Why do we characterise the prescription against unjust enrichment as a legal principle, not as a rule? The two are often distinguished, but the distinction is framed in different ways by different writers. For Dworkin, rules

[55] K Stanton, 'Incremental Approaches to the Duty of Care' in N Mullany (ed), *Torts in the Nineties* (Sydney, The Law Book Co, 1997) 34. The author identifies the need for incremental, pocket-based approaches to the law to remain open and adaptive to social policy so as to retain a degree of forward dynamism. The approach finds resonance in McLachlin J's search for a compromise between principles and categories in relation to unjust enrichment in *Peel* (above n 21).

have a particular dispositive force which principles do not. They apply in an all-or-nothing fashion, setting out consequences which follow automatically from their application, whereas principles provide reasons which argue for a particular result without necessarily dictating it.[56] Both therefore have normative force, but the force of rules in dictating results is especially strong. By contrast, the distinction for Raz lies not in terms of a proposition's dispositive power, but in terms of the specificity of the acts which it proscribes. Rules proscribe relatively specific (homogeneous) acts such as smoking (which can only be done in a limited number of ways), whereas principles proscribe highly unspecific acts, such as unreasonable or unjust behaviour, (which can be performed in a wide variety of relatively heterogeneous ways).[57]

Both distinctions are ones of degree and in part at least for this reason, some authors deny that it is helpful to make any formal distinction between principles and rules at all.[58] Nonetheless, on either approach, the proposition that a person should not unjustly enrich himself or herself at another's expense more closely resembles a principle than a rule. This is because it is not generally used dispositively (without regard to lower-level concepts) and because the range of behaviour which it is taken to prescribe is, as Hedley has accurately observed, very diverse.[59] It acts as a higher-level mediator of norms expressed in a wide range of lower-level, distinct legal rules. This means that it supplies arguments for changing existing rules and a way of interpreting them coherently, rather than dictating results in its own right.

Understanding the prescription against unjust enrichment in this way disposes of some of the most powerful criticisms made of it, which relate to

[56] R Dworkin, *Taking Rights Seriously* (London, Duckworth, 1977) 24–26. More generally, Dworkin's preference for principles over rules expresses his rejection of positivist approaches to law and legal reasoning.

[57] Raz (above n 27) 834–39, especially at 838. Acts are relatively specific when 'there are only a small number of generic acts by the performance of which they are performed.' They are unspecific when they can be 'performed on different occasions by the performance of a great many heterogeneous generic acts on each occasion.'

[58] W Twining and D Miers, *How to do Things with Rules*, 4th edn (London, Butterworths, 1999) ch 3, especially 123–24. The authors refer to both as types of rule. They prefer to avoid any black-and-white distinctions between propositions based on dispositive power or specificity, stipulating simply that to qualify as a rule, a proposition must be prescriptive (normative), general, a way of guiding behaviour and must provide one kind of a justifying reason for decision or action. Prescriptions thus appear in a spectrum of dispositive power and specificity, without any particular definitional cut-off point.

[59] Hedley (above n 30). This would be so even if the principle were afforded only the limited scope now suggested by L Smith and Birks, who exclude cases in which gains are made through wrongdoing (above n 8 and below, Part V). This restriction is challenged, but even if it applied, unjust enrichment would still encompass a broad band of behaviour, including the receipt of mistaken payments, the exercise of duress or undue influence, the exploitation of another's incapacity, the extraction of taxes and other imposts through the abuse of lawful authority and even the receipt of necessitous goods or services.

its potential to over-expand liability in an uncontrollable way. In fact, it comes to represent a strategy for tackling one of the most difficult tasks in legal reasoning, which is how to develop the law whilst simultaneously keeping in mind both the particular case and the need for general propositions. Too particular an approach based upon the isolated analysis of legal rules inhibits overall development, by restricting access to very narrow lanes of reasoning. Too much abstraction from the particular instance, on the other hand, leads to the expression of ideas which, whilst true, mean little when it comes to disposing of cases, and which provide excessive space for judicial radicalism and inconsistency. The legal principle of unjust enrichment creates a viable compromise between these positions, by expressing at a higher and more general level the reasons expressed in more particular (and more certain) legal rules.

B. Principles and Legal Categories: Unjust Enrichment as a Category

Accepting that the material which the unjust enrichment principle spans is diverse,[60] how can it be regarded as sufficiently homogenous to constitute a category? The answer is that the various rules which the principle mediates all address the same question about the actionability of gains in private law. Moreover, as we shall see in Part Four, they bear to one another a series of important normative resemblances. They are related via their reasons.

To justify the status of the principle as an interpretative category, I accept that more needs to be done. Most of all, we need to explain how a legal category can tolerate differences between the rules it contains, without itself losing coherence. This in itself requires value-laden thinking about legal taxonomy—an understanding of what makes a *good* interpretative or classificatory system. If a 'good' system collates only rules with minimal differences, then unjust enrichment clearly does not qualify. It falls at the first hurdle and Hedley wins the day.

What, then, constitutes a 'good' system of legal classification? A host of suggestions are made, all of which are virtuous in themselves, but not all of which are entirely consistent with one another. A taxonomy should, it is generally thought, contribute to improving the quality of justice administered in any given system.[61] It should therefore be as simple as possible, both in terms of the concepts it uses and in terms of the ease with which the content of laws can be identified.[62] It should seek to be economical, in the

[60] The diversity of the material covered by unjust enrichment was a main focus of Hedley's attack: (above n 30) Question 1.
[61] McCamus (above n 20) 140.
[62] J Raz, *The Concept of a Legal System*, 2nd edn (Oxford, Oxford University Press, 1980) 143.

sense of avoiding in so far as possible overlaps, repetitions and redundancy of rules.[63] It should be as inclusive of legal material as possible without, on the other hand, being so inclusive as to suffer serious loss of coherence.[64] In general, it should be framed in such a way as to best guide behaviour. This is likely to be achieved if categorisations are made in such a way as to correspond to particular act-situations (things one should and should not do)[65] at a relatively 'basic' level[66] (at not too high a theoretical level), and in such a way as to identify the social purposes and policies[67] served by particular sets of rules. Finally, as Summers intimates,[68] we should, in making our analytical groupings, avoid two dangerous traps. These are the snares of reductionism on the one hand (pretending one thing is another just because this is simpler) and essentialism on the other (assuming that one can never refer to things by the same name, just because they do not share a single characteristic or set of characteristics common to all of them).

This is a long wish-list and we cannot hope to understand law in such a way as to meet every mandate perfectly. Particular priority should, however, be given to two of these in the current context. The first is the concern to ensure that the shape of the law reflects its purposes. This priority flows from the vital connection between theory and practice adverted to in the introduction and referred to again at the start of the next section. It emphasises the importance of the structures of the law respecting its underlying reasons. The second is Summers' point about the dangers of essentialism, because an overly essentialist approach to interpretation is likely to unduly restrict our understanding of what unjust enrichment *means*.

Summers attributes essentialism to Plato, describing it as the assumption that 'all of the diverse things to which any general term is applied must have some defining property or properties in common.'[69] Wittgenstein was its most cogent critic and posited a powerful contrary thesis; that one attributes

[63] *Ibid*, 142–43. See also Birks (n 32) 75, citing Occam's razor: 'entities are not to be multiplied without necessity;' Birks 1999 (n 8) 327: '... no entity can simultaneously be a member of more than one category in more than one series..;' N McBride, 'The Classification of Obligations and Legal Education' in P Birks (ed), *The Classification of Obligations* (Oxford, Clarendon, 1997) 71.
[64] McCamus (above n 20) 140.
[65] Raz (above n 62) 144.
[66] J Penner, 'Basic Obligations' in Birks (above n 63) 91. The author draws on concepts from cognitive science, abstracting the conclusion (at 100) that higher-level theories and concepts are 'not really as powerful in rearranging our moral universe as they are generally thought to be,' in contrast to 'basic' level concepts, which are 'in touch with reality, close to our appreciation of things as they are.'
[67] McCamus (above n 20) 144.
[68] R Summers, 'The New Analytical Jurists' in R Summers, *The Jurisprudence of Law's Form and Substance* (Aldershot, Ashgate Publishing, 2000) 22–25.
[69] *Ibid*, 25.

a common name to things, not because they share a single essence, but because they bear 'family resemblances.' The point is made in a much celebrated passage in the *Philosophical Investigations*, where he discusses what is meant by a game.[70] This bears quoting in full.

> Consider for example the proceedings that we call 'games.' I mean board-games, card-games, ball-games, Olympic games, and so on. What is common to them all?—Don't say: 'There must be something in common, or they would not be called 'games'—but look and see whether there is anything common to them all.—For if you look at them you will not see something that is common to all, but similarities, relationships, and a whole series of them at that...... Look for example at board-games, with their multifarious relationships. Now pass to card-games; here you find many correspondences with the first group, but many common features drop out, and others appear. When we pass next to ball-games, much that is common is retained, but much is lost.—Are they all 'amusing'? Compare chess with noughts and crosses. Or is there always winning and losing, or competition between players? Think of patience. In ball games there is winning and losing; but when a child throws his ball at the wall and catches it again, this feature has disappeared. Look at the parts played by skill and luck; and at the difference between skill in chess and skill in tennis. ... And we can go through the many, many other groups of games in the same way; can see how similarities crop up and disappear.
>
> And the result of this examination is: we see a complicated network of similarities overlapping and criss-crossing: sometimes overall similarities, sometimes similarities of detail.
>
> I can think of no better expression to characterise these similarities than 'family resemblances'; for the various resemblances between members of a family: build, colour of eyes, gait, temperament, etc. etc. overlap and criss-cross in the same way.—And I shall say 'games' form a family.

The lesson we can usefully draw from this, I think, is that cases can rationally be grouped under the same name despite the fact that, individually, they display all sorts of differences.[71] Applying that intuition in the current

[70] L Wittgenstein, *Philosophical Investigations* (Oxford, Blackwell, 1953) 31e–32e. For a general critical analysis of the gaming example and its utility in addressing the 'core' concerns of legal theory, see Halpin (above n 2) ch 7. One point that Halpin makes is that the gaming example tells us much about what 'game' *means* (how the word is used in practice) but does not supply a clear *concept* of what a game *is*. This important insight does not seem to detract from the point being made in the text, below, which is simply that a coherent concept of unjust enrichment (designated as such by reference to the stable inquiry it makes into the actionability of gains in private law) can encompass a diverse range of examples which bear to one another only a series of family resemblances.

[71] This does not of course mean that they *must* be. It might be desirable, for example, to 'essentialise' meanings for some purposes, either scientific or legal. It is always open to us to give a term a more restricted meaning if this promotes particular, valuable ends. The point made, below, is that essentialising the term unjust enrichment to give it a more restricted scope

context, we may *meaningfully* refer to a category of private law based on unjust gain, even though it prescribes a broad spectrum of different types of behaviour ranging from misrepresentation and undue influence, on the one hand, to the infringement of intellectual property rights and breaches of fiduciary duty, on the other. Unjust enrichment law, like tort law, is a *mixed* bag without being an *incoherent* bag. Moreover, whilst the rules which it contains indeed display all sorts of important differences, these should not be allowed to obscure the set of similarities which they collectively share. These similarities, as we shall see in the next section, pertain to their underlying reasons—they are fixed at the deepest level of the rules' motivations. No single one of these reasons, it will be seen, runs through all unjust enrichment cases, but collectively they describe a common set of family resemblances which the rules share.

None of this is to deny that the material which the unjust enrichment bag contains could be repackaged in other bags with different labels, in just the same way that books on library shelves can be reorganised according to author or year of publication. What it does demonstrate, however, is that the unjust enrichment category is, in itself, perfectly coherent—because it asks a coherent question—and that this coherence is not reduced merely by the existence of differences between the rules it contains. Essentialism might have led us seductively to this belief, but essentialism can be a significant barrier to understanding what ideas mean.

It is to reasons and their importance in understanding unjust enrichment that we now turn.

IV. REASONS IN UNJUST ENRICHMENT LAW: PHILOSOPHICAL FOUNDATIONS

A. The Value of Reasons in Understanding Rules

A vital part of the thesis of this article is that our way of understanding laws, as well as the concepts we use to develop that understanding, should adequately reflect its underlying purposes, or reasons. This is because reasons are both the law's fuel and compass. Without them, it will remain static, locked into existing categories of recovery, with no sense of where it should be going. Reasons can extend beyond the rules which they justify and therefore accord the law a forward, dynamic force. This is not to say

(for example by excluding from its ambit cases of wrongdoing) is counter-intuitive from the legal point of view, because it reduces its utility as a reasoning tool, obscures normative connections between cases and contradicts the way in which the concept has been used in practice. However, Birks 1999 (above n 8) 328 argues strongly for the opposite position. In his view, a restricted, if 'unnatural,' approach to the concept of unjust enrichment is necessary to meet another important taxonomic objective: avoiding categorical overlap. See further the discussion at n 113, below, for a response to this argument.

that knowing the purposes of a prescription solves all the problems in defining its precise scope, because, as Twining and Miers observe, 'purposes and reasons are at least as subject to indeterminacy as rules.'[72] Sometimes, in fact, they can show greater indeterminacy than the rule they justify. Indeed, the rule may have been formulated precisely in order to try to overcome the uncertainties which broader reference to its purposes creates. Nonetheless, a clear vision of purposes provides a sense of direction and shape for rules, and this in turn helps us to clarify indeterminacies, formulate coherent approaches to the development of the law and guide individual behaviour.

Understanding the reasons behind rules also helps us to understand many of the difficulties which attend their application and development. The reason for a particular rule may change over time, or it may fall away. Some rules may have more than one underlying reason and these reasons, which align in favour of a particular result in one context, may suddenly be brought into conflict with each other, when the rule is applied to another. Without an appreciation of the relationship between rules and their reasons, resolving many problems of interpretation and development in law would simply be impossible. It would, to use Twining and Miers' vivid metaphor, be the 'way of the baffled medic... prescription without diagnosis, concentration on cures without any understanding of diseases.'[73]

B. Reasons in Unjust Enrichment Law

The unjust enrichment principle is not underpinned by any single reason, but by a number of different reasons.[74] Collectively, these create a set of family resemblances between the various legal rules falling under the principle's rubric, even though no single reason applies in all cases. To borrow another metaphor from Wittgenstein,[75] the normative connections between cases falling beneath the principle resemble those in a rope: they comprise a number of different fibres within it, criss-crossing and overlapping, so as to afford it strength. No single fibre, however, runs through its entire length, so as to explain every unjust enrichment rule.

A complete analysis of reasons in unjust enrichment law is beyond the scope of this article. To make the point about the need for a more pluralist account, it is enough, I hope, to focus on the dominant thesis, which proceeds in terms of corrective justice, and to identify some of its limitations.

[72] Twining and Miers (above n 58) 192.
[73] *Ibid*, 194.
[74] See G Fridman, *Restitution*, 2nd edn (Scarborough, Carswell, 1992) 36–41 (unjust enrichment is underpinned by four values: justice, balance, rationality and reasonableness). The account here differs in obvious respects from Fridman's, but endorses his call to pluralism.
[75] Wittgenstein (above n 70) 32e.

(i) Corrective Justice

Corrective justice maintains that the objective of private law is to set right injustices that have occurred between individuals; between the doers and the sufferers of injustice. The idea is originally derived from Aristotle,[76] though in recent years a number of theorists have developed their own (distinct) versions of it.[77] Modern theories differ in their detail, but share a number of important core features.

Firstly, corrective justice is *restorative*. Its concern is to reinstate parties to their prior, pre-transactional positions, not to place them in new, fairer positions. This means, secondly, that it is generally *backward-looking*, not forward-looking. It eradicates the ills of the past rather than seeking to engineer broad solutions for the future. This is not to say that by making rules to deal with the past, future conduct will not be affected. People may learn of the rules and change their behaviour accordingly. But such effects are not the primary purpose of corrective justice rules; they are merely incidental (though beneficial) consequences. This contrasts with the position in instrumentalist theories of economic efficiency or deterrence, where the focus is entirely on the incentive effects which rules can have. Thirdly, corrective justice is *moral*. Different theorists supply different accounts of this morality, but all of them maintain that as a form of justice, it expresses an ethical idea. Finally, it is *individualistic*: it emphasises the unique responsibility of those who commit injustices to set right the effects of their conduct upon their victims. This means that a claimant's moral claim can only really be answered by his offender and not by his obtaining a remedy from some other source, such as an insurance payment or a state hand-out.[78]

Links between corrective justice and unjust enrichment have been drawn for some time. Writing in the thirteenth century, St Thomas Aquinas associated restitution with the analogous idea of commutative justice.[79]

[76] David Ross (tr), *The Nichomachean Ethics of Aristotle* (Oxford, Oxford University Press, 1954) book V, ch IV.

[77] Weinrib (above n 4); J Coleman, 'Tort Law and the Demands of Corrective Justice' (1992) 67 *Indiana Law Journal* 349; J Coleman, *Risks and Wrongs* (Cambridge, Cambridge University Press, 1992); J Coleman, 'The Practice of Corrective Justice' (1995) *Arizona Law Journal* 15; H Hurd, 'Correcting Injustice to Corrective Justice' (1991) 67 *Notre Dame Law Review* 51; R Wright, 'Substantive Corrective Justice' (1992) 77 *Iowa Law Review* 625; R Epstein, 'Causation and Corrective Justice' (1979) 8 *Journal of Legal Studies* 477; G Fletcher, 'Fairness and Utility in Tort Theory' (1972) 85 *Harvard Law Review* 537; P Benson, 'The Basis of Corrective Justice and its relation to Distributive Justice' (1992) *Iowa Law Review* 515. For an attack upon the view that corrective justice is conceptually and normatively distinct from distributive justice, see R Lippke, 'Torts, Corrective Justice, and Distributive Justice' (1999) 5 *Legal Theory* 149.

[78] This feature is sometimes described in terms of 'correlativity:' Weinrib 1995 (above n 4) ch 5. At one time, this was contested by Coleman, but seems now to be accepted: 'Tort Law' (above n 77) 365–67.

[79] Fathers of the Dominican Province (tr), *The 'Summa Theologica' of St Thomas Aquinas* (London, Washbourne, 1918) Part II, Question LXII, 'Of Restitution.' Note, though, two complications: (a) Aquinas' usage of the term restitution covers cases involving the rectification of

Where one party unjustly takes a thing from another, its restoration, he thought, serves the interest of re-establishing a prior equality between the taker and the person from whom it was taken. It is necessary for the taker's moral salvation.[80] Later, in the seventeenth century, the civilian writer Grotius explained 'quasi-contractual' obligations in similar terms.[81] More recently, a second tentative draft of the American *Restatement of Restitution* mentioned Aristotle's idea in its opening paragraphs,[82] and in 1992, McLachlin J (as she then was) invoked the idea explicitly in a judgment of extraordinary erudition in the Supreme Court of Canada.[83] These ideas have recently been vigorously revived by a number of legal scholars, including Weinrib.[84]

Corrective justice sits comfortably with many of the features of unjust enrichment law. The foundations of restitution in what Lord Mansfield once referred to as the ties of equity and natural justice[85] seem to sit well with its moral agenda. The two-party structure of litigation and the fact that defendants are forced to make restitution to private claimants, rather than to disgorge their ill-gotten gains to the state, emphasise what Weinrib calls the correlativity of its rules and reinforce notions of individual responsibility. Since the ambition of corrective justice is restoration of the pre-transactional *status quo*, it also makes sense that restitutionary rules take account of changes in the position of *both* parties resulting from the private transaction between them. This is currently done via the defence of change of position, counter-restitutionary awards and the provision of allowances

both gain and loss (ie it extends to compensation); (b) he uses the phrase 'commutative justice' to refer generally to justice in private transactions, when others (eg G Fletcher, *Basic Concepts of Legal Thought* (Oxford, Oxford University Press, 1996) 90) have used it to refer to a distinctive, more limited notion of justice in exchange (reciprocity), as depicted by Aristotle in the *Nichomachean Ethics* (n 76) book V, ch V. For an account of the different ways in which Aquinas uses the language of commutative justice, see J Finnis, *Aquinas* (Oxford, Oxford University Press, 1998) 188, note (a).

[80] '*Summa Theologica*,' *ibid*, Second Article: 'restitution ... is an act of commutative justice, and this demands a certain equality. Wherefore restitution denotes the return of the thing unjustly taken; since it is by giving it back that equality is re-established.... Since therefore the safeguarding of justice is necessary for salvation, it follows that it is necessary for salvation to restore what has been taken unjustly.'

[81] Grotius, *Inleiding tot de Hollandische Rechtsgeleertheyd* (1631) 3.1.15, cited in P Birks and G McLeod, 'The Implied Contract Theory of Quasi-Contract: Civilian Opinion Current in the Century Before Blackstone' (1986) 6 *OJLS* 46, 63.

[82] *Restatement of Restitution*, 2nd tentative draft (Philadelphia, American Law Institute, 1983) Introductory Note to ch 1.

[83] *Peel* (above n 21) 804; 165 (McLachlin J).

[84] D Stevens, 'Restitution, Property and the Cause of Action in Unjust Enrichment' (1989) *University of Toronto Law Journal* 258, 325; Barker (above n 3); Weinrib (above n 4); L Smith (above n 4).

[85] *Moses v McFerlan* (1760) 2 Burr 1005, 1012. This reference is not to be taken to suggest that courts have only given effect to restitution within their equitable jurisdiction; indeed some of the most ancient contributions to the field have been made by the common law. It simply means that the field has a moral foundation.

to defendants whose work has contributed in part to the profits they have made. As between equal parties, justice ensures that the transactional gains and losses of both be taken into account, in so far as this is practicable.

Beyond this and at a more detailed level, corrective justice appears to provide a viable explanation of a number of particular legal rules, such as:

- (i) the rule that the change of position defence protects a defendant only against *such losses as the transaction itself has caused him or her*, not against changes caused by other factors, such as earthquakes or financial disasters which would simply make liability 'hard' on him or her in distributive terms[86]
- (ii) the presumption that 'remoter' recipients of gains (those who receive their gains indirectly, not from the hands of the claimant himself) are liable only if tracing rules are able to establish a *clear link between the gains received and property which a claimant originally lost.*[87]
- (iii) the presumption in quantifying restitutionary awards that defendants are liable only for *such part of their gains as are factually attributable* to the injustice done to a claimant,[88] and
- (iv) the general rule that beneficial *changes in the financial position of a claimant which are not attributable* to some infringement of the rights or interests of the defendant are *disregarded* in assessing the latter's liability.[89]

Finally, important work has only recently been done which strengthens the potential of corrective justice to explain two potentially problematic types of unjust enrichment case: (a) cases of strict liability and (b) cases in which the defendant is forced to pay more in 'restitution' than the

[86] Burrows (above n 17) 514. In some jurisdictions, this is evident in the requirement that any change of position be made as a result of 'reliance' on a particular receipt: see New Zealand Judicature Act 1908, RS 22, 107, s 94B, but it pertains even on the wider version of the defence described by Burrows.

[87] As in *Lipkin Gorman* (above n 37). This rule currently appears to apply in both personal and proprietary claims, though suggestions have been made that establishing a causal link between gain and loss (ie a more liberal test) should suffice in personal claims: see D Hayton, 'Equity's Identification Rules' ch 1 in P Birks (ed), *Laundering and Tracing* (Oxford, Clarendon Press, 1995). In either case, the need for a clear connection between gain and loss emphasises what Weinrib would call the correlative nature of the relationship between claimant and defendant which is characteristic of corrective justice.

[88] *Sidell v Vickers* (1892) 9 RPC 152 (CA); *My Kinda Town v Soll* (1983) RPC 15 (Ch D) 57; *Westinghouse Manufacturing v Wagner Electric* 225 US 604 (1912) 615; *Dowagiac Manufacturing v Minnesota Moline Plow Co* 235 US 641 (1915); *Potton v Yorkclose Ltd* [1990] FSR 11 (Ch D). The process of causal attribution is again characteristic of conceptions of responsibility in corrective justice theory.

[89] This stems from the general rejection (in English law at least) of any defence of 'passing on.' See *Kleinwort Benson Ltd v Birmingham City Council* [1997] QB 380. Gains which are so attributable are deducted from the claimant's award via counter-claim or counter-restitution.

claimant lost on the facts. The first case—epitomised in the restitutionary liability of the innocent recipient of a mistaken payment—appears superficially inconsistent with the moral stance of corrective justice theory. How can strict liability, one asks, be moral? In fact, however, there is no inconsistency, provided only that a normative basis for liability can be found. A gain can be 'unjust,' without a defendant's conduct necessarily being 'wrongful' in the sense of being in any way at fault.[90] Lionel Smith has made further, significant advances in explaining how this can be so in an excellent recent article in the *Texas Law Review*.[91] The ethical case for restitution of a mistaken payment lies, for example, in defects attaching to the autonomy of the payer's consent. This is not necessarily to say that corrective justice can provide a moral account of *all* strict liability rules.[92] But it is not, of itself, inconsistent with them.

The second case relates to the instance in which a defendant is made liable for an unjust gain which exceeds the value of the claimant's corresponding factual loss. Here, 'restitution' of the gain appears to put the claimant in a better financial position than he or she was in before the transaction, which seems inconsistent with the restorative philosophy. Such cases are most likely to arise where gains have been made via 'wrongdoing,' rather than as a result of a defective transfer of resources between the parties, but they can also, as Burrows has intimated,[93] occur in the latter type of case. Respective examples are where a defendant infringes another's copyright, so as to make a profit which the owner would never in fact have made, or where a defendant profits by subtracting and then selling the owner's property at a price which the owner would never have obtained. Weinrib shows how restitution in either case aligns with the objectives of corrective justice, properly understood. Key to his argument is the immensely important insight that corrective justice restores prior legal *entitlements*, not simply prior *factual positions*.[94] Forcing the infringer of the

[90] Barker (above n 3) 469–70. Note that both Fletcher (above n 77) and Epstein (above n 77) propose corrective justice models which accommodate cases of strict liability. For criticism of Weinrib's model, on the basis (*inter alia*) that it is 'seemingly' fault-based and is therefore incompatible with strict liability, see M McInnes, 'Unjust Enrichment: A Reply to Prof Weinrib' (2001) 9 *Restitution Law Review* 29.

[91] Smith (above n 4) especially 2141–46.

[92] This is as yet untested. The crux cases seem to be those in which restitution is made on some ground of 'public policy.' Even these might fit within a *formal* conception of corrective justice (see Smith, *ibid*), but the norms expressed would not seem to be deontological. This raises difficult questions as to the compatibility of corrective justice with non-deontological conceptions of 'injustice' which are well beyond the scope of this article. For an argument in favour of such compatibility by an author whose reasoning is generally avowedly instrumentalist, see R Posner, 'The Concept of Corrective Justice in Recent Theories of Tort Law' (1981) 10 *Journal of Legal Studies* 187.

[93] Burrows (above n 17) 28–29.

[94] Weinrib (above n 4). This is another bone of contention for McInnes (above n 90), but it seems to make sense. It is difficult to see why the law would concern itself with protecting factual positions as opposed to legal interests or rights.

copyright or the seller of the property to hand over his or her profits to its owner sets right the injustice done in each case because it makes good the owner's *normative* loss. It restores his or her right. Although the owner is *factually* better off at the end of the story than at the beginning, he or she is no better off than he or she was *entitled* to be at that time.

When these clarifications are accepted, corrective justice comes to explain a high proportion of both structural features and liability rules in unjust enrichment law. Its moral mandate applies both in cases in which gains are made by civil wrongdoing and cases in which one party has unjustly subtracted resources from another. It has the potential (not as yet fully explored) to explain both cases in which liability turns on proof of fault and cases in which liability is strict. It can even explain those cases (which are actually a small proportion) in which defendants are made liable for more profit than the claimant has factually lost, provided that the claimant can show some prior legal entitlement to that profit.

(ii) Beyond Corrective Justice

Nonetheless, there are some cases of 'unjust enrichment' which corrective justice struggles to explain. Most problematic on Weinrib's own reasoning are those in which a defendant is forced to transfer to a claimant the value of a gain which exceeds the latter's *normative* loss (the value of his or her original entitlement). There are a number of examples of this.

In *Attorney General v Reid*,[95] a defendant was forced, via a constructive trust, to yield up properties which he had acquired with bribes taken in breach of his fiduciary duty to his employer. The value of the properties vastly exceeded the value of the bribes and it is hard to see how either corresponded to any normative loss of the employer. Indeed, the employer seems to have been left substantially better off at the end of the story than it was originally entitled to be by virtue of its fiduciary right to the defendant's loyalty. One way of avoiding this conclusion is to argue that the employer had a prior legal right to the bribes by virtue of the maxim that equity regards as done that which ought to be: the employee should have given his bribes to the employer, so the employer is deemed to own them. This argument succeeded on the facts, but is a well-known fiction. An employer's primary right of loyalty cannot include a legal entitlement to monies obtained through its breach. That is a logical nonsense. Moreover, even if the right of loyalty did include the right to the *bribes*, the award of the properties clearly exceeded the value of this and caught value which was partly attributable to the defendant's *own investment acumen*. The result is that it is hard to explain *Reid* as a case in which the court simply 'corrected' the wrong done. It seems to have gone considerably further,

[95] [1994] 1 AC 324.

making an award which would express strong disapproval of the defendant's actions (these were crimes in their own right), prevent him from deriving any further profit from them, and deter others from acting in a similar way.

Reid had a public dimension, but the same point arises in a number of other well-known cases in which parties have been held accountable for the products of pure breaches of fiduciary duty, such as *Boardman v Phipps*.[96] Here, a solicitor was held liable to a trust beneficiary for profits made by innocently using information he had obtained as an agent for the trust. Although some allowance was made for the value of the defendant's own effort in bringing the profit about, the award nonetheless seems to have gone beyond making good any normative loss suffered by the beneficiary. Not only had the defendant's conduct in fact brought all beneficiaries of the trust factual gains, they had no prior right to the trust information as such, nor to the products of the solicitor's investment capital and acumen. Reconstructing their primary rights in this way is again a clever but misguided intellectual trick. In such instances, it seems, courts are guided by policies of general deterrence, not corrective justice. Indeed, from the latter point of view, there seems, on the facts of *Boardman*, to have been no significant immorality or normative imbalance to correct.

A third, topical example is *Attorney General v Blake*,[97] in which the defendant profited by publishing a book containing official information in breach of the terms of his contract of employment. The House of Lords ordered an account of all royalties remaining due to him and, in doing so, made no allowance for his contribution to the book's success. Although the precise reasoning in the case is unclear, the court's purpose seems to have been to deter the breach of certain types of contract in which there is a particularly strong interest in performance.[98] Once again, the amount of the defendant's liability exceeded the amount to which the claimant had any prior private right. The only way of avoiding this conclusion would again be to construe the Crown's primary contractual rights as including the right to all profits flowing from Mr Blake's disclosure, including profits attributable to his authorship of those parts of the book which contained no offending information at all. That is a very tenuous construction. Even if the award made good some normative loss of the Crown which it was hard to calculate or prove, it also set out to provide strong performance incentives. The need for deterrence may have weighed particularly heavily on the court's mind, given that Mr Blake was a well-known traitor to his country. But the court's reasoning is not so confined, and for this reason *Blake* cannot be seen as simply an anomalous by-product of its public law history.

[96] [1967] 2 AC 46. See also *Regal (Hastings) Ltd v Gulliver* [1942] 1 All ER 378; *Snepp v United States* 444 US 507 (1980).
[97] [2001] AC 268.
[98] *Ibid*, 285.

It implements broader incentive policies in private law, akin to those prevalent in cases involving trust.

To the above, we should add a number of cases in both the United Kingdom and United States, entailing the breach of intellectual property rights, in which full accounts of a defendant's profits have been ordered even though at least some of them were probably attributable to his own business acumen, not the infringement.[99] The infringements in most such instances were deliberate and the driving rationale seems to have been that the defendant should simply not be allowed to keep his profit. In the United States, the deterrent basis of this approach has been openly admitted,[100] and elsewhere authors have called for that admission and for the rationalisation of the account of profits remedy along deterrent lines.[101] The cases do not all speak with one voice and some adhere to the corrective rationale of awarding the claimant only such proportion of the defendant's profits as corresponded to his or her normative loss.[102] Nonetheless, it is an oversimplification to suggest that results accord always with the corrective rationale. The truth is that courts are engaged in a more complex balancing act between corrective and deterrent philosophies, weighing the desire to avoid leaving the claimant with a normative windfall, on the one hand, against the desire to deter cynical profiteering, on the other.

The use of restitutionary awards for deterrent purposes appears undeniable in these instances and it has received a further boost in recent times from the English Law Commission, which has recommended extending the availability of restitutionary damages to all cases in which a defendant is guilty of the deliberate and particularly outrageous infringement of another's rights.[103] The purpose of this suggestion appears to be to make available to civil courts a more sensitive deterrent mechanism than punitive damages. It allows them to remove the incentives to engage in serious, cynical forms of private wrongdoing, without going so far as to punish. Moreover, whilst deterrent approaches to the calculation of awards feature mainly, as one might expect, in cases involving wrongdoing, they are not so confined. They also appear in some cases of 'subtractive' or autonomous unjust enrichment, in which the defendant has committed no 'wrong' as such. Where, for example, a defendant adds to the value of that which the

[99] *Matarese v Moore-McCormack Lines Inc* 158 F 2d 631 (1946); *WE Bassett v Revlon Inc* 435 F 2d 656 (1970); *Truck Equipment Service Co v Fruehauf Corporation* 536 F 2d 1210 (1976) 1222–23; *Lever v Goodwin* (1887) 36 Ch D 1; *Edelsten v Edelsten* (1863) 1 De GJ&S 185.

[100] *Truck Equipment Service* (above n 99) 1222; *WE Bassett* (above n 99) 664.

[101] Eg, L Bently, 'Accounting for Profits Obtained by Infringement of Copyright: Where does it end?' (1991) 1 *EIPR* 5.

[102] Eg, *Maier Brewing Co v Fleischmann Distilling Corporation* 390 F 2d 117 (1968); *Blackman v Hustler Magazine* 800 F 2d 1160 (1978), where deliberate wrongdoers were allowed to retain a proportion of the profits of their wrongdoing.

[103] Law Commission Report No 247, *Aggravated, Exemplary and Restitutionary Damages* (1997) recommendation 6.2.

defendant has subtracted from a claimant or obtains profit by exchanging it, s 151 of the *Restatement* indicates that he or she may be liable for the additional value the defendant has added, if he or she obtained the property by duress or fraud, or knew of such duress or fraud, or even (sometimes) obtained it by mistake, if he or she knew about the mistake.[104] The point here is that liability for the extra value applies, even though some of it may be attributable to the defendant's own acumen and even if his or her conduct falls short of constituting an actionable breach of some primary duty.[105]

Canadians may be less concerned by these findings than English lawyers, since there is evidence in Canada that unjust enrichment law has not just been used for corrective purposes, but to implement localised exercises of distributive justice between parties on the break-up of quasi-matrimonial relationships.[106] Canadian judges have shown themselves to be (literally in this instance) less 'conservative' in their use of unjust enrichment law. The appropriateness of using unjust enrichment for re-distributive purposes has rightly been doubted, but there is no denying that from time to time, it has happened. Moreover, although English lawyers wag their fingers, this is at the risk of slight hypocrisy. For if we look to that part of our own law which governs the availability of proprietary remedies, for example, there is evidence that courts have been influenced by considerations which are also distributive in nature, though these have often been hidden from view.[107] Thus, in one case, it is arguable that the House of Lords granted a stop-loss insurer an equitable lien over settlement monies held for the insureds in the United Kingdom, in part because not doing so would have loaded it with the unfair expense of pursuing personal claims against the insureds themselves, many of whom lived abroad.[108] There again, in several notable instances, English courts have refused to recognise a 'remedial' constructive

[104] *Restatement of Restitution* (St. Paul, Minn, American Law Institute, 1937). Comment (d) to this section rationalises at least some of these instances as deterrent or quasi-punitive. See Illustration 9 for the mistake case.

[105] *Ibid*, comment (a) to s 151. Although the section is headed 'Value of Property Acquired by Consciously Tortious Conduct' it is clear from this comment that the quantification rules described apply even where the defendant has committed no tort as such.

[106] Above (n 11). On the relationship between corrective and distributive justice, see Fletcher (above n 79) ch 5; Benson (above n 77).

[107] This is the general conclusion expressed in C Rotherham, *Proprietary Remedies in Context* (Oxford, Hart Publishing, 2002), though the text considers a broad band of proprietary remedies, not simply those which target unjust enrichment. See also D Hayton, 'Constructive Trusts: Is Remedying Unjust Enrichment a Satisfactory Approach' in T Youdan (ed), *Equity, Fiduciaries and Trusts* (Toronto, Carswell, 1989) 205, 215–16 (in some cases, the capacity of a beneficiary to claim a proprietary remedy turns on policy questions relating to third party interests, risk-taking and deterrence); D Wright, *The Remedial Constructive Trust* (Sydney, Butterworths, 1998). For a distributive justice analysis of unjust enrichment law, see Dagan (above n 4).

[108] *Lord Napier & Ettrick v Hunter* [1993] AC 713, 717 (Lord Templeman). This is the analysis of Goff and Jones (above n 19) 88. By contrast, Lord Browne-Wilkinson here premised the lien on the combination of two fictions: an implied promise that the insureds would pay any

trust because of the distributive inequity this might cause for third parties or the defendant's creditors on insolvency.[109] They have expressed the view that if such trusts were ever put into real use in England, such considerations would be taken into account in determining their availability.[110] Beyond this, within the apparently more conservative pattern of tracing rules, there is at least some evidence of results being manipulated in order to avoid otherwise unfair distributive outcomes.[111] Whilst in England distributive reasoning has thus largely been confined to the margins and has borne mainly upon remedial matters rather than on liability rules, it does rear its head from time to time.

More clearly needs to be done to test the limits of corrective analysis, but, whilst it undoubtedly dominates, it seems unlikely to provide a full account of the reasons expressed by the unjust enrichment principle. Sometimes courts have admitted both deterrent and (more rarely) distributive factors in their reasoning, although these tend to bear upon the type or amount of restitution that is given rather than on primary liability rules themselves. Not all reasons apply in all cases. Deterrence concerns are strongest, hence, in cases of deliberate wrongdoing or deliberate exploitation falling short of wrongdoing as such. Sometimes corrective and deterrent reasons may overlap in the same case. This is likely to be so, for example, where some of the profits for which a deliberate wrongdoer is made accountable correspond in part to a normative loss the claimant has suffered and in part to his or her own capital or acumen. Sometimes, the reasons may be brought into conflict, as in *Boardman*, where no normative loss is sustained at all but there is nonetheless a strong case for deterring the future abuse of relationships of trust. Both types of reason span the analytical divide sometimes made between cases of 'autonomous' or 'subtractive' unjust enrichment and unjust enrichment 'by wrongdoing.'

The normative relationship between the various unjust enrichment rules resembles, I ventured to suggest above, Wittgenstein's complex of family resemblances. That is, we cannot pick on any single reason as 'essential' to all unjust enrichment cases, though if we were to try to do so, the corrective

settlement monies received in respect of the insured event to the insurer, and the maxim that equity regards as done that which ought to be, converting the claimant's personal right into a proprietary one.

109 See *Westdeutsche Landesbank Girozentrale v Islington Borough Council* [1996] AC 669, 703–5 (Lord Browne-Wilkinson) (no insolvency issue on the facts); *Re Polly Peck International plc (in administration) (No 2)* [1998] 3 All ER 812.

110 *Ibid.*

111 See eg *Re Oatway* [1903] 2 Ch D 356; *Barlow Clowes International Ltd v Vaughan* [1992] 4 All ER 22. Examples of re-distributive reasoning are not confined to proprietary remedies. There are also traces of such reasoning in some cases dealing with remuneration for pre-contractual services. Lord Denning was a particular fan of this type of approach: see, eg, *Jennings & Chapman v Woodman Matthews and Co* [1952] 2 TLR 409, 414; *Brewer Street Investments v Barclays Wool Ltd* [1954] 1 QB 428, 436–37.

rationale would be the most obvious choice, because it explains both the basic structure of litigation and a high proportion of liability rules. On the whole, distributive reasoning is excluded for practical and constitutional reasons. Nonetheless, the reasons which underpin the various rules imbue the unjust enrichment principle with a rich normative fabric, describing a series of shared purposive connections between the material it spans. Sometimes there are tensions within this fabric, because different strands of reasoning pull in different directions as rules are extended to new contexts. Nonetheless, unjust enrichment law can only coherently be understood through the complementary[112] integration of these different perspectives. It is ethically pluralist—a mixed moral bag.

An important point to realise, which has been made before, is that this does not detract from the coherence of unjust enrichment as a category of rules answering questions about the actionability of gains in private law. Non-essentialist approaches to classification remain coherent approaches to classification. That is the important fruit we harvested from Wittgenstein. Despite its ethical pluralism, unjust enrichment remains a coherent approach to the categorisation and development of private law. It mediates and manages a variety of different, overlapping objectives running through the various rules which target unjust gains.

V. CONCLUSIONS AND IMPLICATIONS

Understanding the nature and function of the general prescription against unjust enrichment entails a non-essentialist approach to legal classification and a clear appreciation of the role which principles play in legal reasoning. Whilst generalisations are dangerous, it seems likely that the concept will, in common law jurisdictions, settle into the role of both classificatory category (principle of interpretation) and normative legal principle, mediating at a higher level the reasons expressed in a broad variety of more detailed (and more 'dispositive') legal rules relating to the actionability of gains in private law. No understanding of unjust enrichment is complete without reference to these reasons, which are more diverse and more complex than has been suggested by corrective accounts, but which nonetheless relate the various cases of unjust gain to one another in a complex series of family ties. The normative and legal aspects of the principle which flow from its expression of these reasons imbue it both with legitimacy (respect for

112 For a full exposition of the concept of complementarity, see Englard (above n 7) ch 5, 85ff: 'The notion of complementarity conveys the idea that the full understanding of physical reality requires the use of two contrasting, mutually exclusive models. Consequently, two or more descriptions of a thing are complementary if each alone is incapable of providing a complete description or explanation of the thing in question and both together provide a complete description.'

precedent) and with a dynamic capacity to guide development within the law, even beyond existing rules.

There is at least one very important implication to this analysis. This is that, whilst there are undoubtedly a number of key differences between cases of unjust enrichment 'by subtraction' and unjust enrichment 'by wrongdoing,'[113] both types of case fall within the 'category' of unjust enrichment law and they are related at a foundational level. Both sets of rules target private gains. Both can express the norms of corrective justice and both can express deterrent rationales (though this is admittedly much rarer in cases of unjust enrichment by subtraction, where liability tends to be strict). Excluding cases of restitution for wrongdoing from the ambit of the unjust enrichment principle, as Birks has recently suggested we should,[114] may therefore yet prove a mistake. More clearly mistaken still are accounts which conceive of the two areas as being underpinned by entirely different normative ideas. In fact, if there is a line along which cases can be separated in normative terms, it is more accurately drawn between cases in which a defendant is made liable only for the claimant's normative

[113] Birks (above n 8). The differences stated are: (a) the fact that limitation periods start to run at different times, (b) the fact that the defence of change of position has no application in cases of wrongdoing, (c) the fact that there is no separate 'unjust factor' in cases of wrongdoing, other than the wrong itself, and (d) the fact that no analytical inquiry is needed in cases of wrongdoing into the questions of whether the defendant was enriched, whether that enrichment was unjust, or whether it was at the claimant's expense, the sole question being whether the 'wrong relied on is one for which a gain-based claim lies.' Birks also raises the objection (e) that any broader approach to unjust enrichment such as that proposed here yields classificatory overlap, because some unjust enrichments are unjust only because a wrong has been done. None of these points seems conclusive against a broad conception of the principle: (a) makes sense, because unjust enrichment is understood, on the current analysis, as grouping a variety of different causes of action, rather than describing any *single* cause of action itself, so that it is unsurprising that these causes of action may accrue at different times; (b) betrays an assumption which is questioned in the text, below; (c) is accepted, but does not provide a basis for excluding cases of wrongdoing from the unjust enrichment category, given that this category comprises all events giving rise to gain-based awards in private law; and (d) may not, I suggest, be true. It may simply be that these analytical questions are answered in different ways in cases of wrongdoing. The defendant must still be enriched for there to be any gain-based claim; that enrichment must still be wrongfully made (and so be unjust) and it must be sufficiently causally related to the wrong (such that it can be said to have been made at the claimant's expense, rather than through his own industry or acumen). Finally, (e) makes a valid point, but stems from a particular approach to categorisation. It must be accepted that any approach which collates causes of action for gain in private law will detail some events which also give rise to compensation in other categories. Nonetheless, this does not, surely, yield any contradiction, provided that those other categories of wrongdoing are confined to the compensation of loss. Furthermore, whilst the avoidance of overlap may be one taxonomic objective (see Part III, above), it may be only one, to be balanced against other considerations, including the need to analyse cases in such a way as to reveal the normative relationship between them. This relationship, I have suggested below, tends to be obscured by the bright line Birks proposes. For a similar view, to the effect that the analytical division between cases of 'substantive' and 'remedial' restitution is unhelpful in so far as it obscures the unity of restitution's 'reason and function across all of its factual settings,' see A Kull, 'Rationalizing Restitution' (1995) 83 *California Law Review* 1191, 1226.

[114] *Ibid.*

loss, on the one hand (where the rationale is corrective), and cases in which his liability exceeds this normative loss (where deterrent ideas tend to take over). This line does not correspond neatly to that between 'wrongs' and 'autonomous' unjust enrichment cases. It is a distinction which works within both 'sub-categories' of case. From this point of view, if the word 'disgorgement' is to be used in contrast to 'restitution' to signify some functional distinction in gain-based awards, it cannot be applied to all cases of wrongdoing, but must rather apply to all (and only) cases in which defendants are made to give 'up' more than the value of the claimant's original right. For this reason, I remain cautiously sceptical of the value of using that distinct terminology to refer to the vast bulk of cases in which defendants are forced to pay over their unjust gains to the claimants whose rights they have infringed. Restitution (giving back) seems neatly to capture the essence of what is going on in most such cases.

The above conclusion returns us, ironically, to the orthodoxy which Birks stated many years ago and which is still maintained by Goff and Jones,[115] namely that both cases of 'subtraction' and cases of 'wrongdoing' fall within the unjust enrichment rubric. The exclusion of the latter cases and their hiving off to the law of civil wrongs has a number of worrying implications and disadvantages, some of which have been highlighted by Burrows.[116] Firstly, it flies in the face of a considerable body of judicial opinion—it contradicts an established judicial understanding of what unjust enrichment means at the very time that this understanding is attaining some degree of acceptance.[117] Secondly, it seems to exclude the possibility of the defence of change of position applying in favour of innocent wrongdoers, when it is as yet unclear that this is desirable.[118] Thirdly, it obscures the common nature of a number of important remedial issues relating to valuation methodology, quantification and proprietary remedies which arise in relation to all restitutionary awards, whether flowing from wrongs or from the subtraction of another's resources. A common analytical approach to these remedial issues is, I have argued elsewhere, beneficial in a number of important respects.[119] Fourthly, the divide bars access, in developing the law of restitution for wrongs, to the dynamic, normative power of the broader principle. This is unfortunate, since of all the areas of

[115] Birks (above n 32) 16–18, 26; Goff and Jones (above n 19) part 2, section 3. For another adherent to this orthodoxy, see further Kull (above n 113). For Kull, as for Burrows, all instances in which restitution is made fall within the rubric of unjust enrichment.

[116] A Burrows, 'Quadrating Restitution and Unjust Enrichment: A Matter of Principle?' (2000) 8 *Restitution Law Review* 257.

[117] *Ibid*, 261–63.

[118] *Ibid*, 264–65. See also P Hellwege, 'The Scope of Application of Change of Position in the Law of Unjust Enrichment' (1999) *Restitution Law Review* 92, 96–100; G Virgo, *The Principles of the Law of Restitution* (Oxford, Oxford University Press, 1999) 727.

[119] K Barker, 'Riddles, Remedies and Restitution: Quantifying Gain in Unjust Enrichment Law' (2001) 54 *CLP* 255.

the law of restitution, it is this one that is currently most in need of rationalisation and which faces something of a reasoning deficit. Access to the reasons which the broader, normative principle expresses can provide a sense of shape and direction to the courts, which may be lacking if their lanes of reasoning are more narrowly constrained. This reasoning impasse was astutely observed by Professor Friedmann in an article in 1998[120] and formed the basis of his own suggestion that the basis of liability for restitution in cases of wrongdoing should be regarded as 'independent' of the wrongs themselves and based upon the protection of a number of distinct, protected interests. The case stated here does not go as far as this (it is not denied, for example, that in such cases the event which generates the restitutionary remedy is the wrong itself), but its practical implications are similar—namely, that one may have access to broader policies of corrective justice, deterrence and public policy underlying the principle, so as to develop existing categories of recovery in a more dynamic way.

Fifthly and somewhat selfishly, hiving off 'wrongs' from cases of 'subtractive' enrichment makes teaching very difficult. This is a pedagogical point which may be of less concern to practitioners, but since the purpose of teaching is to impart understanding, the matter is not as far removed from good practice as it may seem. If Birks' change of heart is accepted, it would seem that we ought now to teach the law of restitution in a variety of different sound bites in different undergraduate courses, which will often be encountered by students in different years. They may learn about restitution for breach of contract and tort early on. Later, they may learn about restitution for equitable wrongs. Later still, if they are lucky, they will learn about restitution in analogous but distinct cases, in which contracts are terminated for fundamental breach or for frustration of a contract, or in cases of mistake or undue influence. Nowhere will their understanding of the law's approach to unjust gains be fully integrated. This is not to say that the task is beyond the great teaching traditions of our law schools, but it will not be easy and one cannot help thinking that something will be lost in the process. This concern is, of course, just another way of expressing the view that in normative terms, much of the law of 'restitution' hangs together.

We return, then, to Socrates' question: what is the force and use of names? The answer he was given was that the use of names is to know the things expressed by them. 'Knowing' here meant 'understanding' and it is hoped that we are now in a position to better understand the nature and function of the unjust enrichment principle in private law, such that some of the controversies relating to its use may now finally settle. Part of this understanding flows from a closer examination of the relationship between unjust enrichment and its underlying reasons—from a deeper inquiry into

[120] D Friedmann, 'Restitution for Wrongs: The Basis of Recovery' ch 9 in Cornish (above n 8) 133.

that which is *named*. But part of it also flows from a re-appraisal of our own attitudes to *naming*—what we mean by principles and what approach—(essentialist or pluralist) we take to interpretation (categorisation). As is so often the case when we encounter a problem in the world, considered thinking reveals that part of the problem probably exists in the world itself and part within ourselves.

6

Unjust Enrichment and Corrective Justice

DENNIS KLIMCHUK*

A NUMBER OF legal theorists have recently argued that the law of unjust enrichment expresses, or exhibits the structure of, corrective justice.[1] I will challenge this view and explore an alternative, according to which the structure of the action in unjust enrichment is distributive, in a particular way. As a post-script I will briefly sketch a defence of the old idea, rejected by many contemporary scholars, that there is something equitable about the law of unjust enrichment.

I. PRELIMINARIES

I contend that the plaintiff's claim that the defendant was unjustly enriched at her expense is not a claim in corrective justice. I aim to defend this by arguing that restitution of money received by mistaken payment is not a matter of corrective justice, as Aristotle understood it. I will pause here to justify this approach, that is, to explain why by defending the second,

* Thanks to the audience at the conference from which this volume derives and to my colleagues in the Moral, Political and Legal Philosophy Research Group at UWO who read and discussed a later draft of this article. Thanks, in particular, to Tracy Isaacs, Stephen Smith, Richard Vernon and Ernest Weinrib, whose comments and criticisms forced me to rethink some of my views and (I hope) improve some of my arguments, and to Gillian Demeyere and Mitchell McInnes with whom I discussed the ideas in this article at length.

[1] See K Barker, 'Unjust Enrichment: Containing the Beast' (1995) 15 *OJLS* 457; E Weinrib, *The Idea of Private Law* (Cambridge, Harvard University Press, 1995) 140–42, 196–99; L Smith, 'Restitution: The Heart of Corrective Justice' (2001) 79 *Texas Law Review* 2115 and M McInnes, 'The Measure of Restitution' (2002) 52 *UTLJ* 163. See also RB Grantham and CEF Rickett, *Enrichment and Restitution in New Zealand* (Oxford, Hart Publishing, 2000) 144 fn 1 and RB Grantham and CEF Rickett, 'On the Subsidiarity of Unjust Enrichment' (2001) 117 *LQR* 273, 275. I endorsed, though did not defend, the claim that the plaintiff's claim for restitution in unjust enrichment is a claim in corrective justice in 'Necessity and Restitution' (2001) 7 *Legal Theory* 59.

narrower claim I take myself to be defending the first, broader one. Why, in other words, mistaken payment? And why Aristotle? I'll take these questions up in turn.

I am focussing on mistaken payment because it is, on all accounts, the paradigmatic case of unjust enrichment. Because I am making a controversial theoretical claim I hope to be as non-controversial as possible when it comes to doctrine. So I will, more specifically, take as my example a case of a payment made under the mistaken belief that it was owed to the payee. I do not mean to suggest thereby that only a 'liability mistake,' as it is called, will ground a claim in unjust enrichment,[2] but rather only that it is the most uncontroversial example of a mistake that will do so. This is because the consensus appears to be that, in contrast with, for example, mistakes concerning the payee's identity or the amount transferred, a liability mistake does not prevent title from passing.[3] This matters because, on some accounts, only if title passes does the law of unjust enrichment have anything to do. If title remains with the payer, some hold, her claim lies in property law. Her request is not that an enrichment be undone, but rather, more simply, that her property be returned to her.[4] But title uncontroversially passes if the plaintiff would not have paid the defendant but for her labouring under a liability mistake. So on all accounts she will have a claim in unjust enrichment, and a claim only in unjust enrichment.

Mistaken payment is taken to be the paradigmatic case of unjust enrichment because it brings the autonomy of the action in unjust enrichment into sharp relief. The defendant has committed no tort, no contract may be imputed to the parties, and—at least in liability mistake cases—the plaintiff cannot invoke her property rights on her behalf. I will, in what follows, make much of the defendant's passivity in mistaken payment cases. Not only is the defendant blameless, she need not have *done* anything. Some 'unjust factors'—that is, features of the impugned transaction to which the plaintiff points to make out her claim—implicate the defendant's conduct in the causal history of the transaction. In such cases a corrective justice account of the defendant's liability may seem more plausible. On the other hand, one might argue that the paradigmatic status of mistaken payment counts against this intuition, because it suggests that we ought to infer instead that the defendant's misconduct as such is inessential to

[2] Though that was at one time law. See *Aiken v Short* (1856) 1 H & N 210 (Ex D) 215.

[3] Grantham and Rickett, *Enrichment* (above n 1) 135–36 and G Virgo, *The Principles of the Law of Restitution* (Oxford, Clarendon Press, 1999) 607–10.

[4] So argue, eg, G Virgo in 'What is the Law of Restitution About?' in W R Cornish *et al* (eds), *Restitution: Past, Present and Future* (Oxford, Hart Publishing, 1998) 312–18 and RB Grantham and CEF Rickett in 'Property and Unjust Enrichment: Categorical Truths or Unnecessary Complexity?' [1997] *New Zealand Law Review* 668. On the other side, see P Birks, 'Property and Unjust Enrichment: Categorical Truths' [1997] *New Zealand Law Review* 623. For an argument questioning the starting points of the debate see P Jaffey, *The Nature and Scope of Restitution* (Oxford, Hart Publishing, 2000) ch 9.

the plaintiff's claim.[5] Thus in, for example, the case of duress, one might argue that is it not the quality of the defendant's behaviour but rather the extent to which it impaired the plaintiff's consent that grounds the latter's claim. I will not pursue this question. Whatever its answer, any acceptable account of unjust enrichment must explain the defendant's liability to make restitution for mistaken payment.

Now, why Aristotle's account of corrective justice? Three reasons. The first is that, so far as I know, everyone who has argued that the law of unjust enrichment expresses corrective justice has had Aristotle's account of the latter explicitly in mind.[6] The second is that, as we will see, liability for unjust enrichment seems, at least at first glance, to be exactly what Aristotle had in mind. The third reason derives from a principal motivation for claiming that the law of unjust enrichment expresses corrective justice. Much of the work done by scholars of the law of unjust enrichment in the last twenty years or so has aimed to displace the idea that the law of unjust enrichment is equitable in the broad, broadly Aristotelian sense of case-by-case justice done between parties when the law has run out, or when its strict application would run afoul of justice.[7] On the contrary, commentators argue, the law of unjust enrichment rests squarely on a well-defined set of legal principles on which plaintiffs may and must rely to make out their claims for restitution. Left open by this analysis, however, is the question of what unites these principles. Lurking in the background are a host of taxonomic questions. There is much debate, for example, concerning where unjust enrichment leaves off and the laws of property, tort, and contract begin, and about the significance of the distinction between unjust enrichment and enrichment by wrongs. The claim that the law of unjust enrichment expresses corrective justice aims to answer the former, justificatory question and (thus) help settle the latter, taxonomic debates.[8] But it can do so only if 'corrective justice' names something more specific than 'justice between the parties,' as it is sometimes characterised.[9] Otherwise, we are back where we started. On Aristotle's account, we will see, corrective

[5] Supporting this line is the fact that some commentators argue that claims that rest on factors that impugn *only* the defendant's conduct, such as free acceptance, do not belong in the law of unjust enrichment properly construed. See Grantham and Rickett, *Enrichment* (above n 1) 238–57, for a detailed consideration of this question.

[6] This is so with everyone cited above in (above n 1). See too the comments of McLachlin J (as she then was) in *Peel (Regional Municipality) v Canada*, [1992] 3 SCR 762, 804; 98 DLR (4th) 140 (SCC).

[7] See Aristotle, *Nicomachean Ethics* 5.10 (*EN*) and Aristotle, *Rhetoric* 1.13.

[8] On the relationship between questions of justification and of taxonomy see S Smith, 'Justifying the Law of Unjust Enrichment' (2001) 79 *Texas Law Review* 2177, 2178–83.

[9] Grantham and Rickett, *Enrichment* (above n 1) 115 fn 1, for example, say that corrective justice is 'concerned to set matters right as between the plaintiff and defendant.' 'To this extent,' they add, 'it draws on Aristotle's formulation.' Aristotle's formulation, however, is importantly narrower than this, as we will see.

justice is narrow in the right way. (It is noteworthy that his one illustration of the application of equity is a case of battery, where it is the strict application of corrective justice that must be tempered.[10]) In short, only if it was in Aristotle's sense that the law of unjust enrichment expressed corrective justice would it matter that it did.

Two final prefatory points. The first concerns terminology. I will take 'unjust enrichment' to name an autonomous action, one sometimes called, following Birks,[11] 'subtractive unjust enrichment.'[12] The contrast is with enrichment by wrong, where owing to an infringement of, say, a property right held by the plaintiff, the defendant realises a gain. 'Restitution' is often used to name the remedy in either sort of case. But when the defendant's gain comes from third parties—as in, for example, a case of infringement of copyright—it is better styled as 'disgorgement,' because here the defendant *gives up* a gain. 'Restitution,' as I will use it, refers to a remedy requiring the defendant to *give back* something to the plaintiff (or its value), and so is the only remedy available for 'unjust enrichment' in the sense in which I will use the latter.[13]

Finally, in this article I consider only the common law 'unjust factors' approach to unjust enrichment, according to which what renders an enrichment unjust is the presence in the transfer through which the defendant received it of an 'unjust factor': in the core cases, a factor that in one way or another impairs the plaintiff's consent to that transfer. Whether the arguments below carry over to the civilian 'legal grounds' approach—according to which an enrichment is unjust (or unjustified) if the defendant lacks a legal ground to retain it—is an interesting question, but one that I will not consider.

II. ARISTOTLE

Aristotle divides justice[14] into two domains: distributive and corrective. Each name what Aristotle calls a 'form' of justice. Distributive justice concerns the allocation of benefits and burdens among the members of a group.

[10] *Rhetoric* (above n 7) 1374a35–1374b2.
[11] P Birks, *An Introduction to the Law of Restitution* (Oxford, Clarendon Press, 1985) 23–25.
[12] That said, I do not mean to commit myself to the view that the category of autonomous unjust enrichment is exhausted by subtractive unjust enrichment. On this question, see L Smith, 'Unjust Enrichment, Property, and the Structure of Trusts' (2000) 116 *LQR* 412.
[13] Here I follow L Smith in 'The Province of the Law of Restitution' (1992) 71 *Canadian Bar Review* 672.
[14] More specifically, 'particular' justice. Particular justice is a subset of justice as a whole. Justice *simpliciter* is virtue insofar as it concerns our interactions with one another. The person who is unjust in the way in which particular justice takes an interest is 'grasping.' She tries to get more than her share. Particular justice, then, concerns the standards of conduct that govern interactions in which one stands to gain or lose something. See *EN* (n 7) 5.1–2.

Distributive justice is done, on Aristotle's account, when each has her due, as determined by the measure of merit appropriate to the group. Thus, for example, upon the dissolution of a business partnership, funds might be divided in accordance with each member's investment;[15] political offices, on Aristotle's telling, ought to be filled in accordance with political virtue.[16]

Corrective justice, by contrast, 'plays a rectifying part in transactions between man and man.'[17] So far as corrective justice is concerned:

> it makes no difference whether a good man has defrauded a bad man or a bad man a good one, nor whether it is a good or a bad man that has committed adultery; the law looks only to the distinctive character of the injury, and treats the parties as equal.[18]

Now, whether someone is a good or a bad person is irrelevant to most questions of distributive justice in modern liberal democracies. The vicious are, for example, no less entitled to health care than are the virtuous. But for Aristotle—on whose account the state is constituted for the sake of the good (that is, virtuous) life—the question, whether someone is a good or a bad person, is a candidate distributive criterion. So his point here is that corrective justice is indifferent to the comparative standing of the parties under distributive justice. All that matters is the character of the injury, that is, the value of the loss one has imposed on the other. No disservice is done to Aristotle's point, then, if we substitute in its formulation wealth for moral merit. So translated, the idea is familiar to private lawyers: the plaintiff's right to *restitutio in integrum* and the quantum of relief to which she is entitled are indifferent to the parties' pre-transactional wealth. The parties are treated as equals in the sense that, for the purposes of setting things right between them, their extra-transactional differences are set aside.

So far, then, Aristotle seems to be describing civil liability as we now understand it. The parallel with unjust enrichment in particular is suggested by an analogy Aristotle uses to elucidate the structure of a claim in corrective justice. To understand this analogy we need to add another element of the contrast between distributive and corrective justice as he draws it. Each, on Aristotle's account, expresses a distinct kind of equality or proportion. Distributive justice is done, as we have seen, when persons unequal in merit receive proportionate shares of the goods to be allocated. Aristotle calls this kind of proportion geometric, because it concerns ratios: if A is twice as meritorious as B and x represents twice as much of the relevant good as y, then distributive justice is done when A gets x and B gets y.

[15] *EN* (above n 7) 5.4, 1131b28–31.
[16] Aristotle, *Politics* 3.9.
[17] *EN* (above n 7) 5.2, 1130b34, translation WD Ross in R McKeon (ed), *The Basic Works of Aristotle* (New York, Random House, 1941).
[18] *EN* (n 7) 5.4, 1132a2–4.

The kind of proportion relevant to corrective justice, by contrast, is arithmetic. Aristotle explains with an illustration (which I here modify in minor detail). Imagine two parties to a transaction, A and B. We can represent their pre-transactional holdings as follows:

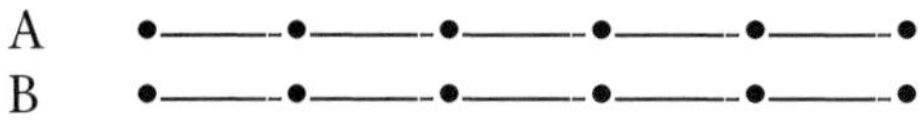

(fig. 1)

and their post-transactional holdings as:

(fig. 2)

Corrective justice is done when the status quo has been restored:

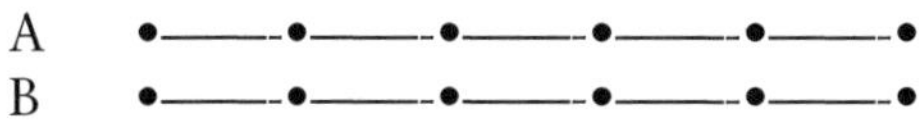

(fig. 3)

Now it might seem that to understand what is going on here we first have to determine what the initial equality of A's and B's lines consists in. But that is, I think, inessential to the analogy, the point of which is to represent the kind of proportion at issue in corrective justice. The analogy shows how the post-transactional disproportion is, in Aristotle's language, arithmetic rather than geometric (as, again, it would be in the case of a maldistribution) because it is a matter of quantity rather than of ratio. The initial equality of A's and B's lines just helps make vivid the crucial point, which is that B's gain corresponds to A's loss. Not only is B up one quantum of holdings and A down one, but B is up one quantum of holdings and A down one for the same reason, namely that B now has one quantum of A's holdings. Conversely, one transaction sets things right, at once depriving B of his gain and restoring to A what she has lost. Thus it does not matter whether 'a good man has defrauded a bad man or a bad man a good one,' because all we need to know to remedy the transaction is internal to it.

Now, the shift from fig. 1 to fig. 2 maps perfectly onto a mistaken payment, just as the shift from fig. 2 to fig. 3 maps perfectly onto the payment by the payee of restitution to the mistaken payer. Hence the attraction of Aristotle's account to scholars of the law of unjust enrichment. More, of course, needs to be said. The shift from fig. 1 to fig. 2 no less represents, for example, A's giving a gift to B, or B's winning over some of A's customers through a successful (and legitimate) advertising campaign. It is not the mere fact of B's gaining at A's expense that triggers the interest of corrective justice. Nor, of course, does it trigger the interest of the law of unjust enrichment: having proven that something of value was transferred from her to the defendant, the plaintiff must then show that the defendant's enrichment is unjust. Now, Aristotle, recall, aimed only to elucidate the *forms* of distributive and corrective justice. As we saw, distributive justice as such is done when each person's benefits and burdens are proportionate to her merit under the relevant criterion. The choice of criterion is a separate question. It is thus, one might argue, no failing of Aristotle's account of corrective justice that it cannot distinguish between gifts and mistaken payments—that it is, in this way, shy of content. It is not meant to do so, or to be otherwise.

So, indeed, argues Kit Barker. 'The crucial idea' in the Aristotelian account, on Barker's reading,

> is that wrongful transactions should be rectified without regard to the respective needs or merits of the individual parties, not that wrongfulness be defined in any particular way. This leaves it open to other theorists to provide alternative definitions of what it is that constitutes 'wrongful' gain or loss, without losing faith with the central intuition that the aims of the law in a given case are 'corrective'.[19]

In the case of unjust enrichment we fill in the content of the scheme whose form is supplied by Aristotle's model with the various unjust factors enumerated by unjust enrichment scholars.

But this, I suggest, makes the concept of corrective justice *too* thin. It is too thin because nothing on this account prevents from being invoked under the name of corrective justice just the sort of equitable considerations restitution scholars have sought to displace. One could, for example, supply as content to the corrective justice framework so construed the criterion Lord Mansfield held to justify recovery of money had and received in *Moses v Macferlan*, namely that such recovery was due if required by the ties of natural justice and equity.[20] That is, one could adopt as the measure of wrong, 'a gain is wrongful if it offends natural justice and equity.' On this account, then, little or no explanatory or justificatory work is done by the form of corrective justice, and most or all of it is done by the catalogue of factors justifying reversing enrichment. We still do not know what—if anything—unites these factors, and that is one of the questions the appeal to corrective justice was meant to answer.

III. ARISTOTLE, TORT AND UNJUST ENRICHMENT

I claim that Aristotle's account of corrective justice is thicker than Barker holds, and that when filled in we will see that restitution of a mistaken

[19] Barker (above n 1) 469.
[20] (1760) 97 ER 676; 2 Burr 1005, 1012.

payment cannot be understood as an instance of corrective justice. To make my point I will briefly leave the law of unjust enrichment to the side and look at the law of torts, which, I will argue, *does* exhibit the structure of corrective justice. Against this background I will return to unjust enrichment.

As many commentators have noted, Aristotle's account of corrective justice seems to make tort liability a puzzle. In many cases tortfeasors realise no gain. And even if they can be reckoned as having gained something—say, liberty—the fortuity of consequences can make the cost of malfeasance vary widely between cases identical from the defendant's perspective. A moment's distraction can cause minor injury or catastrophic loss; a carelessly broken vase may be worthless or priceless. Unjust enrichment, then, looks like the easier case for Aristotle's account—indeed, as Mitchell McInnes suggests, the paradigmatic one.[21]

But it was not Aristotle's paradigm. His examples are what we would now categorise as cases of breach of contract and of intentional torts.[22] The case he discusses in detail is a tort, a battery. How do we make sense, in such a case, of the correlativity between the plaintiff's loss and the defendant's gain that Aristotle's model seems to require? Let's begin with what Aristotle has to say on the question.

> [I]n the case ... in which one has received and the other has inflicted a wound, or one has slain and the other has been slain, the suffering and the action have been unequally distributed; but the judge tries to equalize things by means of the penalty, taking away from the gain of the assailant. For the term 'gain' is applied generally to such cases, even if it be not a term appropriate to certain cases, eg to the person who inflicts a wound—and 'loss' to the sufferer; at all events when the suffering has been estimated, the one is called loss and the other gain.[23]

This is a difficult passage, even for Aristotle. But I think sense can be made of it.[24]

The first thing to note is that Aristotle allows that it is hard to square the idea that a wrongdoer gains by his action with the structure of some kinds of wrongdoing, such as woundings. Yet he continues to say that the defendant's gain plays a role in the analysis of such a case and soon after introduces the

[21] McInnes (above n 1) 194. Smith (above n 1) calls unjust enrichment the heart of corrective justice for similar reasons.
[22] *EN* (n 7) 5.2, 1131a1–9.
[23] *EN* (n 7) 5.4, 1132a7–14.
[24] I am indebted in what follows to both Weinrib's and Stone's work on Aristotle's account of corrective justice. See Weinrib (above n 1) ch 3 and E Weinrib, 'The Gains and Losses of Corrective Justice' (1994) 44 *Duke Law Review* 277, and M Stone, 'The Significance of Doing and Suffering' in G Postema (ed), *Philosophy and the Law of Torts* (Cambridge, Cambridge University Press, 2001) 131–82. My reading differs from both Weinrib's and Stone's on various points. Only one—a point of difference with Weinrib—is relevant here. I draw attention to it below (n 36).

line analogy discussed above. To what, then, could 'the assailant's gain'—to use Aristotle's example—refer? One clue is in the last bit of the passage quoted above: 'when the suffering has been estimated, the one is called loss and the other gain.' This suggests that once the plaintiff's loss is estimated—that is, when the quantum of compensation is fixed—the sum now owed the plaintiff is, while in the defendant's hands, the gain. Perhaps it is at *this* point, then, that A's and B's holdings correspond to the state of affairs illustrated in fig. 2 above.

But this cannot be the whole story. If it were, then the question, 'Did the plaintiff suffer a corrective injustice?', could not be answered until the court determined her remedy. Furthermore—this is the deeper problem—the report of the remedy would be all the answer there would be. This would make the concept of corrective justice hopelessly thin (though thin in a different way than under Barker's interpretation). Let me put the point another way. We need an answer to the question *why* ought the remedy take the form of a payment from the defendant to the plaintiff. The line analogy seems to provide an answer. But if the defendant's gain consists only in his still having, before making compensation, the amount owed the plaintiff, then all the analogy has done is reformulate the question.

Let us return to the passage quoted above. At its beginning Aristotle says that in a case in which 'one has received and the other has inflicted a wound ... the suffering and the action have been unequally distributed.' Now, I am not sure just what, exactly, Aristotle thinks has been unequally distributed. But I think that nonetheless we can see the answer to the puzzle here. Immediately after this passage Aristotle describes the wounder's conduct as the realisation of a gain. So the gain corresponds to the wounding and the loss to the suffering. I say 'corresponds' deliberately. I think we will be led astray if we now ask what exactly, has been gained and what has been lost. Instead the idea, I suggest, is that just as in the line analogy one event could be described as A's losing a quantum of holdings and B's gaining one, the wounding can be described as the defendant's battering and the plaintiff's being battered. The defendant and plaintiff are, respectively, the doer and sufferer of the same wrong.[25] *This* is what anchors the corrective remedy in the wrong.

Let us take an example which corresponds more easily to the architecture of the line analogy. If in taking some chattel *c* from A, B does wrong—again, as Barker emphasises, corrective justice is a form of justice, and as such does not supply the content of 'wrong'—then the remedy can, in effect, be read off the wrong. The relevant correlativity in the transaction, I am suggesting, is not that which obtains between the loss and gain of the quantum of holdings. It is rather that which obtains between the suffering and the

[25] I borrow this crisp phrase from Weinrib and Stone, *ibid*.

doing of the wrong. This relationship is no less manifested in the case of B's wounding of A. It is because the transaction takes this form that 'when the suffering has been estimated' B *now* can be said to have among his holdings something that belongs to A.

This, I suggest, is the only way to make sense of the line analogy in light of Aristotle's examples of cases which attract corrective justice. So tort law can, after all, be reckoned as an expression of corrective justice. But the law of unjust enrichment cannot be. Consider, again, the case of mistaken payment. There are two significant ways, in this context, in which the mistaken transfer of money is unlike, say, a battery. Let me note at the outset that one is *not* that corrective justice requires fault. Perhaps it does. It seems to me, however, that a person imposing an ultra-hazardous risk on another, for example, can be understood to be the agent of the plaintiff's misfortune in a way that respects the structure of corrective justice as I unpacked it above. But we can set this question aside.

The first problem is that, in the case of a mistaken payment, the defendant is not only faultless; again, she need not have *done* anything. That is, in the case of mistaken payment, the doer and the sufferer are the same person. This matters because, as we saw, it is the fact that the same event can be described as a suffering on the plaintiff's part and as a doing on the defendant's part that explains why the remedy—if everything else is in place—takes the form of a transfer for money from the defendant to the plaintiff. But restitution for mistaken payment cannot be anchored that way.

The second problem is, in effect, another side of the first. It is that we cannot describe anything the payee does or refrains from doing in such a way as to identify that feature which, from the payer's perspective, impugns the transaction. That latter feature, it is often said, is that insofar as she was labouring under a mistake, the plaintiff's autonomy was compromised in a way in which the law ought, for that reason, to take an interest.[26] The problem is that nothing that the defendant does counts as an interference with the plaintiff's autonomy. It does not follow from the fact that, but for the plaintiff's autonomy having been compromised, she would not have conferred the benefit on the defendant, that the defendant in any sense

[26] Jaffey (above n 4) 159; H Dagan, 'Mistakes' (2001) 79 *Texas Law Review* 1795, 1798–99. While there is a serviceable sense in which an agent's autonomy is compromised when she chooses under imperfect knowledge, the idea that this is a sense in which the law must take an interest is not obviously true. It can be fairly said that the common law protects autonomy. But, at least in the context of private law, this is just to say that it protects us from others' interference in our doings. It is another matter to say that it protects us from our own mistakes, or that it ought to do so. I do not mean to say that considerations of plaintiff's autonomy will not form part of the best account of justification of restitution for mistaken payment. But I question, for example, Dagan's claim that owing to the sort of compromise of her autonomy a mistaken payee suffers, a liberal law *must* prescribe restitution (Dagan (above n 26) 1799).

brought about her receipt of that benefit. So, again, the defendant is not implicated in the plaintiff's loss in the way that corrective justice requires.

Now, this argument rests on the idea that from the perspective of the law of unjust enrichment the defendant is properly described as being (merely) 'in receipt of' the mistaken payment. So described she is a party to the transaction in only the most attenuated sense. Perhaps, however, this misapprehends the situation. One might argue that at the point at which the defendant becomes aware of her being in receipt of the payment, she is doing something that connects her to the plaintiff's loss in the way corrective justice requires. That is, we can then describe the post-transactional state of affairs at once as the retention of some disputed thing of value x by B and as A's being deprived of x, and this seems to satisfy the correlativity on which claims of corrective justice are grounded.

This argument, however, begs the question. The defendant can be said to 'retain,' rather than merely continue to have, the disputed enrichment—and the plaintiff to be 'deprived' of it, rather than merely to no longer have it—only if the defendant is already under a duty to return it. Anchoring the plaintiff's claim in the defendant's retention of the disputed enrichment is tantamount to explaining the duty to make restitution in terms of *its*—the duty to make restitution's— breach. In terms of Aristotle's analysis, this is akin to holding that the plaintiff's and defendant's holdings correspond to the state of affairs represented in fig. 2 only after 'the suffering has been estimated,' that is, after it is settled what B owes A. But this amounts to holding that it is the estimation of the suffering, rather than the transaction which caused it, that brings about the corrective injustice.[27]

Thus the plaintiff's claim for restitution cannot be understood as a claim that corrective justice be done. Or so, I argue, is the case on Aristotle's account. This matters, I argued above, because only if it was in Aristotle's sense that the law of unjust enrichment expressed corrective justice would it matter that it did. But perhaps I have not yet given the idea a fair hearing, because I have not yet fully unpacked the Aristotelian account. So, I hazard, would argue Ernest Weinrib, at the core of whose influential account of corrective justice is the claim that 'Aristotle's theory of corrective justice is inchoately Kantian.'[28] There is, on Weinrib's telling, a lacuna in Aristotle's account which can be filled in with elements of Kant's legal philosophy (the 'doctrine of right,' in Kant's words) in a way that was anticipated by Aristotle's account. I will consider two arguments in support of the view that unjust enrichment expresses corrective justice that follow

[27] Grantham raises this objection—in somewhat different terms—against the majority analysis in *Roxborough v Rothmans of Pall Mall Australia Ltd* (2001) 185 ALR 335 (HCA) in 'Restitutionary Recovery *Ex Æquo et Bono*' [2002] *Singapore Journal of Legal Studies* 388, 398. McInnes (above n 1) 190–93, makes the same point—again, in somewhat different terms—and raises several more objections to the 'unjust retention' account (as we may call it).
[28] Weinrib (above n 1) 83.

Weinrib's lead on this point, the first making the case with a principle in Kant's legal philosophy, the second with Weinrib's hybrid Aristotelian-Kantian account of corrective justice. In the next section I will sketch Kant's doctrine of right and draw the link between it and Aristotle's account of corrective justice to which Weinrib has drawn our attention. Against that background I will return to unjust enrichment and the question of whether it expresses corrective justice.

Before proceeding, let me note that the reading of Kant's doctrine of right I will outline below departs from Weinrib's both on matters of emphasis and on some substantive issues. Central among the latter is that I do not think that Kant's doctrine of right rests on his account of moral agency. This is the view that, in Weinrib's words, we are 'self-determining' agents, beings capable of acting independently of what Kant calls our inclinations: our desires, wants, needs, and so on. This is a philosophically controversial meta-ethical view, embedded in Kant's even more philosophically controversial metaphysical doctrine of the distinction between the phenomenal and noumenal realms. On my interpretation, the sense of freedom on which Kant's doctrine of right relies is philosophically much more mundane. This has important implications for the justificatory structure of Kantian liberalism.[29] But, at it turns out, it does not affect the link between Aristotle and Kant under consideration here. So while I will trace a different path through Kant's account, I will end up where Weinrib does. I will not here engage the interpretive questions at issue along this path, which are beyond the scope of this article.

IV. KANT

The foundations of what Kant calls the doctrine of right set out the principles that determine the appropriate matter for positive law. Roughly, the law, on Kant's telling, protects us from others' interference with our freedom to pursue our ends, so long as the freedom we claim is consistent with a like exercise by all others. His view is thus liberal in the classical sense: in many cases, what Kant calls the Universal Principle of Right—on which more below—yields results broadly consistent with what is required by Mill's harm principle (though Kant and Mill could hardly be farther apart on questions of justification).

Central to Kant's account is the distinction between duties of right and duties of virtue—that is, between law and morality. Following the tradition

[29] On the question whether Kant's legal and political philosophy is embedded in, or stands free of, his metaphysical views, see T Pogge, 'Is Kant's *Rechtslehre* a "Comprehensive Liberalism"?' and B Ludwig, 'Whence Public Right? The Role of Theoretical and Practical Reason in Kant's *Doctrine of Right*' in M Timmons (ed), *Kant's Metaphysics of Morals: Interpretive Essays* (Oxford, Oxford University Press, 2002), 133–58 and 159–83.

in political philosophy that starts with Hobbes, Kant holds, contrary to Aristotle and his followers, that it is not in the state's purview to enforce virtue. But Kant's argument is not that it is *wrong* for the state to do so, but rather that it is, in a deep sense, *impossible*. We can, I suggest, think of his point as a generalisation of an argument Locke made in the *Letter Concerning Toleration*. One of the reasons the care of souls cannot fall within the magistrate's purview, Locke argued, is that it is in the nature of the understanding that 'it cannot be compelled to the belief of any thing by outward force.'[30]

Kant generalises Locke's point to apply to reasons for actions generally—to, in his language, the ends we set. Which ends one ought to adopt is, on Kant's account, a question for the doctrine of virtue. The various duties of virtue, Kant holds, can all be derived from the duties to adopt two ends: our own perfection and the happiness of others. But while the threat of legal sanction can prompt an agent to *further* an end, it cannot cause her to *adopt* it, for that is something only she can do. Indeed, the attempt to cause an agent to adopt a given end will fail to the extent it appears to succeed, because it will guarantee that the agent's end is avoiding the sanction. So, for example, while one can be compelled to further the well-being of others by being obligated to pay taxes, one cannot be compelled to adopt as one's motivation the furthering of others' well-being. Thus beneficence is a duty of virtue. But the duty to pay taxes could be a duty of right. It is a duty, in Kant's words, for which an external lawgiving—the placing of someone under an obligation to do something under threat of sanction—is possible.[31]

Two important points follow from this analysis. First, because the threat of sanction cannot compel persons to adopt ends, the principle(s) that set the scope of positive law must be formal. Second, the freedom that positive law protects is what Kant calls external freedom, that freedom with which others may interfere by their actions, because only actions—and not reasons for action—can be reached by the threat of sanction. Thus the Universal Principle of Right (UPR) holds that 'An action is *right* if it can coexist with everyone's freedom in accordance with a universal law, or if on its maxim the freedom of choice of each can coexist with everyone's freedom in accordance with a universal law.'[32] From the perspective of right, then, it does not matter whether others approve of the ends I have set, nor whether in setting those ends, I display a virtuous or vicious character. As Aristotle says—here we start to draw the link—'it makes no difference

[30] J Locke, *A Letter Concerning Toleration* (Buffalo, Prometheus Books, 1990) 20.
[31] There is more contained in the idea of an external lawgiving and the conditions of its possibility, but this can be set aside here. I attempt a more complete unpacking of this idea in 'Necessity, Standing and Deterrence' (2002) 8 *Legal Theory* 339.
[32] I Kant, *The Metaphysics of Morals*, translation M Gregor (Cambridge, Cambridge University Press, 1996) 24.

whether a good man has defrauded a bad man or a bad man a good one.' What matters for the purposes of right, instead, is that (to use Aristotle's example) in defrauding A, B has acted in a way that cannot be made into a universal law.

We can now see one way in which, on Weinrib's account, Kant's account fills in a gap in Aristotle's account (I will consider a second below). Aristotle tells us that corrective justice treats the parties to a transaction as equals by ignoring various qualities which set them apart, such as their virtuousness and viciousness. Kant's account fills in this negative definition with a positive account of equality. We are all equal, on Kant's telling, in our capacity to set ends.[33] It is on this—more specifically, on the immunity of this capacity from the effects of external compulsion—that the doctrine of right is grounded.

We are nearly in a position to return to the law of unjust enrichment. One last step. The two arguments in support of the thesis that unjust enrichment expresses corrective justice that I mentioned above rest, respectively, on two elements of Kant's view. I will now draw these out. The first is that UPR forbids us from acting on principles ('maxims' in Kant's words) that cannot be consistent with the freedom of others in accordance with universal law. In short, justice forbids us from making exceptions of ourselves. The second is that it follows from UPR that rights and duties are correlative, in Hohfeld's sense. The boundaries of right are set at the points at which my exercise of freedom is compatible with others', and vice versa. We interact as equals when we respect these boundaries. Wrongdoing consists in crossing these boundaries. A boundary-crossing is at once an invasion of the trespassee's right and a breach of the duty owed her by the trespasser. I will consider the arguments anchored in each of these features of Kant's doctrine of right in the next two sections, respectively.

V. UNIVERSALIZABILITY

The idea on which the first account that I will consider is based, again, is that we treat one another as equals in the sense required by corrective justice when we do not make exceptions of ourselves. The idea is formal, but not thereby bereft of content. We can, for example, make sense of the structure of negligence liability this way. When B breaches a duty of care owed to A, B in effect denies A authority over which costs she (A)

[33] It is in his full account of this capacity that Kant engages the doctrines Weinrib collects under the idea of 'self-determination.' My view is that the argument for UPR does not rely on Kant's, or any other particular, account of moral agency. Even if—to take a view directly opposed to Kant's—we were ultimately slaves to our inclinations, the argument would go through so long as each of us regarded our inclinations as our own.

must bear, and B grants that authority to herself. The argument I am considering here holds that the law of unjust enrichment can be understood in the same way.

No one, so far as I know, quite argues that: (a) liability for unjust enrichment can be understood this way, and (b) showing this shows that the law of unjust enrichment expresses corrective justice. Nicholas J. McBride and Paul McGrath defend an analysis of unjust enrichment along these lines, but do not claim it to be a corrective justice account.[34] Mitchell McInnes, by contrast, casts the idea sketched above as a way to understand the law of unjust enrichment as an expression of corrective justice, but then takes issue with it on the grounds that it (or, in any case, the Kantian approach generally) seems to require us to read a fault requirement into the action in unjust enrichment.[35] Bearing these qualifications in mind, however, we can distil from McBride and McGrath's and McInnes's arguments an account of how the law of unjust enrichment can be reckoned an expression of corrective justice that merits consideration.

McBride and McGrath aim to defend the proposition that '[a]n enrichment is unjust when it is obtained as a result of a disposition of my property which I did not consent to.'[36] Now, this may be questioned on more than one ground.[37] For example, it is hard to square with the doctrines of adverse possession and prescriptive right—and, for that matter, the state's right to collect taxes and levy fines. But let's set this aside. Certainly something is captured by the idea that what impugns the mistaken payment—the case on which McBride and McGrath focus—is the fact that had the payer known what she did not know, she would have acted otherwise, and so that she, in some sense, did not consent to the transfer. Granting this, it follows, McBride and McGrath argue, that the defendant must make restitution:

> If you attempt to keep hold over an asset in your hands, you are invoking a right of ownership over that asset. It is the right to do with one's assets as one pleases. However, in invoking that right, one must concede it to everyone else similarly placed. Therefore, if assets come into my hands, or I retain assets that I would otherwise have expended, as a result of an employment of your property which you did not consent to I cannot assert my right to do with those assets what I please without conceding that you should have been able to exercise a similar right.[38]

Thus, they conclude, I must return the asset.

[34] NJ McBride and P McGrath, 'The Nature of Restitution' (1995) 15 *OJLS* 33, 39,43.
[35] McInnes (above n 1) 187–93.
[36] McBride and McGrath (above n 34) 37.
[37] See L Ho, 'The Nature of Restitution—A Reply' (1999) 16 *OJLS* 517.
[38] McBride and McGrath (above n 34) 39.

McInnes makes a similar argument, but sets it expressly in the context of the Kantian side of the Aristotelian-Kantian account of corrective justice. Imagine A has paid B $500 by mistake.

> By resisting liability, the defendant broadly asserts the right to retain his $500 enrichment until he freely chooses to part with it. Contrary to the Kantian imperative, however, he thereby claims for himself a right that he is unwilling to extend to others. Since the plaintiff's intention in conferring the benefit was vitiated by error, her payment was not truly an instance of self-determining agency. Consequently, if the defendant cannot be forced into an involuntary transaction, the plaintiff cannot be held to hers.[39]

McInnes here follows Weinrib's reading of Kant in invoking as the foundation of the doctrine of right the idea of 'self-determining agency.' And he (as have others) relies on a generous measure of 'involuntariness' according to which one acts involuntarily if one would not have done what one did had one known something one did not know.[40] Each of these ideas is philosophically controversial. But they are, I think, inessential to McInnes's argument, which, in the spirit of a friendly amendment, I will read down at these points. We can recast the argument more modestly as follows. By resisting liability, the defendant broadly asserts the right to retain the $500 enrichment until he freely chooses to part with it. But the plaintiff did not freely choose to part with it in the first place. In Kant's language, the defendant acts on a maxim that cannot be made into a universal law without undoing the grounds upon which he claims the right to the $500. He thus fails to treat the plaintiff as an equal in the sense required by corrective justice. So he must make restitution to her.

While initially attractive, each of these arguments is, I think, flawed. The flaw lies in the description of the right at once asserted and withheld by the defendant: to do with one's property as one pleases (McBride and McGrath), or to keep one's property until one freely chooses to part with it (McInnes). I have two objections in mind, the first more controversial and less telling than the second.

First, it is not obvious that the plaintiff did not do as she pleased with her property, or that she did not freely chose to part with it, in ways in which the law takes an interest. The sorts of un-freedom of choice from whose deleterious consequences one is protected by private law are, ordinarily, either that caused by one's incapacity to choose or that caused by misconduct by the party who stands to benefit from one's choice. In the first case, there is, in effect, no choice to enforce. In the second, enforcing the choice would allow another to profit from her wrongdoing. A mistaken

[39] McInnes (above n 1) 188.

[40] See also, eg, Dagan (above n 26). The *locus classicus* of this view is Aristotle, *EN* (n 7) 3.1.

payment fits under neither category and so is subsumed under neither rationale. First, the plaintiff's capacity is *ex hypothesi* not under question. Indeed, in the case I am taking as paradigmatic—payment made under a liability mistake—the transfer, recall, is sound enough to secure the passage of title from plaintiff to defendant. So in a thin but relatively well-defined sense, the plaintiff's choice *was* intact. Second, the retention of the enrichment by the defendant would not amount to her profiting from a wrongdoing, because she need not have done anything—permissible or impermissible—to have come into its possession in the first place.

Now, there is, of course, a begged question in here. Perhaps the law *ought* to protect us from the consequences of choices such as that made by the mistaken payer on the grounds of their un-freedom. I wonder whether the distinction between mistaken and bad choices is stable enough to support this. But let us set these issues aside. The more telling problem with the view under discussion is internal to it, in the sense that it arises after granting the claim that the plaintiff ought to be protected from the consequences of her choice under the right to do with one's property as one pleases, or the right to keep one's property until one freely chooses to part with it. The problem is that the defendant need not be understood to be asserting either right. In the case on which I am focussing, she need only assert the right to retain that to which she holds title (perhaps 'unless she forfeits it through wrongdoing').[41] The defendant's retention of the payment need not, then, rest on her invoking a right she denies to the plaintiff. So it is not caught by the Kantian prohibition against making an exception of oneself. Thus restitution to the plaintiff is not, on these grounds, required by corrective justice.

VI. DUTY AND RIGHT, GAINS AND LOSSES

The second account begins with the idea that the conception of equality implicit in Aristotle's account and explicit in Kant's expresses itself in a normative order in which rights and duties are correlative. We interact as equals when we respect the boundaries set at the points at which our respective exercises of freedom are compatible with one another; a boundary crossing is at once an infringement of the trespassee's right and a breach of the trespasser's duty to keep within her bounds. The second sense in which Aristotle's theory of corrective justice is inchoately Kantian, on Weinrib's account, is that the correlativity at the heart of Aristotle's

[41] I realise that payment under liability mistake is an easy case for my argument. But, again, it is the paradigmatic case of unjust enrichment. A theory of unjust enrichment must, to be acceptable, account for it. Furthermore, I think the same analysis can be made for other sorts of mistakes and other unjust factors, though the line between the right asserted by the defendant and that asserted by the plaintiff seeking restitution will be thinner in some cases.

account of corrective justice is really the correlativity of duty and right. The correlativity on which rests a claim in corrective justice on Aristotle's account, I suggested above, is that between the doing and suffering of a wrong. 'The doing and suffering of a wrong' describes a relationship better described as the breach of a duty and the infringement of a right.

Consider again Aristotle's example, a battery. There defendant and plaintiff are linked in the way corrective justice requires because the event in which the tort consisted was at once a breach of a duty on the defendant's part and an infringement of a right of the plaintiff's. Now, I argued above that the correlativity of gain and loss illustrated in my figs. 1 to 3 ought to be understood only as an analogy with the relationship between the parties to a transaction that attracts the interest of corrective justice. The point, I argued, was that B's gain and A's loss are two sides of the same coin just as are B's doing and A's suffering of a wrong—or as are B's breach of a duty and the infringement of A's right. Weinrib draws a different connection. There *is*, on his account, a sense in which a wrongdoer (by definition) realises a gain and the victim of the wrong (by definition) bears a loss. The gains and losses at issue, however, are not material. What attracts the interest of justice are departures not from what persons happen to have, but from what they are entitled to have. Such departures, in Weinrib's vocabulary, are *normative* gains and losses.

Now, to what, exactly, do normative gains and losses refer? Weinrib, it seems to me, has two answers. The first is that, in his words, '[c]onsidered normatively, loss refers to the infringement of the plaintiff's right, and gain to the breach of the defendant's duty.'[42] On this account, then, to say of someone that she has enjoyed a normative gain is just to say that she breached a duty; to say that she suffered a normative loss is just to say that a right of hers has been infringed. Elsewhere, however, Weinrib argues that Aristotle 'reads ["gain" and "loss"] back into the relationship [between defendant and plaintiff] from its remedial stage.'[43]

> All that liability under corrective justice requires is that one person have wronged another. The gains and losses in Aristotle's text are nothing but quantitative representations of the doing and suffering of wrong. Properly understood, they refer to surpluses and shortfalls not from what the parties had before the unjust act, but from what the parties ought to have in view of the requirements of corrective justice.[44]

On this account, then, '[t]hey [gain and loss] are not conditions of liability.'[45] I'm not sure that these accounts can be made consistent with one another.

[42] Weinrib (above n 1) 133.
[43] Weinrib (above n 24) 289.
[44] *Ibid.*
[45] *Ibid.*

The first account, again, holds that '[c]onsidered normatively, loss refers to the infringement of the plaintiff's right, and the gain to the breach of the defendant's duty.' On this account, then, the plaintiff's having suffered a normative loss and the defendant's having enjoyed a normative gain *are* conditions of liability.

We can, I think, set this puzzle to the side. What matters for what follows is that B enjoys a normative gain at the expense of a normative loss on A's part when (and only when) B acts in such a way as to breach a duty owed to A that corresponds to an infringement of a right A holds against B. It follows that it is the correlativity of normative gains and losses that marks out cases of corrective injustice. It is immaterial that, for example, a batterer does not (or need not) realise a material gain. Corrective justice takes an interest because the battery can at once be described as an infringement of the plaintiff's right and a breach by the defendant of a duty owed to the plaintiff, and so as a transaction in which one party realises a normative gain corresponding to a normative loss suffered by the other.

Now, it would seem that liability for unjust enrichment is ruled out on this analysis owing to its being strict. Not so, argues Lionel Smith. Smith holds that on the right analysis, the mistaken payer does suffer a normative loss that corresponds to a normative gain on the payee's part. '[W]hen a single transaction, necessarily some kind of transfer, give rise to both a material gain on the part of the defendant and a material loss on the part of the plaintiff,' Smith argues, 'it is not necessary to find that the defendant did anything wrong to characterize that gain and loss as normative. It is enough to find that the plaintiff did not fully consent to the transfer.'[46] It is enough because:

> [i]f the transfer is normatively flawed from the plaintiff's end, then the plaintiff suffers a normative loss. Because the defendant's enrichment is nothing other than the plaintiff's normative deprivation, the defendant's material gain is also a normative gain. Hence, corrective justice is violated, and a duty to make restitution arises without the need to find any breach of duty on the part of the defendant.[47]

Unpacked a bit, the argument, as I understand it, goes like this: Owing to the impairment of her consent, the transfer is for the plaintiff a normative loss; the material loss in which the normative loss is manifested is, at once, a material gain for the plaintiff; just as the plaintiff's normative loss just is her material loss, the defendant's material gain is a normative gain, at the plaintiff's expense. Hence corrective justice requires that the transfer be undone.

[46] Smith (above n 1) 2140.
[47] *Ibid*, 2142.

Elegant as it is, Smith's argument does not, I think, go through. The problem occurs at the first step, in the claim that it follows from the transfer's being 'normatively flawed' from the plaintiff's end that she suffers a normative loss. Notwithstanding the ambiguity in the concepts of normative loss and gain noted above, I cannot see how this is so. A normative loss, again, is a loss relative not to what one happens to have but to what one is entitled to have. Now, one's entitlements in respect of one's holdings consist in claims held against others. So the mistaken payer suffers a normative loss only if, owing to the normative flaw in the transfer, a claim she holds against another fails to be respected. But what could this claim be? The only claim that implicates the payee is the claim for the return of the disputed payment. But that will not do because, as Smith notes, that would beg the question.[48]

My point here might be confused with another, namely that the mistaken payer cannot be entitled, properly speaking, to restitution because such an entitlement would amount to the imposition of a duty to aid. Now, to the extent that it is such a duty, it is difficult to justify in terms of the account of corrective justice on which Smith bases his argument (Weinrib's), because right, on Kant's account, only protects us only from others' interferences with our entitlements (and on this point private common law is largely in agreement). But my point is different and, in a sense, more basic. The problem is that, as Stephen Smith points out, it would follow from Lionel Smith's account that a person suffers a normative loss if she drops a bag of money down a deep hole where she cannot retrieve it.[49] She was, *ex hypothesi*, entitled to the money, but no entitlement she held with respect to it was violated when she dropped it. So she suffered no normative loss. Of course, this is a 'transfer' of money in only a metaphorical sense. But from the plaintiff's perspective the result and the problem are the same: she has lost possession of her money, and she did not intend to divest herself of it as she ended up doing. The normative flaw in each case is the same. By parity of reasoning, the mistaken payer does not suffer a normative loss when she transfers her money to the defendant.

Let me put the point another way. The recipient of a mistaken payment is, in an important sense, akin to a finder. Though she must return it, in taking possession of the chattel, the finder does not deprive the owner of anything she is entitled to. Similarly, though she must return it, by being in receipt of the payer's money, the payee does not deprive the payer of anything she is entitled to. It follows that her being in receipt of the payment cannot constitute a normative gain on her part. Thus the payer's claim for restitution cannot, on this account, be understood as a claim under corrective justice.

[48] *Ibid*, 2127.
[49] Smith (above n 8) 2190.

VII. WEINRIB'S ACCOUNT

I would like, finally, to consider Weinrib's own account, which does not rest on the conceptual framework outlined above, but is also grounded in Aristotle's account of corrective justice. He argues:

> The ultimate basis of ... recovery [in cases such as mistaken payment] is that corrective justice, being in Aristotle's words 'towards another,' assumes the mutual externality of the parties and the consequent separateness of their interests. Accordingly, corrective justice recognizes no obligation to enrich another. The conferral of a benefit is literally within the free gift of the donor as a self-determining agent. Consequently, only if the donor acts in execution of a donative intent is the transfer of the benefit an expression of right. Unilateral transfers, such as mistaken payments, that are not the product of donative intent are juridically ineffective, regardless of the absence of wrongdoing by the donee. Their restitution can therefore be demanded as a matter of corrective justice.[50]

The main idea, as I understand it, is that to allow the mistaken payment to stay in the payee's hands would, owing to the absence of donative intent on the payee's part, be tantamount to enforcing a duty to confer a gratuitous benefit, a duty which corrective justice, on the Aristotelian-Kantian view, does not recognize.

There is, I think, something very important captured in this argument. But it fails to justify its conclusion (below I will say what I think it does capture). Even if it follows from the absence of the payer's donative intent that the payment she makes is not an expression of right,[51] it does not then follow that in being in receipt of the payment the payee violates a right held by the plaintiff. (Put in terms of the framework considered above, nothing in the increase in the defendant's holdings counts as a normative gain to her.) But then there is nothing to anchor the defendant's duty to make restitution. Now, I do not think that Weinrib holds otherwise. He continues:

> In such circumstances, the enrichment itself represents something that is rightfully the plaintiff's. Because its retention by the defendant is an infringement of the plaintiff's right, the defendant has a duty to restore it to the plaintiff. Liability is the juridical confirmation that, by holding on to the factual gain, the defendant breaches a duty that is correlative to the plaintiff's right.

[50] Weinrib (above n 1) 140–41.

[51] I do not see how it can, if by 'right' is meant Kant's conception. On Kant's view, as we have seen, the domain of right is external freedom, that freedom with which others can interfere with their actions and omissions. The mistaken payee has, *ex hypothesi*, suffered no such interference.

However, as we saw above,[52] it begs the question to locate the corrective injustice in the defendant's retention of the benefit. What we need is an account of the antecedent duty to return the benefit. Weinrib's account does not show how that duty is a duty to set right a corrective injustice.

VIII. CONCLUSION TO THE MAIN ARGUMENT

I conclude that the mistaken payer's claim for restitution cannot be understood to be a claim in corrective justice, on Aristotle's understanding. From this I draw the more general conclusion that the law of unjust enrichment does not express or exhibit the structure of corrective justice. The inference to the broader conclusion rests on two claims I discussed at the outset. First, the mistaken payer's claim for restitution is the paradigmatic claim in unjust enrichment. Second, it is only if the law of unjust enrichment expressed or exhibited the structure of corrective justice in Aristotle's sense would it matter that it did. If these are sound then, I believe, the broader conclusion is too.

What now? If we follow Aristotle in holding that corrective and distributive justice collectively exhaust the domain of justice, then we must conclude that the mistaken payer's claim for restitution is a claim in distributive justice. I'm not sure that we should follow Aristotle on this point.[53] However, I suggest, the idea that the mistaken payer's claim for restitution is, in a particular way, a claim in distributive justice merits consideration. Though not, we will see, the whole story, it captures some important features of the structure of the action in unjust enrichment.

IX. THE INTERNAL DISTRIBUTIVE ACCOUNT

In comment (c) to § 1 of the first *Restatement of Restitution*—which sets out its core principle, 'a person who has been unjustly enriched at the expense of another is required to make restitution to the other'—the reporters tell us that an enrichment is unjust only if 'as between the two persons, it is unjust for [the defendant] to retain it.' Let us call this the *Restatement* measure. It may seem to be a tautology, but it is not. There are two substantive claims implicit in it. The first is that the focus of the unjust enrichment inquiry is the post-transactional state of affairs, that is, the state in which the defendant rather than the plaintiff has the disputed thing of value. We can, on this point, contrast unjust enrichment with tort.

[52] See above (n 2) and accompanying text.

[53] Punishment, at least, seems to be a counter-example. Its structure is singular: no where else is C's harming B the remedy for B's wronging A.

In tort it is the event which gives rise to the cause of action that the award of damages seeks to set right.[54]

While important, this first claim is, I take it, uncontroversial. More controversial is the second claim. It is implicit in the use of the locution 'as between the two persons.' As Stephen Perry argues, the invocation of this phrase ordinarily signals that the question of liability at issue is understood to be a matter of what he calls 'localized distributive justice.'

> An argument of this sort is based on a claim of distributive justice because it focuses initially on the loss, which is regarded as a burden to be distributed among a specified group of persons. It is an argument of *localized* distributive justice because the group is limited to the victim and her injurer (or injurers).[55]

An example of this sort of argument from tort law (on which Perry focuses) is found in *Sindell v Abbott Laboratories*. In *Sindell* the plaintiff could prove that it was highly probable that one of the negligent defendants caused her injury, but she could not prove which. The court held that '[t]he most persuasive reasons for finding that the plaintiff states a cause of action is that ... as between an innocent plaintiff and negligent defendants, the latter should bear the cost of the injury.'[56] According to this argument, fault is taken as a kind of tie-breaker, a way out of the evidentiary impasse. The plaintiff's loss is, in effect, taken as sunk, to be distributed according to the measure of fault. The second claim implicit in the *Restatement* measure is that this model describes the structure of the action in unjust enrichment, subject to one modification. The modification is that it is not the cost of a loss but rather a thing of value (money, a good, a service) whose distribution is at issue.

It is important to see in just what sense the structure of the action of unjust enrichment is distributive on this view. In private law theory, distributive justice explanations and justifications of a given legal domain are typically instrumental. One might, for example, defend tort on the grounds of its capacity to efficiently allocate accident costs across the relevant group (or, conversely, urge its abolition on the grounds that some other legal instrument would better realise this goal). But on the view under consideration, the plaintiff's claim in unjust enrichment does not await vindication by proof that the liability rule has positive consequences for some relevant broader group. Nor—it must be emphasised—is the plaintiff's claim that, in light of her and the defendant's extra-transactional holdings, distributive

[54] This is reflected in the fact that the names of the nominate torts pick out both events and the cause of action to which they give rise. A 'battery' for example, could name the event of B's striking A without A's consent, or the action A may thereby bring against B.
[55] S Perry 'The Moral Foundations of Tort Law' (1992) 77 *Iowa Law Review* 449, 461.
[56] 607 P 2d 924 (Calif SC 1980) 936.

justice is best served by the disputed enrichment being returned to her.[57] In other words, the distributive claim is localised in *two* senses. First, it is limited to the parties to the transaction. Second, it rests on a norm whose scope is limited to the structure of the disputed transfer—in the case under discussion something like 'as between a mistaken payer and the payee, the former has the superior claim to the thing transferred.' To emphasise this second point, I will refer to this account as the *internal* (rather than 'localised') distributive justice account.

Two points can be made in favour in the internal distributive account. The first is that it respects the fact—which fact proved the undoing of the corrective justice account—that (to return to the paradigm case) the payee is not the agent of the mistaken payer's misfortune. Secondly, it makes sense of certain features of the substantive principles on which recovery in unjust enrichment are based, features that are not exhibited by the principles on which claims in tort—which, I have argued, are claims in corrective justice—are based. Consider, for example, the duty of care. Such a norm announces in advance what sort of conduct we are entitled to expect of one another. The substantive principles on which unjust enrichment are based differ from such a norm on two measures. First, they apply to holdings or entitlements, rather than to conduct. Second, they apply retroactively—or at least the principle underlying recovery for mistaken payment must, because there is nothing that the payee could have done beforehand to avoid liability. Neither of these features is at odds with the structure of distributive justice. If the contrasting formal properties of the norms enforced by tort—that they (a) prospectively announce (b) standards of conduct—are required by corrective justice, then this argument seems to settle the matter in favour of the internal distributive account. And they are so required, on Aristotle's account, just because on his account the plaintiff and defendant are linked as sufferer and *doer* of the same wrong.

So is the matter settled? Perhaps not. Perhaps, that is, there are properties exhibited by the mistaken payer and payee analogous to that of suffering and doing the same wrong that show their positions to be correlative in the way required by corrective justice.[58] If so, this would show that it is inessential to corrective justice that the norms governing the doctrines that

[57] The point merits emphasis because, arguably, courts sometimes do treat the question whether an enrichment was unjust as shaped, in part, by the parties extra-transactional holdings. On the perils of so doing, see K Barker, 'Rescuing Remedialism in Unjust Enrichment Law: Why Remedies are Right' (1998) 57 *CLJ* 301, 315–16.

[58] Gordley attributes a view something like this to Aquinas. See J Gordley, 'Restitution Without Enrichment? Change of Position and *Wegfall der Bereicherung*' in D Johnston and R Zimmermann (eds) *Unjustified Enrichment: Key Issues in Comparative Perspective* (Cambridge, Cambridge University Press, 2002) 227, 228. I don't think this is what Aquinas held, but I will not pursue the (tricky) interpretive questions here.

exhibit its structure bear the properties exhibited in tort but not unjust enrichment. But I do not think that the positions of mistaken payer and payee can be shown to be correlative in this way. The mistaken payer, again, is akin to someone who has simply lost her money. Of course, that she dropped her money in the defendant's bank account—rather than, say, a garbage can—picks the defendant out as the person from whom to request its return. Their positions are correlative to this point. But no further: that the payer dropped her money in the payee's account does not, in itself, justify the payee's duty to return it. (Bear in mind that in the case under discussion, title has passed.) Put another way, the mistaken payer's claim for restitution is, in effect, a request that the payee insure the payer against her mistakes. But nothing in the transaction serves as consideration for this insurance. The payer's claim must, in that sense, reach beyond the transaction for its justification.

On the other hand, a case can be made that the internal distributive justice account rests, at bottom, on a corrective claim. Here's how. As we saw, the distributive inquiry, according to the internal distributive account, is internal to the transaction in two ways. It is limited to the parties to the transaction, and it is limited to the soundness of the disputed transfer. But—the objection goes—the only thing that could justify thus restricting the scope of the distributive pool and the appropriate distributive criterion is some feature of the transaction itself. And an argument supplying this justification by picking out this feature would show that the mistaken payer's claim for restitution is really a claim in corrective justice. If the arguments of this article are sound, the conclusion to this objection cannot be right. But it nonetheless shows that these explorations have only scratched the surface.[59]

[59] An alternative I have not considered here is Birks's view that the plaintiff's claim for restitution is a claim for the enforcement of a primary right—a right, that is, akin to the right to be free from unconsented physical force, or the right that another perform her contractual obligations—rather than a secondary right, that is, a right triggered by the violation of a primary right, for example, the right to compensation for battery or breach of contract. See P Birks, 'The Concept of a Civil Wrong' in D Owen (ed), *Philosophical Foundations of Tort Law* (Oxford, Oxford University Press, 1995) 31, 48–9, and 'Rights, Wrongs and Remedies' (2000) 20 *OJLS* 1, 28–31. The view is, I think, deceptively simple: it puts at issue many more questions that I can consider here. But I will register one misgiving. While akin to, for example, the right to be free from trespass in that it does not arise from a wrong, the right to restitution is akin to the right for compensation for trespass in that each are a right that another set aright something for the plaintiff. The right to restitution is a primary right of a distinctive sort—a remedial primary right, we might say. To the extent that it is a remedial right, it seems to me, its justification raises just the sort of questions under consideration here. (Birks, I expect, would take issue with this, on the grounds that 'remedy' carries with it a connotation that there is a wrong about that needs to be redressed. I'm not sure this is so. But if it is, I will retract the term. The point remains that the right to restitution, like the right to compensation for a wrong, is a right that another set aright something for the plaintiff. That it is a primary right only deepens the justificatory puzzle.)

X. POSTSCRIPT: UNJUST ENRICHMENT AND EQUITY

I would like to add a final thought. A principal motivation behind the claim that the law of unjust enrichment expresses or exhibits the structure of corrective justice, we saw, is that it provides a response to the worry that the claim that given enrichment is unjust amounts only to the view that it is contrary to equity and conscience. By denying the former I do not mean to affirm the latter. But I do think that it follows from some of the foregoing arguments that there is something equitable about unjust enrichment.

I have two points in mind. The first is that the role of the law of unjust enrichment in private law as a whole can be seen as something akin to the judgment Aristotle described as correcting the application of law when, owing to its universality, it yields an injustice.[60] The point is most easily made with the case I have been treating as paradigmatic. A pays B money under a liability mistake. Title passes. The transaction is, from the perspective of the rest of private law, sound. But it offends justice to leave things as they are. The judgment that the transaction must be reversed rests, I suggested above, on something like the principle that 'as between the mistaken payer and the payee, the former has the superior claim to the thing transferred.' My point here is that the more complete statement of this principle continues 'notwithstanding that the transfer itself was, in a sense, sound.' Of course, there is a begged question here. This analysis relies on treating the rules that yield the result that the transfer is sound—in the sense that title has passed—as exhausting the conditions under which that judgment ought to be made. The analysis, in other words, takes the positive law as found. Perhaps the law of unjust enrichment is only contingently equitable in this first sense. Whether the positive law on this point reflects defensible principles is another question I will not consider here.[61]

The second feature of the law of unjust enrichment that, I suggest, is in some sense equitable concerns the nature of the justification of the principles by which otherwise sound transactions are reversed. Again, I will make my case only in the context of mistaken payment. There, again, the relevant principle is something like 'as between the mistaken payer and the payee, the former has the superior claim to the thing transferred (notwithstanding that the transfer itself was, in a sense, sound).' What justifies this principle? It is on this point that I think Weinrib's analysis of mistaken payments, as I noted above, captures something important. Weinrib's argument, recall, is that the problem with letting the post-transactional state of affairs stand

[60] *EN* (n 7) 5.10, 1137b27.

[61] For a much more fine-grained analysis of the sense in which unjust enrichment is in this sense equitable—in the sense, that is, that it plays a corrective role in private law—see L Smith, 'Property, Subsidiarity, and Unjust Enrichment' in D Johnson and R Zimmermann (eds), *Unjustified Enrichment: Key Issues in Comparative Perspective* (Cambridge, Cambridge University Press, 2002) 588, 610–23.

would be tantamount to enforcing a duty to confer a gratuitous benefit. The common law recognizes no such duty. So why would we not say that restitution was simply required by law? The answer is that refusing restitution would not literally amount to enforcing this duty. Literally enforcing this duty would require imposing a sanction on the payer had she refrained from conferring the benefit in the first place. So strictly speaking, leaving enrichment with the payee would not be contrary to legal principle. But doing so would be in tension with fundamental principles of the common law—with, we might say, the spirit if not the letter of the law. The judgment not to leave the enrichment with the payee, I am suggesting, is equitable in the sense that it is not a question of the strict conformity of a doctrine with legal principle. Perhaps, given its ambiguities, invoking 'equity' here obscures more than it illuminates. But in any case it names a feature of the law of unjust enrichment for which a theory of its foundations must account.

7

Two Theories of Unjust Enrichment

PETER JAFFEY*

I. TWO THEORIES OF UNJUST ENRICHMENT

A. The Strong Theory and the Weak Theory of Unjust Enrichment

IN THIS ARTICLE I will distinguish between two theories that might each be described as a theory of unjust enrichment, which I will refer to as the 'strong theory' and the 'weak theory.' It seems to me that the strong theory is implicitly assumed in most of the restitution and unjust enrichment textbooks. If sound, the strong theory is important. It justifies the recognition of a legal category of unjust enrichment in the sense discussed below. But the strong theory is, in my view, demonstrably false. The weak theory is true, but it is inconsequential: it does not justify the recognition of a legal category of unjust enrichment in any important sense. The two theories tend to be conflated, and the strong theory is often wrongly inferred from the weak theory.

It is clear that there exist claims, arising from the receipt of a benefit by the defendant, to remove the benefit and transfer it to the claimant.[1] An example is the claim to reverse a mistaken payment, which arises from the receipt of the mistaken payment by the defendant. Such a claim might plausibly be described as an unjust enrichment claim. At one time the claim to recover a mistaken payment was classified as a 'quasi-contractual' claim—it was treated as if it were a contractual claim, under the implied contract fiction. Clearly contract was not the true basis of the claim, and the implied contract fiction has been abandoned. The claim was also clearly not a tort claim. At that time claims at common law were, broadly speaking, characterised as either contractual or tortious, and contractual and tortious claims were (and are) understood as being forms of claim for compensation for loss, for

* I am grateful to the participants in the symposium for their comments on this paper.
[1] 'Arising from the receipt of a benefit' means the receipt of the benefit is a condition of the claim.

which the benefit received by the defendant is irrelevant.[2] Thus it is easy, and apparently unobjectionable, to infer that 'unjust enrichment' forms a third category of the common law, distinct from but analogous to contract and tort. But there is an error here, or at least a hidden assumption.

There are different ways of classifying legal claims. The standard means of classification is in terms of the nature of the justification for the claim.[3] One can say that a legal category comprises claims governed by a certain legal principle.[4] For example, one might say that the law of contract is concerned with the application of the principle that agreements should be enforced, and the law of tort with the application of the principle that there is a duty to take reasonable steps to avoid reasonably foreseeable harm (these are intended as illustrative examples; I do not mean to enter into a debate on the nature of these areas of law). This does not mean that the principle is applied directly in every case of contract or tort. Generally there will be more specific rules that govern the particular issue at stake. But the general principle will provide a justification for claims falling into the category and a basis for understanding, interpreting and modifying the rules. It will also generate a framework for dealing with claims falling into the category, which will identify certain characteristic issues that arise in relation to them.

One might object that there could be a recognised legal category without any consensus on a general underlying principle. It might indeed be more accurate to say that a legal category is defined in terms of a certain type of legal problem, concerned with a particular sort of clash of interests between people in certain types of situation, to which the principle offers a solution. For instance, one might say (rather tritely) that contract law is concerned with the problem of how disputes arising from the non-performance of agreements should be resolved, and the principle that agreements should be observed has been recognised as the solution to this problem. In another instance, one might say that tort law is concerned with the extent to which freedom to perform an act should be constrained for the benefit of other people who may be harmed by it, and that the principle that there is a duty to take reasonable care to avoid reasonably foreseeable harm has been recognised as the solution.

[2] A contractual claim is generally understood as either a claim for loss caused by the breach of a duty to perform or as a claim in debt, which is not strictly a claim for breach of duty, although it is sometimes so expressed. The case of contractual reliance loss is discussed below.

[3] I take it to follow that legal categories are mutually exclusive, although a set of facts may generate claims in different categories.

[4] Cf M Moore, *Placing Blame* (Oxford, Clarendon Press, 1997) 18ff. Maybe one should say a set of principles, but it is not necessary to pursue this for present purposes. In adopting an approach along these lines, I take it that I am following the general approach behind the prevailing approach to restitution and unjust enrichment, although as explained below I reject the particular concept of a principle of unjust enrichment.

In the light of this, one can distinguish between the weak and strong theories of unjust enrichment. The weak theory of unjust enrichment asserts that there are claims that arise from the receipt of a benefit by the defendant and that serve to transfer the benefit from the defendant to the claimant. Below, I will refer to these as claims arising from the receipt of a benefit. The weak theory is obviously true, as the claim to reverse a mistaken payment demonstrates, but it is trivial because it says nothing about when a claim should arise, or how the cases should be interpreted, or how the law should be organised or developed. By contrast, the strong theory asserts that there is a legal category of unjust enrichment analogous to contract or tort, ie a 'law of unjust enrichment' in the standard sense identified above. The assertion is not simply that there are claims that arise from the receipt of a benefit, but that all such claims are based on the same principle, the 'principle of unjust enrichment;' or, more broadly, that all such cases raise the same type of legal problem, involving the same types of interest of the parties and the same type of question as to how these interests should be accommodated or which should prevail, so that it makes sense to address them under a common framework and terminology. If the strong theory is true it has (unlike the weak theory) important implications for the structure and content of the law.

The description of a claim as an 'unjust enrichment claim' is ambiguous as between the two theories. An 'unjust enrichment claim' in the weak sense means only that the claim arises from the receipt of a benefit. There is no implication that the claim has any particular basis, or that it has the same basis or falls in the same category as any other such claim. In the strong sense, an 'unjust enrichment claim' is a claim falling in a legal category of unjust enrichment in the sense above and necessarily falling outside other categories of claim, like contract and tort.

The weak theory is consistent with two propositions that are ruled out by the strong theory: (1) that claims arising from the receipt of a benefit—unjust enrichment claims in the weak sense—can fall into different legal categories in the sense explained above; and (2) that these legal categories can include well-recognised legal categories, such as contract.[5] The discussion below provides support for both these propositions.

One might describe the strong theory and the weak theory as the normative and descriptive theories of unjust enrichment. The weak theory is a descriptive theory in the sense that it merely reports that amongst the claims found in the law are some that arise from the receipt of a benefit. The weak theory is non-normative in the sense that it says nothing about the justification for such claims, and therefore offers nothing in the way of

[5] As discussed below, this is clearly true of claims for disgorgement, but is also true of other claims arising from the receipt of a benefit.

guidance in the development of the law or in the resolution of new or controversial cases. On the other hand, the strong theory is normative in this sense. It is a theory about the justification for claims arising from the receipt of benefits, and so it can influence the way cases are decided and the way the law develops.[6]

B. Arguments for the Strong Theory

It is now widely accepted that unjust enrichment claims are to be addressed according to a three-stage test:[7] (1) the defendant must be enriched; (2) the enrichment must have been at the expense of the claimant; (3) the enrichment must be unjust. Different types of case are said to be based on different 'unjust factors.' One might argue that this approach presupposes no more than the weak theory, but it seems clear that it is generally understood in terms of the strong theory. It is taken to imply that unjust enrichment claims, in the weak sense, form a category of law in the sense above, and there is generally understood to be a 'principle of unjust enrichment' that governs the category. 'Unjust factors' are understood to constitute different ways in which an enrichment can be unjust according to the principle. The analysis of claims typically involves the question whether a claim is an unjust enrichment claim rather than a claim in some other category, eg contract or tort. The approach requires that all unjust enrichment claims, in the weak sense, should be brought together through a radical reorganisation of the old case law into a single category under a common framework and common terminology, leading to significant changes in the content of the law. An approach along these lines appears to be adopted in most restitution and unjust enrichment textbooks.[8]

[6] I have not used this terminology generally because these expressions have sometimes been used in other senses.

[7] Or four-stage test, which includes the question whether there is a defence. There are variants of this framework, which it is not necessary to discuss for present purposes.

[8] See eg A Burrows, *The Law of Restitution*, 2nd edn (London, Butterworths, 2002) 15; G McMeel, *The Modern Law of Restitution* (London, Blackstone Press, 2000) 5; G Virgo, *The Principles of the Law of Restitution* (Oxford, Oxford University Press, 1999) 49. Virgo distinguishes between what he describes as the 'formulaic' and the 'normative' approaches to the principle of unjust enrichment (at 52). On the 'formulaic' approach, the principle is merely an 'organising principle' that has no influence in decision-making, which is based on the application of settled rules. On the 'normative' approach, judges apply the principle of unjust enrichment directly to the facts, as it were, so that they have a general discretion. Such a general discretion is open to objection, and seems to have been behind Birks' suggestion that 'the best policy is to make no use of the so-called principle against unjust enrichment;' this would, he thought, '[threaten] to undo the effort taken to make "unjust" look downwards to the cases': P Birks, rev edn, *An Introduction to the Law of Restitution* (Oxford, Clarendon Press, 1989) 19. The idea of an organising principle that determines how the law is classified but has no influence on the way cases are decided surely cannot account for the dynamic aspect of the common

Nevertheless, many writers on unjust enrichment are non-committal with respect to the theoretical basis of the law, and cannot be said to adopt the strong theory explicitly. For example, McKendrick, after emphasising the importance of 'taxonomy,' notes that 'what ... makes a particular enrichment unjust' is a question that 'has not been answered in modern writing on the law of restitution.'[9]

Furthermore, whereas the principles referred to above as standing behind contract or tort have a clear and distinct meaning, it is clear on reflection that the 'principle of unjust enrichment' or the principle that 'all unjust enrichments must be reversed' does not, itself, express a meaningful principle; it is a label for *some* principle, yet to be identified and formulated, that is supposed to lie behind unjust enrichment claims in the weak sense. For example, Johnston and Zimmerman say:[10]

> To state that something amounts to unjustified enrichment is merely a conclusion, that because the enrichment is unjustified it should be returned, restored or made over to the person properly entitled to it. That conclusion is in need of supporting normative argument. But what sort of argument?

Many writers who are implicitly committed to the strong theory, and to a principle of unjust enrichment, do not even attempt to offer any elucidation of the supposed principle. It is surely clear that the three-stage test or an enumeration of supposed unjust factors does not amount to such an elucidation.

It is not easy to identify arguments in the literature to support the strong theory. Some writers appear to conflate the strong theory and the weak theory, or infer the former from the latter. From the recognition that there are claims that arise from the receipt of a benefit, unjust enrichment claims in the weak sense, they infer the strong theory, and they take the exposure of the implied contract fiction to provide support for the strong theory.[11] But the weak theory does not entail the strong theory, and rejecting the strong theory does not entail denying that there are claims that arise from the receipt of a benefit.

law, reflected in its evolution over time. But equally there is surely no question of a wide range of cases being consigned to a judicial discretion. Virgo identifies a 'middle way,' according to which the principle of unjust enrichment plays a guiding role in the development of the law rather than being applied directly to the facts. In fact, this seems to reflect Birks' approach also. In terms of its understanding of the role of an underlying principle, this 'middle way' seems sound, but it says nothing about the supposed principle of unjust enrichment and does not provide a justification of the strong theory.

[9] E McKendrick, 'Taxonomy: does it matter?' in D Johnston and R Zimmermann (eds), *Unjustified Enrichment: Key Issues in Comparative Perspective* (Cambridge, Cambridge University Press, 2002) 628.

[10] D Johnston and R Zimmermann, 'Unjustified Enrichment: Surveying the Landscape' in Johnston and Zimmermann (n 9) 3.

[11] See eg A Burrows, 'Restitution: Where do We Go From Here?' in A Burrows, *Understanding the Law of Obligations* (Oxford, Hart Publishing, 1998).

It has been said that the House of Lords has now recognised a principle of unjust enrichment, which puts an end to any controversy.[12] But although the cases in question may contain a recitation of the three-stage framework and purport to rely on a principle of unjust enrichment, none of them contains a statement of what the principle of unjust enrichment is, and all of them can be perfectly well explained (as discussed below) without the need for the strong theory or for a principle of unjust enrichment.

In the end, the strong theory must be established or refuted by a careful examination of the various unjust enrichment claims, in the weak sense, to see what their justification is. Virgo asserts that the principle of unjust enrichment 'explains earlier cases and can be used to predict results in future cases,' in support of which he directs the reader to the rest of his book.[13] To the contrary, in my view, as soon as one begins to examine particular claims in order to determine what the principle of unjust enrichment might be, it becomes clear that there are different types of claim, based on different principles, and that the strong theory is false. The main part of this article seeks to demonstrate this.[14]

C. Restitution and Unjust Enrichment

I have referred above to claims that arise from the receipt of a benefit and that serve to remove the benefit from the defendant and transfer it to the claimant. The removal of the benefit and its transfer to the claimant is usually described as 'restitution.' The expression 'restitution' is most apt where the benefit takes the form of wealth or property transferred from the claimant, and its removal and transfer to the claimant serves to reverse the transfer. But, as discussed below, in some cases where a claim arises from the receipt of a benefit from the claimant, the claim is not for the reversal of a transfer but for *payment for* the benefit received, for example a benefit resulting from a service performed by the claimant.

[12] Virgo (above n 8) 51. This is rather empty, given the apparent influence of the academic literature on the House of Lords on this issue. The English cases might include *Lipkin Gorman v Karpnale* [1991] 2 AC 548; *Banque Financière de la Cité v Parc (Battersea)* [1999] 1 AC 221; and *Portman Building Society v Hamlyn Taylor Neck* [1998] 4 All ER 202, although they do not all use the expression 'principle of unjust enrichment.' It is in any case open to doubt whether the strong theory of unjust enrichment could be the *ratio* of a decision.
[13] Virgo (above n 8) 52.
[14] The approach adopted here reflects that in P Jaffey, *The Nature and Scope of Restitution* (Oxford, Hart Publishing, 2000), and some of the arguments below are developed further there. Various authors have propounded views opposing what I have described as the strong theory of unjust enrichment or aspects of it, eg S Stoljar, *The Law of Quasi-Contract*, 2nd edn (Sydney, The Law Book Company Limited, 1989); J Dietrich, *Restitution—A New Perspective* (Annandale, Federation Press, 1998); I Jackman, *The Varieties of Restitution* (Annandale, Federation Press, 1998); S Hedley, *Restitution: Its Division and Ordering* (London, Sweet & Maxwell, 2001).

The defendant is liable to pay *some proportion of* the value received. In addition, in other cases involving the removal of a benefit, the benefit did not come from the claimant at all, but from a third party. The strong theory obscures these distinctions, because in all cases it characterises the claim as simply a claim to remove an enrichment, based on a principle of unjust enrichment. In this article, I will refer to unjust enrichment claims in the weak sense or claims arising from the receipt of a benefit without necessarily indicating what the remedial form is, although generally this will be clear from the context.

D. Quadration

Birks' doctrine of quadration holds that there is a relationship of mutual entailment or correspondence between unjust enrichment and restitution: all unjust enrichment claims are restitution claims and vice versa.[15] If 'unjust enrichment claim' is used in the sense of the weak theory, it refers to a claim that arises from the receipt of a benefit and that serves to remove the benefit (or to exact payment for it). If a 'restitutionary claim' refers to any claim for the removal of a benefit (or for payment for a benefit) the doctrine of quadration must follow. This is a simple and inconsequential matter of definition. However, if 'unjust enrichment claim' is used in the sense of the strong theory to refer to a claim based on a principle of unjust enrichment, the doctrine of quadration is simply an assertion of the strong theory itself. It implies that all claims that arise from the receipt of a benefit are governed by the same underlying principle and fall in the same category of law in the sense above.

E. An Intermediate Position

Some writers might object to the analysis advanced above on the basis that, although they recognise a principle of unjust enrichment, they do not accept the strong theory, because they concede that not *all* unjust enrichment claims (in the weak sense) are based on the principle or fall into the category of unjust enrichment. In other words, they recognise that there can be claims arising from the receipt of a benefit that are not based on this principle. This position has been expressed by way of the rejection of the doctrine of quadration.[16]

[15] Birks (above n 8) 17; now repudiated in P Birks, 'Misnomer' in W Cornish and others (eds), *Restitution: Past, Present and Future* (Oxford, Hart Publishing, 1998) but retained by Burrows (above n 8) 5–7.
[16] See eg G Virgo, 'What is the Law of Restitution About?' in Cornish (n 15); Birks (n 15).

There are serious difficulties with this intermediate position, however. As noted above, the 'principle of unjust enrichment' is a supposed principle, the content of which is not apparent on its face, that is taken to account for claims arising from the receipt of a benefit. But once it is acknowledged that there is a particular identified and meaningful principle that can account for a certain type of unjust enrichment claim, in the weak sense, ie a certain type of claim arising from the receipt of a benefit, why should it be supposed that all other such claims are governed by a putative 'principle of unjust enrichment,' which now appears to mean the principle that governs all claims arising from the receipt of a benefit apart from those for which a meaningful underlying principle has actually been identified and formulated? And why call it the 'principle of unjust enrichment,' if it does not account for all claims arising from the receipt of a benefit?

II. EVALUATING THE STRONG THEORY OF UNJUST ENRICHMENT

A. The Raw Material: Unjust Enrichment Claims in the Weak Sense

The discussion below covers various claims that arise from the receipt of a benefit, ie unjust enrichment claims in the weak sense. These include claims to reverse transfers of wealth or property, claims for payment for work done, claims for payment for the unauthorised use of property, and claims to remove the profits of wrongdoing. It is necessary to cover a wide range of claims in order to assess the plausibility of the strong theory. It is inevitable, and not inappropriate, that the emphasis is on the general nature and rationale of the various claims rather than a full exposition of the law governing them.

B. Restitution and Property

(i) Mistaken Payments

Consider first the claim to recover a mistaken payment, which takes the traditional form of money had and received at common law and which under the old implied contract fiction was classified as quasi-contractual. As noted above, this did not indicate the true basis of the claim, which was clearly not contract at all. The claim is now said to be an unjust enrichment claim. This is true in the sense of the weak theory—that the receipt of the transfer is a condition for the claim to arise—but according to the weak theory this says nothing about the basis of the claim. According to the strong theory, the basis of the claim must be the principle of unjust enrichment. The 'unjust factor' is said to be the vitiating factor of mistake. But this does not disclose a principle by virtue of which the mistake and other vitiating factors have the effect of generating a claim. Consider how the mistake is relevant. Because the money transferred belonged to the claimant, it is implicit in his or her right of ownership that he or she should be able to recover the money (or its value) from anyone who received it other than through a valid exercise of his or her power as owner to transfer it. The relevance of the mistake is that by virtue of the mistake the power was not validly exercised—the exercise of the power was vitiated—and so the payment was invalid. Thus a more meaningful characterisation of the claim is that it arises from the claimant's original ownership of the money transferred.[17]

One might express this position by saying that the claim is 'proprietary.' It is necessary to be clear about what is meant by this, because 'proprietary' can be used in two distinct senses. In the first sense, 'proprietary' refers to the *content* of the claim. In this sense, a 'proprietary claim' constitutes an assertion of ownership of property as against the defendant.[18] The contrast is with 'personal claim,' eg a claim for damages or debt. In the second sense, 'proprietary' refers to the *basis* of the claim. It means that the claim arises from the claimant's ownership of the property. The most common usage of 'proprietary' is in the first sense,[19] but it is in the second sense that 'proprietary' is equivalent to 'contractual' or 'tortious' in identifying the basis of a claim. The claim at common law to recover a mistaken payment is personal, and so it is not a proprietary claim in the first sense. It may be that this has led some people to think that it cannot be an ownership-based or proprietary claim in the second sense, but this is clearly not the case.[20]

How can a proponent of the strong theory of unjust enrichment respond to this? One approach is to say that a claim arising from a right of ownership is a particular type of claim governed by the principle of unjust enrichment. This would be consistent with the strong theory.[21] But this approach has not generally been adopted. This is presumably because it is accepted that the protection of ownership is an entirely sufficient basis in itself to account for at least some claims to reverse vitiated transfers, and that it makes no sense to argue that this basis is just a particular form or manifestation of a more

[17] I assume here that money or wealth, meaning intangible transferable value, can be the subject of ownership in the same way as tangible things: this is defended in P Jaffey, 'In Rem Claims to Wealth and Surviving Value' (2002) 55 *CLP* 263.

[18] 'Property' here includes money or wealth: see above n 17.

[19] Because this is often of direct practical significance, particularly in the case where the defendant has become insolvent. In my view, all claims to reverse invalid transfers should in principle be proprietary in the first sense rather than personal: see Jaffey (above n 17).

[20] I have elsewhere tried to distinguish between these two concepts by using 'proprietary' and 'in rem': see Jaffey (above n 17); Jaffey (above n 14).

[21] This is reflected in the idea of an 'unjust factor' of 'retention of title,' advanced by Burrows in the first edition but not the second edition of his textbook: A Burrows, *The Law of Restitution* (London, Butterworths, 1993).

general principle of unjust enrichment that also governs claims that do not concern ownership or wealth or property at all.[22]

Thus the position generally adopted is that there are two types of claim to reverse a transfer arising from a mistake.[23] One is based on the claimant's original ownership (whether or not the claim takes the form of an assertion of continuing ownership), and the other is based on the principle of unjust enrichment. But it is difficult to see either (1) why the claimant's original ownership should be thought insufficient to provide a basis for any claim to reverse a transfer arising from the invalidity or vitiation of the transfer, or (2) on what basis 'unjust enrichment' can constitute a distinct, alternative ground for such a claim. As to the second point, if the claimant validly disposed of the money, what justification for a claim can there be? And if the relevance of the mistake or other vitiating factor is not in vitiating the exercise of the power of transfer, which is an incident of the right of ownership, then what exactly is its relevance, and how exactly does it relate to the supposed principle of unjust enrichment?

Of course, one can reasonably say that the claim based on the claimant's ownership also serves to prevent the unjust enrichment of the defendant; and furthermore that the measure of the claim should be limited to ensure that it does not exceed what is necessary to prevent the defendant's unjust enrichment—ie limited in accordance with change of position[24]—since the effect would otherwise be that the defendant would be left worse off than if he or she had not had the receipt at all, and would thus bear the risk of a net loss, in order to make good a loss from the claimant's estate for which he or she was not responsible. But 'unjust enrichment' here simply refers to the fact that the defendant has received and retains the benefit of a transfer of wealth or property that belonged to the claimant and was not validly transferred, and does not identify a different claim with a different basis.

The view that there is an ownership-based claim to reverse a vitiated transfer, but also an unjust enrichment claim, is a form of the 'intermediate position' criticised above.[25] The fact that a claim to reverse a vitiated payment of money can be based on the right of ownership undermines the strong theory (whether or not the claim is personal), and the natural tendency for the supporter of the strong theory is to retreat to the intermediate position, which retains some distinct role for a supposed principle of unjust

[22] Eg claims for payment for the provision of services. Burrows (above n 8) 13, criticising my own approach in Jaffey (above n 14), does argue that at 'a higher level of generality' the ownership-based claim is 'underpinned by the principle against unjust enrichment.' But Burrows never explains what the principle is, and, furthermore, almost all writers, including Burrows himself, consider that there are in *some* circumstances claims to reverse vitiated transfers based on ownership as *opposed* to a principle of unjust enrichment.

[23] And similarly, it appears, for other vitiating factors.

[24] This effect is also achieved by the rules of tracing: see further Jaffey (above n 17).

[25] Above text at n 16.

enrichment. As pointed out above, the intermediate position is difficult to defend. Since the principle of unjust enrichment is a supposed principle lying behind claims arising from the receipt of a benefit, whose nature is not apparent from the name itself, once a cogent ground is actually recognised that can account for claims to reverse vitiated transfers, what reason is there for insisting that there are also some such claims that are based on a separate 'principle of unjust enrichment,' especially in the absence of any elaboration of the nature of the principle?[26]

(ii) Payment Without Authority

The leading modern English case on the common law recovery of payments—money had and received—is *Lipkin Gorman v Karpnale*.[27] The essence of the case was that a rogue took the claimant's money and, acting without authority,[28] paid it over to the defendant. It is generally said to be an unjust enrichment case—it is said to be one of the cases that recognise a principle of unjust enrichment in English law.[29] But there is no statement of the principle in *Lipkin Gorman*, and the case is consistent with an analysis of the claim as arising from the claimant's original ownership of the money. The main point in issue was whether the money received by the defendant belonged to the claimant.[30] This was understood to be relevant on the basis that if the money did not belong to the claimant then the defendant's enrichment would not have been 'at the expense of the claimant' for the purposes of applying the principle of unjust enrichment, but the decision is entirely consistent with the position that the claim arose from the claimant's original ownership of the money and from the absence of a valid transfer of it. Some writers do indeed consider the claim in *Lipkin Gorman* to be a proprietary

[26] It has been said that the claimant's original ownership of property cannot be the basis for the claim against a recipient because a claim always arises from an event, and 'property is not an event.' This curious argument appears to be due to P Birks, 'Property and Unjust Enrichment: Categorical Truths' [1997] *New Zealand Law Review* 623. It is true that a claim must arise from the occurrence of some event. And it is true that property is not an event. But an event generates a claim by virtue of a legal relation between the parties. The primary legal relation is the relation that subsists before a claim arises and by virtue of which it arises, and the secondary or remedial relation is the claim itself, considered from the claimant's side of the relation. Thus if the defendant has a primary duty, the event that generates the claim is a breach of the primary duty. In the case under consideration, the event generating the restitutionary claim is the invalid transfer of property. But of course this event has this legal effect by virtue of the claimant's ownership—the ownership is the primary relation. It is by virtue of the claimant's ownership that the transfer can be characterised as invalid, and that the claim arises as a result. This is what is meant by saying that the claim is based on the claimant's ownership.

[27] Above (n 12).

[28] See below at n 32.

[29] Eg P Birks, 'The English Recognition of Unjust Enrichment' [1991] *LMCLQ* 330; Burrows (above n 8) 2.

[30] Or was its traceable proceeds.

claim in this sense,[31] although generally they still take the view that there can be two types of claim to reverse an invalid or vitiated transfer, one based on ownership and one on a principle of unjust enrichment. But there is nothing in *Lipkin Gorman* to support such a distinction between two different types of claim.

It seems that writers who consider the claim in *Lipkin Gorman* to be proprietary, meaning ownership-based, rely on the argument that since the money was taken without the claimant's knowledge or permission, there could be no question of his or her having validly transferred ownership, whereas, it is apparently thought, where the claimant makes the transfer himself or herself, even if affected by a vitiating factor like mistake, he or she can make a valid transfer of property even though the vitiating factor generates an unjust enrichment claim. But 'invalidity' cannot be contrasted with 'vitiating factor' as if they were different bases for a claim. As argued above, the significance of a mistake can only be to vitiate the exercise of the owner's power of transfer, so as to invalidate the transfer, just as in the case where the transfer is made without the owner's knowledge or permission. One can say in the latter case that the exercise of the power was vitiated by the fact that it was made without authority from the owner—in other words, the vitiating factor, analogous to mistake, is 'lack of authority.'[32]

The traditional exhaustive division of the common law into contract and tort denied recognition to both prior ownership and unjust enrichment as bases for a claim. In this respect, it is interesting to compare the claim to recover an invalid payment of money with the claim to recover an invalid transfer of goods. The claim to reverse an invalid money payment traditionally took a contractual form under the implied contract theory, and has come to be regarded as based on unjust enrichment. The claim to recover an invalid transfer of goods took the form of the tort of conversion, and, although sometimes the taking or retaining of goods (as of money) will involve a genuine wrong, in general the tort is a fiction just as much as the implied contract was a fiction: just as for money, in principle the claim arises from the receipt of the goods, not from a wrong. It is generally said, however, that conversion is a proprietary tort, and it is sometimes acknowledged that the claim is really concerned with the recovery of property and is not really based on wrongdoing at all.[33] There may be good reason to distinguish between tangible property and money in certain respects, but the basis for the claim in these two types of case is really the same, viz, the

[31] Eg W Swadling, 'A Claim in Restitution?' [1996] *LMCLQ* 63.

[32] This is equivalent to 'ignorance,' which is the expression used by Birks (above n 8) 140–46. This expression fails to capture the true reason for the claim. One might prefer to say that there is simply no exercise of a power of transfer as opposed to a vitiated exercise of the power, but for present purposes the point is that there is no valid exercise of the power.

[33] See eg M Bridge, *Personal Property Law*, 3rd edn (Oxford, Oxford University Press, 2002) 47.

claimant's original ownership of the property or money. However, instead of recognising that the protection of ownership and the prevention or reversal of unjust enrichment are two ways of looking at the same claim, many writers have assumed that they are two distinct bases for a claim, and attempts have been made to identify both types of claim in relation to both invalid transfers of goods and invalid money payments. There has consequently been a futile debate over whether in particular cases the claim to reverse an invalid transfer is an unjust enrichment claim or an ownership-based or proprietary claim.

The same misconceived debate has arisen in equity. The analogous claim in equity to reverse a transfer in breach of trust or fiduciary duty is the equitable proprietary claim.[34] Here 'proprietary' refers to the fact that the claim takes the form of an assertion of ownership of an asset (ie, the first sense above, meaning not a personal claim), but I think it is fair to say that until recently it was also generally understood as proprietary in the other sense also (ie that the basis of the claim is the claimant's original ownership). However, now here also there is a controversy over whether and in what circumstances the claim is an unjust enrichment claim rather than a proprietary claim in this latter sense. The best illustration is provided by *Macmillan v Bishopsgate*,[35] where the issue was the classification of the claim for the purposes of the conflict of laws rules. But nowhere in *Macmillan v Bishopsgate* (or elsewhere) can one find a plausible reason for thinking that there actually are two different categories of claim.

C. Restitution and Contract

(i) Recovery of Contractual Prepayments

Consider now the case where the claimant has made a payment under a valid contract, and the contract has not been fully performed by the defendant. The rule is that the claimant can recover the payment, but traditionally only where the defendant has not performed at all, and not where he has part-performed.[36] The claim arises from the receipt of the payment, and so it is an unjust enrichment claim in the weak sense.[37] The strong theory implies that the claim must be based on a principle of unjust enrichment, and that this is the same principle that governs other unjust enrichment claims in the weak sense, including the claim considered in

[34] Some would say the analogous claim is the claim for knowing receipt, but this is implausible in my view. I have pursued this issue elsewhere: see P Jaffey, 'The Nature of Knowing Receipt' (2001) 15 *Trust Law International* 151.
[35] [1995] 3 All ER 747.
[36] In the traditional language, where there was a 'total failure of consideration.'
[37] But see below n 46.

the previous section. In particular, the strong theory implies that the claim cannot be contractual.

Support for the position that the claim cannot be contractual appears to come from the common understanding that the legal relationship established by a contract consists of a duty to perform the contract and a correlative right to performance. It would appear to follow from this that a contractual claim can only be a claim arising from a breach of duty to perform, and therefore that it must be for compensation for the loss caused by the breach of a duty to perform, ie expectation damages.[38] A claim to recover a payment cannot be explained in this way, because the value of the payment does not correspond to the loss caused by a breach of a duty to perform a contract,[39] and furthermore in some cases where the claim is available—for example on frustration—the defendant clearly has not committed a breach of duty at all.

Thus unjust enrichment theorists have sought an 'unjust factor' to account for the claim, and suppose that they have found it in 'failure of condition.'[40] The argument is that a contractual payment is made subject to the condition that the agreed reciprocal performance will be provided. If the reciprocal performance is not provided, the condition has failed and the claimant is entitled to the repayment of the money. But assume, first, that this condition, that the money will be returned if the reciprocal performance is not provided, is a term of the contract. Then the condition will be binding under the contract and, if the reciprocal performance is not provided, there will be a claim for repayment, but it will be a contractual claim. On the other hand, if the condition is not part of the contract, but the claimant has nevertheless made the payment intending it to take effect subject to this condition, the condition surely cannot bind the defendant. A contracting party must surely be entitled to assume that a payment received by him or her pursuant to the contract is made on the terms of the contract. The recent case of *Roxborough v Rothmans*[41] adopts the failure of condition approach, but it does not show how this objection can be overcome. The court said that there was no implied term in the contract providing that the payment was conditional, but also, inconsistently, that the payment was conditional, even though it was made as a contractual payment.

It seems to me clear that the claim *is* contractual. A contractual claim is a claim that arises from the legal relationship established by agreement

[38] Leaving aside claims for specific performance, and leaving aside debt claims in respect of a sum accrued due under a payment clause.

[39] Except in the sense that there can be a duty to pay a sum accrued due.

[40] This is said to be what is meant by the traditional expression 'failure of consideration.'

[41] (2001) 208 CLR 516. For a discussion of the case along these lines, see P Jaffey, 'Failure of Consideration' (2003) 66 *MLR* 284.

and in response to the fact that the agreement was not performed as agreed. Its justification lies in the principle that an agreement should be fulfilled. Any claim that arises as a result of the fact that a contract was not performed as agreed, and by virtue of this, must be contractual. This is sufficient to justify the conclusion that the claim is contractual. It is easy to show, furthermore, exactly how the claim is justifiable by reference to the contract, in terms of the application of the principle that an agreement should be fulfilled. By virtue of the principle, a contracting party must be entitled to rely on the agreement at the other contracting party's risk, at least with respect to his or her own performance of the contract. In other words, a contracting party should, prima facie, have a claim in respect of loss incurred through his or her performance of the contract. This is consistent with the recognised claim for 'reliance damages,' where a contracting party recovers for expenses incurred in performing the contract. It is surely also a sufficient explanation for a claim to recover a contractual payment. This claim is contractual, but it is not based on the breach of a contractual duty. It is independent of any claims that may arise from such a breach of duty.[42]

It might seem that on this analysis the receipt of a benefit by the defendant is actually irrelevant to the claim, but this is not the case. Imagine a case where the claimant has incurred expenditure in reliance on the contract, but without any benefit accruing to the defendant. If the defendant is liable for the amount of the reliance expenditure, the claimant will be protected from a reliance loss, but the defendant will incur a reliance loss thereby, ie, a loss in the form of his or her liability for the claimant's reliance loss, which results from the defendant's having become bound by the contract. But, on the argument above (and leaving aside the issue of breach of contractual duty), the claimant is responsible for the defendant's loss to just the degree that the defendant is responsible for the claimant's loss, and it would seem fair for them to share the reliance loss between them.[43] To return to the case of the payment from the claimant to the defendant, since the defendant has received the amount of the payment, he or she does not incur any net reliance loss as a result of incurring a liability to repay the whole amount of the payment. Thus the fact that the defendant has received the payment is indeed relevant to the claim.

The position is more complicated where the claimant has made a payment and the defendant has part-performed. First, by way of the part performance, the defendant has also relied on the agreement and so should have a claim for

[42] Recognising that there are reliance claims in contract is not the same as holding that *all* claims in contract are reliance claims, which is the reliance theory of contract. The reliance theory implies that contractual claims are not generally based on breach of duty.

[43] This approach can account for claims arising on frustration and for the so-called 'wrongdoer's claim.' There is room for argument about how to share the loss.

payment for work done in reliance on the contract (as discussed further below), for the same reason that the claimant has a claim to recover the payment. In such a case, if the whole of the claimant's payment is returned to him or her, without deduction, the defendant will end up with an unsatisfied reliance claim. Secondly, the claimant may have received some benefit from the defendant's part performance of the contract, so that his or her net reliance loss is less than the amount of the payment. Thus it would be better to say that, in general, each party has a prima facie reliance claim, and that there should be a resultant net reliance claim for one party that depends on the extent of loss or work done in reliance and the extent of benefit received by the two parties (again leaving aside the issue of breach of duty).[44] The traditional rule is that a contractual payment is recoverable only where the defendant has not performed any part of his or her side of the contract, and this may be understandable in the light of the difficulty of determining what the claim should be. But it is difficult to justify in principle, as is now generally agreed.[45]

The claim to recover a contractual payment is an 'unjust enrichment' claim in the sense of the weak theory, ie, it is a claim that depends (in a certain way)[46] on the receipt of a benefit. According to the strong theory, it follows that the claim must be governed by the principle of unjust enrichment, and it must be the same type of claim as other claims arising from the receipt of a benefit, concerning the same type of interests and having the same type of justification; and in particular it cannot be a contractual claim. But there is no reason to think that the claim is in any way a variant of the claim analysed above as a proprietary or ownership-based claim arising from an invalid transfer, or that these two claims are in some way different applications in different contexts of the same principle. The idea of 'failure of condition' as an 'unjust factor' operating to give rise to a claim on the breakdown of a valid contract is unsustainable. Even assuming that there is something in the idea of a non-contractual claim for failure of condition,[47] it is unclear how this 'unjust factor' is related to the principle of unjust enrichment or how it triggers its operation. On the other hand, it is easy to explain the claim as a contractual claim, protecting the claimant's reliance on the contract.[48]

[44] Subject to any express or implied provision to the contrary in the contract.
[45] Although of course most criticism of the traditional limitation is associated with a completely different understanding of the nature of the claim.
[46] As discussed above, the relationship between the measure of benefit and the measure of recovery is not direct.
[47] I have not considered the separate question whether there can be a non-contractual doctrine of 'failure of condition' that applies in the absence of a contract.
[48] I have not discussed the claim to recover a payment under a void contract. Supporters of the idea of 'failure of condition' as an unjust factor argue that this is the basis for the claim here also, but it is quite implausible that the two claims should have the same basis.

(ii) Payment for Work Done Under a Contract: The Quantum Meruit

The quantum meruit is a claim for payment for work or work and materials, where the amount is not agreed but needs to be assessed as a reasonable sum.[49] One type of case is a claim for payment for work done under a contract, where the contract came to an end before any explicit payment provision was triggered. There are examples of such a claim in the case law.[50] As considered above, it might appear that if such a claim arises it cannot be contractual, on the basis that a contractual claim must be a response to a breach of duty and a quantum meruit cannot be understood as compensation for a breach of a duty.[51] Unjust enrichment theorists have argued that the claim is based on unjust enrichment and arises from the unjust factor of failure of condition. The objection stated above in relation to contractual payments applies here equally,[52] and there are further objections also. A quantum meruit can arise even when the work done has conferred no benefit at all, and such a claim can be explained in terms of unjust enrichment only by way of a brazen fiction.[53] More importantly, a payment is capable of being reversed, and so it is possible for it to be made conditionally, in the sense that if the condition is not fulfilled the payment is not effective and must be reversed. Thus a contractual payment can at least in principle be conditional, if the contract so provides. But work done cannot be reversed, and so cannot be conditional in this sense. The quantum meruit is not the reversal of the work done, but rather payment for it.

By contrast, the approach suggested above works here also: the claim is a contractual reliance claim on the basis set out above. The claimant does work in reliance on the contract and accordingly is (prima facie) entitled to payment for it. The claim serves to satisfy the claimant's 'reliance interest,' where this encompasses both the interest in compensation for reliance loss and the interest in payment for work done in reliance.[54]

It might be thought that an analysis along these lines amounts to reviving the old fiction of implied contract. There is judicial support for the view that if a contract terminates early after the claimant has part-performed, he

[49] One might say that, strictly speaking, the quantum meruit is the measure of payment rather than the claim.
[50] Eg *De Bernady v Harding* (1853) 8 Exch 822.
[51] See above n 38.
[52] In particular, it is surely clear that someone for whom work is done under a valid contract is liable to pay for it only on the terms of the contract.
[53] An example of such a case is *Planché v Colburn* (1831) 8 Bing 14; see Birks (above n 8) 126.
[54] The satisfaction of the reliance interest thus goes beyond mere compensation for reliance loss. The conventional understanding is that where a contract provides for a lump sum payment it has implicitly ruled out a quantum meruit for part performance: eg *Cutter v Powell* (1795) 6 Term Rep 320. But there is no reason why a lump sum payment clause should necessarily be understood in this way. If it is so construed, it should rule out a claim for payment whether it is understood to be a contractual claim or a claim based on unjust enrichment.

or she is entitled to be paid a quantum meruit only if it is possible to imply a new agreement relating to the part performance,[55] and this did indeed generally amount to a fiction. Resort to this fiction, where a claim appeared justified, seems to have resulted from the assumption that a contractual claim must be either for a debt accrued due under a payment clause or for compensation for a breach of duty. This is what leads to the view that if there is a claim for payment it must be based on a new contract. But the reliance approach demonstrates that a claim for payment for work done under a contract can arise from the contract even if it is not provided for expressly under a payment clause and there has been no breach of contract by the defendant. The analysis suggested here involves no fiction.[56] To the contrary, it is the 'failure of condition' approach that involves a fiction, viz, that contractual performance is made conditionally (and that, in the case of work done, payment for the work done constitutes the reversal of it). The fiction is contrived, like other fictions, to try and make the claim conform to a mistaken framework of analysis, in this case the strong theory of unjust enrichment.

D. The Non-Contractual Quantum Meruit

There are certainly cases where a claim for payment for work done arises that cannot be contractual. For example, there may be cases where work is done by mistake and a claim arises that cannot plausibly be explained as contractual.[57] In addition, a claim for payment for work done in an emergency, where no contract was made first, is allowed in certain circumstances.[58]

Such a claim is an unjust enrichment claim in the weak sense.[59] It arises from the receipt of a benefit in certain circumstances. According to the strong theory, the basis for the claim must be the principle of unjust enrichment, which is also behind other claims that arise from the receipt of a benefit. In the case of work done by mistake, the 'unjust factor' is said to be mistake. But it is unclear what the significance of the mistake is, since it clearly is not the fact that it vitiated the exercise of the owner's power to

[55] Eg *De Bernady* (above n 50).

[56] One might also argue that, since there was no actual provision in the contract for the protection of reliance, the claim must be based on an 'implied term,' and so must be a fiction. But an implied term in this sense, meaning a rule addressing a contingency not governed by an agreed term (a default rule) is not a fiction. The rules concerning damages are in the same position.

[57] A possible example is *Craven-Ellis v Canons Ltd* [1936] 2 KB 403.

[58] Ie in maritime salvage cases. In maritime cases the claim would not technically have been described as a quantum meruit, but it would have been equivalent.

[59] I leave aside the argument that a claim may be available where work is done in the absence of agreement—eg in a necessitous intervention case—but no benefit is actually received.

transfer his wealth or property. To say that the mistake is a condition of the claim surely falls short of explaining its basis, or of explaining the relation of the mistake to a supposed principle of unjust enrichment. Similarly, it is sometimes said that 'necessity' is the unjust factor for the claim arising from work done in an emergency ('necessitous intervention'), but again this does not reveal how 'necessity' relates to the principle of unjust enrichment. Furthermore, it is far from clear why this claim for payment for work done in the absence of a contract and the claims discussed above should be thought of as variants of the same claim, governed by the same underlying principle. On the analysis above, this is clearly not the case. The claim is not a contractual claim, to protect work done or a payment made in reliance on an agreement, and it is not a proprietary claim, arising from a prior right of ownership to reverse an invalid transfer of wealth or property. As considered below, the rationale for the claim, and the relevant considerations, are surely quite different.[60]

One might understand this sort of claim in the following way, although whether or not this approach is sound does not affect the point above—that 'unjust enrichment' does not provide an account at all. The claim is concerned with giving effect to an exchange of benefits, typically payment in return for goods or services. The problem that arises with respect to the exchange of benefits, in the absence of agreement, is that because of variability in taste and wealth it is difficult, if not impossible, to determine whether a particular exchange is mutually beneficial. Thus the usual rule is that prior agreement on the exchange is the pre-condition for a claim for payment for goods or services rendered. The agreement ensures that the exchange is mutually beneficial, or, strictly speaking, that it is not unfair to enforce the exchange on the terms agreed, even if it turns out not to be mutually beneficial because of a misjudgment by one of the parties. However, although contract is the optimum mechanism for regulating exchange, it is not absolutely necessary. Arguably a claim for payment for a benefit conferred may be justified where the following two conditions are satisfied. The first condition is that the claimant who provided the goods and services must not have *chosen not* to contract—ie he or she must not have opted out of the optimum means of ensuring that the exchange is fair to the defendant. For example, he or she must have been unable to contract, or must have mistakenly thought that he or she had already made a contract.[61] The second condition is that it is reasonably practicable to

[60] I have not discussed so-called 'pre-contractual claims,' where the parties are actually in negotiation and so, according to the first condition stated in the text, no non-contractual claim should be available (unless there is mistake). In my view such claims are really based on agreement and so are in the nature of contractual claims, even if they do not satisfy all the standard conditions for contractual liability.

[61] On this approach, this is how the concept of 'officiousness' in unjust enrichment law should be understood.

determine an appropriate measure of payment for the goods or services supplied, so that one can be sure that, despite the absence of agreement, the exchange of payment for goods or services at this price is mutually beneficial. This approach would be consistent with the cases mentioned above where a claim has been allowed.[62]

I have previously described this claim, analysed as suggested above in terms of the two conditions and the analogy with contract, as an 'imputed contract' claim.[63] The claim is not contractual, since it is not based on agreement; but where the law provides for such a claim it is performing the same function as contract law, in the sense of achieving a mutually beneficial exchange, and the measure of payment will generally be what the parties would have agreed on if they had been in a position to negotiate a price. Thus 'imputed contract' claim seems an apt description, and it also emphasises the distinction between this type of claim and the claim to reverse invalid transfers of wealth and property, a distinction that is obscured by the strong theory of unjust enrichment.

It has been objected that this 'imputed contract' analysis resurrects the old 'implied contract' fiction.[64] As mentioned above, the implied contract fiction arose (as other fictions do) as a device for forcing a claim—for example the claim to recover a mistaken payment—into a recognised but inapt category. Such a fiction is objectionable because it provides a spurious basis for the claim, and thereby obviates consideration of the true basis and therefore the appropriate conditions for the claim to arise. In the case of the claim to reverse a mistaken payment, the fiction forestalled consideration of the possibility that the claim was based on the claimant's ownership (or, as some would say, on a principle of unjust enrichment); and notoriously in some cases a claim was denied for a reason that would have been appropriate if the claim had actually been based on agreement but was quite inappropriate given the true basis of the claim.[65] But there is no fiction involved in the analysis above or in the use of the expression 'imputed contract.' There is no suggestion that the claim is based on an actual agreement, and the expression indicates the rationale for the claim rather than obscuring it.[66]

[62] There may be good reasons to distinguish between the two types of case: in the necessitous intervention case, but not the mistake case, the claimant exercises a power to impose a liability on the defendant.

[63] Jaffey (above n 14) chs 3 and 4.

[64] Eg K Barker, 'Review Article' [2001] *Restitution Law Review* 232, 236; Burrows (above n 8) 13.

[65] Eg *Sinclair v Brougham* [1914] AC 398; *Phillips v Homfray* (1883) 24 Ch D 439.

[66] In other words, 'imputed contract' makes an analogy, not a fiction. J Edelman, *Gain-Based Damages* (Oxford, Hart Publishing, 2002) 41 misinterprets 'imputed contract' to mean 'inferred contract.' To say that an agreement is inferred where there is clearly no actual agreement, express or implied, is to use a fiction.

E. Restitution, Wrongdoing and 'Restitution for Wrongs'

'Restitution for wrongs' or 'unjust enrichment for wrongs' is generally recognised as a category of the law of unjust enrichment.[67] It appears to consist of claims in respect of benefits received as a result of a wrong, as opposed to claims like the claim to recover an invalid transfer or for payment for work done, which do not depend on a wrong by the defendant. In fact, the cases that have been described as examples of restitution for wrongs involve various types of claim, and the strong theory obscures the differences between them.

(i) Disgorgement

A claim for disgorgement is a claim for the benefit made through a wrong, based on the principle that a wrongdoer should not benefit from the wrong.[68] The claim has sometimes been recognised, for example in the form of an account of profits or a constructive trust in equity, and possibly also exemplary damages at common law.[69] It is clearly a claim whose measure depends on benefit received, and so is an unjust enrichment claim in the weak sense. It is often thought of as the archetypal case of unjust enrichment.

The principle that a wrongdoer should not profit through his or her wrongdoing is quite different in character from an ordinary principle of private law, like the principle that an agreement should be performed, or the principle that there is a duty to take reasonable steps to avoid reasonably foreseeable harm. The function of an ordinary principle of private law is to determine when a claim should arise and how it should be remedied, in the sense of correcting the injustice to the claimant. But disgorgement is not concerned with when a claim should arise or how it should be remedied in this sense (and thus it is, strictly speaking, inapt to refer to disgorgement as a remedy). Disgorgement is a response to wrongdoing in general, including

[67] Birks (above n 8) ch X; Burrows (above n 8) 25–31. In the now conventional exposition due to Birks, 'restitution for wrongs' is to be distinguished from 'autonomous unjust enrichment' or 'restitution for unjust enrichment by subtraction,' which together make up the law of restitution based on unjust enrichment. Cf more recently P Birks, 'Unjust Enrichment and Wrongful Enrichment' (2001) 79 *Texas Law Review* 1767.

[68] As discussed below, a claim arising from a benefit obtained through a wrong is not necessarily based on this principle.

[69] This is not to say that an account of profit or constructive trust always serves to effect disgorgement. Exemplary damages would of course normally be described as a form of punishment, but the rationale in some cases is clearly the removal of the profit of wrongdoing: see eg *Cassell v Broome* [1972] 1 All ER 801, 872-73 (Lord Diplock); see further Jaffey (above n 14) 363–64. It is sometimes said or implied that the waiver of tort cases and the cases of damages in the form of a reasonable licence, considered below, are examples of disgorgement, but this is not the case as discussed below.

breaches of duty in contract or tort, irrespective of the basis of the duty. It promotes the interest of the community as a whole in the fulfilment of legal duties in general, whatever their basis.[70] It operates in general support of ordinary private law principles. In this it is like punishment. Indeed, disgorgement is really no more than a component of punishment: punishment must at the least remove any benefit of the wrong if is to make the defendant worse off for having committed the wrong. It follows that if there is a law of unjust enrichment, analogous to contract or tort, and based on an ordinary private law principle of unjust enrichment, the principle that a wrongdoer must not benefit from his or her wrong cannot be a manifestation or application of this principle and so cannot be a part of a law of unjust enrichment in this sense.

It is surely right that a wrongdoer should be deprived of his or her profits, but the principle is not consistently recognised in the law.[71] In my view, this lack of consistency is attributable to the 'procedural problem': because disgorgement is designed, like punishment, to promote the public interest, rather than to provide a remedy to the claimant, the defendant should be afforded procedural and evidential safeguards beyond those normally provided in civil proceedings. For the same reason, the transfer of the benefit to the claimant is a windfall to the claimant and ideally the legal system should not dispense windfalls. This suggests that disgorgement is not appropriate in civil proceedings, unless these concerns are outweighed by the need to give effect to the disgorgement principle in the absence of other means of doing so. This difficulty accounts for the inconsistent position of the courts.[72]

'Restitution for wrongs' seems generally to be understood to be something along the lines of disgorgement in the sense above.[73] It is also thought of as being a part of the law of unjust enrichment, but, as the argument above shows, it cannot be correct to think of it as a part of a category of unjust enrichment law governed by a principle of unjust enrichment. The effect has been to obscure the distinctive 'quasi-punitive' aspect of disgorgement. In addition, it is not very apt to use the expression 'restitution' to refer to disgorgement, which does not necessarily return a transfer to the claimant or restore him or her to the original position. These errors are induced by the strong theory of unjust enrichment. It is the strong theory that implies that disgorgement must be governed by the same principle as

[70] This formulation of the function of disgorgement is neutral as between deterrence and desert.
[71] In particular there is a division between law and equity: the common law has traditionally been averse to disgorgement in the form of exemplary damages, whereas equity has not hesitated to effect disgorgement by way of an account or constructive trust.
[72] See further Jaffey (above n 14) 374–83.
[73] See eg Burrows (above n 8) 455.

other claims arising from the receipt of a benefit, and it is the strong theory that blurs the distinction between returning a transfer and stripping the defendant of a benefit, which are not the same thing, although they may sometimes be equivalent in effect.

(ii) The Use Claim or 'Restitutionary Damages'

If the defendant uses the claimant's property without permission, the claimant is generally entitled to a reasonable payment for the unauthorised use.[74] This claim traditionally took the form of a claim for damages for trespass, but it is not a claim for compensation. The measure of reasonable payment for use does not correspond to the loss inflicted; indeed the unauthorised use of property may cause no loss at all. It is nowadays often described as a claim for 'restitutionary damages.' It is thought to be a pecuniary remedy for the wrong of trespass, the measure of the claim being the value to the defendant of the unauthorised use. A more helpful and more neutral term is 'use claim.'[75]

This claim is generally not distinguished from disgorgement in the category of 'restitution for wrongs.'[76] But it is not a disgorgement claim. A claim for disgorgement in respect of the profit made through a wrong is quite distinct from a claim for reasonable payment for unauthorised use. The rationale for the claim for reasonable payment for unauthorised use is not to strip the defendant of a benefit received, in order to uphold the community's interest in compliance with legal duties, and the measure of the claim is not such as to do so. 'Reasonable payment' will generally correspond to some proportion of the benefit received, not the whole benefit,[77] as would be appropriate for disgorgement. The rationale of the claim is to secure to the owner of property the use-value of the property, which means, where the property is used to provide a benefit, such proportion of the value of the benefit as is attributable to the use of the property, as opposed to that attributable to other factors like the effort and expertise of the user. This can be assessed as the sum that would have been agreed on as a licence fee, and expressed as a notional licence fee.[78]

[74] Eg *Ministry of Defence v Ashman* [1993] 2 EGLR 102; *Strand Electric & Engineering v Brisford* [1952] 2 QB 246.

[75] 'Claim under the user principle' was used by Nicholls LJ in *Stoke City Council v Wass* [1988] 3 All ER 394, 402.

[76] See eg Virgo (above n 8) ch 16.

[77] *Wrotham Park Estates v Parkside Homes* [1974] 2 All ER 321, 341 (Brightman J).

[78] *Ibid*. Thus the claim can also be aptly described as based on 'imputed contract.' Furthermore, although generally an unauthorised use of property will be wrongful, this need not be the case, and thus the claim for reasonable payment is not actually based on the wrong. The claim arises from the unauthorised use, whether or not it happens also to be wrongful. For example, if the defendant takes a horse without permission in an emergency it is likely that no wrong has been committed but that the defendant should still pay for the use. The argument is expressed more fully in Jaffey (above n 14) ch 4.

Again, the strong theory militates against a proper understanding of the use claim. Because the claim arises from the receipt of a benefit, the assumption is that it must be based on a principle of unjust enrichment, and this obscures the fact that the claim arises from an element of the claimant's ownership of the property.[79] Also, because the strong theory induces the assumption that the appropriate claim is always for the removal of the unjust enrichment, it obscures the fact that the claim is not for the full value of the benefit received, and so is distinct from disgorgement,[80] and also the fact that it is not a claim to reverse a transfer from the claimant.[81]

(iii) Waiver of Tort

Consider the case where the claimant has made an invalid payment to the defendant (in the sense discussed earlier), and the defendant procured the vitiating factor, or took advantage of it, in order to secure the payment to himself or herself. In principle, this is surely wrongful, and the claimant should have an alternative claim for compensation for the wrong. Several types of case can be understood as specific examples of such a claim. For example, deceit wrongfully causes a transfer by mistake, intimidation wrongfully causes a transfer under duress, and trespass or conversion wrongfully causes a transfer without authority. A claim for compensation for the wrong will for most purposes be equivalent to a claim to reverse the transfer:[82] the remedy in both cases will be a payment from the defendant in the amount of the invalid payment. These must be alternative claims, because they are both designed to restore the claimant's loss through the transfer. The old common law doctrine of 'waiver of tort' gave effect to this limitation by requiring the claimant to waive the claim based on the wrong before he or she could succeed in the claim based on the invalidity of the payment.[83]

The claim to reverse the transfer based on its invalidity is an unjust enrichment claim, in the weak sense, since the claim arises from the receipt of the transfer. It would appear that the claim for compensation for the wrong, although its effect is equivalent to reversing the transfer, cannot be understood as an unjust enrichment claim, because the defendant's liability for compensation, and its measure, are not dependent on whether

[79] Cf the discussion above of claims to reverse invalid transfers.
[80] Recent cases concerning breach of contract display this confusion, including *Attorney General v Blake* [2001] 1 AC 268.
[81] Sometimes the unauthorised use is conceived of as effecting a transfer from the owner to the unauthorised user: see eg Edelman (above n 66), but this is evidently not literally the case.
[82] But the compensation claim will necessarily be personal.
[83] The claims had to be pursued in different sets of proceedings, so one had to be waived. Analysis of the doctrine is complicated by problems concerning the nature of conversion: see further Jaffey (above n 14) 369.

the defendant received the transfer. But actually this is not always the case. The problem that arises in connection with compensation is how to measure the loss. Where the compensation is for the loss of a tangible thing transferred to the defendant, the best way to overcome any difficulty in determining the value of the thing transferred, where the thing is still in the defendant's estate, is to require the defendant to return it. There seems no obvious reason why such a remedy should not be justified as a response to the wrong, quite apart from whether the transfer was invalid.[84] Then the claim, or at least the form of the remedy, depends on the fact that the defendant received a certain form of benefit, and one might say that the claim is, in the weak sense, an unjust enrichment claim, even though the claim is also no more than a claim for compensation in tort. Thus this case is a further refutation of the strong theory of unjust enrichment.

III. CONCLUSION

The weak or descriptive theory of unjust enrichment is that there are claims that arise from the receipt of a benefit. This is true but it is trivial, because it does not provide any justification for the claim, and therefore no basis for a category of law equivalent to contract or tort. The strong or normative theory of unjust enrichment holds that claims that arise from the receipt of a benefit are governed by a single principle of unjust enrichment and so form a legal category analogous to contract and tort. The strong theory appears to be accepted in many of the restitution and unjust enrichment textbooks. But the strong theory is wrong. There are various types of claim that arise from the receipt of a benefit, based on different principles, and in the different cases the benefit is relevant to the claim in different ways. There is no 'principle of unjust enrichment,' unless this is used arbitrarily to refer to one of these various principles that generate a claim from the receipt of a benefit. The strong theory has forced together, under a common framework, types of claim that are actually distinct, and raise different issues, and should be governed by different principles. At the same time it has obscured the fact that some such claims are contractual or are based on the claimant's original right of ownership, and it has thereby caused artificial divisions in the law of contract and the law of ownership.

In determining whether a claim arises from the receipt of a benefit in certain circumstances, it is unhelpful to ask whether there is an 'unjust factor.' This presupposes the strong theory, presupposes that the claim will be analogous to other claims arising from the receipt of a benefit, and rules out the possibility that the claim may be fully explicable as a claim arising from the ownership of property or wealth or in contract.

[84] It does not amount to saying that the claimant still owns the property transferred.

The various claims arising from the receipt of a benefit do not all generate a claim to *remove* a benefit. Sometimes the claim is *for payment for* the benefit, which gives effect to an exchange of payment for benefit, not the removal of the benefit. Also, sometimes the claim for removal of the benefit is a claim to reverse a transfer, but this is not always the case. These distinctions are lost in the undiscriminating use of the expression 'restitution' to refer to all claims arising from the receipt of a benefit. Again, this error has been induced by the strong theory, which holds that all claims arising from the receipt of a benefit are governed by a principle of unjust enrichment and that that principle generates a claim for restitution.

8

Enrichment Revisited

MITCHELL McINNES*

I. INTRODUCTION

USING THE APPEARANCE of Professor Birks' text[1] as a benchmark, it can be seen that unjust enrichment scholarship has undergone a dramatic transformation in the past two decades. In the period immediately following 1985, the focus of inquiry was on foundational questions: what is unjust enrichment? what is restitution? and so on. The goal largely consisted of mapping the basic shape and scope of the subject. It was oddly exciting stuff, despite—or perhaps because of—the fundamental nature of the exercise. Consequently, while the subject historically had been the domain of relatively few specialists, it began to attract far more attention. Articles, texts, monographs and collections increasingly appeared in greater numbers. Today, the subject commands its own law review and has become a staple of leading journals. *Goff & Jones*[2] retains its place of pride, but no longer monopolizes the reference shelf.[3]

* I would like to thank Mysty Clapton, Lanna Tsimberg and Linda Smits for their comments on earlier drafts of this article. Research was supported by funding from the Law Foundation of Ontario.

[1] P Birks, *An Introduction to the Law of Restitution* (Oxford, Oxford University Press, 1985).

[2] G Jones, *Goff and Jones: The Law of Restitution*, 6th edn (London, Sweet and Maxwell, 2002).

[3] PD Maddaugh and JD McCamus, *The Law of Restitution* (Aurora, Canada Law Book, 1990); GHL Fridman, *Restitution*, 2nd edn (Scarborough, Carswell, 1992); A Burrows, *The Law of Restitution*, 2nd edn (London, Butterworths, 2002); K Mason and JW Carter, *Restitution Law in Australia* (Sydney, Butterworths, 1995); G Virgo, *The Principles of the Law of Restitution* (Oxford, Oxford University Press, 1999); RB Grantham and CEF Rickett *Enrichment & Restitution in New Zealand* (Oxford, Hart Publishing, 2000); P Jaffey, *The Nature and Scope of Restitution* (Oxford, Hart Publishing, 2000); C Cato, *Restitution in Australia & New Zealand* (Sydney, Cavendish Press, 2000); S Hedley, *A Critical Introduction to Restitution* (London, Butterworths, 2001); A Tettenborn, *The Law of Restitution in England & Ireland*, 3rd edn (London, Cavendish Press, 2002); S Hedley and M Halliwell (eds), *The Law of Restitution* (Butterworths, London, 2002).

Treatises abound.[4] And every year sees the publication of at least one symposium.[5]

The change, however, has been more than quantitative. There is a natural temptation, born of habit, to say that it has been qualitative, but that impulse must be resisted. It would improperly suggest that the early material somehow was inferior or insignificant. And that suggestion would directly run counter to the theme of this article. The real shift, rather, has been one of complexity. Many of the current debates are highly abstract, highly technical or both. Two examples will suffice. In 1997, Professor Burrows suspected that the literature might tend, 'for better or worse ... to become more theoretical and to move further away from ... practical scholarship.'[6] That prediction has come true, at least in part. Although none stand guilty of 'crossing the line from practical to impractical,' recent essays have begun the task of exploring restitution's philosophical foundations.[7] The second illustration involves various attempts to settle the relationship between unjust enrichment and property, particularly at the intersection of law and equity. There is burgeoning literature, often as difficult as it is

[4] In addition to the materials cited below, see H Dagan, *Unjust Enrichment: A Study of Private Law & Public Values* (Cambridge, Cambridge University Press, 1997); J Dietrich, *Restitution: A New Perspective* (Sydney, Federation Press, 1998); A Skelton, *Restitution & Contract* (Oxford, Mansfield Press, 1998); IM Jackman, *Varieties of Restitution* (Sydney, Federation Press, 1998); G Panagopoulos, *Restitution in Private International Law* (Oxford, Hart Publishing, 2000); T Krebs, *Restitution at the Crossroads: A Comparative Study* (London, Cavendish, 2001); P Birks, *The Foundations of Unjust Enrichment: Six Centennial Lectures* (Wellington, Victoria University Press, 2002); J Edelman, *Gain-Based Damages: Contracts, Tort, Equity & Intellectual Property* (Oxford, Hart Publishing, 2002).

[5] M McInnes (ed), *Restitution: Developments in Unjust Enrichment* (Sydney, Law Book Company, 1996); F Rose (ed), *Failure of Contracts: Contractual, Restitutionary and Proprietary Consequences* (Oxford, Hart Publishing, 1997); W Cornish *et al* (eds), *Restitution: Past, Present & Future* (Oxford, Hart Publishing, 1998); F Rose (ed), *Restitution and Banking Law* (Oxford, Mansfield Press, 1998); M McInnes and R Chambers (eds), Symposium on Restitution (1999) 37 *Alberta Law Review* 1; EJH Schrage (ed), *Unjust Enrichment: The Comparative Legal History of the Law of Restitution* (Berlin, Duncker and Humblot, 1999); F Rose (ed), *Restitution & Insolvency* (Oxford, Mansfield Press, 2000); Symposium: Restitution and Unjust Enrichment (2000) 1 *Theoretical Inquiries in Law* 1; EJH Schrage (ed), *Unjust Enrichment & The Law of Contract* (London, Kluwer Law, 2001); Symposium: Restitution and Unjust Enrichment (2001) 79 *Texas Law Review* 1763; D Johnston and R Zimmerman (eds), *Unjustified Enrichment: Key Issues in Comparative Perspective* (Cambridge, Cambridge University Press, 2002); Symposium: Second Remedies Discussion Forum: Restitution (2003) 36 *Loyola of Los Angeles Law Review* 777.

[6] A Burrows, 'Restitution: Where Do We Go From Here?' (1997) 50 CLP 95, 115–16, reprinted in *Understanding the Law of Obligations: Essays on Tort, Contract and Restitution* (Oxford, Hart Publishing 1998) 99, 118–19.

[7] E Weinrib, 'The Gains and Losses of Corrective Justice' (1994) 44 *Duke Law Journal* 277; E Weinrib, 'Restitutionary Damages as Corrective Justice' (2000) 1 *Theoretical Issues in Law*; M McInnes, 'The Law of Unjust Enrichment: A Reply to Professor Weinrib' [2001] *Restitution Law Review* 29; LD Smith, 'Restitution: The Heart of Corrective Justice' (2001) 79 *Texas Law Review* 2115; S Smith, 'Justifying the Law of Unjust Enrichment' (2001) 79 *Texas Law Review* 2177; K Barker, 'Unjust Enrichment: Containing the Beast' (1995) 15 *OJLS* 457; NJ McBride and P McGrath, 'The Nature of Restitution' (1995) 15 *OJLS* 33; L Ho, 'The Nature of Restitution: A Reply' (1996) 12 *OJLS* 517.

important, on tracing,[8] constructive trusts,[9] resulting trusts,[10] accessory liability[11] and so on.[12]

There is no denying the tremendous value of that scholarship. Complex problems require complex investigations. At the same time, however, it sometimes seems that attention shifted too quickly from fundamentals. The task of defining the constituent elements of the cause of action has yet to be completed. When is the defendant *enriched*? When is an enrichment *at the plaintiff's expense*? And when is an enrichment *unjust* and hence reversible? Those questions have not been entirely passed by,[13] but neither do they continue to hold the attention they deserve. That especially is true of the first issue. Although it necessarily lies at the heart of restitutionary doctrine, the idea of enrichment is something of a mystery. Too often, it is approached intuitively. And while various tests have emerged, they have not been explained, clearly and consistently, by reference to any unifying rationale. The result is confusion and, ultimately, injustice.

The primary thesis of this article is that enrichment is best understood in terms of freedom of choice. More precisely, the defendant should be considered enriched only to the extent that he chose to accept the risk of financial responsibility for a benefit or, in the circumstances, had no choice to make. While that proposition is not entirely novel, an examination of the caselaw reveals that it has not been expressed frequently, forcefully or fully enough. It therefore must be revisited in detail.

[8] LD Smith, *The Law of Tracing* (Oxford, Oxford University Press, 1997); C Rotherham, *Proprietary Remedies in Context* (Oxford, Hart Publishing, 2002) ch 5.

[9] G Elias, *Explaining Constructive Trusts* (Oxford, Oxford University Press, 1990); DM Wright, *The Remedial Constructive Trust* (Sydney, Butterworths, 1998).

[10] R Chambers, *Resulting Trusts* (Oxford, Oxford University Press, 1997); P Birks and F Rose (eds), *Restitution and Equity: Resulting Trusts and Equitable Compensation* (London, Mansfield Press, 2000).

[11] P Birks, 'Receipt' in P Birks and A Pretto, *Breach of Trust* (Oxford, Hart Publishing, 2002) 213; LD Smith, 'Unjust Enrichment, Property and the Structure of Trusts' (2000) 116 LQR 412.

[12] See especially P Birks, 'Property and Unjust Enrichment' [1997] *New Zealand Law Review* 623; RB Grantham and CEF Rickett, 'Property and Unjust Enrichment: Categorical Truths or Unnecessary Complexity?' [1997] *New Zealand Law Review* 668.

[13] The idea of 'the plaintiff's expense' has re-surfaced in the context of three-party situations: P Birks 'At the Expense of the Claimant: Direct and Indirect Enrichment in English Law' and D Visser, 'Searches for Silver Bullets: Enrichment in Three-Party Situations' in D Johnston and R Zimmerman (eds), *Unjustified Enrichment: Key Issues in Comparative Perspective* (Cambridge, Cambridge University Press, 2002) 493, 526.

Likewise, the third element of unjust enrichment has been brought back into focus by the suggestion that restitution may be available not because there is a positive reason to reverse a transfer of wealth, but rather unless there is a juristic reason for the defendant's gain: *Campbell v Campbell* (1999) 173 DLR (4th) 270 (Ont CA); *Garland v Consumers' Gas Co* (2001) 208 DLR (4th) 494 (Ont CA); *Westdeutsche Landesbank Girozentrale v Islington LBC* [1996] AC 669 (HL); *Kleinwort Benson Ltd v Lincoln CC* [1999] 2 AC 349 (HL); cf Krebs (above n 4); M McInnes, 'Unjust Enrichment—Restitution—Absence of Juristic Reason' (2000) 79 *Canadian Bar Review* 459; LD Smith, 'The Mystery of Juristic Reason' (2000) 12 *Supreme Court Law Review* 211.

This article also has a secondary thesis: a proper appreciation of the nature of enrichment is critical to understanding the subject as a whole. Once it is recognized that the first element of the action in unjust enrichment serves to safeguard the defendant's autonomy, it becomes relatively easy to resolve a number of contentious issues. Some of those issues obviously are enrichment-related, but others are not. For present purposes, the discussion necessarily is brief. Illustrations are drawn from three areas:(i) the operational basis of the defence of change of position, (ii) the quantification of restitution, and (iii) the defendant's role in the reasons for restitution (ie the unjust factors).

Two more points must be made by way of introduction. First, the discussion focuses on Canadian law. In many respects, Canadian unjust enrichment compares unfavourably with its counterparts elsewhere,[14] largely because of a lack of analytical rigour and a disturbing tendency to fall back on broad notions of 'fairness' and 'equity.' Those problems, moreover, often affect the judiciary's approach to the issue of enrichment. Nevertheless, Canadian law also contains the seeds of an unusually advanced conception of enrichment, thanks largely to the efforts of the current Chief Justice.[15] Consequently, this is one area in which other jurisdictions can profitably look to Canada.

Finally, this article is concerned with the action in unjust enrichment that invariably triggers the response of restitution. It is not concerned, at least directly, with the various species of civil wrongdoing that are capable of triggering the response of disgorgement. There undeniably is overlap between those two areas, particularly with respect to the identification of the defendant's gain. The distinction nevertheless is drawn for a couple reasons. One is the desire to keep the discussion close to a suitable length. The other, much more important, is the belief that notwithstanding occasional similarities, there are fundamental differences between the two types of claims. It is undesirable to collapse restitution and disgorgement for essentially the same reasons that it is undesirable to collapse restitution and compensation. Restitution is a function of the defendant's gain *and* the plaintiff's loss.[16] It has no more in common with disgorgement (which is concerned exclusively with the defendant's gain) than it does with compensation (which is concerned exclusively with the plaintiff's loss). Nothing should be done to obscure that point.

[14] M McInnes 'Reflections on the Canadian Law of Unjust Enrichment: Lessons From Abroad' (1999) 78 *Canadian Bar Review* 416; M McInnes, 'The Canadian Principle of Unjust Enrichment: Comparative Insights into the Law of Restitution' (1999) 37 *Alberta Law Review* 1.

[15] See especially *Peel (Regional Municipality) v Canada* [1992] 3 SCR 762; 98 DLR (4th) 140 (SCC) (herein cited to DLR); *Peter v Beblow* [1993] 1 SCR 980; 101 DLR (4th) 621 (SCC) (herein cited to DLR).

[16] M McInnes, 'The Measure of Restitution' (2002) 52 *University of Toronto Law Journal* 163, 180–86. As discussed below (n 21), that proposition is more secure in Canada than elsewhere.

II. AUTONOMY AND ENRICHMENT

The principle of unjust enrichment has strong intuitive appeal. In the typical case, the plaintiff involuntarily confers a benefit upon the defendant. Because of a mistake, she has lost something that she should have and he has gained something that he should not have. Liberal instinct, fed on a fundamental belief in individual autonomy, presumes that she should get it back. It demands respect for her right to control the allocation of her own resources. If she disposes of an asset with an intention to do so, she should, of course, be held to that decision. But by the same token, the plaintiff should be entitled to retrieve (the value of) something that she did not truly choose to give up.

Respect for the plaintiff's autonomy must not, however, be taken too far. The principal danger of the action in unjust enrichment is too much restitution. There is a risk that the defendant will be adversely affected by liability. Despite doing nothing wrong, he may be worse off after trial than he was before enrichment. To avoid that possibility, he too must be accorded a principled right to control the allocation of his resources. There are various means of serving that goal. Some premise liability upon the defendant's participation in the reason for restitution (ie the unjust factor). As explained below, that tactic tends to tip the scales of justice against the plaintiff in a way that unnecessarily denies relief. The preferable approach is to protect the defendant's autonomy through the notion of enrichment. And that goal is best achieved by employing a three-stage analysis at the first element of the action in unjust enrichment:

1. did the defendant receive an *objective benefit*?
2. can the defendant plead *subjective devaluation*? And
3. can the plaintiff *satisfy the defendant's freedom of choice*?

A. Objective Benefit

In one sense, the concept of enrichment is quite broad. It can encompass virtually any type of gain, including money, land, goods and services. Its scope is immediately limited, however, by the fact that a gain generally[17] is relevant only if it constitutes an *objective* benefit. The defendant normally cannot be considered enriched unless he received something of market value. As McLachlin J explained, '[t]he word "enrichment" ... connotes a tangible benefit.'[18] 'Tangible' in this instance refers not to the capacity for

[17] An exception is discussed below under the rubric of 'subjective overvaluation.'
[18] *Peel* (above n 15) 155.

physical touch, but rather to the capacity for monetary valuation.[19] Canadian law therefore 'has consistently taken a straightforward economic approach to the first two elements of the action in unjust enrichment.'[20]

The insistence upon market value and a 'straightforward economic approach' to the issue of enrichment is justified by the nature of restitutionary relief. The defendant is required to 'give back' the benefit that he received from the plaintiff. Moreover, he generally is required to do so personally, rather than proprietarily. Liability usually takes the form of an obligation to pay a sum of money that represents the value of the enrichment. Consequently, as a practical matter, the courts must have some reliable means of measuring the gain for the purposes of quantifying relief. If the cause of action is to operate above the level of intuitive justice, the definition and calculation of an enrichment cannot be left to judicial discretion. And while market value admittedly entails a range of dollar figures in some situations, the basic concept does provide sufficiently clear guidance.

The focus on monetary value is further justified by the nature of the underlying cause of action. As discussed below, liability for unjust enrichment generally is strict. In most cases, the defendant is held responsible simply because he received an involuntary transfer from the plaintiff and not because he did anything wrong. As a result, unlike a person who has broken a contractual promise or committed a tort, he does not warrant mistreatment. Unjust enrichment should, at worst,[21] be a zero-sum event. The defendant should never be required to give back more than he got.[22]

[19] Were it otherwise, restitutionary relief would not, contrary to established precedent, be available with respect to services.

[20] *Peter* (above n 15) 645.

[21] Restitution is measured by the highest amount common to the defendant's gain *and* the plaintiff's loss. Accordingly, despite receiving an enrichment, the defendant should be relieved of liability to the extent that the plaintiff did not truly suffer a deprivation: M McInnes, 'At the Plaintiff's Expense: Quantifying Restitutionary Relief' (1998) 57 *CLJ* 472. That issue usually arises when a business purportedly becomes liable for a tax. After paying money to the government, the business recoups its loss by raising the prices that it charges it customers. The defence of passing on holds that relief may be denied to the extent that the relevant expense ultimately was borne by the customers: *Air Canada v British Columbia* [1989] 1 SCR 1161, 1202; 59 DLR (4th) 161, 194 (SCC). Anglo-Australian courts, however, have rejected the defence on the basis that the plaintiff need merely prove that it was the immediate source of the defendant's gain and not that it ultimately suffered any loss: *Kleinwort Benson v Birmingham CC* [1996] 4 All ER 733 (CA); *Kleinwort Benson v South Tyneside MBC* [1994] 4 All ER 972 (QB); *Commissioner of Revenue (Vic) v Royal Insurance Australia Ltd* (1994) 182 CLR 51 (HCA); *Roxborough v Rothmans of Pall Mall Australia Pty Ltd* (2002) 76 ALJR 203 (HCA). See also M McInnes, 'Enrichments, Expenses and Restitutionary Defences' (2002) 118 *LQR* 209; M McInnes, 'Passing On in the Law of Restitution: A Reconsideration' (1997) 19 *Sydney Law Review* 179; F Rose, 'Passing On' in P Birks (ed), *Laundering and Tracing* (Oxford, Oxford University Press, 1995) 261.

[22] Aside from the fact that it generally does not involve wrongdoing, the action in unjust enrichment is limited to the response of restitution by the elements of enrichment and corresponding deprivation: McInnes (above n 16) 186.

While perhaps redistributed, the totality of his wealth should be the same both before the event of unjust enrichment and after the response of restitution. Take a simple example. The defendant initially had $5000 cash and a debt of $2000, for a net worth of $3000. If the plaintiff involuntarily discharged his debt, she might be entitled to $2000 in restitution. In satisfying that judgment, the defendant would be required to rearrange his assets, but his net worth would remain the same: $3000 (all cash and no debt). It would be different, however, if relief was available with respect to intangible benefits, such as love and affection, that cannot be translated into monetary terms.[23] In that case, since the defendant did not receive anything of *economic* value, liability necessarily would worsen his financial position. He would be required to give up money even though he did not receive money or money's worth.

(i) Pure Services

The need for a restorable benefit has led some commentators to claim that restitutionary relief cannot be awarded on the basis of 'pure services'—ie services that neither create a marketable residuum nor leave the recipient with exchange value.[24] On that view, an enrichment *can* be recognized if the plaintiff's services provided the defendant with a new asset (eg if she built a boat for him) or improved the market value of an existing assets (eg if she painted his boat).[25] In such circumstances, the defendant can, if necessary, sell the new or improved item in order to obtain the money needed to satisfy judgment. In contrast, a benefit purportedly *cannot* be recognized if the plaintiff's services failed to leave behind something of market value. That would be true, for example, if she performed a

[23] The problem is not that love and affection do not create a physical residuum, but rather that the courts will not recognize such benefits as marketable commodities. Love and affection cannot, for instance, constitute contractual consideration. In that sense, they are distinguishable from other types of services (eg lectures and massages) which similarly do not provide the recipient with a physical residue, but which are quantifiable in the marketplace. Consequently, as discussed below, if the defendant chose to assume the risk of financial responsibility for the second type of service (or, in the circumstances, had no choice to make), he may be considered enriched even if he has nothing to show for the plaintiff's efforts.

[24] J Beatson, *The Use and Abuse of Unjust Enrichment* (Oxford, Clarendon Press, 1991) ch 2; Grantham and Rickett (above n 3) 60–61. While denying the possibility of a claim in unjust enrichment, Grantham and Rickett do accept that pure services may have market value and may be capable of supporting *some other* form of liability (preferably one leading to compensation for reliance loss).

[25] An enrichment can also be recognized if the plaintiff's services save the defendant a necessary expense (eg by discharging a legal obligation on his behalf). In such circumstances, the defendant does not *positively* receive a marketable residuum from the plaintiff. He does, however, *negatively* receive such a benefit insofar as he is spared the need to expend existing resources in fulfilment of the underlying obligation. He can use those existing resources instead to make restitution: Beatson (above n 24) 33.

concert or gave a lecture.[26] In such circumstances, the defendant does not have anything from which he can generate the money needed to make restitution.[27]

That thesis has intellectual appeal and it certainly could provide the basis for some principle of unjust enrichment. It does not, however, represent Canadian law. The leading cases of *Deglman v Guaranty Trust Co*[28] and *Pettkus v Becker*[29] are proof to the contrary. In each instance, the plaintiff performed a number of household services, including some that did not leave marketable residue.[30] The defendant nevertheless was liable in full. Those decisions reveal a significant feature of the Canadian concept of enrichment. While courts insist upon an objective benefit, they are content with the *receipt of market value*—they do not further require proof of the *retention of exchange value*. Consequently, relief may be awarded even if the defendant is unable to either: (i) provide restoration *in specie*, (ii) or satisfy judgment on the basis of a financial gain that he could realize from the plaintiff's efforts. It may be enough that he received pure services, such as an increase in human capital (eg when a capable student receives a lesson) or even an ephemeral experience (eg when an audience listens to a concert). That view certainly comports with common practice. One startling consequence of accepting the objection to pure services is that many of the things for which people regularly pay do not constitute enrichments, or at least do not fall within the scope of the action in unjust enrichment. The masseuse, the hairdresser, the teacher, the taxi driver, the entertainer—in many cases, even the lawyer—would be incapable of demanding restitutionary relief.

(ii) Time of Receipt

Accepting that services, including pure services, can constitute objective benefits, it remains necessary to identify their moment of receipt. While it

[26] There may be a difference between a concert and a lesson. The former presumably does not raise the listener's human capital in the sense of providing him with the intellectual wherewithal to generate wealth. The latter may or may not raise the student's human capital, depending upon his abilities as a pupil. The attentive law student can earn an income from what he was taught, but his inattentive classmate cannot. Those who are opposed to recognizing pure services as enrichments are split on the issue. While Beatson contemplates restitutionary relief where the defendant's human capital is increased (above n 24) 23, 30–31, 35–36, Grantham and Rickett (above n 3) 61, appear to insist upon the receipt of a marketable residuum that is *separate* from the defendant himself.

[27] Logically extended, the same reasoning should apply to the provision of consumed goods, as when the plaintiff provides sustenance to a person suffering from an incapacity. By the time of trial, the digestive process has run its course and there is no marketable residuum. In fact, however, restitutionary relief is available in such circumstances. Grantham and Rickett (above n 3) 227, explain many of those cases on compensatory grounds.

[28] [1954] SCR 725; [1954] 3 DLR 785 (SCC).

[29] [1980] 2 SCR 834; 117 DLR (3d) 257 (SCC) (herein cited to DLR).

[30] Nor did the plaintiff's services invariably save the defendant a necessary expense.

may be possible to award relief even in the absence of a marketable residuum, the defendant should not be held liable unless and until he has received something. When, however, are services received?[31] The centre-piece of that debate is *Planché v Colburn*.[32] The defendant engaged the plaintiff to write a children's book about ancient armour. After the plaintiff researched and wrote a portion of the text, but before he delivered any pages, the defendant broke the contract by stating that it no longer intended to go forward with the publication. The author then successfully claimed the value of his services on a *quantum meruit*—he received restitution for unjust enrichment.[33] That decision is controversial insofar as it appears to hold the defendant liable even though he never actually received an objective benefit in the form of a manuscript. On that view, there simply was nothing to give back. Canadian courts nevertheless have relied upon *Planché* in awarding restitutionary relief[34] and that decision may, indeed, be defensible.[35] The mere fact that the defendant in *Planché* did not receive anything that he could restore *in specie*, or from which he could realize a financial gain, was not necessarily fatal to the issue of enrichment. The cases on pure services are proof of that proposition. Assume a variation on the facts. Although he had not yet decided to publish a book on ancient armour, the defendant wanted to prepare for that contingency and therefore asked the plaintiff to research the topic. The parties agreed at the outset that the production of a manuscript or report would be addressed separately if and when the need arose. The plaintiff performed the services, but the defendant refused payment because the contract was, for some reason, unenforceable. Restitution might be available, notwithstanding the absence of any physical product, on the basis that the defendant had received the plaintiff's time and effort. And that enrichment, which consisted of the research itself, would have been received from time to time as the work was done.

[31] The issue is much simpler, of course, with respect to money, land and goods. The defendant is enriched when he actually acquires the property.

[32] (1831) 5 Car & P 57, 172 ER 876, aff'd (1831) 8 Bing 305, 131 ER 305.

[33] Many commentators prefer to analyze *Planché* (above n 32) as a case in which the plaintiff was awarded reliance damages under a cause of action in breach of contract: Jones (above n 2) 22–23; Burrows (above n 3) 17, 343; Grantham and Rickett (above n 3) 166. And indeed, that would seem the simpler solution. It does not, however, accurately reflect the reasons for judgment. The court employed a restitutionary approach. Furthermore, the contractual analysis would be inapplicable if the services were not rendered pursuant to an enforceable agreement. In that situation, the defendant could be held liable, if at all, only under the action in unjust enrichment.

[34] *Oberholtzer v Exploits Oilskins Originals Inc* [2000] NJ No 173 (Nfld PC) (QL); *Kuny v Wigle*, [1994] AJ No 331 (Alta PC) (QL). See also *Brenner v First Artists' Management Ltd* [1993] 2 VR 221, (Vict SC) 258; *Independent Grocers Co-Operative Ltd v Noble Lowndes Superannuation Consultants Ltd* (1993) 60 SASR 525 (SA SC); GE Palmer, *The Law of Restitution* (Boston, Little Brown and Co, 1978) § 4.2.

[35] See also P Birks, 'In Defence of Free Acceptance' in A Burrows (ed), *Essays on the Law of Restitution* (Oxford, Clarendon Press, 1991) 105,140–41; Maddaugh and McCamus (above n 3) 39; Tettenborn (above n 3) 10.

Returning to the actual facts of *Planché*, there is no reason why a different conclusion is required by the mere fact that the parties initially expected the plaintiff's research to culminate in a marketable residue. The anticipated manuscript would have constituted an enrichment, but so too did the underlying services.[36] And on that view, the defendant arguably began to receive the latter as soon as the plaintiff commenced performance. At that point, even though he subsequently abandoned the project, the publisher had command of the author's labour.[37]

The possibility that services may be received even before an anticipated end product is transferred admittedly entails certain complications. First, it requires a court to determine whether the defendant sought both the plaintiff's services and their end product (eg research and a printed manuscript) or merely the end product (eg a printed manuscript). If the latter, but not the former, he presumably would be immune to a claim based on the services themselves. Second, even if the defendant sought both services and their end product, a court must determine whether the plaintiff's actions were merely preparatory and hence non-recoverable (eg walking to a library), or whether they constituted part performance and hence were recoverable (eg conducting research).[38]

B. Subjective Devaluation

Objective benefit is broadly defined. If unqualified, it would be practically intolerable. There would be too much restitution. A person would be at risk of liability any time that he received something of market value. Moreover, such an approach would be irreconcilable with a basic tenet of our legal system. As Justice McLachlin has explained, the common law 'was founded on a philosophy of robust individualism which expected every person to look out after his or her own interests and which place[d] a premium on the right to choose how to spend one's money.'[39] And while it is true that '[c]ommon law man has lost the rougher edges of his individualism,'[40] Canadian courts

[36] *BP Exploration Co (Libya) Ltd v Hunt (No 2)* [1979] 1 WLR 783, 802 (QB) (prospecting services may constitute a benefit in themselves, even if they do not discover minerals).

[37] Palmer (above n 34) § 4.2. Burrows (above n 3) 18, draws a distinction between services that are intended to create an end product and those that are not. The former, he says, are received only when part of the end product is transferred to the defendant, whereas the latter are received as soon as the plaintiff starts performance. In either event, however, the plaintiff is working for the defendant once performance begins. And moreover, in some situations, the end product may be relatively unimportant to the parties. People pay for balloon animals, not so much because they want the end products, but rather because they enjoy the creative process.

[38] Jones (above n 2) 23, 514 ('such fine distinctions are unattractive').

[39] Peel (above n 15) 152–53.

[40] P Birks, *An Introduction to the Law of Restitution*, rev edn (Oxford, Clarendon Press, 1989) 121.

remain vigilant to protect freedom of choice. They do so through the concept of *subjective devaluation.*

That phrase was coined by Birks[41] and only recently began to appear in the caselaw.[42] The underlying principle, however, is long-standing. Having received an objective benefit, the defendant has always been entitled to argue that, regardless of the market's perception of his purported enrichment, he did not *choose* to place value on it and therefore should not be held responsible. It is important to stress the nature of that plea. The defendant need not deny the objectively beneficial nature of his receipt. Nor, more significantly, is he required to prove that he did not personally feel enriched.[43] He only has to show that he did not freely assume financial responsibility for his gain.[44] Consequently, as one Canadian judge observed, it may be possible to resist an action in unjust enrichment by turning to the claimant and saying, 'it is not your job to make my choices.'[45] Take a simple example. Before going on vacation, the defendant left his car at the plaintiff's garage for an oil change. By mistake, however, she performed extensive repairs. Upon returning home, the defendant might concede that the car's market value has been enhanced and admit that he is delighted by the improvement. Without more, however, the plaintiff's claim should fail. 'Liabilities are not to be forced upon people behind their backs any more than you can confer a benefit upon a man against his will.'[46]

C. Satisfying the Defendant's Freedom of Choice

To satisfy the requirement of an enrichment, the plaintiff consequently must do more than establish the provision of an objective benefit. She must also overcome the plea of subjective devaluation by satisfying the court that

[41] *Ibid*, 109.
[42] *Gidney v Shank* [1995] 5 WWR 385 (Man QB) 400, rev'd on other grounds [1996] 2 WWR 383 (CA); *Olchowy v McKay* [1996] 1 WWR 36 (Sask QB) 46; *Club 7 Ltd v EPK Enterprises Ltd* (1993) 15 Nfld & PEIR 271 (Nfld SC TD) 315; *Ministry of Defence v Ashman* [1993] 2 EGLR 102 (CA) 105.
[43] Some authorities suggest that the plea of subjective devaluation is overcome if the defendant personally felt enriched: *Olchowy* (above n 42) 46. That approach is unacceptable insofar as it fails properly to respect the underlying principle of freedom of choice. There is a fundamental difference between recognizing the beneficial nature of a receipt and being willing to assume financial responsibility for it. For instance, while most car owners would be quite happy to have a new paint job, few are willing to pay for that service.
[44] The label 'subjective devaluation' is, for that reason, somewhat misleading. The important point is not the defendant's personal *valuation* of a benefit, but rather his personal *choice* to accept the risk of financial responsibility for it.
[45] *Magical Waters Fountain Ltd v Sarnia (City)* (1990) 74 OR (2d) 682 (Ont CA) 691 (Gautreau J), rev'd on other grounds (1992) 91 DLR (4th) 760. See also JRM Gautreau, 'When Are Enrichments Unjust?' (1989) 10 *Advocates' Quarterly* 258, 261 ('The choice of how to invest one's time, effort and money should not be forced on one. Freedom of choice is the dominant consideration in these cases.').
[46] *Falke v Scottish Imperial Insurance Co* (1886) 34 ChD 234 (CA) 248.

liability would not intolerably infringe upon the defendant's freedom of choice. To do so, she must demonstrate either that he chose to assume the risk of financial responsibility for an enrichment, or that, given the very nature of the benefit, there was no choice to make. Broadly speaking, there are three possibilities: (i) request, (ii) free acceptance, and (iii) incontrovertible benefit.

(i) Request

The defendant may be enriched if he received something that he requested. Having actually exercised a choice, he cannot complain that liability would intolerably infringe upon his autonomy. That basic proposition is incontestable. It is, nevertheless, subject to certain qualifications.

(a) Contract The fulfilment of a request usually occurs within a contractual context. The parties' agreement may be express or it may be genuinely implied. In either event, the plaintiff generally is required to pursue her remedies in contract. The action in unjust enrichment cannot be used to override a contractual allocation of risk.[47] Restitution therefore is confined to situations in which the agreement somehow can be overcome or set aside. The parties may have tried, but failed, to create a valid contract.[48] They may have created a contract that is valid, but unenforceable.[49] They may have created an enforceable contract that was subsequently discharged for breach.[50] Or they may have created a contract that did not address the allocation of a particular risk.[51]

(b) Acceptance of Financial Responsibility Even within the context of a claim in unjust enrichment, a mere request should not invariably preclude a plea of subjective devaluation. A request is relevant only insofar as it demonstrates that the defendant chose to accept the risk of financial responsibility for his benefit. Granted, that usually is the case. A request normally indicates not only a desire to receive something, but also a willingness to pay for it. Sometimes, however, the second conclusion cannot be drawn. A person at a festival might ask an on-site tattoo artist for a temporary image in the reasonable belief that the service was being provided free. If so, he should not be considered enriched by her work. As might be expected, it is difficult to find cases directly on point. The proposition nevertheless is supported by the general structure of the action and, more specifically, by the defence of change of position. A recurring theme throughout unjust enrichment is that a person cannot be held responsible

[47] *Pettkus* (above n 29) 274.
[48] *Clarke v Moir* [1987] 82 NSR (2d) (NS CA).
[49] *Deglman* (above n 28).
[50] *McElheran v Great Northwest Insulation Ltd* [1995] NWTR 120 (CA).
[51] *Roxborough* (above n 21).

for an act that was the product of an impaired intention. As explained below, it is for that reason that the plaintiff can recover a mistaken payment and that, notwithstanding proof of a prima facie claim, the defendant is relieved of liability to the extent that he incurred an exceptional expenditure in the honest, but erroneous, belief that he was entitled to retain an enrichment. A request that was unaccompanied by the anticipation of payment should be ineffective in the same way. As to hidden consequences, an apparent choice is really no choice at all.

(c) Extent of Enrichment It further follows that even if the defendant's conduct imports both a desire to receive a benefit and willingness to pay for it, he should be considered enriched only to the *extent* indicated by his request.[52] Suppose that the defendant asks the plaintiff to repair his house at a price of $10,000. She performs the service, but then discovers that the apparent contract is unenforceable for want of some formality. She also discovers that she had entered into a bad bargain because the market value of her work was actually $15,000. If she brings a claim for restitution, she undoubtedly can establish the defendant's enrichment on the basis of his request. Nevertheless, the defendant should be allowed partial recourse to subjective devaluation. He assumed financial responsibility for the repairs, but only at the lower price. He did not exercise his freedom of choice with respect to the additional $5000. Unfortunately, as discussed below,[53] courts frequently overlook that fact. They often disregard the terms of the defendant's contractual request and, without full analysis, measure relief by reference to market value alone.

(d) Reprehensible Seeking Out The recipient of a requested benefit normally is considered enriched because, in seeking out a benefit, he demonstrated a willingness to pay for it. As Professor Burrows has noted, however, that test does not properly work with respect to some wrongdoers.[54] The defendant may have requested—indeed demanded—a benefit, knowing that payment normally would be expected, but intending to take it for free. A fugitive may compel medical services at gun point or, less dramatically, a thief may steal a car from a rental agency. An enrichment nevertheless can be found. The defendant cannot rely on his own reprehensible conduct to disregard the usual incidents of the marketplace.

(e) Part Performance Difficulties may also arise if the defendant merely receives part of a requested benefit. He is apt to argue that he accepted financial responsibility only on the assumption that he would get *everything* that he wanted. That may be true in the case of an 'entire contract.'

[52] If the parties did not agree on a price, the defendant can, in the absence of evidence to the contrary, be assumed to have agreed to pay market value. Likewise if the parties agreed to a 'reasonable' price: *Pavey & Matthews Pty Ltd v Paul* (1986) 162 CLR 221 (HCA).
[53] Section III(B)(ii).
[54] Burrows (above n 2) 24–25.

The parties may have agreed that payment would be due only *when* and *if* the project was completed. Such an arrangement has the capacity to create injustice insofar as it may allow a party to retain a substantial benefit without liability in either contract or unjust enrichment. And while it is certainly possible for a person to contract out of the right to restitution,[55] the courts should be slow to reach that conclusion.[56] That issue is discussed elsewhere.[57] For present purposes, the relevant question is somewhat narrower. It pertains not to the ultimate right to relief, but rather to the existence of an enrichment. Can a person subjectively devalue a benefit received in partial fulfilment of a request?

That question is often answered in the negative. If a person pays part of a requested sum, restitution may be available if the reason for the payment later fails.[58] That is not surprising. As discussed below, the receipt of *any* money invariably constitutes an incontrovertible benefit. More interestingly, restitution may be available if the defendant, having requested a non-monetary benefit, prevents the plaintiff from completing the project after she has partially performed.[59] The defendant cannot avoid liability by insisting that he chose to accept financial responsibility only if he received full performance. Were it otherwise, he would be able to retain a non-contractual benefit, without any payment, simply by stopping the plaintiff before she finished.

According to the orthodox view, however, the result is different if the roles are reversed such that performance is interrupted by the person who partially performed a service.[60] In that situation, restitution normally is denied. Although the reasons vary, it is sometimes suggested that part performance does not provide an enrichment.[61] That proposition is untenable

[55] *Cutter v Powell* (1795) 6 Term Rep 320, 101 ER 573 (KB); M Dockray, '*Cutter v Powell*: A Trip Outside the Text' (2001) 117 *LQR* 664.
[56] *Campbell Albo Low Ltd v Black* (1995) 26 OR (3d) 111 (GD).
[57] Maddaugh and McCamus (above n 3) 443–446; Burrows (above n 3) 354–359; *Kemp v McWilliams* (1978) 83 DLR (3d) 544 (Sask CA).
[58] That is true whether the ultimate failure of the transaction is attributable to the payor or the payee: *Dies v British & Intl Mining & Finance Corp* [1939] 1 KB 724; *Stephenson v Bromley* [1928] 4 DLR 735 (Man CA); *Rowland v Divall* [1923] 2 KB 500; *Gibbons v Trapp Motors Ltd* (1970) 9 DLR (3d) 742 (BC SC). In other words, even a party who breaks a contract by refusing to pay the full price normally is entitled to restitution. Of course, he may be subject to a counterclaim for breach of contract.
[59] Indeed, restitution may be available even if the defendant was not left with anything of value. *Planché* (above n 32) is authority for that proposition. On one view, the defendant enjoyed the benefit of the plaintiff's labour, even though his subsequent actions rendered those services fruitless. Moreover, it may be that the defendant is *estopped* from pleading subjective devaluation in such circumstances. Having represented that he would pay for performance, and having thereby induced the plaintiff into action, he may not have the right to falsify his representation by denying the enriching nature of her efforts: Virgo (above n 3) 88–91, 94.
[60] *Sumpter v Hedges* [1898] 1 QB 673 (CA); B McFarlane and R Stevens, 'In Defence of *Sumpter v Hedges*' (2002) 118 *LQR* 569.
[61] M Garner, 'The Role of Subjective Benefit in Unjust Enrichment' (1990) 10 *OJLS* 42.

as a general rule. As previously explained, an objective benefit may be received from the time that performance commences. Moreover, while part performance occasionally leaves the recipient with nothing of practical value, that is not always true. Suppose that the defendant asked the plaintiff to build a house. She laid the foundation, but was unable to complete the project. The defendant can legitimately assert that *none* of his request has been effectively fulfilled if, because of the circumstances, he must hire someone else to both re-lay the foundations and finish the structure.[62] However, he cannot legitimately deny that *part* of his request has been fulfilled if, because the initial work need not be repeated, he only has to hire someone else to build on top of the existing foundations.[63] Unless he is considered enriched to that extent, he ultimately will receive full performance at a reduced price.[64]

(f) Subjective Overvaluation The final difficulty associated with request concerns, for want of a more elegant phrase, *subjective overvaluation*. The element of enrichment usually requires the plaintiff to override the defendant's attempt to subjectively devalue an objective benefit. An interesting question will arise, however, if the requested services were not objectively beneficial or, going further, if they were objectively detrimental. Take an extreme example. The defendant, an eccentric billionaire, arranges for one of his houses to be razed by the plaintiff, a demolition expert. Can the defendant be considered enriched despite losing something of great value? As always, the essential question is whether or not liability would intolerably curtail freedom of choice. And in that regard, there is no danger in recognizing an enrichment if the defendant received the very thing that he requested, even if no reasonable person would have agreed with his choice.[65] Autonomy includes the right to be perverse. Not surprisingly, it is

[62] *Bradley v Horner* (1957) 10 DLR (2d) 446 (Ont CA).

[63] The enrichment presumably should be measured by the difference between the cost of the complete job and the cost of completing the job. Suppose that the defendant asked the plaintiff to build the house for a total price of \$50,000. After laying the foundation, she was unable to do any more. The defendant then paid another contractor \$40,000 to finish the structure. The enrichment that he received from the plaintiff should be valued at \$10,000. That is true even if, in the normal course of events, the foundation and the top-structure would count equally toward the total price. The defendant should not be penalized by the fact that additional transaction costs were necessitated by the need to deal with two parties, rather than one. *Vis a vis* the plaintiff, the defendant chose to assume financial responsibility to a maximum of \$50,000.

[64] Once again, even if the party in breach successfully claims restitution, the innocent party is entitled to claim contractual relief if the benefit was conferred pursuant to an enforceable agreement.

[65] Cf M Garner 'Benefits: For Services Rendered—Commentary' in McInnes *Restitution: Developments in Unjust Enrichment* (above n 5) ch 6; Burrows (above n 3) 24.

difficult to find cases directly on point. However, as an Australian judge explained, the concept of a benefit:

> ... must be seen from the perspective of the recipient who is, after all, the person to be charged. It may be that for some idiosyncratic reason a defendant seeks performance of work which another would see as without benefit or, indeed, a positive dis-benefit ... But where a person requests another to do something, it is not unreasonable for the law to conclude that the former sees some benefit in its performance, however wrong this may be on an objective basis and for the law to act upon the perception of the recipient.[66]

It might be objected that the defendant cannot be enriched because, in the absence of an objective benefit, he has nothing that he can give back. That argument is sufficiently overcome, however, by pointing to the cases in which restitution is awarded with respect to pure services. As previously explained, Canadian law has rejected the proposition that an enrichment is premised upon the retention of a marketable residuum.

Finally, it admittedly may be difficult to assess the value of the enrichment in a case of subjective overvaluation. That problem will not arise if the defendant's request was accompanied by the quotation of a price. And even in the absence of a stated amount, a court may be able to resolve the issue by reference to prevailing values. That will be true if, despite creating an objective detriment in the circumstances, the plaintiff provided a *type* of service that is readily available in the market. The court will be without such guidance, however, if there is neither a stated price nor a market for the plaintiff's services. In that situation, a court might simply assume that the defendant's enrichment coincides with the plaintiff's expenses.

(ii) Free Acceptance

To establish an enrichment, the plaintiff must overcome the defendant's subjective devaluation. Request is a relatively simple concept because it proceeds by proof that the defendant *actively* exercised his freedom of choice. The test of 'free acceptance,' in contrast, recognizes an enrichment on the basis of *passive* conduct. The operative phrase was coined by Goff and Jones,[67] who today state that the defendant:

> ... will be held to have benefited from the services rendered if he, as a reasonable man, should have known that the plaintiff who rendered the services expected to be paid for them, and yet he did not take a reasonable opportunity open to him to reject the proffered services.[68]

[66] *Brenner* (above n 34) 258 (Byrne J).
[67] R Goff and G Jones, *The Law of Restitution* (London, Sweet and Maxwell, 1966) 30.
[68] Jones (above n 2) 20.

That test has been adopted, with slight modifications, into Canadian law. Although it first appeared in *Pettkus v Becker*,[69] it is applicable in both family[70] and commercial matters.[71]

The role of free acceptance is best explained by a simple example.[72] The defendant delivers his car to the plaintiff's garage for a tune-up. He notices that she has mistakenly begun to perform a much more valuable service. He knows that she expects payment accordingly, but he remains silent until the job is done. His acquiescence indicates little about his perception of the objective benefit. He might have accepted the service because he felt that it was personally enriching. But so too he might have remained silent because he was entirely indifferent to the work. In the circumstances, however, that distinction is irrelevant. The significance of free acceptance lies not in its ability to identify subjective benefits, but rather in its ability to overcome the defendant's freedom of choice. It demonstrates that he passively assumed financial responsibility for his receipt. In effect, he had an obligation to reject a benefit for which he was unwilling to pay. Having failed to do so, he is taken to have voluntarily accepted the risk of liability.[73]

[69] *Pettkus* (above n 29) 274.

[70] In fact, in family cases, the courts often simply assume that the defendant was enriched and then apply the test of free acceptance to satisfy the third element of the action in unjust enrichment. Free acceptance nevertheless is often the best explanation for the defendant's enrichment: *Sorochan v Sorochan* [1986] 2 SCR 38; 29 DLR (4th) 1 (SCC) (herein cited to DLR); *Clarkson v McCrossen Estate* (1995) 122 DLR (4th) 239 (BC CA); *Davidson v Kuzonski* (1990) 37 ETR 297 (BC SC); *Forrest v Price* (1992) 48 ETR 72 (BC SC); *King v Andrews* (1992) 48 ETR 125 (Ont GD); *McDougall v Gesell* (1999) 140 Man R (2d) 161 (Man QB); *Wilgosh v Puchalski* (1999) 132 Man R (2d) 299 (QB).

[71] *Brisebois v Modern Music Co* (1993) 50 ETR 305 (Ont GD) (QL); *Gill v Grant* (1988) 30 ETR 255 (BC SC). Once again, the courts often intuitively find enrichments that are best explained on the ground of free acceptance: *Hiscock v Nolan* (1993) 109 Nfld & PEIR 302 (Nfld SC); *Hesjedal v Granville Estate* (1993) 109 DLR (4th) 353 (Sask QB); *Sharwood & Co v Municipal Finance Corp* [1998] OJ No 4907 (GD). A number of older cases more understandably employ the theory, but not the name, of free acceptance: *Tannenbaum & Downsview Meadows Ltd v Wright-Winston Ltd* [1965] OR 1 (Ont CA).

[72] Principles governing request apply *mutatis mutandis* to free acceptance. For instance, the defendant should be considered enriched only to the *extent* of his free acceptance. Consequently, if he acquiesced in the receipt of a benefit that carried market value of $5000, but only because he reasonably believed that the plaintiff expected to receive payment of $4000, he should not be held liable for the greater amount.

[73] Acquiescence in the receipt of a benefit does not invariably result in restitution. Liability may be denied if the plaintiff officiously foisted upon the defendant a benefit that she knew had not been requested. So too if the plaintiff did not expect payment. Free acceptance cannot create liability with respect to a benefit that was provided with a gratuitous intention. Finally, even if the defendant knew of the plaintiff's non-gratuitous intention, he will not be caught by the principle of free acceptance unless he failed to use a *reasonable opportunity* to reject a benefit. Although that requirement is seldom contentious, it does serve an important function. The concept of free acceptance imposes a burden upon the defendant to positively reject something for which he does not wish to pay. Given the importance of choice, that obligation of affirmative action is tolerable only because it is subject to an overriding limitation of reasonableness: *Cyvel International Corp v Janif* (1984) 18 CLR 82 (BC Co Ct).

While Canadian courts frequently apply the test of free acceptance, their judgments reveal little appreciation of its controversial nature. Enrichment is based upon autonomy. But in that regard, it is one thing to find that a choice was made through request, and quite another to conclude that the defendant exercised his volition by doing nothing at all. Moreover, given its fundamentally individualistic orientation, the common law generally refuses to impose liability on the basis of mere passivity.[74] Possibly for that reason, English courts have refrained from endorsing the concept of free acceptance.[75]

The controversial nature of the Canadian position runs even deeper. The plaintiff can establish the existence of an enrichment by proving either: (i) that the defendant knew that she expected payment, or (ii) that a reasonable person in the defendant's position would have known that she expected payment. The former branch, which turns upon *subjective knowledge*, is relatively less troublesome. Although it requires a policy decision to impose liability on the basis of mere passivity, it is not entirely inconsistent with the underlying value. It is plausible to say that the defendant actually exercised a choice if he failed to reject a benefit for which he *knew* payment was expected. The analysis becomes much more difficult, however, if the defendant merely had *constructive knowledge* of the plaintiff's expectation.[76] Regardless of what he *should have known*, the defendant could not *truly* have chosen to assume financial responsibility if, in fact, he was unaware of the possibility of doing so. Accordingly, since autonomy is the paramount consideration under the first element of the action in unjust enrichment, free acceptance should be limited, in principle, to cases of actual knowledge (including recklessness and wilful blindness).[77] Constructive knowledge should be irrelevant. An accurate account of Canadian law nevertheless must recognize that courts occasionally do rely

[74] *Felthouse v Bindley* (1862) 11 CBNS 869, 142 ER 1037; cf Tettenborn (above n 3) 18.

[75] Burrows (above n 3) 20–23; cf Birks (above n 35) 128–132.

[76] In *Peter* (above n 15) 635, Cory J discussed free acceptance in the context of the third element of unjust enrichment, having assumed, without analysis, that the defendant had been enriched. He affirmed that the test is objective and further held that, at least in a cohabitational context, it should be presumed proven in the absence of evidence to the contrary.

[77] The timing of such knowledge can vary with the nature of the enrichment. Since they cannot be restored *in specie*, the defendant should be held to have freely accepted services only if he had knowledge of the plaintiff's expectation of payment *before* she conferred the benefit. Subsequent knowledge should not suffice because, having received services, the recipient no longer has the option of rejecting them. In contrast, goods may subsist for an extended period. And so long as they have not deteriorated or been consumed, the recipient may enjoy the capacity for restoration. Accordingly, despite being initially unaware of the plaintiff's expectation of payment, the defendant can properly be put to a choice *after* he acquires knowledge of her non-gratuitous intention: *Sumpter* (above n 60) (liability for construction materials provided by the plaintiff and subsequently used by the defendant). Unfortunately, Canadian courts have not been attentive to those distinctions and occasionally have awarded relief with respect to services that the defendant received without knowledge of the plaintiff's expectation of payment: *Pettkus* (above n 29).

upon the broader test. Those cases can be defended, if at all, on policy grounds.[78] The defendant anomalously may be denied recourse to subjective devaluation, not because he actually exercised a choice, but rather because he was unreasonably imperceptive.[79]

(iii) Incontrovertible Benefit

Leaving aside anomalies created by the over-extended concept of free acceptance, restitutionary enrichments generally are a function of the *defendant's conduct*. Regardless of the precise nature of the benefit, liability is possible because he exercised a choice to assume financial responsibility for it.

Exceptionally, however, the plaintiff may overcome the plea of subjective devaluation, without regard to the defendant's conduct, by pointing to the *nature of the benefit itself*. That is true if he received an *incontrovertible benefit*. Once again, while the terminology is relatively new,[80] the underlying principle is well-established. As Justice McLachlin explained, if a benefit is not clear and manifest, it generally would be 'wrong to make the defendant pay, since he or she might well have preferred to decline the benefit if given a choice.' An incontrovertible benefit, however, is 'not the antithesis of freedom of choice,' but rather 'exists when freedom of choice as a problem is absent.'[81] That is because such a benefit is 'demonstrably apparent and not subject to debate or conjecture.'[82] There are several possibilities.

[78] Unfortunately, even if the threshold issue of liability can be explained on policy grounds, the measure of relief frequently awarded in free acceptance cases remains controversial. Perhaps because the test of free acceptance is based on the defendant's awareness of the plaintiff's *reasonable expectation* of payment, there is a tendency, especially in cohabitational cases, for courts to improperly calculate relief so as to fulfil the plaintiff's expectation: discussed below at Section III(B)(iii).

[79] The plaintiff is protected from the defendant's unreasonable lack of perception in other areas of private law: *Hadley v Baxendale* (1854) 9 Exch 341, 156 ER 145; *Overseas Tankship (UK) Ltd v Morts Dock and Engineering Co Ltd., The Wagon Mound (No 2)* [1967] 1 AC 617 (PC).

[80] *Park Lane Ranch Ltd v Fleetwood Village Holdings (Phase II)* (1980) 17 RPR 35 (BC SC) 44; *Republic Resources Ltd v Ballem* [1982] 1 WWR 692 (Alta QB) 705; *Magical Waters Fountains Ltd* (above n 45) 691; *Gidney* (above n 42) 397; *Olchowy* (above n 42) 46; *Halifax (City) v Nova Scotia (Attorney General)* (1997) 163 NSR (2d) 360 (NS CA) 369; *Sharwood & Co v Municipal Financial Corp* (2001) 197 DLR (4th) 477 (Ont CA).

[81] *Peel* (above n 15) 159, in part quoting Gautreau (above n 45) 270–71. It is important to stress the nature of the concept. Contrary to a common misperception, incontrovertible benefit is *not* an independent cause of action: cf *Gill* (above n 71) 272; *Wettstein v Wettstein* [1992] BCJ No 1026 (SC); *Alyea v South Waterloo Edgar Insurance Brokers Ltd* (1993) 50 CCLI 266 (Ont GD) 274; *Lavigne v Dak Enterprises Ltd* [1996] BCJ No 196 (SC) § 30; cf *Sharwood & Co* (n 80) 487. To say that the defendant received an incontrovertible benefit merely is to say that he undeniably was enriched. It does not reveal who provided that enrichment, nor does it indicate any reason for reversing the transfer. A gift of $500 is an incontrovertible benefit because it is not 'subject to debate or conjecture.' But, of course, being a gift, it need not be returned. Furthermore, incontrovertible benefit is only one of several means by which the plaintiff can overcome subjective devaluation. It is not, as some courts have said, the *exclusive* test of enrichment: *Toronto Dominion Bank v Bank of Montreal* (1995) 22 OR (3d) 362 (GD) 375; *GJV Investments Ltd v Katz* [1993] BCJ No 466 (BC SC).

[82] *Peel* (above n 15) 159.

(a) Money The receipt of money is an incontrovertible benefit. Since it is the very means by which the law recognizes and expresses value, money cannot be subjectively devalued.[83] It is always valuable and, moreover, it is equally valuable regardless of who holds it. A $5 bill is worth precisely as much in the defendant's hands as in the plaintiff's. And finally, because of its fungibility, money can be effectively restored even if the defendant no longer holds the same notes and coins that he received from the plaintiff. One $5 bill is as good as the next.[84]

(b) Services The analysis is more complicated when the defendant receives services, rather than money. Services are not invariably valuable, nor are they equally valued by everyone. Regardless of the fact that a shoeshine may have a market price of, say, $5, the defendant may place less value, or no value at all, on that type of service. Furthermore, unlike money, services are not fungible and cannot be restored *in specie*. As Baron Pollock famously said, 'One cleans another's shoes; what can that other do but put them on?'[85]

As a result, judges are reluctant to characterize services as incontrovertible benefits. There is a very real danger of imposing liability despite the fact that, if presented with a timely opportunity to do so, the recipient might have refused to assume financial responsibility for the work in question. Consequently, although the cases have yet to be expressly rationalized along such lines, it appears that the plaintiff must demonstrate that her services provided the defendant with the *equivalent of a monetary benefit*. Two possibilities have been recognized: (i) discharge of a necessary expense, and (ii) realization of a financial gain.[86]

(1) Necessary Expense Services constitute an incontrovertible benefit to the extent that they anticipate a necessary expense. The defendant cannot deny that he has been enriched if the plaintiff has discharged an obligation on his behalf. That is true if she provided money and eliminated a monetary debt (eg a contractual duty to pay rent) or if she performed work and eliminated a non-monetary debt (eg a statutory duty to clear a blocked sewer). In either event, it is *as if* she gave the defendant money itself. Being relieved of a $5000 burden essentially is the same as receiving $5000.[87] Consequently, liability leaves the defendant none the worse for wear.

[83] *BP Exploration Co (Libya) Ltd* (above n 36) 799 *per* Goff J ('Money has the peculiar character of a universal medium of exchange. By its receipt, the recipient inevitably is benefited.'); *Sharwood & Co* (above n 80) 485; *Halifax* (above n 80) 370.

[84] Exceptions exist. For instance, even if it qualifies as currency, an old or unusual coin may be worth more than its face value.

[85] *Taylor v Laird* (1856) 25 LJ Ex 329 (Exch) 332. The same observations apply, *mutatis mutandis*, with respect to goods that have been consumed. The retention of unconsumed goods generally is caught by the concept of free acceptance, as previously discussed.

[86] *Peel* (above n 15) 161.

[87] *Carleton (County) v Ottawa (City)* [1965] SCR 663; 52 DLR (2d) 220 (SCC); *Peter* (above n 15) 644; *Peel* (above n 15); *Davey v Municipality of Cornwallis* [1931] 2 DLR 80 (Man CA); *Halifax* (above n 80); *JBC Consulting Inc v Gray* (2000) 47 OR (3d) 212 (SCJ).

The resources that he could have used to discharge the underlying debt can be used instead to satisfy the plaintiff's judgment. And while it is true that he has no choice but to effect restitution, it is also true that he had no choice but to honour his original debt.

There is, however, need for caution. First, it is important to stress that the defendant is enriched only to the *extent* that he was saved a necessary expense. The focus at this stage of the inquiry therefore is not upon the expense that the plaintiff incurred, but rather upon the expense that the defendant was spared. Suppose that while the plaintiff paid $5000 to discharge the defendant's original obligation, he could have achieved the same result himself at a cost of only $3000. Perhaps the underlying burden consisted of a monetary debt that he could have satisfied at less than face value (eg because he held a right of set-off against his landlord).[88] Or perhaps it pertained to a service that he could have personally performed at a cost below market value (eg because he was capable of un-blocking a sewer himself and therefore had no need to hire someone for that job). In either event, notwithstanding the generally incontrovertible nature of his benefit, he should be entitled to subjectively devalue the enrichment by $2000. The law must respect the fact that he initially enjoyed an option as to whether he would spend $5000 or $3000 in discharge of the burden.

Even more fundamentally, the defendant should not be considered enriched at all (at least under this heading) unless he was saved a *necessary* expense. Given the ultimate focus of the inquiry, the italicized word must not be defined in a way that intolerably undermines freedom of choice. It certainly should not be enough that most reasonable people would consider a particular expenditure to be highly desirable or even inevitable. While the defendant cannot demand every indulgence, he must be allowed, to a substantial degree, to dissent from common perceptions.

In that regard, a distinction must be drawn between *legally* necessary expenses and *factually* necessary expenses. The former are relatively simple. True, it occasionally is difficult to determine whether or not the defendant was indeed legally obliged to pay money or perform services.[89] However, once that question has been answered in the affirmative, an enrichment can be readily recognized.[90] A legal obligation is usually narrowly prescribed in terms of content and timing.[91] Taxes, for instance, must be paid in a specified amount by a specified date. Moreover, while it is true that some legal obligations are never fulfilled, it would be perverse for a

[88] Cf *Boulton v Jones* (1857) 2 H & N 564, 157 ER 232 (Exch).

[89] *Peel* (above n 15); *Metropolitan Police District Receiver v Croydon* [1957] 2 QB 154 (CA).

[90] *Carleton* (above n 87) (plaintiff discharged defendant's statutory obligation to care for indigent person); *Davey* (above n 87) (plaintiff discharged defendant's statutory duty by burying unidentified body).

[91] Timing may be important. For instance, if the plaintiff discharged the defendant's debt before it was due, he might be able to prove that it would have been financially advantageous for him to postpone payment. If so, judgment for the full amount of the plaintiff's payment

court to countenance the possibility of non-compliance. The defendant should not be heard to say that he would have ignored his legal duty.[92]

A factually necessary expense is much more difficult to establish. Strictly speaking, of course, nothing is absolutely necessary. A person is free to refuse the necessities of life.[93] The law generally excludes extreme choices, however, by disregarding 'unrealistic or fanciful possibilities of ... doing without.'[94] Consequently, a person who improperly occupies a house cannot subjectively devalue that benefit by pointing to the possibility of living on the street.[95] Likewise, a person suffering from an incapacity, due to infancy, mental disability or intoxication, may be liable for restitution after being provided with food, clothing or shelter.[96] More controversially, a person who attempts suicide may be considered enriched by the receipt of emergency medical treatment, at least if he can be presumed to have acted with an impaired intention.[97] The identification of factually necessary

would deprive the defendant of the opportunity that he would have enjoyed to profitably invest money pending payment of the original debt: cf *RBC Dominion Securities Inc v Dawson* (1994) 111 DLR (4th) 230 (Nfld CA) (rejecting the relevance of timing *per se* but without investigating the financial implications of accelerating repayment).

[92] Suppose that the defendant was indebted to his mother for $5000. If the plaintiff discharged that obligation, the debtor should not be allowed to argue that he could have taken advantage of his parent's desire for harmonious relations by cynically refusing repayment. It would be different, of course, if the mother had actually forgiven the debt.

[93] *Malette v Shulman* (1990) 67 DLR (4th) 321 (Ont CA).

[94] Birks (above n 40) 120.

[95] Cf *Ministry of Defence v Ashman* [1993] 2 EGLR 102 (CA); *Ministry of Defence v Thompson* [1993] 2 EGLR 107 (CA) (discussed in the context of a claim to disgorgement under the cause of action for trespass to land). The facts of both cases were substantially similar. The defendant was married to a man who, because he was in the military, was entitled to housing at a substantially reduced rate. After her husband moved out on his own, the defendant was legally obligated to vacate the premises. She nevertheless remained in possession on the ground that she could not afford alternative accommodation on the open market and therefore was waiting for the local government to provide her with subsidized council housing. The Ministry of Defence sought to recover the full market value of the military quarters. It succeeded in part. The defendant could not entirely deny that she had been enriched. After all, she had been saved the necessary expense of paying for shelter. She was, however, entitled to partially subjectively devalue her benefit by arguing that she merely had been saved the necessary expense of *subsidized rent*, rather than *market rent*. That conclusion is open to debate. It is true, on the one hand, that the defendant would not have paid full market value in the normal course of events. It was beyond her means. But it is also true, on the other hand, that if she had been physically removed from the military accommodation, she would have been required to find some alternative pending the availability of council housing. In such circumstances, it is difficult to calculate the saved expense because it is not clear how the defendant, if pressed by the exigency, would have resolved the problem created by a lack of subsidized accommodation.

[96] *Re Rhodes, Rhodes v Rhodes* (1890) 44 ChD 94 (CA) (recognizing an enrichment, but refusing liability on the basis that the services were provided as a gift).

[97] The analysis is further complicated if the patient died despite receiving competent care. Even in that instance, however, an enrichment may be established by assessing the necessity at the time of emergency, rather than the time of trial. Immediately after sustaining a potentially fatal gunshot wound, for instance, no reasonable person would deny the need for treatment. Moreover, in cases of doubt, the law should, on policy grounds, favour a rule that encourages intervention: *Matheson v Smiley* [1932] 2 DLR 787 (Man CA).

expenses therefore can begin by proceeding by analogy to the rules that govern the enforceability of contracts concerning the provision of 'necessaries' to incapacitated parties.[98]

Leaving aside the necessities of life, however, it is unclear how far the courts will go in the recognition of incontrovertible benefits.[99] There is no obvious answer and, in formulating an appropriate rule, the courts will be required to weigh a number of considerations. Most significantly, they will have to balance the traditional desire to protect freedom of choice against the fact that, in practice, many expenditures, if not strictly necessary, are effectively compelled by circumstance.[100] Without resolving the issue, McLachlin J canvassed several possibilities in *Peel v Canada*. She referred at one extreme to an 'inevitable expense'[101] and at the other to a cost that the defendant 'would likely have paid.'[102] The former is unacceptable insofar as it suggests a complete lack of flexibility. Given the competing values, the defendant should not be able to defeat the plaintiff's claim for unjust enrichment merely by pointing to a slight chance that he would not have incurred the expense in the normal course of events. The second proposal is even less palatable. It suggests that the defendant could be exposed to the risk of liability simply because he *probably* would have incurred an expense. A bare probability, however, admits of a 49% chance to the contrary—a chance that intolerably undermines the notion of freedom of choice. In the final analysis, it appears that the concept of a factual necessity unfortunately is not susceptible to precise definition. The courts will be required to proceed cautiously while bearing in mind the nature of the exercise.

(2) Realization of a Financial Gain An incontrovertible benefit can also be recognized if the plaintiff provided the defendant with something from which he realized a financial gain. Once again, freedom of choice is the touchstone. Suppose that the plaintiff repaired the defendant's chattel and thereby raised its value from $5000 to $7000. At that point, he could plausibly argue that he should not be held liable because he did not voluntarily assume financial responsibility for the work. That argument certainly would be lost, however, if he subsequently sold the property in its improved state for $7000. The sale proceeds would be attributable to both the original

[98] Birks (above n 40) 121. See generally SM Waddams, *The Law of Contracts*, 4th edn (Toronto, Canada Law Book, 1999) ch 18.
[99] The courts occasionally have taken a very relaxed approach: *Cyvel International Corp* (above n 73) (defendants said to be incontrovertibly benefitted by the installation of house siding that they intended to acquire in the future *if* financing was available).
[100] The reality, for instance, is that some types of companies simply will not do without the services of managing director: *Craven-Ellis v Canons Ltd* [1936] 2 KB 403 (CA).
[101] Lord Goff and G Jones, *The Law of Restitution*, 3rd edn (London, Sweet and Maxwell, 1986) 21–22.
[102] M McInnes, 'Incontrovertible Benefits and the Canadian Law of Restitution' (1990) 12 *Advocates' Quarterly* 323.

condition of the thing *and* the repairs. Consequently, having turned the plaintiff's services into money, it is *as if* the defendant received $2000 in cash from her. And, as always, money is immune to subjective devaluation.

Although that analysis must be correct, it is surprisingly difficult to find conclusive authority. The effect of the leading English case, *Greenwood v Bennett*,[103] is qualified. The notion of realization of a financial gain does, however, enjoy stronger support in Canada. It was favourably discussed, without being applied, by the Supreme Court of Canada in *Peel v Canada*.[104] The Ontario Court of Appeal expressly stated that it would have been prepared to impose liability in *Sharwood & Co v Municipal Financial Corp*[105] if, *inter alia*, the defendant had derived a profit from the plaintiff's services. Likewise, in *Olchowy v McKay*,[106] while relief ultimately was

[103] [1973] 1 QB 195 (CA). The facts can be simplified for present purposes. The defendant car dealer owned a Jaguar that was valued at between £400 and £500. In preparation for its sale, he agreed to pay Searle £85 to make minor repairs. Instead of fixing the car, Searle drove it into the ground and then wrongfully sold it to a third party for £75. The third party then sold it at the same price to the plaintiff, who proceeded to spend £226 on repairs. After Searle's misconduct was detected, the police seized the car and, since both the plaintiff and the defendant claimed ownership, commenced interpleader proceedings. The trial judge awarded the car to the defendant and rejected the plaintiff's claim for reimbursement of his expenses. While an appeal was pending, the defendant sold the vehicle, as originally intended, for £400. The Court of Appeal unanimously varied the trial decision. It confirmed that the Jaguar belonged to the defendant, but it also found that the plaintiff was entitled to £226 as reimbursement for his expenses. Unfortunately, the judges split on the reasons for the latter conclusion. Cairns LJ held, and Phillimore LJ seemed to agree, that the plaintiff only enjoyed a *passive* claim. His right to relief was premised upon the fact that the defendant had recovered the vehicle through legal proceedings: *Peruvian Guano Co v Dreyfus Brothers & Co* [1892] AC 166 (HL); *Mayne v Kidd* (1951) 1 WWR 833 (Sask CA). Cairns LJ expressly stated that the dealer would have avoided liability altogether if he had re-acquired the Jaguar through his own efforts. On that view, reimbursement effectively was the price the defendant had to pay for the court's help. In contrast, Lord Denning MR expressly recognized that the plaintiff could, if necessary, have *actively* claimed restitution. The defendant would 'not be allowed unjustly to enrich' himself, even if he did not invoke the court's jurisdiction on his own behalf. Lord Denning's analysis is more compelling. The defendant undeniably was enriched, either because he realized a financial gain from the plaintiff's services, or because those services saved him an expense that was, given his intention to sell the car, factually necessary. Finally, although the defendant's benefit was £325 (insofar as the value of his car was increased from £75 to £400), the plaintiff's corresponding deprivation was only £226. Restitution was properly limited to the lesser amount. The plaintiff could not get back more than he actually lost.

[104] Above (n 15).

[105] Above (n 80) 482–83. The defendant contractually agreed to pay a success fee if the plaintiff was able to arrange 'debt or equity financing' on its behalf. To that end, the plaintiff introduced the defendant to several banks, but financing never occurred as anticipated and the parties' agreement was terminated. The defendant then sold its assets to one of the institutions to whom it had been introduced. The plaintiff insisted that it was entitled to be paid for its services. The court rejected that claim on the ground that the sale (which was a different type of transaction than 'debt or equity financing' and hence was not within the scope of the contract) would have occurred in any event and therefore was not causally related to the plaintiff's efforts. In other words, while the defendant had realized a financial gain, it did not do so on the basis of the plaintiff's services.

[106] Above (n 42) 46–47. See also *Kraft v Kraft* [1999] BCJ No 288 (PC) (QL) (land made saleable through creation of culvert); *Hill Estate v Chevron Standard Ltd* (1992) 83 Man R (2d) 58 (CA) 70 (enrichment resulting from services that created a profitable oil well); cf *Republic Resources Ltd* (above n 80) (oil well was not, and was not likely to be, placed into production).

denied on other grounds,[107] an enrichment was recognized after the defendant profitably harvested a crop that the plaintiff had planted. And in *Park Lane Ranch Ltd v Fleetwood Village Holdings (Phase II)*,[108] the court found that the services of a realtor provided an incontrovertible benefit to a mortgagee insofar as they resulted in the building's sale price being increased by $200,000.

Accepting that the realization of a financial gain can overcome the plea of subjective devaluation, the exact scope of that principle remains to be defined. Most significantly, it has yet to be determined whether the defendant is enriched only if he *has* realized a financial gain, or whether it is sufficient that he received services from which he *could* realize a financial gain. That issue arose in *Gidney v Shank*.[109] The plaintiff bought a dilapidated canoe for $100. After spending considerable time and $800 on repairs, he raised its value to $1900. The canoe was then seized by the RCMP and returned to the defendant, from whom it had been stolen years earlier. The plaintiff, who had been unaware of the theft, brought an action in unjust enrichment for the value of his efforts and expenses. Justice Beard allowed the claim.[110] She said that where 'a canoe is unusable as a water craft before the repairs and becomes useable as a result of the repairs ... [the] improvement qualifies as an incontrovertible benefit as earlier defined.'[111] That meaning of that statement unfortunately is obscured by the fact that her earlier definition of 'incontrovertible benefit' referred to both 'necessary expenses' and 'realizable financial gains.' It is difficult to accept, however, that the repairs fell within the former category. The owner of a badly damaged boat is not required, legally or factually, to fix it. Beard J therefore presumably relied on the fact that the defendant *could* realize a financial gain by selling the canoe in its improved condition, even though he had not *actually* done so.

Was the decision in *Gidney* correct? As always, the issue turns on freedom of choice and the extent to which the defendant should enjoy control over his own resources. The defendant began the episode with value of $100,

[107] McLellan J improperly denied relief on the basis that the parties did not share a 'special relationship': discussed below at Section III(C)(iii)(a).
[108] Above (n 80) (the court also found an enrichment on the basis of the defendant's request or free acceptance).
[109] Above (n 42).
[110] With respect to the second and third elements of the cause of action, Beard J held that the defendant suffered a corresponding deprivation through the provision of services and the payment of money, and that the defendant's enrichment was unjust because the plaintiff had acted in the mistaken belief that he owned the canoe. While accepting the trial judge's findings on the issues of enrichment and deprivation, the Manitoba Court of Appeal relieved the defendant of responsibility on the ground that he did not share a relationship with the plaintiff under which he had requested or accepted the improvements: [1996] 2 WWR 383. The purported requirement of a 'special relationship' is discussed below at Section III(C)(iii)(a).
[111] Above (n 42) 400.

in the form of a decrepit canoe. Even if he was held responsible for the full amount of the financial gain that he could realize from the plaintiff's repairs,[112] he would still have $100 in value at the end of the story. The totality of his wealth would not be diminished, but it would be forcibly re-allocated. Instead of a canoe worth $100, he would have a canoe worth $1900 and a debt worth $1800. Moreover, in order to satisfy judgment, he would be forced to expend resources in a way that he had not anticipated. If he wished to keep the canoe, he would have to forgo other assets (eg personal savings). Alternatively, if he was unable or unwilling to deploy other assets, he would be required to sell the canoe in its improved state. With the sale proceeds, he could discharge his $1800 debt to the plaintiff and, if he wished, attempt to replace the original item with the remaining $100. Of course, in the circumstances, that last transaction seems implausible. There is no market for decrepit boats. Consequently, the defendant might be left with something that he never chose: $100 in cash, rather than a canoe worth $100. Admittedly, that may not seem a hardship on the facts of *Gidney*, precisely because the property was so undesirable at the outset. Significantly, however, the same line of reasoning might require the defendant in another situation to liquidate an irreplaceable asset to which he was profoundly attached. And in any event, freedom of choice is generally defined by the right to choose—sensibly or perversely as the individual sees fit.

Canadian courts have yet to conclusively decide whether or not the defendant's freedom of choice can be overridden upon proof of a *realizable* financial gain. There is no logically compelling answer. A resolution of the issue requires an assessment of practical considerations and, ultimately, a political choice. The possibilities, as found in the academic literature, run a wide range.[113] At one extreme, Professor Birks insists that the defendant should not be considered enriched unless he has already *realized* a financial gain from the plaintiff's services.[114] While defensible, that rule does put the plaintiff at the defendant's mercy. He can defeat her claim merely by retaining the improved item until the trial has ended or the limitation period has expired. For that reason, Professor Burrows suggests that an enrichment should also be recognized if it is *reasonably certain* that the defendant will realize a financial gain.[115] Lord Goff and Professor Jones

[112] The trial judge actually limited recovery to $806, as reimbursement of the plaintiff's out-of-pocket expenses. She denied remuneration for his services because the evidence was incomplete.

[113] Canvassed in M McInnes, 'Incontrovertible Benefits in the Supreme Court of Canada' (1994) 23 *Canadian Business Law Journal* 122. Time has passed by several earlier proposals. Professor Klippert, for instance, rejected the concept of realization of a financial gain on the ground that the defendant generally cannot be enriched unless he chose to receive a benefit: GE Klippert, *Unjust Enrichment* (Toronto, Butterworths, 1983) 56–61. Canadian courts have moved well beyond that position.

[114] Birks (above n 40) 121–24.

[115] Burrows (above n 3) 19.

endorse a test that is both more lenient and more complicated. They begin with the proposition that the defendant is enriched if he received a *readily realizable* financial gain. In their opinion, it usually is 'not unreasonable' to compel the defendant to sell the improved property in order to satisfy judgment.[116] It is otherwise, however, if the property in question is unique, for the defendant should not be forced to sacrifice something that is irreplaceable.[117] Finally, Professors Maddaugh and McCamus generally agree with *Goff and Jones*.[118] In their view, a *realizable* financial gain generally should suffice, unless liability would create a hardship for the defendant. In that situation, they favour the imposition of an equitable lien that would be enforceable only if the defendant actually realized a profit from the plaintiff's services.[119]

(c) Specific Restitution While seldom recognized as such, the receipt of property should qualify as an incontrovertible benefit *if* the plaintiff seeks specific restitution.[120] The plaintiff's burden, as always, is to overcome the plea of subjective devaluation. She must prove that liability would not intolerably dictate the defendant's allocation of resources. Services are problematic precisely because they cannot be restored *in specie*. Restitution can be effected only substitutionally through the payment of money, with the result that the defendant must give up something to which he prima facie is entitled (ie resources that were not directly acquired from the plaintiff). The situation is much different, however, if the plaintiff provided the defendant with property that he still (traceably) retains and that she wants returned. Since she is not claiming monetary relief, there is no need to assess

[116] Jones (above n 2) 24, 238.

[117] *Ibid*, 238; cf G Jones, 'Restitutionary Claims for Services Rendered' (1977) 93 *LQR* 273, 293 (arguing that an enrichment should be recognized if the defendant has disposable funds with which to satisfy judgment—the defendant's freedom of choice can be infringed, so long as he is not required to sacrifice unique property).

Jones (above n 2) 25, 29, similarly rejects the second branch of incontrovertible benefit where services improve real property, on the basis that every parcel of land is unique. That position is difficult to sustain in absolute terms. First, Canadian law no longer views *every* parcel of land as unique: *Semelhago v Paramadevan* [1996] 2 SCR 415; 136 DLR (4th) 1 (SCC). Second, if an enrichment can be recognized with respect to unique chattels when disposable funds are available, it is not clear why the same exception should not apply in the case of land. Third, the argument from freedom of choice is attenuated if the defendant intended to sell his property in any event. And finally, there is no reason to refuse relief if the defendant not only *could*, but actually *has*, realized a financial gain from the plaintiff's services: *Olchowy* (above n 42); *Hill Estate* (above n 106).

[118] Maddaugh and McCamus (above n 3) 43–44, 101–2.

[119] That view finds support in *Re Gareau Estate* (1995) 9 ETR (2d) 25 (Ont GD). The amount secured by the lien presumably would depend upon the gain that the defendant actually realized, rather than upon the gain that he could have realized by selling the property either at the time of receipt or at the time of trial. Consequently, the value of the plaintiff's remedy would normally depreciate over time, along with the value of the property. See also AG Spence, 'In Defence of Subjective Devaluation' (1998) 48 *McGill Law Journal* 889, 918.

[120] Birks (above n 40) 130; Burrows (above n 3) 16; Chambers (above n 10) 95.

the value of that property.[121] More significantly, since she is asking to recover the very thing that he should not hold, there is no danger of improperly overriding the defendant's autonomy. He should not enjoy *any* freedom of choice with respect to the disposition of the very item that he must give back.

The preceding analysis is, however, subject to several qualifications. First, it presumes that the plaintiff is entitled to proprietary relief. In fact, restitution normally is available only in personal form. The defendant is required to give back the monetary value of his enrichment, rather than the enrichment itself. The exceptional circumstances in which a court will order restoration *in specie* cannot be explored in this article.[122] For present purposes, it is enough to say that the defendant's retention of the property (or its traceable proceeds) is a necessary, but not sufficient, condition. Consequently, the plaintiff cannot invariably avoid the hurdle of subjective devaluation by simply claiming proprietary relief.

Second, it is important to distinguish the situation currently under discussion from the situation in which the plaintiff acquires rights over a particular piece of property as a result of conferring a *different* form of enrichment upon the defendant. In *Pettkus v Becker*,[123] for instance, the court imposed a constructive trust over a farm because its legal owner had received beneficial services. Lothar Pettkus received one thing (ie labour), but was required give up another (ie land). Consequently, since she was not seeking specific restitution, Rosa Becker overcame the plea of subjective devaluation by other means (ie free acceptance).

Third, there is a debate as to whether or not the defendant can be enriched by the *possession* of property to which the plaintiff retains *title*. The operative question, as phrased by Professors Grantham and Rickett, is 'whether the requirement of enrichment is ... factual or legal.'[124] Suppose

[121] That point occasionally is overlooked. *Soulos v Korkontzilas* is illustrative: [1997] 2 SCR 217; 146 DLR (4th) 214 (SCC). The defendant, a real estate agent, breached a fiduciary duty by buying a property that he should have made available to the plaintiff, his principal. The plaintiff sought the imposition of a constructive trust and offered, in return, to indemnify the defendant for any losses or expenses that he incurred in connection with the property. In a dissenting opinion, Sopinka J believed that such relief was premised upon an 'unjust enrichment,' and therefore required proof that the defendant had received a 'pecuniary advantage.' That burden could not be discharged because the value of the land had depreciated after its purchase: 241–42; see also 224 *per* McLachlin J. Given the nature of the plaintiff's claim, however, the actual *value* of the property should have been irrelevant. Any concern for the defendant's freedom of choice was sufficiently met by the plaintiff's willingness to accept relief on terms. The question therefore was whether the defendant was enriched by the possession of property with which he could satisfy judgment *in specie*. The answer should have been in the affirmative.

[122] R Chambers, 'Constructive Trusts in Canada' (1999) 37 *Alberta Law Review* 173; R Chambers, 'Resulting Trusts in Canada' (2000) 38 *Alberta Law Review* 378.

[123] Above (n 29).

[124] Above (n 3) 61.

that the defendant steals the plaintiff's car.[125] From a factual perspective, he clearly is enriched and she clearly is deprived: he has use of the vehicle and she does not. From a legal perspective, however, the theft is irrelevant, at least in one sense. The plaintiff continues to enjoy ownership even though the defendant has possession. It therefore has been suggested that the first element of the action in unjust enrichment cannot be satisfied because, unless property has passed, the defendant gains, and the plaintiff loses, nothing.[126] That proposition is debatable. As a practical matter, the plaintiff certainly is interested in title, but her more immediate concern, as she walks to work, pertains to the enjoyment of the vehicle. The value of a car consists largely in its use. Moreover, as a matter of precedent, the existence of an enrichment does not invariably depend upon proof that the defendant received title to something. That proposition is demonstrated by every case in which restitution is awarded for services. There is no reason why a different rule is required merely because property is involved. The better view, therefore, may be that the plaintiff's retention of title does not preclude recognition of an enrichment.[127]

III. RELATED ISSUES

The primary purpose of this article is to demonstrate that the concept of enrichment is best understood as a function of the defendant's freedom of choice. That exercise is important in itself. It provides a coherent explanation for the first element of the action in unjust enrichment and, in doing so, offers resolutions for several long-standing, enrichment-related debates. Significantly, however, recognition of the true essence of enrichment also affects a number of other issues. The remainder of this article briefly explores three such issues: (i) the nature of the defence of change of position, (ii) the quantification of restitution, and (iii) the defendant's role in the reason for restitution.

A. Change of Position

If the plaintiff establishes the three elements of unjust enrichment, she prima facie is entitled to restitution. The defendant nevertheless may be able to

[125] Likewise, for instance, if the plaintiff paid money pursuant to a fundamental mistake that prevented property from passing to the defendant.
[126] W Swadling, 'A Claim in Restitution?' [1998] *LMCLQ* 63; Grantham and Rickett (above n 3) 61–63; cf RB Grantham and CEF Rickett 'Restitution, Property and Ignorance—A Reply to Mr Swadling' [1998] *LMCLQ* 463 (accepting that the defendant is enriched but arguing that the claim in unjust enrichment is subverted to a claim in property).
[127] Birks (above n 12) 654; A Burrows, 'Proprietary Restitution: Unmasking Unjust Enrichment' (2001) 117 *LQR* 412, 419; M McInnes, 'Restitution, Unjust Enrichment and the Perfect Quadration Thesis' [1999] *Restitution Law Review* 118, 123–27.

avoid liability by successfully pleading a defence. Change of position is by far the most important possibility.

Change of position traditionally was relevant only as an element of estoppel. The defendant was required to prove that he experienced a detrimental change of position as a result of relying in good faith upon the plaintiff's representation of the validity of the enrichment. That defence was both under-inclusive and over-inclusive. Unless he could attribute his change of position to the plaintiff's representation, the defendant was held liable for the full value of his initial enrichment, even if he honestly evacuated all or most of that gain (eg by irretrievably paying it to a charity[128]). In contrast, if he was able to establish the elements of estoppel, he was relieved of all responsibility, even if the detrimental reliance affected only part of his enrichment.[129]

Given the clumsiness of the estoppel defence, it was inevitable that change of position would emerge as an independent plea, stripped of the need for a causative representation and effective *pro tanto*.[130] That development nevertheless was a long time coming. The House of Lords waited until 1991[131] and the High Court of Australia a year later.[132] In that sense, at least, the Supreme Court of Canada was unusually advanced. In 1975, Martland J held in *Rural Municipality of Storthoaks v Mobil Oil Canada Ltd* that the defendant will be relieved of liability to the extent that he in good faith 'materially changed [his] circumstances as a result of the receipt of the [benefit].'[133] Unfortunately, the law has not developed much further since. A number of issues are outstanding.[134] Most significantly, the precise basis of the defence remains open to debate.

Generally speaking, there are two possibilities. According to the first, a change of position is relevant insofar as it demonstrates that, notwithstanding the plaintiff's prima facie claim, the defendant's enrichment was not

[128] *Baylis v Bishop of London* [1913] 1 Ch 127 (CA).

[129] *Avon County Council v Howlett* [1983] 1 All ER 1073 (CA); cf *National Westminster Bank plc v Somer Intl* [2002] 1 All ER 198 (CA) (allowing estoppel to operate *pro tanto*).

[130] It is unclear if the defence of estoppel has survived the emergence of the independent plea of change of position. Although a number of lower courts have suggested that the newer defence displaces the older one (*RBC Dominion Securities Inc* (n 91) 237; *Empire Life Insurance Co v Neufeld Estate* (1998) 4 CCLI (3d) 278 (BC SC)), the Supreme Court of Canada has left the issue open: *Kenora Hydro Electric Commission v Vacationland Dairy Co-operative* [1994] 1 SCR 80; 110 DLR (4th) 449 (SCC). The English Court of Appeal has declined the invitation to abolish the defence of estoppel: *Scottish Equitable plc v Derby* [2001] 3 All ER 818; *National Westminster Bank plc* (above n 129).

[131] *Lipkin Gorman (a firm) v Karpnale Ltd* [1991] 2 AC 548 (HL).

[132] *David Securities Pty Ltd v Commonwealth Bank of Australia* (1992) 175 CLR 353 (HCA).

[133] (1975) 55 DLR (3d) 1,13.

[134] For instance, it has yet to be determined whether the defence can be based on an *anticipatory* change of position, as when the defendant incurs an exceptional expenditure in reliance upon an enrichment that he correctly predicted he would receive in the future. The Privy Council recently answered that question in the affirmative: *Dextra Bank & Trust Co v Bank of Jamaica* [2002] 1 All ER (Comm) 193, noted in McInnes, 'Enrichments, Expenses and Restitutionary Defences' (above n 21).

truly *unjust*. The defence operates as a flexible instrument of fairness. There is some support for that view. In *Storthoaks* itself, Martland J held that the defendant 'may defend himself by everything which shows that the plaintiff *ex aequeo et bono* is not entitled to the whole of his demand,'[135] and suggested, as one instance of that principle, that it would be 'inequitable' to require restitution of an enrichment upon which the recipient detrimentally relied. As similar view was expressed in *RBC Dominion Securities Inc v Dawson*. After receiving a mistaken payment from the plaintiff, the defendant incurred a number of exceptional expenditures, including the purchase of a chesterfield that she otherwise would not have acquired. While holding that she continued to be 'enriched' by the retention of the furniture that 'replace[d] the money,' the court relieved her of responsibility for that benefit on the broad basis that 'Equity [was in her] favour.'[136]

That approach should be rejected for at least two reasons. The first is uncertainty. Conceived as an injustice-related defence, change of position entails a broad judicial discretion to determine, having regard to all of the circumstances of the individual case, the extent to which it would be 'fair' and 'equitable' to hold the defendant liable. Litigation, on that view, becomes something of a lottery. Because different judges inevitably 'balance the equities' differently, results are inherently unpredictable. Unjust enrichment slides into the sort of 'well-meaning sloppiness of thought'[137] that historically inhibited its development. That danger finds ample expression in New Zealand, where a statutory formulation of the defence allows the defendant to escape liability if 'in the opinion of the Court, having regard to all possible implications ... it is inequitable to grant relief.'[138] So too in those Canadian cases in which judges have attempted to assess the parties' relative 'equities.'[139] Significantly, the lesson of those experiences recently led the Privy Council to repudiate the first conception of change of position, which Lord Goff castigated as 'hopelessly unstable.'[140]

More importantly for present purposes, the injustice-related view of the defence should also be rejected on the ground that it fails to carry through,

[135] Above (n 133) 14, quoting *Moses v Macferlan* (1760) 2 Burr 1005, 1010, 97 ER 676, 679. Martland J also relied upon the *Restatement of the Law of Restitution, Quasi-Contracts and Constructive Trusts* (St Paul, American Law Institute 1937) § 142(1) ('The right of a person to restitution from another because of a benefit received is terminated or diminished if, after the receipt of the benefit, circumstances have so changed that it would be inequitable to require the other to make full restitution.').

[136] Above (n 91) 239. See also *AJ Severnsen Inc v Village of Qualicum Beach* (1982) 135 DLR (3d) 122 (BC CA).

[137] *Holt v Markham* [1923] 1 KB 504 (CA) 531.

[138] *Judicature Act 1908* s 94B. See *Thomas v Houston Corbett & Co* [1969] NZLR 151 (CA); *National Bank of New Zealand Ltd v Waitaki International Processing (NI) Ltd* [1999] NZLR 211 (CA); RB Grantham and CEF Rickett 'Change of Position and Balancing the Equities' [1999] *Restitution Law Review* 158.

[139] *Durand v Highwood Golf & Country Club* (1998) 240 AR 320 (Prov Ct).

[140] *Dextra Bank & Trust Co* (above n 134).

in a principled manner, with the promise of autonomy. The element of enrichment protects the defendant's freedom of choice in connection with the *initial receipt* of a benefit. The plaintiff's prima facie right to restitution requires proof that the defendant either chose to assume the risk of financial responsibility, or had no choice to make. That protection will be largely illusory, however, unless it can extend to *subsequent events*. As always, the central concern is that liability may improperly override choice. And from a practical perspective, that concern is most pronounced at the time of trial, rather than the time of enrichment. The defendant is really only interested in the question of liability to the extent that it ultimately translates into a judgment. Consequently, he requires assurance that he will be held responsible only to the extent that: (i) he acquired a benefit that was a reflection of his autonomy, *and* (ii) he did not experience a causally-connected involuntary dis-enrichment. That assurance is most effectively provided through the alternative conception of change of position. The defence should operate not by denying the defendant's *unjust* enrichment, but rather by denying his unjust *enrichment*.

Though perhaps obscure when stated in the abstract, those propositions can be easily illustrated through a simple example. The defendant owned shares in the plaintiff company. Due to a clerical error, the company mistakenly paid a dividend of $10,000. In the honest belief that he was entitled to retain that money, he incurred four expenditures. The first two would not have occurred but for the receipt of the dividend. The defendant spent $4000 on a party for his friends and $3000 on a computer. He also spent $2000 on a trip to Edmonton that he previously intended to purchase with other resources. Finally, after learning of the plaintiff's error, the defendant spent the remaining $1000 on a weekend spa that he would not have considered but for the fact that he received the mistaken payment.[141]

At the time of payment, the plaintiff was entitled to recover $10,000. Since money is an incontrovertible benefit, the defendant undeniably was enriched in that amount. And since, if he had known of the plaintiff's claim, he could have achieved restitution by returning his enrichment *in specie* (or, because of the fungibility of money, by handing over notes of the same value), the defendant could not have complained that liability would infringe his freedom of choice.

That situation, however, subsequently changed. While the party may have given the plaintiff a great deal of pleasure, it did not leave anything with which he could satisfy judgment. Liability for the full amount of the initial enrichment consequently would be unfair. It would intolerably override his

[141] It is assumed, for the sake of simplicity, that the defendant paid for the various expenses with the *same* money that he received from the plaintiff. The analysis would be no different, however, if he used other resources for those purposes and retained possession of his initial enrichment *in specie*. Change of position is not concerned with tracing property, but rather with the evacuation of value.

freedom of choice. Granted, when spending the $4000, the defendant acted voluntarily in a narrow sense. He knew that he was trading *those* bills for *that* party. But on a more significant level, his apparent intention was vitiated by his erroneous belief in the validity of the plaintiff's payment. He was willing to blow part of his enrichment on a party *precisely because* he thought that the dividend represented a legitimate windfall. On that view, as compared with his pre-enrichment position, the expenditure did not leave him worse off. Significantly, however, the defendant never chose to assume financial responsibility for the party in the belief that he thereby would be required to deplete his own pre-existing resources. If he had been told, the moment before incurring the expense, that he was about to create a situation that would entail: (i) repayment of $10,000 to the plaintiff, *and* (ii) payment of $4000 on a party, he would have canceled the event and sent his friends home. It therefore follows, as a function of the law's concern for autonomy, that liability must be reduced by at least $4000.[142]

The analysis is more complicated with respect to the computer that the defendant bought before learning of the plaintiff's claim. As with the party, he will argue that he did not truly assume financial responsibility for the expense. His apparent intention was vitiated by his error. The purchase occurred only because he believed that he was entitled to retain the apparent windfall. The two expenditures nevertheless are distinguishable. The money spent on the party is irretrievably gone. The computer, in contrast, continues to represent something of value. It falls under the second branch of incontrovertible benefit.

If the defendant has *actually realized* a financial gain by re-selling the computer, he certainly should be held liable. He once again would be in possession of money, which, as always, is immune to subjective devaluation.[143] The answer is less clear, however, if the computer merely represents a *realizable* financial gain. Is the defendant's freedom of choice sufficiently respected by the fact that he *could*, through re-sale, generate funds with which to satisfy judgment? Just as that question has split the courts when raised in connection with the recognition of a prima facie enrichment, so too it has divided opinion when asked in connection with change of position. Although the issue has never been properly analyzed, defendants

[142] As a matter of integrity, the plaintiff must accede to that argument. As discussed below (Section III(C)(i)), the plaintiff's claim in unjust enrichment is based on the assertion that it should not be held liable for the consequences of *its own* mistake. The prima facie right to restitution arose because the original payment was not truly a function of free choice. But by the same token, the plaintiff must be prepared to relieve the defendant of responsibility for the consequences of *his* mistake.

[143] Of course, the defendant generally should be held liable only for the price realized upon re-sale (eg $2500) even though the computer initially cost more (ie $3000). The analysis would be different, however, if, after learning of the plaintiff's claim, the defendant intentionally sold it for less than market value (eg $2000 instead of $2500). In that case, he could be held responsible for his own decision to sell at a discount.

sometimes are,[144] and sometimes are not,[145] held responsible for the retention of realizable financial benefits. The latter position is difficult to defend. It may be appropriate to deny liability if the plaintiff provides services that enhance the value of an asset already in the defendant's possession. The defendant can forcefully argue that he should not be forced to sell pre-existing property. The situation is much different, however, if the defendant, having received money from the plaintiff, incurred an exceptional expense by purchasing an asset. The notion of freedom of choice is much attenuated. At worst, the defendant will be required to satisfy judgment by selling an asset that he never would have acquired but for his unjust enrichment.

The proper treatment of the $2000 spent on the trip to Edmonton is simpler. The defendant once again will attempt to draw an analogy to the party. And indeed, there are important parallels. In each instance, the defendant acted in good faith, and in each instance, he is left with nothing from which he can satisfy judgment. Nevertheless, while change of position applies with respect to the party, it must fail with respect to the trip. The core issue, as always, is freedom of choice. And whereas the defendant would not have thrown the party if he had known of the plaintiff's claim, he intended to visit Edmonton in any event. Liability for the $2000 accordingly is consistent with his autonomy. He expected to pay for the trip with pre-existing resources. He instead used the money received from the plaintiff. He therefore can re-direct his pre-existing resources toward judgment. Restitution leaves him none the worse for wear.

Finally, even though the remaining $1000 was spent: (i) in a way that left behind nothing of value, and (ii) on an expenditure that would not have arisen but for the initial enrichment, the defendant cannot plead change of position with respect to the spa weekend. Since he incurred that expense *after* he learned of the plaintiff's mistake, a court will hold that he did not act in *good faith*. More to the point, he is liable because he freely chose to assume financial responsibility for the expense. He knew, at the operative moment, that the cost of the spa would have to come from his own pocket.

B. Quantification of Restitution

Restitution is the only principled response to unjust enrichment. The cause of action requires proof of an enrichment, a corresponding deprivation and an unjust factor. The defendant received from the plaintiff something that he should not be allowed to keep. He therefore must give *it* back to her.

[144] *Sullivan v Lee* (1994) 95 BCLR (2d) 195 (BC SC); *Empire Life Insurance Co* (above n 130); *Lipkin Gorman* (above n 131) 560.
[145] *RBC Dominion Securities Inc* (above n 91).

Stated in the abstract, that proposition is relatively uncontroversial. Its application, however, occasionally creates difficulty.

The problem begins with a basic question: precisely what is 'it' that the defendant must return to the plaintiff? The answer, only rarely, is the very thing that he acquired from her. Proprietary restitution is the exception rather than the rule, even if the defendant received and retained something that he could restore *in specie*.[146] Instead, the defendant almost always is required to give back the *value* of his enrichment. Liability, in other words, entails a personal obligation to pay money.

The amount of that monetary obligation must accurately reflect the elements of the underlying action.[147] Because of the need for a corresponding deprivation, the plaintiff cannot recover more than she actually lost, regardless of the size of the defendant's gain.[148] More importantly for present purposes, regardless of the size of the plaintiff's loss, the defendant cannot be held responsible for more than he actually gained. And significantly, the gain that informs the quantification of relief must be the same gain that constitutes the operative enrichment. The law's concern for the defendant's autonomy must run throughout the unjust enrichment analysis. It would be futile to safeguard his freedom of choice when examining the threshold issue of liability, only to ignore it when calculating relief. Consequently, while objective market value may provide a point of departure, the final figure must reflect the notion of subjective devaluation and the means by which the plaintiff satisfied the defendant's freedom of choice. That proposition sometimes is overlooked. The offending cases can be divided into three groups.

(i) No Enrichment

In the first type of case, the defendant is held liable to return the objective value of his gain even though he did not truly receive *any* enrichment. *Estok v Heguy*[149] is illustrative. The parties attempted to create an agreement for the sale of the defendant's land. In the honest belief that he had become the owner, the plaintiff deposited a 'substantial amount of manure' on the property, thereby changing 'pasture to crop bearing soil.' The purported contract was then struck down for lack of *consensus ad idem*. The plaintiff claimed restitution and won.

The court's error consisted of equating objective benefit with legal enrichment. Although the market value of the land had been enhanced by the addition of the fertilizer, the plaintiff could not properly overcome the

[146] That is never the case, for instance, when an enrichment takes the form of services.
[147] McInnes (above n 16).
[148] That point is most clearly recognized in Canada: above (n 21).
[149] (1963) 40 DLR (2d) 88 (BC SC). See also *T & E Development Ltd v Hoornaert* (1977) 78 DLR (3d) 607 (BC SC).

defendant's plea of subjective devaluation. The owner had neither requested the manure, nor freely accepted it with knowledge that payment was expected. Both parties believed that the plaintiff was acting entirely on his own behalf. Nor did the defendant receive an incontrovertible benefit. The manure did not represent a necessary expense. Given that he used the land for pasture, the defendant was 'satisfied with the previous tilth.' Furthermore, the defendant had not actually realized a financial gain from the plaintiff's work by selling the land in its improved state for an increased price. And finally, even if an enrichment can be recognized on the basis of a realizable financial gain (which is a dubious proposition in the context of land[150]), there is nothing in the reported decision to suggest that the defendant still intended to sell the property *and* would be able to do so while the fertilizer continued to constitute a saleable improvement. As a result, the court's decision was unfairly one-sided. It fully respected the plaintiff's freedom of choice by allowing him to recover the value of a mistakenly conferred benefit. But at the same time, it entirely ignored the defendant's autonomy by holding him responsible despite his total lack of volition.

(ii) Extent of Enrichment

In the second type of case, the court calculates restitution by reference to the *full* objective value of a benefit even though the plaintiff only *partially* overcame the defendant's plea of subjective devaluation. That error may arise in a number of ways. Some involve incontrovertible benefits. The plaintiff may have discharged a necessary expense, but only by incurring greater costs than the defendant would have incurred achieving the same result. Or the plaintiff may have performed services that improved property, but only by spending more money than the defendant could realize by selling the item in its enhanced state.

Typically, however, the operative error arises in connection with requested (or freely accepted) services.[151] The paradigm case begins with a contract. The bargain is a bad one from the plaintiff's perspective insofar as she has agreed to provide services at a price below market value. She nevertheless proceeds with performance. Before the project is completed, however, the defendant commits a breach that allows the plaintiff to discharge the agreement. She now enjoys an option.[152] She could claim compensation for breach of contract, but if she did so, her measure of relief would be

[150] Above (n 116).

[151] McInnes (above n 16) 210–18; M McInnes, 'Contractual Services, Restitution and the Avoidance of Bad Bargains' (1995) 23 *Australian Business Law Review* 218; N Rafferty, 'Contracts Discharged Through Breach: Restitution for Services Rendered by the Innocent Party' (1999) 37 *Alberta Law Review* 51; Skelton (above n 4).

[152] Waddams (above n 98) ch 16; *Komorowski v Van Weel* (1993) 12 OR (3d) 444 (Gen Div).

capped by the terms of the contract. That would be true whether she sought expectation damages or reliance damages.[153] She therefore pleads unjust enrichment: (i) the defendant was enriched by the receipt of requested services, (ii) she suffered the corresponding deprivation because she performed the work, and (iii) her intention was impaired insofar as she intended for him to retain that benefit only if he fulfilled his side of the contract. Remarkably, she can thereby avoid the consequences of her bad bargain. The leading cases, both in Canada[154] and abroad,[155] indicate that restitution will be calculated on the basis of true market value and without regard to the terms of the parties' dealings.

The problem once again stems from the judicial tendency to confuse objective benefits with legal enrichments. As a general rule, the defendant should not be held liable for more than a *pro rata* share of the total contract price. There is, of course, no question of enforcing the contractual terms *per se*. By committing a serious breach, the defendant lost the right to insist upon the protection of the contract. Nevertheless, in the context of the restitutionary claim, he should enjoy the protection normally offered by the principle of unjust enrichment. More specifically, he should be entitled to turn to the plaintiff and say, 'it is not your job to make my choices.'[156] And as always, the plaintiff should be required to overcome that plea of subjective devaluation by demonstrating that the defendant chose to assume financial responsibility for his benefit or in the circumstances had no choice to make.

At a threshold level, the plaintiff can discharge that burden by simply pointing to the defendant's (contractual) request. In the circumstances, that request obviously imports both a desire to receive a benefit and a decision to pay for it. Significantly, however, it also contains an inherent limitation. The defendant chose to have the benefit at the contractual rate; he did not choose to have it at market value. Accordingly, whether the plaintiff pleads unjust enrichment or breach of contract, the defendant should be entitled

[153] *Bowlay Logging Ltd v Domtar Ltd* (1982) 135 DLR (3d) 179 (BC CA).

[154] *McElheran* (above n 50) 122 ('[I]n the event of repudiation the innocent party may sue for damages or claim *quantum meruit* for the value of the services rendered prior to repudiation. This may result, in the case of an unprofitable bargain, in higher recovery under a *quantum meruit* basis for part performance that what would have been paid for complete performance.'); *Lindsay v Sutton* [1947] OWN 951 (HCJ); *Van Wezel v Risdon* [1952] 7 WWR 646 (Alta SC) 659; *O'Brien v Buffalo Narrows Airways Ltd* (1998) 171 Sask R 217 (QB).

[155] *Slowey v Lodder* (1901) 20 NZLR 321 (CA), aff'd [1904] AC 442 (PC); *DeBenardy v Harding* (1853) 8 Exch 822 (Exch); *Brooks Robinson Pty Ltd v Rothfield* [1951] VLR 405; *Renard Constructions (ME) v Minister for Public Works* (1992) 26 NSWLR 234 (CA); *Iezzi Constructions Pty Ltd v Watkins Pacific (Qld) Pty Ltd* (1995) 2 Qd R 350 (CA); *Rover International Ltd v Cannons Film Sales Ltd* [1989] 1 WLR 912 (CA) (restitutionary relief not limited by terms of void contract); *Boomer v Muir* 24 P 2d 570 (Cal App 1933); *United States v Zara Contracting Co* 146 F 2d 606 (2d Cir CA 1944); *Re Montgomery's Estate* 6 NE 2d 40 (NY CA 1936).

[156] *Magical Waters Fountain Ltd* (above n 45) 691.

to rely upon the choice that he expressed through the terms of the discharged agreement.[157] In the context of the restitutionary claim, he should, notwithstanding his request, be entitled to subjectively devalue his benefit down to the *pro rata* contractual price.

The analysis is different, however, if an enrichment is established not by a request (or free acceptance), but rather by an incontrovertible benefit. In the former situation, the plaintiff overcomes subjective devaluation by relying upon the defendant's own conduct — ie his contractual expression of a choice. Restitution therefore must be calculated by reference to the terms of the discharged agreement. There is no other ground upon which the defendant can be held responsible. An incontrovertible benefit, in contrast, is based not upon the defendant's conduct, but rather upon the nature of the benefit itself. It is 'demonstrably apparent and not subject to debate or conjecture.' It 'exists when freedom of choice as a problem is absent.'[158] Consequently, the defendant's preferences, as disclosed by the terms of the discharged agreement, are irrelevant. His enrichment should be measured by reference to the market value of the benefit itself.[159] That is true if the incontrovertible benefit arose from the realization of a financial gain. Regardless of what he expected to pay for the plaintiff's services, the defendant cannot subjectively devalue the receipt of money. $100 is worth $100, even if it is the product of a service for which the recipient expected to pay $60. Likewise if the incontrovertible benefit arose from the discharge of a necessary expense.[160] Unless he can prove that he otherwise would have satisfied the obligation at a discount (eg by persuading a third party to enter into the same bad bargain as the plaintiff), the defendant cannot deny the full market value of the plaintiff's services. $100 worth of services is worth $100, even if the recipient contractually expected to receive them for $60.

[157] As it sometimes is said, relief should be subject to a 'contractual ceiling' if the plaintiff pleads breach of contract and to a 'valuation ceiling' if she pleads unjust enrichment: A Burrows, 'Free Acceptance and the Law of Restitution' (1988) 104 *LQR* 576, 587–88; P Birks, 'Restitution After Ineffective Contracts: Issue for the 1990s' (1990) 2 *Journal of Contract Law* 227, 230–33; Birks (above n 35) 135–37.
[158] *Peel* (above n 15) 159.
[159] The paradigm case occurs when the plaintiff provides the defendant with money, rather than services. In such circumstances, restitution is measured by the full market value of the gain, even if the defendant contractually expected to receive the money in exchange for something of lesser value: *Bush v Canfield* 2 Conn 485 (CA 1818); *Jay Trading Corp v Ifax Export & Import Ltd* [1954] 2 DLR 110 (NS SC); *Wilkinson v Lloyd* (1845) 7 QB 27.
[160] There is need for caution on that point. Maddaugh and McCamus (above n 3) 429 (emphasis added), argue in favour of a general presumption that the defendant 'wanted or *needed*' contractually requested services, such that if he had not extracted unusually favorable terms from the plaintiff, he 'would have been *obliged* to [pay] the market price under a less profitable arrangement with someone else.' On that view, the provision of contractual services prima facie always constitutes an incontrovertible benefit. That proposition should be rejected on a number of grounds: McInnes (above n 16) 217–18. Most significantly, it intolerably overrides the defendant's freedom of choice. Necessity is but one reason for entering into a contract. Most agreements surely are a function of choices, not needs.

(iii) Wrong Measure of Relief

The preceding categories involved errors of application. The courts tried to award restitution, but mis-calculated the amount of the defendant's obligation. The final category involves a more fundamental error. The courts occasionally intend to respond to the action in unjust enrichment with something other than restitution.

That problem unfortunately is obscured by two factors. The first is semantic. Judges often use 'compensation,' 'restitution' and 'disgorgement' loosely and even synonymously,[161] rather than as distinct terms of art. On those occasions, it may be difficult to know exactly what they had in mind. Second, a single award may have more than one effect. For instance, because it involves the restoration of a benefit, true restitution inevitably contains elements of both compensation (insofar as the plaintiff receives reparation for her loss) and disgorgement (insofar as the defendant is required to give up his gain). In light of those considerations, it is important to classify remedies not on the basis of judicial language, nor on the basis of incidental effects, but rather on the basis of intended *purpose*. What goal did the court have in mind when issuing a particular order? Was it trying to repair a loss (ie compensation)? Reverse an unjustified transfer of wealth (ie restitution)? Strip an ill-gotten gain (ie disgorgement)? Or something else (eg punish the defendant)?[162]

To reiterate, restitution is the only coherent response to unjust enrichment. Although that proposition is a function of the principle as a whole, it is possible for present purposes to focus the issue more narrowly on the element of enrichment. The gist of the plaintiff's action is that she provided the defendant with a benefit that he cannot retain. In itself, the fact that the plaintiff unjustifiably suffered a loss may be unfortunate, but it does not provide any reason as to why the defendant, as opposed to someone else, should be required to provide relief. The defendant is brought into the juridical relationship only by reason of his corresponding enrichment. That benefit explains both why, and the extent to which, he can be held responsible.

Against that backdrop, it is relatively easy to recognize the error that persistently occurs under the rubric of 'restitution' in the family law context.

[161] 'Compensation' meaning restitution: *Peter* (above n 15) 633, 634, 636, 649, 650. 'Restitution' meaning compensation: *Canson Enterprises Ltd v Boughton & Co* [1991] 3 SCR 534; 85 DLR (4th) 129, 137–38, 141, 145, 157–59 (SCC). 'Restitution' meaning disgorgement: *Lac Minerals Ltd v International Corona Resources* [1989] 2 SCR 574, 616; 61 DLR (4th) 14, 76 (SCC). 'Disgorgement' meaning restitution: *Air Canada v Ontario (Liquor Control Board)* [1997] 2 SCR 581,600; 148 DLR (4th) 193, 213 (SCC).

[162] In *Air Canada*, both the Ontario Court of Appeal and the Supreme Court of Canada suggested in *dicta* that punitive damages may be available under the action in unjust enrichment: (above n 161), aff'g (1995) 126 DLR (4th) 301.

The issue has been explored in detail elsewhere[163] and therefore need merely be outlined. The facts follow an established pattern.[164] A couple cohabitates for many years. Although both work hard, the woman's contribution leaves no traceable product. She devotes substantial labour to the operation of the family home and possibly meager earnings to transitory benefits like groceries and heating. The man, in contrast, focuses on outside employment and, moreover, uses that income to purchase lasting benefits. Title to all of the significant assets (eg the house and the car) are taken in his name alone. Consequently, when the relationship eventually breaks down, there is an intolerable disparity in terms of financial well-being. She is destitute, while he enjoys the fruits of their joint efforts. The judicial instinct to re-distribute the property along more equitable lines is irresistible. It merely requires an appropriate vehicle.

Although the underlying problem is common to all cultures, different jurisdictions have addressed it through different techniques.[165] Leaving aside legislative interventions, Canadian law has, since 1980,[166] employed the action in unjust enrichment. Superficially, at least, it seems a natural fit. As a result of the cohabitational relationship: (i) the defendant received a substantial benefit, (ii) the plaintiff suffered a corresponding deprivation, and (iii) there is a reason to reverse that transfer of wealth insofar as he knew (or should have known) that she expected recompense for her contribution.

There nevertheless remain remedial difficulties. Restitution cannot do what needs to be done. It inevitably involves a restoration of the *status quo ante*. The defendant must simply give *back* to the plaintiff what he received from her—nothing more. Such relief is entirely acceptable in a commercial context and even in a non-intimate family setting.[167] It borders on the offensive, however, if used to redress the aftermath of a cohabitational breakdown. The plaintiff did not enter into her relationship with the defendant with a view to being treated as hired help. To the contrary, both parties presumably believed that they were creating a unique form of lifelong partnership in which benefits and burdens would be shared equally. Their shared focus was on the future, not the past. Accordingly, while the question is usually avoided at the outset in the interest of harmonious relations, if the parties had been asked how their accumulated wealth should be distributed in the event of separation, they very likely would have agreed on a roughly equal split.

[163] McInnes (above n 16) 204–10.

[164] See *Pettkus* (above n 29); *Peter* (above n 15).

[165] J Mee, *The Property Rights of Cohabitees: An Analysis of Equity's Response in Five Common Law Jurisdictions* (Oxford, Hart Publishing, 1999).

[166] *Pettkus* (above n 29).

[167] *Deglman* (above n 28) (although the nephew expected to receive his aunt's house in exchange for his domestic services, his remedy was limited to the market value of his services).

Given the nature of the underlying relationship, the most appropriate remedy in such circumstances is one that fulfills mutual expectations. Both parties contributed to the venture on the unspoken assumption that, if the situation fell apart, they would share equally. If, upon dissolution, they cannot amicably implement that outcome, then the law should do so on their behalf. And, in fact, that typically is the response that Canadian courts provide in the name of 'restitution.'[168] In a particularly candid judgment, Cory J conceded that the goal in the family context was not to 'closely scrutinize the contributions made by each party,' but rather to 'achieve a fair result,' having regard to 'common sense,' 'the nature of the relationship' and especially the parties' expectations.[169]

Significantly, however, whether that species of expectation relief is conceived as a form of prospective compensation (as in contract) or as something *sui generis*, it is *not* restitution. The defendant cannot satisfy his obligation by merely putting the plaintiff *back* into the condition that she enjoyed before the relationship began. He must instead move her *forward* to the position that she expected to enjoy after the breakup. As a result, he may be held liable for an amount that exceeds the value of his gain.[170]

[168] Not infrequently, Canadian courts employ a third approach in which relief is awarded pursuant to a seemingly unfettered discretion. The goal is not to effect restitution, nor even to fulfil expectations, but rather to simply do justice, as perceived on the particular facts of the case: *Nowell v Town Estate* (1997) 35 OR (3d) 415 (CA). The effect is wholly unprincipled and 'well nigh unrecognizable' as a function of unjust enrichment: *Hubar v Jobling* (2000) 195 DLR (4th) 123 (BC CA)135 (Southin JA).

[169] *Peter* (above n 15) 639–40. The judicial inclination to award relief in proprietary form further reinforces the tendency to fulfil expectations. The imposition of a constructive trust is premised upon a number of factors, including the plaintiff's reasonable expectation that she would receive an interest in the defendant's property: *Peter* (above n 15) 637, 652; *Sorochan* (above n 70) 12. In the circumstances, the distinction between the appropriate 'quantum of recovery (strictly no more than the gain at the plaintiff's expense) and the [proprietary] mode of recovery' is 'too delicate ... for forensic realities': 'Proprietary Rights as Remedies' in P Birks (ed), *The Frontiers of Liability* vol 2 (Oxford, Oxford University Press 1994) 214, 222.

[170] In the context of the action in unjust enrichment, the best defence of expectation relief might lie along the following lines. The essence of enrichment is the defendant's freedom of choice. He can be held liable only if, and to the extent that, he assumed financial responsibility. He can exercise his autonomy by requesting or freely accepting services with knowledge of the plaintiff's expectation of payment. Furthermore, as a result of the concept of *subjective overvaluation* (discussed above at Section II(C)(i)(f)), he may assume financial responsibility in an amount that exceeds the objective value of his benefit. Consequently, in a cohabitational case, the defendant may assume responsibility for the fulfilment of the plaintiff's expectation, even if satisfaction of that expectation involves something in excess of market value.

There are, however, a number of problems with that analysis. (1) Leaving aside the family law decisions for which an explanation is being sought, it does not appear that any cases have actually been decided on the basis of subjective overvaluation. Support for that concept is theoretical, rather than precedential. (2) Even if they accept the general viability of subjective overvaluation, the courts might refuse on practical grounds to apply that concept where the defendant's valuation is not assessed by reference to something relatively specific and hence manageable (eg current market value of similar services, cost of the plaintiff's performance), but rather by reference to a relatively open-ended exercise to be conducted many years after

Restitution is limited to 'tangible' benefits.[171] The expectation that arises in a cohabitational relationship, in contrast, is the accumulated product of both tangible contributions (eg money and household services) and intangible contributions (eg love and commitment). Its value consequently tends to be greater than the former factor alone.[172]

C. The Reason for Restitution

The final issue for consideration pertains to the defendant's role in the reason for restitution. The essence of the argument can be stated briefly. To reiterate,

the provision of the services (ie division of such assets and liabilities as may exist if the parties' cohabitational relationship eventually dissolves). (3) Most significantly, even if the concept of subjective overvaluation allows the court to conclude that the defendant's enrichment is equal to the value of the plaintiff's expectation, restitution must still be capped by the value of the plaintiff's corresponding deprivation. The defendant cannot be held liable for more than he was enriched, but neither can the plaintiff recover more than she actually lost. And whereas the legal notion of enrichment reflects objective values as mediated by the defendant's autonomy, the element of deprivation is exclusively objective. The role of the second element of unjust enrichment is not to protect the plaintiff's freedom of choice, but rather more simply to identify the source of the defendant's gain. Consequently, the plaintiff cannot enhance her position by arguing that she chose to feel deprived by an amount that exceeds market value. Moreover, given the need for 'tangible' gains and losses (*Peel* (above n 15) 155), she cannot, for the purposes of unjust enrichment, feel deprived at all with respect to contributions like love and affection.

171 *Peel* (above n 15) 155.

172 A good example is provided by *Peter* (above n 15). The plaintiff, who was virtually penniless, moved into the defendant's house, along with her four children and his two children. Over the next twelve years, she cared for the extended family, tended to the property and occasionally worked outside the house as a cook. The defendant worked in the construction industry and was frequently absent from home. Both parties contributed to the purchase of groceries and household supplies, but the defendant paid the vast majority of the expenses. He also paid off the remainder of his mortgage within two years. On the basis of her meagre outside income, the plaintiff was able to purchase another small property. When the relationship eventually broke down, the defendant retired on a war veteran's pension and moved into a houseboat. At that point, he still held exclusive title to the cohabitational property.

The plaintiff sued in unjust enrichment. The Supreme Court of Canada responded by imposing a constructive trust that gave her sole beneficial ownership of the home. That remedy may be explicable as fulfillment of the parties' expectations. It is possible, given the very significant 'intangible' benefits that the plaintiff brought to the relationship, that the parties, if asked in a timely way, would have agreed upon such a result. Nevertheless, that remedy clearly exceeded the value of the defendant's actual enrichment. Since the court was willing to off-set enrichments (eg by crediting the defendant for having provided food and shelter to the plaintiff and her children), the claimant should have been limited under the action in unjust enrichment to the amount by which the defendant's enrichment was greater than her own. And in that regard, it is almost inconceivable that the plaintiff's restitutionary entitlement could equal the value of the house. Regardless of how hard she works, a single woman with four children, minimal savings and marginal job skills cannot normally acquire clear title to two residential properties in little more than a decade. That is precisely why the division of cohabitational property is such a powerful feminist issue.

the great danger of unjust enrichment is too much restitution—liability may intolerably infringe the defendant's freedom of choice. There are two principal strategies for containing that danger. The first involves the element of enrichment. The defendant is placed at risk only if he chose to assume financial responsibility for his benefit, or had no choice to make given the very nature of that gain. The second strategy involves the reason for restitution. The defendant can be held liable only if he caused, or somehow was complicit in, the events that led the plaintiff to confer the enrichment.

The first approach is preferable insofar as it more sensitively addresses the core concern. There is, however, an even more fundamental point: as a general rule, the law must select one strategy *or* the other. Protecting the defendant's autonomy at both the first *and* third stages of the action in unjust enrichment is worse than redundant. It inevitably leads to decisions in which worthy claimants unnecessarily are denied relief. Consequently, having satisfied the defendant's freedom of choice in connection with the element of enrichment, the plaintiff should not be *required* to do so again in connection with the unjust factor.

(i) Strict Liability

The analysis begins with the fact that liability in unjust enrichment normally is strict.[173] Narrowly construed, that statement means that the reason for reversing a transfer of wealth does not involve the defendant's breach of an obligation.[174] For present purposes, however, the position can be put more broadly. Assuming proof of an enrichment and a corresponding deprivation, the grounds for relief normally proceed without reference to the recipient's participation, acquiescence or knowledge. Most significantly, there is no attempt at the third stage of analysis to safeguard the defendant's autonomy. While volition usually lies at the heart of the unjust factor, it generally is examined only from the plaintiff's perspective. The reason for restitution consists of the fact that, regardless of the nature of the defendant's conduct,

[173] P Birks, 'The Role of Fault in the Law of Unjust Enrichment' in W Swadling and G Jones (eds), *The Search for Principle* (Oxford, Oxford University Press, 1999) 235; McInnes (above n 7).

[174] 'Strict liability' is an ambiguous phrase. As used in tort, for instance, it refers to a situation in which the defendant is held responsible for non-intentionally and non-carelessly committing a wrong. In such circumstances, the defendant's breach of a primary obligation (eg to refrain from converting the plaintiff's property) gives rise to a secondary obligation (eg to pay compensatory damages to the plaintiff). As used in the law of unjust enrichment, however, 'strict liability' refers to a situation in which the defendant is held responsible even though he did not commit any wrong. There is only ever a primary obligation (ie to provide restitution), which the plaintiff enforces directly against the defendant. There is no question of a breach or a secondary obligation.

the plaintiff acted with an impaired intention. Because it takes the notion of choice seriously, the law recognizes the claimant's right to reverse a transfer that was not truly voluntary.

Strict liability is well established in the paradigm case of a mistaken payment. Despite older authorities[175] and occasional lapses to the contrary,[176] it is clear that the cause of action in unjust enrichment is complete once the defendant receives money from the plaintiff.[177] It is irrelevant that he is unaware of his gain or her error.[178] That conclusion is easily reached in a case of mistaken payments because of the nature of the enrichment. Since money is an incontrovertible benefit, the recipient's freedom of choice obviously is never in issue (except insofar as it concerns a defence like change of position). Nevertheless, while more controversial, the same regime should apply whenever the plaintiff demonstrates that she did not truly intend to confer a benefit upon the defendant, even if that benefit consisted of services.[179] Regardless of the precise form of the enrichment, the plaintiff's claim will never reach the third stage analysis unless she already has shown that the defendant received something for which he chose to assume a risk of financial responsibility, or had no choice to make. Consequently, in considering the specific reason for restitution, a court can generally focus on the plaintiff's volition, without regard to the defendant's.

[175] *Royal Bank v The King* [1931] 2 DLR 685 (Man QB) 713 (the defendant is liable for the return of a mistaken payment only if he was 'in some way party to the mistake, either as inducing it, or as responsible for it, or connected with it').

[176] *Pinnacle Bank NA v 1317414 Ontario Inc (cob Jay-B Conversions)* [2002] OJ No 281(CA); *David E Funston Merchandising Ltd v JE Gidney Enterprises Ltd* (1997) 120 Man R (2d) 133 (QB); *Evergreen Spray Service Ltd v Ingram-Cotton* (1995) 17 CCEL (2d) 228 (Alta Prov Ct); *Howe v Laurentian Life of Canada* (1995) 161 NBR (2d) 368 (QB TD). There is an anomalous requirement of fault in the context of the 'knowing receipt' of trust property: discussed below at Section III(C)(iii)(b).

[177] Consequently, limitation periods run (*Michelin Tires (Canada) Ltd v Canada* (2001) 271 NR 183 (FCA)), and interest accrues (*Air Canada* (above n 161) 213), from the time of the defendant's receipt and not from the time that he learns of the plaintiff's claim. It occasionally is suggested that liability arises only once the defendant is aware of his unjust enrichment and refuses to provide restitution: *Roxborough* (above n 21); Smith (above n 7); McBride and McGrath (above n 7) 38; EJ Weinrib, *The Idea of Private Law* (Cambridge, Harvard up, 1995) 134, 141. That position is, however, contrary to precedent and principle: McInnes (above n 16) 188–93; R Grantham 'Restitutionary Recovery: *Ex Æquo et Bono*' [2002] *Singapore Journal of Legal Studies* 388, 398–99.

A slight variation in the analysis occurs if the plaintiff's intention was impaired in the sense of being *qualified*, rather than *vitiated*: discussed below at Section III(C)(ii)(c). In that case, the action in unjust enrichment crystallizes, and the restitutionary obligation arises, only if and when that event fails to materialize.

[178] *Air Canada* (above n 161); *Central Guaranty Trust Co v Dixdale Mortgage Investment Corp* (1994) 121 DLR (4th) 53 (Ont CA).

[179] *Carleton* (above n 87) (restitution available with respect to both money that the plaintiff mistakenly paid and services that it mistakenly rendered in discharge of the defendant's statutory obligation to care for an indigent person).

(ii) The Defendant's Participation — Principled Reasons for Restitution

The fact that restitutionary liability generally is strict does not mean that there is anything inherently wrong with a reason for restitution that implicates the defendant.[180] That point can be demonstrated through four examples.

(a) Fraud and Duress The defendant's conduct or knowledge is sometimes relevant, even when the law technically responds to the plaintiff's impaired intention. That is true, for instance, in a case of fraud or duress. Lack of volition can arise in a variety of ways. The plaintiff may pay money to the defendant because of her own spontaneous mistake. But so too she may confer the enrichment upon him because he tricked her or put a gun to her head. In any event, the essential fact is that her action was not truly a function of her autonomy. Spontaneous mistake, fraud and duress are important primarily from an evidentiary perspective because they explain *why* the plaintiff's intention was vitiated—not because they constitute distinct unjust factors in themselves.[181]

(b) Mental Incapacity In a case of fraud or duress, liability is imposed on the basis of the plaintiff's vitiated intention *even though* the defendant was responsible for that vitiation. The law would have been satisfied with *any* proof of impairment. The plaintiff simply chose to support her claim with evidence of the defendant's misconduct. In other circumstances, however, the law defensibly goes further and *requires* proof of the defendant's participation even if the plaintiff has shown that she did not truly intend to confer an enrichment upon him. That may be true when impairment is a product of mental incapacity. While lack of volition due to infancy is sufficient in itself to trigger relief,[182] the rule is different when involuntariness is attributable to old age. In the latter case, restitution is available only if the defendant had notice of the plaintiff's impairment.[183] Significantly, the purpose of that rule is not to protect the defendant's autonomy, but rather to avoid the infantilization of seniors. A pure rule of strict liability would inhibit people from dealing with the very old, just as they hesitate to deal with the very young.

(c) Qualified Intention It appears that the defendant similarly must be implicated if the plaintiff's intention is impaired in the sense of being qualified

[180] It sometimes is suggested that any element of fault is problematic within the law of unjust enrichment because, at least in theory, breach of an obligation invariably is capable of supporting responses other than restitution: P Birks, 'Rights, Wrongs and Remedies' (2000) 20 *OJLS* 1, 33; P Birks, 'Equity in the Modern Law: An Exercise in Taxonomy' (1996) 26 *University of Western Australia Law Review* 1, 40. The better view, however, is that whether or not its third stage of analysis involves an element of fault, the action in unjust enrichment can trigger only restitution. Any other response is incoherent given the requirement of an enrichment and a corresponding deprivation: McInnes (above n 16) 181–83.
[181] Grantham and Rickett (above n 3) 185–88.
[182] *R Leslie Ltd v Shiell* [1914] 3 KB 607.
[183] *Hart v O'Connor* [1985] AC 1000 (PC); *Permaform Plastics Ltd v London & Midland General Insurance Co* [1996] 7 WWR 457 (Man CA).

rather than vitiated. *Vitiation* negates the initial intention to transfer an enrichment. Mistake is the paradigm. The plaintiff confers a benefit on the defendant as a result of an error. Significantly, the claimant must show that her error pertained to *existing state of affairs*.[184] That requirement has important implications. The requisite error obscures the fact of its own existence, with the effect that the plaintiff normally cannot knowingly accept its risk.[185] And for the same reason, it would be self-defeating for the law to require proof that she notified the defendant, at the time of enrichment, that she might seek recovery in the future.[186]

The analysis is different if an enrichment is provided pursuant to a *qualified* intention. In that situation, the plaintiff fully intends the defendant to have the benefit at the outset. However, she also intends for him to retain it only if some specified event happens. Restitution is available (under the traditional, but misleading, label of 'failure of consideration') if the condition fails *and* if the defendant was aware of the conditional nature of his enrichment.[187] While occasionally questioned, the latter requirement is consistent with the law's concern for autonomy. Significantly, however, the rule does not reflect a desire to safeguard the defendant's freedom of choice,[188] but rather a desire to take seriously the plaintiff's volition. A qualification does not involve a mistake, but rather a misprediction. It is an error as to a *future state of affairs*. And, as the plaintiff must appreciate, the future is inherently incertain. Consequently, she assumes a risk of error. She can shift that risk onto the defendant if she informed him of the operative condition at the outset. Otherwise, she must accept responsibility for her actions.

(d) Free Acceptance Finally, and perhaps most interestingly, the defendant's conduct is legitimately relevant to the reason for restitution in a case of free acceptance. As previously explained, that concept provides a means by which the plaintiff can overcome a plea of subjective devaluation.

[184] Cf *Kleinwort Benson Ltd* (above n 13).

[185] Restitution will be denied, however, if 'money is intentionally paid without reference to the truth or falsehood of the fact,' such that the plaintiff means to 'waive all inquiry into it, and that the person receiving the payment shall have the money at all events, whether the fact be true or false': *Brisbane v Dacres* (1813) 5 Taunt 143, 152; 128 ER 641, 645. See also S Arrowsmith, 'Mistake and the Role of 'Submission to an Honest Claim' in A Burrows (ed), *Essays on the Law of Restitution* (Oxford, Oxford University Press, 1991) 17.

[186] Essentially the same analysis applies if the plaintiff's intention was vitiated by, say, fraud or duress, rather than spontaneous mistake. The defendant obviously knows of any vitiating factor of which he is the author. In other situations, however, he may be the recipient of a benefit that a third party improperly induced the plaintiff to transfer. Nevertheless, liability should not be premised upon proof that he had notice of the underlying defect. The same factor that vitiated the plaintiff's intention and caused the enrichment quite likely precluded her from providing such notice. Moreover, to reiterate the primary thesis of this article, while it may be true that the defendant was entirely innocent, it also is true that his autonomy is adequately protected through the element of enrichment and its related defences.

[187] Birks (above n 1) 219; Grantham and Rickett (above n 3) 148.

[188] The defendant's autonomy is no more in need of protection in a case of qualified intention than it is in a case of vitiated intention.

The defendant is said to have exercised a choice to assume financial responsibility for a non-monetary benefit if, despite knowledge that payment was expected, he failed to reject the plaintiff's services. Significantly, however, free acceptance can establish not only an *enrichment*, but also an *unjust* enrichment.[189] The unjust factor consists of the defendant's bad conduct—ie his unconscientious decision to retain the benefit without payment and thereby frustrate the plaintiff's expectation. Consequently, whether it pertains to the element of enrichment or to the element of injustice, free acceptance is very much a function of the defendant's autonomy.

While troubling in a number of respects,[190] the concept of free acceptance does not create any particular problems in the present context. It does not require the plaintiff, having overcome the defendant's autonomy in connection with his enrichment, to *additionally* do so in connection with the unjust factor. Instead, it provides a means by which, on the basis of the *same* proof, she can establish both the first *and* third parts of her action.[191] Consequently, there is no danger that she will be improperly denied relief despite proving that she provided the defendant with a benefit for which he accepted financial responsibility.

(iii) The Defendant's Participation—Unprincipled Reasons for Restitution

There are, however, several lines of authority that do fall afoul that danger. In a number of situations, the defendant's freedom of choice is *doubly* protected. The plaintiff is *required* to overcome his autonomy in *one way* for the purpose of establishing of enrichment and in *another way* for the purpose of establishing a reason to reverse the impugned transfer of wealth. Not surprisingly, the additional hurdle can prove fatal to an otherwise meritorious claim. The discussion focuses on two rules: (i) one requiring proof of a special relationship, and (ii) the other requiring proof of knowing receipt.

(a) Special Relationship The concept of a 'special relationship' was introduced into Canadian law by the Ontario Court of Appeal's decision in *Nicholson v St Denis*.[192] St Denis agreed to sell a building to Labelle. Title

[189] The dual nature of free acceptance was noted by Goff and Jones when first articulating the concept. They said that the defendant 'will be held to have benefited from the services rendered' and that '[m]oreover, in such a case, he cannot deny that he has been *unjustly* enriched': R Goff and G Jones, *The Law of Restitution* (London, Sweet and Maxwell, 1966) 18. Dickson J's formulation of free acceptance closely echoed, but did not cite, *Goff and Jones: Pettkus v Becker* (n 2) 275.

[190] Above at Section II(C)(ii).

[191] In theory, there is no reason why free acceptance must be used, if at all, as both a test of enrichment *and* an unjust factor. It should possible, for instance, to overcome subjective devaluation by proving an incontrovertible benefit and to then rely upon free acceptance only for the purpose of establishing a reason for restitution. In practice, however, claimants naturally prefer to use the same proof twice.

[192] (1975) 57 DLR (3d) 699(Ont CA).

was not to be transferred until the price was paid in full, but Labelle was allowed to take immediate possession. Upon doing so, he contractually requested Nicholson, the plaintiff, to apply aluminum and rock siding to the premises. Although that work was done, Labelle paid only $150 against the total price of $1978. He also defaulted on his payments under his contract with St Denis. Nicholson successfully sued Labelle for breach of contract, but because of the defendant's financial problems, judgment could not be satisfied. Anticipating that possibility, Nicholson also sued St Denis in unjust enrichment on the basis that, as the owner of the improved property, he had received the benefit of the work. The trial judge invoked a seemingly unfettered discretion to act 'in accordance with good conscience'[193] and allowed the claim despite the fact that St Denis had no knowledge of the plaintiff's services until after the project was finished.

MacKinnon JA allowed St Denis' appeal. In doing so, he examined the general scope of the action in unjust enrichment and suggested:

> ... that in almost all of the cases the facts established that there was a *special relationship* between the parties, frequently contractual at the outset, which relationship would have made it unjust for the defendant to retain the benefit conferred on him by the plaintiff ... This relationship in turn is usually, but not always, marked by two characteristics, firstly, knowledge of the benefit on the part of the defendant, and secondly, either an express or an implied request by the defendant for the benefit, or acquiescence in its performance.[194]

As frequently interpreted by subsequent courts, that sort of 'special relationship' is an 'essential nexus,' the '*sine qua non* of success,'[195] without which a restitutionary claim must fail.[196]

[193] (1974) 48 DLR (3d) 344, 350.
[194] *Ibid*, 701–02 (emphasis added).
[195] *McLaren v The Queen* [1984] 2 FC 899 (TD) 905.
[196] *Agrium v Chubb Insurance Co of Canada* [2002] AJ No 685 (QB); *Elmford Construction Co v South Winston Properties Inc* (1999) 45 OR (3d) 588 (SCJ); *Alyea v South Waterloo Edgar Insurance Brokers Ltd* (1993) 50 CCEL 266 (Ont Ct Gen Div). A number of other decisions appear to be to the same effect, albeit ambiguously so: *Nu-Way Kitchens Ltd v Smallwood* (2000) 187 Nfld & PEIR 251 (Nfld SC); *Turf Masters Landscaping Ltd v TAG Developments Ltd* (1995) 143 NSR (2d) 275 (CA); *Robert D Sutherland Architects Ltd v Montykola Investments Inc* (1995) 142 NSR (2d) 137 (SC).

In some instances, the courts require proof of a 'special relationship' by a different name. In *Campbell* (n 13) 283, the Ontario Court of Appeal held that restitutionary relief is invariably premised upon 'bilaterality,' in the sense that the defendant must have requested a benefit from the plaintiff. To allow relief otherwise, Borins JA said, 'would effect the result of enabling the plaintiff to unilaterally constitute [the defendant's] obligation. In my view, liabilities are not to be forced upon people without their consent, and without their knowledge'; critiqued in McInnes (above n 13).

A distinct, but similar, line of thought can be traced to *Peter* (above n 29) 645. McLachlin J addressed the question of which enrichments are 'unjust' and hence reversible. She said that the 'test is flexible' and that 'the factors to be considered vary with the situations before the court,' such that 'different factors may be more relevant in a ... claim for unjust enrichment between different levels of government, than in a family case.' However, she then cited *Pettkus* and stated that '[i]n every case, the fundamental concern is the legitimate expectation of the

That proposition is flawed in a number of ways.[197] Most significantly for present purposes, it excessively protects the defendant's interests at the plaintiff's expense. The root of the problem is obvious. All of the relevant cases involved the provision of services, rather than the payment of money. And true enough, in such circumstances, restitution usually is possible only

parties'; cf *Peel* (above n 15) 153, 164. That statement has been interpreted to mean that restitution is *never* available unless it accords with the parties' reasonable expectations. In other words, a shared belief that a benefit would be the subject of repayment is not merely *one factor among many* that may be capable of triggering restitution. It is, rather, an *invariable prerequisite* to relief: *Canada (Attorney General) v Confederation Life Insurance Co* (1995) 24 OR (3d) 717 (Gen Div) 771–72; *Smithson v Bock Estate* [1999] 1 WWR 243 (Alta QB) 259; *Baltman v Melnitzer (Trustee of)* (1996) 43 CBR (3d) 33 (Ont Gen Div) 42; *Re Collett & Brown Ltd* (1996) 11 ETR 164 (Ont Gen Div) 179; *Regnier v O'Reilly* (1997) 39 BCLR (3d)178 (SC) 184; *Toronto Airports Authority v Air Canada* [1999] OJ No 2532 (SCJ) § 112 *Clarkson* (above n 70) 251; *Campbell* (above n 13) 281.

[197] First, it simply is not universally true. At least at law, a mistaken payment can be recovered regardless of the existence of a special relationship between the parties: discussed above at Section III(C)(i).

Second, even if the observations made in *Nicholson v St Denis* are confined to case involving services, rather than money, it is important to note that they were offered in *dicta*. The plaintiff's claim for restitution was, in fact, rejected on entirely orthodox grounds. The defendant had not received an enrichment. Since he learned of the plaintiff's services only after they had been rendered, he clearly did not exercise a choice, through request or free acceptance, to assume financial responsibility for them. Nor did the plaintiff's work constitute an incontrovertible benefit. Aluminum and rock siding is not a necessary expense; the defendant had not actually realized a financial gain by selling the property in its improved state for an enhanced price; and even if an enrichment can be found on the basis of a realizable financial gain (which is debatable, especially with respect to services rendered to land), it does not appear that the court was provided with any evidence as to the value added by the plaintiff's services. Furthermore, even if there had been an enrichment, there was no reason for restitution. The defendant, unaware that the services were being performed, could not have freely accepted them. Moreover, the plaintiff's intention was not impaired in a relevant way. He did not, for instance, act in the mistaken belief that the property was his. To the contrary, he voluntarily agreed to exchange his services for Labelle's bare promise of future payment. And, as generally recognized, restitution should not be permitted to cut across contractual boundaries: *Rathwell v Rathwell* [1978] 2 SCR 436; 83 DLR (3d) 289, 306 (SCC); *Nu-Way Kitchens Ltd* (n 196); *Turf Masters Landscaping Ltd* (above n 196); *Hussey Seating Co (Canada) v Ottawa (City)* (1997) 145 DLR (4th) 493 (Ont Gen Div); *McLaren* (above n 195). Among the reasons for that rule is the fact that a contract is the creation of autonomous agents. The parties are free to allocate risks between themselves as they choose. Nicholson could have demanded pre-payment in full, just as he could have taken steps to secure his right to payment by means of a mechanic's lien. He chose instead to rely on Labelle's credit. That obviously was a bad decision, but not one that could be remedied by restitution. Nicholson was properly required to bear responsibility for his own choice.

Finally, even approached on its own terms and confined to cases involving services, the *dicta* in *Nicholson v St Denis* does not support the proposition that a special relationship is the '*sine qua non* of success.' MacKinnon JA's comments were qualified. He referred to 'almost all of the cases' and said that the operative relationship 'is usually, but not always' marked by the defendant's knowledge and request or acquiescence. He also discussed, seemingly with approval, *Greenwood v Bennett* (above n 103), in which the defendant received an incontrovertible benefit, in the form of a realized financial gain, after selling a vehicle that the plaintiff had repaired. That case was distinguished on the basis that the plaintiff had acted in the mistaken belief that he was improving his own property. Unlike the claimant in *Nicholson*, he had not chosen to incur the risk of non-payment.

if the defendant participated in the provision of the benefit. Significantly, however, the better explanation for that requirement pertains not to the reason for restitution, but rather to the element of enrichment. Services, unlike money, do not by their very nature invariably overcome freedom of choice. Consequently, the plaintiff must displace the defendant's subjective devaluation by showing that he actually chose, by means of request or acquiescence, to assume financial responsibility for her work. In such circumstances, relatively little harm is done if the law then requires the plaintiff, at the third stage of analysis, to show that she provided the enrichment within the context of a special relationship. She already has established such a relationship in connection with the defendant's enrichment. And moreover, the unjust factors that would most naturally apply (ie qualified intention and free acceptance) are roughly equivalent to the broad notion of a special relationship. Accordingly, while the reasoning could be clearer, the results should be the same.

Sometimes, however, the requirement of a special relationship will lead to injustice. Once again, the explanation stems from a proper understanding of the element of enrichment. While services normally cannot constitute an enrichment unless the defendant actually chose to assume financial responsibility for them, they exceptionally may create an incontrovertible benefit, without regard to his conduct. And in such circumstances, while the plaintiff may be able to establish a commonly accepted unjust factor (eg mistake), she may not be able to show that she shared a special relationship with the defendant. If so, the purported rule in *Nicholson v St Denis* will improperly deprive her of restitution.

Olchowy v McKay is illustrative.[198] In the mistaken belief that he had purchased a piece of land, the plaintiff cleared the property of rocks and planted canola seed at a cost of $3889 plus labour. The defendants, who knew of the operative mistake, silently watched the services being rendered and then bought the land for themselves. At the end of the growing season,

[198] Above (n 42). *Gidney* (above n 42), is to similar effect. The plaintiff innocently purchased a canoe that had been stolen from the defendant. He spent considerable time and money repairing it. After the boat was seized by the police and returned to the defendant, the plaintiff sued for restitution. The trial judge allowed the claim on the basis that the defendant had received an incontrovertible benefit (in the form of a realizable financial gain), which the plaintiff had conferred by mistake. The Manitoba Court of Appeal overturned that decision. Huband JA stated:

> In my view, there was a juristic reason for the enrichment, namely, that there was no relationship between [the parties] … and consequently [the defendant] had no knowledge that [the plaintiff] was investing time and money in the canoe. [The defendant] had neither consented nor acquiesced to that investment.
>
> …
>
> In the cases where unjust enrichment is found to exist, and where a remedy is provided, it would be inequitable for the defendant to retain the benefit. But that is because the defendant knew, or should have known of, the plaintiff's efforts and either consented or acquiesced to what the [plaintiff] was doing … But in the present case, there is nothing to bind the conscience of [the defendant].

they harvested the crop and sold it for $4386. As McLellan J found, the defendants undeniably received an incontrovertible benefit. Their financial gain was not merely realizable, but actually realized. The plaintiff's goods and labour had been turned to account. In effect, it was as if he had provided the defendants with money, rather than services. Relief nevertheless was denied on the basis of *Nicholson v St Denis*.[199] The judge stressed that the parties did not share a 'special relationship' because the defendants 'neither requested the services nor did they persuade the [plaintiff] to continue cultivation, fertilizing and seeding.'[200]

The result in *Olchowy v McKay* is indefensible. Indeed, it epitomizes the notion of unjust enrichment: the defendants literally were allowed to reap what the plaintiff had sown. Admittedly, since they had not yet acquired ownership at the operative time, they had no choice but to accept the creation of the crop. It may even be true, as a matter of sound agricultural practice, that they were practically compelled to harvest the canola. The critical fact, however, is that having done so, and having deducted reasonable remuneration for their own efforts, the defendants held money that was directly attributable to the plaintiff's mistaken services. And, of course, they could not subjectively devalue that enrichment. The only remaining question should have been whether or not there was a reason to reverse the impugned transfer of wealth. And in that regard, it should have been sufficient that, given his mistaken belief in ownership, the plaintiff's intention in creating the crop was vitiated. The mere absence of a special relationship should not have justified the defendants' retention of the money.

(b) Knowing Receipt In the event of a breach of trust, the beneficiary's primary claim lies against the trustee. Exceptionally, however, it may be possible to bring an action against a stranger—ie someone outside the formal trust relationship.[201] There are three possibilities.[202] The stranger may be sued as a trustee *de son tort* if he purported to administer trust property as a trustee. He may be sued for *knowing assistance* if he participated in a fraudulent breach of trust with actual knowledge of the underlying breach.[203]

[199] McLellan J also held that there was a juristic reason for the defendants' enrichment insofar as the Torrens system provided them with indefeasible title to the property that they had purchased. The plaintiff, however, was not claiming an interest in the land, but rather a personal judgment for the value of his services.

In a small concession, the plaintiff was awarded $428 under the *Improvements Under Mistake of Title Act*: RSS 1978, c I–1. That statute provides relief for 'lasting improvements' to land that are induced by an error of title. The judge held that while the cultivation of a crop did not qualify, the clearing of rocks did.

[200] Above (n 191) 57.

[201] The various possible actions are discussed in M McInnes, 'Knowing Receipt and the Protection of Trust Property' (2002) 81 *Canadian Bar Review* 171.

[202] *Barnes v Addy* (1874) 9 Ch App 244 (CA) 251–52.

[203] *Air Canada v M & L Travel Ltd* [1993] 3 SCR 787; 108 DLR (4th) 592 (SCC); cf *Royal Brunei Airlines Sdn Bhd v Tan* [1995] 2 AC 378 (PC); *Twinsectra Ltd v Yardley* [2002] 2 AC 164 (HL).

And finally, he may be sued for *knowing receipt* if he beneficially acquired trust property. The first two types of claim are species of wrongdoing for which the defendant generally is held liable for compensation.[204] In contrast, at least in Canada,[205] the action in knowing receipt is an equitable species of unjust enrichment that invariably triggers the response of restitution.

The leading case is *Citadel General Assurance Co v Lloyds Bank Canada*.[206] Citadel General Assurance hired a company called Drive On to collect insurance premiums on its behalf. Under the terms of that arrangement, the agent was to hold the money in trust pending payment over to the insurer. Drive On and its parent company, IWC, both held habitually overdrawn accounts at Lloyds Bank. On instructions from IWC, the bank made nightly transfers from the subsidiary's account (which held the insurer's trust funds) to the parent's account. That scheme constituted a breach of trust: Drive On, as trustee, allowed funds beneficially belonging to Citadel, as beneficiary, to be dissipated. Financial problems continued to mount for IWC and Drive On, and both were eventually forced out of business. Because it was still owed more than $600,000, Citadel sued Drive On for breach of trust. That claim was successful, but given the defendant's insolvency, judgment could not be satisfied. The insurer then turned its attention to the bank.

The bank had not purported to administer the trust property and therefore could not be liable as a trustee *de son tort*. Furthermore, there was a finding at trial that while the bank *should have known* that it was participating in a breach of trust, it did not have *actual knowledge* of that impropriety, and therefore could not be liable for knowing assistance. Relief consequently was possible, if at all, only on the basis of the bank's receipt of the insurer's trust funds.

In the Supreme Court of Canada, LaForest J held that a claim for knowing receipt requires proof of two elements: (i) a beneficial receipt of trust funds, and (ii) a reason to reverse the impugned transfer. The first requirement was satisfied even though the trust funds initially were transferred from Drive On's account to IWC's. Since IWC's account was overdrawn, every deposit effectively provided the bank with the benefit of repayment on an

[204] Exceptionally, if the defendant received a benefit from either the plaintiff or a third party, he may be held liable for disgorgement: *Warman International Ltd v Dwyer* (1995) 182 CLR 544 (HCA); *Fyffes Group Ltd v Templeman* [2000] 2 Lloyd's LR 643 (QB).

[205] Elsewhere, knowing receipt traditionally has been viewed as another species of accessory wrongdoing: *Belmont Finance Corp v Williams Furniture Ltd (No 2)* [1980] 1 All ER 393 (CA); *Bank of Credit & Commerce Intl (Overseas) Ltd v Akindele* [2000] 4 All ER 221 (CA). There is, however, growing support for the view that the plaintiff should also enjoy a *strict liability* claim in unjust enrichment: Birks (above n 11); Lord Nicholls, 'Knowing Receipt: The Need for a New Landmark' in WR Cornish *et al* (eds), *Restitution: Past, Present & Future* (Oxford, Hart Publishing 1998) 213; cf *Twinsectra Ltd* (n 203) 194 (per Lord Millett).

[206] [1997] 3 SCR 805; 152 DLR (4th) 411 (SCC). See also *Gold v Rosenberg* [1997] 3 SCR 767; 152 DLR (4th) 385 (SCC).

outstanding loan. The second element of the claim was more contentious. Justice LaForest recognized two lines of authority. One required proof of the defendant's actual knowledge of the trustee's breach; the other could be satisfied by proof of constructive knowledge.

In resolving that debate, LaForest J drew a distinction between knowing assistance, which is 'concerned with the furtherance of fraud,'[207] and knowing receipt, which he saw as a claim in unjust enrichment:

> More is expected of the recipient who, unlike the accessory, is necessarily enriched at the plaintiff's expense. Because the recipient is held to this higher standard, constructive knowledge ... will suffice as a basis for liability ... This lower threshold of knowledge is sufficient to establish the "unjust" or "unjustified" nature of the recipient's enrichment.[208]

Significantly, however, he was unwilling to lower the standard even further by adopting a test of strict liability:

> [Strict liability] may establish an unjust deprivation, but not an unjust enrichment. It is recalled that a plaintiff is entitled to a restitutionary remedy not because he or she has been unjustly *deprived* but, rather, because the defendant has been unjustly *enriched*, at the plaintiff's expense. To show that the defendant's enrichment is unjustified, one must necessarily focus on the defendant's state of mind, not the plaintiff's knowledge or lack thereof. Indeed, without any constructive or actual knowledge of the breach of trust ... [it] would be unfair to require a recipient to disgorge a benefit that has been lawfully received [209]

The rule regarding knowing receipt suffers from the same sorts of defects that affect the supposed requirement of a special relationship.[210] Most significantly, it unfairly tips the balance in the defendant's favour by overzealously protecting his freedom of choice. And once again, the root of the problem can be traced to a failure to appreciate the role of enrichment.

Strict liability would indeed be 'unfair' if, as LaForest J suggests, it meant that the plaintiff was entitled to restitution merely because she involuntarily

[207] Above (n 206) 432.
[208] *Ibid*, 434.
[209] *Ibid*, 435.
[210] As the cases cited in *Citadel* (above n 206) demonstrate, the requirement of knowing receipt is not unprecedented. Traditionally, however, it generally was confined to the situation in which a beneficiary alleged that a stranger committed an *equitable wrong* by improperly receiving trust property. The same rule did not extend to claims in *law*, nor to claims in *unjust enrichment*. It therefore is unfortunate that LaForest J couched his comments in universal terms. There is a danger that they will be taken to mean that 'bad conscience [is] a condition of all restitutionary claims' in Canada: Birks (above n 12) 635. It is virtually inconceivable, however, that the Court intended to create such a rule. A mere three months before deciding *Citadel*, it expressly rejected the suggestion that 'one must necessarily focus on the defendant's state of mind' in order to establish an unjust enrichment: *Air Canada* (above n 161).

transferred a benefit to the defendant. The unfairness would stem from lack of respect for the recipient's autonomy. He might be required to restore the value of a benefit for which he did not choose to assume financial responsibility, and that was not, by its very nature, enriching. So too, he might be held liable if, after receiving an undeniable enrichment, he honestly and irretrievably evacuated it (eg by giving it anonymously to charity). Consequently, despite a lack of wrongdoing, the defendant might be hurt by restitution.

LaForest J's analysis is, however, built upon an invalid premise. The defendant is amply protected even under a regime of strict liability. He cannot be considered enriched unless he received a benefit that he requested or freely accepted, or that is incontrovertible. And even if the plaintiff prima facie establishes the existence of an enrichment, the defendant may be able to reduce or avoid liability by pleading a dis-enriching defence. Change of position is the most obvious possibility, but in the context of a claim for the receipt of trust property, *bona fide* purchase may prove even more effective.[211] In any event, when the principle of unjust enrichment is considered as a whole, it is clear that the defendant is not in any danger. It is also clear that *Citadel*'s requirement of knowing receipt unnecessarily prejudices the plaintiff.

Take a simple example. The defendant arranges a vacation worth $2000. He has $2000 in his mattress with which he intends to pay. He innocently receives $2000 that the plaintiff's trustee had stolen from her trust fund. The defendant uses *that* money to pay for his holiday and therefore still has $2000 in his mattress. According to *Citadel*, he is not liable under the equitable species of unjust enrichment because he did not receive the trust funds with knowledge of the misappropriation.[212] That result is unjustifiable.

[211] Stated in general terms, the defence of *bona fide* purchase applies if the defendant in good faith paid a third party to receive a benefit from the plaintiff. Unlike change of position, which operates *pro tanto, bona fide* purchase is a complete defence. Nevertheless, it too may operate by negating the plaintiff's prima facie proof of an enrichment. Respect for contractual principles may preclude a court from comparing the value of the enrichment that the defendant received with the value of the consideration that he provided in exchange. Consequently, by operation of law, *bona fide* purchase may necessarily entail a complete dis-enrichment. There is, however, an alternative conception of the defence that denies relief on policy grounds and without regard to the issue of enrichment. *Bona fide* purchase may have effect simply because the law wishes, as a matter of fairness and commercial efficacy, to occasionally create exceptions to the general rule of *nemo dat quod non habet*. Because of the need to ensure that money flows freely through the market, a *bona fide* purchase clears title to stolen funds and protects the recipient from liability: compare P Birks and C Mitchell, 'Unjust Enrichment' in P Birks (ed), *English Private Law* (Oxford, Oxford University Press 2000) 525, 617–19, 626–27; Grantham and Rickett (above n 3) 320–29; K Barker, 'After Change of Position: Good Faith Exchange in the Modern Law of Restitution' and P Birks, 'Overview: Tracing Claiming and Defences' in P Birks (ed), *Laundering and Tracing* (above n 21).

[212] Moreover, although a victim of misappropriated trust property theoretically enjoys several avenues of relief, the plaintiff may find that they are all ineffective: McInnes (above n 201). The facts do not disclose an action in trustee *de son tort* or knowing assistance. Nor could the

The rule in *Citadel* allows the defendant far too much, and the plaintiff far too little,[213] leeway in determining the allocation of their respective resources. The plaintiff is unable to recover the value of a benefit that was taken from her without her consent. At the same time, the defendant enjoys a windfall. He began the episode with $2000 and the expectation that he would return from his vacation penniless. Nevertheless, because he cannot be ascribed with fault, he is permitted to have both his holiday at the plaintiff's expenses *and* the continued use of the money in his mattress.[214]

A much better balance would be struck between the parties' interests if the requirement of knowing receipt was dropped in favour of a model of strict liability. The defendant was unjustly enriched at the plaintiff's expense: (i) he received $2000 in cash; (ii) she suffered a corresponding deprivation; and (iii) her lack of consent constitutes a sufficient reason to reverse that transfer of wealth. Moreover, he has no defence to her claim. Although he used the misappropriated funds to pay for his holiday, he did not thereby sustain a relevant change of position. He intended to take the same vacation in any event. Consequently, the imposition of liability would properly respect each party's freedom of choice. Since the plaintiff did not choose to dispose of $2000, she can get that amount back. And since the defendant did choose to spend $2000 on a trip and return home penniless, restitution effectuates his chosen state of affairs.

IV. CONCLUSION

Despite the trend toward increasing complexity in restitutionary scholarship, it is necessary to revisit the basic concept of enrichment. Courts and commentators must more clearly recognize that the core issue is freedom of choice. It is not enough for the plaintiff to prove that she conferred an objective benefit upon the defendant. She must also overcome his right to subjective devaluation by showing that he either assumed the risk of financial

plaintiff assert a proprietary claim to recover the stolen trust funds *in specie*. The defendant no longer holds the money or its traceable proceeds. Moreover, even if the plaintiff could trace the funds into the hands of someone else, such as the travel agent with whom the defendant dealt, she almost certainly would be met by a defence of *bona fide* purchase or change of position. Finally, although the trustee would be liable for breach of trust, he may be judgment-proof or impossible to locate.

[213] Admittedly, the plaintiff did not have the right to direct the disposition of property held in trust for her benefit. She should, however, have the right to demand recovery of misappropriated funds by means of a strict liability claim in unjust enrichment.

[214] The last clause in that sentence is not intended to suggest that the plaintiff should have a proprietary right to the money in the defendant's mattress, but rather, more loosely, that in the absence of other resources, he should use that money to discharge his personal obligation to provide her with restitution.

responsibility or had no choice to make. Appreciation of that point will help to resolve a number of long-standing debates regarding the precise scope of enrichment. It will also affect several other aspects of the action in unjust enrichment. It will clarify the nature of the defence of change of position. It will better ensure the proper calculation of restitutionary relief. And perhaps most significantly, it will reveal the harmful redundancy that typically occurs when a reason for restitution is formulated with a view to protecting the defendant's freedom of choice.

9

Planting Another's Field: Unrequested Improvements Under Jewish Law

ERNEST J. WEINRIB*

I. THE CASE OF THE PLANTED TREES

AT SOME POINT in the early third century of the Common Era, a man in Babylonia went into another's field and, without the owner's permission, planted trees there. The question then arose: under Jewish law was the owner liable for this unsolicited improvement to his property? The case was brought before Rav, the pre-eminent Jewish jurist of the time. The Talmud gives the following account of the proceedings:

> A man came before Rav. Rav said to the owner of the field, 'Go and make an assessment for him.' The owner said, 'I do not want the trees.' Rav said, 'Go and make an assessment for him, and he shall have the lower hand' [that is, on the standard interpretation, the improver shall be entitled to the lesser of his expenses or what the owner would pay to have the trees planted]. The owner said, 'I do not want the trees.' Subsequently, Rav saw that the owner had built a fence around the field and was guarding it. Rav said to the owner, 'You have revealed your view that you are pleased with the trees. Go and make an assessment for him, and he shall have the upper hand.'[1]

This ancient incident brings together features familiar to modern students of the law of restitution. On one side is the improver, who claims remuneration for the benefit, albeit unrequested, of the planted trees. On the other side is the owner, who (anticipating the modern notion of subjective devaluation)[2]

* I am grateful to Murray Rosenthal for his assistance in reviewing the Jewish legal texts, and to Dr. Arye Edrei of the Buchmann Faculty of Law, University of Tel Aviv, for his comments.

[1] *Babylonian Talmud*, Baba Mezia 101a (throughout this article the translations are my own). On Rav, see EE Urbach, *The Halakha: Its Sources and Development* (Israel, Massada, 1986) 295–302.

[2] P Birks, *An Introduction to the Law of Restitution* (Oxford, Clarendon Press, 1985) 109–16.

repeatedly denies that this is a benefit that he wants. Rav, adjudicating the dispute, indicates the measure of the owner's payment with various formulations, but makes a decisive ruling only when the owner's behaviour shows that he was satisfied with the trees after all. Pervading the whole account is familiar tension between the owner's freedom to determine the use of his own property and the prevention of enrichment at the improver's expense.

Rav's treatment of the planting of these trees represents one of the fundamental building blocks of the Jewish law of unrequested improvements. In this article I want to set out the influence of this story, the legal context in which it is situated, the effect on Jewish law of competing interpretations of it, and, more generally, some of the conceptual possibilities about the treatment of unrequested benefits that cluster around the story and its associated doctrinal material.[3]

This article thus contributes to the burgeoning comparative literature that the revival of restitution in the common law world has stimulated.[4] From the standpoint of the common law, this literature has an obvious attraction. Although the modern common law of restitution has antecedents that stretch back several centuries, only within the last decades have scholars and courts made a sustained effort to develop a set of distinct principles of unjust enrichment. Attention to the sophisticated older European traditions about unjust enrichment not only exposes further possibilities of analysis, but also contributes to the intellectual self-consciousness necessary for productive reflection about unjust enrichment as a juridical concept. However, scholars of restitution have had little opportunity to consider Jewish law, as is understandable given its obscurity and inaccessibility. Nonetheless, as the episode involving Rav indicates, issues of unjust enrichment have engaged the attention of the leading figures of the Jewish legal tradition for almost two millennia. This makes Jewish law the locus for the world's oldest uninterrupted and continuing discussion of unjust enrichment.

Being of such extended duration, the Jewish legal tradition has produced a jurisprudence about unrequested benefits that is extraordinarily complex. The dictum about the common law—that it has been 'fined and refined by

[3] For a brief treatment from an economic perspective contending that Jewish law converges with efficiency, see A Levine, *Free Enterprise and Jewish Law: Aspects of Jewish Business Ethics* (Jersey City, Ktav Publishing, 1980) 78–83. See also I Warhaftig, 'Yored Lesadeh Haveiro Shelo Birshut' (1986) 13 *Shnaton HaMishpat HaIvri* 65.

[4] Especial attention has been paid to German law. See eg, T Krebs, *Restitution at the Crossroads: A Comparative Study* (London, Cavendish Publishing, 2001); G Dannemann, 'Unjust Enrichment by Transfer: Some Comparative Remarks' (2001) 79 *Texas Law Review* 1837; BS Markesinis, W Lorenz and G Dannemann, *German Law of Obligations: A Comparative Introduction to the Law of Contracts & Restitution* (Oxford, Clarendon Press, 1997) 710–816; R Zimmermann, 'Unjustified Enrichment: The Modern Civilian Approach' (1995) 15 *OJLS* 403; R Zimmermann, *The Law of Obligations: Roman Foundations of the Civilian Tradition* (Oxford, Oxford University Press, 1990) 834–901.

an infinite number of Grave and Learned Men'[5]—is even more apposite to the development of Jewish law. But because this long history has been accompanied by wide geographical dispersion and a largely decentralized structure of legal authority, legal doctrine has often been fluid and evolving within the stable framework provided by the Talmud, the system's basic text. Accordingly, although the jurisprudence of unrequested improvements originates in the brief Talmudic segment that centers on Rav's case, centuries of commentaries, responsa, and codifications have produced varied understandings of the legal elements of the problem and different suggestions of how those elements are to be combined. To examine, or even refer to, all the possibilities is beyond the scope of this article. I hope, instead, to highlight what seem to me to be the main approaches and to excavate their conceptual underpinnings. My especial focus is on the perennial interplay between the improver's claim and the owner's freedom.

The article, accordingly, proceeds in the following stages. Section II explains the different measures of remuneration ('having the upper hand' and 'having the lower hand') to which, in the opinion of subsequent commentators, the Talmudic account of Rav's case refers. These different measures are tied to the suitability of the property to the activity of the improver. As section III then outlines, the notion of suitability was the basis of the earliest conception in Jewish law of what we would term 'incontrovertible benefit.' The basic idea was that the owner of a field that was suitable for planting trees could be compelled to pay for them on the higher measure because the owner would not be averse to having the field brought to its optimal use. This idea depended on interpreting Rav's case as involving a field that was not suitable for trees. Section IV outlines the collapse of this interpretation of Rav's case in favour of the view that, regardless of whether the field was or was not suitable for planting trees, owners retained their liberty to reject the improvement. Nonetheless, simultaneous with this collapse, a different basis for incontrovertible benefit arose, from which modern commentators derived two different conceptions of the conditions under which the owner could not reject an improvement. Finally, section V offers some brief concluding reflections.

II. THE MEASURES OF REMUNERATION

Rav's case appears in a section of the Talmud, extending to less than twenty lines, that deals with unrequested improvements. The section discusses two situations in which the improver acts for the owner's benefit but without the owner's permission. In the first, the improver plants trees in another's field,

[5] T Hobbes, *A Dialogue between a Philosopher and a Student of the Common Laws of England,* J Cropsey (ed), (Chicago, University of Chicago Press, 1971) 55.

and the Talmud discusses the quantum that the owner is to pay for this improvement. In the second, the improver rebuilds another's dilapidated structure, and the Talmud discusses the improver's right to remove his materials. Rav's case is the final element in the discussion of the first of these situations.

The Talmud's conclusion in the first situation is that the amount to be paid by the owner depends on whether the field was 'suitable for the planting of trees.'[6] Where trees are a more profitable use of the field than the crops that otherwise would be there, the improver is entitled to a higher level of remuneration. Rav formulated the different levels of remuneration in terms of whether the improver had 'the upper hand' or 'the lower hand.'[7] What precisely he meant by this was a matter of dispute among subsequent commentators.

By the middle ages the most accepted view was as follows.[8] The practice was that persons who were employed by others to plant on their behalf were paid a proportion, determined by local custom, of the appreciation in the yield produced by their efforts. The unrequested improver, of course, had not been employed by the owner. Nonetheless, if the field was suitable for trees, the improver got either his expenses or the customary share of the yield, whichever was greater. By being entitled to the more advantageous of these alternative measures of remuneration, the improver 'had the upper hand.'

The reason for this treatment of a field that was suitable for trees is that the planting of trees brought the field to its optimal use. Accordingly, the improver did what the owner would have done in any case, and therefore the owner can be treated as if he wanted the trees planted. To arrive at the improver's remuneration, 'one assesses how much a man would give to have this field planted.'[9] Such an owner would have been willing to allot to

[6] *Babylonian Talmud*, Baba Mezia 101a.
[7] *Ibid.*
[8] Rashi (Rabbi Solomon Yitzhaki, France, 11th century) on 'gilita adaatech deniha lach,' Babylonian Talmud, Baba Mezia 101a; Ramban (Rabbi Moses ben Nahman, Spain, 13th century), *Milhamot HaShem* on Baba Mezia 101a; Rosh (Rabbi Asher ben Yehiel, Germany and Spain, 13th–14th century) on Baba Mezia, ch 8, 22. This view was described by Rashba, who disagreed with it (see below n 14), as held by most of the commentators, see Rashba (Rabbi Solomon ben Abraham Adret, Spain, 13th century), *Hiddushei HaRashba* on Baba Mezia 101a. Rabbi Joshua ben Alexander HaKohen Falk (Poland, 16th–17th century), *Sefer Meirat Einayim* on Shulhan Aruch 375, 17 summed up the view as follows: 'Know that according to the opinion of Rashi and the Rosh in several places that 'he has the upper hand' means that if the appreciation exceeds the expenditure he takes part of the appreciation like the other planters in the city, and if the expenditure exceeds the appreciation, he takes all the expenditure even though the owner got no benefit from it.' There were many controversies concerning the details of this and similar approaches. What distinguishes these approaches from the minority view mentioned below (n 17) is that they involve a comparison of expenditure and appreciation. *Encyclopedia Talmudit*, v. 23 s.v. 'Yored lenichsei haveiro shelo midaato', ch 2, gives a catalogue of the various interpretations.
[9] Samuel's formulation of the improver's remuneration in *Babylonian Talmud*, Baba Mezia 101a.

the improver a share of the yield in accordance with the usual practice of the locality. Moreover, if the planter's expenditures exceeded his prospective share of the yield, the owner would have at least reimbursed those expenditures; otherwise the trees would not have been planted, because the improver would not have agreed to do it at a loss.[10] Therefore, once one treats the owner as desiring the improvement, the improver becomes entitled to the expenses or the planter's customary share of the appreciation, whichever is the greater.

If the field is not suitable for planting trees, the situation is different. Although the owner has benefited, the trees do not represent the optimal use of the field, so that the reason for treating the owner as wanting the improvement falls away. All that remains is the benefit itself, which is valued as the lesser of the cost of creating it and the appreciation that accrues from it. On the one hand, the value transferred from improver to owner is the value of the efforts expended in improving the property. On the other hand, the improver's expenditure does not enrich the owner beyond the appreciation in the yield; indeed, if the improver could charge the owner for expenses that exceed the value that his efforts added to the yield, he would be impoverishing rather than enriching the owner. Accordingly, the increase in the yield's value functions as a ceiling in the calculation of the quantum of the benefit received by the owner from the improver. Hence, the classic explanation of what it means for the improver to have the lower hand is that 'if the appreciation is greater than the expenditure, he gets the expenditure, and if the expenditure is greater than the appreciation he gets no more than the appreciation.'[11]

For improvements to non-agricultural properties such as buildings, where the notion of a yield was not relevant, the notional comparison of expenditure and appreciation worked in a slightly different way. Having the lower hand gave the improver the lesser of the expenditure and the increased value of the property.[12] However, the improver who had the upper hand was entitled to what the owner would have paid to have the work done, even if this exceeded the increase in the value of the property. The difference between the lower and the upper hand is that in the former the appreciation set the upper limit of the improver's remuneration, whereas in the latter improvers were entitled to the cost of the improvement without limit.[13]

[10] Falk (above n 8) observes about Rav's award of the upper hand to the improver: 'If he had not planted the field, the owner himself would have planted it and expended this amount on it.'
[11] Rashi on 'yado al hatahtona,' *Babylonian Talmud*, Baba Mezia 101a.
[12] The same rule is mentioned by the Roman jurist Celsus in his treatment of inadvertent improvements; Justinian, *Digest* 6.1.38 (Celsus).
[13] Alfasi (Rabbi Isaac Alfasi, Morocco, 11th century) *Sefer HaHalachot*, on Baba Mezia 101a; Rabbi Yosef Haviva (Spain, 15th century) *Nimukei Yosef* on Alfasi, Sefer HaHalachot, on Baba Mezia 101a.

Thus, the accepted view of the contrast between the improver's having the lower hand and having the upper hand involves a difference in the principle on which the remuneration is assessed. When the improver has the upper hand, the assessment is quasi-contractual. Because the improvement moves the property to its optimal use and is thereby equated to one that the owner desires, the assessment is based on a reconstruction of what the owner would have agreed to pay an improver to achieve the desired improvement. In contrast, when the improver has the lower hand, the assessment is restitutionary. Because the planting of trees benefits the owner without moving the property to its optimal use, the confidence in the owner's desire for the improvement is absent. What matters then is not what the owner would have agreed to pay, but rather the value of the benefit that was transferred to the owner through the improver's efforts.

Some commentators in the middle ages found the accepted interpretation of the 'upper hand' implausible regardless of whether the expenditure or the appreciation was greater.[14] If the share of the appreciation was greater than the improver's expenses, the accepted view, by giving him the customary share of the appreciation, treated him like a person who had been hired to plant the trees. But this, so the objection went, treated a non-consensual transaction as if it were a consensual one. Moreover, giving the improver more than he expended meant that what the improver received exceeded the benefit that was attributable to him.[15] On the other hand, awarding the improver his expenses, no matter how large they were, even if those expenses exceeded the appreciation in the yield's value, would also entail having the owner pay for more than he benefited. The most that could be awarded to the improver is the expenses up to the value of the appreciation, since anything above that is a loss that the improver inflicted on himself.[16] The accepted view of 'the upper hand', in other words, remunerated the improver on a contractual measure despite the non-existence of a contract, while failing properly to measure the benefit that was the basis of the improver's claim.

Instead these commentators suggested a different view of the contrast between having the upper and the lower hand. What mattered for them was not the comparison of expenditure and appreciation, but different ways of measuring the expenditure.

[14] Rezah (Rabbi Zerahia Halevi Gerondi, France, 12th century), *Hamaor Hagadol* on Alfasi, Sefer HaHalachot on Baba Mezia 101a; Rashba (n 8); see also Rabbi Yosef Karo (Israel, 16th century), *Beit Yosef*, Hoshen Mishpat 375, 3.

[15] As Rashba (above n 8) puts it: '[on the standard view] the owner gives him what the planters of the city get, meaning, even more than the expenditure; this view is surprising, for on what basis will the owner give the improver more than the latter has benefited him?' Rashba is presumably assuming that the enrichment that the improver can claim consists only in the amount that quantifies his efforts, not in a share of the yield's appreciation, since the yield belongs to the owner unless he freely parts with it.

[16] Rezah (above n 14).

> The meaning of 'he has the upper hand' is as in the superior kind of hiring, when a man says to his fellow, 'Build on this land of mine, or plant this field of mine, so that I myself won't have to bother with it,' for this certainly is of conspicuous benefit to him. And the meaning of 'he has the lower hand' is as with the inferior kind of hiring, when the inferior workers treat it cheaply.[17]

The owner for whose field the planting of trees is the optimal use can be presumed to want the work done and to be willing to hire a more able contractor and pay him at a high rate to have the planting properly executed. The owner benefits by being spared the trouble of attending to this desired project himself; in particular he does not have to bother with bringing in various workmen to attend to the various stages of the work.[18] In contrast, the owner for whose field the planting of trees is not optimal would be satisfied to have it done at the minimal cost using the cheapest labor. The benefit consists simply in having someone put trees where there were none before. Thus, according to this view the benefit received by the owner varies with the kind of field he has. With respect to both kinds of field, the analysis is oriented to the enrichment that accrued to the owner, and the amount of the remuneration is conceptualized in what we would consider to be restitutionary terms.

We can now return to Rav's case and set it into its Talmudic context. The Talmud introduces the case to show Rav's view of the remuneration to be paid to the improver. Immediately before the Talmud's account of the incident, the Talmud mentions an apparent dispute between Rav and his contemporary Samuel with respect to the unsolicited planting of trees. Rav had said that the planter has the lower hand, whereas Samuel had said that the planter receives what the owner would have been willing to pay to have the field planted. The Talmud then cites an opinion that these sages do not disagree; their stated views simply apply to different kinds of fields: Rav's statement applies to a field not suitable for planting, whereas Samuel's statement applies to a field suitable for planting. That Rav does not disagree with Samuel is inferred from the incident that came before him, where Rav envisages two measures of remuneration, the 'lower hand' that the Talmud had previously attributed to him and 'the upper hand' that is equivalent to the view attributed to Samuel. In dealing with the tree-planting, Rav makes three interventions. He first orders remuneration but without specifying its measure, to which the owner replies that he does not want the improvement. He then orders remuneration with the improver having the

[17] *Ibid.*

[18] As Ritva explained in glossing Rezah's idea, 'One estimates how much a person would be willing to pay to someone who will undertake to do this as a single project, so that the owners will not have to bother with it by arranging for workmen to come and go; for a person would gladly pay a lot of money for this.' Ritva (Rabbi Yom Tov ben Abraham Eshvili, Spain, 13–14th century), *Hiddushei HaRitva* on Baba Mezia 101a.

lower hand, which is the measure appropriate to a field that is not suitable for planting. The owner then repeats his insistence that he does not want the improvement. Finally, when Rav notices that the owner, by fencing and guarding the trees, has demonstrated that he wants them despite his earlier denials, Rav tells him to remunerate the improver with the improver having the upper hand, that is, at the higher level appropriate to a field suitable for planting.

III. INCONTROVERTIBLE BENEFIT

The special significance of a field that is suitable for planting is reminiscent of the common law's notion of an incontrovertible benefit. An incontrovertible benefit is one that would not have been declined even if the owner would have had the opportunity to choose.[19] For the determination of whether an improvement is incontrovertible, the nature of the improved property and the necessary or optimal use of it are relevant.[20] Jewish law takes the suitability of a field for the planting of trees as paradigmatic of optimal use; what is necessary to produce this optimal use then becomes the measure of the improver's remuneration, as the party who 'has the upper hand.'

To equate the field's suitability for trees with the incontrovertibility of the benefit at common law would, however, be premature. The incontrovertibility of the benefit goes to the owner's liability to make restitution of an unrequested benefit. In contrast, our discussion of the kinds of field has gone not to owner's liability but to the measurement of the improver's remuneration. To this point the upper hand and the lower hand function merely as default rules for quantifying what the improver receives for the improvement. Whether the owner can be legally compelled to pay is another issue.

In the Jewish legal literature this issue arises in the following way. The short Talmudic section on unrequested improvements deals with two problems. The first is the remuneration of the person who plants trees without the owner's permission. The second is whether a person who reconstructs a dilapidated building without the owner's position can change his mind and remove his materials. The answer that the Talmud gives is that the improver can remove building materials from a structure but not trees from a field.[21] There are two reasons for this. The first, applicable only to the land of

[19] *Peel (Regional Municipality) v Canada* [1992] 3 SCR 762, (1993) 98 DLR (4th) 140 (SCC) 156.

[20] *LAC Minerals Ltd v International Corona Resources Ltd* [1989] 2 SCR 574, (1989) 61 DLR (4th) 14 (SCC) 53 (LaForest J): 'on the assumption that he Corona had acquired the Williams property, it would of necessity have had to develop the mine.'

[21] *Babylonian Talmud*, Baba Mezia 101b.

Israel, is that the special value of settling the land would be undermined by removing the trees. The second is that because trees are nourished by the earth, removing them would weaken the owner's soil. But what if it is the owner, not the improver, who wants the trees or the building materials removed? Can the owner reject the improvement by telling the improver to take his materials and go? The Talmudic text does not explicitly deal with this issue.

In the absence of explicit treatment, post-Talmudic commentators looked to the implications of the Rav story. Two features of this story attracted their attention. First, Rav told the owner to 'go and make an assessment for him and he shall have the lower hand.'[22] This mention of the lower hand indicates that the field in question was not suitable for planting trees. Second, when the owner then repeated his statement that he did not want the improvement, Rav did nothing in the face of this apparent defiance until the owner revealed his true sentiments by fencing and guarding the trees. From Rav's failure to compel the owner to obey him, commentators concluded that, so far as that particular field was concerned, the owner was within his rights to refuse the improvement, at least until his conduct contradicted his professed rejection.

Having thus determined that the field was not suitable for planting trees and that no obligation to pay arose from an improvement to such a field, the commentators reconstructed the various stages in the Rav incident as follows.[23] When the case was brought to Rav initially, he did not know whether the field was suitable for planting or not. He accordingly required an assessment without indicating whether the improver was to have the upper or the lower hand. When the owner declared that he did not want the trees, Rav inferred that the owner was unwilling to pay on the higher measure for having trees planted in a field that was not suitable for that use. Rav therefore told him that he should pay only on the lower measure, as was appropriate for a field not suitable for trees. The owner then repeated his assertion that he did not want the trees. Rav interpreted this as implicitly requiring the improver to remove the trees. Thus, Rav's inaction in the face of the owner's statement led to the conclusion that that the owner of a field that was unsuitable for trees could require the improver to remove the improvement. Subsequently, by fencing in and guarding the trees, the owner revealed that he did want them after all. This expression of the owner's desire allowed the field to be treated as if it was one that was suitable for planting. Rav accordingly ordered him to pay for the trees on the higher measure.

[22] Above (n 1).

[23] Ramban, *Hiddushei HaRamban* on Baba Mezia 101a; Rashba (above n 8); *Nimukei Yosef* (above n 13); Ritva (above n 18).

Accordingly, on this interpretation, the owner could refuse to accept the trees if the field was not suitable for that use. Although the trees might well be a benefit from an objective point of view, the freedom of the owner of such a field to assert that he preferred not to have them was untrammeled.

The converse, however, also obtained. This interpretation emphasized that the field in Rav's case was not suitable for planting. Had the field been suitable for that purpose, the owner would not have been able to refuse the trees and would have had to pay for them on the higher measure. Just as Rav finally compelled the owner who fenced and guarded the trees to pay, with the improver having the upper hand, so the owner of a suitable field could be forced to accept and pay on the higher measure for trees planted without his authorization.

It is worth emphasizing the radical nature of this conclusion from the standpoint of the common law. Common lawyers are familiar with—and often troubled by—cases where the owner is made to pay for an improvement by someone who mistakenly thought he owned the object improved.[24] This interpretation of Rav's case, however, imposes on the owner an obligation to remunerate the improver who *knowingly* plants trees in another's field, provided that the field is suitable for planting. The improver in Rav's case did not make a mistake of title or of any other kind.[25]

This contrast between the common law and Jewish law reflects differing premises about the volunteer. The common law views a person who improves property that he or she knows belongs to another as a volunteer who is making a gift. The improver's expectation of remuneration merely indicates that in bestowing this gift, the improver is also taking the risk that the owner will pay for it. The common law sees no reason to reverse the gift or reallocate the risk through an award of restitution.[26] Because the improver knows that only owners have the right to determine the condition of what they own, the improver is taken to know that the improvement cannot obligate the owner to pay for it. Hence the improvement counts as nothing more than a donative act. However, when the benefit is conferred by mistake, the argument that the improver was acting with

[24] *Greenwood v Bennett* [1973] 1 QB 195 (CA); *Gidney v Shank* [1995] 5 WWR 385 (Man QB), reversed [1996] 2 WWR 383 (Man CA); P Matthews, 'Freedom, Unrequested Improvements, and Lord Denning' [1981] *CLJ* 340.

[25] Moreover, the liability obtains even where Jewish law sees no difficulty in detaching the improvement from the improved property. The Talmud itself indicates that building materials can be detached from a reconstructed building, at least at the instance of the builder. Nonetheless, on the argument to this point, if the ruined building had been suitable for reconstruction, the owner would be legally compelled to remunerate the stranger for restoring the building. Compare the suggestion of Richard Sutton that the owner should owe restitution if he or she could have allowed the improver to remove the improvement; R Sutton, 'What Should be Done for Mistaken Improvers?' in P Finn (ed), *Essays on Restitution* (Sydney, Law Book Co, 1996) 252–54.

[26] Birks (above n 2) 101–3; G Virgo, *The Principles of the Law of Restitution* (Oxford, Clarendon Press, 1999) 39–40.

donative intent evaporates. Then the issue becomes whether it is truly a violation of the recipient's freedom to compel payment and thus to treat the recipient as accepting the benefit. When considered as an incontrovertible benefit, for example, the improvement is one where—given the nature of the property, its necessary or optimal uses, or the owner's plans for it—the owner can be viewed as having every reason consistent with his or her own autonomy to accept it.[27]

In contrast, Jewish law does not assume that the improver who knowingly acts on another's property does so with donative intent. 'We do not say that simply because he went down into another's field, his intention was just to give a gift.'[28] The general principle relevant to all unrequested benefits is that 'if any person does an action or benefit for another, one cannot say to him that "you did it for me gratuitously because I did not ask you to do it," but one must give him his remuneration.'[29] The person who planted the trees did so in order to get paid by the owner.[30] Jewish law treats this as a purpose worth giving effect to. Rather than disqualifying him as a volunteer or an officious intermeddler, the improver's knowing operation on another's property is the basis of his claim, which is inescapable (on the present interpretation of the Rav story) when the property is suitable for the improvement.

In this context both the common law and Jewish law are individualistic, but they exhibit different conceptions of individualism.[31] For the common law, the individualism resides in the institution of property and in the juridical construction of the social understandings to which property gives rise. Because the improver can be taken to know that only owners have the right to change the condition of their property, the improver is understood as giving a gift and, accordingly, is not eligible for restitution. For Jewish law, the individualism resides in giving effect to the improver's non-altruistic motivation. In the absence of evidence of a donative intent, improvers are treated as forwarding their own self-interested purposes.

From the standpoint of the common law, the approach of Jewish law has a paradoxical implication. Whereas for the common law the improver's knowledge of another's ownership weakens the improver's case, for Jewish

[27] Incontrovertible benefit is usually understood as negating the possibility of subjective devaluation by the defendant and thus going to the existence of the enrichment, see Birks (above n 2) 116. My account here varies from this understanding. My reasons for varying would involve an extensive exploration of the normative structure of unjust enrichment, which I hope to set out on another occasion. My purpose here is simply to say enough to render intelligible the terms of my contrast between the common law and Jewish law.

[28] Rashba, *Hiddushei HaRashba* on Nedarim 33b.

[29] Rema (Rabbi Moses Isserles, Poland, 16th century), *Shulhan Aruch*, Hoshen Mishpat 264, 4.

[30] Ramban, *Milhamot HaShem* on Baba Batra 4b.

[31] For a provocative comparison of Jewish and American law in another restitutionary context, see H Dagan, *Unjust Enrichment: A Study of Private Law and Public Values* (Cambridge, Cambridge University Press, 1997) 50–7, 109–29.

law this knowledge strengthens it. The improver's claim to be remunerated on the higher measure presupposes that the improver has acted to improve another's land, for only if the improver's intention was to have another pay for his work can he be paid what (in Samuel's words) 'a man would give to have this field planted.'[32] Accordingly, if he mistakenly thought that he was working his own land, he can be remunerated only on the lower measure, even if the field is one that was suitable for planting trees.[33]

The absence in Jewish law of the common law notion of a volunteer exposed owners to the possibility that, if their property was suitable for the improvement in question, they would be compelled to pay the improver for effecting it. How could this apparent indifference to the autonomy of owners to determine the use of their own property be justified? This question did not present itself explicitly; for those who interpreted the Rav story to lead to this result, the Talmudic origin of the rule was justification enough. Nonetheless, three general observations are in order.

First, the premise was that, if the field was suitable for planting, the improver was doing something that the owner wanted done. 'The person who knowingly improves another's field thinks that the owners are pleased with it.'[34] Conversely, the owner has no liability for the improvement if he has warned the improver not to do the work. A ruling to this effect in the thirteenth century included the comment that this was 'in order to prevent everybody from forcing someone else to plant and to build.'[35] Owners could protect their autonomy over their property by telling improvers that they did not want the contemplated improvement.

Second, some commentators based the higher measure of remuneration on a notion of acquiescence. 'Because the field was suitable for planting and the owners knew and kept quiet, it is certain that they were pleased with his work, and he is like a person who made the improvement with their knowledge.'[36] When this explanation of the improver's having the upper hand is combined with the owner's inability to refuse the improvement, the picture that emerges is not unlike the recent suggestion of a common law

[32] Above (n 9).

[33] Ramban, *Hiddushei HaRamban*, on Baba Mezia 40a; Rivash (Rabbi Isaac ben Sheshet, Spain, 14th century), *Responsa of the Rivash*, 515. This resembles the rule in Roman law, that if I improved another's property thinking it was my own, I have no actio negotiorum gestorum for reimbursement, 'because I did not intend to obligate anyone to me' (*Digest* 10.3.14.1).

[34] Rivash (above n 33) 515.

[35] Rashba, *Responsa of the Rashba* 4, 54.

[36] Ritva (above n 18); *Nimukei Yosef* (above n 13); compare also *Nimukei Yosef* on Alfasi, Sefer HaHalachot, on Baba Batra 4b; Rosh on Baba Batra 7. For a different view of the significance of the owner's silence, see S Albeck, *Dinei Hamamonot Batalmud* (Jerusalem, Dvir, 1976) 193. Albeck suggests that the silence operates as a retrospective consent once the owner discovers the improvement. This implies the effectiveness of a protest made against an improvement discovered after being completed, which seems inconsistent with the view of Ritva and *Nimukei Yosef* that the owner can be compelled to accept the improvement if the land is suitable for planting trees.

doctrine of free acceptance.[37] On the one hand, the improver acts (and is assumed by Jewish law to act) not gratuitously but with the expectation of payment. On the other hand, the owner, knowing this and allowing the work to proceed without protest, cannot subsequently treat the improvement as undesired, especially since the improvement is consonant with the optimal use of the property. This notion of acquiescence can be regarded as an extension of the owner's power to warn away the potential improver: because at any moment the owner's protest puts an end to the potential improver's claim, omission to make the protest can be construed as free acceptance of the improvement.[38]

Third, because liability is not confined to situations where the 'the owners knew and kept quiet,'[39] a more comprehensive basis for liability must be postulated. The common law notion of incontrovertible benefit is a formulation, applicable to Jewish law, of this more comprehensive basis. Given that liability depends on the status of the land as suitable for planting trees, the improvement must be regarded as a benefit that the improver has no reason not to accept. By bringing the land to its optimal use, the improver has done what the owner wants done and, accordingly, what the owner cannot repudiate when done by another. It is not merely that the improver has made the owner better off in some general way; if that were all that were necessary, owners on this reading of the Rav story would be liable—as they are not—for improvements even to land that was not suitable for planting trees. Rather, the land's suitability for trees frames the legal construction of what owners can be assumed to want. By differentiating their wealth into specific pieces of property that have particular characteristics, owners can be regarded as signaling the terms on which they are prepared to accept improvements. Thus, although one cannot conclude that they are willing to remunerate an improver for producing general increases in their wealth (such increases might take forms incompatible with owners' specific projects), having property of a certain sort can be taken to indicate their willingness to have this property developed in accordance with its optimal use. An improvement consonant with the specific nature of a piece of property is a benefit that the law assumes the owner has no reason to reject. On this view, the nature of the property itself indicates what the owner of the property wants and is willing to pay for, thereby supposedly reconciling the owner's freedom of choice with the improver's entitlement to remuneration.

[37] Birks (above n 2) 277–79; P Birks, 'In Defence of Free Acceptance' in A Burrows (ed), *Essays in the Law of Restitution* (Oxford, Clarendon Press, 1991) 105.
[38] Writing several centuries later than the authorities mentioned above (n 36) and without referring to those texts, Maharit (Rabbi Yosef of Trani, Turkey, 17th century), *Responsa of the Maharit*, I, 106, denied that an owner could incur liability for an unsolicited improvement by knowing about it and keeping quiet. He contended that, unlike fencing and guarding, silence does not constitute a manifestation of the owner's view that he is pleased with the improvement.
[39] Above (n 36).

An example of such reasoning appears in a responsum of the early seventeenth century.[40] The author is commenting on the view of an earlier authority that, whereas the owner of a field suitable for planting trees could be compelled to accept the improvement, the owner of a dilapidated structure that was suitable for building could not.[41] He finds the argument in the earlier authority convoluted,[42] but he suggests that the distinction between an improved field and an improved structure might be supported in a more straightforward way:

> Even the commentators who differed about whether we listen to the owner of a field suitable for planting when he says 'Take your trees and go' can acknowledge that we do listen to the owner of a house even though it is suitable for rebuilding. And the reason for this is that in the case of a field suitable for planting trees it is well known that a field of trees is worth more than a field of grain, and an unplanted field is available for being planted with trees, and because the improvers have made the field more valuable, one needs to give restitution for this surplus. But in the case of courtyards and fields, even if they are suitable for building, nonetheless not every person is ready to squander his wealth and to busy himself with buildings, which impoverish their owners, as the Talmud says, 'Repair and you will not have to rebuild.'[43]

The difference is that improving a field by planting trees in it is an unequivocal benefit, but improving a dilapidated structure involves a commitment to continuing efforts and expenditures that the owner might not want. Fields thus signal the acceptability of improvements in a way that buildings do not.

In sum, Rav's case was initially interpreted as allowing the owner of the field to repudiate the improvement only if the field was not suitable for the planting of trees. It was because Rav was dealing with a field of this sort

[40] Maharit (above n 38).
[41] *Nimukei Yosef* (above n 13).
[42] The convoluted argument in *Nimukei Yosef* is based on three elements. The first is that the implication of Rav's case is that the owner of a field suitable for planting trees cannot refuse the improvement but the owner of a non-suitable field can. The second is the Talmud's explicit statement at Baba Mezia 101b that the improver can remove his materials in the case of a building but not in the case of a field. The third is that the early post-Talmudic Babylonian academies were of the view that there was reciprocity between the owner and the improver, in that the owner can have the materials removed in any situation in which the improver can have them removed. From this the *Nimukei Yosef* argued that it followed from the first of these considerations that issue of removal mentioned by the Talmud applied only to properties that were suitable for the improvements (since we know from Rav's case that owners could have improvements removed from properties that were not suitable); that it further followed from the second and third of these considerations that the owner can have the improvement removed only in the case of suitable buildings but not of suitable fields; and that it further followed from the first of these considerations, that such removal could apply even to buildings that were suitable for rebuilding, but not to fields that were suitable for planting trees.
[43] The reference is to *Babylonian Talmud*, Yevamot 63a: 'Rav Papa said: "... P lug the hole and you will not have to repair; repair and you will not have to rebuild; for whoever engages in building becomes poor."'

that the owner could with impunity declare that he did not want the improvement, even after Rav had told him to pay on the lower measure. The owner, however, would have been compelled to remunerate the improver if the field had been suitable for trees. In this liability of the owner one can discern the Jewish equivalent of the common law notion of incontrovertible benefit.

IV. THE DEMISE AND REBIRTH OF INCONTROVERTIBLE BENEFIT

Although this interpretation of the Rav's case attempts to bring the improver's claim for remuneration into harmony with the owner's freedom of choice, the truth is that the optimal use of the field can serve only as a rough surrogate for the desires of the owner. It is easy to imagine cases in which planting trees in a field used for grains interferes with the owner's autonomy, even though it increases the owner's wealth. The owner may be leading a life that is interwoven with the field's unimproved state: he may want to feed himself and his family with grain grown by his own hands, or he may be knowledgeable about growing grain but not about managing trees, or he may simply be unable to afford the improvement.[44] Thus, although non-optimal, the particular use may satisfactorily match his particular projects, which would be disrupted by the obligation to accept the improvement imposed by a stranger. If the owner could not reject the improvement, 'it would turn out that any person could compel another to transform his field into an orchard and his courtyard into buildings.'[45]

In the fourteenth century, Rosh, a leading authority in Jewish law, proposed a different interpretation of Rav's case that avoided this result.[46] As we have seen, the accepted view until then was that Rav was dealing with a field that was not suitable for planting, as is indicated by his ordering the owner to pay on the lower measure; the fact that Rav did not react to the owner's assertion that he nonetheless did not want that improvement led to the inference that the owner of a field not suitable for trees could not be compelled to pay the improver. Rosh contended that this reading of the incident was mistaken.

Rosh made two interpretive arguments. The first argument noted that Rav twice told the owner to pay, not specifying the measure of remuneration the first time and specifying the lower measure the second time. If the field was one that was not suitable for planting, the first order would have

[44] These examples are taken from Rabbi Abraham Karelitz (Lithuania and Israel, 1878–1953), *Hazon Ish*, Hoshen HaMishpat, Baba Batra 2, 3.
[45] Maharit (above n 38) and Karo (above n 14) 375, 2 (citing the students of Rashba).
[46] Rosh (above n 8).

implied remuneration on the lower measure, thus making the second order a pointless repetition of the first. In Rosh's view, the field in question was one that was indeed suitable for planting trees, and the owner had the right, even for such a field, to refuse the improvement. When Rav told the owner to pay on the lower measure, he was not implying that the field was not suitable for planting. He was merely saying that 'if the owner acquiesces in the improvement, let him pay the improver so much.'[47] In other words, Rosh thought that Rav was merely proposing a settlement that might appeal to both parties: to the owner, because he would be getting the improvement for which his field was suited at a lower price than if he employed someone to plant the trees, and to the improver because he would get something for the trees instead of having to remove them.

Rosh's second argument noted that after Rav saw that the owner had fenced in and guarded the trees, Rav compelled the owner to pay on the higher measure. This disposition creates a puzzle if one thinks that the field in question was not suitable for planting. Remuneration for planting a non-suitable field should have been on the lower rather than the higher measure. To be sure, the owner's actions can be taken to show that his earlier denial that he wanted the trees was untruthful; but, given that the level of remuneration depends on the status of the land, it is hard to see why the fact that he really does want the trees should change the amount he has to pay for them. If, however, the field was suitable for planting trees (as Rosh thought), then the mystery about the award on the higher measure disappears.

With this transformation of the story, any semblance of liability for an incontrovertible benefit falls away from it. Rav's inaction after the owner repeated that he did not want the improvement shows that an owner could not be compelled to accept an improvement even if that improvement accorded with the optimal use of the property. All that the difference between the upper and the lower hand does is mark the different default measures of remuneration

> if the owner is willing to keep the seedlings in his field. But if he is not willing to keep them, he can tell the improver to take his seedlings and go even if the field is suitable for planting trees, for he can say that 'as far as I am concerned, it is more satisfactory for me to have a field of grain' ... It makes no sense at all for the owner of the field to have to pay the improver as a hired planter when he does not want the seedlings.[48]

In the story the owner ends up paying on the higher measure, but this is because, having shown through his actions that he wanted to keep the trees, he became liable to pay at the appropriate default level. If he really had not

[47] *Ibid.*
[48] *Ibid.*

wanted the trees, he could have insisted that the improver remove them even though his field was suitable for planting. Rosh thus sees the story as reflecting the unbridled freedom of the owner to determine the use of his own property. In Rosh's interpretation of the case, what is paramount is the autonomy of the owner, not the status of the land.

Although Rosh's interpretation of Rav's case became the accepted one, it turned out not to be the end of the notion of incontrovertible benefit in Jewish law. For simultaneously with shutting off this avenue involving the planting of fields, Rosh opened or kept open another involving the building of structures.

Because of the Talmud's omission to deal with the matter expressly, disagreement had arisen among Rosh's predecessors about the right of the owner to refuse an improvement that consisted in the building or rebuilding of a structure, even if this structure was the land's optimal use.[49] This right to refuse the improvement, if it existed, would be expressed by the owner's telling the improver to remove his materials, thus restoring both parties to the position they were in before the improver's activities. One of the strands in this disagreement was the view that the owner had no such right, because building materials lose part of their value by being incorporated into a structure. Accordingly, by ordering the improver to remove his materials, the owner would be harming the improver rather than merely restoring the status quo.[50]

This disagreement stands in the background of Rosh's treatment of the owner's right to refuse the improvement. So far as fields were concerned, Rosh championed the view that even if the field was suitable for planting

[49] For one facet of this disagreement, see above (n 41).

[50] Ravad (Rabbi Abraham ben David, France, 12th century), Comments on Alfasi, Sefer HaHalachot, on Baba Mezia 101a, in *Shitah Mekubetzet* on Baba Mezia 101a. The Talmud had dealt expressly only with the instance of the improver who wanted to remove his materials; it had been silent about whether the owner could order the materials removed. The rule stated in the Talmud was that the improver could remove his materials in the case of a structure but not in the case of a field, see above (n 21). The early post-Talmudic Babylonian academies were of the view that whatever rule about removal applied to the improver also applied to the owner, with the result that the owner of the structure could order the improver to remove the materials; but see above (n 42). Ravad contested this view. The controversy is summed up by Ravad's follower Meiri (Rabbi Menahem ben Solomon, France, 13th century), *Beit HaBehirah* on Baba Mezia 101a, as follows:

> The Talmud does not mention what the rule is if the owner of the land tells the improver to take his wood and stones. The heads of the academies agreed to treat the improver and the owner equally, and because the improver can say 'I am taking my wood and stones,' so the owner can say 'Take your wood and stones.' Nonetheless, the greatest of the commentators disagree with this, because in the latter case there is a great loss. When the improver says 'I am taking my wood and stones,' we listen to him because he is waiving his loss. But in the case of an owner who says 'Take your wood', it is appropriate to say that we do not listen to him but we allow the improver to occupy the structure until the owner reimburses his expenses or gives him what we assess for him.

trees, owners did not have to keep the trees if they did not want them. Structures, however, were different from trees. In the case of trees, the Talmud had ruled that the improver could not remove his trees, because once they received nutriments from the earth, their removal would weaken the owner's soil.[51] This ruling does not apply to the *owner's* requesting the removal of the trees, because the owner can decide to accept the weakening of his own soil. Nor is this weakening something about which the improver can complain; the improver gets his trees back unimpaired. However, the situation is reversed if the improvement involves building materials. In this case it is the *improver* who suffers from the depreciation of his materials. If the improver wishes to remove the materials and accept this loss, the owner cannot complain—which perhaps accounts for the Talmud's ruling that improvers can remove building materials but not trees. But the owner cannot impose a loss on the improver by requiring the materials to be removed.

Accordingly, Rosh ruled that although owners could not be forced to accept trees, they could be forced to accept structures. However, instead of merely adopting the conclusion that the owner could not require the improver to suffer a loss by removing the building materials, Rosh also outlined the conditions under which this conclusion applied. Rosh insisted that the consideration of the harm to the improver not be at the expense of harm to the owner. He therefore asserted that the owner was barred from having the improvement removed only if the improvement did not cause him a loss. Thus, commenting on the view that the owner causes a loss by requiring removal of the building materials from a rebuilt ruin, he remarked:

> This consideration makes sense where the owner was not using the ruin and he had his own place, because it is appropriate to build a structure like this when it does not impair the owner's livelihood, because [if the owner then requests removal of the materials] he is really seeking a pretext to inflict loss on the improver, and so we do not listen to him.[52]

On the surface Rosh's reasoning seems delictual rather than restitutionary. His reason for preventing the owner from having the materials removed is that owner cannot gratuitously inflict loss on the improver,[53] rather than that the improver is entitled to have the owner give restitution for a benefit. Nonetheless, in this context the delictual cannot be disentangled from the restitutionary. Rosh's formulation sets out what he regards as the conditions in which the owner is not adversely affected by—and therefore cannot

[51] Above (n 21).
[52] Rosh on Baba Mezia, ch 8, 23.
[53] Rosh's statement that the owner seeks a pretext to inflict loss on the improver is presumably related to the recognition in Jewish law of a doctrine of abuse of rights. On this doctrine, see A Kirschenbaum, *Equity in Jewish Law: Formalism and Flexibility in Jewish Civil Law* (New York, Yeshiva University Press, 1991) 185–252.

complain about—the improvement. Under these conditions, the owner's freedom to determine the use of his own property no longer obtains, and the owner must pay for the improvement on the higher measure. Although the reasoning is not explicitly restitutionary, it has a restitutionary dimension.

This restitutionary dimension reflects the principle implicit in Rosh's formulation. Rosh's view is that owners can be compelled to keep the improvement when it does not leave them worse off than they would otherwise have been. An owner who is left worse off by the improvement could hardly be described as 'seeking a pretext to inflict loss on the improver'; by having the materials removed in those circumstances all that the owner would be doing is avoiding his or her own loss. In other words, only if the improvement can be regarded as a benefit that the owner has no reason to reject does the preclusion against inflicting loss on the improver get off the ground. In this way, incontrovertible benefit, which was expelled in Rosh's account of trees, returns in his treatment of buildings.

But what counts as an incontrovertible benefit in this line of reasoning? Given that Rosh holds that planting trees in a suitable field does not obligate the owner to pay for the improvement, incontrovertible benefit can no longer refer to the optimal use of the property. What sort of benefit, then, is implicit in Rosh's thinking? Modern authorities who have addressed this question have offered a restrictive and an expansive suggestion.

The restrictive suggestion appears in the codification of Rabbi Yehiel Michal HeLevi Epstein.[54] The owner could not refuse a benefit

> where the court sees that it is necessary for the builder to build in this place according to the owner's circumstances and the circumstances of the city, and the owner himself himself would have built there, and the builder built it properly, in a way that the owner himself would not have improved upon.[55]

The benefit must be accepted only when the improver merely anticipates what the owner necessarily and inevitably would have done. This consideration is independent of the optimal use of the property. An owner can tell the improver to remove trees planted even in a field suitable for trees, because it is always possible that the owner prefers to grow grain.[56] The fact that the field is suitable for trees does not make trees necessary. As long

[54] Rabbi Yehiel Michal HaLevi Epstein (Poland, 1829–1908), *Aruch HaShulhan*, Hoshen Mishpat 375, 10–16 (1892).

[55] *Ibid*, 11. By 'the circumstances of the owner' Epstein means that the owner has to be able to afford the improvement. If the owner does not have the resources to pay for the improvement, the owner can require the improver either to remove the materials (*ibid*, 12) or to buy the property at its pre-improved value (*ibid*, 14–15). By 'the circumstances of the city' Epstein means that the building has to be conform to the standard of the locality. As the earlier codifications said about building in a courtyard, 'he should build a useful building appropriate to that courtyard as is the custom of that place.' Maimonides, (Egypt, 12th century), *Mishneh Torah*, Laws of Robbery and Loss, 10, 6; Rabbi Joseph Karo, *Shulhan Aruch*, Hoshen Mishpat 375, 7.

[56] Epstein (above n 54).

as the owner can plausibly point to some other use for the property than the one exemplified by the improvement, the improvement can be rejected. Epstein thus allows the improver to interfere with the owner's freedom to determine the use of the property only when that interference matches what the owner would do in any case.

Epstein illustrates the distinction between necessary and unnecessary improvements with a responsum authored by Rosh himself. This instructive responsum is worth quoting almost in full:[57]

> Reuben owned some houses, but travelled away from his city. Simeon came and lived in them and saw that the house was tottering and about to collapse. He reconstructed it and reinforced it and saved it from the danger of falling and plastered and panelled it. When Reuben returned, he wanted to evict Simeon from his house, saying that his initial entry was unauthorized. Does Reuben have to reimburse Simeon ... ? Answer: Because it was tottering and close to collapsing, Reuben cannot evict him until he reimburses all the expenditures that Simeon made to reinforce the house and save it from collapsing, but what Simeon built that was not necessary, like making rooms and plastering and panelling, he did for his own benefit, and Reuben does not have to pay him for that but he tells him 'Take your wood and your stones,' and this assessment will be according to builders who will determine what Simeon had to expend to avoid the house's collapse, and they will assess him, and when Reuben gives this to Simeon, then Simeon will vacate Reuben's house.
>
> The questioner asked further, Let our rabbi teach us: why do we not take into account the usefulness of the construction apart from the danger of collapse, especially since the houses had previously been plastered, and beneath the plaster the wall was mouldy and tottering, and Simeon had to destroy the plaster in order to fix the wall, and he fixed it to its previous state, and he fixed gates and windows and leaky roofs and locks? The answer: For any construction that is not to deal with the danger that the building could not continue to exist and remain standing and be kept from collapsing out of decay, why should we obligate the owner to pay? He can say, 'I do not want to spend my money on it, because the house could continue to exist without this construction. If you built it for your benefit, take your wood and your stones.'

This responsum draws a sharp distinction between the existence and the condition of the improved object. One cannot be sure that the owner wants a change in an object's condition, even if the improvement restores the object to the previous condition from which it deteriorated. The fact that the house had previously been plastered and that the plaster had to be removed to save the house from collapsing does not mean that the improver can charge the owner for replastering. The owner is therefore free to insist that the improver undo this aspect of the renovation, even though, since

[57] The responsum is available in the work of Rosh's son, Rabbi Jacob ben Asher (Spain, 14th century), *Tur Hoshen Mishpat*, 375.

plaster cannot be reused, this causes the improver a loss. However, the owner can be compelled to pay for those aspects of the renovation that preserved the house. This benefit is incontrovertible, so that it would be abusive for the owner to make its conferral the reason for harming the improver. As Epstein remarks in glossing the responsum, 'The court determines whether it was necessary for the owner to do this, and makes an assessment for him with the improver having the upper hand, because although the improvement was without authorization, the improver nonetheless conferred a benefit on him, and so why should he suffer a loss?'[58] Rosh, and Epstein following him, think that one can safely ascribe to owners a desire to have their properties preserved, so that then they have no legitimate reason to harm improvers by compelling the removal of the materials. Because the owner necessarily realizes a benefit from the preservation of the property, the improver is entitled to be reimbursed for the expenses entailed in achieving that end. This responsum shows that, although in the case of structures Rosh did not nullify the notion of incontrovertible benefit (as he did in the case of trees), he narrowed the basis for the improver's claim to circumstances in which the interference with the owner's freedom of choice is not significant, because the owner is merely paying for work that in any case had to be done if the structure was to be saved from collapsing.

So much for Epstein's narrow construction of incontrovertible benefit. In contrast stands the more expansive view of Rabbi Abraham Karelitz.[59] Karelitz's argument is that the owner must accept and remunerate the improver at the higher level for any improvement that increases the value of the property, unless the owner has a bona fide reason for not accepting it. Whereas Epstein restricts what common lawyers would think of as the benefit's incontrovertibility to what was necessary in the circumstances, Karelitz broadens it to include whatever adds value without genuine inconvenience to the owner.

Karelitz's view of the circumstances under which the improvement must be accepted arises from a reconceptualization of what it means to say that a field is suitable for planting trees. A field is considered suitable for planting not because trees are its optimal use, but because a field with trees is worth more than a field with grain. In his view, the difference between a plantable and non-plantable field is simply a matter of the objectively higher economic value of the former. If the improvement increases the value of the field, the owner is assumed to want the improvement and must remunerate the improver at the higher rate. Similarly, if the owner reveals that he actually wants the improvement—as was the case with the owner who fenced and guarded the trees in the dispute that came before Rav—then the owner must

[58] Epstein (above n 54) 375, 12.
[59] Karelitz (above n 44).

pay on the higher measure even if improvement does not add value to the property. What is decisive is the benefit to the owner, whether that benefit is manifested in the increased value of the property or in conduct revealing the owner's desire for the improvement even though it does not increase the property's value.

To this notion of benefit objectively manifested through value or conduct, Karelitz adds an important qualification: an owner who has a bona fide reason for not wanting an improvement that increases the property's value can refuse to pay and can have the materials removed. This qualification too involves an objective inquiry into the circumstances and motivations of the owner. Karelitz would have had little sympathy for the suggestion that the possibility of the owner's subjective devaluation of the benefit immunizes the owner from liability.[60] For Karelitz Jewish law does not, and never did, attach any significance to the owner's rejection of the benefit on the strength of 'private reasons of his own.'[61] The freedom of the owner to determine the use of his or her property is not absolute; it must reflect a plausible reason for rejecting a benefit that increases the value of the property. 'Everything is according to what appears to the eye of the judge, as to whether the increased value is truly not to the benefit of the owner, or whether the owner is just saying so to put the improver off.'[62] Karelitz reinterprets even the dispute between Rosh and his predecessors about whether the owner of a plantable field had to accept the trees as involving not a difference of legal principle but a distinction on the facts. Rosh's predecessors, who held that the owner of a field suitable for planting could be compelled to pay for the improvement, were merely referring to a situation where

> the owner has no excuse or reason for why he would not want to plant the field, and we see his response 'Take your seedlings' as being merely for the sake of angering the improver, as if to say 'Neither I nor you will get anything,' or as evading payment; but if we see that it is actually the truth that he does not want the seedlings and he wants them uprooted, then we treat him as having field that is not suitable for planting.[63]

Similarly, when Rosh allows the owner to reject the improvements, he is dealing with a situation in which the owner has a genuine reason for preferring his land in an unimproved state.

Karelitz accordingly regards Rosh's statement about the rebuilt ruins[64] as illustrative of these principles. It will be recalled that Rosh held that, although the owner generally could have the improvement removed, the

[60] See Birks (above n 2).
[61] Karelitz (above n 44), second paragraph.
[62] *Ibid*, Baba Kama 22, 6.
[63] *Ibid*, Baba Batra 2, 3.
[64] Above (n 52).

owner of a ruin rebuilt without authorization could not order the improver to remove his materials if he was really seeking a pretext to inflict loss on the improver. Karelitz noted that Rosh indicated two circumstances that presented genuine reasons for not wanting the rebuilt structure. The first was that the owner was already using the ruin for something else, so that the pre-existing use could be taken as a manifestation of his genuine desires concerning the property. The second was that the rebuilding impaired his livelihood, which Karelitz interpreted as meaning that the owner could not afford to pay for the improvement. If, however, despite such considerations, the owner moved into the rebuilt ruin and began to live there, this conduct could be taken as a manifestation of his acceptance of the benefit, triggering an obligation to remunerate the improver on the higher measure.[65]

In sum, Jewish law refers to three different conceptions of what common lawyers regard as incontrovertible benefit. The earliest is that the owner can be compelled to accept an improvement that moves the property to its optimal use. This conception was destroyed by Rosh, who held that, regardless of the nature of the property, the owner is at liberty to order the improver to remove the improvement. In qualifying this with the observation that the right to order the removal of building materials cannot be turned into a pretext to cause loss to the improver, Rosh allowed incontrovertible benefit to be reborn. One form of this rebirth was the stringent view that the owner was barred from rejecting the improvement only if the improvement was necessary. The other form was the more liberal view that the owner had to accept any improvement that increased the value of the property, except if the owner had a genuine reason for rejecting it.

V. CONCLUSION

In this article I have traced the main lines in the development of the Jewish law governing unrequested improvements. The point of departure for this development is the story in the Talmud of Rav's dealings with the owner whose field was planted with trees. From this story emerge subsequent discussions of the difference between having the upper and the lower hand, of the significance of an improvement that puts the property to its optimal

[65] Karelitz (above n 44) 2, 6. Karelitz's view has one additional complexity that I wish merely to mention for the sake of completeness. Having reconceptualized the suitability for planting trees in terms of an increase in the property's value, Karelitz was faced with the difficulty of explaining why the Talmud and the legal tradition to this point distinguished between fields that were or were not suitable for planting trees. For on Karelitz's view what matters ultimately is not the kind of field it is but whether the owner receives a benefit manifested either through value or conduct. Karelitz's solution to this difficulty was that even if the owner did not want the improvement and had genuine reason to reject it, the owner might nonetheless be willing to put up with it. Then whether the field was suitable for planting trees (that is, in Karelitz's view, whether the trees increased the value of the land) would determine the rate of the improver's remuneration, see Karelitz (above n 44) 3, 4.

use, and of the conditions under which the owner could be compelled to accept the benefit.

At first blush, the Talmud's account of the trees planted in another's field and the jurisprudence that flows from it might, from the standpoint of the common law, seem peculiar on a number of grounds. The most important of these is that throughout the Talmudic passage Rav seeks, with eventual success, to have the owner pay for the improvement. In the eye of the common law, this solicitude for the improver seems misplaced. By planting trees in what he knew was another's field, the improver was the most unappealing of restitutionary claimants, a mere volunteer or officious intermeddler. Conversely, the owner should surely be able to determine for himself whether to plant trees in his own field. Right from the beginning Rav's assumption that the owner should be assessed for the trees seems eccentric.

A second peculiarity is that Jewish law gives the knowing improver a preferential position over an innocent one. Only the improver who knows that the property being improved belongs to another can claim remuneration on the higher measure, which under some circumstances gives the improver a share of the yield and under other circumstances allows the improver to recover expenditures in excess of the property's increased value. This is because the basis of such remuneration is what the owner would have paid to have the improvement, a quasi-contractual measure that presupposes that the improver is rendering a service to someone else rather than merely being mistaken about the extent of one's own ownership.

A third peculiarity is that situations in which the materials for the improvement (the trees in the field example, the wood and stones in the building example) can be removed are paradigmatic for the discussion of unsolicited improvements. English law encapsulates its concerns in Chief Baron Pollock's famous question—'One cleans another's shoes; what can the other do but put them on?'[66]—because it assumes that the benefit has been irretrievably entangled in the owner's property. Jewish law, in contrast, expresses the owner's rejection of the benefit through the owner's telling the improver to 'take your materials and go.' In part this reflects the idea that even after the materials have been affixed to the owner's land or structure, the owner acquires property in them only on signaling acceptance of the improvement by offering to pay.[67] More deeply, however, it reflects a commitment to restoring the parties to their positions before the improvement, or at least to preventing the owner from ostensibly rejecting the benefit while continuing to enjoy it. When the Jewish jurists turned their attention to unremovable benefits (the classic example was dyeing someone else's wool), they adopted an approach similar to the one that governed

[66] *Taylor v Laird* (1856) 156 ER 1203 (Ex D).
[67] Rashba (above n 8).

removable ones: the owner had to pay unless there was reason to suppose that the improvement was not in fact a benefit.[68]

Perhaps from the perspective of systems other than the common law, some of these peculiarities might not seem all that eccentric after all. The possibility of removing an enrichment for which the owner is not liable was mentioned by the Roman jurist Celsus in the second century, is present in contemporary German law, and has been suggested for the common law as well.[69]

Be that as it may, the differences between Jewish law and the common law mask an important similarity. Although the particular moves about unrequested improvements in each system diverge, these moves respond to the same challenge. When dealing with unrequested benefits, any rational system of private law must reconcile the owner's freedom to determine the use of his or her property with the improver's claim that that the owner should not be unjustly enriched at the improver's expense. This in turn requires attention to two issues. The first issue is whether the improvement is a gift from the improver to the owner; if it is, the improver has no reason to complain that the owner's use of it is unjust. The second issue is whether, even assuming that the improvement was not a gift, acceptance of the improvement can reasonably be imputed to the owner; if it can, there is no injustice in compelling the owner to pay the improver. The first of these issues directs us to consider whether the improver has acted with donative intent; the second directs us to consider the conditions under which an unrequested benefit would nonetheless be consistent with the autonomy of owners with respect to their own property. Taken together, these two issues vindicate the conception of private law as a realm of freedom by insisting that, in the transfer of a benefit from the improver to the owner, both its bestowal and its receipt are the expression of the free will of the parties.

The law's treatment of these two issues, although of course based on the specific events of the transaction in question, is a matter not of fact but of juristic construction. It involves not merely ascertaining what happened but working out the relevant legal categories and ascribing meaning in their light to the conduct of the parties. Different legal systems, while addressing the same issues, can nonetheless reasonably differ in their construction of the legal categories, or in the meaning they ascribe to the parties' conduct, or in their understanding of the relationship between conduct and categories.

The contrasting attitudes toward donative intent in the common law and in Jewish law provide a dramatic illustration of this. Both the common law

[68] Rabbi Jacob Lorbeerbaum (Poland, 1760–1832), *Netivot HaMishpat* on Shulhan Aruch 375; Karelitz (above n 44) 2, 6.

[69] DA Verse, 'Improvements and Enrichment: A Comparative Analysis' [1998] *Restitution Law Review* 85, 88, 102–3.

and Jewish law concern themselves with whether a knowing unsolicited improvement is to be construed as a gift, but they elaborate different answers. Because the common law imputes to the parties the awareness that only the owner can determine the use of what is owned, the common law includes the taking of a risk of being remunerated within its conception of the improver's donative intent, with the result that volunteering or intermeddling becomes a fatal obstacle to the improver's claim. Jewish law does not regard the improver as a risk-taker but looks more single-mindedly at the intent or the presumed intent of the improver, who is therefore assumed not to have acted with donative intent. As a result, the only substantial barrier in Jewish law against liability for unrequested improvements is the second issue of determining the conditions under which acceptance of the improvement can reasonably be imputed to the owner.

It is, accordingly, hardly surprising that the Jewish law, over the eighteen centuries of its recorded discussions of unrequested improvements, has on this issue elaborated the variety of views outlined in this article. These discussions direct attention either to the optimal use of the property being improved, or to the necessity for the improvement, or to the genuineness of the owner's reason for not welcoming the increase in the property's value. The common law, in contrast, both because of the relative youth of its law of restitution and because of the filtering effect of the issue of volunteering, is only at the beginning of a similar elaboration of its parallel idea of incontrovertible benefit. However, with the intense interest that the law of restitution is now enjoying in the common law world, we common lawyers can perhaps already sympathize with the observations expressed by the distinguished author of a sixteenth century responsum about unrequested improvements: 'I do not have time to go on at length about these matters, because there are many controversies and the questioner is pressing.'[70]

[70] Maharashdam (Rabbi Samuel de Medina, Salonika, 16th century), *Responsa of the Maharashdam*, Hoshen Mishpat 327.

10

Unrequested Benefits in German Law

THOMAS KREBS

I. INTRODUCTION

SHORTLY AFTER THE Second World War, a construction company wanted to develop some land in Frankfurt by building an office block on it. The site next to it was still covered by the rubble of a bombed out building. The company would have liked to use that site for storing materials, but was refused permission to do so by the owner. It went ahead anyway, removed the rubble and used the land by putting up a building shed and storing building materials. The building work completed, the owner of the adjacent site took the company to court. The *Landgericht* Frankfurt awarded him DM 7,774.51 plus interest. The company's first appeal was successful. In the view of the appeal court, it was entitled to a counter-claim based on its work in removing the rubble from the land, thereby completely extinguishing the owner's restitutionary claim for a reasonable sum in respect of rental. The company appealed to the *Bundesgerichtshof* (*BGH*) which restored the original judgment: the value of the company's work in removing the rubble was not to be taken into account. In other words, the company had no claim to restitution of any benefit conferred on the owner by clearing the land.[1]

This result is clearly correct. It can be reached in two ways: the most straightforward approach is to argue that no restitutionary claim ever came into existence. In the terminology of the common law, this amounts to saying that there is simply no reason for restitution on these facts. The restitutionary claim never gets off the ground because there is no unjust factor which the defendant can rely on. A system which, like German law, hides the substantive reasons for restitution behind an abstract formula such as 'absence of legal ground' or 'absence of juristic reason' finds it more difficult

[1] BGHZ 39, 186 (25 March 1963).

to reach the correct result at this early stage. In such a system the company in the example might well overcome the first hurdle by showing that it conferred a benefit on the owner which is not supported by any legal ground recognised by the law. It might still fail at the second hurdle, of course, namely when the court asks whether and to what extent the owner of the land can be said to have been enriched by the clearing of the rubble. This may raise a plethora of difficult questions. Should the owner be required to account for the objective value of the work? Should it matter that he would have been able to carry the work out more cheaply himself? If he intended to sell the land, should he be compelled to account for the difference in value between the land in its current cleared state and in its previous state? Should the company be entitled to lead evidence that the owner intended to sell the land? Should the owner possibly even be required to sell the land, or to put it to some profitable use (which would, in turn, render the work carried out by the defendant valuable for him)?

In this chapter, I shall argue that it is vital to keep the two inquiries separate. It is comparatively easy to decide whether a reason for restitution exists, and where no such reason can be found the complex issues concerned with the enrichment of the benefited party are avoided. It is only where there is a reason for restitution that these issues need to be addressed at all. It thus makes sense to look at the two questions separately. First, what is the basis of the restitutionary claim? Second, in what circumstances should a defendant, faced with a restitutionary claim based on a positive reason for restitution, be entitled to claim that the benefit received does not constitute an 'enrichment' for him?

German law is instructive for English law, which could easily be on the brink of adopting civilian structures, and may be even more instructive for Canadian law, where the reception of civilian structures into the law of unjust enrichment has already happened.

II. THE BASIS OF THE RESTITUTIONARY CLAIM

It is striking that Weinrib, in his fascinating contribution to this volume, takes the existence of a restitutionary claim largely for granted. It will be remembered that his article is mainly focused on a case decided by the preeminent third century Jewish jurist Rav, 'reported' in the Babylonian Talmud.[2] The case involved a man planting trees in another man's field. The inquiry is focused exclusively on whether and to what extent the owner of the field could be said to have been benefited by the trees; this question is

[2] Babylonian Talmud, Baba Mezia, 101a. Professor Weinrib is entitled to the gratitude of the unjust enrichment community for drawing this fascinating source to our attention and for making it accessible to those of us not versed in ancient Hebrew.

answered by asking whether the field was suitable for planting trees and whether the owner chose to adopt the man's action—eg by fencing off the land. The prior question whether the improver should be entitled to any restitutionary claim at all does not seem to arise. In fact, the source does not even address the questions which would be relevant to this prior inquiry. Why did the man decide to plant the field? Did he think he was planting his own field? Or did he feel that, in the absence of other employment, he would make himself useful by planting trees in the owner's field, expecting to be remunerated? Did the owner know that this was going on? If so, did he try to stop it? None of these questions are taken to be relevant, at least not at this first stage of the inquiry.

Where a legal system bases restitutionary claims on a negative requirement, such as the absence of a juristic reason for an enrichment, this is understandable. Let us take the Canadian *Pettkus v Becker*[3] formula as an example. According to the Supreme Court of Canada a plaintiff needs to show three things:

(1) an enrichment;
(2) a corresponding deprivation; and
(3) the absence of any juristic reason for the enrichment.

There seems to be no express requirement that the enrichment must be 'unjust.' As such, provided there is an enrichment which is unsupported by either: (a) an underlying obligation, or (b) donative intent, restitution will follow provided a corresponding deprivation can be found.[4] Much if not most of the work is thus left to requirements (1) and (2), work that is very necessary in order to restrict the otherwise extremely wide restitutionary claim based on (3), the absence of any juristic reason.

A. The Taxonomy of the Modern German Law of Unjust Enrichment

§ 812 I of the German Civil Code, the *Bürgerliches Gesetzbuch* (*BGB*), is strongly reminiscent of the *Pettkus v Becker* formula:

Wer durch die Leistung eines anderen oder in sonstiger Weise auf dessen Kosten etwas ohne rechtlichen Grund erlangt, ist ihm zur Herausgabe verpflichtet. (…)	He who obtains something through somebody else's performance or in another way at his expense without a legal cause is obliged to make restitution to the other. (…)

[3] [1980] 2 SCR 834; 117 DLR (3d) 257, 274 (SCC).
[4] J Neyers, 'Understanding Unjust Enrichment: An Introduction' ch 1, 1–2.

As in Canadian law, an enrichment is thus considered unjust if it lacks a 'legal cause' or 'juristic reason.' In most cases, this will mean that a benefit has been transferred under a supposed legal transaction which has turned out to be void or not to have existed at all. § 812 I will then sort out the restitutionary consequences by ordering the defendant to make restitution of the benefit received.

The problem with § 812 I is, however, that it is considerably wider than this. As Markesinis, Lorenz and Dannemann point out, the main dilemma with general clauses 'is that with them one tends to get more than one has bargained for: their wording will often cover more than it should. The main attention within legal systems based on general clauses will, therefore, be geared towards excluding certain categories from the application of the general rule.'[5] One of the devices used to narrow down § 812 I was to interpret the words '*auf dessen Kosten*' ('at his expense') to require a corresponding deprivation on the part of the claimant.[6] With the development of a more sophisticated taxonomy of the law of unjust enrichment this rather arbitrary restriction has been abandoned, culminating in Esser's famous dictum that we are dealing with the law of unjust *enrichment*, not the law of unjust *disenrichment*.[7] To put it in a different way, the claimant has a right to restitution, not to compensation.

The provision in § 812 I is today narrowed down by categorising the different enrichment claims according to the manner in which the enrichment came about. This differs sharply from the common law typology which appears to be based upon positive reasons for restitution such as mistake, duress and failure of consideration. The modern German taxonomy was developed in the thirties and fifties by Wilburg and von Caemmerer in order to narrow down the scope of the general enrichment action which might otherwise have led to an uncontrollable extension of liability.[8] This taxonomy, now enjoying overwhelming academic and judicial recognition, draws a bright line between cases in which the enrichment comes to the defendant by a performance made by the plaintiff and a minority of other cases in which it does not. One could say that this modern taxonomy takes out the 'easy' cases (in which the enrichment is conferred by some sort of performance, or, in German, *Leistung*) and bundles them together under the label *Leistungskondiktion*. These cases are 'easy'

[5] BS Markesinis, W Lorenz and G Dannemann, *The German Law of Obligations*, vol 1 (Oxford, Oxford University Press, 1997) 713.

[6] See F Schulz, *AcP* 105 (1909) 478; M Planck, *Schuldrecht II*, 4th edn (1928) 1624.

[7] J Esser and HL Weyers, *Schuldrecht Besonderer Teil*, 4th edn (1984) 403.

[8] W Wilburg, *Die Lehre von der ungerechtfertigten Bereicherung nach östereichischem und detuschem Recht* (Graz, Leuschner & Lubensky, 1934); E von Caemmerer, 'Bereicherung und unerlaubte Handlung' in *Festschrift für Rabel*, vol 1 (Tübingen, Mohr, 1954) 333. Cf R Zimmermann and J du Plessis, 'Basic Features of the German Law of Unjustified Enrichment' [1994] *Restitution Law Review* 14, 24.

because performances are aimed at certain ends, often the discharge of an existing legal obligation. If a supposed underlying obligation is void because of a provision of the general law of obligations, the reason of the invalidity will also furnish the reason for restitution. This elegantly takes the pressure off the law of unjust enrichment and leaves the material questions to be worked out by the general law.[9] On the other hand, if the legal obligation which the performing party means to discharge does not exist at all, it is clear that he was mistaken. The substantive reason for restitution is thus mistake. This becomes particularly clear in § 814. This reads:

Das zum Zwecke der Erfüllung einer Verbindlichkeit Geleistete kann nicht zurückgefordert werden, wenn der Leistende gewußt hat, daß er zur Leistung nicht verpflichtet war, oder wenn die Leistung einer sittlichen Pflicht oder einer auf den Anstand zu nehmenden Rücksicht entsprach.	That which has been performed for the purpose of discharging a liability cannot be demanded back if the performing party knew that he was under no liability to perform, or if his performance was pursuant to a moral duty.

The restitutionary claim is thus excluded where the transferor cannot be said to have been mistaken. In other words, the enriched party is allowed to keep the benefit.

The more difficult cases are those which do not involve any performance. These are broadly categorised as cases *not* based on performance (*Nichtleistungskondiktionen*), or cases in which the defendant was enriched 'in another way,' and then further subdivided according to the manner in which the benefit found its way to the defendant. The most common sub-categorisation distinguishes between cases of *Eingriff* (which can be translated, albeit clumsily, as interference or encroachment), *Rückgriff* (restitution where the claimant has validly discharged the defendant's debt to a third party) and *Verwendung* (restitution where the claimant has expended his own assets and/or labour on property belonging to the defendant). The corresponding claims are referred to as *Eingriffskondiktion, Rückgriffskondiktion* and *Verwendungskondiktion*. Following the lead of Birks and Chambers, who suggested a diagram for the common law of unjust enrichment in 1997,[10] the modern taxonomy can be expressed in diagrammatic form as follows:

[9] Cf T Krebs, 'In Defence of Unjust Factors' in D Johnston and R Zimmermann (eds), *Unjustified Enrichment—Key Issues in Comparative Perspective* (Cambridge, Cambridge University Press, 2002) 76, 85–92; for greater detail see T Krebs, *Restitution at the Crossroads: A Comparative Study* (London, Cavendish Publishing, 2001) chs 10, 11 and 14.

[10] P Birks and R Chambers, *Restitution Research Resource 1997* (Oxford, Mansfield Press, 1997) 3.

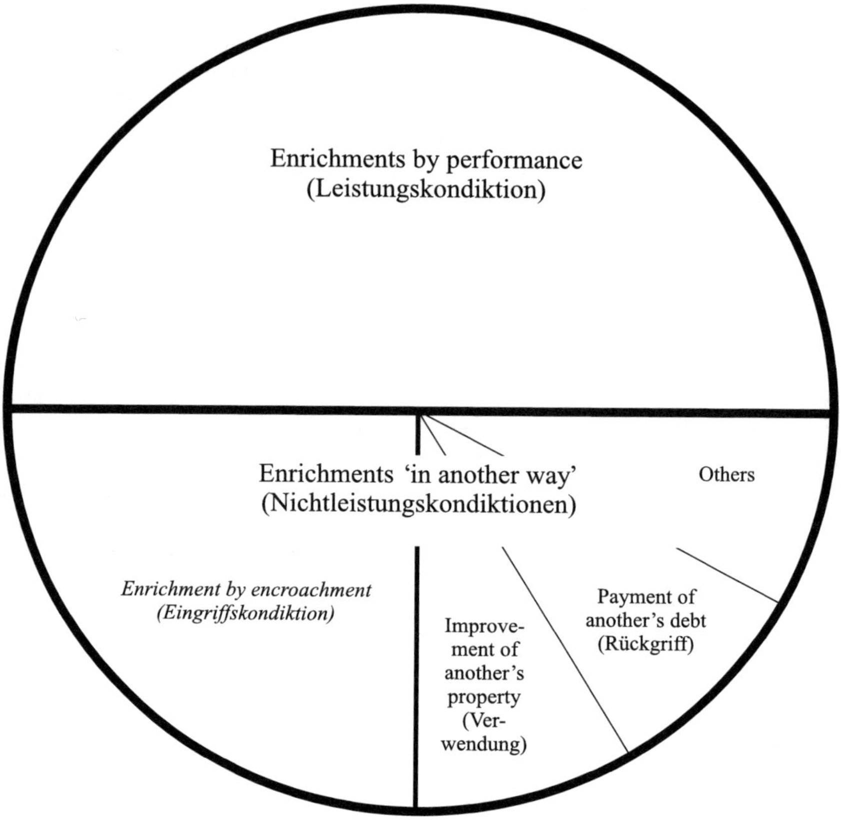

Thus, where the defendant has obtained a benefit by trespassing on the plaintiff's land or by infringing the plaintiff's copyright, he will be open to a claim based on the *Eingriffskondiktion*. There has been an interference with the plaintiff's rights without his consent. This does leave open the question, however, which rights will give rise to restitutionary claims in such circumstances. This question is answered by reference to the attribution of rights under the general law: has the enrichment been obtained by infringing a legally protected right belonging to the plaintiff? This test is read into the requirement 'without legal ground' by translating that phrase to mean 'contrary to the attribution by the general law' (*Zuweisungswidrigkeit*).[11]

The *Rückgriffskondiktion*, based on the valid discharge of another's debt, is extremely rare, mainly because in most cases the payment of another's debt will constitute a performance to that person and allow the payer to recover on the basis of the *Leistungskondiktion* if the performance has failed.

[11] D Reuter and M Martinek, *Ungerechtfertigte Bereicherung* (1983) 241.

The final category of restitutionary claims, the *Verwendungskondiktion*, has been even more problematical in this respect. Both the initial example involving the clearing of rubble from the claimant's land and Weinrib's example of planting trees in another's field would be put in this category by German law. The focus of the remaining discussion will be on this particular restitutionary claim.

B. The *Verwendungskondiktion*

(i) *The Verwendungskondiktion in the Context of the BGB*

It should be pointed out at the outset that the importance of the *Verwendungskondiktion* is limited because of a number of special rules found elsewhere in the *BGB*. One very large category of cases is covered by special rules relating to the relationship between the owner and possessor of a thing, whether it be movable or immovable. These are to be found in §§ 987 ff *BGB*. If these rules apply, the general law of unjust enrichment contained in §§ 812 ff *BGB* is excluded. In fact, our initial example was solved by the *BGH* applying these special rules: according to § 996, a *mala fide* possessor (ie a possessor who knows that he is not in lawful possession) cannot demand restitution in respect of improvements made by him where these improvements were merely useful, but not necessary. The clearing of the land might have been useful, but it was certainly not necessary. As such, the company's counter-claim was excluded. It would be beyond the scope of this chapter to discuss these highly technical provisions of the *BGB* in any detail. Suffice it to say that the courts have generally preferred to apply them in a way that emphasises the owner's right to dispose of his property as and how he pleases, and this has certainly had a knock-on effect on the general law of unjust enrichment.

(ii) *The Verwendungskondiktion and Substantive Reasons for Restitution*

It was briefly explained above that the German law of unjust enrichment is ultimately based on substantive reasons for restitution, at least where the most common restitutionary claims such as the *Leistungs-* and the *Eingriffskondiktion* are concerned. It is not quite as obvious where any such reason is to be found when it comes to the *Verwendungskondiktion*. The requirements of the claim are said to be an enrichment of the claimant at the defendant's expense which has come about by a *Verwendung* on the part of the defendant—ie by the defendant expending his labour and/or property on improving the claimant's property. There seems to be no obvious requirement that the claimant be mistaken in effecting the improvement, or that any other factor be present which would be regarded as a reason for restitution in the common law world.

This problem with the *Verwendungskondiktion* was first identified in von Caemmerer's essay 'Bereicherung und unerlaubte Handlung' in 1954.[12] The main theme of this seminal essay was the endorsement of the taxonomy suggested some 20 years previously by Wilburg[13] and the identification of substantive grounds for restitution in the general German law. When it came to the *Verwendungskondiktion*, von Caemmerer was content to highlight the issue without expressing his own view: should restitution only be available where the improver was labouring under some kind of misapprehension? The alternative would be to allow the claim notwithstanding the absence of a substantive reason for restitution but to limit it drastically to those cases in which the defendant has been incontrovertibly benefited.

Some commentators, notably Reimer in his influential monograph on the enrichment issue, take the latter view.[14] In Weinrib's example, therefore, Reimer would proceed along the same lines as the eminent Jewish jurist Rav, allowing the improver a restitutionary claim notwithstanding the absence of a proper reason for restitution but asking to what extent the owner can be said to be benefited by the 'improvement.' Similarly, Reimer would approach our initial example (clearing a plot of land from rubble) in the following way:[15] the restitutionary claim is generally available because the owner has been saved the cost of clearing the land himself at the company's expense without a juridical reason. The case must therefore be decided by asking whether the owner can be expected to realise the increased value of the land. In weighing up the relatively small appreciation of the land on the one hand and the gross disregard for the owner's rights by the company on the other, Reimer concludes that the company has no restitutionary claim on the basis that the owner has not been enriched. On this approach, much pressure is placed on the 'enrichment' stage of the inquiry. The bulk of Reimer's monograph seeks to identify a set of criteria that can be used to determine adequately when a defendant can be said to have been 'enriched' without jeopardising his individual autonomy. It is interesting to note that Reimer rejects the modern typology of German enrichment law first proposed by Wilburg and von Caemmerer. His work thus provides further support for the argument here advanced, namely that the wider the boundaries of restitutionary claims are drawn, the more pressure will be placed on the 'enrichment' inquiry, and the more workable

[12] Von Caemmerer (above n 8).

[13] Wilburg (above n 8).

[14] J Reimer, *Die Aufgedrängte Bereicherung: Paradigma der 'negatorischen' Abschöpfung in Umkehrung zum Schadensersatz* (Berlin, Duncker and Humboldt, 1990) 139 f.

[15] *Ibid*, 139. Reimer argues that the *BGH* was wrong to hold a claim based on §§ 812 ff to be excluded by § 996 *BGB*. As such, the solution of the case according to the general rules of unjust enrichment law is of significance to his argument.

criteria will be needed to help decide when a party can be said to have been enriched.

At least in cases in which the owner has sold the improved property or otherwise realised the benefit, Canaris adopts a very similar approach, conflating the 'unjust' and the 'enrichment' inquiries. In such cases, he generally allows the enrichment creditor to succeed. Thus, where a person restores and sells somebody else's painting, he should, according to Canaris, be able to deduct the increase in value due to the restoration when asked to account to the owner for the value of the painting, notwithstanding the fact that the improver fully knew that the painting belonged to somebody else, and in the absence of any other substantive reason for restitution.[16] Canaris makes this subject to one important qualification, however, which he bases on the general requirement of good faith: where the improver makes the improvement with the intention of asking for restitution, his claim will be barred. Any other solution would effectively compel the owner to contract with the improver.[17] It is, in fact, quite difficult to think of cases lacking a substantive reason for restitution in which Canaris's qualification would not bar the restitutionary claim.

The dominant view amongst German commentators is that the restitutionary claim should be barred from the start in cases in which there is no substantive reason for restitution other than the mere fact that the defendant's property was improved.[18] There is, however, far less agreement on how this result is to be achieved in the context of the *Verwendungskondiktion*. § 814 *BGB* is often taken as a valuable indicator of the right direction. It will be recalled that this provision excludes the *Leistungskondiktion* if the performing party knew that he was not obliged to perform—in other words, if he was not mistaken. The provision does not apply to the *Verwendungskondiktion* because it is limited to cases in which 'a performance is made in order to discharge a liability.' Yet the same idea could be said to apply in a situation in which an improvement is made to property which the improver knows does not belong to him and which he knows has not been requested by the owner. A look at the minutes of the drafting commissions of the *BGB* confirm that enrichment law was meant to reverse *unintended* shifts of wealth from claimant to defendant.[19] On this basis, Klauser argued in 1965 that where the claimant pursued his own interests in making the improvements, in full knowledge of the true situation, his

[16] K Larenz and CW Canaris, *Lehrbuch des Schuldrechts II/2, Besonderer Teil*, 13th edn (München, Beck, 1994) 287.
[17] *Ibid.*
[18] E von Caemmerer, *Festschrift Rabel* [1954] 367; Scheying, *AcP* 157, 371, 389 f; Klauser, NJW 1965, 515, 518; Staudinger-Lorenz, Vorbem zu § 812, no 46, 53 f; Reuter and Martinek (above n 11) 545.
[19] Motive II, 833.

restitutionary claim should be barred by analogy with § 814.[20] Lorenz, in his influential commentary on German enrichment law, agrees that, in parallel to the rules governing owner and possessor, the restitutionary claim should only be available where the claimant was labouring under a 'misapprehension of the facts,' again tying this result to § 814.[21]

Most writers, however, refuse to base the exclusion of restitution in such cases directly on § 814. They identify the basis of that provision to be the prohibition of a *venire contra factum proprium*, roughly the civilian equivalent of estoppel. This prohibition is then applied to the *Verwendungskondiktion*, leading generally to the same result: the restitutionary claim is excluded.[22]

In sum, it is clear that German law struggles with the wide formulation of § 812 I in these cases. The negative formulation 'without legal ground' makes it difficult to justify the exclusion of restitution in cases in which an improvement is made to property belonging to the defendant without reference to any underlying obligation or transaction. German law thus has to find reasons to block the claim in circumstances where a system based on positive reasons for restitution would deny restitution from the start.

English law, so long as it can still be said to be based on positive reasons for restitution or 'unjust factors,' thus takes much of the pressure off the enrichment inquiry. Where the defendant cannot be said to have been incontrovertibly benefited, the unjust factors will generally have much to say when it comes to deciding whether a defendant has been enriched. If the restitutionary claim is based on duress, for instance, it will generally be easy to hold the defendant liable for the objective value of the benefit received, based on Burrows' 'reprehensible seeking out' test.[23] If the unjust factor is failure of consideration, the test to be applied will usually be his 'bargained for' test.[24] If there is an independent, defendant-sided unjust factor called 'free acceptance' or 'unconscientious receipt,' it will be applied to both the 'unjust' and the 'enrichment' stages of the inquiry.[25]

Problems remain in cases based on mistake. The advantage of the English approach, however, is that cases in which the claimant cannot be said to have been mistaken are ruled out from the start. The inquiry can thus be focused on those cases in which a benefit in kind has been conferred on a defendant by mistake (given that the receipt of money will 'incontrovertibly benefit' the recipient).

[20] Klauser, NJW 1965, 515, 518.
[21] Staudinger-Lorenz, Vorbem zu §§ 812 ff, no 46.
[22] Cf von Rittberg, *Die aufgedrängte Bereicherung* (1969), 106 ff; Reuter and Martinek (above n 11) 545.
[23] A Burrows, *The Law of Restitution*, 2nd edn (London, Butterworths, 2002) 24, 25.
[24] *Ibid*, 23, 24.
[25] See P Birks, 'In Defence of Free Acceptance' in A Burrows (ed), *Essays on the Law of Restitution* (Oxford, Clarendon Press, 1991)105; cf Burrows (above n 23) 402.

The system based on unjust factors is, however, threatening to break down both in England and in Canada. Arguably, Canada has ventured further down that road than England. The *Pettkus v Becker* formula adopts civilian language without the civilian superstructure needed to keep the resulting wide bases for restitutionary claims in check. This, as has been pointed out above, puts a lot of pressure on the 'enrichment' stage of the inquiry. Similarly, in England, cases such as *Westdeutsche Landesbank v Islington*,[26] *Guinness Mahon v Kensington and Chelsea*[27] and *Kleinwort Benson v Lincoln*[28] have moved the law much closer to the civilian model. Again, a typology similar to that identified for German law by Wilburg and von Caemmerer has yet to be developed here. This means that, again, the 'enrichment' inquiry, along with the defence of change of position, will have to absorb much of the pressure, at least until a suitable typology can be developed.

III. THE ENRICHMENT INQUIRY—DEVALUATION AND REVALUATION

German law provides for the extent of the restitutionary claim in §§ 818 ff. If there is prima facie liability under § 812, the claim will be directed primarily at whatever has been received. In other words, German law will normally order specific restitution. Thus, if the claimant has mistakenly transferred a valuable painting to the defendant, he will not be confined to restitution of the painting's value in money—he will get the actual painting back. This restricts the scope for subjective devaluation considerably, because the plea that he does not value the benefit received will obviously not help a defendant who is still in a position to return it *in specie*.

§ 818 both extends and restricts this prima facie claim. § 818 I extends the claim to the value of the user of the benefit received and to any substitute which the defendant has obtained following the destruction or loss of the benefit itself (in particular, to any monetary compensation or claims to monetary compensation). § 818 III contains the disenrichment defence, the German version of the defence of change of position. The restitutionary claim is excluded to the extent that the recipient is no longer enriched. Finally, § 818 II provides for restitution of the value of the benefit in circumstances where specific restitution is not possible because of its nature (eg it consists of a service rendered by the claimant) or for some other reason. The crucial question here is what the *BGB* means by 'value,' particularly when it comes to unrequested benefits. A car is given a full service instead of the requested minor repair. A building is built on the defendant's land

26 [1994] 4 All ER 890 (QB and CA).
27 [1999] QB 215 (CA).
28 [1999] 2 AC 349 (HL).

without his knowledge. Trees are mistakenly planted on the defendant's field. To be exposed to a restitutionary claim would mean that the defendant would have to pay for something which he never requested or wanted. The problem is referred to as '*aufgedrängte Bereicherung*' ('imposed enrichment') in the German literature. There is substantial agreement that the enrichment debtor cannot in all cases be compelled to make restitution of the objective value of the benefit received, as this might unduly restrict his autonomy. That, however, is as far as it goes. There is a myriad of different views, and even where commentators agree in the result they rarely agree on how that result can best be reconciled with the *lex scripta* of the *BGB*. I will confine myself to referring to one example from the (sparse) case law and to outlining some of the most influential academic theories.

In a case decided in 1956,[29] the *BGH* came up with an innovative and ingenious approach to the problem. The claimant had held a contractual licence to use the defendant's land for breeding poultry. By the terms of the licence, he was allowed to erect suitable small buildings on the land. If he wanted to build larger buildings he needed to obtain the defendant's written permission. All small buildings were to pass into the defendant's ownership at the expiration of the licence, the defendant accounting to the claimant for the increased value of the land (to be determined by an independent surveyor). The claimant erected a very large building without obtaining the defendant's permission. As a result of the ensuing dispute, the parties brought the licence to a premature end. The claimant demanded restitution of the value of the building, or at least of the difference in value of the land with and without the building. The *BGH* pointed out that the building had been erected unlawfully, without the consent of the owner of the land. As such, the defendant had a right, based on § 1004 *BGB*, to demand that his land be restored to the state it would have been in without the unlawful interference on the part of the claimant. This right could, according to the *BGH*, be used as a defence to a claim in unjust enrichment.

While this solution is ingenious, it clearly cannot be applied to all cases involving 'imposed' enrichments. In particular, it is clearly unsuitable for cases involving services. For this reason, academic writers have sought solutions of more general applicability, basing these on § 818 II or § 818 III or both.

Canaris, it will be remembered, would generally allow all claims where the benefit received has been realised,[30] along the same lines as the common law 'incontrovertible benefit' test. Where the benefit has not been realised, Canaris distinguishes between bad faith and good faith claimants. If the claimant knew that he was acting unlawfully in improving the

[29] BGHZ 23, 61 (21 December 1956).
[30] Canaris (above n 16).

defendant's property, his claim should, according to Canaris, generally be barred. On the other hand, a good faith claimant (ie a claimant who believed that he had every right to improve the defendant's property) should be entitled to restitution of the objective value of the improvement notwithstanding the fact that there will be interference with the defendant's personal autonomy. Canaris even goes so far as to say that a bad faith claimant will in some circumstances be entitled to demand that the defendant realise the benefit conferred, and again bases this on the general principle of good faith in § 242. Thus, where a high rise building has been built on the defendant's land, he cannot leave it empty merely to avoid accounting to the claimant for rent received. Canaris concedes that the subjective interest of the defendant must be respected to a great degree, so that, for example, a defendant cannot be compelled to sell a beloved painting only to realise its increased value following its restoration by the claimant.[31]

Canaris goes further than most German writers in subordinating the defendant's interest in private autonomy to the claimant's interest in obtaining restitution. The dominant view is certainly more willing to accommodate the defendant's interests, and this is also supported by the attitude taken by the *BGH* in the example above.[32] The view that probably is now dominant interprets the 'value' referred to in § 818 II subjectively. In the words of Lieb, 'the creditor is limited to recover only as much as the debtor can realise from the benefit received.'[33] This subjective view of value is ultimately based on § 818 III, read in conjunction with § 818 II. There is, however, considerable uncertainty over the practical implications of a subjective view. There are a number of possibilities:

1. The recipient might be allowed to retain any benefit received unless he decides to realise it by selling or otherwise profitably using the improved piece of property. Thus, if the owner of a car that has been the subject of extensive repairs decided to sell it, he would have to account to the improver for the increased price achieved as a result of the repairs. This would appear to reflect the preferred solution in the common law world. The problem with this solution, however, is that it might lead to fortuitous results depending on the time at which the owner decides to sell. If he sold the car before the action, he would have to account for the full increase in value.[34] If he waited until afterwards, he would most likely be able to retain the benefit. Some German commentators argue that the enrichment claim should lie dormant

[31] *Ibid*, 290 f.
[32] Above (n 29).
[33] MünchKomm-Liebs, § 812, no 262.
[34] The same point is made by Burrows with reference to the incontrovertible benefit test: (above n 23) 19.

until realisation of the benefit.[35] This solution has obvious difficulties. It enables the enrichment creditor to modify his behaviour so as to minimise his restitutionary liability. It also causes difficulty when it comes to limitation periods: does the claim accrue at the time of the enrichment, or at the time the enrichment is realised?

2. This has led some German commentators to modify the claim so as to allow the court to assess the actual and probable benefit which will accrue to the owner as a result of the improvement. How likely is it that the owner will decide to sell the improved property, or to derive profit from it in some other way—eg by renting out a building erected by the improver on the owner's land?[36] This would appear to be in broad agreement with the test suggested by Burrows for English law.[37]
3. The dominant view in Germany appears to be as follows. The owner of the improved piece of property is prima facie entitled subjectively to devalue the benefit—in other words, to claim that to him, subjectively, the benefit is not valuable. This right, however, is normatively qualified (*normativ eingeschränkt*): can the owner be expected, in the light of all the circumstances of the individual case, to sell the improved piece of property or to use it profitably so as to realise the benefit conferred by the improver?[38] If this is the case, he will be obliged to make restitution of the objective value of the improvement. The standard applied is thus neither purely objective nor purely subjective. In effect, the dominant view asks how a reasonable person *having the owner's characteristics and preferences* could be expected to behave in the circumstances.

While both German law and English law thus respect the recipient's right to decide for himself how to spend his money, German law, at least as far as the dominant view in the literature is concerned, generally appears to be more inclined to protect the improver's interest in restitution. There is nothing wrong with this, in my view. In the end it is just a matter of emphasis. It is important, however, to stay focused on the reason for restitution: the improver's interest in restitution is much less worthy of protection where no reason for restitution is recognised by the law in the first place. Where the improver knows that he has no business interfering with the owner's

[35] Cf J Esser, E Schmidt and J Köndgen, *Fälle und Lösungen, BGB Schuldrecht*, 3rd edn (1971) 94.
[36] Cf Koller, *DB* 1974, 2385, 2458.
[37] Above (n 34).
[38] MünchKomm-Lieb, § 812, no 264.

property, he should not be entitled to assert any kind of restitutionary claim. The owner's enrichment, if any, is simply not unjust in those circumstances. This is obvious where, as in Weinrib's example, the improver is intent on charging the owner for an improvement which he knows the owner has not requested. Any other solution, as Canaris points out, would amount to forcing the owner to contract with the improver.[39] Where the claimant makes the improvement in his own interest, but in full knowledge of the facts, it normally will be open to him to communicate with the owner and enter into a contract which then regulates the restitutionary consequences of any improvement.

Once the need for a reason for restitution is accepted—as it is by the dominant view in Germany, albeit in a roundabout way—the German approach to the enrichment issue becomes much more acceptable. On the one side there is now a claimant who has spent money or effort conferring a benefit on a defendant and who has a strong claim to restitution based upon a legally recognised reason for restitution. On the other side there is a defendant who has clearly been enriched and who, merely to avoid his restitutionary liability, chooses to subjectively devalue. Take the example of a claimant who has built a luxury villa on the defendant's land, mistaking the defendant's plot for his own adjacent land. Neither party previously used his land in any way and the plots are of identical size. The more flexible German approach leads to the correct result: the defendant would be required to transfer his land to his neighbour in exchange for the latter's land.

The common law's reluctance to introduce this kind of flexibility reflects a general preference for remedial simplicity. Common lawyers realise that justice comes at the price of uncertainty. In any but the clearest cases (of which the above example may be one), it would be all but impossible to predict the outcome of any action brought by the improver. The owner would lead evidence as to his own preferences and predilections, introduce witness statements outlining his projected uses of the improved property, and explain why the improvements are useless to him in the circumstances. The improver would no doubt put forward evidence to the contrary. In the end, it would be for the court to decide on criteria that would be very difficult to articulate. Advising clients on their prospects in any litigation would be well nigh impossible and settlements would become less likely. The tension between certainty and equity is obviously present in both systems. It may well be a sweeping generalisation, but on the whole it is probably correct to say that the common law will generally err on the side of certainty, with a corresponding preference for equity in civilian jurisdictions.

[39] Canaris (above n 16).

IV. CONCLUSION

If we ask what lessons for the common law can be drawn from the German experience, the following points suggest themselves.

1. The importance of identifying substantive reasons for restitution cannot be overestimated, particularly where unrequested benefits are concerned. Contrary to appearances, German law cannot do without positive reasons for restitution. The *Verwendungskondiktion* is no exception, although this is probably more controversial than in the context of other restitutionary claims in German law. Common law jurisdictions should be aware of this. Negative requirements for restitution, such as 'absence of juridical reason' or 'absence of consideration,' are too wide and put too much pressure on the 'enrichment' stage of the inquiry.
2. In looking at the German law on subjective devaluation, it is important to appreciate that many cases are not decided on the basis of the general law of unjust enrichment but on the basis of specialised rules relating to the relationship between owner and possessor and *negotiorum gestio*. While discussing those rules in detail would have been beyond the scope of this chapter, it generally is noticeable that the courts tend to lay considerable stress on the autonomy of the recipient of the benefit in applying those provisions.
3. In the law of unjust enrichment proper, the general view in Germany appears to give more weight to the improver's interest in restitution, to the detriment of the recipient's freedom to dispose of his property as and how he pleases. Whether this is relevant in practice is open to serious doubt, given the extreme dearth of decided cases on the subject. The difference between the German approach and the common law approach is explicable by the different legal cultures, in particular the common law preference for remedial simplicity and certainty.

11

Tracing and Unjust Enrichment

ROBERT CHAMBERS

I. FOLLOWING, TRACING, AND CLAIMING

IN *THE LAW of Tracing*, Dr Lionel Smith usefully distinguished three different concepts: following, tracing, and claiming.[1] We follow assets, trace value, and claim rights. For example, if I stole your car and sold it, you could follow the car into the buyer's hands and sue the buyer for conversion. That does not involve tracing. You have followed an asset and claimed your right to possess that asset. If I stole your money instead and bought a car, something different happens. You could follow your money into the hands of the car dealer, but there would probably be no point. If the dealer was a *bona fide* purchaser of the money, you would have no claim to that money or against the dealer.[2] However, you could trace your value from the money into my new car and claim beneficial ownership of the car. I would hold the car in trust for you because I acquired it using your value.[3]

Tracing is the process of tracking the location of value when one asset is exchanged for another.[4] The law of tracing tells us when the value of one asset has been used to acquire another asset. That task is easy when one asset is simply traded for another. It becomes more difficult when value from several different sources gets mixed together and then used to buy several different assets. The law of tracing provides the rules that determine whose value was used to acquire which assets.

The title of this article is somewhat misleading. It is concerned not with the tracing rules that identify the location of value, but with the claims that are made when the tracing process is complete. It does not deal with all

[1] LD Smith, *The Law of Tracing* (Oxford, Clarendon Press, 1997) 6–14.
[2] *Miller v Race* (1758) 1 Burr 452; 97 ER 398; D Fox, 'Bona Fide Purchase and the Currency of Money' (1996) 55 *CLJ* 547.
[3] *Black v S Freedman & Co* (1910) 12 CLR 105 (HCA); *Re Kolari* (1981) 36 OR (2d) 473 (Dist Ct).
[4] *Boscawen v Bajwa* [1996] 1 WLR 328 (CA) 334; Smith (above n 1) 15; S Evans, 'Rethinking Tracing and the Law of Restitution' (1999) 115 *LQR* 469, 470.

possible claims, but only those which depend on tracing value into some asset. Therefore, a more accurate title would be 'Claims Based on Tracing and Unjust Enrichment.' This article deals with two basic questions. First, if you can trace your value through one or more exchange transactions into some asset, and then make a claim to that asset, what is the source of your claim? Secondly, why do you have a right to a specific asset when your only link to that asset is the fact that it was acquired using your value? I do not doubt that you can and should have a right to it. However, the source of that right needs to be identified and understood.

Unjust enrichment appears in the title because the thesis of this article is that many claims based on tracing are created by unjust enrichment. The claim exists because the new asset was acquired at the claimant's expense without the claimant's consent. Some claims based on tracing are created by consent or a statute and others may be responses to wrongdoing. However, in the absence of consent, statutes, or wrongdoing, unjust enrichment provides the best explanation for the claim. This assertion is controversial because the House of Lords recently declared, in *Foskett v McKeown*,[5] that claims based on tracing are not part of the law of unjust enrichment, but part of the law of property. This article asserts that this dichotomy is false. While some claims are not part of the law of unjust enrichment and some are not part of the law of property, many belong to both. In other words, many claims based on tracing are property rights created by unjust enrichment.

II. CLAIMING CONFUSION

The sources of rights dependent on tracing are not well understood. In *Foskett v McKeown*, a trustee misused trust assets to pay the premiums on his life insurance policy and then killed himself. The House of Lords decided that the trust beneficiaries could trace their value into the death benefit paid by the insurer and claim part ownership of that benefit. I believe the source of that right was unjust enrichment. The death benefit was purchased using value taken from the trust without consent. There was an enrichment of the life insurance beneficiaries, a corresponding deprivation of the trust beneficiaries, and an absence of juristic reason for that enrichment. However, in *Foskett v McKeown*, the majority of law lords said that the claim was not created by unjust enrichment.

According to Lord Millett, 'The transmission of a claimant's property rights from one asset to its traceable proceeds is part of our law of property, not of the law of unjust enrichment.'[6] This tells us what rights existed, but not why.

[5] [2001] 1 AC 102 (HL).

[6] *Foskett* (above n 5) 127; see also P Matthews, 'The Legal and Moral Limits of Common Law Tracing' in P Birks (ed), *Laundering and Tracing* (Oxford, Clarendon Press, 1995) 23, 35–37, 66–70.

The trust beneficiaries had property rights to the death benefit. Those property rights are part of the law of property, just as the trust beneficiaries' personal rights are part of the law of obligations. This does not tell us why those rights arose, except to eliminate unjust enrichment as a possible source.

There are two difficulties with the notion that claims dependent on tracing are part of the law of property and not of the law of unjust enrichment. First, property and unjust enrichment are not opposing concepts. Property is a kind of right, while unjust enrichment is a source of rights.[7] Property rights, like personal rights, can be created by consent, wrongdoing, unjust enrichment, or other events, such as detrimental reliance or statutes.[8] What we need to know is which of these events create the rights that depend on tracing.

Secondly, tracing is not restricted to the law of property. Value can be traced into and through personal rights. For example, a bank account is not a property right, but a debt due from a specific person.[9] It is a desirable form of value primarily because it is not property. The account holders do not have to worry about the destruction or theft of their money, but have happily exchanged the risks and burdens of ownership for a bank's promise to pay, because the bank is a person that will almost certainly pay its debts. The ability to trace value into and through bank accounts means that claims based on tracing are not just part of the law of property, but also part of the law of banking.

In *Foskett v McKeown*, value was traced through a contract of insurance. In the years between the payment of the insurance premiums with stolen trust money and the payment of the death benefit, the value consisted of the trustee's personal rights under a contract of insurance. So, claims based on tracing are also part of the law of insurance. Of course, it is completely unhelpful to divide the law of tracing up in this way. The tracing of value involves a set of common principles that applies regardless of the nature of the value or the area of law which governs it. This is also true of the claims that depend on tracing. Whether personal or proprietary and regardless of context, those claims can be created by consent, wrongdoing, unjust enrichment, or other events.

III. SOURCES OF CLAIMS BASED ON TRACING

All claims based on tracing share a common trait. In each case, the claimant had a right to an asset, that asset was exchanged for another asset, and the

[7] P Birks, 'Property, Unjust Enrichment, and Tracing' (2001) 54 *Current Legal Problems* 231, 238–41; P Birks, 'Property and Unjust Enrichment: Categorical Truths' [1997] *New Zealand Law Review* 623, 627–28; LD Smith, 'Unjust Enrichment, Property, and the Structure of Trusts' (2000) 116 *LQR* 412, 413.

[8] P Birks, *English Private Law* (Oxford, Oxford University Press, 2000) xlii; R Chambers, *An Introduction to Property Law in Australia* (Sydney, LBC Information Services, 2001) 236–37.

[9] *Foley v Hill* (1848) 2 HLC 28; 9 ER 1002 (HL).

claimant thereby acquired a right to the new asset. The link between the two assets is value. The tracing process, whether simple or complex, shows that the value of the original asset was used to acquire the new asset.[10] That link between those two assets forms the basis for the claimant's right to the new asset, because it shows that the new asset was acquired at least partly at the claimant's expense. The cost of acquiring the new asset was met by disposing of the claimant's rights to the original asset. In essence, the new asset was purchased using the claimant's value.

The claimant's right to the new asset depends on tracing the claimant's value into that asset, but that fact alone does not explain why that right arises.[11] Something more is required. In many cases, the additional element was consent. The exchange was authorised on the basis that the claimant would acquire rights to the new asset. In other cases, the additional element was provided by statute. Regardless of consent, the claimant had a statutory right to the new asset. In the absence of consent or a statute, some other justification is needed. Wrongdoing can explain many of the remaining cases. If the disposition of the original asset was a wrongful use of the claimant's value, the claimant's entitlement to the new asset can be explained as a response to that wrong. However, that does not account for all the cases.

Claims based on tracing are possible even in the absence of consent, statutes, and wrongdoing. Therefore, they must be created by unjust enrichment or some other event. Unjust enrichment provides a perfectly satisfactory explanation. However, it is important first to consider other possible explanations, especially since the House of Lords rejected the connection between unjust enrichment and property claims based on tracing. Three alternatives are discussed: (1) that a right based on tracing is not a new right, but the continuation of a pre-existing right that has become attached to a new asset, (2) that a normal feature of all property rights is a right to the proceeds of sale of those rights, and (3) that a right to the proceeds of sale of property rights is one of the ways in which those rights are enforced. Each of these three possibilities might be used to support the argument that claims based on tracing belong to the law of property and not to the law of unjust enrichment. However, they turn out to be unsatisfactory or incomplete.

A. Consent

Rights based on tracing can be created by consent. For example, we could make a personal property security agreement in which I grant you security over my assets and over any proceeds from the sale of those assets.

[10] Smith (above n 1) 119.
[11] *Ibid*, 299.

Romalpa clauses,[12] which are used by suppliers to retain ownership of raw materials delivered to manufacturers, often provide that the supplier is entitled to the products manufactured from those materials and to the proceeds of their sale unless the price for the raw materials is paid in full. Although tracing is used to identify the proceeds of sale, the supplier's right to those proceeds is created by the contract between the parties.[13]

Another important example is an express trust which gives the trustees powers of investment. When trustees sell trust assets, the trust attaches immediately to the proceeds of sale, whether the sale was authorised or not.[14] If the transaction was authorised by the terms of the trust, the beneficiaries' rights to the proceeds were created by the settlor who created the trust. The trustees received the original trust assets from the settlor in trust for the beneficiaries and then relied on the authority given to them by the settlor to exchange those assets for others. The new assets are held on express trust for the beneficiaries and there is no doubt that this trust was created by the settlor, even though those assets never belonged to the settlor. Tracing the value of the original trust assets into the new trust assets shows that the trust of the new assets was created by the settlor and not by the trustees or anyone else. The identity of the settlor can be important for many reasons, such as taxation, fraudulent preferences or conveyances, or the resulting trust that can arise if the express trust fails. By tracing the value of the original trust assets (and the income from those assets) through various exchange transactions, the continued existence of the trust fund is maintained from the outset even though the individual assets that constitute that fund have been replaced.[15]

Something different occurs if the sale of trust assets was unauthorised. The sale proceeds are held in trust as soon as the trustees receive them,[16] but will cease to be held in trust unless all the beneficiaries ratify the unauthorised investment.[17] If any beneficiaries reject the investment, the trustees will be required to compensate the trust for the loss caused by their breach and will own the new assets beneficially, subject to an equitable lien securing their obligation to pay compensation.[18] The beneficiaries' rights to the sale proceeds are not created by consent. The investment was not authorised by the settlor. If the beneficiaries reject it, their lien arises by operation

[12] Named after *Aluminium Industrie Vaassen BV v Romalpa Aluminium Ltd* [1976] 2 All ER 552 (CA).
[13] S Worthington, *Proprietary Interests in Commercial Transactions* (Oxford, Clarendon Press, 1996) 37–40.
[14] *Foskett* (above n 5) 127.
[15] B Rudden, 'Things as Thing and Things as Wealth' in JW Harris (ed), *Property Problems From Genes to Pension Funds* (London, Kluwer Law International, 1997) 146, 156–57.
[16] *Foskett* (above n 5) 127.
[17] *Wright v Morgan* [1926] AC 788 (PC) 798.
[18] *Foskett* (above n 5) 130–131; R Chambers, 'Liability' in P Birks & A Pretto (eds), *Breach of Trust* (Oxford, Hart Publishing, 2002) 1, 28–32.

of law in response to the breach of trust. If they adopt the investment, it might be argued that they have consented to an *ad hoc* variation of the trust. However, there are two objections to that argument. First, the subsequent ratification of the unauthorised investment by the beneficiaries does not explain why they obtained beneficial ownership of the sale proceeds at the outset when they were probably unaware of the breach of trust.

Secondly, if trust assets were used wrongly to buy land, that land would be held in trust for the beneficiaries even if the original express trust was an oral trust of chattels or money. According to the Statute of Frauds and its descendents in most common law jurisdictions, an express trust of land must be made in writing and signed by the settlor, but trusts arising by operation of law are exempt from that requirement.[19] This suggests that the trust of an unauthorised investment is created not by consent, but by operation of law. Of course, this conclusion merely eliminates consent as a possible source of the trust, but does not identify that source. As discussed below, it can be explained as restitution of either wrongful enrichment or unjust enrichment.

B. Statutes

Rights based on tracing can also be created by statutes. For example, under Canadian personal property security legislation, security interests in assets can become attached to the traceable proceeds of the sale of those assets.[20] The statutes do not define the tracing rules used to identify the proceeds of sale, but create security rights to those proceeds, which arise regardless of consent.

Under matrimonial property legislation, the assets acquired by either spouse during the marriage are shared by them at the end of the marriage. However, the value of certain assets, such as gifts, inheritances, and payments received as compensation for a tort, may be exempt from sharing. That exemption can also extend to the traceable proceeds of the sale of those assets.[21] Tracing is used to identify the proceeds and the statute determines how they will be distributed between the spouses.

C. Wrongs

In *Foskett v McKeown*, the trust beneficiaries' rights to the death benefit were not based on consent or statute. The use of trust assets to pay the

[19] Statute of Frauds 1677 (UK) ss 7, 8; Law of Property Act 1925 (UK) s 53; Statute of Frauds RSO 1990 ss 9, 10; GG Bogert & GT Bogert, *The Law of Trusts and Trustees,* 2nd rev edn (St Paul, West Publishing Company, 1984) [62].

[20] See, eg, Personal Property Security Act RSA 2000 c P 7 ss 1(1)(jj) 28; RCC Cuming & RJ Wood, *Alberta Personal Property Security Act Handbook*, 4th edn (Toronto, Carswell, 1998) 236–62; Smith (above n 1) 41–42.

[21] See, eg, Matrimonial Property Act RSA 2000 c M 8 s 7; Smith (above n 1) 38–40.

trustee's life insurance premiums was unauthorised and clearly in breach of trust. This is typical of many claims based on tracing. Assets were taken without the consent of their beneficial owners and then used to buy other assets. In the absence of consent or a statute, the claim to the new assets must be based on wrongdoing, unjust enrichment, or some other event.

In many cases, the non-consensual use of assets is a wrong, such as a breach of trust, breach of fiduciary duty, fraud, theft, or conversion. Therefore, many claims based on tracing can be explained as responses to wrongdoing. When the traceable proceeds from the sale of misappropriated assets is an enrichment acquired by breaching a duty owed to the claimant, the claimant's right to those proceeds effects restitution of that wrongful enrichment. For example, when trustees misappropriate trust assets and use them to acquire other assets for themselves, they will hold the new assets in trust for the beneficiaries, as discussed above. The trust of the new assets is not created by consent, but is a constructive trust that arises to ensure that the trustees do not profit from their own breach of trust.[22]

There is a temptation to overuse wrongdoing to explain all claims based on tracing that are not created by consent or statutes. For example, in *Chase Manhattan Bank NA v Israel-British Bank (London) Ltd*,[23] the claimant bank paid US$2M to the defendant bank by mistake and was permitted to trace the value of that money and claim beneficial ownership of the proceeds if they could be found. The defendant had done nothing to induce the mistake, which was caused solely by the claimant's own clerical error. Although the claim to the proceeds seems to be created by unjust enrichment, it has been suggested that it may have been created instead by the defendant's unconscionable failure to repay the money when it was notified of the mistake two days later.[24] In *Westdeutsche Landesbank Girozentrale v Islington LBC*, Lord Browne-Wilkinson said:

> Since the equitable jurisdiction to enforce trusts depends upon the conscience of the holder of the legal interest being affected, he cannot be a trustee of the property if and so long as he is ignorant of the facts alleged to affect his conscience, ie until he is aware that he is intended to hold the property for the benefit of others in the case of an express or implied trust, or, in the case of a constructive trust, of the factors which are alleged to affect his conscience.[25]

If this is correct, then the claimant's personal right (at common law) to repayment of the value of the money arises at the outset as restitution of unjust enrichment, while the claimant's property right (in equity) to the

[22] AW Scott & WF Fratcher, *The Law of Trusts,* 4th edn (Boston, Brown & Co, 1989) [202], [508].
[23] [1981] Ch 105.
[24] *Westdeutsche Landesbank Girozentrale v Islington LBC* [1996] AC 669 (HL) 715.
[25] *Ibid*, 705.

traceable proceeds of the money arises later as restitution of wrongful enrichment, but only if the defendant becomes aware of the unjust enrichment and wrongly refuses to repay it.[26] There are several difficulties with this proposition. First, trusts can arise even though the trustees are unaware of the existence of the trust or of the facts giving rise to it. An express trust can be created before the terms of the trust are communicated to the trustees.[27] Although the trustees will not be liable for breach of trust before they are aware of the trust and they will be free to disclaim the trust when they do become aware of it, their knowledge of the trust is not required for its creation.[28] Also, there are many cases in which resulting trusts have arisen without the trustee's knowledge of any of the facts giving rise to it.[29]

Secondly, from the claimant's perspective, there is no difference between a defendant who unconscionably refuses to repay a mistaken payment and one who innocently fails to repay it. In *Chase Manhattan Bank NA v Israel-British Bank (London) Ltd*, the defendant was solvent when it received the money and was later notified of the mistake, but became insolvent without repaying it. If the defendant had become aware of the mistake only after it became insolvent, its failure to repay the money could not have been unconscionable, because repayment would have been an impermissible preference of the claimant over the defendant's other creditors. This happened in *Re Berry*,[30] where the defendants received a mistaken payment and were petitioned into bankruptcy three days later, before the mistake was discovered. This made no difference because a constructive trust arose at the outset when the defendants received the money.

Finally, if claims based on tracing also depended on the state of the defendant's conscience, a great deal of uncertainty would be introduced into the law. The timing of the creation of the claimant's property right to the proceeds may be important for many different reasons, such as the priority of competing claims to those proceeds, liability for taxation, risk of loss, and limitation periods. Apart from the defendant's conscience, all the relevant facts giving rise to the claimant's right exist when those proceeds are first acquired and it is relatively easy to determine precisely when that right arose. If the state of the defendant's conscience becomes an element of the claim, the inquiry is no longer confined to a specific transaction, but may span many years between that transaction and the claimant's assertion of a right to those proceeds.

[26] Birks, 'Property and Unjust Enrichment: Categorical Truths' (above n 7) 664; G Virgo, *The Principles of the Law of Restitution* (Oxford, Oxford University Press, 1999) 631.
[27] *Smith v Wheeler* (1671) 1 Lev 279; 83 ER 406; *Siggers v Evans* (1855) 5 E & B 367; 119 ER 518; *Mallott v Wilson* [1903] 2 Ch 494.
[28] Scott & Fratcher (above n 22) [72]; PJ Millett, 'Restitution and Constructive Trusts' (1998) 114 *LQR* 399, 412.
[29] *Birch v Blagrave* (1755) Amb 265; 27 ER 176; *Childers v Childers* (1857) 1 De G & J 482; 44 ER 810 (CA); *Re Vinogradoff* [1935] WN 68 (CA); *Re Muller* [1953] NZLR 879 (NZ SC); R Chambers, *Resulting Trusts* (Oxford, Clarendon Press, 1997) 205–06.
[30] (1906) 147 F 208 (CA).

Although the Court of Chancery was regarded as a court of conscience and the Chancellor's interventions in early cases were justified on the basis of conscience, equity long ago evolved into a body of law which no longer depends on the consciences of individual litigants, but on the application of general rules.[31] This was demonstrated clearly by *Re Diplock*,[32] in which several charities were required to repay legacies that had been paid to them by mistake. Some of the charities were unaware of the mistake when they spent the money and argued that they could not be liable because they had not acted unconscionably. The Court of Appeal responded as follows:

> It is no doubt true that an equitable claim predicates that the consciences of the defendant must be affected. But we have failed to observe any justification, in the judgments cited, for the suggestion that the state of the defendant's conscience depends upon his knowledge or assumed knowledge that his title to the money paid to him may or may not be defeasible in favour of other interested persons. The test as regards conscience seems rather to be whether at the time when the payment was made the legatee received anything more than, at the time, he was properly entitled to receive.[33]

Clearly, the claim did not depend on unconscionable behaviour by the defendants, who were entirely innocent. If an affected conscience was an element of the claim, then their consciences were deemed to be affected by innocent receipt of a mistaken payment and, as Professor Birks said, 'once conscience is "deemed to be affected" in this way it becomes a fifth wheel on the coach.'[34] There is no longer any need for this sort of pretence and we can now safely admit that equitable claims, including claims based on tracing, can arise in the absence of consent, statutes, and wrongdoing.

There are also cases in which the initial acquisition of assets was wrongful, but those assets or their traceable proceeds could be followed into the hands of innocent donees. For example, in *A-G Hong Kong v Reid*,[35] the defendant received bribes to breach his fiduciary duty to his employer, the claimant. The Privy Council advised that he held those bribes on constructive trust for the claimant from the moment of receipt. The value of those bribes could be followed and traced into lands in New Zealand owned by the defendant's wife and his solicitor. The claimant had property rights to those lands and was therefore entitled to maintain caveats lodged against their titles.

[31] JH Baker, *An Introduction to English Legal History*, 4th edn (London, Butterworths, 2002) 105–11.
[32] [1948] Ch 465 (CA); aff'd *Ministry of Health v Simpson* [1951] AC 251 (HL).
[33] [1948] Ch 465 (CA) 488.
[34] P Birks, 'Trusts Raised to Reverse Unjust Enrichment: The *Westdeutsche* Case' [1996] *Restitution Law Review* 20.
[35] [1994] 1 AC 324, [1994] 1 NZLR 1 (PC).

Claims based on tracing value into assets in the hands of wrongdoers can be explained as rights to restitution of wrongful enrichment. It may be that, in *A-G Hong Kong v Reid*, the defendant's wife and solicitor were accessories to his wrongs and, therefore, the claimant's rights to their lands could be explained that way. It may also be that they held the land on resulting trust for the defendant and that the claimant's property rights attached to the defendant's interest in the lands. However, how would we explain that claim if they had received the money as innocent donees and then used it to buy land? If they had done nothing wrong, the claim could not be justified by the principle that people should not profit from their own wrongs. The claimant's connection to their land would be based, not on their wrongdoing, but on their use of the claimant's value. Although the claimant's initial property right to the bribes was created by the defendant's breach of duty to the claimant, the source of that right becomes irrelevant once that value is traced and followed into the hands of innocent donees and then traced into other assets. The outcome would be the same even if the initial property right had been created innocently (for example, if the defendant had been a resulting trustee who had innocently paid that money to his wife and solicitor).[36]

A large number of claims based on tracing can be explained as responses to the wrongful acquisition of assets, especially because many of them are triggered by the misappropriation of the claimant's assets. However, that explanation only works for claims against wrongdoers. Once those assets are followed into the hands of innocent donees, any further claims based on tracing value into new assets must be explained in some other manner. As discussed below, unjust enrichment provides a satisfactory explanation, since the new assets were acquired by the innocent donee at the claimant's expense without the claimant's consent. Before that argument is made, it is helpful to consider three alternative arguments that claims based on tracing are part of the law of property and not of the law of unjust enrichment: first, that property rights to assets that are sold can continue to exist by attaching themselves to the proceeds of sale, secondly, that property rights to assets include the right to the proceeds of sale of those assets and, thirdly, that property rights to assets are enforced by claiming the proceeds of sale of those assets.

D. Continuing Rights

In *Foskett v McKeown*, Lord Millett said, 'A beneficiary of a trust is entitled to a continuing beneficial interest not merely in the trust property but in its

[36] Birks, 'Property and Unjust Enrichment: Categorical Truths' (above n 7) 661–62.

traceable proceeds also.'[37] By 'continuing beneficial interest,' Lord Millett may have meant only that the right to the proceeds arises at the moment the right to the original assets is extinguished so that, at all times, the beneficiary has a beneficial interest in something. However, it implies that the claim to the proceeds is not a new right, but a continuation of the beneficiary's pre-existing rights. According to this theory, if an asset is sold without the owner's consent, the owner's right to that asset detaches from it and attaches to the proceeds of sale. So long as the owner's value can be traced, the original right persists in relation to the current link in the chain of substitutions. For example, in *Taylor v Plumer*, Lord Ellenborough CJ said:

> [T]he product of or substitute for the thing still follows the nature of the thing itself, so long as it can be ascertained to be such, and the right only ceases when the means of ascertainment fail, which is the case where the subject is turned into money, and mixed and confounded in a general mass of the same description.[38]

When expressed this way, tracing starts to look like following. It appears that the claimant is merely following the same property right that has persisted through a series of exchange transactions and been attached to a series of different things. However, this is contrary to the very nature of property rights. In reality, the claimant is tracing value through those exchange transaction into a series of different rights.[39]

(i) The Nature of Property Rights

A property right cannot be separated from the thing to which it relates. It is a right to a thing, which is enforceable generally against other members of society, and it cannot exist except in relation to some specific thing.[40] By contrast, personal rights are rights enforceable against specific persons that need not relate to any particular things. A property right that relates to nothing in particular is like a personal right that is enforceable against no one in particular. It simply cannot exist.

It is true that the word 'property' is often used in a broad sense to include all kinds of assets, including personal rights such as bank accounts and contracts of insurance.[41] However, whether we use this extended notion of

[37] *Foskett* (above n 5) 127.
[38] (1815) 3 M&S 562, 575; 105 ER 721(KB).
[39] Smith (above n 1) 7–8.
[40] JE Penner, 'The "Bundle of Rights" Picture of Property' (1996) 43 *UCLA Law Review* 711, 742; JE Penner, *The Idea of Property in Law* (Oxford, Clarendon Press, 1997) 111, 152; P Birks, *English Private Law* (Oxford, Oxford University Press, 2000) xxxviii–xxxix; Chambers (above n 8) 7–12.
[41] P Matthews, 'The Legal and Moral Limits of Common Law Tracing' in P Birks (ed), *Laundering and Tracing* (Oxford, Clarendon Press, 1995) 23, 33–35.

property or a general term such as 'assets' to include both personal and property rights,[42] we are describing specific rights that relate either to specific things or to specific persons. Each property right depends on the existence of an identifiable thing that is the subject matter of the right and each personal right depends on the existence of an identifiable person against whom that right can be enforced.

Property rights do not move from one thing to another. They always relate to specific assets. The identity of the subject of the property right is not a matter of indifference. This is why contracts to sell unascertained goods do not pass title at common law.[43] Since property rights can be enforced generally against other members of society, it is important to know exactly which of the seller's goods have been transferred to the buyer.

Also, the nature of a property right depends largely on the nature of the asset to which it relates. A right to possess land is different from a right to possess a dog, which is different from a copyright to a song, which is different from a licence to fish for salmon. For a single property right to continue to exist through the tracing process, not only would it have to hop from asset to asset, it might also have to transform itself each time it landed. A right to prevent others from making copies of a book may need to become rights to vote shares and receive dividends before becoming a right to possess land for a period of time. A property right might also have to become a personal right, such as a debt due from a bank or rights under a contract of insurance. Rights simply do not behave in this way.

The right to traceable proceeds is a new right, which arises when those proceeds are acquired. Everything about the right to the proceeds may be different from the former right to the asset sold. For example, suppose that value from a bank account could be traced into the purchase of land. Tracing began with a personal right to receive payment and ended with a property right to possession of land for some period of time. The debt due from the bank did not transform itself into an estate in land. The estate is a new right. For all purposes (such as property taxation, capital gains, insurable risk, occupier's liability, limitation periods, and priority disputes), that right was acquired when the estate was purchased from the vendor and not when the value used to acquire that estate was added to the bank account. The only connection between the two rights is value.

(ii) The Nature of a Fund

It is easy to forget that claims based on tracing are new rights when a collection of assets is viewed as a fund. When dealing with a pension fund, mutual fund, or other trust fund, most people are more concerned with the

[42] Smith (n 1) 49–50.
[43] *Re Goldcorp Exchange Ltd* [1995] 1 AC 74, 90; [1994] 3 NZLR 385 (PC).

overall value of the fund than with the identity of the individual assets that make up that fund. The main significance of each asset is its capital value or ability to produce income. In other words, the assets in the fund are important, not for their particular characteristics as things, but because they are units of wealth.[44]

A fund can retain a notional identity even though assets are added to and removed from it. For example, a trust fund may be wholly devoted to charity and therefore exempt from taxation or the capital gain of a trust fund may be taxed at regular intervals. The trust fund continues to exist and its beneficiaries have continuing beneficial interests in it regardless of changes to its contents. However, the status accorded to the entire fund does not change the fact that it is a collection of individual assets. It is not a single right to a shifting pool of assets, but a collection of distinct personal and property rights held by the same persons and used collectively for the same purposes. Every single asset in the fund has a separate identity and every sale or purchase of assets has legal significance. When an asset is added to the fund, a new right is acquired and, when an asset is removed from the fund, a right is lost.

The flow of individual assets in and out of the fund is unimportant when the relevant fact is the fund's overall value, for example, because that value is being reported to investors, being taxed, or is the subject of litigation against the fund managers. The individual assets come into focus whenever the rights to those assets are relevant. For example, the priority of competing claims to an asset in a trust fund depends on the nature of the trustees' right to that asset, the date it was acquired, and the circumstances surrounding its acquisition. The overall value of the fund is irrelevant to that issue.

Claims based on tracing depend to some extent on the value of a fund, because tracing value is an element of (or prerequisite for) the claim. This is true even where the claim is made to an asset owned by an individual defendant and, strictly speaking, there is no actual fund in existence. Returning to an example at the beginning of this article, if I stole your money and used it to buy a car, you could claim beneficial ownership of that car because I bought it using your value. If I then traded the car for a boat, you could claim the boat for the same reason. Although I no longer have the car, I have not lost its value. That value was used to obtain the boat and it can be said, for the purposes of your claim, that the value that used to be located in the car is now located in the boat. This is artificial because the car still has value, which now belongs to someone else. However, the removal of the car from my inventory of assets corresponds to the addition of a boat to that inventory. My net wealth remains (more or less) unchanged, but that wealth now resides in a modified collection of assets.

[44] JW Harris, *Property and Justice* (Oxford, Clarendon Press, 1996) 140–42; Rudden (above n 15) 148.

In a sense, your claim based on tracing depends on treating my assets as a fund of value.

The fact that your claim depends on tracing value does not mean that you are free to disregard the separate identity of each of my assets and treat them as a single fund of indistinguishable value. The subject of your claim is a specific asset. Although the creation of your claim depends on tracing value, the existence of your claim depends on the continued existence of the boat and the enforceability of your claim depends on its priority over any competing claims to that boat. If the existence or enforceability of your claim to the boat are called into question, the issue will be resolved by recognising that your right to the boat is a new right arising when I used your value to acquire that boat.

The story would be different if you were not claiming a specific asset. For example, in *Lipkin Gorman v Karpnale Ltd*,[45] a partner in a firm of solicitors misappropriated funds from their client trust account and gambled them away at the defendant's club. The solicitors traced value from the trust account into money in the gambler's hands, followed that money to the defendant, and then claimed restitution of its value from the defendant (as money had and received). Since the solicitors did not claim any particular assets in the defendant's hands, the specific things owned by the defendant were not relevant to their claim. However, the overall value of the defendant's assets was relevant because the defendant had changed its position by paying the gambler on his winning bets. It did not matter which money was paid to the gambler. What mattered was the effect of winning and losing bets on the overall value of the defendant's assets. As Professor Birks said, the solicitor's personal claim to restitution of unjust enrichment depended on the value 'abstractly surviving' and not on the value 'specifically surviving' in the defendant's hands.[46]

E. Incident of Rights

A claim based on tracing may be regarded as a normal incident of property ownership. In an influential essay, Professor Honoré described the rights most commonly associated with ownership, noting that the owner of a thing has a right to sell it and a right to its capital value.[47] Using the American concept of ownership as a 'bundle of rights,'[48] we might say that

[45] [1991] 2 AC 548 (HL).

[46] P Birks, 'Change of Position: The Nature of the Defence and its Relationship to Other Restitutionary Defences' in M McInnes (ed), *Restitution: Developments in Unjust Enrichment* (Sydney, LBC Information Services, 1996) 49, 71.

[47] AM Honoré, 'Ownership' in AG Guest (ed), *Oxford Essays in Jurisprudence* (London, Oxford University Press, 1961) 107, 118–19; reprinted in T Honoré, *Making Law Bind* (Oxford, Clarendon Press, 1987) 161.

[48] Eg, *Union Oil Co of California v State Board of Equalization* 386 P 2d 496 (1964) 500; *Moore v University of California* 793 P 2d 479 (SC Cal 1990) 492, 509.

ownership is a collection of rights that includes the owner's right to the proceeds of sale of an asset. Since ownership of those proceeds would include the same right, the owner of an asset sold without consent can trace its value through any number of substitutions and claim ownership of any asset acquired with that value. Viewed in this way, ownership of a fee simple estate is not just the right to possess land for an indefinite period of time, but also includes the ownership of the proceeds of the sale of that estate and any asset into which that value might be traced.

Value can be traced through rights less than ownership (such as a leasehold estate, bailment, mortgage, lien, easement, profit, or licence), so the right to the proceeds of sale of an asset is a feature not just of full ownership, but of all property rights. Since value can also be traced through bank accounts and insurance contracts, the right to sale proceeds is not just a feature of property rights, but also a feature of personal rights created by contract. If the right to the proceeds of sale of an asset is simply one in a bundle of rights to that asset, then most rights exist in bundles. When we make a contract, we acquire not only the right to performance by the other party as agreed, but also ownership of any asset into which the value of that performance can be traced. Every simple debt is really at least two rights: a right to payment of a sum of money and a right to any asset acquired by reducing or extinguishing that debt.

This reveals one of the flaws of the concept of property as bundles of rights.[49] Dr Penner argues convincingly that the power to sell an asset is not inherently part of our property rights to that asset, but exists because we have the power to make contracts to exploit our resources, including our property rights, other assets, and personal abilities.[50] This explains why we can own and possess things that we are not permitted to sell (such as human tissue and blood, restricted drugs, and prohibited weapons). Although we have the power to sell most of our assets, ownership of an asset does not include ownership of any proceeds of sale of that asset. In jurisdictions (such as Germany) which limit claims based on tracing, people enjoy full ownership of their assets even if they cannot claim ownership of the proceeds of a non-consensual sale.[51] None of this is a criticism of Honoré's essay on 'Ownership,' which is a valuable description of ownership in most societies and was never intended to be a definition of property.

Even if rights based on tracing were inherently linked to the ownership of assets, that would not make them continuing rights. Ownership of the

[49] For criticism of the 'bundle of rights', see JE Penner, 'The "Bundle of Rights" Picture of Property' (1996) 43 *UCLA Law Review* 711; JE Penner, 'Hohfeldian Use-Rights in Property' JW Harris (ed), *Property Problems From Genes to Pension Funds* (London, Kluwer Law International, 1997) 164.
[50] JE Penner, *The Idea of Property in Law* (Oxford, Clarendon Press, 1997) 91–92.
[51] BS Markesinis, W Lorenz, & G Danneman, *The German Law of Obligations: The Law of Contracts and Restitution* (Oxford, Oxford University Press, 1997) vol 1, 756–59; Honoré, 'Ownership' (above n 47) 107, 109.

sale proceeds of an asset is a new right acquired when the asset is sold and not before. The event creating the right to those proceeds is not the same event that created the right to the original asset. For example, suppose I inherited a painting from my grandfather, it was misappropriated, and its value could be traced to a house. If I am entitled to the house, it is not because I inherited it from my grandfather. While my right to the painting was created by consent (my grandfather's will), my right to the house was not. To say that I am entitled to the house because it is the proceeds of the sale of the painting, does not explain why I am entitled to it. In the absence of consent, statute, and wrongdoing, that right must be created by unjust enrichment or some other event.[52]

F. Enforcement of Rights

Another argument, similar to the preceding one, is that claims based on tracing arise as one of the ways in which the law protects property rights. The normal method of protection is a right to the payment of damages from any person who wrongly interferes with a property right (for example, by trespass, conversion, nuisance, or breach of copyright). Sometimes, the owner of an asset can enforce her or his property rights directly by an injunction restraining further interference with those rights or by specific recovery of the asset from someone wrongly in possession of it. Further protection may be provided by permitting the holders of property rights to claim any assets which represent the traceable proceeds of those rights. Like the personal right to payment of damages, the right based on tracing is a new right created as a method of indirectly protecting the original right. Unlike rights to damages, rights based on tracing do not depend on wrongdoing.

If claims based on tracing arise to protect property rights, they also arise to protect personal rights. In other words, they are not just features of property law, but legal responses designed to protect all forms of value at common law and in equity. Claims which arise to protect other rights are normally regarded as remedies for wrongs. They are secondary rights created by the wrongful interference with primary rights.[53] However, as discussed above, claims based on tracing can arise as primary rights in the absence of wrongdoing. In the absence also of consent or a statute, they must be created by unjust enrichment or some other event.

[52] Birks, 'Property and Unjust Enrichment: Categorical Truths' (above n 7) 661.

[53] *Photo Production Ltd v Securicor Transport Ltd* [1980] AC 827 (HL) 848–50; P Birks, 'Rights, Wrongs, and Remedies' (2000) 20 *OJLS* 1, 12; P Birks, 'Three Kinds of Objection to Discretionary Remedialism' (2000) 29 *University of Western Australia Law Review* 1, 4; P Birks, 'Definition and Division: A Meditation on *Institutes* 3.13' in P Birks (ed), *Classification of Obligations* (Oxford, Clarendon Press, 1997) 1, 23–24.

G. Unjust Enrichment

Many claims based on tracing are created by consent, statutes, or wrongdoing, as discussed above. What about the rest? If they are not part of the law of unjust enrichment, as suggested in *Foskett v McKeown*, then they must be created by some unidentified other event. However, they can all be explained as rights created by unjust enrichment. The asset claimed has been acquired by use of the claimant's value and the claimant did not consent to that use of that value. The claimant's sole connection to the new asset is the use of value derived from another asset, to which the claimant had a right. The new asset is an enrichment obtained at the claimant's expense and the absence of consent provides the reason why that enrichment is unjust.[54] Using the Canadian definition of unjust enrichment set out in *Pettkus v Becker*,[55] the defendant is enriched by receipt of the new asset, the claimant has suffered a corresponding deprivation by losing rights to another asset, and the absence of consent means there is an absence of juristic reason for the enrichment. The claimant's right to the new asset is a new right which effects restitution of that unjust enrichment.

Although there may be claims based on tracing created by events other than consent, statutes, wrongdoing, or unjust enrichment, nothing comes to mind. The elements of unjust enrichment are present whenever consent and statutes are absent. The essence of almost all claims based on tracing is that the defendant has acquired at an asset at the claimant's expense.[56] When that is done without the claimant's consent, that asset is an unjust enrichment. If the defendant has breached a duty to the claimant, by misappropriating the claimant's assets without the claimant's consent, then claims based on tracing the value of those assets can be analysed as restitution of either wrongful enrichment or unjust enrichment.

IV. CLAIMS TO RESTITUTION OF UNJUST ENRICHMENT

All rights to restitution of unjust enrichment (whether based on tracing or not) cause the defendant to give up that enrichment or pay for it.[57] No other response is justified, because the defendant has not breached a duty to the claimant, consented to do anything for the claimant, or done anything which might give the claimant any reasonable expectations that ought

[54] P Birks, *An Introduction to the Law of Restitution*, rev edn (Oxford, Clarendon Press, 1989) 140–42; Birks, 'Property and Unjust Enrichment: Categorical Truths' (above n 7) 661; A Burrows, *The Law of Restitution*, 2nd edn (London, Butterworths, 2002) 81.
[55] *Pettkus v Becker* [1980] 2 SCR 834; 117 DLR (3d) 257, 273–74 (SCC) (herein cited to DLR).
[56] Burrows (above n 54) 79.
[57] Birks, *An Introduction to the Law of Restitution* (above n 54) 12–13.

to be fulfilled. The duty to make restitution is created solely by the defendant's receipt of a benefit which the law regards as unjust, usually because the claimant did not intend to enrich the defendant.[58] The adjective 'unjust' does not imply that the defendant has done anything wrong or even anything at all. The passive receipt of an enrichment may be the only thing which connects the defendant to the claimant. Therefore, restitution of unjust enrichment should never leave the defendant in a worse position than if the unjust enrichment had never occurred.[59]

This point is obscured in Canada by a series of cases concerning the division of family assets at the end of a marriage or similar relationship.[60] When the relationship ended, one spouse was the sole owner of the family home, but was required to share it with the other spouse in accordance with the values of their respective contributions to the relationship. The home owner held the home on constructive trust for the claimant because: (a) the home owner had been unjustly enriched by the claimant's services, and (b) the claimant had a reasonable expectation of obtaining an interest in the home.[61] On its own, unjust enrichment does not justify that trust, because the home was not that enrichment. Although the claimant's interest in the home is linked to the value of the unjust enrichment, the trust does not cause the home owner to give up that enrichment or pay for it. The trust is not restitutionary, but 'perfectionary,' meaning that it arises by operation of law to give effect to the claimant's expectations.[62]

By itself, unjust enrichment produces only two types of claims: a right to the enrichment or a right to be paid its value. When a trust is created solely by unjust enrichment, the subject matter of that trust is always the enrichment received by the defendant at the claimant's expense. If the enrichment cannot be given up (for example, because it was a service performed for the claimant), then the only coherent response is to require the defendant to pay for the value of the enrichment. There is no reason why a defendant, who has breached no duties, made no promises, and induced no reasonable expectations, should be forced to give up any assets other than the enrichment. Although trusts of other assets can be justified by other events, they cannot be explained as restitution of unjust enrichment.

[58] *Ibid*, 100–03.

[59] M McInnes, 'The Measure of Restitution' (2002) 52 *University of Toronto Law Journal* 163, 181–83.

[60] *Pettkus* (above n 55); *Sorochan v Sorochan* [1986] 2 SCR 35; 29 DLR (4th) 1 (SCC) (herein cited to DLR); *Peter v Beblow* [1993] 1 SCR 980; 101 DLR (4th) 621 (SCC) (herein cited to DLR).

[61] *Pettkus* (above n 55) 274; *Sorochan* (above n 60) 12; *Peter* (above n 60) 633; P Parkinson, 'Beyond *Pettkus v Becker*: Quantifying Relief for Unjust Enrichment' (1993) 43 *University of Toronto Law Journal* 217, 245–48.

[62] G Elias, *Explaining Constructive Trusts* (Oxford, Clarendon Press, 1990) 157; R Chambers, 'Constructive Trusts in Canada' (1999) 37 *Alberta Law Review* 173, 197–203; McInnes (above n 59) 204–10.

Claims based on tracing can effect restitution of unjust enrichment in four different ways: (A) personal claims to the value of assets, (B) liens securing personal claims to the value of assets, (C) beneficial ownership of assets, and (D) powers to obtain the beneficial ownership of assets. The first two methods of restitution cause defendants to pay for the value of unjust enrichments and the last two cause them to give up those enrichments.

A. Personal Claims

Many personal claims to restitution of the value of unjust enrichment do not depend on tracing. The claimant does not need to trace if the enrichment received by the defendant is a service performed by the claimant or an asset transferred by the claimant. In either case, the same thing both enriches the defendant and deprives the claimant and there is no need to trace value to connect the enrichment to the deprivation.

Personal claims can depend on tracing in two different ways. First, if the enrichment is an asset which previously did not belong to the claimant, tracing will be needed to show that the asset was obtained by the defendant at the claimant's expense.[63] Secondly, the defendant may be entitled to the defence of change of position if the traceable proceeds of the enrichment are dissipated without any benefit to the defendant.

(i) Tracing Value to the Assets Received by the Defendant

In *Lipkin Gorman v Karpnale Ltd*,[64] discussed above, the claimants had a personal right to restitution of the value of the money that had been taken from their client trust account by their partner, Mr Cass, and gambled away at the defendant's club. The asset taken from the claimants was a debt due from their bank, as represented by the balance of their trust account. Mr Cass reduced that debt by drawing cheques on the trust account and depositing those cheques in other accounts. He then withdrew cash from those other accounts and paid it to the defendant. The defendant conceded that the claimants could trace their value from their trust account into the cash paid to the defendant.[65]

Since the claimants were not claiming a property right, they did not have to show what happened to the money after the defendant received it. However, their claim that the defendant was unjustly enriched at their expense depended on showing that they had a property right to the money when it was paid to the defendant. Tracing allowed them to do this.

[63] Burrows (above n 54) 79.
[64] *Lipkin* (above n 45).
[65] *Ibid*, 559, 572.

As Lord Goff said, 'there is no doubt that, even if legal title to the money did vest in Cass immediately on receipt, nevertheless he would have held it on trust for his partners, who would accordingly have been entitled to trace it in equity into the hands of the [defendant].'[66] However, the claimants chose not to rely on their equitable property right to the money. Instead, they based their claim on their common law right to the cash, which was established by tracing the value withdrawn from their bank account.[67]

If assets are misappropriated from a trust and transferred to a stranger, the beneficiaries of the trust have a property right to those assets and any assets into which their value might be traced, subject to the defence of *bona fide* purchase. They may also have a personal claim against the stranger for the value of those assets, if the stranger knew or ought to have known about the breach of trust.[68] In that case, the stranger is said to be 'liable to account as a constructive trustee' for 'knowing receipt' of the trust assets or their traceable proceeds.[69] The same rules and terminology apply to the recovery of the value of assets misappropriated from a corporation, even though the assets were not held in trust before their misappropriation, but belonged to the corporation beneficially. If the misappropriation is a breach of fiduciary duty by a corporate director, officer, or employee, the corporation is entitled to sue the recipient for 'knowing receipt' in a court of equity.[70]

The claim based on knowing receipt of misappropriated trust or corporate assets is a right to restitution. The recipient is required to give up the value of an asset received at the claimant's expense. However, there is an ongoing debate over whether it is restitution of wrongful enrichment or of unjust enrichment. Some judges and lawyers believe the claim can be made only against recipients who are at fault,[71] while others believe that recipients can also be strictly liable (subject to the defences of *bona fide* purchase and change of position) on the basis of unjust enrichment.[72] In any event, to establish that a knowing recipient has been enriched at the expense of the claimant, it may be necessary to trace the value of assets misappropriated from the claimant into assets transferred to the recipient. The claimant

[66] *Ibid*, 572.
[67] *Ibid*, 574; Smith (above n1) 332; Burrows (above n 54) 89–92.
[68] *Citadel General Assurance Co v Lloyds Bank Canada* [1997] 3 SCR 805; 152 DLR (4th) 411(SCC) (herein cited to DLR).
[69] LD Smith, 'Constructive Trusts and Constructive Trustees' (1999) 58 *CLJ* 294, 299; Burrows (above n 54) 196.
[70] *Belmont Finance Corp v Williams Furniture Ltd (No 2)* [1980] 1 All ER 393 (CA) 405.
[71] *Re Montagu's Settlement Trusts* [1987] 1 Ch 264 (Megarry V-C); S Gardner, 'Knowing Assistance and Knowing Receipt: Taking Stock' (1996) 112 *LQR* 56, 91; LD Smith, 'Unjust Enrichment, Property, and the Structure of Trusts' (2000) 116 *LQR* 412, 436.
[72] PJ Millett, 'Tracing the Proceeds of Fraud' (1991) 107 *LQR* 71, 81; Lord Nicholls, 'Knowing Receipt: The Need for a New Landmark' in WR Cornish *et al* (eds), *Restitution Past, Present and Future: Essays in Honour of Gareth Jones* (Oxford, Hart Publishing, 1998) 231; P Birks, 'Receipt' in P Birks & A Pretto (eds), *Breach of Trust* (Oxford, Hart Publishing, 2002) 213; Burrows (above n 54) 202–03.

can then establish an equitable property right to those assets. Since the claim for knowing receipt is a personal claim for the value of the assets received, the claimant does not have to trace that value beyond the moment of receipt.

(ii) Change of Position

The defence of change of position shows that a defendant who has received an unjust enrichment is no longer enriched to the same extent when the claim for restitution of that unjust enrichment is made. The claim for restitution is reduced to the value of the enrichment that still survives when the claim is made. A personal claim for restitution does not depend on the survival of any particular assets, but on the 'abstract survival' of the value of the enrichment as part of the defendant's overall wealth.[73]

Change of position can occur in two different ways. First, defendants can incur additional expenses in reliance on their apparent entitlement to unjust enrichment. For example, their new-found wealth could lead them to make an exceptional gift to charity or an unplanned trip to Las Vegas. If they were then required to make restitution of the full value of the enrichment received, they would be left in a worse position than if the unjust enrichment had never occurred. Since the receipt of unjust enrichment on its own does not justify inflicting any harm on the defendants, the claim for restitution will be reduced or eliminated to ensure that the addition and removal of the unjust enrichment has no effect on their wealth.[74]

Secondly, the loss or destruction of the enrichment can count as a change of position, even if the defendants do not rely on their apparent entitlement to it. For example, if I paid you $100 by mistake and a thief stole your wallet with that $100 the next day, you would no longer enriched. The theft of your wallet and money does not count as a change of position, but the theft of the enrichment does. If I had not paid you by mistake, you would not have had that $100 in your wallet when it was stolen. Therefore, if you then have to make restitution to me, you will be left in a worse financial position than if the unjust enrichment had never occurred. This can be tricky, because the loss of the enrichment itself does not always mean that defendants will be worse off if they have to make restitution. For example, if you would have withdrawn $100 from your bank machine if I had not paid you by mistake, you are still enriched despite the theft of your wallet, because your money would have been stolen instead of mine. Also, if you spend my $100 on your weekly groceries, you are still enriched even though you no longer have the money. The essential question is whether the enrichment itself was dissipated without benefit to the defendants before they

[73] Birks (above n 46) 49, 52.
[74] See, eg, *RBC Dominion Securities Inc v Dawson* (1994) 111 DLR (4th) 230 (Nfld CA).

became aware of the unjust enrichment and had a reasonable opportunity to return it to the claimants.[75]

Tracing may become relevant at this stage. If the destruction of an asset can be a change of position, then the destruction of its traceable proceeds should also qualify. For example, suppose I gave a $100 bill to you by mistake and you used that bill to buy your morning coffee, received $97 in change from the annoyed server, and then had your wallet stolen. If the theft of the $100 bill would have counted as a change of position, then the theft of the traceable proceeds of that bill should also count. As with the destruction of the enrichment received from the claimant, the destruction of its traceable proceeds will not always count as a change of position. For example, if the defendant used an unjust enrichment to buy a painting which was later destroyed by fire, there is no change of position if the defendant would have purchased the painting in any event.

B. Liens

In some cases, the claimant's right to restitution of the value of an unjust enrichment is secured by an equitable lien over the assets into which that value can be traced.[76] The lien is a property right to a specific asset, but it is different from property rights which cause defendants to give up enrichments. The lien does not give the claimant a right to take that asset from the defendant, but exists solely to make it more likely that the claimant's personal right to restitution will be satisfied. The defendant's primary obligation is to pay for the value of the unjust enrichment and the defendant is free to use any of her or his assets to meet that obligation. Once the obligation is performed, the lien ceases to exist. The claimant will have recourse to the asset subject to the lien only if the defendant fails to perform the obligation to pay for the value of the unjust enrichment.

A lien is subordinate to the obligation it secures. Although it is limited by the current value of the asset to which it is attached, the lien is measured, not by the value of that asset, but by the value of the obligation. Fluctuations in the value of the asset do not affect the value of the lien, unless the value of the asset dips below the value of the obligation secured by the lien. The sole purpose of the lien is to make it more likely that the obligation will be performed. Therefore, a lien is restitutionary if it secures an obligation to make restitution and is compensatory if it secures an obligation to pay compensation.

[75] American Law Institute, *Restatement of the Law of Restitution* (St Paul, American Law Institute Publishers, 1937) [142]; R Nolan, 'Change of Position' in P Birks (ed), *Laundering and Tracing* (Oxford, Clarendon Press, 1995) 135, 150–51; Birks (above n 46) 49, 61–62.

[76] See, eg, *Re Hallett's Estate* (1879) 13 Ch D 696 (CA).

Appearances can be deceiving. A lien is not restitutionary just because it attaches to the traceable proceeds of a misappropriated asset. For example, if trustees make an unauthorised investment of trust assets, the beneficiaries are faced with a choice: they can either ratify the investment and add those assets to the trust or reject the investment and require the trustees to compensate the trust for the loss caused by the breach of trust.[77] If the investment is rejected, the beneficiaries will have a lien on the unauthorised investment to secure the trustees' obligation to pay compensation. This lien appears to be restitutionary, because it attaches to the traceable proceeds of the trust assets, but it is really compensatory. The trustees become the beneficial owners of the unauthorised investment, subject only to the lien which secures their obligation to pay compensation.[78]

A lien which secures an obligation to pay for the value of an unjust enrichment attaches to an asset which is related to that enrichment. Often the value of the enrichment can be traced to the asset or resides in it in some other way. For example, the claimant may have improved the defendant's land or paid the defendant's mortgage.[79] However, the asset subject to the lien need not be the enrichment. For example, when a purchaser of land pays a deposit to the vendor, the purchaser may have a right to restitution of that deposit if the contract cannot be performed. That right will be secured by a purchaser's lien on the land, even though the value of the deposit cannot be traced into the land.[80]

C. Beneficial Ownership

There are two types of restitution which compel the defendant to give up the unjust enrichment and not just pay for its value. The first, discussed here, is beneficial ownership of that enrichment, usually under a constructive or resulting trust, but sometimes at common law. The second, discussed in the next section, is a power to obtain beneficial ownership, usually through rescission or rectification, but possibly through tracing as well.

(i) Trusts

In some cases of unjust enrichment, restitution is effected by creation of a trust for the claimant. As soon as the defendant receives legal ownership of the

[77] *Foskett* (above n 5) 130–31.

[78] R Chambers, 'Liability' in P Birks & A Pretto (eds), *Breach of Trust* (Oxford, Hart Publishing, 2002) 1, 30–32.

[79] *Lac Minerals Ltd v International Corona Resources Ltd* [1989] 2 SCR 574; 61 DLR (4th) 14, 53 (SCC); *Calverley v Green* (1984) 155 CLR 242 (HCA) 263; Smith (above n 1) 352.

[80] *Rose v Watson* (1864) 10 HLC 672; 11 ER 1187 (HL); *Whitbread & Co Ltd v Watt* [1902] 1 Ch 835 (CA); *JAR Leaseholds Ltd v Tormet Ltd* [1965] 1 OR 347; (1965) 48 DLR (2d) 97 (CA); *Lehmann v BRM Enterprises Ltd* (1978) 88 DLR (3d) 87 (BC); Worthington (above n 13) 226–27.

enrichment, a trust arises to remove beneficial ownership of that enrichment from the defendant and transfer it to the claimant. In some cases, the trust co-exists with a personal right to restitution of the value of the unjust enrichment and, in others, it is the sole method of restitution. For example, in *Re Berry*[81] and *Chase Manhattan Bank NA v Israel-British Bank (London) Ltd*,[82] discussed above, the claimants had personal rights to be paid the value of the money they had mistakenly paid to the defendants. However, those claims were adversely affected by the insolvency of the defendants, so the claimants turned to their equitable claims to beneficial ownership of that money or the assets into which its value could be traced. In each case, the mistaken transfer of an asset created two distinct rights to restitution: a property right to that asset and a personal right to its value.

In *Hodgson v Marks*,[83] the claimant had a property claim to restitution of a house, but no personal claim to its value. She had transferred her house to her lodger, intending that he would hold the house in trust for her. That intention to create a trust could not create an express trust, because it was not expressed in writing as required by section 53 of the Law of Property Act 1925 (UK). However, the lodger held the house on resulting trust for the claimant from the moment of receipt, because her ineffective intention to create a trust proved 'that the transfer was not intended to operate as a gift.'[84]

Of course, there are many cases in which the claimant had no property right to restitution of an unjust enrichment, but only a personal right to be paid its value. It can be difficult to tell when a claimant is entitled to restitution of the actual enrichment, either instead of or in addition to a right to restitution of its value. This uncertainty is exacerbated in Canada by the misleading connection between constructive trusts of the family home and restitution of unjust enrichment, as discussed above. I believe there are two requirements for every property right to restitution of the unjust enrichment itself.

First, the enrichment must be an asset which is capable of being the subject matter of a property right.[85] If the enrichment consists of services performed or goods consumed, there is no asset to which a property right might attach. Although these things may have great value, they cannot be transferred to the claimant and the only possible form of restitution is by payment of their value.[86] All kinds of assets can be held in trust, including personal rights such as bank accounts. However, some forms of value cannot be the subject of a trust or of any other kind of property right. For

[81] *Re Berry* (above n 30).
[82] *Chase Manhattan Bank NA* (above n 23).
[83] [1971] Ch 892 (CA).
[84] *Ibid*, 933 (Russell LJ).
[85] Burrows (above n 54) 69.
[86] See, eg, *Deglman v Guaranty Trust Co of Canada* [1954] SCR 725; [1954] 3 DLR 785 (SCC) (herein cited to DLR).

example, a university degree or professional qualification can be highly valuable, but it is a recognition of the training and attributes of its holder and is not an asset that can be transferred or held in trust.[87] In cases where one spouse has helped the other earn a professional qualification and a substantially higher earning potential, the enrichment consists of the services performed and money spent on tuition, books, travel, and living expenses while that qualification was obtained. However, even if the qualification could be regarded as the unjust enrichment, it could not be held in trust for the claimant.

Secondly, if the enrichment consists of an asset that can be transferred to the claimant, property restitution is possible but will not be permitted if the defendant acquires full beneficial ownership of that asset before the right to restitution arises.[88] In almost all of the cases in which the claimant had a property right to an unjust enrichment, that right arose immediately when an asset was transferred to the defendant. The defendant was unjustly enriched by receipt of that asset, possibly because it was transferred by mistake,[89] under duress,[90] or in response to undue influence.[91] The defendant may have obtained the asset by taking advantage of some factor which affected the claimant's ability to make decisions.[92] In some cases, the claimants were completely unaware of the unauthorised transfer of their assets to the defendants.[93] Also, resulting trusts can arise when it is proved or presumed that a transfer was not intended as a gift.[94] In some of these cases, a trust arose at the outset, returning beneficial ownership to the claimant immediately. In others, the claimant immediately acquired a power to recover beneficial ownership of the asset (as discussed in the next part). At no time did the defendant acquire unfettered beneficial ownership of the asset, free of the claimant's right to recover it.

There are some exceptions, such as *Re Ames' Settlement*,[95] in which a father had settled £10,000 in trust upon his son's marriage for his son for life, with the remainder for his son's wife and their children. When the son's marriage was annulled 18 years later, the trust fund resulted to the father's estate, because the purpose for creating the trust had failed. Although the father's right to restitution did not arise until many years after the fund was transferred to the trustees, it was a property right because they never obtained full beneficial ownership of the fund. This sets *Re Ames' Settlement*

[87] *Caratun v Caratun* (1992) 96 DLR (4th) 404 (Ont CA).
[88] Burrows (above n 54) 68–69; Chambers (above n 29) 148–153.
[89] *Blacklocks v JB Developments (Godalming) Ltd* [1982] Ch 183.
[90] *Barton v Armstrong* [1976] AC 104 (PC).
[91] *Barclays Bank plc v O'Brien* [1994] 1 AC 180 (HL).
[92] *Louth v Diprose* (1992) 175 CLR 621 (HCA).
[93] *Malory Enterprises Ltd v Cheshire Homes (UK) Ltd* [2002] Ch 216 (CA).
[94] *Hodgson* (above n 83); Chambers (above n 29) 12–27.
[95] [1946] Ch 217.

apart from most cases of failure of consideration, in which the claimant paid money to the defendant with no strings attached to the defendant's use of that money. When the consideration for the payment later failed, the claimant had a personal right to repayment of the value of the money, but no property right to the money itself.[96]

If the defendant receives an asset which only later turns out to be an unjust enrichment, the method of restitution will depend on the extent of the defendant's right to that asset in the intervening period. If the defendant became the full beneficial owner of the asset and was therefore free to spend, consume, or even destroy it, the continued existence of that asset (or its traceable proceeds) when the claimant obtains a right to restitution is merely fortuitous. However, if the defendant never obtains full beneficial ownership of the asset, the claimant may be entitled to property restitution of it even though the enrichment was not unjust when the asset was first transferred to the defendant.

This is demonstrated by two cases that are distinguishable from each other only by one significant difference. In *Moseley v Cressey's Co*, subscribers paid deposits to purchase shares from a company, in response to a prospectus which stated, 'Deposit returned if no allotment made.'[97] The company was placed in receivership before those shares were issued. Although the subscribers had rights to restitution, they were only personal rights which had little or no value against the insolvent company. The company had obtained unfettered beneficial ownership of the subscribers' deposits before their rights to restitution arose. As Page Wood VC said, 'payment to the company's bankers to the account of the company made the monies *ipso facto* part of the company's assets.'[98]

The same thing happened in *Re Nanwa Goldmines Ltd*, except the application form for the company's shares said that the deposits would 'be retained in a separate account' until the conditions for issuing those shares were met.[99] The company became insolvent before those shares could be issued, but the subscribers had property rights to restitution, because the company never obtained full beneficial ownership of their money before their rights to restitution arose. The company's promise to keep their money in a separate account made all the difference. Harman J said, 'I cannot but think that the whole object of making such a promise was to indicate that it would be kept apart and separate, not mixed with the company's monies, until the board saw whether the conditions were fulfilled.'[100]

[96] *Chillingworth v Esche* [1924] 1 Ch 97 (CA); *Guardian Ocean Cargoes Ltd v Banco do Brasil SA* [1994] 2 Lloyd's LR 152 (CA).
[97] (1865) LR 1 Eq 405, 408.
[98] *Ibid*, 409.
[99] [1955] 1 WLR 1080 (Ch D) 1081–1082.
[100] *Ibid*, 1084.

(ii) Ownership at Common Law

In almost every case in which the claimant immediately acquired beneficial ownership of an unjust enrichment, the defendant received legal title to the enrichment and held it in trust for the claimant. *FC Jones & Sons v Jones* is a notable exception.[101] After a partnership committed an act of bankruptcy, one of the partners paid £11,700 of partnership money to his wife (the defendant) by cheques drawn on a partnership account. She deposited the cheques in her account with a commodity broker, which increased in value to £50,760. She then drew cheques on that account to transfer the money to another account with R Raphael & Sons plc. The trustee in bankruptcy for her husband's partnership claimed the full balance of the account at Raphael & Sons. The trustee was the beneficial owner of that account, but not because the defendant held her account in trust for the trustee. The court decided that the trustee was the legal owner of the accounts into which the partnership money had been deposited. Millett LJ said:

> If the cheques had passed the legal title to the defendant but not the beneficial ownership, she would have received the money as constructive trustee and be liable to a proprietary restitutionary claim in equity. ... But the defendant was not a constructive trustee. She had no legal title to the money. She had no title at all. ... The chose in action, which was vested in the defendant's name but which in reality belonged to the trustee, was not a right to payment from the brokers of the original amount deposited but a right to claim the balance, whether greater or less than the amount deposited; and it is to that chose in action that the trustee now lays claim.[102]

When the trustee in bankruptcy was appointed, he became the legal owner of the partnership assets retroactively to the date of the act of bankruptcy. Therefore, although everyone concerned thought that the partners had legal title to their assets when the money in the partnership account was paid to the defendant, the trustee was the legal owner of the account from which that money was paid. The trustee was able to trace that value into the defendant's accounts and claim legal beneficial ownership of those accounts.

As Dr Smith notes,[103] the trustee's legal ownership of the accounts in the defendant's name could have had potentially drastic consequences for third parties. Millett LJ said, 'the trustee was entitled at law ... to the money in the defendant's account at Raphaels and able to give them a good receipt for the money. The defendant never had any interest, legal or equitable, in any of those moneys.'[104] If Raphael & Sons had paid all the money to the

[101] [1997] Ch 159 (CA).
[102] *Ibid*, 167, 170.
[103] Smith (above n 1) 329–30.
[104] *FC Jones* (above n 101) 170.

defendant, why would that have been any different from paying the money to a complete stranger? Perhaps Raphael & Sons would have been protected by the defence of change of position, for paying money in good faith to the person apparently entitled to the money, just like the defendant in *Lipkin Gorman v Karpnale Ltd*.[105] If not, payment to the defendant would not have affected the balance owed to the trustee, who could have later claimed payment of the full amount that should have been in the account.

The trust may provide a better mechanism for dealing with this problem, because the defendant would be the legal owner of the account as everyone believed, but would hold that debt in trust for the trustee. Raphael & Sons would not be liable for allowing the defendant to withdraw money from that account unless it knew this was a breach of trust, and could not be liable for knowing receipt unless it received the money for its own benefit (for example, by setting off the balance in the account against a debt owed by the defendant).[106] People who received money paid out of that account would take it free of the trust so long as they were *bona fide* purchasers.

A trust was used in this situation in *Sharp v McNeil*,[107] in which a partner had secretly used partnership assets to buy land for his sister. When the partners became insolvent, the curator of their estate claimed that land. Townshend CJ said, 'The law is not so helpless as to leave the party wronged without a remedy, and it holds the person to whom such a conveyance has been made as a trustee for the rightful owner. In other words a resulting trust follows.'[108] Trusts are also used when money is stolen. Although the thief obtains only possession and not legal ownership of the stolen cash, beneficial ownership will pass from the victim to anyone who receives it as a *bona fide* purchaser, including a bank. The thief would then hold the bank account and any other traceable proceeds of the stolen money in trust for the victim.[109]

(iii) Claims to Recover Assets

There is a significant difference between a right to restitution of assets that used to belong to the claimant and a right to restitution of a new asset into which the claimant's value has been traced. The claim to recover an asset which used to belong to the claimant does not involve tracing value from one asset to another. The claimant's right to the asset is based not on the defendant's use of the claimant's value, but on the claimant's previous right to that asset. The asset is an enrichment received by the defendant at the

[105] *Lipkin* (above n 45).
[106] *Citadel General Assurance Co* (n 68); *Karak Rubber Co Ltd v Burden* [1972] 1 WLR 602 (Ch D) 623–24.
[107] (1913) 15 DLR 73 (NSSC); aff'd (1915) 70 DLR 740 (SCC).
[108] *Sharp v McNeil* (1913) 15 DLR 73 (NSSC) 75.
[109] *Merchants Express Co v Morton* (1868) 15 Gr 274; *Black* (above n 3); *Re Kolari* (above n 3).

claimant's expense and that enrichment is unjust usually because the claimant did not really intend to transfer beneficial ownership of the asset to the defendant.

The claimant can recover an asset transferred to the defendant in three different ways: through rescission or rectification or under a trust. Rescission and rectification can give claimants the power to recover the beneficial ownership of assets, as discussed in the next section. In some cases, the defendant may hold the asset in trust for the claimant from the moment of receipt. This occurred in *Re Berry*[110] and *Chase Manhattan Bank NA v Israel-British Bank (London) Ltd*,[111] discussed above, in which the claimant paid money to the defendant by mistake. It also occurred in *Hodgson v Marks*,[112] also discussed above, in which the claimant transferred her house to her lodger, who held it on resulting trust for her from the outset.

A claim to recover an asset after title has passed to the defendant is different from a claim to recover an asset by a claimant who retained title, but lost possession to the defendant.[113] For example, if I stole your car and sold it to the defendant, you could follow your car into the defendant's hands and claim your better right to possess it. Your claim is based not on unjust enrichment, but on your pre-existing ownership of the car, which was probably acquired by consent (through a sale or gift) and continues to exist despite my theft and sale to the defendant. If you claim damages for trespass or conversion, your right to payment is created not by unjust enrichment, but by the defendant's wrongful interference with your better right to possession. Your claims can be described as restitutionary, because the defendant is required to give up the car or its value, but they are not restitution of unjust enrichment.[114]

Claims to recover assets that used to belong to the claimant are new rights created by unjust enrichment, but they can be mistaken for continuing rights.[115] This is because the claimant had beneficial ownership of the asset before the impugned transaction and, immediately upon transferring title to the defendant, obtained either beneficial ownership of the same asset under a trust or the power to obtain beneficial ownership of it through rescission or rectification. If the asset is held in trust from the moment of

[110] *Re Berry* (above n 30).
[111] *Chase Manhattan Bank NA* (above n 23).
[112] *Hodgson* (above n 83).
[113] Burrows (above n 54) 81.
[114] P Birks, 'Misnomer' in WR Cornish *et al* (eds), *Restitution Past, Present and Future: Essays in Honour of Gareth Jones* (Oxford, Hart Publishing, 1998) 1; P Birks, 'Unjust Enrichment and Wrongful Enrichment' (2001) 79 *Texas Law Review* 1767, 1771–76.
[115] See, eg, RB Grantham & CEF Rickett, *Enrichment and Restitution in New Zealand* (Oxford, Hart Publishing, 2000) 310; CEF Rickett & RB Grantham, 'Resulting Trusts—A Rather Limited Doctrine' in P Birks & F Rose (eds), *Restitution and Equity* (London, Mansfield Press, 2000) 39.

transfer to the defendant, the claimant will continue to be its beneficial owner despite the transfer of legal title. However, the claimant does not retain a pre-existing right, but acquires a new right to recover the asset.[116] Prior to the transfer, the claimant had beneficial legal ownership and, after the transfer, has beneficial equitable ownership or the legal or equitable power to acquire beneficial ownership. The equitable ownership or power did not exist before the transfer to the defendant. As Lord Browne-Wilkinson said in *Westdeutsche Landesbank Girozentrale v Islington LBC*:

> A person solely entitled to the full beneficial ownership of money or property, both at law and in equity, does not enjoy an equitable interest in that property. The legal title carries with it all rights. Unless and until there is a separation of the legal and equitable estates, there is no separate equitable title. Therefore to talk about the bank 'retaining' its equitable interest is meaningless. The only question is whether the circumstances under which the money was paid were such as, in equity, to impose a trust on the local authority. If so, an equitable interest arose for the first time under that trust.[117]

The recovery of assets which used to belong to claimants is the purest form of restitution of unjust enrichment. Claimants and defendants are restored to their previous positions, because the claimants recover the very things they have lost and the defendants merely give back something which should not have been transferred to them or retained by them for their own benefit. So long as the claimants pay the transaction costs, the defendants are in no worse position than if the unjust enrichment had never occurred. Since the defendants are not being asked to pay for their enrichment, its value to them or in the market-place is irrelevant. From a defendant's perspective, the claimant's right to recover an asset is the least intrusive form of restitution.

Like other forms of restitution, recovering an asset from the defendant may involve complications and difficult issues. The question whether an enrichment is unjust can be complex, but this affects all forms of restitution of unjust enrichment equally. However, unlike personal claims for the value of unjust enrichment, claims to recover assets can affect, and be affected by, competing rights to those assets acquired by other persons. Although recovery of an asset avoids the problem of valuing the enrichment objectively and subjectively,[118] it does not remove the problem of its effect on the value of

[116] *DKLR Holding Co (No 2) Pty Ltd v Commissioner of Stamp Duties* (NSW) (1982) 149 CLR 431; Chambers (above n 29) 102–04. Although Worthington calls this a 'retained proprietary interest' in Worthington (above n 13) 118,119 she does not use this expression to mean that the claimant retains a pre-existing interest in the asset, but says, 'A "retained" interest indicates only that the holder has, continuously, some form of proprietary interest in the asset, although the interest may change over time: eg, legal ownership may be followed by an equitable security interest.'
[117] *Westdeutsche Landesbank Girozentrale* (above n 24).
[118] Birks, *An Introduction to the Law of Restitution* (above n 54) 130.

the defendant's overall wealth. Defendants may incur debts or make other expenditures in reliance on their apparent entitlement to the assets claimed. Restitution should not leave a defendant in a worse position than if the unjust enrichment had never occurred. Therefore, the claimant's right to recover an asset should be subject to the defence of change of position (for example, by a lien on the asset for the value of the defendant's reliance expenditures).[119]

(iv) Claims to New Assets

Claims to new assets based on tracing are different from claims to recover assets that used to belong to the claimant. They do not restore the *status quo ante*. The defendant does not give back an asset, but must give up an asset to which the claimant had no previous right. This needs some explanation. Why do claimants have property rights to assets when their only connection to those assets is the use of their value?

As discussed above, the claimant can acquire rights to the defendant's assets by consent, statutes, or wrongdoing. No previous connection to those assets is required. However, when the claim is based solely on unjust enrichment, the only possible response is restitution of that enrichment or its value. Why is a claim based solely on the use of the claimant's value not restricted to restitution of that value? By tracing, the claimant can point to a specific asset and say, 'There is my value.' This justifies a personal claim for that value and a lien over the asset to secure the defendant's obligation to pay it. However, there is no reason to compel an innocent defendant to give up that asset unless it is the unjust enrichment. The claimant's ownership of that asset arises, not because it is a repository of the claimant's value, but because it is an unjust enrichment received by the defendant at the claimant's expense.

When tracing value through a series of exchange transactions, on each exchange, the receipt of the proceeds is an unjust enrichment. In other words, each link in the chain is a separate occurrence of unjust enrichment. The chain starts with an asset belonging to the claimant or, more accurately, with an asset to which the claimant has some right (whether full beneficial ownership or some lesser right). That right was probably created by consent (such as a sale, gift, mortgage, or declaration of trust), but it need not be. The initial right might have been created by statute, wrongful enrichment, unjust enrichment, or some other event. It does not matter.

When the initial asset is sold without the claimant's consent, the claimant acquires a right to the new asset which is received by the defendant as the

[119] American Law Institute (above n 75) [178]; Nolan (above n 75) 135, 175–85; P Birks, 'Overview: Tracing, Claiming and Defences' in P Birks (ed), *Laundering and Tracing* (Oxford, Clarendon Press, 1995) 289, 319–22; Birks (above n 46) 49, 55–56; Burrows (above n 54) 527–29.

proceeds of sale. This is a new right created by unjust enrichment. The defendant acquired the new asset at the claimant's expense because the defendant used the value of the claimant's right to the initial asset to pay for the new asset. Essentially, the claimant paid all or part of the purchase price for the new asset. If the new asset is exchanged for another asset, the process repeats. The second new asset was purchased for the defendant by the claimant, who paid for it by involuntarily exchanging her or his rights to the first new asset. So long as the claimant's value remains identifiable under the tracing rules, this may occur over and over again until the claimant finally asserts a right to the asset at the end of the chain.

Equitable rights to the ownership of assets based on tracing value used without consent are, in the words of Dr Smith, 'functionally identical to purchase-money resulting trusts.'[120] Many resulting trusts arise because the claimant transferred an asset to the defendant without intending to make a gift, as in *Hodgson v Marks*,[121] discussed above. Many others arise because the claimant purchased an asset for the defendant without intending to make a gift. Essentially, the beneficiary of a purchase-money resulting trust is tracing the value of the purchase money into its traceable proceeds and claiming beneficial ownership of those proceeds. The claim depends on the proof or presumption that the claimant did not intend to make a gift to the defendant.

In most resulting trust cases, the claimant is aware that the defendant has acquired the new asset at the claimant's expense, but this is not essential. For example, in *Goodfellow v Robertson*, the claimant suffered from an 'unsoundness of mind.'[122] His land was sold and the proceeds were used to buy land for his father-in-law, who held it on resulting trust for the claimant even though the claimant may have lacked the capacity to consent to the transaction. Spragge C said:

> [I]t is a trust resulting by operation of law, and it does not seem to be necessary to prove that the money was advanced by its owner in order to its application in the purchase of land. If such proof were necessary, an assenting mind on his part would necessarily have to be shewn; and in the case of the money of a lunatic, the rule could not apply. In nearly all the cases certainly the money was advanced by the nominal purchaser for the purpose of making the purchase; but there are some cases in which this was not the case; *Ryall v Ryall* was one of these.[123]

Ryall v Ryall[124] is one of the earliest cases to make the connection between tracing and resulting trusts. The claimants were legatees of a testator's

[120] Smith (above n 1) 357.
[121] *Hodgson* (above n 83).
[122] (1871) 18 Gr 572, 574.
[123] *Ibid*, 575.
[124] (1739) 1 Atk 59; 26 ER 39; (1739) Amb 413; 27 ER 276 (herein cited to Atk).

estate. The executor used estate assets to purchase land in his own name and then died. Legal title to the land passed to the executor's heir at law and the claimants brought a bill against him to have their legacies paid out of that land. Lord Hardwicke LC said:

> Courts of equity have been very cautious how they follow money which has been laid out in land, because it has no ear-mark.... But in the present case I think it is necessary there should be an inquiry, whether part of the assets of the testator have been laid out in the purchase of an estate? Because if it should plainly appear that they have been so laid out, they ought to be restored to the personal estate of the testator ... and the means of coming at this by way of resulting trust is excepted out of the statute of frauds; if the estate is purchased in the name of one, and the money paid by another, it is a trust notwithstanding there is no declaration in writing by the nominal purchaser.[125]

Tracing was also connected to the resulting trust in *Merchants Express Co v Morton*.[126] The proceeds of a train robbery in the United States were traced to the purchase of a hotel in Toronto and the victim of the robbery obtained an injunction restraining the sale of the hotel. According to Spragge VC, that right was based on 'the principle of resulting trust arising from the purchase of property by one with the moneys of another, and upon the principle of the Court following moneys or other property; and fastening upon them in favour of the true owner.'[127] In *Re Kolari*,[128] a bank teller stole money from her employer and it was traced into the purchase of a car, which the teller held in trust for her employer. Stortini DCJ said that 'a resulting trust arises where property is obtained by fraud or theft.'[129]

There is a theory that purchase-money resulting trusts do not effect restitution of unjust enrichment because they are created by the presumed intention to create a trust. Megarry J discussed this theory in *Re Vandervell's Trusts (No 2)*[130] and the best arguments in its favour have been made by Mr Swadling.[131] However, it cannot explain the cases discussed above and many others in which it was clear that the claimants did not intend to create trusts for themselves.[132] Also, it does not explain why an unwritten intention to create a trust of land should take effect as a resulting trust if it

[125] *Ibid*, 59–60.
[126] (1868) 15 Gr 274.
[127] *Ibid*, 278.
[128] *Re Kolari* (above n 3).
[129] *Ibid*, 478.
[130] [1974] Ch 269.
[131] WJ Swadling, 'A New Role for Resulting Trusts?' (1996) 16 *Legal Studies* 110; WJ Swadling, 'A Hard Look at *Hodgson v Marks*' in P Birks & F Rose (eds), *Restitution and Equity* (London, Mansfield Press, 2000) 61.
[132] *Lane v Dighton* (1762) Amb 409; 27 ER 274; *Williams v Williams* (1863) 32 Beav 370; 55 ER 145; *Vandervell v Inland Revenue Commissioners* [1967] 2 AC 29 (HL); *Brown v Brown* (1993) 31 NSWLR 582 (CA); Chambers (above n 29) 19–27.

fails to create an express trust because of non-compliance with the Statute of Frauds or its descendents. These problems do not arise when the resulting trust is understood as a trust arising by operation of law in response to an absence of intention to make a gift.

The resulting trust was explained this way in *Air Jamaica Ltd v Charlton*,[133] which involved the surplus funds of an invalid pension trust. Lord Millett gave the advice of the Privy Council:

> Like a constructive trust, a resulting trust arises by operation of law, though unlike a constructive trust it gives effect to intention. But it arises whether or not the transferor intended to retain a beneficial interest—he almost always does not—since it responds to the absence of any intention on his part to pass a beneficial interest to the recipient.[134]

Potter LJ said something similar in *Twinsectra Ltd v Yardley*:

> Express trusts are fundamentally dependent upon the intention of the parties, whereas the role of intention in resulting trusts is a negative one, the essential question being whether or not the provider intended to benefit the recipient and not whether he or she intended to create a trust. The latter question is relevant to whether the provider succeeded in creating an express trust, but its relevance to the resulting trust is only as an indication of lack of intention to benefit the recipient ...[135]

(v) Payment of the Purchase Price

The claimant will not obtain beneficial ownership of an asset based on tracing unless the claimant's value is traced into the purchase of that asset. It is not sufficient merely to trace that value into the improvement of an asset or the payment of a mortgage over it. If the defendant owned the asset before the value was traced into it, then that asset is not the unjust enrichment. The unjust enrichment consists instead of the increased net value of that asset to the defendant, either because its market value has increased or because the amount that would be paid to a mortgagee on its sale has decreased. Unjust enrichment on its own cannot justify the obligation to surrender an asset which was acquired independently of that unjust enrichment. The claimant should have a personal claim for the value of the improvement, secured by a lien over the improved asset, which leaves the defendant free to use other assets to make restitution of the value of the unjust enrichment.

[133] [1999] 1 WLR 1399 (PC).

[134] *Ibid*, 1412; also see PJ Millett, 'Restitution and Constructive Trusts' (1998) 114 *LQR* 399, 401–02.

[135] [1999] Lloyd's Rep Bank 438 (CA) [81]; rev'd [2002] UKHL 12; [2002] 2 AC 164 (HL).

It is sometimes suggested that the payment of a mortgage can be treated as equivalent to payment of the purchase price. As Dr Mee explained in *The Property Rights of Cohabitees*,[136] Irish courts have declared the existence of resulting trusts of family homes based on contributions to mortgage payments. However, since those contributions can consist of domestic services which added to the overall economic well-being of the family, such claims are not based on tracing value into the home. They are perhaps better explained as a perfectionary trust giving effect in part to intentions to share the home.

Another approach is Dr Smith's concept of tracing backwards through the payment of debts (such as a bill for goods purchased earlier, an overdrawn bank account, a monthly credit card bill, or a mortgage payment).[137] He suggests that the claimant should have a right to the assets that were purchased previously by incurring that debt:

> Payment of a debt is just the delayed payment of the price for something acquired earlier. In determining whether enrichment traceably survives, it is not permissible to stop part way at the payment of the debt; it is necessary to move forward to the traceable proceeds, acquired earlier, and to determine what has become of those proceeds.[138]

This proposal certainly has merit and has received some favourable judicial and academic attention.[139] Courts do not worry about small gaps between the purchase of an asset and the payment of the purchase price. Dr Smith gives the example of a thief buying a car and paying for it with stolen money the next day. The delayed payment would not prevent the victim of the theft from tracing the value of the money into the car. Yet, if title to the car passed to thief when the contract of sale was made, the money was used to pay a debt and its value must be traced back into the asset purchased by incurring that debt the day before.

If it is also possible to trace value back through the payment of debts over much longer periods of time, then the payment of a mortgage could be traced into the purchase of the mortgage asset. However, established law does not permit this. In *Calverley v Green*, the High Court of Australia said that it was 'understandable but erroneous to regard the payment of mortgage instalments as payment of the purchase price of a home.'[140] In that case, the claimant was entitled to reimbursement of the money he had paid for the defendant's share of the mortgage payments, possibly with a lien over the home for that amount, but those payments did not affect their beneficial

[136] J Mee, *The Property Rights of Cohabitees* (Oxford, Hart Publishing, 1999) 67–68.
[137] LD Smith, 'Tracing into the Payment of a Debt' (1995) 54 *CLJ* 290; Smith (above n 1) 146–52.
[138] Smith (above n 1) 151–52.
[139] *Bishopsgate Investment Management Ltd v Homan* [1995] Ch 211 (CA) 216–17; *Foskett* (above n 5) 315; Burrows (above n 54) 103–04; Virgo (above n 26) 653.
[140] *Calverley* (above n 79) 257(Mason and Brennan JJ).

ownership of the home under a resulting trust. Their shared ownership of the home was determined when the home was purchased, based on their contributions to the purchase price either through the down payment or by incurring liability under the mortgage.

In any event, a claimant who makes a payment due on a mortgage would probably rather have a right to repayment of that value, secured by a lien over the mortgaged asset, than a beneficial interest in that asset. The value of the unjust enrichment is the full value of the mortgage payment, because that was a necessary expense saved by the defendant. However, not all of that value can be traced back into the purchase of the asset. A large portion of most mortgage payments is consumed by interest or credit charges. Since the asset was purchased with the principal amount borrowed, the only portion of a mortgage payment that can be traced into the purchase is the reduction of principal.

If it is possible to trace back through the payment of a debt into the purchase of an asset acquired by incurring that debt, the claimant's right to that asset is based on a delayed contribution to the purchase price. This does not mean that the claimant's right to that asset arises when it was purchased. Between the date of purchase and the date on which the debt was paid with the claimant's value, the claimant had no connection to the asset and no interest in it whatsoever. The claimant's right to trace value into that asset would not change that fact retroactively. For all purposes, including the priority of competing claims to that asset, the claimant's interest arises when the claimant's value is used to pay that debt, and not before.

If claims based on tracing value through debts are permitted, they must not be used to obscure the essential distinction between the purchase of an asset and the improvement or maintenance of its value. The claimant is allowed to claim beneficial ownership based on tracing and unjust enrichment because the claimant can point to a specific asset and say, 'I bought that for you' or 'You and I bought that together.' A claimant who traces value into a mortgage payment made several years after the initial purchase cannot make the same claim. The possible methods of restitution depend on whether the asset is an unjust enrichment received by the defendant at the claimant's expense or merely the location of the value of an unjust enrichment.

It is not always easy to distinguish these two situations from each other. When the payment of the purchase price follows shortly after the purchase, the payment of that debt is part of the purchase transaction. Money is paid to the vendor in exchange for the asset and the order of payment and transfer of title is irrelevant. However, when the purchase price is borrowed from a third party, payment of that debt becomes a separate transaction. For example, when an asset is purchased by using a credit card, payment of the ensuing credit card debt is not part of the purchase transaction. Similarly, when a home is purchased with the aid of a mortgage to the bank, payment of the purchase price to the vendor and payment of that mortgage to the bank are different transactions. A claimant who pays these debts on behalf of a defendant are not contributing to the purchase price.

The distinction between purchase and loan is blurred when a vendor accepts delayed payment of the purchase price over an extended period of time. For example, if a vendor sells land under an agreement for sale over 25 years, this is essentially no different from a transfer of title at the outset with a mortgage back to the vendor for 25 years, which becomes no different from a mortgage to a bank for 25 years. At some point, the vendor ceases to be a vendor and becomes a secured lender.[141] Repayment of the debt to the vendor should not necessarily be equated to payment of the purchase price for tracing purposes.

D. Powers

A claimant can have a right to recover an asset which was transferred to the defendant, without having beneficial ownership of that asset. There are powers to recover assets through rescission or rectification and there may also be powers to obtain ownership of new assets through tracing. Although these powers are not ownership, they are property rights to specific assets that are enforceable generally against other members of society, subject to competing property rights acquired for value and without notice of them.

A power to obtain ownership of an asset through rescission, rectification, or tracing is similar in some respects to an option to purchase, which is also a property right less than ownership. A person with an option to purchase land has the power to obtain ownership of that land, because the exercise of that option will create a specifically enforceable contract to purchase the land. As Martland J said in *Canadian Long Island Petroleums Ltd v Irving Industries Ltd*, 'forthwith upon the granting of the option, the optionee upon the occurrence of certain events solely within his control can compel a conveyance of the property to him.'[142] It is this unilateral power to obtain beneficial ownership which makes the option to purchase a property right. For the same reason, powers to obtain ownership of an asset, through rescission, rectification, or tracing are also property rights.

Rights to recover assets through rescission or rectification are not based on tracing. They lead to recovery of an asset that used to belong to the claimant and there is no need to trace value into any new assets. A discussion of those rights may seem out of place in an article dealing with claims based on tracing. However, it is helpful to compare those powers to recover assets to the power to obtain new assets through tracing, especially because it is not yet clear that there are restitutionary powers based on tracing.

[141] See NY Chin, 'Relieving Against Forfeiture: Windfalls and Conscience' (1995) 25 *University of Western Australia Law Review* 110.
[142] [1975] 2 SCR 715; 50 DLR (3d) 265, 277 (SCC).

(i) Rescission

There are many cases in which the claimant had transferred an asset to the defendant, but had a right to rescind that transaction and thereby recover that asset. If the claimant has a common law right of rescission, exercising that right can cause legal ownership of the asset to revert to the claimant. For example, in *Car & Universal Finance Co Ltd v Caldwell*,[143] the claimant was induced by fraud to sell his car. He discovered the fraud the next day and rescinded the contract of sale, thereby recovering legal ownership of the car from the purchaser. Since the contract of sale was the event which caused legal title to pass from the claimant to the purchaser, the rescission of that contract caused legal title to jump back to the claimant. If legal title to an asset was transferred by deed, then rescission of that deed at common law would cause that title to return to the claimant.[144]

Rescission will not cause legal ownership to revert to the claimant if title passed to the defendant by registration. The claimant's election to rescind will cause beneficial ownership to return to the claimant, but the defendant will continue to be the legal owner of the asset (holding it on trust for the claimant) until the register is rectified. Also, if the claimant has only an equitable right to rescind a transaction (for example, because of undue influence or an innocent misrepresentation), the claimant's exercise of that right will not affect legal title to the recoverable asset, but will create a trust for the claimant.[145]

Whether legal or equitable, the right to rescind a transaction and thereby recover an asset is itself a property right to that asset, which can be enforced against people who receive the asset as donees or with notice of that right.[146] Until the claimant elects to rescind the transaction, he or she is not the beneficial owner of the recoverable asset, but has a power to obtain beneficial ownership of the recoverable asset.[147] As discussed below, the equitable right to rescind is sometimes called a 'mere equity' to indicate that it is easily defeated by competing equitable property rights acquired for value and without notice of the right to rescind.

[143] [1965] 1 QB 525 (CA).
[144] *Barton v Armstrong* [1976] AC 104 (PC).
[145] *Allcard v Skinner* (1887) 36 Ch D 145 (CA); *Lonrho plc v Fayed (No 2)* [1992] 1 WLR 1 (Ch D) 11–12; *El Ajou v Dollar Land Holdings plc* [1993] 3 All ER 717(Ch D) 734, rev'd [1994] 2 All ER 685 (CA); PJ Millett, 'Restitution and Constructive Trusts' (1998) 114 *LQR* 399, 416.
[146] *Stump v Gaby* (1852) 2 De GM&G 623; 42 ER 1015; *Gresley v Mousley* (1859) 4 De G&J 78; 45 ER 31; *Dickinson v Burrell* (1866) LR 1 Eq 337; *Melbourne Banking Corp v Brougham* (1882) 7 App Cas 307 (PC); *Hunter BNZ Finance Ltd v CG Maloney Pty Ltd* (1988) 18 NSWLR 420; *Latec Investments Ltd v Hotel Terrigal Pty Ltd* (1965) 113 CLR 265 (HCA); *Breskvar v Wall* (1971) 126 CLR 376 (HCA).
[147] Birks, *An Introduction to the Law of Restitution* (above n 54) 66; Birks, 'Property and Unjust Enrichment: Categorical Truths' (above n 7) 637–48; R Nolan, 'Dispositions Involving Fiduciaries: The Equity to Rescind and the Resulting Trust' in P Birks & F Rose (eds), *Restitution and Equity: Resulting Trusts and Equitable Compensation* (London, Mansfield Press, 2000) vol 1, 119, 132.

(ii) Rectification

There are two situations in which a claimant can have a right to recover an asset through rectification. The first occurs when a transaction causes the transfer of an asset that was not supposed to be included in the transaction.[148] The claimant, who transferred the asset to the defendant by mistake, has an equitable right to rectify the transaction to make it correspond to their agreement and thereby recover that asset. Secondly, when a property right is transferred from the claimant to the defendant by registration of a forged document, the register can be rectified to delete that registration, thereby restoring legal title to the claimant.[149] In this situation, there is no agreement between the parties and the transfer occurred without the knowledge of the claimant. There is a mistake in the sense that the registrar believed that the document submitted for registration was genuine. However, the enrichment of the defendant is unjust, not because of the claimant's mistake, but because of the claimant's ignorance of the transaction.[150]

In both situations, the claimant has a power to recover an asset from the defendant and therefore has a property right to that asset. The right to rectify a mistake in a transaction (like an equitable right to rescind a transaction) is sometimes called a 'mere equity.' This label derives from Lord Westbury LC's famous *obiter dictum* in *Phillips v Phillips*, where he spoke of 'circumstances that give rise to an equity as distinguished from an equitable estate—as for example, an equity to set aside a deed for fraud, or to correct it for mistake.'[151]

The term 'mere equity' is potentially misleading, because it is used sometimes to indicate that a claimant has only a personal right to an asset.[152] However, when a claimant has an equitable right to rectify (or rescind) a transaction and thereby recover an asset from the defendant, the claimant has an equitable property right to that asset, which can be enforced generally against other members of society, including someone who purchases legal title to the asset with notice of the claimant's right.[153] In that situation, the term 'mere equity' indicates that the property right is not an equitable estate, meaning that it is not beneficial ownership. It also indicates that it is more fragile than most equitable property rights. While all equitable property rights are subject to legal property rights acquired subsequently by *bona fide* purchasers, mere equities are also subject to equitable property rights

[148] *Taitapu Gold Estates Ltd v Prouse* [1916] NZLR 825; *Blacklocks* (above n 89); *Tutt v Doyle* (1997) 42 NSWLR 10 (CA).

[149] *Malory Enterprises Ltd v Cheshire Homes (UK) Ltd* [2002] EWCA Civ 151; [2002] Ch 216.

[150] Birks, *An Introduction to the Law of Restitution* (above n 54) 140–46; Burrows (above n 54) 182–85.

[151] (1862) 4 De GF&J 208, 218; 45 ER 1164.

[152] *National Provincial Bank Ltd v Ainsworth* [1965] AC 1175 (HL).

[153] *Blacklocks* (above n 89).

acquired subsequently for value and without notice of them.[154] Similarly, a common law right to rescind a transaction and thereby recover an asset is a relatively fragile legal property right to that asset, which is subject to the defence of *bona fide* purchase (unlike most legal property rights).[155] Professor Birks said, 'No one has yet had the nerve to speak of a "mere common law."'[156] However, if an equitable property right to recover an asset through rescission continues to be called a 'mere equity,' how should we describe the common law version of that right?

(iii) Tracing

Like the rights to recover assets that used to belong to the claimant, the rights to obtain new assets into which the claimant's value can be traced should include both immediate beneficial ownership and the power to obtain ownership. However, the existence of restitutionary powers based on tracing is not clearly established. The property right in *Lipkin Gorman v Karpnale Ltd*,[157] discussed above, may be such a power. Even if it does not already exist, a power may be the best way to deal with cases in which the claimant has property rights both to an asset and to its traceable proceeds.

In *Lipkin Gorman v Karpnale Ltd*, the claimants traced value from their client trust account into the money that their partner, Mr Cass, gambled away at the defendant's club. They had a personal right to restitution of that value from the defendant, because they had a common law property right to the money which the defendant received from Cass. However, Cass had legal ownership of the money withdrawn from the trust account. Therefore, the claimants had some other kind of legal right, described by Dr Smith as 'a proprietary right, less than ownership, which does not carry with it a right to immediate possession; hence it will not generate liability in conversion.'[158] This right might best be explained as a legal power to obtain ownership of that money.[159] Professor Burrows explained it as follows:

> The money withdrawn from the account by Cass was owned by Cass not by the firm of solicitors.... [I]f the money was traceable from the firm's property, the firm could have claimed against Cass a proprietary right to that traceable property. To that extent, Cass' title to the money was defeasible: that is, it was vulnerable to being defeated by the firm's (restitutionary) proprietary rights to

[154] *Latec Investments Ltd* (above n 146).
[155] *Hunter BNZ Finance Ltd v CG Maloney Pty Ltd* (1988) 18 NSWLR 420 (SC NSW); Chambers (above n 8) 393–95.
[156] Birks, 'Property and Unjust Enrichment: Categorical Truths' (above n 7) 638.
[157] *Lipkin* (above n 45)
[158] Smith (above n 1) 337.
[159] P Birks, 'The English Recognition of Unjust Enrichment' [1991] *LMCLQ* 473, 478–79; Birks, 'Overview: Tracing, Claiming and Defences' (above n 119) 289, 310–11; Birks, 'Property and Unjust Enrichment: Categorical Truths' (above n 7) 662–63.

> the traced money. And that defeasibility was sufficient for the claimant firm to establish that traceable money paid over to the club by Cass was at the firm's expense rather than at the expense of Cass. It did not matter that the firm had not actually asserted its (restitutionary) proprietary rights to the money while it was in Cass' hands.[160]

A power based on tracing may be especially useful in cases where the claimant has property rights both to the original asset and to the traceable proceeds of its sale. When the defendant sells the claimant's asset, the claimant's property rights to that asset may be destroyed by the defence of *bona fide* purchase. In that case, the claimant may have a personal claim to its value and a property claim to the proceeds of sale. However, the claimant's property right to the original asset will continue to exist if it is a legal property right and none of the exceptions to *nemo dat* apply or if the buyer had sufficient notice of that right, whether it is legal or equitable.[161] If that right survives, the claimant will have a choice between two alternative property rights: a continuing right to the original asset and a new right to the sale proceeds. The question is, what sort of rights exist before the claimant makes that choice?

Unless it is affected by the defence of *bona fide* purchase, the claimant's right to the original asset will continue to exist unchanged by the defendant's sale of that asset. If the claimant was the beneficial owner of the asset before the sale, the claimant remains its beneficial owner after the sale and can assert that right against the purchaser. If the claimant also acquired beneficial ownership of the sale proceeds when the asset was sold, this would lead to a strange situation in which the claimant's overall wealth had temporarily increased by the value of those proceeds until the claimant decided whether to claim the original asset or the proceeds.[162]

The solution to this problem is to say that, so long as the claimant retains a right to the original asset, the claimant has only a power to obtain beneficial ownership of the proceeds of its sale. If the claimant elects to enforce her or his right to the original asset, the power to obtain ownership of the proceeds is lost. If the claimant elects to take ownership of the proceeds, this ratifies the defendant's sale to the purchaser (without forgiving the defendant's wrongful actions, if any) and causes ownership to pass directly from the claimant to the purchaser.[163] At the same time, it converts the claimant's power over the sale proceeds into beneficial ownership of those proceeds.

There are, and will continue to be, many cases in which the claimant obtains at the outset beneficial ownership of the assets into which the

[160] Burrows (above n 54) 90–91.
[161] Chambers (above n 8) 379–95 (*nemo dat quod non habet*), 408–14 (notice).
[162] Birks *An Introduction to the Law of Restitution* (above n 54) 91–93; Birks, 'Property and Unjust Enrichment: Categorical Truths' (above n 7) 662.
[163] Smith (above n 1) 291–92, 324.

claimant's value can be traced. As discussed above, all purchase-money resulting trusts fall into this category and so do *Foskett v McKeown*[164] and *FC Jones & Sons v Jones*.[165] How do we distinguish between those cases which should give rise to immediate beneficial ownership of the proceeds of sale and those which should give rise only to a power to obtain ownership? That could depend on whether the claimant has a choice between a right to the original asset and a right to its sale proceeds.[166] However, that distinction is not without difficulties.

Lipkin Gorman v Karpnale Ltd[167] has been explained as a common law power over the traceable proceeds and yet the claimants did not have an election between two different property rights. Their right to the full balance of their client trust account was irretrievably lost when Mr Cass withdrew money from that account. Lord Goff explained the claimants' right to the proceeds of that account in terms which suggest that an election was involved: 'Of course, 'tracing' or 'following' property into its product involves a decision by the owner of the original property to assert his title to the product in place of his original property.'[168] However, the claimants' decision did not involve a choice to abandon their rights to their original property. Without such a choice, the claimants merely had a decision whether to pursue their right to the proceeds or not. This is no different from any other legal or equitable rights, since the enforcement of rights almost always involves the right holder's decision to assert them. Unless people are under a duty to exercise their rights (for example, because they are trustees of those rights) or they are incapacitated and someone else is exercising their rights on their behalf, they are free not to exercise them.

In *Foskett v McKeown*,[169] the claimants had immediate beneficial ownership of the traceable proceeds of the assets misappropriated from their trust fund, even though they were faced with an election. They could ratify the improper investment and add it to the fund or reject the investment and demand compensation from the trustees (secured by a lien over the investment). Pending the election, the claimants were beneficial owners of the improper investment, but that ownership would be lost if even one beneficiary elected to reject it.[170] However, the claimants' election involved a choice between a personal claim to compensation and a property claim to restitution. They were not choosing between alternative claims to different assets. Their rights to the original assets misappropriated from the trust fund were lost when those assets were paid to the insurance company,

[164] *Foskett* (above n 5).
[165] *FC Jones* (above n 101).
[166] Smith (above n 1) 322–25.
[167] *Lipkin* (above n 45).
[168] *Ibid*, 573.
[169] *Foskett* (above n 5).
[170] *Wright v Morgan* [1926] AC 788 (PC) 798.

which was a *bona fide* purchaser of those funds. This may explain why the claimants had immediate beneficial ownership of the proceeds, subject to divestment by election, rather than a power to obtain beneficial ownership by election.

Finally, the equitable right to recover assets through rectification is usually viewed as a power to obtain beneficial ownership, as discussed above, but the claimant is not really faced with an election. The right to rectify a transaction arises because the transaction did not conform with the underlying contract between the claimant and the defendant. Since they were both unaware of the error in the transaction, they are both entitled to rectify it. This is different from cases of rescission, in which the claimant entered the transaction by mistake, under duress or undue influence, or as a result of unconscionable exploitation of the claimant's weakness. The transaction is binding on the defendant unless and until the claimant chooses to exercise the right to rescind it.[171] Therefore, the claimant has a unilateral choice between enforcing the transaction or rescinding it. The power to recover an asset through rescission becomes beneficial ownership if and when the claimant elects to rescind. There is no similar election to rectify which might mark a transition from power to beneficial ownership. This is perhaps why a claimant who can recover an asset through rectification might be regarded as the beneficial owner of that asset from the outset.[172]

V. CONCLUSION

It is not surprising that so many areas of uncertainty and contention are encountered when examining the laws which govern the various claims based on tracing. The tracing of value occurs in so many different areas of law, including banking, corporate law, crime, family law, insurance, land law, partnerships, personal property security, sales, trusts, and unjust enrichment. Tracing used to be a much more difficult subject before the publication of Dr Lionel Smith's book on the subject just a few years ago. We can now talk meaningfully about tracing and make real progress in the many different areas of law in which it occurs. It is this new-found ability to see the common principles connecting the tracing of value in different contexts that exposes the many issues that have become the subject of new debates.

What does surprise is that some of these contentions are still about the most fundamental of legal concepts. This is especially true of the sources and nature of property rights based on tracing. However, this is just one aspect of the wider uncertainty over the proper roles of personal and property

[171] PJ Millett, 'Restitution and Constructive Trusts' (1998) 114 *LQR* 399, 416.
[172] *Blacklocks* (above n 89); American Law Institute (above n 75) [160], 650.

rights to restitution, which in turn is merely part of an even greater uncertainty over the connections between obligations and property that run through all of private law. Claims based on tracing are not exclusive to the law of property nor are they excluded from the law of unjust enrichment. They may be personal or property rights and they may be created by consent, wrongdoing, unjust enrichment, or other events.

In the absence of another apparent source, such as consent or a statute, unjust enrichment provides a perfectly satisfactory explanation of claims based on tracing. This is because the claimant's right is created by the defendant's use of the claimant's value without the claimant's consent. A claim based on tracing is always a new right which arises when one asset is exchanged for another. If that claim is created by unjust enrichment, it arises to effect restitution of that enrichment or its value. No other response is justified. Since the sole basis of the claim is the enrichment of the defendant at the claimant's expense, defendants should be left in no worse position than if they had never been unjustly enriched. They should not be forced to surrender assets other than the unjust enrichment (except through the normal execution process that applies to all judgment debts) nor should they have to pay more than the value of the surviving enrichment.

A claim to restitution of an unjust enrichment is different from a claim to restitution of its value. Tracing can lead to both forms of restitution. It is easy to understand why the claimant should have a right to restitution of the value of the unjust enrichment, because the claim is based on the defendant's use of the claimant's value. Since the tracing rules show that the claimant's value is located in a particular asset, it is also easy to understand why the claimant might have a lien over that asset. The lien does not compel the defendant to give up that asset, but attaches to it solely for the purpose of securing the defendant's obligation to pay for that value.

Tracing can also lead to a property right to restitution of the enrichment itself, which is either beneficial ownership of the asset into which the claimant's value is traced or a power to claim that ownership. This right is not justified merely by the conclusion that the claimant's value is located in that asset. There is no reason why the defendant should be compelled to give up that asset unless it is the unjust enrichment which the defendant received at the claimant's expense. The claimant's beneficial ownership of that asset is justified because the claimant paid all or part of its purchased price. In essence, the claim is (or arises for the same reason as) a purchase-money resulting trust.

Personal and property rights to restitution behave in different ways, even if those two rights are created by the same unjust enrichment. The personal right is enforced against a specific person (the defendant). It depends not on the continued existence of any particular asset, but on the continued enrichment of the defendant as measured by the effect of that enrichment on the defendant's overall wealth. So long as the defendant's wealth remains swollen by the value of the unjust enrichment, the claimant has a right to payment of the amount by which it is swollen. Personal restitution does not restore specific assets to the claimant, but reduces the defendant's wealth by the value of the surviving enrichment.

In contrast, property rights to restitution relate not to specific persons, but to specific assets. The value of the right depends on the value of the asset subject to that right and not on the defendant's overall wealth.[173] The property right follows the asset and can be enforced against other members of society who obtain that asset, subject to the normal rules for determining the priority of claims to it. If the asset is sold or exchanged, the claimant may be able to trace its value into another asset and assert a new property right to restitution of the new asset.

When an unjust enrichment creates both a property right to that enrichment and a personal right to payment of its value, those two rights to restitution are similar to each other in two respects when they come into existence. First, they are both enforceable against the same person, because the defendant has been unjustly enriched by the receipt of the asset which is subject to the claimant's property right. Secondly, both rights have the same value, because the defendant's wealth is swollen by the value of that asset. However, those two rights may soon diverge. If the asset is transferred, the claimant's personal right and property right may be enforceable against different persons and, if the asset changes in value, those two rights may have different values. This divergence is not surprising because personal rights and property rights are fundamentally different and behave in different ways. The personal right is linked to a specific person and the property right is linked to a specific asset. That person (and her or his overall wealth) may go in an entirely different direction from that asset (and its market value).

Despite these essential differences between personal and property rights to restitution, they share an important trait. Since both kinds of rights are created by unjust enrichment, they are only justified to the extent that the defendant remains unjustly enriched. Therefore, they should both be subject to the defence of change of position. Even though a personal claim for restitution does not depend on the existence of any particular assets, the destruction of the enrichment itself or its traceable proceeds may count as a relevant change of position which reduces the personal claim. Conversely, even though a property claim for restitution does not depend on the wealth of the defendant, a reduction of that overall wealth may count as a relevant change of position which should limit the claimant's property right to restitution of the enrichment.

There is one final point concerning restitution and disgorgement. Dr Smith and Dr McInnes have each argued that we should refer to the giving back of unjust enrichment as restitution, but refer to the giving up of wrongful

[173] *FC Jones* (above n 101).

enrichment as 'disgorgement.'[174] They make strong arguments in favour of changing the current practice of describing both responses as restitution. However, claims based on tracing cast doubts on this proposal. A personal claim for the value of unjust enrichment is always restitution, because value has flowed from the claimant to the defendant in some form and the defendant is compelled to give back that value. The defendant pays money to the claimant, not to reverse an earlier payment made by the claimant, but to transfer the value of an unjust enrichment back to the claimant. For example, if the claimant performs $3,000 worth of services for the defendant and the defendant pays $3,000 to the claimant as restitution of their value, the defendant has given back the value which flowed from the claimant as an unjust enrichment. It does not matter that the claimant never had that money before or even that sum of money before. The money is merely a measure of value and its payment is merely the standard way to transfer value.

Property rights to restitution function differently. If an unjust enrichment is an asset transferred from the claimants to the defendant and they recover that asset (through rescission, rectification, or a trust), the defendant has made restitution by giving that enrichment back to them. However, if the claimants trace their value into a new asset and claim beneficial ownership of that asset, they are not recovering an asset that used to belong to them. The defendant is not giving something back, but giving something up. That asset is not transferred to the claimants as a repository of value. Property restitution causes the defendant to give back or give up a specific asset regardless of its objective or subjective value. In other words, a property right to an unjust enrichment is restitution when the claimants recover an asset, but disgorgement when it is based on tracing their value into a new asset.

In his recent book, *Gain-Based Damages*, Dr Edelman demonstrated convincingly that there are two different measures of damages awarded in response to wrongful enrichment. He 'uses the term "restitutionary damages" to refer to a monetary award which reverses a transfer of value' and contrasts this with 'disgorgement damages,' which are 'based on the actual profits made by a defendant,' regardless of whether there has been a transfer of value from the claimant to the defendant.[175]

I am happy to refer to all legal and equitable responses to unjust enrichment or wrongful enrichment as restitution, because all of them cause the defendant to give up an enrichment or pay for its value. This recognises that these responses are created by different events and are measured in different ways, but all of them achieve the same basic goal. This use of the

[174] LD Smith, 'The Province of the Law of Restitution' (1992) 71 *Canadian Bar Review* 672; Smith (above n 1) 297–98; McInnes (above n 59) 185–86.
[175] J Edelman, *Gain-Based Damages* (Oxford, Hart Publishing, 2002) 66, 72.

term 'restitution' corresponds to the normal use of the term 'compensation' to refer to a variety of different responses which require the defendant to pay for the value of a loss suffered by the claimant. The obligation to pay compensation can be created by different events, such as breach of contract, tort, breach of trust, or breach of a statute, and the claimant's loss may be measured in different ways, depending on the source of the claimant's right to compensation. Despite their differences, all these rights to compensation achieve the same basic goal of causing a defendant to pay for a claimant's loss, just as all rights to restitution cause a defendant to give up or pay for an enrichment.

If judges and lawyers do adopt a practice of describing 'giving back' as restitution and 'giving up' as disgorgement, they must remember that restitution is not confined to unjust enrichment and disgorgement is not confined to wrongful enrichment. A defendant may be required to give back an enrichment or its value (as restitution of unjust enrichment), give up an enrichment into which the claimant's value has been traced (as disgorgement of unjust enrichment), give back the value of an enrichment wrongly taken from the claimant (as restitution of wrongful enrichment), or give up a profit obtained by breaching a duty to the claimant (as disgorgement of wrongful enrichment).

12

Disgorgement for Breach of Contract and Corrective Justice: An Analysis in Outline

PETER BENSON

I. INTRODUCTION

THE QUESTION THAT I wish to discuss is whether gain-based damages for breach of contract can ever be compatible with the fundamental character of the contractual relation. There appears to be an emerging view in the case law and in legal scholarship that such damages can be given in certain circumstances.[1] According to this view, a defendant's gain can be the measure of damages where the plaintiff has the requisite interest in the defendant's performance. The central case is where the plaintiff's interest is such that specific performance would be the appropriate remedy. Suppose a contract for the sale of a unique object and the defendant,

[1] Among English and Commonwealth judicial decisions, the most important and most instructive is *Attorney General v Blake* [2000] 4 All ER 385 (HL). Both the majority speech of Lord Nicholls and the dissenting speech of Lord Hobhouse are particularly interesting and thoughtful. Another important decision is that of the Supreme Court of Israel in *Adras Building Material v Harlow & Jones* 42(1) PD 221, translated in (1995) 3 *Restitution Law Review* 235. The majority judgments of Levin and Barak JJ, by making disgorgement generally available, go further than the emerging view and cannot be justified on the analysis I propose here. The dissenting opinion of Ben-Porath V-P, however, is consistent with the emerging view and with my suggested justification. There is an already substantial and still growing body of academic literature that advances the emerging view. I refer here only to such instructive discussions as RJ Sharpe and SM Waddams, 'Damages for Lost Opportunity to Bargain' (1982) 2 *OJLS* 290; SM Waddams, 'Profits Derived from Breach of Contract: Damages or Restitution' (1996/7) 11 *Journal of Contract Law* 115; LD Smith, 'Disgorgement of the Profits of Breach of Contract: Property, Contract and "Efficient Breach"' (1994) *Canadian Business Law Journal* 121; and J Beatson, 'What Can Restitution Do for You?' (1989) 2 *Journal of Contract Law* 65. The thoughtful discussion by Daniel Friedmann (D Friedmann, 'The Efficient Breach Fallacy' (1989) 18 *Journal of Legal Studies* 1) makes disgorgement generally available and so goes further than the emerging view or what can be justified on the basis of the argument presented in this essay. The most carefully articulated academic analysis opposing disgorgement for breach of contract is E Weinrib, 'Punishment and Disgorgement as Contract Remedies' (2002) 78 *Chicago-Kent Law Review* 101.

in breach of contract, sells the object to a third party or uses it in some way to his or her profit. Here, the emerging view holds that the profit may in principle set the measure of damages. The fact that the plaintiff may not have been able to put the object to such a use, or gained so profitably, would not necessarily stand in the way of such recovery. At the same time, this view emphasizes that gain-based damages should *not* be available unless the plaintiff does have this kind of interest, irrespective of whether a breach is 'deliberate.' Therefore, in ordinary commercial contracts, where substitutes for the promised subject matter are obtainable and expectation damages would be adequate, a defendant's profit or savings should not be the basis of recovery. The fact that the defendant could not have gained in this way but for the breach would be irrelevant. Can this emerging view, both in what it allows and in what it denies, be justified from the standpoint of a general theory of contract? I shall approach this question from the theoretical perspective through which I have previously tried to explain the main doctrines of contract law.[2] From the start, I should emphasize that I understand contract law as coming under corrective rather than distributive justice. And so the question is: can disgorgement of gain ever be the measure of damages for breach of contract, consistent with a conception of contract as corrective justice?

To focus discussion, I want first to identify the most fundamental difficulties that stand in the way of affirming the emerging view. In my opinion, there are two such difficulties, and they are fully recognized in both the judicial decisions and legal scholarship that propose this view.

The first difficulty is whether disgorgement for breach of contract may properly be characterized as a measure of *compensation*. More specifically, if compensation implies reparation for loss caused and where a breach neither interferes with the plaintiff's actual or contemplated use of the thing promised nor affects its value, how can disgorgement of the defendant's gain qualify as a measure of compensation?

The second difficulty concerns the specific character of contractual rights in contrast with proprietary interests. While it is well established that disgorgement of gain may be an appropriate measure of recovery for interference with property rights, the question is whether there is some basic difference between property and contractual rights that rules out this remedy when the latter are violated. In other words, does the fact that contractual rights are *in personam* rather than *in rem* preclude disgorgement as a measure of recovery?

To answer these questions, I shall proceed in the following manner. Before discussing the possibility of gain-based damages for breach of contract, I want to consider the less contentious issue of gain-based damages

[2] See P Benson, 'The Unity of Contract Law' in P Benson (ed), *The Theory of Contract Law: New Essays* (Cambridge, Cambridge University Press, 2001) 118–205.

for violations of property rights. Understanding why disgorgement can be appropriate in this situation, we can then deal with the more difficult question of contract. Accordingly, I shall first ask how disgorgement for violation of property rights may properly be understood as compensation. What is presupposed in viewing it as such? I will then consider contract to see whether, on the assumption that contractual rights are *in personam*, they are different from property rights in such a way that absolutely precludes their remedial protection by disgorgement. I will try to show that they are not.

II. DISGORGEMENT AND PROPERTY

The starting point for understanding property rights is a fundamental distinction between ownership and property.[3] *Ownership* entails a right against and exclusive of another to possess, determine the use of, and to alienate an object that is external to the person. *Property* is a distinct and definite mode of *acquiring* ownership. Contract is taken as a second and different mode of acquiring ownership. Thus property and contract are the same insofar as both entail the idea of ownership. They differ in the way ownership is acquired and therefore in the way ownership operates as between persons. We arrive at the specifically proprietary character of acquisition by understanding the fact that, in property, what is acquired is a right against the world—a right *in rem*. More exactly, one acquires a right against anyone and everyone who does not already have a prior and superior exclusive right to the object. What are the presuppositions of such a right?

First, and most fundamentally, the object to be acquired must be *unowned*. We must suppose that no one is in a rightful exclusive relation of ownership vis-à-vis others with respect to the object. In keeping with the pervasive and limited idea of responsibility in private law that is reflected in the principle of no liability for nonfeasance,[4] we further suppose that no one is injured or suffers a wrong just by the fact that another acquires the object.

[3] I have presented this view in more detail in P Benson, 'The Philosophy of Property' in J Coleman & SJ Shapiro (eds) *The Oxford Handbook of Jurisprudence and Philosophy of Law* (Oxford, Oxford University Press, 2002) 752–814. This distinction is found in Kant who differentiates the question of rightfully *having* something as one's own from the question of how one can rightfully *acquire* something of one's own. The first is discussed in Part I, Chapter I of the *Doctrine of Right* whereas the second is taken up in Chapter II of the same Part. See, I Kant, *The Metaphysics of Morals* in *Practical Philosophy (1797)*, M Gregor (tr and ed), (Cambridge, Cambridge University Press, 1996) 401–10, 411–36. Hegel certainly recognizes this distinction as well, see GWF Hegel, *The Philosophy of Right,* TM Knox (tr), (Oxford, Oxford University Press, 1996).

[4] The distinction between misfeasance and nonfeasance is a fundamental, and indeed an organizing, feature of private law. As Francis Bohlen wrote, 'no distinction [is] more deeply rooted in the common law and more fundamental.' See F Bohlen, 'The Moral Duty to Aid Others as a

Because the rights of no one else are engaged—the object is acquired in the condition of being unowned—anyone can acquire the object without securing the prior consent of others. Property acquisition does not require the participation, concurrence, or agreement of others. In other words, one may rightfully acquire something unowned by one's unilateral act. And since, by supposition, no one else already owns it, such acquisition *must* be good as against any and every one who comes after. They have no basis in rights for complaint. The class of persons against whom this right applies is indefinite except for the qualification that its members all share the same feature of not already having prior ownership with respect to it.

Now it is uncontroversial in law that property acquisition can only be effected via a person's external acts. Let me try to unpack this in light of the fundamental condition of property acquisition; namely, that it is acquisition with respect to something that is simply unowned.

First, there must be an *act*. To acquire something that is unowned by anyone, one must *do* something. If the right of ownership inhered in persons simply in virtue of their existence, as distinct from their acts, nothing could be conceived as unowned and to be acquired. Property ownership is categorically distinct from the right of bodily integrity. From the fact that the object to be acquired as property must be acquired in the condition of being unowned, it also follows that the object must be something that exists in time and space as an entity that is independent of the existence of anyone. It must not be possible to assimilate or reduce it to an aspect of anyone's body. Thus the thing to be acquired must be a single corporeal object. Now, if a right of ownership, which essentially and irreducibly entails *a definite relation to others*, is to be acquired by one's acts with respect to corporeal objects, the act necessary for acquisition must be one *that can reasonably be understood by others as unilaterally depriving the object of its independent existence*. More specifically, there must be an act which, so far as others are concerned, brings the object under one's control; that is, an act which enables others reasonably to conclude that one can, at will and without

Basis of Tort Liability' (1908) 56 *University of Pennsylvania Law Review* 217, 219. To prevent misunderstanding, I should emphasize that the distinction between misfeasance and nonfeasance, as I think it is best understood, is *not* the same as the difference between acts and omissions; nor does it turn on the presence or absence of factual causation. An omission (such as a failure to perform in breach of contract) may be misfeasance and an act (such as intercepting the flow of percolating water) may be nonfeasance. Moreover, failure to rescue another may constitute a cause of resulting injury on the 'but-for' test of factual causation. Yet, in the absence of a special relationship between them, it is still treated in law as a case of nonfeasance. There is nonfeasance whenever the defendant's act or omission interferes with or otherwise affects something that does not come under the plaintiff's exclusive rights as against the defendant. By contrast, misfeasance is an act or omission that *does* injure something that is in law under the plaintiff's exclusive right as against the defendant. Clear and helpful judicial presentations of this distinction are found in Lord Diplock's speech in *Home Office v Dorset Yacht* [1970] AC 1004 (HL) 1027 and Chief Judge Cardozo's decision in *HR Moch Co v Rensselaer Water Co* 159 NE 896 (NYCA 1928).

their participation, bring the object into contact with one's body and thus into one's physical possession,[5] thereby negating its independent existence. Hence the legal requirement of first occupancy. Only in this way can a difference be introduced that is relevant to relations of ownership among persons when the thing to be acquired is unowned. One does not acquire such an object in virtue of the fact that one wants, wishes for, or needs it. The merely inward assertion in thought or imagination that one has taken something under one's control cannot affect relations of ownership vis-à-vis others. Indeed, even an announcement to others that one has done so would not in itself be sufficient. Property acquisition requires an external act of the appropriate kind.

The external act of occupancy that accomplishes property acquisition is, in effect, an act which *actually and presently* treats an object as one's own. Hence the conclusion that it is only insofar as one does something that can count as a present and complete exercise of ownership that one acquires ownership. Further, the meaning and compass of property are contained in the act that establishes it. I have argued elsewhere that, conceptually, the external act that establishes ownership may be analysed as an act of taking possession, use, and alienation of the object of ownership.[6] The right of ownership thereby acquired consists in a right to possess, to determine the use of, and to dispose of the thing owned.

What is the immediate and necessary consequence of property acquisition so far as the relation of ownership among persons is concerned? Briefly stated, it is that others no longer have the liberty (as distinct from a right)[7] to make or treat the object as their own. The object is no longer available for their appropriation. Correlatively, they can do nothing through their unilateral acts that can change the proprietor's ownership in the object. Simply by possessing, using or alienating the thing as he or she determines, a proprietor can do no wrong to others and enjoys an immunity against them, no matter what they do. This immediate consequence of acquisition is presupposed by, but not quite yet the same as, a right not to be injured in one's ownership

[5] Note that I characterize the act in terms of a power of bringing the object into one's physical possession, as distinct from actually reducing it to one's physical possession. Continuous physical possession is unnecessary, since the capacity to use something (entailing the power to grasp the thing as one wills) can be a present reality signaled to others whether or not one is actually physically holding it. Moreover, as Kant argued, if continuous physical possession were necessary, there would be no need for a right of property that is categorically distinct from and irreducible to the right of bodily integrity.

[6] See 'Philosophy of Property' (above n 3) 767–77.

[7] It is a liberty rather than a right because, by supposition, prior to its being acquired, the object is ownerless and therefore the normative character of the relations among persons with respect to the object is an absence of rights and duties, hence a liberty rather than a right-claim in the Hohfeldian sense. I should emphasize that because it is merely a liberty and not a right, the fact that acquisition by one cancels the liberties of others with respect to the object acquired is unproblematic so far as the conception of limited responsibility in private law is concerned. There are no grounds of complaint that come under the idea of liability for misfeasance.

through the actions of others. To arrive at this latter right, one must go beyond this mere immunity in the proprietor and absence of liberty in the others and specify certain further normative conditions and requirements. These conditions and requirements are specified by the law of torts.

Property can be violated by any external act on the part of a non-owner that is incompatible with the owner's exclusive right to take possession, use, or alienate the object of property. More precisely, an injury to property rights is any interference with the owner's sole authority to choose to possess, use, or dispose of his or her object. It is of the first importance to emphasize here that it is the owner's exclusive *authority* to determine use, for example, and not any particular use as such to which the owner has decided to put the object, which is the protected interest. Thus, even if an owner is not in the process of actually using his or her object in a particular way, another injures the owner's right by putting it to a use which he or she, and *not* the owner, chooses. The fact that the owner would not or could not use it in this way is irrelevant. The act represents a usurpation of the authority to determine use which belongs solely and exclusively with the owner. Where violations consist in the non-owner taking possession of, using, or alienating the thing, such acts *in and of themselves* constitute injuries to the owner's right of property. This is true whenever an act constitutes an intentional tort. Intentional tort presupposes that the wrongdoer has at least taken possession of another's thing,[8] quite apart from whether he or she puts it to some particular use or whether the owner was in the process of using it in a particular way. An act that constitutes an intentional tort *necessarily* imports injury to the proprietary rights of another.

Just as the right of property is, and must be, embodied in definite powers (to possess, use, and alienate) with respect to a particular determinate object for it to be a right, so injury to that right is, and must be, expressible in determinate terms. Whatever the right is, so must the injury be, and vice versa. For the injury represents the doing of something the determination of which rightfully belongs exclusively to the proprietor. It represents precisely, and

[8] This is not true of negligence. I argue in 'Philosophy of Property' (n 3) 792–99, that negligence is distinct from intentional tort (and from breach of contract) insofar as it involves an avoidable act that interferes with the owner's actual use of his or her thing or impairs its value but that falls short of taking possession of it. Negligence is not actionable without loss. There must be interference with actual use or value because the defendant's act does not per se usurp the owner's sole authority to take possession of, use, or alienate the thing. On the view that I am suggesting, intentional tort represents fully and explicitly what injury is whereas negligence and unjust enrichment (understood as independent of fault) represent injury at an implicit stage of analysis. In terms of conceptual and normative import, negligence and unjust enrichment are implicitly what intentional tort and breach of contract are fully. The former point to, and are understood in the light of, the latter. The distinction between implicit and explicit is conceptual and normative. I do not pretend to have elaborated, let alone explained, it here. I try to do so in a preliminary and limited way in 'Philosophy of Property' (above n 3). In my opinion, this distinction is relevant not only to the analysis of the different kinds of wrong but also to a rational classification of the different substantive bases of liability in private law.

is identical in content with, what belongs to the plaintiff as owner. For example, in every case of intentional tort, the defendant must have taken possession of the plaintiff's thing. This is the qualitative determinate existence of the injury. Now the explicit and developed character of injury is that it consists in taking what belongs to another.[9] For the right of property is not so much a right to a thing as the exclusive authority to exercise certain definite powers with respect to it. And it is interference with this authority that makes the defendant's action an injury. Accordingly, it is essential that the injury be represented in a way that reflects the fact that it is a taking by one (the defendant) that is taken from another (the plaintiff).[10] Moreover, since normatively what the defendant takes is, and must be, identical in content with what the plaintiff is deprived of, the injury must be represented as a 'taking by' that is identical to the 'taken from.'

The analysis of injury in terms of a 'taking by' and a 'taken from' is developed one step further and expressed in terms of the idea of correlative gain and loss: gain corresponds to the 'taking by' and loss to the 'taken from.' On the view that I am suggesting, gain and loss are the way the two-sided character of injury is given a satisfactory determinate form. Being correlatives, the defendant's gain and the plaintiff's loss are understood as not only equal in value but as one and the same thing viewed from two different sides. Thus, by representing injury in terms of correlative gain and loss, we make explicit, first, that the injury entails two distinct sides, a taking by and a taken from; and, second, that the two sides are identical, inasmuch as they are quantitatively comparable (hence share the very same qualitative character) and indeed are quantitatively identical. In general, *identity* between two irreducibly *distinct* sides is, and can only be, represented as *equivalence*. Correlative gain and loss is thus the determinate form that injury to property takes when its normative character is made explicit.

Moreover, the role of legal remedies in private law—whether damages or specific performance—is, I wish to suggest, to cancel the injury in such a way that supposes the injury to entail, and indeed that makes explicit that it does entail, correlative gain and loss. Unless the injury can be so conceived, a remedy is not available. And it *is* so conceived as long as the injury is understood and analysed as a violation of the right of ownership, in the way suggested above.

To prevent misunderstanding, my claim here is *not* that the law first identifies or determines correlative gains and losses in quantitative terms and then cancels them via the legal remedy of damages or specific performance. Rather, the sole quantitative task that is performed by the law in assessing

[9] This characterization of wrong is not explicitly true of negligence which, in contrast to intentional tort, represents the idea of injury only implicitly, see above (above n 8).

[10] Interestingly, this is how Aristotle illustrates the operation of corrective justice in involuntary transactions. See, Aristotle, *Nichomachean Ethics*, T Irwin (tr), (Indianapolis, Hackett Publishing Company, 1985) v.

the measure of the remedy is ordinarily limited to giving the injury a *single* quantitative measure: *either* the plaintiff's loss (flowing from interference with actual or contemplated use of the property or from impairment of its value) *or* the defendant's gain (profits or savings made by wrongfully using or disposing of the property). The first may be styled 'loss-based' damages; the second, 'gain-based.' In determining either of these measures, the law will *not* ordinarily assess, or even refer to, (in the first case) an actual gain that is correlative to the plaintiff's financial loss or (in the second case) an actual loss that is correlative to the defendant's gain.

Nevertheless, the single quantum of the loss or gain that is assessed as the measure of the injury is the quantitative representation *of an injury*. But an injury, I have suggested, is, and must be, identical in content with the property right it violates; the injury must be viewed as something that belongs to the proprietor alone. Therefore, the measure of injury, whether it is the plaintiff's loss or the defendant's gain, must be taken as rooted in a normative conception in which the injury is analysed as a 'taking by' and a correlative 'taken from.' This normative fact is reflected in the very operation of the legal remedy which, whether by an award of damages or by an order of specific performance or injunction, nullifies the injury by requiring the defendant to transfer the measure of the injury's value (whether it be the plaintiff's loss or the defendant's gain) to the plaintiff: this quantum is taken or subtracted from the defendant's resources—what belongs to him or her—and is given or added to the plaintiff's. The operation of the legal remedy thus makes explicit the normative analysis of the injury (with its idea of correlative gain and loss) that must be presupposed.[11]

So long as the loss or gain can be conceived as a *quantitative determination of injury*, the remedy that cancels it, whether by repairing the plaintiff's loss or by disgorging the defendant's gain, comes under a single regulative principle. It fulfils the aim of putting the party injured in the same position as he or she would have been if he or she had not sustained the wrong.[12]

How in particular do restoration of loss and disgorgement of gain illustrate this single principle? Here it is crucial to recall that the owner's legally protected interest is his or her *exclusive authority to determine the purposes* to which the object is put. It is not limited to any particular use as such, let alone to physical possession. Both reparation of loss and disgorgement of gain are to be understood in this light.

[11] This account of the relation between injury, on the one hand, and gain and loss, on the other hand, shares certain important features with Ernest Weinrib's instructive analysis of gain and loss in E Weinrib 'The Gains and Losses of Corrective Justice' (1994) 44 *Duke Law Journal* 277. Without going into the differences and similarities between his account and my own, I wish merely to note that the view that I have outlined here does not rest on the distinction between 'normative' and 'material' gains or losses as presented in his article. This difference has important, even if subtle, implications for our respective accounts.

[12] This formulation is taken from Lord Blackburn in *Livingstone v The Rawyards Coal Company* (1880) 5 App Cas 25 (HL) 39.

Take first an award of damages representing the financial loss sustained by a plaintiff as a result of defendant's interference with his or her foreseeable use of his or her property. Let us also suppose that this interference has not produced any identifiable financial gain for the defendant. According to the analysis of injury as well as of gain and loss that I have suggested, the plaintiff's financial loss is the determinate quantitative measure of the injury. Because the injury is with respect to a proprietary right, it can, and indeed must, be conceived as entailing a correlative taking and taken from or, in quantitative terms, a gain and a loss. On this analysis, the financial loss suffered by the plaintiff represents the value of the defendant's wrongful interference with the plaintiff's exclusive authority to determine the uses to which his or her property is to be put. The measure of the value happens in this case to be set by the plaintiff's loss. In the assumed circumstances, the loss represents the value of what has been taken by the defendant at the plaintiff's expense. Although it is a financial loss sustained by the plaintiff alone and unconnected to any actual financial gain made by the defendant, it is not in any way more, or differently, the value of what has been taken from the plaintiff than it is the value of what the defendant has taken: it is the value, simultaneously and identically, of what the defendant has taken and of what has been taken from the plaintiff. From a normative point of view, the injury is both of these correlatives at once.

The same analysis applies where the defendant gains a profit from his or her violation of the plaintiff's property right. Suppose circumstances where the defendant takes the plaintiff's property and uses it in a way that was not within the plaintiff's capacity or interest to pursue. Let us even assume that the defendant made use of the property during a period when the plaintiff would not have put it to any particular use. While the defendant gained from the misappropriation, we suppose that the plaintiff did not suffer any immediate financial loss as a result therefrom. This is a case of profit without financial loss.[13] Here again, it would be open to a court in the appropriate circumstances to construe the defendant's profit as the measure of the injury and the value of the defendant's usurpation of the plaintiff's exclusive authority to determine the uses to which his or her property is put. As such, the defendant's profit would be the value of what has been taken from the plaintiff no less than of what has been taken by the defendant.

[13] The circumstances I have in mind are found *Edwards v Lee's Adm'r* 96 SW 2d 1028 (Ken CA 1936) and has been referred to on a number of occasions in the House of Lords. See eg, the speech of Lord Nicholls in *Blake* (above n 1) 390 and, earlier, that of Lord Shaw in *Watson, Laidlaw & Co Ltd v Pott, Cassels and Williamson* (1914) 31 RPC 104 (HL) 119. Where the injury manifests itself in both an actual gain to the defendant and an actual loss to the plaintiff, the plaintiff should have the option of suing for one or the other measure of damages, assuming that suing for both would lead to over-compensation. This is recognized in the so-called 'waiver of tort' cases, see eg, *United Australia Ltd v Barclays Bank Ltd* [1941] AC 1 (HL).

One might think of an award of damages calculated on the wrongdoer's profit as representing what in fairness the plaintiff was entitled to exact from the wrongdoer as the price of his or her consent[14] or, alternatively, as treating the wrongdoer's profit *as made for the benefit of the owner*.[15] Here again it is crucial to distinguish 'profit' as a measure of the injury from the gain that is correlative to loss, which are the two sides of injury, normatively conceived. The profit or actual gain that is the measure of damages is not the same thing as the gain that refers to the defendant's taking: the former is the *value* of the injury and therefore also the value of both the gain and correlative loss.

I have argued that reparation of the plaintiff's loss and disgorgement of the defendant's gain both come under a single regulative principle, the aim of which is to put the party injured in the same position as he or she would have been if he or she had not sustained the injury. Is it appropriate to characterize this principle as one of compensation? In one sense, the answer must surely be yes. If compensation is contrasted with punishment, then, on the foregoing analysis, both measures of recovery are compensatory in character since neither transfers to the plaintiff a windfall that is not owed directly by the defendant to the plaintiff. At the risk of repetition, it must be emphasized that neither measure is intrinsically more justified by or more reflective of the aim of canceling the injury. The plaintiff's (actual) loss and defendant's (actual) gain *just* represent alternative measures of the single idea of injury: they are identical in terms of their normative significance. They stand in the very same relation to the principle of reparation of civil injury under corrective justice, which is non-punitive and, this sense, compensatory in character. If, however, it is insisted that the term 'compensation' be restricted only to remedies that repair the plaintiff's loss,[16] then it must also be recognized that, with this usage, 'compensation' does not, and cannot, designate the highest regulative principle for private law remedies under corrective justice.

The foregoing analysis of injury, measure of the injury, and correlative gain and loss has been presented in relation to the right of property. I began the discussion of property by drawing attention to a distinction that I think is basic to understanding property rights, namely, the distinction between ownership and property. Property, I suggested, is to be understood as a definite and specific mode of acquiring ownership. Does the foregoing analysis of

[14] This is how it is understood by Sharpe and Waddams (above n 1) 296–97. This approach has been approved by the House of Lords in *Blake* (above n 1) 394 (Lord Nicholls). Note that the idea of lost opportunity is not intended to refer to an actual or even a hypothetical lost opportunity. It is rather a purely normative conception, as is the equitable approach referred to below (above n 15).

[15] This is the view taken in Equity. See eg, *Lake v Bayliss* [1974] 2 All ER 1114 (Ch D).

[16] This is the way Lord Nicholls understands the term in *Blake* (above n 1) 392–93. It is also presupposed by Peter Jaffey in his incisive piece, P Jaffey, 'Restitutionary Damages and Disgorgement' (1995) *Restitution Law Review* 30.

injury reflect the specifics of property acquisition, in contrast to the idea of ownership as such? The fact that ownership is acquired as property entails that the object of the right is a thing (as opposed to an action) that can subsist independently of persons and, further, that injury can be done by (indefinitely) anyone and everyone who comes after the one who first occupied the thing. However, that the injury is, and indeed must be, normatively conceived as a taking that is constituted by the two correlative sides of gain and loss reflects the fact that it is an injury *to ownership*, and all that the latter entails. That the plaintiff has an exclusive authority to determine the purposes to which his or her thing is put, that this authority is further specified in terms of possession, use, and alienation, and that the wrong must consist in the defendant usurping this exclusive authority by acting in a way that amounts to taking possession, using, or disposing of the plaintiff's thing, all pertain to the meaning of ownership as such, not the particular proprietary mode of acquiring it.

This conclusion, that the analysis of disgorgement for violations of property rights rests on the idea of ownership, is crucial to the fundamental question of this essay: can disgorgement be a measure of contract damages if we suppose that contract rights, although *in personam* and not *in rem*, come under corrective justice and that contract remedies are compensatory, that is, non-punitive, in character? My contention will be that while contract is distinct from property as a different mode of acquiring ownership, it shares at a fundamental level with property the very same idea of ownership. Consequently, the foregoing analysis of disgorgement should be applicable in circumstances of breach of contract where appropriate. I now turn to this question.

III. DISGORGEMENT AND CONTRACT

The starting point of any analysis of contract is the fact that the law presents the standard remedies for breach of contract, namely, an award of expectation damages or an order of specific performance, as compensatory in character. From the legal point of view, this is taken as a fixed point and absolutely fundamental. Yet, as I have discussed elsewhere, this premise of the law is by no means self-evident.[17] In making the standard remedies

[17] In the twentieth century, this problem was posed most clearly and forcefully in L Fuller and W Perdue, 'The Reliance Interest in Contract Damages' (1936) 46 *Yale Law Journal* 52, 52–55. I discuss the Fuller and Perdue argument in earlier essays beginning with P Benson, *Toward a Pure Theory of Contract* (LLM Thesis, Harvard Law School, 1983) and more recently in P Benson, 'Contract' in D Patterson (ed), *A Companion to Philosophy of Law and Legal Theory* (Oxford, Blackwell's Publishers, 1996) 24, 24–29; 'The Unity of Contract Law' (above n 2) 118–38; and P Benson, 'The Expectation and Reliance Interests in Contract Theory: A Reply to Fuller and Perdue' in J Gordley (ed), *Symposium: Fuller and Perdue* (2001) *Issues in Legal Scholarship*: Article 1 <http://www.bepress.com> (19 June 2003).

available, the law aims to put the plaintiff in the position he or she would have been in had the defendant performed as promised. These remedies appear to give the plaintiff what was promised (or its value). But, the question immediately arises, in what way does the failure to keep one's promise deprive the promisee of what is already his or her own? In other words, how is a breach of promise to be construed as an interference with something that presently comes under the plaintiff's exclusive right as against the defendant? We must be able to say that, prior to and independently of performance, the plaintiff has, in some sense, an exclusive authority to possess, use, or alienate the thing promised and that non-performance of the promise is incompatible with that authority. Otherwise, the breach cannot be viewed in law as an injury and the standard remedies cannot possibly be understood as compensatory as character. Unless the plaintiff has this entitlement, the imposition of such remedies compels the defendant to confer a gift on the plaintiff. And this is directly contradictory with the pervasive and fundamental idea of responsibility in private law which is reflected in the formulation of liability for misfeasance only.[18]

The standard remedies of expectation damages and specific performance can be compensatory on one condition *only*: at, and indeed through, contract formation, and therefore prior to and independently of the moment of performance, the plaintiff acquires an exclusive ownership right as against the defendant with respect to the latter's promised performance. While this right, as contractual and *not* proprietary, must be *in personam*, it must at the same time have the essential character and features that mark ownership as the fundamental juridical idea that demarcates the metes and bounds of responsibility in private law. Is there an account of contract formation that shows how this is possible?

In the history of legal thought, there is at least one model of understanding contract that seems suited to provide this account. This model, for want of a better term, I shall call 'contract as a transfer of right.' I shall not argue here that it is the only such model in past or present contract theory. Moreover, as I shall indicate, there are distinct and competing versions of it, so that the model of contract as transfer constitutes a family of differing theories of contract, which nonetheless share certain important features. Let me now try to identify those features.

First, and foremost, accounts of contract as transfer take as contract's fundamental feature the fact that it is *derivative* acquisition: what is acquired by one is *already* owned by another. More exactly, contractual, as opposed to proprietary, acquisition is derivative in the sense that it is acquisition from, and with the participation of, the owner, and the object acquired is acquired by one *in the condition of being owned by the other*,

[18] Fuller and Purdue (above n 17) 56, fn 7 understood the challenge to the expectation measure in this way.

rather than as ownerless. There is a qualitative difference between property and contract as modes of acquisition. The fact that contract is derivative acquisition implies that acquisition is effected by and through two external manifestations of will or choice, not just one; and each of these acts must entail an exercise of the right of ownership—appropriation on the one side and alienation on the other. The existence and interpretation of these acts is to be determined from a standpoint that is suitably and reasonably reflective of the interaction between the parties in keeping with the fundamentally bilateral character of acquisition by contract.[19] The requirement of publicity that is appropriate to contract is different from that in property acquisition. Whereas in the latter, the acts must be public vis-à-vis (indefinitely) anyone who might come after, in contract the requisite acts must be public as between the two parties only. This difference fits with the difference between real and personal rights respectively.

Further, these acts of appropriation and alienation must be mutually related in a definite way. First, the acts must be such that mutual relatedness obtains just in virtue of and through these acts alone. To satisfy this requirement it would seem that the acts must be sequential in time, with the first being given on condition that the second is done in response to it. There is a second (normative) conceptual requirement.[20] If the object of the contract is to be acquired by one party *in the condition of being owned* by the other, it must be the case that the acts of ownership be construable as simultaneous, such that it is possible to represent the act of appropriation by one as operative only insofar as this is also true of the act of alienation by the other, and vice versa. One side is, and is understood, only in and through its relatedness to the other. The fundamental and irreducible unit of analysis is the integrated unity of these acts.

To prevent misunderstanding, it should be noted that the idea of transfer is not meant to imply that one party's right of ownership is simply and straightforwardly transferred to the other—as if ownership were a sort of thing that can be handed from person to person. The one who acquires is not invested by the other with the exclusive authority that marks ownership. Rather, each party, just in virtue of being a juridical person with a capacity for rights and therefore with a capacity for ownership, has the inherent moral powers to exercise rightful possession, use, and alienation consistently with the equal rightful powers of others. By appropriating in response to the other's decision to alienate, a party is exercising this inherent individual moral power that belongs to him or her independently of what anyone, including the other party, does or judges. What the model of contract as transfer supposes is that for contractual acquisition, in contrast to the case of property, this exercise of ownership is not sufficient by itself

[19] This is reflected in the so-called objective test for contract formation at common law.
[20] It is Kant who first set out this requirement, see Kant (above n 3) 424.

to effect a change in ownership. As I have said, not only must the one party voluntarily yield the object of the contract into the power of the other—such alienation being itself an exercise of the right of ownership—but the two sides must be mutually related in the way that I suggested above. At the same time, it should be emphasized that in this process of mutually-related acts, the ownership that is given up and the ownership that is acquired are one and the same: an exclusive authority to possess use, and alienate a determinate object, where this authority is not defined in terms of, or restricted to, any particular purpose. And since, in contract, the object alienated is the same as that acquired, there is a complete identity between the two sides. It is the fact that identical ownership of the same object is acquired by one party through and in relation to this object being yielded by the other that makes it appropriate to think of contract on the model of a transfer between two parties.

Contractual acquisition, I have suggested, must be analysed as taking place at the moment of contract formation, if the standard legal remedies for breach are to be conceived as compensatory in character. Indeed, this acquisition must be complete and final at formation. It follows that performance or delivery cannot affect one iota the contractual analysis. So far as *contractual* acquisition goes, performance or delivery *merely* represents a physical event that exhibits the promisor's respect for the promisee's already and fully established right. Here enters the distinction between contractual rights, which are *in personam* insofar as they hold *only* as between the parties, and proprietary rights, which are *in rem* in that they hold against (indefinitely) anyone and everyone. Performance or delivery does not affect in any way the rights *in personam* that are acquired at contract formation. It *does* alter, however, the rightful relation vis-à-vis non-contracting parties by giving a party the kind of physical possession essential to establish a right in property against others. Thus, while contract formation gives rise to rights personal as between the parties, performance gives a party a real right as against the world.

On the approach that I am suggesting, *both* personal and real rights are taken as rights of ownership. Their difference lies in how ownership is acquired and as against whom it operates. It is important to note here that there is a further possible way in which they may differ, at least according to one version of the transfer model. According to this model, first systematically presented by Kant,[21] in addition to the differences just noted, property and contract have substantively distinct *objects*: whereas the object of property is a (corporeal) thing existing apart from persons in time and space, the object of contract is an act, more specifically the act of performing

[21] See Kant (above n 3) 421–27. John Austin takes a similar view, see J Austin, *Lectures on Jurisprudence*, 4th edn, R Campbell (ed), (London, J Murray, 1879) Vol I, Lecture XIV. More recently, Ernest Weinrib has presented Kant's view in E Weinrib (above n 1) 111–17.

a promise. On this view, contract formation and delivery give the promisee different objects and establish different juridical relations of ownership even between the two contracting parties. Contract formation gives the promisee a personal (ownership) right with respect to the promisor's act of performing his or her promise; by contrast, delivery gives the promisee a real (ownership) right against everyone, including the promisor, with respect to the corporeal thing that is delivered. According to this version of the transfer model, the *kind* of ownership that obtains as between the two contracting parties changes upon performance: the promisee obtains rightful possession of something new and additional as against the promisor.

It is worth noting here that there is a quite different interpretation of the relation between formation and performance. According to this alternative view, perhaps best associated with Hegel, performance produces *no* change whatever in the relations of ownership *as between the contracting parties.* The object of contract is not the act of performing the promise as such, because this act is nothing other than the promisor's will to yield or alienate his or her property and this will belongs, and can only belong, to the promisor alone with whom it remains as constituting one side of the relation with the promisee. Rather, the object of the contract is the thing promised, which may be a service or an object. Substantively, property and contract differ only inasmuch as contractual acquisition makes possible another's service as an object in addition to corporeal things, whereas property acquisition can only be of corporeal things.[22] It is worth repeating that the service, just like the thing, is the object of, and so categorically distinguished from, the act of alienation (the promise).

Formally and conceptually, what is crucial according to this second view is that in contract, acquisition is determined by the parties' interaction; that is, by the mutually-related acts of alienation and appropriation which, by hypothesis, must be *ad idem*. The acquisition of ownership, and so the object acquired, are construed in terms that are thoroughly transactional. This is the fundamental difference between contract and property. Moreover, this second version of the transfer model holds that performance does not contribute positively in any way to the normative relation of ownership between the two contracting parties: as between them, performance is a purely physical occurrence which demonstrates that the promisor has not interfered with the ownership rights of the promisee acquired at contract formation. The change that performance *does* produce is to the

[22] A person, we suppose, may voluntarily externalize his or her power of action in particular acts or services which can then be alienated to another. The former's consent is, however, essential. Hence, an act or service can be the object of a contract because contract is bilaterally consensual. Property, on the other hand, is unilateral acquisition in which the consent of others is excluded as a normatively operative factor. Hence property acquisition can only entail the appropriation of an already separated external object existing in time and space—a corporeal thing.

rightful relations between the promisee and *third parties*, who are now under a duty of non-interference with the *property* of the promisee.

In this article, I shall not discuss in more detail or evaluate these competing versions of the transfer model.[23] Rather, I want to see whether disgorgement for breach of contract is a possible legal remedy on either version.

To begin, I wish to emphasize the point that according to both approaches to the transfer model, the right that the promisee acquires at formation is a right of ownership, entailing therefore the right to possess, use, and alienate the object of ownership.[24] We must keep in mind here the distinction between ownership, on the one hand, and modes of acquiring ownership (property and contract), on the other hand. At contract formation, then, a promisee acquires, as against the promisor, ownership of, and thus a right to possess, use, and alienate, a definite object, always in accordance with the terms agreed-upon by the parties. Recall here that unless the promisee is deemed to have ownership of a definite object (whether the promised performance or something else), we cannot understand a breach as an injury or the standard remedies for breach as compensatory.

If a promisee acquires at contract formation a right of ownership as against the promisor, the promisee has, as against the promisor, a complete and full right to possess, use, or alienate an object from that point on, as determined by the terms of the parties' agreement. This right is to be *exercised* at the moment of performance, again in accordance with the agreed-upon terms. It follows that, at the agreed-to time for performance, a promisee is entitled to say as against the promisor: I may rightfully possess, use, or alienate a definite object from which you are now excluded. The promisee alone, and *not* the promisor, has the (juridical) moral authority to determine what is done with or to this object. Non-performance by the promisor interferes with, and represents a usurpation of, the promisee's exclusive authority.

At this point, it is necessary to introduce a factual difference that bears importantly on the question of disgorgement. The object of the contract may be unique, so that there is nothing reasonably available that can serve as a substitute for it, or it may be just one like others of a certain kind which are reasonably available to the parties. Whether an object is unique or not must ultimately be decided in accordance with the objective test of contract formation and therefore to be gathered from a reasonable interpretation of

[23] I do so in a preliminary way in 'The Unity of Contract Law' (above n 2) 135–37.

[24] The different aspects or incidents of the right of ownership are protected under the different headings of damages that are available for breach of contract. To illustrate, the nominal damages that are given for breach as such may be viewed as damages for interference with the right to possess apart from financial or other loss; expectation damages may be seen as restoring the value of what is promised; and consequential loss damages can be viewed as protecting actual or contemplated use of the thing promised so long as this use is reasonably foreseeable at contract formation.

the terms, subject matter, and purpose of the contract, construed in light of the transaction's context and the parties' reasonable assumptions.

Now where the object is *not* unique, the defendant does not breach the agreement just because he or she fails to deliver this or that particular, identifiable, object. To see this, suppose the defendant promises to sell the plaintiff a certain quantity of goods which, while they are readily available elsewhere on the market, happen to be stored at the defendant's warehouse. Instead of delivering these goods, the defendant sells them to a third party and purchases the same number of substitute goods at a better price, which the defendant then delivers to the plaintiff. Unless the contract, reasonably interpreted, requires the defendant to deliver those specific goods that are in storage at the warehouse, the defendant has committed no breach. Now suppose that instead of replacing the sold goods, the defendant does nothing at all and simply decides not to perform. Clearly there has been a breach. However, the fact that the defendant has sold the stored goods is *not* as such a violation of the plaintiff's right. The contract does not give the plaintiff a right to any particular set of goods of the requisite kind. Rather, the breach consists in the fact that the defendant has failed to deliver *some* set of goods of the required kind and number. Selling the stored goods to a third party does not amount to a misappropriation of something which rightfully belongs to the plaintiff. The legal remedy that would reflect the kind of wrong done, then, would be expectation damages representing the difference between the contract price for the goods and the market price at the time of breach. Such damages would ensure that the plaintiff receives both the value of what was promised and the means of payment to go out to the market and obtain possession of what was promised.[25]

Suppose now that the defendant is able to sell to a third party the stored non-unique goods at a profit, compared to both the contract and going market prices. Suppose also that this profit is made possible by the fact that the defendant has not delivered the stored goods. However, because the non-delivery of *these* goods is not as such a breach, the profit does not flow from the breach and so cannot possibly represent the value of the injury to the plaintiff's contractual rights. The sale of the stored goods to a third party does not amount to a misappropriation of anything coming under the plaintiff's exclusive rights as against the defendant. The profit obtained through this sale cannot be construed as in any way belonging to the plaintiff. By selling the non-unique goods, the defendant is disposing of something that comes under his or her own rights; whatever benefit the defendant

[25] While this conclusion may be in accord with efficient breach analysis, the route by which it is reached is entirely different. I should add that if the breach interferes with reasonably foreseeable uses to which the plaintiff intended to put the articles, thereby causing further loss, this can be remedied, of course, by damages given for consequential loss under the principle articulated in *Hadley v Baxendale* (1854) 9 Ex 341.

obtains thereby represents his or her own use and value, to which the plaintiff, no differently than anyone else, has no claim.[26]

Where, by contrast, the subject matter of the contract is unique, a different analysis applies. This different analysis is necessary, not because the remedy of specific performance may be available in such circumstances, but rather in virtue of the way the right is determined with respect to its object when that object is unique. Suppose then that by the terms of their contract, the plaintiff is entitled to delivery of *these* specific goods stored in the defendant's warehouse. As against the defendant, the plaintiff can rightly say that at the time performance is due, he or she may exercise the right to possess, use, and alienate these determinate objects in accordance with the agreed-upon terms. Once again, the defendant sells them for a profit to a third party. In contrast to the previous scenario involving non-unique goods, this sale as such *does* constitute a complete and sufficient breach of contract. By selling these goods to a third party, the defendant interferes with the plaintiff's exclusive authority to dispose of them. As between the two parties—and between them only[27]—there is a misappropriation by the defendant of what belongs to the plaintiff and, as suggested in the discussion of property, the profit can in principle represent the value of the injury to the plaintiff's exclusive right. Here, then, a case may be made in principle for the availability of disgorgement or gain-based damages as a remedy for breach of contract. In this instance, and as between plaintiff and defendant, there would be no basic juridical difference between this contractual wrong and a wrong (intentional tort) against a property right.

Both versions of the transfer model illustrate this analysis. It seems clear that this would be true of the version which holds that the object of the contract is a service or thing promised. The service or thing may be unique and where this is the case, a plaintiff should not necessarily be limited to the standard remedies of expectation damages or specific performance but should in principle be able to claim disgorgement or gain-based damages, where appropriate and applicable. By contrast, it might appear at first blush that the disgorgement analysis cannot apply if the object of the contract is taken to be the act of performance itself, as the alternative version of the transfer model holds. If the promised performance, as opposed to the thing to be delivered, is the object of the plaintiff's contractual rights, it might seem that in *no* circumstances would the defendant's use or disposal of the thing, say, by selling it to a third party, infringe the plaintiff's rights. It would, in

[26] I should note that this analysis is found in Smith (above n 1) 136. The plaintiff could claim lost profit that he or she would have obtained had there been no breach, under the head of consequential loss. But this is no longer disgorgement.

[27] It cannot be emphasized enough that the analysis proposed here holds *only* as between the two contracting parties and has no direct application to the plaintiff's relation with third parties.

other words, always be a case of the defendant disposing of something that comes under the defendant's, not the plaintiff's, rights. What the defendant does with the thing would have no bearing on the plaintiff's contractually protected interests since the plaintiff's sole right is to the performance.

To assess this line of argument, it is necessary to consider more closely the relation between performance and thing. *Every* contractual performance consists in a *determinate* act and its determinacy lies not only in the circumstances (time, place, and so forth) of performance but also in the object, whether thing or service. In this sense, act and object are inseparable. This is not to say that the particular content of the object is, in its particularity, legally relevant to the act's determinacy. The point is rather that the act is not definite and therefore cannot be a legally operative factor unless reference is made to its having some determinate content.[28] To speak or think of the act apart from an object is to deprive it of legal reality and significance. Such an act certainly lacks the determinate existence that is necessary to its playing a role in external interactions or transactions between persons. In specifying the act that is owed to the plaintiff, we cannot avoid making reference to the object that makes it determinate.

Now where the thing to be delivered is non-unique, the defendant's disposal of it does not, and indeed cannot, directly implicate his or her duty to perform. The defendant's performance does not consist in delivering any specific set of goods. The act's determinacy is not linked to any specific object in particular. Accordingly, the analysis suggested above for non-unique items applies and disgorgement should not be available as a remedy. But what if the thing is unique? In this case, the act's determinate character *is* linked to the delivery of specific goods. The act that is owed to the plaintiff is an act-to-deliver-goods *x*. If we adopt the standpoint of this version of the transfer model, we must say that it is *this* act which the plaintiff acquires as against the defendant at the time of contract formation. Correspondingly, it is this act which the defendant is no longer free to use or to dispose of as he or she sees fit. But, by selling the specific goods to a third party, the defendant has done the very thing which is now under the rights of the plaintiff. The act of selling to the third party is identical to the act which has been already transferred to the plaintiff. This act no longer belongs to the defendant to do as he or she wishes. Selling to a third party represents a misappropriation by the defendant of what belongs exclusively to the plaintiff. Profit which the defendant obtains thereby can be construed

[28] At common law, this necessary reference to the content of the object is established as a legal requirement through the doctrine of consideration. There must be a content that is of value in the eye of the law and that either confers a benefit on the promisor or imposes a detriment on the promisee. The value of the performance—indeed its very legal character as performance—is determined by and through the consideration that it embodies. I discuss the role and rationale of consideration in detail in my essay 'The Unity of Contract Law' (above n 2) 154–84.

as the value of the injury to the plaintiff's contractual rights. Thus, disgorgement may be given consistently with this version of the transfer model as well.

IV. CONCLUSION

Here then is an outline of an analysis of how disgorgement for breach of contract can be understood within the larger framework of the theory of contract law and of private law itself. The standpoint of corrective justice has been presupposed throughout. The proposed analysis suggests that what I have referred to as the emerging view—which holds that disgorgement may be appropriate in cases where specific performance is in principle available[29]—may be plausible from a more general point of view. While I have not argued that the situation of unique subject matter is the sole instance where disgorgement may be justified as a remedy for breach of contract, it is perhaps the central case and it may provide important guidance in determining whether there are other instances where 'the plaintiff [has] a legitimate interest in preventing the defendant's profit-making activity and, hence, in depriving him of his profit.'[30]

[29] 'In the same way as a plaintiff's interest in performance of a contract may render it just and equitable for the court to make an order for specific performance or grant an injunction, so the plaintiff's interest in performance may make it just and equitable that the defendant should retain no benefit from his breach of contract.' *Blake* (above n 1) 397.
[30] *Ibid*, 398.

13

Characterisation of Unjust Enrichment in the Conflict of Laws

STEPHEN G.A. PITEL*

I. INTRODUCTION

THE AIM OF several of the articles in this book, and indeed of much recent scholarship in this area, is to define and organize the law of unjust enrichment and to distinguish it from other areas of law. This aim is laudable, for several reasons. At times, some of those reasons can seem somewhat abstract, seeking cohesion or structural elegance as an end in itself. Many of those reasons, though, are highly practical. Without clear parameters there is a greater risk of inconsistent decisions from the courts. Mapping the boundaries of unjust enrichment makes the law more intelligible to students, academics, lawyers and judges.

These reasons become even more important in cases which raise the issue of choice of law. Choice of law rules determine what legal system a court will use to resolve a dispute with foreign elements. Consider a payment, based on a mistaken view of the law, by an English corporation to a New Zealand corporation. The English corporation would want to bring an action in unjust enrichment to recover the money paid. Suppose that New Zealand law denied recovery if the mistake was in accordance with a settled view of the law, shared by those operating in the area, that was later found to be incorrect.[1] Suppose also that English law considered such a settled view irrelevant and allowed recovery.[2] It would therefore be of vital importance to know whether New Zealand or English law would be

* This article is based on a chapter of my doctoral dissertation. I am grateful to G Virgo, my supervisor, and to J Neyers for their comments. I am also grateful for funding received from Gonville & Caius College in the form of a WM Tapp studentship, and from the Overseas Research Student Awards Scheme.

[1] See the New Zealand Judicature Act 1908, RS 22, 107, s 94A(2).

[2] See *Kleinwort Benson Ltd v Lincoln County Council* [1999] 2 AC 349 (HL), where the majority (Lords Goff, Hoffmann and Hope) rejected a defence to the claim based on a settled understanding of the law.

applied to resolve the claim. The answer to that question is provided by a choice of law rule for unjust enrichment. Such a rule might, for example, state that the claim is governed by the law of the place where the defendant was enriched.[3]

The importance of choice of law for unjust enrichment is increasing. Unjust enrichment claims are now coming before the courts with increased frequency. Moreover, changes in modern life and business have increased the number of cases which involve a foreign element, a connection to a country other than the one in which the litigation takes place. Fewer and fewer cases are wholly domestic. In the words of Lord Millett:

> Cases on Restitution with a foreign element are now coming before the courts with increasing frequency. As a result judicial pronouncements on the subject are multiplying. But the judges are on uncharted waters with little to guide them ... There is a real need for academic work on the subject of Restitution in the Conflict of Laws.[4]

In a very practical way, choice of law for unjust enrichment is impossible without a clear understanding of the law of unjust enrichment and the boundaries between it and other areas of law. These boundaries may not matter much in an entirely domestic context,[5] but they are crucial to choice of law. In order to know which choice of law rule to apply one must identify the cause of action or issue under consideration. For each cause of action or issue there will be a choice of law rule which determines the applicable law. An issue which could be viewed, for example, as one of succession or one of matrimonial rights raises the question of which choice of law rule to apply, that for succession or that for matrimonial rights.[6] This is the problem of characterisation. Accordingly, choice of law for unjust enrichment requires as a starting-point a well-defined law of unjust enrichment.

This article is divided into three main sections. The first briefly outlines the current law on characterisation, the process through which choice of law rules are selected and applied. The second proposes a definition of the

[3] It should be stressed that this rule—using the place of enrichment—is only an example. In fact, there is considerable debate as to the appropriate choice of law rule for unjust enrichment. Recent contributions to that debate, which is beyond the scope of this article, include G Panagopoulos, *Restitution in Private International Law* (Oxford, Hart Publishing, 2000); PM North and JJ Fawcett, *Cheshire and North's Private International Law*, 13th edn (London, Butterworths, 1999) ch 20; L Collins (ed), *Dicey and Morris on the Conflict of Laws*, 13th edn (London, Sweet & Maxwell, 2000) ch 34 and J Bird, 'Conflict of Laws' in S Hedley and M Halliwell (eds), *The Law of Restitution* (London, Butterworths LexisNexis, 2002).

[4] Lord Justice Millett, 'Jurisdiction and Choice of Law in the Law of Restitution' in TK Sood *et al* (eds), *Current Issues in International Commercial Litigation* (Singapore, The Faculty of Law of the National University of Singapore, 1997) 204.

[5] One important area where these boundaries will matter in a domestic context is that of limitation periods, which are often different for different causes of action.

[6] This was the issue in *Anton v Bartolo* (1891) Clunet 1171. See North and Fawcett (above n 3) 37.

law of unjust enrichment to be used in the characterisation process. The third analyses the parameters of unjust enrichment, looking at the boundaries between it and contract, wrongs and property. Throughout the article, the focus is on English law, though some Canadian and Australian law is considered for comparative purposes.

II. CHARACTERISATION

Choice of law rules link a cause of action or issue with a particular legal system by means of a connecting factor. In order to apply a choice of law rule, the first step is to identify the cause of action or issue involved. A dispute about what the cause of action or issue is will become a dispute about which choice of law rule to apply. The process of determining which choice of law rule to apply is called characterisation.[7]

As an illustration of this problem, consider a claim to recover for services performed in a situation of necessity, such as rendering life-saving aid at the scene of an accident. This claim could fall within one of four different choice of law rules. It could be characterised as a claim in (i) contract, based perhaps on an implied request, (ii) tort, based perhaps on the defendant's role in creating the emergency situation, (iii) unjust enrichment, using necessity as an unjust factor or (iv) its own special legal category with its own choice of law rule. To the extent that these different choice of law rules point to different applicable laws, either the claimant or the defendant will have an interest in making characterisation an issue in order to have the claim governed by a particular law.

Characterisation raises two central issues. First, there is debate about what is characterised. Second, there is debate about whether characterisation is done with reference to the *lex fori*, the *lex causae* or some other legal framework.

A. What is Characterised

English courts have not attempted a coherent answer to the question of what is characterised. In *Macmillan Inc v Bishopsgate Investment Trust Plc (No 3)* the three members of the Court of Appeal variously referred to characterising the issue, the judicial concept or category, the question in the

[7] This process can also be called classification. On characterisation generally see North and Fawcett (above n 3) 34–45; JG Collier, *Conflict of Laws*, 3rd edn (Cambridge, Cambridge University Press, 2001) 13–19; CMV Clarkson and J Hill, *Jaffey on the Conflict of Laws* (London, Butterworths, 1997) 483–99; Collins (above n 3) 33–45; J-G Castel, *Canadian Conflict of Laws*, 5th edn (Toronto, Butterworths, 2002) [3.1]–[3.13].

action and the relevant rule of law.[8] This is not sloppiness, for in certain situations all of these different answers can be correct. The editors of *Dicey and Morris* suggest that issues, sets of facts and legal rules can all be characterised.[9] There is room to doubt whether facts are characterised, since the issues in any dispute are unknown until legal rules are applied to the facts.[10] It is also unhelpful to say that connecting factors are characterised. It is analytically clearer to consider the interpretation of connecting factors, such as determining the meaning of domicile or the place of enrichment, as an entirely separate question.[11] Beyond this, causes of action, issues and legal rules are all characterised in different situations.

The difference between characterising a cause of action and an issue is well illustrated in *Macmillan*. The claimant asserted that its cause of action was 'restitutionary.' The Court of Appeal did not disagree, but went on to decide that the central issue in the dispute was whether the transferees of the shares the claimant sought to recover were *bona fide* purchasers. The court therefore did not apply the claimant's suggested choice of law rule, which was that the obligation to restore the benefit of an unjust enrichment was governed by the place of the enrichment, which it argued was England. The court instead applied the choice of law rule that issues of ownership of shares were governed by the *lex situs* of the shares, the place of incorporation of the company, which was New York. Staughton LJ held 'the rule of conflict of laws must be directed at the particular issue which is in dispute, rather than at the cause of action which the claimant relies on.'[12] This is unobjectionable, and properly recognizes that different aspects of a dispute can be governed by different applicable laws.

Nevertheless, it is likely that courts will continue to characterise causes of action as well as legal issues, as it is appropriate to do so in cases where no issues of subdivision arise. Indeed, to have a choice of law rule for a legal category such as contract or tort is to proceed on the understanding that each issue which goes towards establishing the cause of action is governed by the same applicable law.

The debate over what is characterised has an additional dimension because of the dichotomy between substance and procedure. Under English law matters of procedure are governed by the law of the forum, English law. Determining what is substantive law and what is procedure is thus part

[8] [1996] 1 All ER 585 (CA) 589, 591 (Staughton LJ), 604 (Auld LJ), 614 (Aldous LJ).
[9] Collins (above n 3) 34–35. See also D McClean, *Morris: The Conflict of Laws*, 4th edn (London, Sweet & Maxwell Ltd, 1993) 418.
[10] JD Falconbridge, *Essays on the Conflict of Laws*, 2nd edn (Toronto, Canada Law Book Company, 1954) 58, 69; AH Robertson, *Characterisation in the Conflict of Laws* (Cambridge, Mass, Harvard University Press, 1940) 61–63; C Forsyth, 'Characterisation Revisited: An Essay in the Theory and Practice of the English Conflict of Laws' (1998) 114 *LQR* 141, 147.
[11] Castel (above n 7) [3.12] suggests that connecting factors are characterised, and see also Clarkson and Hill (above n 7) 494–95. McClean (above n 9) 417 disagrees.
[12] *Macmillan* (above n 8) 596.

of the process of characterisation.[13] In these situations, though, what are characterised are not causes of action or issues but rather particular legal rules. Forsyth argues that in all situations only legal rules are characterised, but in doing so he chiefly relies on cases concerning this distinction between substance and procedure. Furthermore, he admits that characterising causes of action amounts to the same thing as characterising rules.[14] Because characterisation involves both dividing law into separate categories and dividing all law as either substantive or procedural, it is impossible to generalize about what is being characterised.

Characterisation problems can be divided into two stages, further complicating the issue. In the first stage, the cause of action or issue is characterised in order to determine which choice of law rule to apply. The choice of law rule then indicates the applicable law. The second stage involves determining which rules from the whole of the relevant legal system comprise the law applicable to the dispute.[15] For example, a cause of action may be characterised as being in tort and the choice of law rule may indicate that the law of France is the applicable law. This does not mean, however, that the entirety of French law is applicable to the dispute. Only the French law of tort is applicable, and so the characterisation process must determine which French legal rules are part of that law.[16] Once again, causes of action, issues and legal rules are all characterised in different situations.

B. The Approach to Characterisation

The second debate concerns whether characterisation is done with reference to the *lex fori*, the *lex causae* or some other legal framework. At first, the issue of what law is used for the characterisation process seems unusual, since the most straightforward answer is that the court can only characterise with reference to its own law. Just as the choice of law rules are those of the forum, the process of interpreting those rules to determine what causes of action or issues they cover would also use forum law. This is the

[13] For an example of this kind of characterisation in the succession context, see *Re Cohn* [1945] Ch 5.

[14] Forsyth (above n 10) 146–50; CF Forsyth, *Private International Law*, 2nd edn (Cape Town, Juta & Co, Ltd, 1990) 66. See AV Levontin, *Choice of Law and Conflict of Laws* (Leyden, AW Sijthoff, 1976) 136; O Kahn-Freund, 'General Problems of Private International Law' (1975) 143 *Recueil des Cours* 139, 371. Clarkson and Hill (above n 7) 485 argue that characterising legal issues, as raised by the facts, and characterising rules amount to much the same thing.

[15] On this process, see North and Fawcett (above n 3) 35–36; Falconbridge (above n 10) 51–53; J O'Brien, *Conflict of Laws*, 2nd edn (London, Cavendish Publishing Limited, 1999) 95–99.

[16] As *Re Cohn* (above n 13) and *Re Maldonado's Estate* [1954] P 223 (CA) illustrate, at this second stage the characterisation can concern either the distinction between substance and procedure (as in the former) or the difference between two legal categories (as in the latter).

view of the editors of *Dicey and Morris*.[17] The idea that characterisation should be done according to the *lex causae*, the law which the choice of law rule is itself trying to identify, has been widely criticized as entirely circular. In addition, it breaks down if the competing applicable laws do not include the law of the forum and the competing legal systems each characterise the cause of action or issue differently, leaving no answer to the question of which is to be preferred.[18]

One of the reasons *lex fori* characterisation seems straightforward is that thus far the focus has been on characterising causes of action or issues familiar to English law. However, causes of action or issues unknown to English law also have to be characterised when raised in proceedings in England. For example, suppose German law recognizes a cause of action unknown to English law. If in English proceedings a claimant seeks to rely on that German law, that cause of action must be characterised so that an English choice of law rule can determine whether the applicable law is indeed German. Using a *lex fori* characterisation, English law would consider the function or nature of the claim and determine the closest analogy under English law.[19]

Critics of *lex fori* characterisation take a more comparative view. They recognize that international agreement on a series of legal categories is impossible and that each jurisdiction will perform its own characterisation. However, they argue that domestic categories should be adjusted for purposes of choice of law so as to better accommodate foreign legal systems. Kahn-Freund and others call this the enlightened *lex fori*.[20] A classic example of this approach is the English choice of law rules on property, which do not use the domestic distinction between real and personal property but which instead use the distinction between immovable and movable property used by many other legal systems.[21] While some variation from a purely domestic characterisation is to be welcomed, this is still very much an approach dominated by the *lex fori*. In the difficult cases where competing applicable laws use different legal institutions to accomplish the same

[17] Collins (above n 3) 42–45.

[18] D McClean, *Morris: The Conflict of Laws*, 5th edn (London, Sweet & Maxwell Ltd, 2000) 495; Collins (above n 3) 36; Collier (above n 7) 16; Clarkson and Hill (above n 7) 490–91; Kahn-Freund (above n 14) 372. Forsyth addresses additional problems with *lex causae* characterisation, such as those of cumulation and gap: (above n 10) 152.

[19] For example, German law recognizes contracts of inheritance. There is no directly comparable legal institution in English law, but using a functional analysis it seems likely that the closest analogy would be to a will and the law of succession rather than to contract law: Kahn-Freund (above n 14) 376. See also Clarkson and Hill (above n 7) 487–88.

[20] Kahn-Freund (above n 14) 374–77; Forsyth (above n 10) 153–54. Lipstein is a leading advocate of this approach: see K Lipstein, 'Characterization' in *International Encyclopedia of Comparative Law* (Tübingen, Mohr Siebeck / Dordrecht, Martinus Nijhoff Publishers, 1999) vol III (Private International Law), 5–7 and also K Lipstein, *Principles of the Conflict of Laws, National and International* (The Hague, Martinus Nijhoff Publishers, 1981) 96–97.

[21] North and Fawcett (above n 3) 39; Collier (above n 7) 19.

end result, for example one using contract and the other using tort to handle the same kind of claim, no amount of enlightenment will resolve the conflict.[22] Each system can be expected to maintain its own characterisation according to its own law.

The debate over which law governs the characterisation process continues into the second stage of characterisation. In *Re Maldonado's Estate* the Court of Appeal, having determined the law applicable to an issue of intestate succession to movables was Spanish law, looked to what Spanish law considered to be within that legal category.[23] While the first stage of characterisation used the *lex fori*, the second stage used the *lex causae*. This approach to the second stage can create considerable problems. Suppose an issue is characterised by English law as part of the law of tort and by Spanish law as part of the law of contract. An English court will apply the choice of law rule for tort. If the applicable law is Spanish and the *lex causae*, Spanish law, is used for the second stage of characterisation, the focus will be on ascertaining what Spanish law considers to be its tort law. This will not properly address the issue, because, as noted at the outset, Spanish law characterises that issue as contractual.

To avoid the problem in *Re Maldonado's Estate*, and in keeping with the overall analysis of the approach to characterisation thus far, the *lex fori* should be used for both the first and second stages of characterisation. This approach will at times be sensitive to differences between legal systems, as in its treatment of the types of property, but it is firmly grounded in the legal system's own internal divisions of law.

C. Characterisation Fundamentals

Lipstein's conclusion that the 'process of subsuming claims formulated in accordance with one legal system under one of several rules of the conflict of laws of the forum by way of interpreting each in terms of the other is the essence of characterisation' illustrates its considerable complexity.[24] However, such complexity can be substantially simplified by proper pleadings. Causes of action and issues should be identified with precision so as to facilitate identification of the correct choice of law rule. Claims should be made in the alternative where appropriate so that each cause of action can be analysed separately. In the earlier example of a claim to recover for services rendered in an emergency situation, each possible alternative claim should be pleaded. This will minimize arguments about whether the claim can only be characterised as being in contract, tort, unjust enrichment or another legal category. If it is arguable that the claim as pleaded could fall

[22] Kahn-Freund (above n 14) 378.
[23] Above (n 16).
[24] Lipstein 1981 (above n 20) 95–96.

within the legal category under consideration, it is unlikely that a court would refuse to give effect to the claim as characterised by the claimant. Instead the court would apply the relevant choice of law rule to each of the alternative causes of action and let the applicable law determine whether such a claim can be made out. In contrast, litigants who plead claims without due precision deserve the characterisation disputes that result.

As far as the law of unjust enrichment is concerned, the most important lesson of this analysis of characterisation is the need, under English law, to be able to identify those causes of action, issues or rules which are part of that law so that the choice of law rules for unjust enrichment can be applied in the appropriate cases. At the first stage of characterisation, a court must be able to characterise a cause of action or issue as being in unjust enrichment. At the second stage, a court must be able to identify those rules of the applicable law, English or foreign, which are part of the law of unjust enrichment.

III. UNJUST ENRICHMENT

The precise nature of the cause of action in claims about unjust enrichment is critical to characterisation. While the law of unjust enrichment can be viewed in many different ways, the approach adopted here is to analyse it as a separate cause of action.

A. A Cause of Action

To advocate a cause of action in unjust enrichment, two main challenges must be answered. First, critics of unjust enrichment do not accept that it can conceptually unite any body of law, much less amount to a cause of action. Second, some supporters of unjust enrichment nonetheless see it as something less than a cause of action, viewing it as only a concept or principle which helps to unify other causes of action previously thought to be unrelated. These challenges bear directly on the development and application of appropriate choice of law rules for this area. If unjust enrichment does not unite a body of law, then the focus should instead be on developing specific choice of law rules for, say, claims to recover money paid by mistake and other discrete types of claim. Further, if unjust enrichment is only a unifying concept or principle, the choice of law rules for those causes of action within its ambit will likely be more diverse and divergent than if it is itself a cause of action.

(i) The First Challenge

One part of the first challenge is about whether any single principle can be said to underlie any specific part of the law of obligations. Initially focusing on the supposed distinctions between contract and tort, Atiyah argued that contract is about more than giving effect to the parties' intentions and protecting expectations. He thus rejected the idea that distinctions could be drawn between areas of the law of obligations based on underlying principles.[25] On this theory, the principle that unjust enrichment should be reversed is as much an element of the law of contract as it is of any other part of the law of obligations. Hedley has continued this argument, claiming that the law of obligations cannot be divided into contract, tort and unjust enrichment by reason of each having a separate underlying principle.[26] For Hedley, unjust enrichment cannot identify and separate part of the law of obligations from any other part. More recently, he has argued that the cases others have tried to explain using unjust enrichment are better accommodated by expanding the current boundaries of contract, tort and property law.[27]

In contrast, Burrows argues that courts and academics now recognize that the principle of unjust enrichment underpins a certain body of law, drawing together cases previously thought to be unconnected.[28] This body of law is the law of unjust enrichment. Contract, tort and unjust enrichment are not contextual areas of law like employment law and family law. To be coherent each must be united by its own underlying principle.[29] Burrows has argued that the threefold division of the law of obligations is satisfactory, with underlying principles separating 'at least most of the law' into contract, tort and unjust enrichment.[30] Atiyah's arguments about whether these underlying principles are exclusive has not impaired the recognition of contract and tort as separate parts of the law of obligations. The cores of the law of contract and the law of tort are clear, regardless of any dispute about the exclusivity of the relevant underlying principle, and there is no reason to think the core of the law of unjust enrichment cannot be just as clear.[31]

[25] PS Atiyah, 'Contracts, Promises and the Law of Obligations' in PS Atiyah, *Essays on Contract* (Oxford, Clarendon Press, 1986) 42, 48–50. In response see P Birks, 'Restitution and the Freedom of Contract' [1983] *CLP* 141.

[26] S Hedley, 'Unjust Enrichment as the Basis of Restitution—An Overworked Concept' (1985) 5 *LS* 56, 58; S Hedley, 'Contract, Tort and Restitution; or, On Cutting the Legal System Down to Size' (1988) 8 *LS* 137, 141; S Hedley, 'Ten Questions for 'Unjust Enrichment' Theorists' [1997] 3 *Web Journal of Current Legal Issues* under question three; S Hedley, 'Restitution: Contract's Twin?' in F Rose (ed), *Failure of Contracts* (Oxford, Hart Publishing, 1997) 247–51. See also SJ Stoljar, *The Law of Quasi-Contract*, 2nd edn (Sydney, The Law Book Company Limited, 1989) 1; SM Waddams, 'Restitution as Part of Contract Law' in A Burrows (ed), *Essays on the Law of Restitution* (Oxford, Clarendon Press, 1991).

[27] S Hedley, *Restitution: Its Division and Ordering* (London, Sweet & Maxwell Limited, 2001) 224–28, 231–32. He makes similar arguments in S Hedley, *A Critical Introduction to Restitution* (London, Butterworths, 2001) 21–22, 25, 47–49, 60, 66–67.

[28] A Burrows, 'Restitution: Where do We Go From Here?' [1997] *CLP* 95, 96.

[29] See Hedley, 'Ten Questions' (above n 26) under question one.

[30] A Burrows, 'Contract, Tort and Restitution—A Satisfactory Division or Not?' (1983) 99 *LQR* 217, 253–55. See also WA Seavey and AW Scott, 'Restitution' (1938) 54 *LQR* 29, 31–32.

[31] See P Birks, 'Unjust Enrichment—A Reply to Mr Hedley' (1985) 5 *LS* 67, 69.

Critics of unjust enrichment also take another approach, arguing that it does not bring together everything that is neither contract nor tort.[32] Stoljar, for example, argued that cases involving unsolicited services could not be explained by unjust enrichment but rather by unjust sacrifice, which does not focus on enrichment by the defendant.[33] The point is arguable, mainly turning on the extent to which services are considered as enrichment,[34] but it does not diminish unjust enrichment if in the end it does not eliminate all residual aspects of the law of obligations.

Despite these challenges to the utility of unjust enrichment as a principle, it has been accepted in the English courts. Time has not dated Lord Wright's dictum in *Fibrosa v Fairbairn*, as it is now clearer than it was in 1943 that

> any civilized system of law is bound to provide remedies for cases of what has been called unjust enrichment or unjust benefit, that is to prevent a man from retaining the money of or some benefit derived from another which it is against conscience that he should keep.[35]

While civilian and mixed legal systems have long recognized the law of unjust enrichment as part of the law of obligations,[36] formal recognition came slowly in the common law world, particularly in England.[37] However, in 1991 the House of Lords held that the law of unjust enrichment was part of English law. In *Lipkin Gorman v Karpnale Ltd* both Lord Templeman and Lord Goff accepted that the claimant's claim was founded on unjust enrichment and could only succeed if it established that the defendant was unjustly enriched at the expense of the claimant.[38]

The House of Lords has since recognized and approved of the law of unjust enrichment on several occasions.[39] For example, in *Banque Financière de la Cité v Parc (Battersea) Ltd*, Lord Steyn stated that 'unjust

[32] Three recent challenges to unjust enrichment in this vein are IM Jackman, *The Varieties of Restitution* (Sydney, The Federation Press, 1998), J Dietrich, *Restitution—A New Perspective* (Sydney, The Federation Press, 1998) and P Jaffey, *The Nature and Scope of Restitution* (Oxford, Hart Publishing, 2000).

[33] Stoljar (above n 26) 1, 250. See also P Watts, 'Restitution—A Property Principle and a Services Principle' [1995] *Restitution Law Review* 49, 50–51, 81; Hedley 1985 (above n 26) 60–66.

[34] J Beatson, *The Use and Abuse of Unjust Enrichment* (Oxford, Oxford University Press, 1991) 38, 44; P Birks, *Restitution—The Future* (Sydney, The Federation Press, 1992) 103.

[35] [1943] AC 32 (HL) 61.

[36] B Dickson, 'Unjust Enrichment Claims: A Comparative Overview' [1995] *CLJ* 100, 111ff.

[37] For an explanation of this slow development, see Lord Goff and G Jones, *The Law of Restitution*, 6th edn (London, Sweet & Maxwell, 2002) 5–11; P Birks, *An Introduction to the Law of Restitution* (Oxford, Clarendon Press, 1989) 4–5, 34–39.

[38] [1991] 2 AC 548 (HL) 559 (Lord Templeman), 578 (Lord Goff).

[39] See, eg, *Woolwich Equitable Building Society v IRC* [1993] AC 70 (HL) 196–97 (Lord Browne-Wilkinson), *Westdeutsche Landesbank Girozentrale v Islington London Borough Council* [1996] AC 669 (HL) 710 (Lord Browne-Wilkinson) and *Kleinwort Benson Ltd v Lincoln County Council* [1999] 2 AC 349 (HL) 371–72 (Lord Goff, with whom the other Law Lords agreed on this point).

enrichment ranks next to contract and tort as part of the law of obligations. It is an independent source of rights and obligations.'[40] As far as authority is concerned, unjust enrichment now has a firm base of support.

(ii) The Second Challenge

Recognition of unjust enrichment as part of English law does not mean it is a cause of action. As Lord Escher explained, a cause of action is 'every fact which it would be necessary for the claimant to prove, if traversed, in order to support his right to the judgment of the Court.'[41] In other words, a cause of action is a factual situation which entitles a claimant to a remedy.[42] At issue is whether unjust enrichment comes within this definition.

During the past ten years the law of unjust enrichment has been defined with increasing precision. Part of that process has involved defining unjust enrichment as a cause of action with three elements.[43] A claimant will succeed in a claim to reverse unjust enrichment if it can show (i) that the defendant has been enriched, (ii) that the enrichment is at its expense and (iii) that it would be unjust for the defendant to retain the enrichment.[44] Each of these elements is in turn further refined, particularly the third. Far from being an open-ended invitation to the court to do justice in the particular case, the third element has developed into a series of unjust factors, like mistake and duress, on which the claimant must base its claim in order to recover.

Returning to the definition of a cause of action for unjust enrichment, two of the facts which would entitle a claimant to a remedy are (i) that the defendant has been enriched and (ii) that the enrichment is at the claimant's expense. Each of these facts, which are identified in quite general terms, will have to be proven, and to prove them the claimant will have to rely on further, more specific facts which will vary from case to case. A defendant

[40] [1999] 1 AC 221 (HL) 227. The other Law Lords did not expressly agree with Lord Steyn, but some did discuss the case, at least in part, in unjust enrichment terms: see Lord Clyde, 237.

[41] *Read v Brown* (1889) 22 QBD 128 (CA) 131. This definition was approved in *Coburn v Colledge* [1897] 1 QB 702 (CA) and in *Central Electricity Board v Halifax Corporation* [1963] AC 785 (HL) 800 (Lord Reid). The rules of court do not define a cause of action: The Civil Procedure Rules 1998, SI 1998 No 3132. See also K Mason and JW Carter, *Restitution Law in Australia* (Sydney, Butterworths, 1995) 73–75, 970ff.

[42] *Letang v Cooper* [1965] 1 QB 232 (CA) 242–43 (Diplock LJ); *Republic of India v Indian Steamship Co Ltd* [1993] AC 410 (HL) 419 (Lord Goff). See also P Birks, 'Rights, Wrongs and Remedies' (2000) 20 *OJLS* 1, 25.

[43] Many formulations of the cause of action in English law actually list four elements, the fourth being the absence of a successful defence to the claim. Defences to claims in unjust enrichment, especially change of position, are increasingly important in the analysis of the cases. However, causes of action are not generally formulated to include the absence of a defence as an element.

[44] Birks (above n 37) 7; A Burrows, *The Law of Restitution*, 2nd edn (London, Butterworths, 2002) 15; Goff and Jones (above n 37) 17; Mason and Carter (above n 41) 10, 38. See also *Banque Financière* (above n 40) 227 (Lord Steyn).

can be enriched in many different ways, but that does not invalidate defining the cause of action in terms of the more general fact of the defendant's enrichment.[45] The facts which make up the definition of a cause of action are necessarily general.

Further, that it would be unjust for a defendant to retain a benefit is a legal conclusion, not a matter of fact. The underlying facts behind the third element of the cause of action are therefore those pointing to the ground or basis supporting the conclusion that it would be unjust for the defendant to retain the enrichment. Again, different factual grounds or bases can suffice, but that is no reason for treating each such ground or basis as part of a unique cause of action. The alternative would be separately to recognize a cause of action to reverse unjust enrichment based on mistake, a cause of action to reverse unjust enrichment based on duress, and so on for each possible ground. This needlessly multiplies the causes of action. Each type of unjust factor can be accommodated within the more general cause of action, provided that in pleading the cause of action the unjust factor is clearly identified in each case.[46]

At the heart of this issue is the role of the unjust factors, particularly as acknowledged by the courts. Some of those who urge the acceptance of unjust enrichment as a general cause of action play down the role of these factors. They argue that the principle of unjust enrichment can allow a claimant to recover even when its claim is not based on an accepted unjust factor.[47] Support for this approach can be drawn from Canadian law, under which the third element of the cause of action for unjust enrichment is not the establishing of a particular unjust factor but rather the absence of any juristic reason for the enrichment.[48] This shifts the focus, at least in theory, away from consideration of unjust factors to consideration of reasons why the defendant should be allowed to retain the enrichment.

In contrast, most of those who see unjust enrichment as only a unifying concept are committed to the accepted unjust factors. For them, unjust enrichment draws together decided cases and explains their results but it

[45] By analogy, to succeed in a cause of action in nuisance the plaintiff must prove an unreasonable interference with the enjoyment of land. There are many possible forms of unreasonable interference, involving noise, smells, radio interference and so on, but each is not part of a separate cause of action.

[46] J Edelman, 'Money Had and Received: Modern Pleading of an Old Count' [2000] *Restitution Law Review* 547, 569–70. See also G Virgo, *The Principles of the Law of Restitution* (Oxford, Oxford University Press, 1999) 55–57.

[47] Goff and Jones (above n 37) 15–16; G Jones, 'A Topography of the Law of Restitution' in PD Finn (ed), *Essays on Restitution* (Sydney, The Law Book Company Limited, 1990) 3.

[48] *Pettkus v Becker* [1980] 2 SCR 834, 848; (1980) 117 DLR (3d) 257 (SCC) 273–74 (Dickson J). See also GB Klippert, *Unjust Enrichment* (Toronto, Butterworths, 1983) 27–28; PD Maddaugh and JD McCamus, *The Law of Restitution* (Aurora, Canada Law Book Inc, 1990) 27. German law is similar, looking not to specific grounds of restitution but instead to an absence of legal justification for the enrichment: see K Zweigert and H Kotz, *Introduction to Comparative Law*, 3rd rev edn (Oxford, Clarendon Press, 1998) 540–41.

does not go further. Unjust enrichment may be a principle but it is not a cause of action in its own right. To support their position, critics of a general cause of action to reverse unjust enrichment argue that it has not been endorsed in the case law.[49]

However, there is a middle ground, in the form of a general cause of action that is closely linked to the unjust factors. Support for this position is found in the recognition by the courts that the existing unjust factors are not a closed list and that new factors can be identified as the law develops.[50] A cause of action in unjust enrichment can, and should, be accepted without disregarding the unjust factors. Not only can this be done without adopting the Canadian approach,[51] but that approach may be a false alternative in any case. Both Smith and McInnes, leading experts on the Canadian law of unjust enrichment, have recently argued that even within the Canadian formulation the unjust factors have played a role that is very similar to their role in English law.[52] In addition, Jones argues that acceptance of a more general, widespread notion of unjust enrichment is dependent on giving firm and meaningful content to the ground for restitution.[53]

There is growing judicial support for unjust enrichment as a cause of action in English law. In *Foskett v McKeown*, Lord Millett, with whom the other Law Lords agreed, specifically referred, though in *dictum*, to a cause of action to reverse unjust enrichment.[54] This is consistent with similar recognition in *Baltic Shipping Co v Dillon*, a case about total failure of consideration in which two judges of the High Court of Australia referred to the action as being in unjust enrichment.[55] It also parallels recent academic

[49] Birks (above n 37) 22–25; W Swadling, 'Restitution and Unjust Enrichment' in *Towards a European Civil Code* (Nijmegen, Martinus Nijhoff Publishers, 1994) 268; PA Butler, 'Viewing Restitution at the Level of a Secondary Remedial Obligation' (1990) 16 *University of Queensland Law Journal* 27, 34, 45; P Gallo, 'Unjust Enrichment: A Comparative Analysis' (1992) 40 *AJCL* 431, 431, 465.

[50] In *Pavey and Matthews Pty v Paul* (1987) 162 CLR 221 Deane J (at 256–57) called unjust enrichment a 'unifying legal concept' which explained a variety of distinct types of cases but added that it also assisted in determining whether to reverse an unjust enrichment 'in a new or developing category of case.' See also *James More & Sons Ltd v University of Ottawa* (1974) 5 OR (2d) 162 (HCJ) and *Woolwich* (above n 39) which created a new unjust factor, *ultra vires* demands by public authorities.

[51] For a different view, see A Burrows and E McKendrick, *Cases and Materials on the Law of Restitution* (Oxford, Oxford University Press, 1997) 92, where the authors appear to equate the idea of a general cause of action with adoption of the Canadian formulation. See also Burrows (above n 44) 48–51.

[52] LD Smith, 'The Mystery of "Juristic Reason"' (2000) 12 *Supreme Court Law Review* (2d) 211; M McInnes, 'Absence of Juristic Reason: *Campbell v. Campbell*' (2000) 79 *Canadian Bar Review* 459. Smith argues that Canadian law should expressly shift its focus to a positive reason for reversing an enrichment. Both argue that unjust enrichment is an independent cause of action.

[53] G Jones, 'The Law of Restitution: The Past and the Future' in Burrows (above n 26) 3.

[54] [2001] 1 AC 102 (HL) 129. The House of Lords held that the claim in this case was to vindicate property rights, not to reverse unjust enrichment.

[55] (1993) 176 CLR 344 (HC) 375, 379 (Deane and Dawson JJ).

support for this conclusion.[56] These developments, coupled with the logic of the arguments above, provide a sufficient basis to treat unjust enrichment as an independent cause of action.

B. Unjust Enrichment and Restitution—Terminology Problems

The law of unjust enrichment and the law of restitution are not the same, although for many years leading academics claimed that they were. It has been repeatedly observed that restitution refers to a remedy or, more generally, a response to causative events.[57] In this sense it is parallel to compensation, another remedy, or punishment, another response. Similarly it has long been appreciated that unjust enrichment refers to a causative event, parallel to a breach of contract, a tort or a breach of an equitable obligation.[58] In terms of definition, then, academics did not claim unjust enrichment and restitution were the same thing. However, they claimed that unjust enrichment was the only causative event which could lead to restitution as a remedy and that restitution was the only remedy for unjust enrichment.[59] Birks called this the 'quadration' of unjust enrichment and restitution.[60] The most obvious example of this quadration was the repeated assertion that restitution belonged alongside contract and tort as a third part of the law of obligations.[61] Such a claim only makes sense if restitution is a synonym for unjust enrichment.

Quadration caused many problems. Most of these flowed from the meaning of restitution. In its ordinary meaning restitution means the act of restoring, and in the context of a legal remedy the restoring of something to someone. Technically one cannot restore to someone something which he or she did not originally have. However, this technicality was not enough to prevent the rise of a broader meaning of restitution. This broader meaning

[56] P Hellwege, 'The Scope of Application of Change of Position in the Law of Unjust Enrichment: A Comparative Study' [1999] *Restitution Law Review* 92, 94; P Birks, 'Private Law' in P Birks and F Rose (eds), *Lessons of the Swaps Litigation* (London, Mansfield Press, 2000) 26–27, 40.

[57] P Birks, 'Restitution and Wrongs' (1982) 35 *CLP* 53, 53; Birks (above n 37) 9; P Birks, 'The Independence of Restitutionary Causes of Action' (1990) 16 *University of Queensland Law Journal* 1, 4; Stoljar (above n 26) 1; Virgo (above n 46) 3.

[58] Birks (above n 37) 26; Birks (above n 31) 71; Birks 1990 (above n 57) 21–22.

[59] Goff and Jones (above n 37) 3, 14; Burrows (above n 44) 1, 5–6; A Tettenborn, *The Law of Restitution in England and Ireland*, 3rd edn (London, Cavendish Publishing Limited, 2002) 1; A Burrows, 'Understanding the Law of Restitution: A Map Through the Thicket' (1995) 18 *University of Queensland Law Journal* 149, 149; Lord Justice Millett, 'Restitution and Constructive Trusts' (1998) 114 *LQR* 399, 408.

[60] Birks (above n 37) 17.

[61] Burrows and McKendrick (above n 51) 1; Burrows (above n 59) 150. Similarly, Hedley's contrary argument that restitution is a miscellaneous category consisting of 'the left-overs of the law' only makes sense if by restitution he means something other than a type of response: Hedley, 'Ten Questions' (above n 26) in the introduction.

contrasted compensation, a remedy based on loss suffered by the claimant, with restitution, a remedy based on removing gain from the defendant and transferring it to the claimant.[62] This meaning was broader in that it mattered not that the claimant never originally had what was being transferred. The category of restitutionary remedies consequently includes much more than just those remedies which restore something to someone.

Quadration demanded that everything encompassed by this broader meaning of restitution had to be explained in terms of unjust enrichment. The central illustration is the well-known divide identified by Birks and supported by many others between unjust enrichment by subtraction and unjust enrichment by wrongdoing.[63] In unjust enrichment for wrongs the focus was on remedies, not causes of action. Yet Birks imposed the same three-part structure of an unjust enrichment by subtraction claim on cases involving wrongs. This required considerable manipulation of the structure. The 'at the expense of' element became, in the wrongs context, shorthand for the wrong having been done to the claimant, something which was already part of the independent cause of action based on the law of wrongs. Moreover, the unjust factor was simply that a wrong had been committed.[64] Beatson and Smith challenged the artificiality of this approach,[65] but it was widely adopted by academics.

In addition, quadration required a confusing treatment of property claims. First, substantial parts of the law of property, which seemed to involve straightforward restitutionary remedies, had to be carved out of the law of restitution so that the law of unjust enrichment did not include, as a mere subset, the law of property. Claims based on pre-existing property rights were simply said to be excluded from restitution.[66] Next, and even more troublesome, claims based on property rights which were not pre-existing but rather which arose on transfer of the property, which were viewed as part of the law of restitution, then had to be explained in terms of unjust enrichment. This eventually led commentators to advocate, as unjust factors, ignorance and, even more awkwardly, retention of the claimant's property without consent, in order to bring these claims within the structure of the law of unjust enrichment.[67]

[62] A Kull, 'Rationalizing Restitution' (1995) 83 *California Law Review* 1191, 1212–13. See also Birks (above n 31) 70.
[63] Birks (above n 37) 26. By 'wrongs,' Birks refers primarily to torts and breaches of equitable obligations, although breaches of contract could also be included.
[64] Birks 1982 (above n 57) 62–63; Birks 1990 (above n 57) 12; Burrows (above n 44) 25–26, 44; Burrows and McKendrick (above n 51) 89, 569–70.
[65] Beatson (above n 34) 3, 20, 24; LD Smith, 'The Province of the Law of Restitution' (1992) 71 *Canadian Bar Review* 672, 683–87, 694. See also S Hedley, 'Unjust Enrichment' [1995] *CLJ* 578, 594.
[66] Birks (above n 37) 13–15; Mason and Carter (above n 41) 94, 98–99.
[67] A Burrows, *The Law of Restitution* (London, Butterworths, 1993) ch 13. Burrows has since abandoned the latter unjust factor: A Burrows, 'Quadrating Restitution and Unjust Enrichment: A Matter of Principle?' [2000] *Restitution Law Review* 257, 259; Burrows (above n 44) 61.

C. Rethinking Quadration

Two relatively recent cases have prompted considerable rethinking. In the first case, *Macmillan*, the claimant sought a declaration that it was beneficially entitled to certain shares which had been nominally transferred to the defendants and then pledged, without the claimant's consent, to several banks as security for loans.[68] The parties disputed whether this issue was governed by English law or the law of New York. The claimants argued, and the Court of Appeal accepted, that their claim was 'restitutionary.' It is difficult to understand what this means, since restitution is a response and not a cause of action. At a minimum it would seem to mean that the claimants were seeking a restitutionary remedy. Yet the Court of Appeal recognized that the case had nothing to do with a cause of action in unjust enrichment.[69]

In the second case, *Attorney General v Blake*, a former employee of the SIS who had passed information to the USSR wrote a book about his experiences.[70] The government sued him to prevent him receiving the proceeds of the book, arguing, *inter alia*, that he had breached his contract of employment. There was a clear breach of contract but because, as the government conceded, the information in the book was no longer confidential, it had suffered no loss and therefore could recover only nominal damages. The House of Lords considered the question of whether the court could award restitutionary damages for breach of contract. For the majority Lord Nicholls held that '[i]n a suitable case damages for breach of contract may be measured by the benefit gained by the wrongdoer from the breach.'[71] In so doing he made no reference to unjust enrichment. This decision makes it clear that a restitutionary remedy can be awarded for breach of contract.

While there is some debate about whether *Macmillan* is about restitution at all, as opposed to the law of property,[72] taken together these two cases establish that restitutionary remedies are not confined to claims in unjust enrichment. In the wake of these cases quadration has been rejected by Birks, one of its leading advocates for many years.[73]

[68] Above (n 8).
[69] *Ibid*, 605 (Auld LJ), 615 (Aldous LJ). See also G Virgo, 'Reconstructing the Law of Restitution' (1996) 10 *Trust Law International* 20, 21.
[70] [2001] 1 AC 268 (HL).
[71] *Ibid*, 283–84. Lords Goff and Browne-Wilkinson agreed, as did Lord Steyn in concurring reasons. Lord Hobhouse dissented.
[72] W Swadling, 'A Claim in Restitution?' [1996] *LMCLQ* 63; J Bird, 'Restitution's Uncertain Progress' [1995] *LMCLQ* 308.
[73] P Birks, 'Misnomer' in WR Cornish and others (eds), *Restitution—Past, Present and Future* (Oxford, Hart Publishing, 1998) 7; P Birks, 'The Burden on the Bank' in F Rose (ed), *Restitution and Banking Law* (Oxford, Mansfield Press, 1998) 191; P Birks, 'Annual Miegunyah Lecture: Equity, Conscience, and Unjust Enrichment' (1999) 23 *Melbourne University Law Review* 1, 4–5, 11. While Birks changed his position before the House of Lords decided *Blake* (on 27 July 2000), he had the benefit of the Court of Appeal's decision in that

The most important result of the recognition that restitutionary remedies are an available response to claims beyond those in unjust enrichment is the ability to discard the fiction of unjust enrichment by wrongdoing. Of course wrongs can trigger restitutionary remedies, but it is now possible to recognize that these cases have nothing to do with unjust enrichment.[74] It is now possible, in other words, to confine unjust enrichment to what has previously been described as unjust enrichment by subtraction.

D. Terminology Solutions

The rethinking of quadration has led to several proposals on how to organize the law in this area. One idea is to accept that the law of restitution has two parts, one substantive and one remedial. The substantive part is the law of unjust enrichment. The remedial part is the restitutionary remedies that can be awarded not only for causes of action based on unjust enrichment but also for causes of action based on breach of contract, wrongs and other causative events.[75] McInnes has argued that these two parts are linked by the underlying theory of unjust enrichment. His analysis on the second part is that restitutionary remedies require a defendant to give up an enrichment where it would be unjust to retain it. These remedies therefore share characteristics with the substantive cause of action.[76]

However, a two-part analysis of the law of restitution is not helpful. In the context of the substantive cause of action, unjust has a specific meaning. It explains why an otherwise legal transfer of benefits is reversed. The situation in the context of restitutionary remedies for wrongs is quite different. Here the defendant is a wrongdoer and the law must determine which wrongs will trigger this type of remedy. To claim such remedies should be awarded to avoid injustice is either empty rhetoric, adding nothing to the analysis, or makes one of two mistakes. The first is to attempt to use the same meaning of unjust in these two different contexts. The second is to

case (16 December 1997). That court had indicated that restitutionary damages could be awarded for breach of contract in exceptional cases: [1998] Ch 439.

[74] Birks notes that every wrong which leads to a restitutionary remedy can be described in the language of unjust enrichment, but 'that language does not alter the fact that the causative event is the wrong': Birks, 'Misnomer' (above n 73) 14. In other words, one trigger of restitution need not, and should not, be redescribed in terms of another trigger. Virgo makes a similar point in distinguishing the substantive sense of unjust enrichment from a purely descriptive sense: G Virgo, 'What is the Law of Restitution About?' in Cornish (above n 73) 310–11, and Virgo (above n 46) 8–9.

[75] P Birks and R Chambers, 'The Restitution Research Resource' [1997] *Restitution Law Review Supplement* 1, 2; Birks (above n 34) 1–2.

[76] M McInnes, 'The Structure and Challenges of Unjust Enrichment' in M McInnes (ed), *Restitution: Developments in Unjust Enrichment* (Sydney, LBC Information Services, 1996) 35. See also JD McCamus, 'Restitution and the Supreme Court: The Continuing Progress of the Unjust Enrichment Principle' (1991) 2 *Supreme Court Law Review* (2d) 505, 541.

attempt to formulate an additional meaning for the same word, which is bound to cause confusion. There is no benefit in using the analysis which has developed for unjust enrichment by subtraction to determine when restitutionary remedies should be available for wrongs.

Another approach is to change the meaning of restitution, restricting it to the law based on liability for unjust enrichment, including remedies. Restitutionary remedies would be only those in response to unjust enrichment. Different terms would have to describe gain-based remedies for breaches of contract, civil wrongs or other causative events. Never again could there be restitution without unjust enrichment. This is a revised quadration, more restricted in scope. Advocating this redefinition, Kull argues that '[i]f a unitary definition of restitution is preferable to a complex one, then—logic and accuracy permitting—we should avoid describing restitution as a remedial alternative for liabilities not founded on unjust enrichment.'[77]

Central to this approach is the notion of disgorgement. At present restitution can refer to the defendant's both giving back and giving up value to the claimant.[78] However, if the latter of these is instead called disgorgement, and only the former is called restitution, a more limited form of quadration between unjust enrichment and restitution is again possible.[79] The remedy for breach of fiduciary duty, for example, would be disgorgement and it would not have to be explained in terms of unjust enrichment.

This new, smaller quadration may be unrealistic. It does have the benefit of clarity and precision, using two different terms to describe two different kinds of remedy.[80] However, for better or worse, the legal community has become used to referring to gain-based remedies as restitutionary.[81] It would be a difficult task to convince courts to stop the current use of restitution terminology in cases of breach of fiduciary duty or breach of confidence. Moreover, introducing disgorgement to preserve quadration still leaves unanswered the more fundamental question of why quadration should be preserved. Contract and tort operate as parts of the law of obligations without any quadration between right and remedy, and there is no reason why unjust enrichment cannot do so also.

In addition, even if restitution and disgorgement are identified as separate remedies, there is still no quadration between restitution and unjust enrichment. This is because, as Edelman has recently argued, both restitution and disgorgement are possible remedies for wrongs such as torts or breaches of equitable duties. Accordingly, even if restitution is the only

[77] Kull (above n 62) 1223.
[78] P Birks and C Mitchell, 'Unjust Enrichment' in P Birks (ed), *English Private Law* (Oxford, Oxford University Press, 2000) vol 1, 591.
[79] Smith (n 65) 695–99; M McInnes, 'Restitution, Unjust Enrichment and the Perfect Quadration Thesis' [1999] *Restitution Law Review* 118, 120–22.
[80] J Edelman, *Gain-Based Damages* (Oxford, Hart Publishing, 2002) 65, 80, 83, 244–45.
[81] P Birks, 'The Law of Restitution at the End of an Epoch' (1999) 28 *University of Western Australia Law Review* 13, 20–23. See also Virgo (above n 46) 4–5.

remedy for unjust enrichment, it is still incorrect to claim that all restitution must be based on unjust enrichment.[82]

The most sensible solution is to accept that restitutionary remedies cut across different causes of action and cannot be confined to claims in unjust enrichment. The primary focus should be on the cause of action to reverse unjust enrichment.[83] Moving back to the choice of law context, it is lamentable that the authors of *Cheshire and North*, in choosing to devote considerable space to these issues for the first time, focused heavily on restitution and not unjust enrichment.[84] Also unfortunate is reference by the editors of *Dicey and Morris* to choice of law for restitutionary claims.[85] The law of restitution, to the extent that it is collected together, is only about remedies.[86] Nowhere is this shift in focus more important than in developing and applying choice of law rules for this area of the law. Choice of law rules focus on the cause of action, not the remedial response. There are no choice of law rules for compensation and there should be none for restitution.

IV. CHARACTERISATION OF UNJUST ENRICHMENT

The relatively recent emergence of unjust enrichment as a discrete part of the law of obligations and the lack of an established body of case law using the modern terminology means that the boundaries between unjust enrichment and other areas of law such as contract, tort and property are still being worked out. The earlier analysis of characterisation has demonstrated that these boundaries need to be as clear as possible so that the appropriate choice of law rule is applied in each case.[87]

A. Unjust Enrichment and Wrongs

Thus far in this article wrongs has had an expansive meaning, collectively referring to a wide range of causative events including tort, breach of equitable obligations and breach of contract. The last of these is at this stage better analysed as a separate part of the law of obligations, but tort and equitable breaches will still be considered together as wrongs.

82 Edelman (above n 80) 38, 78.
83 Birks, 'Misnomer' (above n 73) 4–5. See also Elias, 'About a "Proper Law of a (Restitutionary) Remedy"' [1998] *Denning Law Journal* 85, 95.
84 North and Fawcett (above n 3) ch 20 entitled 'Restitution.'
85 Collins (above n 3) 1486. This is even more confusing because the editors entitle ch 34 'Restitution' but then formulate a choice of law rule entirely in the language of unjust enrichment: R 200, 1485. The editors further fail to distinguish between unjust enrichment and wrongs when they argue that their rule should be used for breach of confidence claims because those claims are 'restitutionary' in nature: 1486.
86 Virgo (above n 46) 3.
87 For a recent discussion of this issue, see Panagopoulos (above n 3) 47–94.

The recognition that restitution as a remedy can flow from causative events other than unjust enrichment has greatly assisted in clearing away much of the confusion surrounding the divide between unjust enrichment and wrongs. Wrongs can lead to restitution but this has nothing to do with unjust enrichment.[88] In the past, many academics have claimed that the causes of action for breach of confidence and breach of fiduciary duty are part of the law of restitution. As properly understood, that law is only about remedies. These equitable claims are part of neither the law of restitution nor the law of unjust enrichment. They are part of the law of wrongs. The difficult question of what wrongs trigger restitutionary remedies, rather than compensation, is not part of the law of unjust enrichment. It is to be answered by the law of wrongs and the law of restitution.[89]

In stark contrast, the authors of *Cheshire and North* have recently advocated that we need a special choice of law rule for restitution for wrongdoing.[90] The authors arrive at this solution as a result of unwarranted despair about the correct analysis of such claims under English domestic law, seemingly too overwhelmed by the debate in the area to adopt a rational solution. Their proposal cannot be supported. It entirely fails to focus on the cause of action involved and needlessly emphasizes the nature of the remedy being sought. The separation of unjust enrichment and wrongs is now sufficiently clear that difficult questions of characterisation should be rare. Claims based on wrongs can be distinguished from unjust enrichment claims and the various choice of law rules for wrongs, which include separate choice of law rules for tort and for breaches of equitable obligations, can be applied to those claims. There is no need for a special rule in this area.

It is important to be aware that there will be factual situations which give rise to both a claim to reverse unjust enrichment and a claim based on a wrong.[91] For example, as a result of misrepresentations about the true extent of a debt a borrower pays a lender £1,000 more than is owed. The borrower can sue in tort, relying on the misrepresentation. If the lender has invested the money wisely it might have increased, and the borrower might seek a restitutionary remedy to deprive the lender of the gain. This has

[88] Edelman (above n 80) 34, 36, 41.

[89] Dissent on this issue might come from Beatson, who has argued that where a defendant takes or uses the plaintiff's property the restitutionary claim available is generated by the receipt of the property, not the wrong. On this theory the restitutionary theory depends not on the wrong but on 'the wrongful acquisition of a benefit': Beatson (above n 34) 208, 242–43. It is not easy to recast this argument in unjust enrichment terms. Possibly much of what Beatson considers is covered by the availability of an alternative claim in unjust enrichment, provided an accepted unjust factor is identified. Beyond this, it is difficult to appreciate why conventional notions of wrongs should be recast into receipt-based language which nonetheless still has to focus on 'wrongful' acquisition. For views similar to Beatson's, see D Friedmann, 'Restitution for Wrongs: The Basis for Liability' in Cornish (above n 73) 134–35.

[90] North and Fawcett (above n 3) 694.

[91] Birks 1982 (above n 57) 54–57, 69; Birks (above n 34) 21–24. See *United Australia Ltd v Barclays Bank Ltd* [1941] AC 1 (HL).

nothing to do with unjust enrichment. However, the borrower can also sue in unjust enrichment, relying on the unjust factor of mistake. In the latter case, no reliance needs to be placed on the wrong committed by the lender. The claim is entirely independent.[92] To avoid errors of characterisation, either or both claims must be clearly pleaded.

B. Unjust Enrichment and Contract

At one level it is easy to separate unjust enrichment and contract. While a contract is effective, it governs the relationship between the parties. There is little, if any, room for an unjust enrichment claim while the contract remains effective.[93] Mead has considered the possibility of an employee bringing an unjust enrichment claim for services rendered while his or her contract of employment remains binding. He concludes that the employee might succeed if either the contract did not govern the period of work in issue or the work done was outside the scope of the contract.[94] However, neither is a case of unjust enrichment within a contractual context. Both are illustrations of a separate unjust enrichment claim outside the scope of a binding contract.

If a contract is breached the law of contract will determine the consequences.[95] On the other hand, when a contract ceases to be effective, because it is repudiated, void *ab initio*, avoided or frustrated, there is considerable debate about the respective roles for the law of contract and the law of unjust enrichment. At a minimum, a key feature of the common law is that the consequences of an ineffective contract are not always addressed by the law of contract. Rather, they are sometimes left to the law of unjust enrichment.[96]

[92] For another example, see Birks and Mitchell (above n 78) 527. See also Edelman (above n 80) 93–94, 202–3.
[93] *Pan Ocean Shipping Co Ltd v Creditcorp Ltd* [1994] 1 All ER 470 (HL) 473–74 (Lord Goff). See also Burrows (above n 44) 323, 333.
[94] G Mead, 'Restitution Within Contract?' (1991) *LS* 172, 184–85. See also J Beatson, 'The Temptation of Elegance: Concurrence of Restitutionary and Contractual Claims' in W Swadling and G Jones (eds), *The Search for Principle: Essays in Honour of Lord Goff of Chieveley* (Oxford, Oxford University Press, 1999) 151–54.
[95] It can be argued that the contract claim does not exclude a concurrent claim in unjust enrichment, but this is difficult to accept if the contract remains valid: see E McKendrick, 'Total Failure of Consideration and Counter-Restitution: Two Issues or One?' in P Birks (ed), *Laundering and Tracing* (Oxford, Clarendon Press, 1995) 224–31; SA Smith, 'Concurrent Liability in Contract and Unjust Enrichment: The Fundamental Breach Requirement' (1999) 115 *LQR* 245. A broad view of concurrent claims in unjust enrichment based on failure of consideration could amount to recasting all breach of contract claims as unjust enrichment claims, with no real separation of the elements of each claim.
[96] The separation between these two areas of the law is crucial to choice of law, because there is no certainty that the law governing the ineffective contract will be the same as that governing the unjust enrichment claim. It is not obvious that claims to address the consequences of contracts void *ab initio* or illegal contracts must be governed by the law of those contracts. See, for example, *Baring Brothers v Cunninghame District Council* [1997] CLC 108 (Court of Session: Outer House).

The boundary between contract and unjust enrichment was considered in *Kleinwort Benson v Glasgow City Council*.[97] In that case, which concerned jurisdiction under Article 5 of the Modified Convention allocating jurisdiction within the United Kingdom,[98] the House of Lords considered a claim in unjust enrichment to address the consequences of interest rate swap contracts which had, in previous judicial proceedings, been held to be void *ab initio*. The majority of the House of Lords confirmed the independence of the unjust enrichment claim, which was not, in the language of the Convention, founded on a contract. The claimant was not seeking a contractual remedy, flowing from the void contract. The claimant was required to proceed with a separate claim to reverse unjust enrichment in order to recover.

By extension, supported by the reasoning in *Kleinwort Benson*, in a case where the validity of a contract is still in issue the claimant is required to advance two separate causes of action. The first would be in contract, for a declaration that the contract is void, and the second would be in unjust enrichment, to address the consequences of the invalid contract. These two causes of action must be properly distinguished for characterisation purposes.

The same approach applies to virtually any unjust enrichment claim in a contractual context. Two causes of action are required, one in contract to set the contract aside and a second in unjust enrichment seeking a restitutionary remedy. For example, to recover benefits conferred under a contract entered into under undue influence, the contract must first be set aside, as a result of a successful contractual claim, and then, in the absence of the contract, the claimant can proceed with a claim in unjust enrichment.[99] The fact that undue influence is both central to setting aside the contract and provides the ground of restitution should not obscure the two independent causes of action at work in such cases.[100]

[97] [1999] 1 AC 153 (HL).

[98] The Modified Convention, Sch 4 of the Civil Jurisdiction and Judgments Act 1982 (c 27), applied the framework of the Brussels Convention, more formally the Convention on Jurisdiction and the Enforcement of Judgments in Civil and Commercial Matters (1968), forming Sch 1 of the Civil Jurisdiction and Judgments Act 1982 (c 27); consolidated version at OJ C027 26/01/1998 at 1, to the separate parts of the United Kingdom. See now the Civil Jurisdiction and Judgments Order 2001, SI 2001/3929, Sch 2, para 4, and EC Council Regulation 44/2001, [2001] OJ L12/1.

[99] See K Barker, '*O'Brien*, Notice and the Onus of Proof' in Rose (above n 73) 84–85. Goff and Jones advocate an unjust enrichment analysis for the various types of ineffective contract, whether void, illegal, frustrated or discharged through breach: Goff and Jones (above n 37) 485–95. Burrows (above n 44) 338–43, agrees. However, frustration cases may be less clear because they raise a further issue, namely whether the non-contractual claim can be entirely explained by unjust enrichment or whether it also involves other elements such as loss apportionment: see Virgo (above n 46) 376, 388.

[100] Zweigert and Kotz (above n 48) 556–57. For a very different view, see D Friedmann, 'Valid, Voidable, Qualified, and Non-Existing Obligations: An Alternative Perspective on the Law of Restitution' in Burrows (above n 26) 263, 276. Friedmann argues, in the context of voidable contracts, that the basis for a restitutionary remedy is the fact of the contract's avoidance.

This separation into two causes of action is clear enough to dispose of most cases, but the remedy of rescission following an ineffective contract still presents considerable characterisation problems. This question used to focus on whether rescission was a restitutionary remedy,[101] but with the recognition that restitutionary remedies can have triggers other than unjust enrichment, such as contract, this is no longer determinative. The issue is whether rescission can be considered a contractual remedy, governed by choice of law rules for contract, or instead should be seen as a shorthand way of expressing the separate cause of action in unjust enrichment.

In Stoljar's view, restitutionary remedies following contractual breakdown are nothing more than remedies in contract. He included rescission alongside damages and specific performance and rejected the notion of unjust enrichment claims based on total failure of consideration.[102] This narrow view of the scope of unjust enrichment is at odds with *Kleinwort Benson*, *Westdeutsche* and many other cases which have recognized total failure of consideration as an unjust factor.[103]

At the other end of the spectrum are those like Birks who argue that rescission belongs to the law of unjust enrichment.[104] While it is arguable that the way in which the law determines whether rescission is available is quite similar to the analysis of a cause of action in unjust enrichment,[105] at this stage it cannot be stated with certainty that rescission should be characterised as involving a separate cause of action in unjust enrichment arising on the failure of a contract. Rescission has historically been analysed as a contractual remedy and, absent widespread change of view, is likely to continue to be characterised as part of the law of contract. Until this issue is resolved, it would be wise to advance alternative claims in both contract and unjust enrichment.

While unjust enrichment and contract need to be separated, the House of Lords' favourable comments on the availability of restitutionary damages for breach of contract in *Blake* is the clearest indication yet that there is no such separation between contract and restitution.[106] Wholly separate from unjust enrichment, claims in contract can trigger restitutionary remedies. For choice of law purposes, however, such claims would be classified as contractual and would use the choice of law rules for contract.

C. Unjust Enrichment and Property

There is considerable debate about the relationship between the law of unjust enrichment and the law of property. Many academics argue that

[101] Burrows and McKendrick (above n 51) 141; Mason and Carter (above n 41) 87.
[102] Stoljar (above n 26) 222.
[103] Above (n 97) and (n 39) respectively.
[104] P Birks, 'Unjust Factors and Wrongs: Pecuniary Rescission for Undue Influence' [1997] *Restitution Law Review* 72, 78.
[105] See Burrows (above n 44) 337.
[106] Above (n 70).

these two areas of the law cannot be separated, arguing that claims to reverse unjust enrichment can be proprietary as well as personal. Others argue that unjust enrichment claims can only be personal so that clear separation is possible.

Birks has argued against the separation of these two areas of the law and in doing so has proposed an intricate structural analysis which focuses on the divide between causative events and responses. To Birks, the causative events in our legal system are consent, wrongs, unjust enrichment and a miscellaneous category of other events. Responses include compensation and restitution.[107] Controversially, Birks includes property as a response and not a causative event. He therefore argues that unjust enrichment and property cannot be separated because the two are not in the same series, just as contract and compensation cannot be separated.[108] Birks thus creates a framework which he and others can use as a basis for the argument that unjust enrichment claims can lead to proprietary remedies.

However, Birks' treatment of pure proprietary claims within this framework is cause for concern. Having argued that property is a response, he is forced in each case to identify a causative event which can give rise to property rights. In *Macmillan*, which the Court of Appeal held was not about unjust enrichment, Birks identifies as the causative event 'receipt of another's thing,' which falls into his other event category.[109] This quickly begins to look artificial.

It is a fair observation that the pure act of owning something is not a causative event which gives rise to any response. Something further is required. But consent, by itself, does not give rise to a response either. Consent is shorthand for a broader causative event which includes both the agreement and some further act which gives rise to a dispute, such as non-performance. Similarly, property embodies not simply the act of owning but also some further event which interferes with that act.

Birks' argument that property is a response and not an event has been strongly criticised.[110] Grantham and Rickett, for example, argue that property has a dual nature and thus can be either a causative event or a response depending on the circumstances.[111] This may emerge as the better view, but

[107] Birks, 'Misnomer' (above n 73) 7–9.

[108] P Birks, 'Property and Unjust Enrichment: Categorical Truths' [1997] *New Zealand Law Review* 623, 627–31.

[109] Above (n 8); Birks (above n 108) 657; Birks, 'Misnomer' (above n 73) 21–26.

[110] See Virgo (above n 46) 592–97 and Virgo (above n 74) 307, 312. Virgo's reference is to the 'vindication' of property rights, but the infringement of or interference with property rights might better parallel the other causative events. See also K Barker, 'Rescuing Remedialism in Unjust Enrichment Law: Why Remedies are Right' [1998] *CLJ* 301, 324–25; RB Grantham and CEF Rickett, 'Property and Unjust Enrichment: Categorical Truths or Unnecessary Complexity' [1997] *New Zealand Law Review* 668, 671, 675.

[111] RB Grantham and CEF Rickett, *Enrichment and Restitution in New Zealand* (Oxford, Hart Publishing, 2000) 25. See also J Stevens, 'Restitution or Property? Priority and Title to Shares in the Conflict of Laws' (1996) 59 *MLR* 741, 744–45.

it does not resolve the issue of the dividing line between property and unjust enrichment, since at a minimum it allows for the possibility of a proprietary response to a claim in unjust enrichment.[112] The analysis must therefore delve deeper.

Those who argue against separation focus on a particular kind of claim, labeled a restitutionary proprietary claim. The label is rooted in quadration and is therefore somewhat unhelpful when focusing on unjust enrichment.[113] Relabeled, a proprietary unjust enrichment claim is one which is not based on pre-existing property rights. It is based on new proprietary rights which are created to reverse unjust enrichment. The unjust enrichment aspect of the claim comes from the fact that each of the three elements of the cause of action to reverse unjust enrichment must be made out. The proprietary aspect of the claim comes from the proprietary remedy which is granted.

In support of this type of claim, Birks contends that some unjust enrichment claims will have a proprietary element and will lead to proprietary remedies while others will not. Birks and others have long contended that proprietary claims not based on pre-existing property rights but rather to reverse unjust enrichment are claims in unjust enrichment and are not either claims based on interference with property rights, a causative event Birks rejects anyway, or claims in the other events category.[114]

On the other hand, those who favour separation of unjust enrichment and property argue that both cases dealing with pre-existing property rights and cases where supposedly new property rights are created are all part of the law of property and have nothing to do with unjust enrichment.[115] For all of the supposed focus on the elements of a claim to reverse unjust enrichment, it is the law of property which determines whether the claimant has a proprietary interest. For example, in cases of mistaken transfer, it is the law of property which determines whether the mistake has been so fundamental

[112] Grantham and Rickett see *Chase Manhattan Bank NA v Israel-British Bank (London)* [1981] Ch 105 as such a case, although it does not mention unjust enrichment: *ibid*, 31.

[113] Any future judicial or academic use of the phrase 'restitutionary proprietary claim' could trigger a question as to the sense in which 'restitutionary' is used, particularly as to whether such a claim involves the substantive cause of action to reverse unjust enrichment.

[114] Birks (above n 108) 632ff; Birks 1990 (above n 57) 23; P Birks, 'Establishing A Proprietary Base' [1995] *Restitution Law Review* 83, 92. See also P Watts, 'Property and "Unjust Enrichment": Cognate Conservators' [1998] *New Zealand Law Review* 151, 158–62; LD Smith, 'Unjust Enrichment, Property, and the Structure of Trusts' (2000) 116 *LQR* 412, 428–29; Panagopoulos (above n 3) 61–62. For two more extreme views, see D Stevens, 'Restitution, Property, and the Cause of Action in Unjust Enrichment: Getting By With Fewer Things' (1989) 39 *University of Toronto Law Journal* 258, 286 which argues 'that claims for the return of specific material or notional objects are just a special case, even the paradigm case, of the unjust enrichment claim;' and R Chambers, *Resulting Trusts* (Oxford, Clarendon Press, 1997), which argues that a resulting trust should be the chief remedy for unjust enrichment claims.

[115] See Virgo (above n 74) 312, 318–19. See also LD Smith, 'Tracing and Electronic Fund Transfers' in Rose (above n 73) 126–31.

as to prevent title passing.[116] These aspects of the law of property have long been separate from the elements of a claim to reverse unjust enrichment. This separation has led some, like Virgo, to argue that the only possible remedy for an unjust enrichment claim is personal, not proprietary.[117]

English law, having created the distinction between legal and equitable title, has long been comfortable with treating claims about either as property claims. The equitable title which arises in the context of a flawed transfer, whether retained or created, does not require explanation in terms of the reversal of unjust enrichment.[118] It can be explained as part of the law of property.[119] Moreover, retention of title by the claimant seems to negate the first element in an unjust enrichment claim, namely that the defendant has been enriched. The claimant's ownership, legal or equitable, would seem to preclude an unjust enrichment claim.[120] Further, one of the key unjust factors Birks relies on when including such claims within unjust enrichment, ignorance, has not been accepted by the courts. These arguments point to greater separation of unjust enrichment and property.

At least some support for a clear separation between unjust enrichment and property can be found in recent English cases. In *Foskett v McKeown* Lord Millett, with whom the other Law Lords agreed, held that the claim advanced by the claimants was 'to vindicate their property rights, not to reverse unjust enrichment.'[121] While this is a strong statement, it is not at all clear whether it covers only the facts of the instant case or is intended as a broader comment on this issue. It is unarguable that some cases will involve pure property claims and not unjust enrichment, but this does not mean that no unjust enrichment claim can be proprietary.[122]

[116] See WJ Swadling, 'Restitution for No Consideration' [1994] *Restitution Law Review* 73, 81–82. Compare the similar approach under German law: C Zulch, 'Bona Fide Purchase, Property and Restitution: *Lipkin Gorman* v. *Karpnale* in German Law' in WJ Swadling (ed), *The Limits of Restitutionary Claims: A Comparative Analysis* (London, The United Kingdom National Committee of Comparative Law, 1997) 106.

[117] Virgo (above n 46) 11–17, 592–97. See also G McMeel, *The Modern Law of Restitution* (London, Blackstone Press Limited, 2000) 397–98.

[118] In *Westdeutsche* (above n 39) 706 Lord Browne-Wilkinson held that the bank, paying under a contract it thought was valid but which was void, did not retain equitable title to the money. However, for the contrary position see S Worthington, *Proprietary Interests in Commercial Transactions* (Oxford, Clarendon Press, 1996) 1–23; W Swadling, 'The Law of Property' in P Birks and F Rose (eds), *Lessons of the Swaps Litigation* (London, Mansfield Press, 2000) 265–67. Those who believe that an equitable interest can or should be retained would generally treat the claim as based on a pre-existing proprietary interest and hence as a pure property claim in no way involving unjust enrichment.

[119] See Grantham and Rickett (above n 110) 682; RB Grantham and CEF Rickett, 'Restitution, Property and Mistaken Payments' [1997] *Restitution Law Review* 83, 84–87.

[120] W Swadling (above n 49) 273; E Bant, '"Ignorance" as a Ground of Restitution—Can it Survive?' [1998] *LMCLQ* 18; N Segal, 'Cross-Border Security Enforcement, Restitution and Priorities' in F Rose (above n 73) 112. For the opposite view, see Birks (above n 108) 654.

[121] Above (n 55) 129; see also 108, 110 (Lord Browne-Wilkinson) and 115 (Lord Hoffmann).

[122] Similar analysis can be applied to *Box v Barclays Bank* [1998] Lloyd's Rep Bank 185, discussed in G Virgo, 'Unpacking Proprietary Restitutionary Claims' [1999] *Company, Financial*

There is a middle ground between the competing positions. It is possible to distinguish between a proprietary claim and a proprietary remedy. This distinction is a notable feature of some common law systems, like Canada and Australia, yet it has not found favour in England. To the extent that such a distinction is accepted, to a greater or lesser degree, one could accept both that unjust enrichment claims are wholly separate from proprietary claims and that unjust enrichment claims can, in certain cases, give rise to proprietary remedies. However, English law has not been enthusiastic about the remedial flexibility this entails, as is well illustrated by its unfavourable reaction to the remedial constructive trust used extensively in North America.[123] For example, English law refuses to see *Chase Manhattan* as a personal claim to reverse unjust enrichment in which the court granted a proprietary remedy.[124]

The debate about whether unjust enrichment and property are separate areas of law is ongoing, and it will take further judicial decisions to clarify the issue. Yet the result has great implications for choice of law. If there is such a claim as a proprietary unjust enrichment claim, characterisation could become more complex. Separation, on the other hand, leaves property claims to be resolved by an established set of choice of law rules for property.

As with wrongs, it should be noted that there are cases in which the claimant will be able to choose between alternative claims, one in property based on continued ownership and one in unjust enrichment in which continued ownership is not asserted.[125] The latter claim, personal in nature, depends on establishing an accepted unjust factor such as mistake or total failure of consideration.

V. CONCLUSION

The very idea of choice of law for restitution has to be abandoned. Choice of law rules must be formulated for the cause of action to reverse unjust enrichment. Those choice of law rules should focus on the three elements of

and Insolvency Law Review 119, and to *Portman Building Society v Hamlyn Taylor Neck* [1998] 4 All ER 202 (CA), discussed in RB Grantham and CEF Rickett, 'Trust Money as an Unjust Enrichment: A Misconception' [1998] *LMCLQ* 514.

123 See, eg, *Re Polly Peck International Plc (No 2)* [1998] 3 All ER 812 (CA) where the court held that the applicants had no hope of a proprietary remedy in the circumstances because an English court would not impose a remedial constructive trust. However, this hostility was somewhat tempered by Mummery LJ's observation that in the circumstances not even the Supreme Court of Canada would have imposed such a trust. See also Millett (above n 59) 399; Virgo (above n 46) 635–37.

124 Above (above n 112); *Westdeutsche* (above n 39) 714 (Lord Browne-Wilkinson).

125 See Birks (above n 108) 625–26, where he argues that the plaintiff in *Macmillan* (above n 8) could have pleaded such an alternative claim; Watts (above n 114) 159–61.

the cause of action: the enrichment of the defendant, the expense of the claimant and the unjust factor justifying the reversal. The characterisation process, by which the correct choice of law rule is selected, has to differentiate between unjust enrichment claims and other types of claim. It will do so according to the law of the forum. The scope of the law of unjust enrichment therefore must be as clear as possible, allowing claims to be characterised with a minimum of difficulty. While the gradual rejection of quadration has greatly clarified the line between unjust enrichment and wrongs, the line between unjust enrichment and property remains blurred and will not likely be clarified for some time. As a result, claims in this area must be clearly pleaded, in the alternative if necessary, to avoid errors of characterisation.

14

Restitution on Dissolution of Marital and Other Intimate Relationships: Constructive Trust or Quantum Meruit?

JOHN D. McCAMUS

I. INTRODUCTION

IF A HISTORY of the Canadian law of restitution is to be written, it seems likely that the year 1954 will attract the historian's attention. In that year, the Supreme Court of Canada rendered its decision in *Deglman v Guaranty Trust*[1] in which the court embraced the American unjust enrichment theory as the foundation of restitutionary claims, at least those from the common law or quasi-contractual side. The decision is well known to Canadian lawyers. A nephew, Constantineau, had provided personal services to his aunt on the faith of the latter's undertaking that she would leave a residential property to him in her estate. When the aunt died, and it became apparent that she had failed to fulfill this undertaking, the nephew advanced a claim against the estate. As the aunt's undertaking had not been recorded in writing, a claim to enforce the arrangement failed on the basis of the Statute of Frauds.[2] However, the nephew's alternate claim in quantum meruit, for the value of the services rendered, enjoyed success. Although the defendant had urged that the 'implied contract' that necessarily underlay a quantum meruit claim would be inconsistent with the fact of an existing but unenforceable agreement, the Supreme Court of Canada rejected the 'implied contract' explanation for restitutionary relief and granted recovery on the basis that the estate had been unjustly enriched. The nature of the injustice is clear. The nephew provided services in the expectation of reward. The enrichment of the aunt and, in due course,

[1] [1954] SCR 725; [1954] 3 DLR 785 (SCC).
[2] Today, see for example RSO 1990 c S.19.

of her estate in refusing to compensate him for the services rendered was self-evidently unjust.

If, as a result of *Deglman*, 1954 can be considered to be a watershed year for Canadian restitutionary law, no less significance will be attached to the year 1980, the year of the decision of the Supreme Court of Canada in *Pettkus v Becker*.[3] By strange coincidence, 1954 was also the year in which Lothar Pettkus and Rosa Becker had separately emigrated from central Europe to Canada. They each arrived in Montreal, where they met in 1955. Shortly thereafter they began living together and, apart from a brief separation in 1972, they lived together until their relationship dissolved in 1974. In the early period of their relationship, they both earned wages. The fact that Ms Becker devoted her earnings to household expenses enabled Mr Pettkus to amass savings, which were used by him to acquire a farm property in Quebec, title to which he took in his own name. The couple worked together in the farming business and, with its proceeds, bought two additional properties which were located, felicitously from our historian's perspective, in Ontario. Fortune smiled again on the Canadian common law when the couple moved to one of the Ontario properties before their separation in 1974.

Ms Becker, believing that she was entitled to claim a share in the properties which, from her perspective, had been acquired through 'joint effort and teamwork' with Mr Pettkus, asserted a claim to this effect. The legal foundations of the claim were not promising. The claim was novel. Worse still, the Supreme Court of Canada had recently turned down a claim made in similar circumstances by a farming wife upon the dissolution of a lengthy marriage, in *Murdoch v Murdoch*.[4] In that case, the court had applied English doctrine to the effect that the only relief potentially available to achieve such a result, the awarding of a resulting trust, was available only where the parties had formed a common intention that the properties, though vested solely in one spouse, were to be held beneficially by that spouse on behalf of both of them in some proportion or other.[5] Relying on a suggestion to this effect made by Laskin J in his dissenting opinion in *Murdoch*, the plaintiff argued in *Pettkus* that even in the absence of such a common intention, a constructive trust could be imposed in order to prevent the unjust enrichment of the defendant. Apart from the novelty of the claim, this argument faced the additional hurdle that the Supreme Court of Canada had not yet clearly indicated that the American unjust enrichment analysis provided the proper foundation for the Canadian law of constructive trust. To be sure, unjust enrichment had been held in *Deglman* to constitute the proper foundation for common law claims of the

[3] [1980] 2 SCR 834; (1980) 117 DLR (3d) 257 (SCC).
[4] [1975] 1 SCR 423; (1973) 41 DLR (3d) 367 (SCC).
[5] *Pettitt v Pettitt* [1970] AC 777 (HL); *Gissing v Gissing* [1971] AC 886 (HL).

quasi-contractual variety, but it had not yet been plainly determined that the unjust enrichment principle provided the correct explanation for restitutionary claims drawn from equitable roots. Contemporary restitution scholars no doubt held their breath as the fate of the unjust enrichment analysis on the equity side appeared to have become inextricably linked with the fate of an argument proposing a radical reformulation of the doctrine applied in *Murdoch*. Though it was true that a similar argument had been articulated by Dickson J in one of the opinions making up the majority, favouring relief, in *Rathwell v Rathwell*,[6] the rest of the *Rathwell* majority grounded relief on traditional resulting trust analysis. The prospects for the unjust enrichment constructive trust could not have appeared overly promising.

In the event, of course, the equity shoe dropped. On behalf of a majority of the court in *Pettkus*, Dickson J opined that '[t]he principle of unjust enrichment lies at the heart of the constructive trust.'[7] Further, the majority held that regardless of the plaintiff's difficulty in establishing a common intention resulting trust, an unjust enrichment constructive trust could be imposed in order to prevent the unjust enrichment of Mr Pettkus. That the decision was a close one is apparent from the opinions delivered in *Pettkus*. The adoption of the unjust enrichment rationale for constructive trust was opposed by three of the six common law trained members of the court, who felt that the common intention resulting trust was available on the facts of *Pettkus* and that recognition of the unjust enrichment rationale was either unnecessary or undesirable. It is generally accepted, however, that the decision in *Pettkus* has definitively and affirmatively answered the important question of whether the Supreme Court of Canada's recognition of the importance of unjust enrichment analysis for quasi-contractual claims would be matched by a similar recognition in the context of equitable restitutionary claims.

However, the reasoning in support of the actual claim allowed in *Pettkus*—for the granting of proprietary rights in assets held by one spouse which could be said to be the product of joint effort and teamwork—raised a host of difficult questions, the answers to which were at best hinted at in Dickson J's majority opinion. What are the elements of the new cause of action? Is the claim contingent upon a finding that a particular asset or, more generally, surplus wealth in some form has been acquired or produced through joint effort and teamwork? Must there be a direct connection, in some sense, between the plaintiff's contribution to the teamwork and the targeted asset? Is the claim contingent upon a showing that the plaintiff had a 'reasonable expectation' of acquiring a proprietary interest in a particular asset? Is the relief afforded invariably proprietary in nature or does there

[6] [1978] 2 SCR 436; (1978) 83 DLR (3d) 289 (SCC).
[7] Above (n 3) 847; 273.

exist a role for non-proprietary relief in cases of this kind and, if so, in what measure? Clear answers to most of these questions have not yet emerged in the Canadian case law.

The Supreme Court of Canada returned to consider them in *Peter v Beblow* in 1993.[8] In this case, the court plainly indicated that relief in a *Pettkus* type of claim was not exclusively proprietary in nature. Indeed, a majority of the court indicated as a more general matter that proprietary relief should be granted only where monetary compensation is 'inadequate' for some reason. The Supreme Court of Canada has not returned to a consideration of the *Pettkus* claim in more recent years and, accordingly, the decision in *Peter* is of considerable significance in assessing the current status of the *Pettkus* claim in Canadian law. This article briefly attempts such an assessment, placing emphasis on the relationship between proprietary and personal relief as alluded to by the court in that case.

II. THE ELEMENTS OF THE *PETTKUS v BECKER* CAUSE OF ACTION

In *Pettkus*, it is clear that Dickson J saw his task as one of solving a problem presented by the requirement, established by the traditional law of resulting trust, of demonstrating a common intention to hold property beneficially. It would appear that he was much influenced by the critique of the traditional English doctrine mounted by Waters in a note in the *Canadian Bar Review*.[9] Waters suggested that if to grant relief in these cases the courts were required to find such an intention, they would very likely do so, albeit sometimes on a slender or perhaps non-existent evidentiary basis. At the same time, he suggested, there exists the risk that a stricter application of the traditional doctrine will produce results which are inconsistent with what would seem to be a just result. The solution proposed by Waters to this problem was to abandon the search for 'phantom intent' and impose constructive trust relief in order to avoid the unjust enrichment that would otherwise accrue to the spouse with title. In *Pettkus*, Dickson J adopted this proposal. At the same time, however, it appears that Dickson J sought to replace the common intention test with a test requiring that the claimant have a reasonable expectation of acquiring an interest in the target asset and that such an expectation was, in the circumstances of the case, a reasonable one. Thus, he described the relationship between the parties in the following terms:

> Miss Becker supported Mr Pettkus for 5 years. She then worked on the farm for about 14 years. The compelling inference from the facts is that she

[8] [1993] 1 SCR 980; (1993) 101 DLR (4th) 621 (SCC).
[9] D Waters, 'Matrimonial Property Disputes—Resulting and Constructive Trusts—Restitution' (1975) 53 *Canadian Bar Review* 366.

> believed that she had some interest in the farm and that that expectation was reasonable in the circumstances. Mr. Pettkus would seem to have recognized in Miss Becker some property interest, through the payment to her of compensation, however modest. There is no evidence to indicate that he ever informed her that all her work performed over the nineteen years was being performed on a gratuitous basis. He freely accepted the benefits conferred upon him through her financial support and her labour.[10]

Dickson J summarized the point as follows:

> ... I hold that where one person in a relationship tantamount to spousal prejudices herself in the reasonable expectation of receiving an interest in property and the other person in the relationship freely accepts benefits conferred by the first person in circumstances where he knows or ought to have known of that reasonable expectation, it would be unjust to allow the recipient of the benefit to retain it.[11]

In addition to these reasonable expectations, Dickson J held that the claimant must establish a causal connection between the contribution made and the target asset. This did not present any difficulty on the present facts, in his view. He explained as follows:

> There is a clear link between the contribution and the disputed assets. The contribution of Miss Becker was such as enabled, or assisted in enabling, Mr Pettkus to acquire the assets in contention. For the unjust enrichment principle to apply it is obvious that some connection must be shown between the acquisition of property and corresponding deprivation.[12]

Although Dickson J emphasised the importance of a contribution to the 'acquisition' of property, this point was later clarified in *Sorochan v Sorochan*,[13] a case in which a farm couple worked together on a farm property brought into the marriage by the husband. The Supreme Court of Canada held that the causal connection test would be met where the claimant spouse had contributed not to the acquisition of property but rather to its 'preservation, maintenance or improvement.'[14]

Observers have tended to be rather critical of the *Pettkus* 'reasonable expectation' test.[15] It is not clear that the test identifies a necessary element in a claim of this kind nor, indeed, is it clear that the test was met on the

[10] *Pettkus* (above n 3) 849; 274.
[11] *Ibid.*
[12] *Ibid*, 852; 277.
[13] [1986] 2 SCR 38; (1986) 29 DLR (4th) 1 (SCC).
[14] *Ibid*, 50; 10.
[15] See, eg, M McInnes, 'Reflections on the Canadian Law of Unjust Enrichment' (1999) 78 *Canadian Bar Review* 416, 428–31 (characterizing the reasons in *Pettkus* as a 'distortive exercise in judicial legislation' at 429).

very facts of *Pettkus* itself. Certainly, Mr Pettkus had a clear view of the matter. According to the court it was apparent that Mr Pettkus took a negative view of Ms Becker's entitlement. He put title to the properties in his own name. When she raised the idea of marriage, he rejected it. He never regarded her as his wife. Their finances were completely separate except for a joint account for retail sales of farm produce. Ms Becker conceded that there was no express arrangement for sharing economic gain. When the couple briefly separated in 1972, Mr Pettkus threw $ 3,000 on the floor and told Ms Becker to take the money, an old Volkswagen car and 40 beehives and 'get lost.'[16] From this incident, as the above passage indicates, Dickson J felt able to infer the existence, on Mr Pettkus' part, of an understanding of a reasonable expectation on the part of Ms Becker that she would receive an interest in properties which he no doubt regarded as his alone. There does not appear to have been direct evidence, however, that Ms Becker provided services in the reasonable expectation of acquiring title. If Ms Becker had consulted a lawyer, of course, she would have received no encouragement in her alleged belief that she was entitled to an interest in the properties held by Mr Pettkus. Thus, the requirement of a reasonable expectation of entitlement to an interest appears to be quite artificially applied in *Pettkus* itself.

It is not clear why the reasonable expectations test was introduced in the reasoning in *Pettkus*. In his earlier formulation of the cause of action in *Rathwell v Rathwell*,[17] Dickson J made no reference to the necessity of establishing such a 'reasonable expectation.' Although the basis of the claim was not considered at length in Dickson J's reasons in *Rathwell*, the reasoning is strongly suggestive of a doctrine which rests on a theory of frustration of the marital venture. The relationship between married parties is such that the provision of services or other benefits does not signal any need to ascertain with precision the terms and conditions on which they are being rendered. Hence, the claimant will be unable to establish the existence of the common intention required by traditional resulting trust doctrine. As Dickson J explained:

> The property is acquired during a period when there is marital accord. When this gives way to discord, problems arise in respect of property division. There is seldom prior express agreement. There is rarely implied agreement or common intention, apart from the general intention of building a life together. It is not in the nature of things for young married people to contemplate the break-up of their marriage and the division, in that event, of assets required by common effort during wedlock.[18]

[16] *Pettkus* (above n 3) 840–41; 268.
[17] Above (n 6).
[18] *Ibid*, 447–48; 301.

Proceeding on the basis of understandings or assumptions about a shared future which may or may not be articulated, the dissolution of the marriage constitutes what might be referred to as a frustration of the venture. As in the context of frustrated contracts, a surprising event has created a situation in which one party has received an unanticipated windfall. In the absence of a clear understanding between the parties as to what should happen with respect to the wealth produced by their joint labour—and, as Dickson J noted, young married couples are unlikely to apply their minds to an appropriate division of assets upon a possible eventual dissolution of their marriage—it would be unjust to allow the spouse with title, typically the husband, to in effect enrich himself through the appropriation to himself of wealth produced by the other spouse's effort or, in other words, to reap what he has not sown. Dickson J reasoned as follows:

> ... [I]t is clear that only through the efforts of Mrs Rathwell was Mr Rathwell able to acquire the lands in question ... it would be unjust, in all of the circumstances, to allow Mr Rathwell to retain the benefits of his wife's labours. His acquisition of legal title was made possible only through 'joint effort' and 'team work.'[19]

Moreover, Dickson J opined that if a married couple did contemplate an appropriate division of assets upon dissolution of their marriage, they would likely expect a division of assets of the kind imposed in *Rathwell*, a sharing of the assets produced by their joint effort. A similarly realistic view was set out by Cory J in *Peter* in the following terms:

> ... [I]t is unlikely that couples will ever turn their minds to the issue of their expectations about their legal entitlements at the outset of their marriage or common-law relationship. If they were specifically asked about their expectations, I would think that most couples would probably state that they did not expect to be compensated for their contribution. Rather, they would say, if the relationship were ever to be dissolved, then they would expect that both parties would share in the assets or wealth that they had helped to create. Thus, rather than expecting to receive a fee for their services based on their market value, they would expect to receive, on a dissolution of their relationship, a fair share of the property or wealth which their contributions had helped the parties to acquire, improve, or to maintain.[20]

Cory J did not go on to suggest that in cases where the parties have not in fact applied their minds to this question of relief, it therefore cannot be awarded. Indeed, it was his assumption that the *Pettkus* claim is available

[19] *Ibid*, 461; 310.
[20] Above (n 8) 1022–23; 639.

in such circumstances. Cory J proposed, in effect, a default rule to the effect that parties in marital and similar relationships will be presumed, in the absence of evidence to the contrary, to have an expectation that on the dissolution of their relationship jointly produced wealth will be shared. Although Cory J did not articulate this point, the factual foundation for such a default rule surely is that the parties to marital and equivalent relationships view themselves as partners, not only in an emotional sense but in an economic sense as well, at least with respect to some of the assets of the marriage. Whatever the status of legal title to the particular asset, such parties are likely to see themselves as creating wealth in a common enterprise that will assist in sustaining their relationship, their well-being and their family life. Parkinson has usefully referred to this state of mind as a 'sharing intention.'[21] Parties to an intimate relationship that manifest a sharing intention are less likely to be concerned about matters of title or the preservation of a separate accounting of monies earned and spent. In many such relationships, one party may rely on the expectations engendered by their mutual sharing intention to withdraw from the wage-earning workforce in order to devote full-time attention to the raising of their children. In the context of such relationships, as Cory J suggested in the quotation above, couples who do not consciously address the matter would, if asked, likely articulate an expectation of fair sharing on dissolution of the relationship.

A similar defence of the 'fair sharing on dissolution default rule' has been provided by Rotherham.[22] As he points out, the principal objection to this approach rests on absolutist conceptions of private property and freedom of contract that insist that property cannot be transferred without consent. As Rotherham argues, however, the justifications for this conception of property—that it rewards labour, thereby promoting autonomy, virtue and efficiency—have little purchase in the context of intimate relationships. Such relationships are characterized by a sense of collective rather than individual welfare, a sense that the parties' interests are inextricably linked, an emotional environment in which the legalities of individual property entitlement appear irrelevant and a lack of planning for the eventuality of separation. Such relationships create opportunities for exploitation and unfairness upon dissolution. Parties to such relationships do not bargain rationally to ensure that their efforts are rewarded by property entitlements. Indeed, cultural attitudes still weigh against such negotiations. The justification for a default rule of the kind adopted in *Pettkus*, then, is that such a rule gives effect to the set of entitlements that rational decision-makers would have devised with respect to dissolution.

[21] P Parkinson, 'Beyond *Pettkus v Becker*: Quantifying Relief for Unjust Enrichment' (1993) 43 *University of Toronto Law Journal* 217.
[22] C Rotherham, *Proprietary Remedies in Context* (Oxford, Hart Publishing, 2002) 220–30.

In sum, a powerful case can be made for relief in the absence of actual 'reasonable expectations' of acquiring a proprietary interest, and that case is made, in good measure, by Dickson J in *Rathwell* and Cory J in *Peter*. However, the reasonable expectations requirement cannot easily be made to disappear from Canadian law. One possible explanation for its introduction in *Pettkus* is the nature of the relationship of the parties in *Pettkus* as opposed to that in *Rathwell*. In *Rathwell*, the parties were married. In *Pettkus*, they were not. Perhaps it is not surprising that in the context of a so-called common law relationship, the court sought evidence of a 'sharing intention.'[23] In the context of married couples, a 'sharing intention' is very likely to be present.[24] In the context of unmarried couples, however, especially if the relationship is one of short duration, it is less obvious that a 'sharing intention' will be present. Thus, in *Peter*, Cory J analysed at length the specifics of the relationship of the unmarried couple, the sharing of their income, the creation of a home environment for their children and the duration of the relationship.[25]

Accordingly, the key to understanding the recovery awarded for the *Pettkus* claim would appear to be that the court was satisfied that the parties were engaged in a common venture in which they expected to share the benefits flowing from the wealth that they jointly created. Ms Becker, at least, had such an expectation and, in the court's view, Mr Pettkus should have been aware of it. A preferable reading of *Pettkus*, then, is not that Ms Becker had the precise expectation of obtaining a legal interest in certain properties, but rather that given the long-term and *quasi-marital* nature of the relationship with Mr Pettkus, Ms Becker had a 'sharing intention' of which Mr Pettkus ought to have been aware. The court believed Ms Becker when she asserted that she had such an expectation and it would not appear unfair to Mr Pettkus to conclude that although he did not share this view, he should have appreciated that Ms Becker believed their relationship to be one in which they were jointly producing wealth for their mutual benefit.

There may be other circumstances, however, that may provide a basis for finding the presence of a 'sharing intention.' Thus, the fact that the parties have 'pooled their assets'[26] or that their 'lives and their economic well-being were fully integrated'[27] might indicate the presence of such an intention. The fact that a common law relationship is a lengthy one may be of some assistance.[28] The fact that one of the parties to the relationship makes

[23] Parkinson (above n 21) 242–44.
[24] Parkinson cites empirical studies which support this conclusion, as well as those suggesting that the phenomenon is less common in the relationships of unmarried couples: (above n 21) 240–41.
[25] Above (n 8) 1014; 633.
[26] *Ibid.*
[27] *Pettkus* (above n 3) 850; 276.
[28] *Ibid*: 'Mr Pettkus and Miss Becker lived as man and wife for almost 20 years.'

the financial sacrifice of giving up paid employment in order to maintain the matrimonial home or take the leading role in raising the children of the couple also appears suggestive of such an intent. In short, the 'reasonable expectations' test appears to provide an incomplete account of the kinds of evidence that might give rise to a finding that the couple in question, or at least one of them, has a 'sharing intention.'

If the reasonable expectations requirement remains controversial, however, there is one important point which appears to be more straightforward. In *Pettkus* itself and the other decisions of the Supreme Court of Canada considering the *Pettkus* cause of action, it is apparent that the claim relates to surplus wealth generated through the joint effort and teamwork of married couples and others in similar relationships. Thus, if in *Pettkus* itself the facts were that the asset held in the male partner's name had so deteriorated in value as to be virtually worthless at the time of the dissolution of the relationship, it is clear that the *Pettkus* claim would not be available. In other words, the *Pettkus* claim is to be distinguished from the kind of claim, brought in *Deglman*,[29] where services have been provided on the faith of an undertaking by the recipient that they will be paid for or that the claimant will be compensated in some fashion for their provision. When that undertaking proves to be unenforceable, the claim in quantum meruit is allowed in order to prevent the unjust enrichment of the recipient. Such claims do not typically arise in the context of married couples, it appears, for the reason indicated in the earlier quotation from the opinion of Cory J in *Peter*. Married couples normally do not have expectations of compensation for services rendered during marriage on a fee-for-service basis.

It is important to note, however, that the fee-for-service quantum meruit claim may shade into fact situations like the one in *Pettkus*, if the relationship between the parties commences on a fee-for-service basis but evolves into a relationship more closely resembling a marital bond. In the typical fact pattern of the housekeeping cases, an elderly gentleman, who may not be able to afford to both maintain his home and pay for domestic services, gives an undertaking to a woman who agrees to provide such services on the faith of his undertaking that the home will be left to her in his will or, more vaguely, that she will be 'looked after' or 'provided for' after his death. In such circumstances, the services are, as in *Deglman* itself, being provided on the basis of an expectation of compensation, and quantum meruit claims are normally allowed when the undertaking to compensate is not fulfilled. As *Rowe v Public Trustee*[30] demonstrates, such an expectation of 'compensation' could be reasonably generated by a promise of marriage, as this is equivalent to a promise that the service provider will, in some sense, be 'looked after.' The key to recovery in quantum meruit in a case

[29] Above (n 1).
[30] (1963) 38 DLR (2d) 462 (Ont HCJ).

like *Rowe*, however, is not the romantic relationship of the parties but rather the fact that services are being provided on the faith of an undertaking that the supplier of the services will be materially rewarded for them. As we shall see, it is not entirely clear that the division between the *Pettkus* cause of action and the cause of action exemplified in the housekeeping cases has been clearly preserved in the reasoning of the court in *Peter*.

III. SEVERING REMEDY FROM THE CAUSE OF ACTION: *PETER v BEBLOW*

In *Pettkus*, the Dickson J majority appears to have assumed that if relief is to be available, it is to be in the form of the constructive trust. This assumption, if it was made, may have arisen from the simple fact that the court was remedying a gap in the jurisprudence created by the common intention requirement of the traditional resulting trust. Following Laskin J's suggestion in *Murdoch*, the claim was framed and, no doubt, argued in the metre of constructive trust. Be that as it may, it is not self-evident that relief in a proprietary form is always appropriate in the context of the *Pettkus* cause of action. Thus, the suggestion by the court in *Sorochan* that a distinction must be drawn between the existence of the cause of action and the separate question of whether a proprietary remedy would be appropriate in the particular circumstances was a welcome clarification. In *Peter*,[31] the Supreme Court of Canada returned to consider this issue.

In this case, an unmarried couple had cohabited for about twelve years, each party bringing into the relationship children from previous marriages. The female plaintiff, apart from a winter job in a bakery and part-time summer work as a cook, looked after the home in which they lived and cared for both sets of children while they remained at home. She also undertook various projects which contributed, albeit modestly,[32] to the maintenance and preservation of their home, a house owned by the male defendant. The plaintiff also contributed financially to the household expenses. The plaintiff's principal contribution, however, was in the form of domestic services which, in the court's view, saved the defendant 'the expense of hiring a housekeeper and someone to care for the children.'[33] Indeed, prior to cohabiting with the plaintiff, the defendant, a grader operator whose work

[31] Above (n 8). For discussion, see TG Youdan, 'Resulting and Constructive Trusts' in Special Lectures of the Law Society of Upper Canada 1993, *Family Law: Roles, Fairness and Equality* (Scarborough, Carswell, 1994) 169.
[32] See *Peter* (above n 8) 1024; 640: the plaintiff 'painted the fence, planted the cedar hedge, installed the rock garden and built the chicken coop.'
[33] *Ibid* (Cory J). See also *ibid*, 1003; 654 (McLachlin J): plaintiff's efforts 'saved the respondent large sums of money.'

regularly required him to be away from home for periods of time, had retained the services of a housekeeper. As a result of these saved expenses, the court held, the defendant was able to pay off the mortgage on his house and purchase a van and houseboat.[34]

The trial judge had allowed the plaintiff's claim in unjust enrichment, holding that the defendant ought to have known of the plaintiff's reasonable expectation that she would be compensated, and awarded her a constructive trust over the home. The principal issue on appeal was whether domestic services, as such, could provide a basis for constructive trust relief. For the defendant, it was argued that such services did not establish the necessary causal link to the property. On this point, the court was unanimous. Both McLachlin J, for the majority, and Cory J, in a minority concurring opinion, rejected the suggestion that domestic services could not provide the necessary link. For Cory J, this conclusion followed from the holding in *Pettkus* that an indirect financial contribution could ground constructive trust relief.[35] For McLachlin J, a broader point was at issue. The defendant had argued that since domestic services should be considered to 'arise from natural love and affection' and since the plaintiff had 'voluntarily assumed the role of wife and stepmother,' the plaintiff's domestic services could not give rise to unjust enrichment.[36] For McLachlin J this argument rested on the notion that domestic services are not worthy of recognition, a notion which she described as 'a pernicious one that systematically devalues the contributions which women tend to make to the family economy.'[37] Rejection of the defendant's submissions thus had the effect of granting 'legal recognition of the value of domestic services.'[38] It is thus clearly established in *Peter* that contributions in the form of domestic services may indirectly contribute to the acquisition, maintenance or preservation of assets and thus provide a basis for an unjust enrichment claim.

There are, however, a number of issues touched upon in *Peter* that remain more elusive. First, it is unclear whether the majority opinion in *Peter* advances the law beyond the position established in *Pettkus* that indirect contributions—ie those that permit the other party to amass savings—can ground constructive trust relief. In *Pettkus*, it will be recalled, the contributions made by the plaintiff to the household expenses were financial. In *Peter*, the principal contribution was in the form of domestic services, albeit services that the other party would otherwise have had to hire someone to provide. The saved expense constitutes the benefit. It may be asked, then, whether domestic services will count as a contribution to the creation of

[34] *Ibid*, 1021; 638 (Cory J), 1003; 654 (McLachlin J).
[35] *Ibid*, 1020; 638.
[36] *Ibid*, 989–90; 645.
[37] *Ibid*, 993; 647–48.
[38] *Ibid*, 994; 648.

surplus wealth only where it can be shown, as in *Pettkus* and *Peter*, that the plaintiff's contribution enabled the other party to amass savings by relieving that party of an expense that would otherwise have been incurred. If so, *Peter* appears, as Cory J suggested, to be merely an application of the *Pettkus* principle.

The point may be tested by considering the following hypothetical cases. Would an unjust enrichment occur in the context of a cohabiting and childless couple if one spouse stays at home and provides domestic services, or could the other spouse argue that, if not cohabiting, he or she would have looked after himself or herself and would not have retained a personal housekeeper? Can a similar defence be raised in the context of a cohabiting couple with their own children and a similar division of responsibilities? The court has not yet had occasion to plainly answer these questions. As others have suggested,[39] however, it may be that in the latter context at least an argument could be made that were it not for the decision of one spouse to stay at home and provide domestic and child care services, the couple would have been required to share the expense of hiring someone to provide some level of service of this kind. If it cannot be established, however, that the defendant has been saved an expense, it would appear that *Pettkus* would not apply as the defendant has not been unjustly enriched.[40]

Second, the court in *Peter* elaborated on the point made in *Sorochan* that the question of whether unjust enrichment has occurred should be distinguished from the selection of the appropriate remedy, whether proprietary or personal. In *Peter*, the majority of the court articulated a presumption in favour of non-proprietary relief. For McLachlin J, the constructive trust should not be awarded where a monetary award is sufficient.[41] Further, some guidance was offered as to when proprietary relief in the form of the constructive trust would be appropriate. McLachlin J indicated that in a family setting, a monetary award is normally insufficient where 'the claimant's efforts have given her a special link to the property.'[42] Since, in a *Pettkus* claim, the plaintiff must show a causal connection with an increase in the

[39] See B Hovius and T Youdan, *The Law of Family Property* (Toronto, Carswell, 1991) 135.

[40] Less plausibly, it has been suggested that recovery may be generally grounded on a presumption that where couples decide that one spouse will forgo paid employment to provide domestic services, this decision rests on a joint belief that this arrangement will 'maximize their economic resources.' See M Neave, 'Three Approaches to Family Property Disputes—Intention/Belief, Unjust Enrichment and Unconscionability' in T Youdan (ed), *Equity, Fiduciaries and Trust* (Toronto, Carswell, 1989) 254. The point was put colourfully by Lord Simon in his 1964 Holdsworth Lecture, 'With All My Wordly Goods' at the University of Birmingham ('The cock-bird can feather his nest precisely because he is not required to spend most of his time sitting on it'), quoted by McLachlin J in *Peter* (above n 8) 993; 647. Although this is undoubtedly true in some cases, this view appears to ignore the economic realities of many salaried and other wage-earning spouses, whose incomes are not increased by such arrangements, and the fact that such decisions may often be taken for other reasons.

[41] *Peter* (above n 8) 997; 650.

[42] *Ibid*.

defendant's assets and, in theory at least, a reasonable expectation of receiving an interest in the assets, the existence of a 'link' may be readily established. On the other hand, it is clear that McLachlin J was suggesting that constructive trust relief is appropriate only where a particularly strong link to the asset is shown, as where the claimant has made a 'substantial and direct'[43] rather than an indirect contribution to the target asset. Another reason why a monetary award might appear insufficient, for McLachlin J, is that difficulties in enforcing a merely personal award are anticipated.[44] Cory J, on the other hand, did not appear to adopt the proposition that constructive relief is available only if monetary relief is found to be insufficient. Further, in his view, the necessary link can be established by an indirect contribution.[45] For Cory J, 'the choice between a monetary award and a constructive trust will be discretionary and should be exercised flexibly.'[46]

On its facts, *Peter* was a case in which the plaintiff's direct contributions to the property appear to have been very modest. Nonetheless, the trial judge's award of a constructive trust was upheld by both McLachlin and Cory JJ. McLachlin J's view that the contribution needs to be direct and substantial to justify a constructive trust remedy might appear to suggest that the provision of domestic services which enable the other spouse to amass savings and buy assets would not attract that form of relief. In *Peter,* however, McLachlin J supported the trial judge's decision on the basis that the claimant's contributions may be considered to have a 'link' to all of the assets of the 'family enterprise,' thus suggesting that in a marriage-like setting, at least, an indirect contribution may be sufficiently 'linked' to the assets to provide a basis for constructive trust relief.[47] By different doctrinal routes, then, McLachlin and Cory JJ both came to the conclusion that a contribution to wealth acquisition through the provision of domestic services may ground a constructive trust.

Third, the opinions in *Peter* raise a new complication concerning the measure of relief applicable in cases of this kind. For both McLachlin and Cory JJ, the issue was whether an award, be it monetary or constructive trust, should be calculated according to a 'value received' or a 'value surviving' measure. These terms were borrowed by the court, perhaps indirectly,[48] from Birks[49] and require brief explanation. These terms were devised by

[43] *Ibid.*
[44] *Ibid*, 999; 652.
[45] *Ibid*, 1020; 638.
[46] *Ibid*, 1023; 640.
[47] *Ibid*, 1001–03; 653–54.
[48] The terms are also employed by Neave (above n 40) 255, an article referred to by both McLachlin and Cory JJ in their opinions in *Peter*.
[49] PBH Birks, *An Introduction to the Law of Restitution* (Oxford, Clarendon Press, 1985) 75–77.

Birks to refer generically to two different measures of relief that can be awarded in restitution cases. The apparent point of the exercise was to attempt to find concepts that could simplify and replace the sometimes bewildering list of measures: quantum meruit, quantum valebat, money had and received, money paid, constructive trust, accounting and so on. 'Value received' is the normal measure. It is based on an assessment of the value of the money, goods or services that the defendant has received. This measure ignores whatever may have happened to that value after the receipt. That is, it is irrelevant whether the money received, for example, was lost, stolen or invested in securities which have appreciated in value. The defendant's liability is for the value at the time of receipt. Exceptionally, however, and typically in the context of equitable proprietary claims, the claimant, in order to recover, must identify his or her property in the hands of the defendant and will be entitled only to what can be so identified. As Birks has said, in such a case the plaintiff is entitled to 'what is left'[50] or the value surviving. In such a case, subsequent events such as loss or theft of the asset or substitution of a new asset for the old may become very material. As Birks concedes,[51] the phrase 'value surviving' may mislead slightly because 'what is left' may be an asset—for example, securities acquired through breach of a fiduciary duty—that has appreciated in value. For Birks, then, a claim for 'value received' could never be proprietary. In a proprietary claim, the claimant must identify a *res* in the defendant's hands and 'what has happened' to the *res* is relevant.[52] By way of contrast, however, personal claims or, as the court called them in *Peter*, 'monetary claims,' could, in principle at least, be in either measure. Thus to return to the example of the defaulting fiduciary and the improperly-acquired securities, the fiduciary might be determined to hold the securities on a constructive trust, being the proprietary or in rem claim, or be subjected to an accounting of profits, which could include the appreciated value of the securities, being the personal or in personam claim. Both of these claims are in the value surviving measure.

Returning to the matrimonial property context, in *Peter* the court employed these phrases to refer to, on the one hand, the value of the target asset, for example, the matrimonial home, as value surviving and, on the other, to the value of money, goods or services provided by the claimant as value received. The true choice between the value received and the value surviving measures depends, to some extent, on the true nature of the *Pettkus* claim, a matter considered above. In *Peter*, however, Cory J and McLachlin J appear to have considered the claim to be one for a fair share in the surplus value created by joint effort and then asked whether the claim should be calculated in the received or surviving measure. Both appear to

[50] *Ibid*, 75.
[51] *Ibid*, 76.
[52] *Ibid*, 77.

have accepted the possibility of a quantum meruit value received claim. Cory J noted that the constructive trust is traditionally calculated on a value surviving basis but indicated that he saw no reason why it could not be calculated on a value received or 'quantum meruit' basis.[53] McLachlin J disagreed with this approach. In her view, the constructive trust must be calculated only on a value surviving basis for both doctrinal and practical reasons. Where the claim is for an interest in property, in her view one must 'determine what portion of the value of the property claimed is attributable to the claimant's services.'[54] Moreover, this approach avoids the complications of balancing benefits and detriments said to be inherent in the value received approach. Further, McLachlin J stated that value surviving 'arguably accords best with the expectations of most parties; it is more likely that a couple expects to share in the wealth generated from their partnership, rather than to receive compensation for the services performed during the relationship.'[55] For McLachlin J, then, value received is reserved for monetary awards. It is important to note, however, that McLachlin J did not plainly assert that a monetary award could only be made in the value received measure, though this might be thought to be implicit in her analysis. On the other hand, if, as McLachlin J suggests, merely monetary awards should be made unless they are insufficient for some reason and, further, that value surviving normally accords with the parties' expectations, it is surely preferable that monetary awards can be made in the value surviving measure. Provincial appellate courts, however, have differed on this point.[56]

In considering the choice between value received and value surviving, *Peter* touched obliquely and inconclusively on the more fundamental question of whether the claimant spouse might have, as an alternative to the claim for a share of the surplus wealth held by the other spouse resulting from their joint effort, a simple claim for the value of domestic services rendered on a quantum meruit basis, regardless of whether surplus wealth has been created. Acceptance of this possibility would be a substantial departure

[53] *Peter* (above n 8) 1025; 641. On this view, we assume, one would calculate the value of the services rendered and impose an equitable charge or lien on the targeted asset for the amount in question.

[54] *Ibid*, 999; 651. Presumably these remarks are limited to the matrimonial property context. In principle, the equitable lien can provide equitable proprietary relief for a fixed sum rather than a proportionate share of the target property in the context of a restitutionary claim. It is not entirely clear why such relief could not be made available in a matrimonial property claim where, for example, value received was considered to be the appropriate measure but problems in enforcing the judgment were anticipated.

[55] *Ibid*, 999; 651–52.

[56] Such relief has been awarded in the following cases: *Pickelein v Gillmore* [1997] 5 WWR 595 (BCCA); *Shannon v Gidden* (1999) 178 DLR (4th) 395 (BCCA); *Hubar v Jobling* (2000) 195 DLR (4th) 123 (BCCA); *Nasser v Mayer Nasser* (2000) 130 OAC 52 (Ont CA), leave to appeal to SCC refused [2000] SCCA No 206 (QL). *Cf Bell v Bailey* (2001) 203 DLR (3d) 589 (Ont CA), holding that such relief is precluded by *Peter*.

from the *Pettkus* claim, as it would appear to retrospectively, on the occasion of dissolution of the relationship, transform domestic services provided by either spouse without expectation of payment in return into services rendered on a fee-for-service basis. If, as seems likely, the injustice perceived in these cases is that of profiting by acquiring surplus wealth at the other's expense, the granting of such relief would be inconsistent with the underlying theory of liability. Thus, although Cory J referred to the possibility of 'quantum meruit'[57] and McLachlin J referred to the possibility that parties might expect to receive 'compensation for the services performed during the relationship,'[58] it appears correct to interpret such references within the context of a *Pettkus* claim for a share of surplus wealth produced through joint effort. Thus read, the opinions in *Peter* suggest that in a *Pettkus* claim it may be appropriate to make an award based on the value of the services rendered by the claimant which contributed to the creation of the surplus. Such awards have occasionally been made.[59] It has been suggested that such an award is appropriate where 'the unjust enrichment is an uncompensated but measurable contribution to the defendant's general estate that is not reflected in a particular property.'[60] As we have seen, however, the majority in *Peter* suggested that if, in such a case, the assets could be considered to constitute a 'family enterprise,' full value surviving constructive trust relief could be appropriate.

IV. STRIKING THE BALANCE BETWEEN PROPRIETARY AND PERSONAL REMEDIES

By plainly severing considerations relating to the cause of action from remedial issues, *Peter* offers the prospect for the development of a more coherent jurisprudence surrounding the *Pettkus* claim. The clear statement that proprietary relief is not necessarily available in such a case is a constructive one. Moreover, the suggestion that courts can refer to the reasons offered by LaForest J in *Lac Minerals*[61] for selecting the proprietary remedy of constructive trust in the fiduciary duty context points them to a potentially useful source of guidance in attempting to discern the relative roles of proprietary and personal relief in the context of the *Pettkus* claim. On the other hand, the analysis in the opinions in *Peter* runs the risk of creating potential confusion in subsequent cases. In particular, the suggestion that the fundamental remedial choice in this context is between a constructive

[57] *Peter* (above n 8) 1025; 641.
[58] *Ibid*, 999; 652.
[59] See, eg, *Ledrew v Ledrew* (1993) 46 RFL (3d) 11 (Ont Gen Div); *Bell* (above n 56).
[60] *Pickelein* (above n 56) 609 (Huddart JA).
[61] *Lac Minerals Ltd v International Corona Resources Ltd* [1989] 2 SCR 574; (1989) 61 DLR (4th) 14 (SCC).

trust over a targeted asset or, on the other hand, a quantum meruit for the value of services rendered is problematic. After exploring this difficulty, I will return to a consideration of the circumstances in which proprietary and personal relief might be appropriate.

A. The False Dichotomy of Constructive Trust and Quantum Meruit

In *Peter*, both McLachlin and Cory JJ considered constructive trust and quantum meruit to be the alternative measures of relief available in a *Pettkus* claim. As noted above, this choice was treated somewhat differently in the two opinions but both judges appear to be in agreement that relief might be calculated in either the value received or the value surviving measure. There are two difficulties with this approach. First, it is difficult to see what role, if any, the traditional common law quantum meruit claim could play in the *Pettkus* context. The claim appears to rest on a right to share in the surplus wealth created by joint effort and teamwork rather than, as in cases like *Deglman,* a right to claim for services rendered in the expectation of compensation. A fee-for-service claim does not likely accord with the expectations of the parties. As McLachlin J noted in *Peter*:

> ... A 'value survived' approach arguably accords best with the expectations of most parties; it is more likely that a couple expects to share in the wealth generated from the partnership, rather than to receive compensation for the services performed during the relationship.[62]

Indeed, it seems most unlikely that married couples or others in similar circumstances would expect, on the dissolution of their relationship, to engage in a massive accounting of the value of services rendered, presumably by both parties, with a view to rendering a tally enabling the provider of the lion's share of the services to bring a claim for the net value of services rendered, at the market rate. This prospect of duelling quantum meruits, with its incentives for micro-accounting and keeping track of services rendered, appears inconsistent with and possibly undermining of relationships in which services are surely provided without any expectation of compensation in this sense. In short, the quantum meruit measure of recovery appears to be inconsistent with the fundamental nature of the *Pettkus* claim. Thus, if the only remedial choice in such a claim is between the proprietary relief of constructive trust and the common law remedy of quantum meruit, it would appear that only the constructive trust remedy would be available in a genuine *Pettkus* claim.

[62] Above (n 8) 999; 651–52.

The second problem with the proposed choice between constructive trust and quantum meruit is that it ignores the possibility that an in personam or personal remedy in the value surviving measure in the form of an accounting of profits is a plausible alternative to the constructive trust in a *Pettkus* claim. Neither McLachlin nor Cory JJ appears to have admitted of this possibility, though if there is to be a significant alternative personal remedy to constructive trust in this context it must surely be a remedy of this kind. A *Pettkus* claim is a claim for a share in the profits or surplus wealth generated by joint effort and teamwork. It is inherently a 'value surviving' claim. If a personal remedy is to be possible in this context, it is surely a personal remedy for a share of that wealth. Therefore, a richer range of remedial options should be considered to be available in the context of a *Pettkus* claim and, more particularly, an accounting of profits should be considered to be the in personam remedial alternative to the proprietary constructive trust.

B. When Would the Constructive Trust be the Appropriate Remedial Choice?

In attempting to identify the circumstances in which the constructive trust remedy appears to be particularly appropriate, it is important to distinguish between its appropriateness as against the defendant spouse and its appropriateness as against third party creditors. While it is certainly arguable that the constructive trust remedy will be appropriate, at least in some circumstances, where the contest is exclusively one between the spouses, it is very difficult to articulate a ground on which the claimant spouse should gain a priority, through the medium of constructive trust, over the creditors of the defendant.

With respect to the first point, the approach taken by McLachlin J in *Peter* may prove to be fruitful. Having affirmed that a finding that the plaintiff is entitled to a remedy for unjust enrichment does not necessarily imply that constructive trust relief will be available, McLachlin J went on to observe that 'for a constructive trust to arise, the plaintiff must establish a direct link to the property which is the subject of the trust by reason of the plaintiff's contribution.'[63] At a later point in her opinion, she indicated that '[w]here a monetary award is insufficient in a family situation, this is usually related to the fact the claimant's efforts have given him or her a special link to the property, in which case a constructive trust arises.'[64] Such a link is very likely to be established, of course, with the matrimonial home. Indeed, it is in the context of a claim to an interest in the matrimonial home

[63] *Ibid*, 995; 649.
[64] *Ibid*, 997; 650.

that the constructive trust claim may appear to be at its strongest.[65] As *Pettkus* itself demonstrates, however, there may be other factual situations in which the claimant's direct connection with the acquisition or maintenance of a particular asset, such as a parcel of land, may suggest that the just result is to force co-ownership upon the unjustly enriched spouse. In the absence of such circumstances, however, it is far from clear that constructive trust relief is appropriate. If the defendant spouse has, with savings accumulated as a result of the financial and other contributions made by the claimant, acquired a houseboat or fishing lodge which the claimant has never visited, it is difficult to see why monetary compensation in the form of a partial accounting of profits would not be an adequate form of relief.

Rotherham has persuasively argued that the 'causal connection' or direct link test for proprietary relief is 'transcendental nonsense.'[66] Certainly in the Canadian context it merely appears to restate the nature of the claim, rather than to identify a reason why the particular remedy of constructive trust is appropriate. Once one accepts, as the Supreme Court of Canada did in *Peter*, that indirect contributions—such as the provision of domestic services or other beneficial services that save the other party expenses—support a *Pettkus* claim, the existence of a 'causal connection' seems to support proprietary relief in *every* case. After all, there is no claim unless one can show that the plaintiff's contribution produced wealth in the defendant's hands. Rotherham prefers a test of 'psychological connection' with the property. The home, of course, is the asset to which the spouses will most likely have an emotional attachment. This may be especially so with a stay-at-home mother. As Rotherham states:

> In the context of the division of property on the breakdown of intimate relationships, plaintiffs may quite reasonably have formed such strong psychological attachments to the assets in question that the parties' proprietary rights should be adjusted to reflect this.[67]

There is much force in this point—consider, for example, the matrimonial home or Ms Becker's connection to the bee farm—and yet, simply asking the question, 'how emotionally attached does the claimant feel to this property?' is a test that will be difficult to apply. Moreover, the remedy—a partial share of the asset—does not fully vindicate the sentiment. It may be, therefore, that the test is better focussed on the nature of the contribution and its connection to the asset. Where there is a strong connection, the psychological link is also likely to be present. In other words, the direct connection test may usefully function as a surrogate for identifying

[65] A point made persuasively by Rotherham (above n 22) 235–38.
[66] *Ibid*, 233.
[67] *Ibid*, 237.

circumstances where a strong psychological sense of attachment or 'ownership' is likely to be present.

As far as third party creditors are concerned, various arguments have been made in favour of priority for the claimant spouse.[68] To the extent that the claimant has created or enhanced the value of an asset, it might be viewed as an unearned windfall to which the ordinary creditors of the defendant should have no claim. On the other hand, the acceptance of risk argument does not do full justice to trade creditors who may well have relied on credit reports based to some degree on registered ownership of assets. Further, though creditors may determine with relative ease the fact of marriage, other intimate relationships are less easily detected. More importantly, however, the very nature of the *Pettkus* claim is that the defendant spouse has been unjustly enriched by retaining all of the surplus wealth created by joint effort and teamwork. The claims of the creditors should be taken into account, surely, in calculating the extent of that surplus. If, as LaForest J observed in *Lac Minerals,* one of the principal considerations in determining whether a constructive trust should be awarded is whether the granting of a priority in insolvency is appropriate,[69] the application of this consideration in the present context would weigh heavily against constructive trust relief.

V. CONCLUSION

The role of the unjust enrichment principle in the context of matrimonial property disputes has been controversial in common law Canada, as it has in other common law jurisdictions. Nonetheless, the *Pettkus* line of authority clearly establishes a right to recover, on the part of the spouse without title a portion of the surplus wealth accumulated by a married couple as a result of their joint effort and teamwork. The spouse without title is entitled to recover that portion of the surplus wealth that is attributable to or caused by his or her contribution, whether financial or otherwise. The contribution may be direct, as where the financial or other contributions have directly enabled the acquisition, preservation or maintenance of a particular asset, or indirect, as where the claimant's efforts have enabled the spouse with title to amass savings which have been used to acquire the assets in question. Such claims reverse the enrichment achieved by the spouse with title at the expense of the claimant. Such claims are not restricted to married couples. They are available to others in similarly intimate relationships who have contributed to the acquisition of surplus wealth.

[68] They are briefly analysed in Ontario Law Reform Commission, *Report on Family Property Law* (Toronto, Ministry of the Attorney General, 1993) 46–49, 139.
[69] Above (n 61) 678; 51.

Although the Supreme Court of Canada in *Pettkus* indicated that such a claim would be available only where the claimant has 'reasonable expectations' of acquiring a proprietary interest in the asset in question, this requirement is unsatisfactory for a number of reasons. Spouses in married and similarly intimate relationships are unlikely to consciously formulate such expectations. Their claims may nonetheless be meritorious. Thus, in *Pettkus* itself, the requirement appears to have been applied quite artificially. An explanation for recovery which is preferable to that of 'reasonable expectations' was articulated by Dickson J in *Rathwell* and Cory J in *Peter*. In those cases, Dickson and Cory JJ suggested that spouses were unlikely to address or plan for the consequences of the dissolution of the relationship. Their expectation is that their relationship will last. Moreover, such planning or negotiation may be inimicable to their ongoing relationship. Nonetheless, it is likely that if parties in such circumstances were to address these issues, they would likely be able to agree that surplus assets would be fairly distributed in light of the contribution of the respective parties to their acquisition. The *Pettkus* cause of action thus serves as a default rule, reflecting the expectations of reasonable parties, around which parties may bargain should they choose to do so. This default rule seems particularly appropriate in the context of a married couple, where such parties normally have a 'sharing intention' and an expectation that their relationship will endure. With respect to couples that are not married, however, the default rule seems appropriate only if the relationship of the parties is similar to that of a married couple in the sense that there exists a 'sharing intention.' Thus, the proper explanation for the emergence of the 'reasonable expectations' standard in *Pettkus* may be that the couple in that case was unmarried. In *Rathwell*, a case involving a married couple, the 'reasonable expectations' standard was not articulated or applied. In the absence of agreement to the contrary, it may be assumed that a married couple has the 'sharing intention' which provides the necessary foundation for the default rule.

The *Pettkus* claim, then, provides a remedy for the exploitation that might otherwise occur in intimate relationships when surplus wealth, created by the contributions of both parties, ends up in the hands of one of them. This claim is very different from the more traditional restitutionary claim available in circumstances where services have been provided on the faith of an understanding that the provider will be compensated. Thus, in *Deglman*, the nephew who provided services on the faith of the aunt's unenforceable oral undertaking to compensate him by leaving him property in her will was entitled to recover in quantum meruit for the value of services rendered on the faith of this unenforceable undertaking. Claims for the value of services rendered on a fee-for-service basis are unlikely to arise in the context of marriage or similar relationships. Domestic services are simply not provided on such a basis in the normal course of such relationships.

However, the *Deglman*-type claim could arise in the context of promises to marry, where a person provides services on the faith of an undertaking that he or she will be rewarded by the financial consequences of marriage.[70] Similarly, it is possible to imagine circumstances in which a spouse might provide services that the recipient would otherwise have had to pay for, in the expectation of similar financial rewards or security.[71] As a general matter, however, the prospect of what has been referred to here as 'duelling quantum meruits' appears inconsistent with the nature of and the expectations of the parties to marital and similar relationships. Thus, the suggestion in *Peter* that once the *Pettkus* line of authority is applicable, the remedial choice then available to the court is either constructive trust for a share of the surplus assets or a claim of quantum meruit for the value of services rendered appears to be inconsistent with the general nature of the *Pettkus* claim. Rather, the appropriate remedial choice would appear to be that between proprietary relief in the form of the constructive trust and in personam relief in the form of an accounting of profits.

Although the earliest cases in the *Pettkus* line of authority appear to have assumed that constructive trust was the only form of relief available in these cases, the Supreme Court of Canada has more recently indicated that a choice is to be made between proprietary and personal relief. The court touched upon the difficult question of when, if ever, proprietary relief in the form of the constructive trust would be appropriate in *Peter*. McLachlin J suggested that the constructive trust was appropriate where in personam was inadequate for some reason and, more particularly, where 'the claimant's efforts have given him or her a special link to the property.'[72] As Rotherham has suggested, however, it may be that the most convincing reason for awarding a constructive trust would be that the claimant has developed a strong psychological attachment to the asset in question. The asset to which this consideration would most obviously apply is the matrimonial home. This is also the asset to which the claimant spouse is very likely to have a 'special link.' Thus, it may well be that the direct connection test suggested by McLachlin J in *Peter* will serve as a proxy for identifying cases in which a strong psychological connection is present. With respect to third party creditors of the spouse with title, however, it is difficult to articulate a convincing rationale for imposing constructive trust relief. If, as appears to be the case, the theory of the claim is that the claimant has contributed to the surplus wealth generated by the couple, the surplus should surely be determined after the claims of the creditors have been satisfied.

70 *Rowe* (above n 30).
71 See, eg, *Georg v Hassanali* (1989) 18 RFL (3d) 225 (Ont HCJ) (where the female plaintiff spent ten years managing an apartment building owned by the defendant).
72 Above (n 8) 997; 650.

15

Legitimating 'Legitimate Expectations': A Case Study on Filial Responsibility; Can Parents Recover for Supporting Their Children at University?

JEFF BERRYMAN*

I. INTRODUCTION

IN AT LEAST two iterations of the principles that govern unjust enrichment in Canada, McLachlin J has stressed the need to determine that the parties' legitimate or reasonable expectation was that a benefit was conferred on the assumption that it would be paid for or returned in some way.[1] McLachlin J has also suggested that the development of restitution in Canada should follow a middle or third way.[2] It should be cognizant of existing doctrine, but also mindful of general principles so as to be adaptive to new situations; it should chart a path between the Scylla of doctrinal formalism and the Charybdis of unrestrained discretion. Within that model, Professors Mitchell McInnes and Lionel Smith, two of Canada's leading restitution theoreticians, have argued for greater emphasis on choosing and defining the right unjust enrichment doctrine for Canada. Their fear is that our current path leads only to idiosyncratic and 'palm tree' justice. While not disagreeing with them, I wish to argue that when measured against its

* I wish to thank my research students, Damien McCotter and Jennifer Lalonde, for their assistance in preparing this essay.

[1] *Peter v Beblow* [1993] 1 SCR 980; 101 DLR (4th) 621, 645 (SCC) (herein cited to DLR) and *Peel (Regional Municipality) v Canada* [1992] 3 SCR 762; 98 DLR (4th) 140, 164 (SCC) (herein cited to DLR).

[2] *Peel* (above n 1) 153. See also L Smith, 'The Mystery of "Juristic Reason"' (2002) 12 *Supreme Court Law Review* 211, 241 and G Virgo, *The Principles of the Law of Restitution* (Oxford, Clarendon Press, 1999) 54.

adaptive abilities, the current emphasis on general principle, particularly in determining legitimacy of expectations, provides more scope. In Part II, I sketch out some of these arguments. In Part III, I offer a 'straw person'—an exploration of how a parent could recover for support of a child at university—to demonstrate the adaptive properties of 'legitimate expectations.' In Part IV, I suggest that in Canada, the genie having escaped the bottle, it will not be easily recaptured in terms of the change in analytical thinking that Smith and McInnes call for. Time more profitably could be spent looking for indicia of McLachlin J's 'legitimate expectations.'

II. REASONS FOR RESTITUTION

McInnes and Smith have both taken to task the current direction of Canadian restitution law.[3] In particular, they are concerned at the apparently amorphous concept of 'juristic reason' as developed by Canada's Supreme Court. Both contrast Canada to the United Kingdom, ultimately concluding that there is greater coherence in the United Kingdom position and recommending that Canada follow the trodden path.

Both Smith and McInnes have performed masterful service in analysing jurisdictional differences and identifying what is at stake. The Canadian 'juristic reason' formulation appears to shift the onus to the defendant to prove that there is a juristic reason for *keeping* a transfer of wealth.[4] Both Smith and McInnes have pointed out, however, that this has not in fact been the situation and that the onus of proof ultimately remains with the plaintiff to prove all elements of the case.[5] Of course, Dickson J never intended the 'absence of juristic reason' formula to be used in a strictly literal sense. In another part of his judgment he spoke of the fact that retention of the benefit would have to be 'unjust.'[6] Smith suggests that reasons for keeping transfers of wealth may be grouped under the following headings:

[1] Legislation as juristic reason.[7]
[2] Rules of property law.

[3] L Smith (above n 2); M McInnes, 'The Canadian Principle of Unjust Enrichment: Comparative Insights into the Law of Restitution' (1999) 37 *Alberta Law Review* 1; M McInnes, 'Reflections on the Canadian Law of Unjust Enrichment: Lessons from Abroad' (1999) 78 *Canadian Bar Review* 416 and M McInnes, 'The Measure of Restitution' (2002) 52 *University of Toronto Law Journal* 163.

[4] As an aside, I wonder if it would be profitable to consider the development of unjust enrichment as how it embodies both biological and social conditioning. Absence of juristic reasons, or looking at reasons to keep enrichments, seems intuitively in keeping with biological behaviour that focuses primarily upon the individual's preservation of self; whereas acts of altruism are learned through social conditioning and therefore must be explained and justified.

[5] Smith (above n 2) 228 and McInnes, 'Reflections on the Canadian Law of Unjust Enrichment' (above n 3) 421.

[6] *Pettkus v Becker* [1980] 2 SCR 834; 117 DLR (3d) 257, 273–74 (SCC) (herein cited to DLR).

[7] Most recently applied by the Ontario Court of Appeal in *Mack v Canada (Attorney General)* (2002) 60 OR (3d) 737(CA); leave to appeal to SCC dismissed April 24, 2003 (without reasons), [2002] SCCA No 476.

[3] Intention to give.
[4] Contract.
[5] Policy:
  (i) Legitimate expectations that the benefit provided will be compensated.
  (ii) Submission or compromise.
  (iii) Public policy.
[6] Officiousness.

In contrast to 'juristic reason,' the approach adopted in the United Kingdom requires the plaintiff to prove that the enrichment was 'unjust' and therefore *reversible*. For English scholars this engages a search for 'unjust factors' the presence of which justifies restitution. Smith suggests the following, although this is not an exhaustive list:

[1] Mistake of law or of fact.
[2] Free acceptance.
[3] Failure of basis—ie as in a failure of contract formation or of consideration.
[4] Compulsion.
[5] Public policy.[8]

Smith then evaluates both approaches against three criteria; better results, better fit, and better doctrine. Ultimately, Smith accepts only the last criteria as relevant. By better doctrine he asks which approach will best ensure that like cases are treated alike. Better doctrine: (1) provides clarity on the basic grounds of liability, (2) provides for the exclusion of incidental or officious benefits, (3) prevents the redistribution of risks consensually assumed, and (4) provides security of receipt in appropriate cases. Smith then asserts that there is much more doctrinal clarity in looking for reasons to reverse enrichments than in attempting to find reasons to keep enrichments.

Smith has set a modest goal for the law: doctrinal clarity. He does not assert that one approach has a monopoly on achieving better justice, only that the latter has a better chance of avoiding idiosyncratic or 'palm tree' justice. While I do not disagree with Smith, I do doubt that the latter approach provides greater coherence because it is inherently better doctrine. Rather,

[8] The public policy here is not of the same ilk as that under the former classification of reasons for keeping enrichments. This public policy is far more circumscribed. As Virgo states, to consider it otherwise would be to see this unjust factor open the door to restitution being granted whenever 'circumstances of receipt were considered unjust.' Virgo (above n 2) 124.

it may be better because there is simply that much more of it. In fact Smith, together with other Canadian scholars, notably Maddaugh and McCamus,[9] Fridman,[10] and Waters,[11] have done much to provide a framework built upon Canadian jurisprudence sketching the doctrinal parameters of the juristic reason approach and thereby giving it the coherence Smith states it lacks.

McInnes is much more strident in his criticism of the Canadian approach. In his own words:

> Generally, however the Supreme Court of Canada's approach to the principle of unjust enrichment is marked by a lack of analytical rigour; in many instances the Court has distorted precedent and principle in order to achieve desired ends. In that respect, the influence of the cohabitational property cases can not be understated. Not only has the Court's jurisprudence in that area established a host of questionable rules, it has created an environment in which unjust enrichment often appears to be perceived simply as a malleable means of securing situational fairness.[12]

McInnes, who is not alone in his criticism,[13] also critiques the cohabitation cases. He suggests that fairness may well dictate that some accommodation should be made for the unfortunate party (usually the woman) found in the predicament of a common law cohabitation relationship, but insists that unjust enrichment is not the appropriate vehicle to attain that result. If it were, 'free acceptance' would be the unjust factor.[14]

The concept of free acceptance has been notoriously troublesome, perhaps most notably in the context of family dissolution.[15] The concept abrogates the role of freedom of choice by the recipient and forces expenditures which, left to his or her own free will, the recipient would not necessarily have made or given priority above other expenditures at the time. Unlike the return of money, un-requested services provided to the recipient cannot be returned, nor does the recipient necessarily place the value on those services

[9] PD Maddaugh & JD McCamus, *The Law of Restitution* (Aurora, Canada Law Book, 1990).
[10] GHL Fridman, *Restitution*, 2nd edn (Toronto, Carswell, 1992).
[11] DWM Waters, *The Law of Trusts in Canada*, 2nd edn (Toronto, Carswell, 1984).
[12] McInnes, 'The Canadian Principle of Unjust Enrichment' (above n 3) 37.
[13] T Krebs, *Restitution at the Crossroads: A Comparative Study* (London, Cavendish, 2001) 262; P Birks, 'Mistakes of Law' (2000) 53 *CLP* 205, and RB Grantham and CEF Rickett, *Enrichment & Restitution in New Zealand* (Oxford, Hart Publishing, 2000) 9.
[14] McInnes also suggests that in the facts of *Pettkus*, (above n 6) the enrichment could also give rise to an argument based on incontrovertible benefit. However, such an action could not substitute for the identification of an unjust factor. McInnes suggests that some Canadian courts have wrongly allowed incontrovertible benefit to become a freestanding cause of action. McInnes 'The Canadian Principle of Unjust Enrichment' (above n 3) 34, fn 178.
[15] See the arguments discussed in Grantham and Rickett (above n 13) 243 and G McMeel, *The Modern Law of Restitution* (London, Blackstone Press, 2000) 217.

equivalent to either their market value or the value placed on them by their provider (subjective devaluation). In family dissolution cases, free acceptance requires the provider to prove the reasonableness of her expectation in being compensated. This is made problematic where the actions of the recipient demonstrate that he does not share the notion of joint family wealth and selfishly keeps all acquired property and wealth in his own control. The actions of the recipient in disavowing any joint ownership must shake the reasonableness of the provider's intention and result in the provider having assumed the risk of non-compensation for continuing to provide those same services (act officiously). Further problems occur depending upon whether the provider's claim is to share jointly in the accumulated surplus wealth made while together or to have an *in personam* claim for *quantum meruit*. If the latter is favoured, then the provider will be a general judgment debtor. If the former is preferred, then the claim will be effectively extinguished if the assets that the parties acquired during their relationship declined in value.[16]

For many of the above stated reasons, McInnes concludes that Rosa Becker should not have been able to bring herself within existing unjust enrichment doctrine. Herein lies a paradox. For the sake of doctrinal clarity, we are asked to embrace an approach to unjust enrichment, or at least a classificatory schema, that cannot accommodate the cohabitation cases that have been instrumental in the development of our basic understanding of unjust enrichment in Canada, the fairness of which have not been questioned even by those who challenge the courts' reasoning.[17] It would be easy to dismiss the cohabitation cases as raising distinct issues concerned with social policy.[18] But such an approach, I suggest, is a little disingenuous. Canadian courts have not distinguished the cohabitation cases from other areas of unjust enrichment. In fact, there is almost universal acceptance of the *Pettkus* criteria as embodying powerful legal principles (the analogy to tort law's duty of care principle as derived from *Donoghue v Stevenson*[19] is noted by Fridman in this collection of essays[20]). Any elucidation of these principles, as in *Peter*, is quickly applied in other divergent claims based on unjust enrichment.

[16] See Maddaugh & McCamus (above n 9) 660, and J McCamus's essay in this collection, Ch 14.
[17] We are also asked to embrace what some consider dubious doctrinal categories, eg free acceptance.
[18] In a case comment on *Peter* (above n 1), J McLeod has described the Supreme Court's approach as engaging in 'social engineering' and wonders whether this is best done through private law or better left to legislative reform as a part of public law. By conferring on unmarried people cohabitating rights found in legislation for married couples, the court has withdrawn the possibility that people may freely choose to cohabit with full knowledge of its legal consequences and desiring those same results. JG McLeod, (1993) 44 RFL (3d) 396.
[19] [1932] AC 562 (HL).
[20] See also Smith (above n 2) 213.

The test of doctrine, in addition to the criteria advanced by Smith, cannot be divorced from perceptions of what is just and fair. A hallmark of the common law, in addition to doctrinal clarity and maintenance of the rule of law, is that its direction and adaptation has been achieved through a case-by-case approach. Meticulous attention to facts comes before legal argument.[21] Disputes arise from an individual's perception of facts and sense of injustice or grievance. Lawyers transform these into evidence and legal arguments. They choose whatever legal tools are available. Judges determine facts and transform legal tools into doctrine. Where there is a widespread disconnect between individual perceptions of injustice and doctrine, the law is brought into disrepute. The experience over the advance of a matrimonial property scheme is that very story.

One of the last iterations of Canada's unjust enrichment doctrine was given by McLachlin J in *Peter*.[22]

> This court has consistently taken a straightforward economic approach to the first two elements of the test for unjust enrichment. ... It is in connection with the third element—absence of juristic reason for the enrichment—that such considerations may more properly find their place. It is at this stage that the court must consider whether the enrichment and detriment, morally neutral in themselves, are 'unjust.' ...
>
> What matters should be considered in determining whether there is an absence of juristic reason for the enrichment? The test is flexible, and the factors to be considered may vary with the situation before the court. For example, different factors may be more relevant in a case like *Peel,* a claim for enrichment between different levels of government, than in a family case. ...
>
> In every case, the fundamental concern is the legitimate expectation of the parties: *Pettkus*. In family cases, this concern may raise the following subsidiary questions:
>
> (i) Did the plaintiff confer the benefit as a valid gift or in pursuance of a valid common law, equitable or statutory obligation which he or she owed to the defendant?
> (ii) Did the plaintiff submit to, or compromise, the defendant's honest claim?
> (iii) Does public policy support the enrichment?[23]

Peter is illustrative of this approach. The plaintiff had lived in a common law relationship with the defendant for twelve years. During that time, she had contributed household and domestic services by looking after the defendant, his two children, as well as her own four children. The relationship

[21] LaForest J has stressed the importance of a detailed factual examination in *Lac Minerals Ltd v International Corona Resources Ltd* [1989] 2 SCR 574; 61 DLR (4th) 14 (SCC) (herein cited to DLR), a case determining whether a fact-based fiduciary relationship exists and whether a constructive trust should be awarded as an appropriate remedy.

[22] Above (n 1).

[23] *Peter* (above n 1) 645.

deteriorated, particularly after all the children left home. The plaintiff moved out of the family home and commenced an action seeking an interest in the family home by way of constructive trust or financial compensation based on the unjust enrichment of the defendant.

McLachlin J, applying the unjust enrichment principle, quickly found an enrichment and a corresponding detriment. The simple fact that prior to the defendant entering into the cohabitation arrangement he had paid for a domestic servant to care for his children and perform other household tasks was clear evidence of his enrichment. In addition, the defendant, freed of the need to pay for domestic services, was able to pay off his mortgage at an enhanced rate. The fact that the plaintiff had provided these services without compensation was seen as incurring a corresponding deprivation or detriment.[24] Turning to the third element, the defendant argued that the domestic services were provided either as a gift or pursuant to a recognized legal obligation. In an earlier ruling of the Supreme Court of Canada, the court had held that a common law spouse owed no duty at common law, in equity or statutorily to perform domestic services for her partner.[25] Nor did the Court accept that acting out of a motivation of natural love would turn the provision of services into a gift without a legitimate expectation of sharing in the property of the relationship once, and if, terminated. Turning to any public policy considerations that would support an enrichment, the only argument proffered was the suggestion that it was distasteful to place a price upon services provided through love and affection and then make the recipient of these non-financial and indirect contributions pay recompense. This argument was rejected as being untenable in contemporary Canadian society because it 'systematically devalues the contributions which women tend to make to the family economy' and has 'contributed to the feminisation of poverty.'[26]

Both Smith and McInnes argue that the unjust factor in this and similar cases is free acceptance. If the test of free acceptance is a subjective one, ie that it requires proof that the defendant knew that the benefit was not provided gratuitously, then rarely will it operate in the cohabitation or family sphere. Cory J succinctly stated the obvious:

> The test put forward [from *Pettkus*] is an objective one. The parties entering a marriage or a common law relationship will rarely have considered the question of compensation for benefits. If asked, they might say that because they loved their partner, each worked to achieve a common goal of creating a home and establishing a good life for themselves. It is just and reasonable that

[24] Cory J, who rendered the other opinion in *Peter* (above n 1) concluded that upon proof that one party had been enriched by the efforts of the other, it was 'virtually automatic' to conclude that a corresponding deprivation had been incurred by the other party.
[25] *Sorochan v Sorochan* [1986] 2 SCR 38; 29 DLR (4th) 1 (SCC).
[26] *Peter* (above n 1) 647.

> the situation be viewed objectively and that an inference be made that, in the absence of evidence establishing a contrary intention, the parties expected to share in the assets created in a matrimonial or quasi-matrimonial relationship, should it end.[27]

If the test for free acceptance is an objective one as asserted by Cory J[28] (ie it is sufficient that a reasonable person in the defendant's shoes would have realized that the plaintiff had not provided the benefit gratuitously), then the inquiry is quite different and is not dependent upon any characterization of the particular defendant's conduct as being unconscientious.[29] Rather, the inquiry then becomes one of how to determine the 'legitimacy' of a plaintiff's expectations, which does incorporate broad notions of justice and fairness.[30]

Much is made of McLachlin J's middle path or third way that seeks as its *objective* to reconcile general principles with established categories of recovery. However, its *goal* is to give us a way to adapt existing doctrine to contemporary circumstances. The former objective is subservient to the latter goal.

III. EXPECTATIONS AND LEGITIMATE EXPECTATIONS

In this part I offer three factual examples coupled with a sense of injustice. The examples are deliberately chosen to provoke debate on what turns an 'expectation' into a 'legitimate expectation.'

[a] Chinese parents incur significant expense in sending their first-born child to university with the expectation, in keeping with a cultural custom of filial piety, that their son will take care of them in their elder years. The son later disavows any such responsibility. Can the parents recover any of the benefits bestowed upon their son?

[b] Parents with two children finance and support the elder child's university education. Tragically, both die before their younger daughter commences university, although she harbours the same

[27] *Ibid*, 635.

[28] Goff & Jones takes this position. See G Jones, *Goff & Jones: The Law of Restitution,* 6th edn (London, Sweet & Maxwell, 2002) 20. Virgo disputes it. See Virgo (above n 2) 83.

[29] See G Tolhurst, in S Hedley and M Halliwell (eds), *The Law of Restitution* (London, Butterworths, 2002) §19.65 fn 2.

[30] McInnes argues that 'free acceptance' or 'unconscientious' behaviour can only be based on subjective grounds. The defendant must know of the claimant's expectation of payment for the proffered services and is under a duty to reject or disabuse the claimant of that expectation. For McInnes the cohabitation cases can only be accommodated in a category of 'policy-based reasons' as an 'unjust factor.' This category is to be circumscribed so as not to allow an unbridled judicial discretion. McInnes, 'The Measure of Restitution' (above n 3).

expectation that her parents would have financed her university education. Under the parents' wills their estate is divided equally between the children. Can the estate's representatives recover benefits bestowed by the deceased upon the older child to create a more equitable distribution of the estate?

[c] Lower income parents support and finance their children's university education. Both children become well-established professionals. Can the parents now recover for the support of their children expended while they were at university?

As presently understood, Canadian law would not provide a cause of action in any of the above examples, and yet, I would argue, the claims are not completely fanciful. In the first example, there is already some recognition given to cultural filial piety in our law. In the case of wrongful death, parents of children from ethnic communities in which filial piety is practised have been able to receive enhanced compensation under the provisions for loss of dependency or for loss of care, guidance and companionship.[31] It seems ironic that compensation flows from a third party in recognition of this cultural expectation where he or she has caused the principal holder of the obligation's death, yet the holder himself is not liable for its non-fulfilment. Similarly, in the first and third examples our law recognizes a general obligation owed by a child to provide support for a parent.[32] The genesis of these provisions was the English poor laws and the desire by legislatures to

[31] See for example Ontario's Family Law Act RSO 1990 c F-3 s 61. Most of the cases under these provisions deal with claims brought by children or a surviving spouse of a deceased or injured parent or spouse. The usual approach to claims brought by a parent for loss of a child is to allow very modest amounts of compensation for pecuniary losses. This approach is justified on the basis that the cost of raising a child, which will no longer be borne, offsets any pecuniary gain the parents could have expected from the child in later life. See S Waddams, *Law of Damages* (Toronto, Canada Law Book, looseleaf edn) ¶6.220. However, for cases where claims based on filial piety have enhanced the compensation paid to parents see *Lai v Gill* [1980] 1 SCR 431(SCC), *Fong Estate v Gin Bros Enterprises Ltd* [1990] BCJ No 1138 (QL) (BCSC), *Lian v Money* [1994] 8 WWR 463, appeal allowed in part [1996] 4 WWR 263 (BCCA), and *Sum Estate v Kan* (1995) 8 BCLR (3d) 91, appeal dismissed (1997) 44 BCLR (3d) 250 (BCCA). In the latter case the court accepted expert evidence called by both sides to the effect that at a minimum the financial contribution of a child to its parents would be between 10% and 20% of a child's gross income. See also *Ayeras v Front Runner Freight Ltd* [1998] BCJ No 1803 (QL)(BCSC), and *To v Toronto Board of Education* (2001) 55 OR (3d) 641 (CA). In *Yu v Yu* (1999) 48 MVR (3d) 285 (BCSC) the court insisted that an enhanced award based on filial piety could only be sustained where there was clear evidence that the child would have followed the traditional practice. Nor are these cases confined to claims brought by parents of Asian descent, see *Mafhani v Laing* (1981) 9 ACWS (2d) 144 (BCSC) (East Indian descent) and *Ayoub v Dreer* [2000] 24 CCLI (3d) 96 (Ont SCJ) (Palestinian descent).

[32] See for example Ontario's Family Law Act RSO 1990 c F-3 s 32:

> Every child who is not a minor has an obligation to provide support, in accordance with need, for his or her parent who has cared for or provided support for the child, to the extent that the child is capable of doing so.

minimize indigents claiming welfare from the state.[33] These provisions usually condition a successful claim on the fact that the parent did actually provide either care or support during childhood, and then move to a balance test of parental need measured against a child's capacity to pay. Parents cannot enhance their own lifestyle just because their children have been successful. Nor does the child have to forsake its own spouse and children, who keep first priority, in order to support a parent.[34] Of course, neither statutory provisions on filial responsibility nor the cultural dimensions of filial piety seek to make a direct financial nexus between the amount a parent can claim and that provided by the parent during the child's dependency. In the case of the second example, our law currently recognizes the right of a dependent child to make a claim under the Succession Law Reform Act[35] for an additional payment from the estate where insufficient provision has been made. The court is given a broad discretion to consider a multitude of factors in quantifying the amount to be paid. However, this claim does nothing to enrich the estate by those who have benefited prior to the testator's demise.

Could and should a restitution action be maintained in any of these examples? Approached from existing doctrine, the problems seem insurmountable. No matter whose list of 'unjust factors' you choose, none of the examples appear to come within their parameters. End of story. However, if the examples are approached through the lens of McLachlin J's exploration in *Peter*, one is more sanguine.

Parental support towards a child's university education may come in many forms. The payment of money used by the child to pay tuition and living costs is an obvious one. However, a child may also be supported by parents when living at home by the provision of domestic services or by the use of computers, cars and so on. In any case, the support can be positioned within the principles of restitution to fairly easily show that a benefit has been conferred. The usual benefit from a parent is cash and a direct monetary contribution confers an incontrovertible benefit.[36] However, in the second

[33] A useful survey of American provisions on filial responsibility is provided by T Kline, 'A Rational Role for Filial Responsibility Laws in Modern Society' (1992) 26 *Family Law Quarterly* 195. Kline argues that despite the widely held view that such laws are an anachronism in a modern welfare state, there may be valid reasons for supporting such provisions as a way to deal with chronic poverty experienced by many elderly persons, particularly, where a changing demography will result in a higher proportion of elder persons.

[34] For a comprehensive review of the Canadian law see the judgment of Burnyeat J in *Newson v Newson* (1998) 53 BCLR (3d) 191(BCSC) and T Hainsworth, *Ontario Family Law Act Manual*, 2nd edn (Toronto, Canada Law Book, looseleaf edn) 32§1.02.

[35] RSO 1990 c S 26.

[36] An incontrovertible benefit has been defined by McLachlin J in *Peel* (above n 1) 159 as:

> ... an unquestionable benefit, a benefit which is demonstrably apparent and not subject to debate and conjecture. Where the benefit is not clear and manifest it would be wrong to make the defendant pay, since he or she might well have preferred to decline the benefit if given a choice.

type of case, the supply of services, there are additional concerns about whether a benefit has in fact been rendered. The child may not value the benefit the same way as the parent who provided it. The benefit's value is subject to the notions of subjective devaluation. Equally, money paid or services rendered by the parent constitute a corresponding deprivation. The first two elements of a restitution claim are found. The third requirement, absence of juristic reason, is more problematic.

Does the parent confer the benefit as a valid gift or in pursuance of a valid common law, equitable or statutory obligation, which he or she owes to the child?

There is a legal statutory obligation to provide support to an unmarried child attending full-time post secondary education and who has not withdrawn from parental control. In Ontario, the Family Law Act[37] accords a right to a dependent child to bring an action for support against both parents provided the child is attending a full-time program of education and has not withdrawn from parental control.[38] The level of support is determined on the basis of the student's need and the parents' ability to pay. This statutory obligation has a number of limitations. Full-time study imposes an obligation to make real and genuine efforts at completing the program. 'Withdrawn from parental control' is a defence to such a claim brought by a child where the child has made a free and voluntary withdrawal from parental control and has decided to strike out on life on his or her own. The amount of the claim is assessed on a combination of ability to pay and demonstrable need, but much of this assessment has been standardised in a child support table, although still subject to a court discretion to deviate from the table.[39] The interaction of this statutory obligation and unjust enrichment does not necessarily lead to the negation of the latter claim. The contributions provided by parents may be in excess of what would be required to meet the statutory obligation. There is also a high likelihood that the student will fall within the defences, particularly where they have

[37] RSO 1990 c F-3 s 31:

(1) Every parent has an obligation to provide support, for his or her unmarried child who is a minor or is enrolled in a full time program of education, to the extent that the parent is capable of doing so.
(2) The obligation under subsection (1) does not extend to a child who is sixteen years of age or older and has withdrawn from parental control.

Similar legislative provisions exist in the other Provinces of Canada.

[38] Under the Federal Child Support Guidelines enacted pursuant to the Divorce Act RSC 1985 c 3 (2nd supp) s 26.1 as amended by, SC 1997 c 1 s 11, upon divorce both parents are still liable, subject to a court's discretion, to provide support to a child attending post-secondary education, even where the child has passed the age of majority. See JC MacDonald, *Law and Practice Under the Family Law Act of Ontario* (Toronto, Carswell, looseleaf edn) 33§4.6(e), and JC MacDonald & LK Ferrier, *Canadian Divorce Law and Practice*, (Toronto, Carswell, looseleaf edn) 15§89.

[39] See Hainsworth (above n 34) 31§1.02, G3§9.01.

left home. Funds paid or services rendered that met the statutory obligation would not constitute a 'benefit' under the unjust enrichment claim, but any surplus could.[40]

Does parental support constitute a gift? Typically, a parent will say to a child, 'I will pay this amount to put towards your university education.' This declared intention, coupled with actual delivery, constitutes a valid gift. In this exchange there is no suggestion that the gift is qualified by the child either repaying the parent or agreeing to provide some assistance to the parent once the child has graduated and become established. Other legal forms exist if it is the parent's true intent to create that type of relationship. The parent could, for example, create a contractual loan relationship, or other bilateral contract in which the child agrees to provide some level of support once established after graduating. Such agreements would need to rebut the presumption that family arrangements do not create legal contracts if enforcement became an issue.[41]

The essential requirement of an unjust enrichment action in these circumstances is the need to find that the parent has legitimate expectations of repayment. Normally, the presence of a contract would indicate this requirement, and only where there had been a failure of consideration or other defect in contractual formation would a restitution action exist. But contract is not the only source of legitimate expectations. The matrimonial/cohabitation property cases demonstrate that 'societal expectations' alone can be a source of 'legitimate expectations,' and once identified, can be imposed on the parties regardless of any knowledge requirement.[42] Arguments concerning the avoidance of the feminisation of poverty and the societal expectation that domestic services provided by women go undervalued, even where provided out of a motive of love and affection, operate to vitiate 'voluntary giving' as a 'juristic reason.' Against that backdrop, what arguments can be made to vitiate 'voluntary giving' as a

[40] R Scane makes a similar argument with respect to spousal support payments. See R Scane, 'Relationships "Tantamount to Spousal" Unjust Enrichment, and Constructive Trusts,' (1991) 70 *Canadian Bar Review* 260, 273.

[41] Historically a presumption of advancement lay between fathers to child of any property settled on the child. The presumption did not equally apply to property settled by a mother. This presumption has been criticized by the Supreme Court of Canada as 'embodying any credible inference of intent.' See *Rathwell v Rathwell* [1978] 2 SCR 436; 83 DLR (3d) 289 (SCC). In any case it does not apply to the payment of money. See N Le Poidevin, J Mowbray, E Simpson and L Tucker, *Lewin on Trusts,* 17th edn (London, Sweet & Maxwell, 2000) 9–11.

[42] The transformation in the law's attitude to matrimonial property from *Murdoch v Murdoch* [1975] 1 SCR 423; (1973) 41 DLR (3d) 367 (SCC), where the woman plaintiff had laboured many years as a ranch hand and received no part of the joint property on the basis that she had simply performed the services of a wife without expectation of receiving any interest in land, to *Pettkus* (above n 6), where the wife had laboured extensively in building up the couple's apiary business and was given a constructive trust interest over the property, can only be explained by the change in attitudes towards matrimonial and cohabitation arrangements and the status of women within those arrangements over the same period.

'juristic reason' where a parent supports a child through university? In the matrimonial/cohabitation cases there is now an assumption that the effort of both spouses is towards accumulation of joint family wealth and that a gift made out of love and affection needs to be scrutinized to ensure an actual and exclusive donative intent.[43]

Can arguments be made to suggest that parental support of a child through university is something less than an act of pure altruism?

An easier case can be made in those cultures that maintain strong links of filial piety. In Chinese, Japanese, Korean, Cambodian and other Asian cultures the concept of filial piety still maintains a strong vitality. Filial piety covers a gamut of social practices from showing affection and respect, through to compensating for care. Two theories underlie this practice. One focuses upon the internalized norms of what constitutes moral and socially acceptable behaviour in ethnic Chinese communities, the second focuses upon the intergenerational exchange of resources and power. 'Child rearing is viewed as a process of social investment with an expectation of delayed repayment, in the Chinese term, "Bau-Da" (Payback).'[44] Even where ethnic Chinese have immigrated to North America and have thus been exposed to more individual and atomistic western values, filial piety is still practised. However, it would appear that some of the social practises undergo commodification. Rather than living together as an extended family, children will provide monetary support to purchase housing and domestic services.[45] An unjust enrichment claim brought by parent against child would be one way of legally recognizing such a duty. This raises the interesting issue how far broad common law doctrine should be adaptive to particular ethnic or cultural beliefs to advance our pluralistic society. If the strengths of filial piety are strongest in Asian communities should evidence of such a phenomenon be used to imbue legitimate expectations concerning the act of providing support towards university education of a child by its parents?[46]

Absent an ethnic or cultural difference, can a case be made to suggest that parental support of a child through university is something less than an act of pure altruism? The cohabitation cases are illustrative. In *Peter*,

[43] This is a direct inversion of the old law that assumed the wife's contribution was a gift made out of love and affection and that some form of intent (some courts called this a phantom intent) had to be found to impose a resulting, implied, or constructive trust.

[44] P Lan, 'Subcontracting Filial Piety: elder care in Dual-Earner Chinese Immigrant Households in the Bay Area' Working Paper 21 (April 2001) <http://workingfamilies.berkeley.edu/papers.html> (02 June 2003).

[45] *Ibid.* See also K Sung, 'Filial Piety in Modern Times: Timely Adaptation and Practice Patters' paper given at the 1997 World Congress of Gerontology: Aging Beyond 2000: One World One Future. <http://www.cas.flinders.edu.au/iag/proceedings/proc0030.htm> (02 June 2003).

[46] Asian immigration now accounts for approximately 50% of all Canadian's immigrants per year. People who claim to be of Asian descent now constitute 8% of Canada's total population, but 17% of the Province of British Columbia.

McLachlin J and Cory JJ highlighted the work of Professors Neave, Hovius and Youdan who had documented the change in public policy on the value of a woman's contribution to a family unit and how lack of recognition had contributed to the 'feminisation of poverty.' Canada's policy with respect to the funding of post-secondary education is also undergoing a rapid transformation.

Up until the early 1990s post-secondary education in Canada was almost universally provided through publicly funded universities requiring relatively modest contributions by way of fees from students. Of course, students who moved away from home to attend university bore the cost of housing and living expenses. During the 1990s most provincial governments, as a result of confronting fiscal deficits, shifted the burden of post-secondary education onto the shoulders of students and those who supported them. University fees increased. In some professional programs fees were completely deregulated resulting in annual tuition fees of around $ 20,000. Over the period of the last twenty years, while median family income has remained stable, undergraduate tuition has risen over 150%, and over 200% for professional programs.[47] The cost to complete a four-year undergraduate program if enrolled in 2002 is now estimated to be $ 60,000 and in twelve years time will be $ 86,000.

It is clear that a larger burden of educational costs has been shifted from governments to students and parents. Indicators of this trend are the increase in student indebtedness and default under student loan guarantees,[48] and the change in the portion of student fees as a part of university operating costs reported by universities. That parents are expected to shoulder part of this burden has been both internalized by students and parents as well as externalized by governments in policy changes. In a recent survey by Statistics Canada on trends in post secondary education, over 63% of students and graduates of post secondary institutions report that they received money from parents or partners that they did not have to pay back.[49] The same survey also demonstrated that no matter what the household income, the vast majority of parents wanted their children to attend post secondary education although less than half save for that eventuality.

Governmental policy changes have also reinforced the idea that parents should actively provide for their children's post-secondary education.

[47] Statistics Canada, *Youth in Transition Survey* (2000) <http://www.statcan.ca> (02 June 2003).
[48] Statistics Canada, *Student Debt* (30 July 1999) The Daily <http://www.statcan.ca/Daily/English/990730/d990730b.htm> (02 June 2003). Between 1991 and 1996 the consolidated debt of all students who held Canada Student Loans (a government sponsored loan and debt guarantee scheme) grew 70.6%, for an average indebtedness of $ 7,725 from $ 6,810 per student. The rate of loan default over the same period grew from 17.6% to 21.8%.
[49] See also J Oderkirk, 'Presentation to the Conference on Access to Post Secondary Education: Facts and Gaps, Statistics Canada' (April 2002) <http://www.cprn.com/work/apse_e.htm> (02 June 2003).

In 1998 the Federal Government introduced its widely touted 'Education Budget.' This saw the introduction of the Registered Education Savings Plan (RESP) whereby parents were encouraged to make regular contributions into a savings plan specifically for their children's post-secondary education. The government matches contributions at 20% up to a maximum of $400 per annum. Investment returns in an RESP are taxed only when withdrawn by the student, and then at the much lower tax rate of the student. Under the government's student loan scheme, student eligibility, and the amount that can be borrowed, is dependent upon the income levels of his or her parents where one of them is claiming the student as a dependent for tax purposes. Although the parent gains some tax relief where the student is claimed as a dependent, this is also recognition that the student's post-secondary education is to be financially supported by the parent. Yet another tax policy allows the student to transfer unused tax credits from tuition and living expenses while attending university to his or her parent to be used on the parent's income tax return. Again, this policy reinforces the notion that parents bear some responsibility for their children's post-secondary education. The presence of such policies must influence the characterisation of the 'voluntary' nature of any payments or support made by parents toward their children's education.

Drawing a parallel with the cohabitation cases may be tenuous. There, the change in societal values concerning the valuation of domestic services and the economic power imbalance of cohabitation relationships was accompanied with sufficient political pressure to bring about legislative intervention. It is, however, interesting to note that the initial rejection by Canadian courts of unjust enrichment arguments in cohabitation cases became something of a lightening rod for subsequent legislative changes. The backlash over earlier rulings spurred the courts later on to advance the remedial constructive trust based on unjust enrichment in areas where the legislation did not reach, namely common law and same-sex relationships. The case for suggesting that funds advanced by a parent for university education should be regarded as a loan or is accompanied with the expectation of return rather than a gift does not present the same stark comparison. Nevertheless there is one common feature, and that is that the decision to advance is made within the context of a relationship that is marked by intimacy, emotion, love and affection; not usually the best companions for rational decision-making. It is perhaps this feature that legitimates legal intervention. While it is always open for a parent and student to use existing legal instruments to structure their relationship concerning university education, the circumstances cloud judgment and make recourse to such legal instruments unlikely even though they represent the most rational course of action.

An important function of the common law is the setting of 'default rules' where behaviour will not lead to the most rational or desirable outcome.

Are there good social policy reasons for creating a regime that suggests a loan rather than a gift? Governmental policies that have downloaded the cost of university education onto students and those who support them have resulted in an increase in student indebtedness. As between parent and child how should this debt be organized? If the parent gifts money to the child this will obviously lower the child's indebtedness. If the parent refuses, the child will have to increase its indebtedness. Because students have little if any stable income they are naturally bad credit risks and the cost of borrowing reflecting the risk of loan default is high. Government policies in Canada seek to ameliorate these risks but there is still a high incidence of default.[50] The cost of default is borne by the community at large because it consumes government revenues that could have gone to direct support of post-secondary education without the intermediary of a defaulting debtor. The cost of default is also borne by the student in that subsequent attempts to borrow will incur denial of a loan or higher costs of borrowing. If the parent borrows the money to give to the child, the cost of borrowing is lower, based upon the better security risk of the parent and the lower risk of default on the loan. If a parent is treated as the child's banker the cost of borrowing for the child should be lower, the likelihood of default lower, and the incidence of forgiveness of debt higher. It would appear to be fiscally desirable to encourage both gifting and *loaning* by a parent to a child to support university education.[51] In setting a default position perhaps the latter should now be preferred over the former.

Of course there are many other issues that make the award of unjust enrichment problematic in my examples. Would a change of position defence be available to the child? In the first example, is recognition of a cultural obligation inconsistent with other fundamental Canadian values? What shape would a remedy take and when would it be imposed? These

[50] Prior to 2001 Government policies were aimed at guaranteeing the risk of default to private loan providers. However, even with these guarantees many banks withdrew from the scheme because of the cost of administration and the high rate of default. Government assumed the direct burden of loan support in 2001.

[51] Because there is objective evidence that shows a child's income stream benefits from a university education I stop at supporting the encouragement of loaning for this single purpose. Apart from the intrinsic value of a university education there is ample evidence demonstrating the indirect fiscal benefits that flow to a university graduate no matter what program they have been enrolled in. In one study from British Columbia the rise in earnings for a graduate as against a person who simply completed high school was of a 15% to 20% magnitude. The study also shows that a graduate will pay an additional $ 50,000 in taxes to the government across his or her working life as a result of enhanced earning power. B Allen, *Paid in Full: Who Pays for University Education in BC* (Canadian Centre for Policy Alternatives). In a recent report issued by the United States Bureau of Statistics it was reported that a person with a post-secondary qualification will on average earn slightly less than twice as much as a person without the qualification over their income earning lifetime. Further, a person graduating with a professional degree will earn four times as much. United States Census Bureau, *The Big Payoff: Educational Attainment and Synthetic Estimates of Work-life Earnings* (July 2002) <http://www.census.gov/prod/2002pubs/p23–210.pdf> (02 June 2003).

are similar questions to those posed during the development of an unjust enrichment remedy in the cohabitation cases. In addition, more would need be known of the specific factual context surrounding my examples if they were real cases. A sense of injustice or grievance exists subjectively as an expectation of return. Whether this expectation is legitimately or reasonably held raises a wider inquiry.

In essence I am suggesting that the notion of giving in the context of parents who support their child at university should be subject to greater scrutiny and that the assumption of a voluntary gift as a juristic reason explaining the transfer should not be automatically presumed. Social and policy arguments were marshalled against the assumption that a woman who acts through love and affection when performing tasks that support her husband's endeavours has abandoned any expectation of remuneration on dissolution of the relationship. Likewise, I have suggested reasons why parental advancement may also carry with it expectations of some return by way of restitution. Such a suggestion is consistent with the traditional wariness of the law to altruistic behaviour as something that has to be explained.[52] It echoes similar disputes over classification between gifts or loans made by parents to their children on marriage when there is a subsequent separation requiring a division of matrimonial property;[53] and disputes over contributions made by a claimant against a deceased's estate for services rendered prior to the deceased's demise.[54] The common feature in all these situations is that the decision to give is made in an environment that is replete with emotions of love and affection, but not to a level that would traditionally be regarded as sufficient to impair decision-making ability.

The issue of parental support of children is part of a wider debate now taking place over the transfer of inter-generational wealth. It is propitious that these issues should be debated. Changes in mortality rates and Canada's demography will mean that by the year 2026 the number of persons aged 65 and over will exceed those aged under 19.[55] There is also growing evidence of significant levels of unfunded pension liabilities to sustain this aging population.[56] Ensuring economic stability for an aging population

[52] For example the insistence of delivery coupled with donative intent to constitute a valid gift; the emphasis on bargain in exchange and resistance of equity to assist a volunteer; and the presumption of resulting and constructive trust when the property of one person is entrusted into another's keeping.

[53] See the comments of L Wolfson, 'How to Make Gifts to Children' (1998) 33 RFL (4th) 153.

[54] A Gesser, 'Disrespecting your elders or getting what is rightfully yours? Unjust enrichment in estate litigation' (1997) 17 *Estate and Trust Journal* 37.

[55] Statistics Canada, Population projections for 2026, CANSIM II, table 052–0001.

[56] E Church, 'Pensions: A Report on Business Investigation' *The Globe & Mail* (Toronto, Canada, 12 May 2003) s B1. Canada is not alone in experiencing these difficulties. See E Pfanner, 'European workers take to the streets to protest planned cuts in pensions. *International Herald Tribune* (Paris, France, 10 May 2003) 12.

has already resulted in governmental amendment to the rates of contribution of the Canadian Pension Plan. Clearly, inter-generational wealth is a social issue to be managed, not only by governments, but also by courts for those who resort to private ordering through litigation.

IV. INDICIA OF LEGITIMATE EXPECTATIONS

Whether one believes that an action in unjust enrichment should be accorded parents who support their child's university education is secondary to the process by which that decision should be made. One approach would occur under the rubric of explicit recognition of the policy-based reasons sketched above as constituting an unjust factor. But this is to invite the label of judicial activism and threaten to usurp the role of the legislator. The second approach is through recognition of the importance accorded in Canadian law to legitimate or reasonable expectations, either because they displace the validity of a gift as constituting a juristic reason, or because they validate free acceptance as an unjust factor.

Reasonable expectation denotes both a descriptive classification, as in identifying actual expectations of a claimant which are known to the other party and which are reasonably held or relied upon; and a prescriptive classification, as in identifying an entitlement which a claimant is reasonably entitled to expect regardless of whether the other party was aware of that expectation or not. Finn and Smith characterize reasonable expectations, particular those that fall into the latter category, as a contrivance that can 'enhance the reach and contrive the direction of a particular rule or doctrine.'[57] It is not the simple notion of an expectation, no matter how reasonably held, that justifies enforcement. Rather, it is the recognition of reasonable expectations in the context of established doctrine, here the constituent elements of an unjust enrichment claim, that justify recognition of the claimant's entitlement. While this may prescribe some limits on a claimant it still begs the question of how a court undertakes the task of identifying reasonable or legitimate expectations. Admittedly, this is not a question easily answered. However, an analogy can be drawn to the work of La Forest J in *Lac Minerals Ltd v International Corona Resources Ltd*[58] determining criteria to establish fact-based fiduciaries.

La Forest J acknowledged his indebtedness to Finn's scholarly work on the fiduciary principle, and it is apposite to quote from his work just as La Forest J did.

[57] P Finn & K Smith, 'The Citizen, the Government and "Reasonable Expectations"' (1992) 66 *Australian Law Journal* 139, 141.
[58] Above (n 21).

> The critical matter in the end is the role that the alleged fiduciary has, or should be taken to have, in the relationship. It must so implicate that party in the other's affairs or so align him with the protection or advancement of that other's interest that foundation exists for the 'fiduciary expectation.' Such a role may generate an actual expectation that the other's interests are being served. This is commonly so with lawyers and investment advisers. But equally the expectation may be a judicially prescribed one because the law itself ordains it to be the other's entitlement. And this may be so either because the party should, given the actual circumstances of the relationship, be accorded that entitlement irrespective of whether he has adverted to the matter, or because the purpose of the relationship itself is perceived to be such that to allow disloyalty in it would be to jeopardise its perceived social utility.[59]

In another judgment La Forest J stressed the importance accorded the reasonableness that one party could expect the other party to act or refrain from acting in a way such as to adversely affect its interests.[60] When applying this approach to the case before him, La Forest J undertook a meticulous examination of the actual relationship between the parties to determine whether any trust and confidence had developed between them; a review of the industry practice associated with sharing of information between geologists of competing mining companies; and the degree to which one party shared confidences with the other and why particular legal vehicles were not employed to ensure the maintenance of those confidences. Perhaps not surprisingly, La Forest J has been criticized for accepting into his doctrine identifying fact-based fiduciaries the concept of reasonable expectations, leading to the imposition of fiduciary duties even where the fiduciary is unaware of those expectations raised in the claimant.[61] There is a fear of too many relationships being characterized as fiduciary, just as there is a fear of too much unjust enrichment being accorded. However, the work of La Forest J does add credence to the notion that dialogue on what constitutes a reasonable expectation can happen within principled doctrinal analysis.

As demonstrated by La Forest J in *Lac Minerals*, focussing upon legitimacy or reasonableness of expectations opens up different but comparable avenues of inquiry. What is the source of the plaintiff's subjective expectation that either money should be returned or services provided should be compensated? How has the plaintiff sought to obtain that result when advancing the money or providing the service? In particular, what legal vehicle existed to affect the plaintiff's desired result? If the plaintiff has consciously chosen a particular legal vehicle why has it failed? Alternatively,

[59] P Finn, 'The Fiduciary Principle' in T Youdan (ed) *Equity, Fiduciaries and Trusts* (Toronto, Carswell, 1989) 64. Quoted by La Forest J in *Lac Minerals Ltd* (above n 21) 648.
[60] *Hodgkinson v Simms* [1994] 3 SCR 377; 117 DLR (4th) 161 (SCC).
[61] L Smith, 'Fiduciary Relationships—Arising in Commercial Contexts—Investment Advisors: *Hodgkinson v Simms*' (1995) 74 *Canadian Bar Review* 714.

why did the plaintiff fail to avail him or herself of that legal means at the time? The last question may reveal a disconnection between the actions of a rational decision maker and the actual actions of the plaintiff; action taken only because the plaintiff was in a relationship of intimacy, emotion, love and affection which affected the quality of rational decision-making. But this disconnection can only be revealed by analysing what actions a rational decision-maker would have taken in similar circumstances. Does the rational decision maker then, for example, consider the cultural values of one particular ethnic community, or the economic determinism of the most efficient way to fund household debt associated with post-secondary education, or the sociological impact of how domestic work is valued in a relationship? Can one meaningfully look at the legislative direction in comparable areas? Answers to these question may be difficult and require extensive evidence—that is a burden a claimant must assess when considering the economics of litigation—but they are capable of rendering rational decisions that can distinguish when a claimant's entitlement is to be recognized and when it is not. For example, evidence of cultural filial piety, and the extent that it is practiced in a particular community or by a claimant, is just as capable of proof as an 'industry practice' concerning the sharing of information amongst mining geologists was in *Lac Minerals*.

Identifying a person's 'expectations' is an easy task resolved simply by calling on the person to communicate the same. Identifying 'reasonable' or 'legitimate' expectations moves from the subjective and descriptive to the objective and prescriptive. This is a task entertained in many areas of the law, often with little appreciation of how the normative standard that it entails has been derived. The sole source of legitimacy cannot simply be extrapolation from established legal doctrine, although clearly that factor remains very important.[62]

V. CONCLUSION

In John McCamus's contribution to this collection, he laments that 'the reasonable expectations requirement cannot easily be made to disappear from Canadian law'.[63] Rather than deploring this development I argue that we

[62] The argument made here is that 'reasonable expectation' fulfils an important substantive component of the test to determine absence of juristic reason, or where free acceptance can be raised as an unjust factor. However, 'reasonable expectation' can also be engaged in a lesser role as creating an evidential presumption that enables a claimant to readily establish the absence of a gift, or that the defendant was aware of the claimant's expectations of return or remuneration. R Scane alludes to this function being performed by reasonable expectations in the cohabitation cases. See R Scane, 'Relationships "Tantamount to Spousal," Unjust Enrichment and Constructive Trusts' (1991) 70 *Canadian Bar Review* 260, 277.

[63] J McCamus, 'Restitution on Dissolution of Marital and Other Intimate Relationships: Constructive Trust or Quantum Meruit' ch 14 in this volume.

should embrace the challenge it raises for identifying the process through which expectations turn into legitimate or reasonable expectations. This is not an easy task but I believe it offers more fruitful inquiry then trying to recap the genie of 'reasonable expectations.'[64] The difficulty for doctrinal purists is that they are required to argue either that the Supreme Court of Canada came to the 'just' result in the cohabitation cases, but that their doctrinal analysis does not stand rigorous scrutiny, or that the cohabitation cases, all admittedly of central importance to the development of unjust enrichment in Canada, are to be contained and marginalized in some policy-based legal ghetto. Perhaps the real answer to this paradox lies in questioning the doctrine we are asked to embrace. McLachlin J's formulation in *Peters* of Dickson J's three unjust enrichment principles, and Smith's restatement[65] of the same, which incorporate 'legitimate expectations' as an integral part of the action, seems more consistent with McLachlin J's third way.

[64] My colleague, L Rotman makes a similar plea for recognition of 'good conscience' as a standard bearer for the imposition of a constructive trust. L Rotman, 'Deconstructing the Constructive Trust' (1999) 37 *Alberta Law Review* 133.
[65] Above (n 2).

16

The Relation of Unjust Enrichment to Other Legal Concepts

STEPHEN WADDAMS

THE TWO ARTICLES by John McCamus and Jeff Berryman have important implications for the classification of legal concepts. Each of them tends to show that the results reached in the Canadian family property cases cannot be derived solely from the concept of unjust enrichment—on the basis of any single principle stated in terms of unjust enrichment the cases either go too far (McCamus), or not far enough (Berryman). The fact that American jurisdictions have not derived similar results from the concept of unjust enrichment strengthens this conclusion.[1]

But it by no means follows that unjust enrichment has been irrelevant. The courts themselves have invoked unjust enrichment as the principal reason for the results reached, and the general concept has evidently been influential. But so also have other legal concepts, notably contract (especially ideas of partnership and joint venture), detrimental reliance, wrongdoing,

[1] See A Kull, 'Comments on the Paper of John McCamus' (presented at the Understanding Unjust Enrichment Symposium, January 2003). As Andrew made clear in his comments, contemporary US decisions will only allow relief to former cohabitants on the basis of unjust enrichment where a defendant retains discrete assets acquired through the plaintiff's extraordinary contributions—preferably made in cash. See *Restatement Third, Restitution and Unjust Enrichment* §28 (Council Draft No 4, 2002); A Estin, 'Unmarried Partners and the Legacy of *Marvin v Marvin*: Ordinary Cohabitation' (2001) 76 *Notre Dame Law Review* 1381. There are other accepted grounds of liability—notably express or implied contract—but these afford relief in an even smaller number of cases, with the result that many former cohabitants are left with neither assets nor viable claims. Recognition of this practical reality is one of the inspirations for Canadian courts to grant relief, stretching the contours of restitution to find a justification. In the United States, where the courts have been less accommodating, the most salient contemporary reform proposal urges that quasi-spousal rights be created directly, whether by statute or judicial decision. The rationale is not that the parties' cohabitation results in the unjust enrichment of the defendant (which by ordinary standards will rarely be the case), but that the plaintiff's status as a former 'domestic partner' gives him or her an entitlement to support that should be recognized as analogous to that of the former spouse. See the *American Law Institute's Principles of the Law of Family Dissolution: Analysis and Recommendations*, ch 6 (2002).

property, and public policy. Each of these is closely interrelated with the others—interrelated, indeed, to such an extent that often they may be said to be mutually reciprocal. Thus the court perceives as wrongful, and as causing an unjust enrichment, the taking of what ought to be treated as the plaintiff's property, but what ought to be treated as the plaintiff's property is that which, when taken, causes an enrichment perceived to be unjust, and which would disappoint expectations perceived to be reasonable. None of these concepts, considered alone, could have justified the claims, but cumulatively they have been effective. It is impossible to doubt that considerations of public policy have also been influential: results reached in 1985 could not have been contemplated 50, or even 15, years earlier. But it need not follow from this that unjust enrichment has not also played a part, as have the other concepts mentioned in this paragraph. Public policy does not exclude the idea of justice between the parties, and so has both influenced and in turn been influenced by the several concepts mentioned, including unjust enrichment.

In a forthcoming study,[2] I attempt to show that many legal issues in Anglo-American private law have been resolved in this sort of manner, that is, not by being allocated to a single concept to the exclusion of others, but by the cumulative and concurrent operation of several. The family property cases, I suggest, constitute one such instance. Another instance, discussed in the present book,[3] is the question of profits derived from wrongdoing. The results reached in those cases by Anglo-American courts in the past cannot be explained solely on the basis of unjust enrichment. As Peter Benson's article notes, concepts of entitlement and ownership have also been of crucial importance.[4] So also have, in many of the cases, considerations of wrongdoing, breach of contract, and public policy.

Another instance, also discussed in the book, is tracing.[5] During discussion of the issue, Lionel Smith lamented the expenditure of intellectual energy on both sides of the dispute over whether tracing is, on the one hand, 'part of' the law of property or, on the other hand, 'part of' the law of unjust enrichment.[6] The tracing cases evidently cannot be explained solely on the ground that they vindicate prior property rights, yet they certainly have something to do with proprietary concepts: as Lionel Smith put it, 'property is part of the picture.'[7] When the author of the leading book on the subject[8] doubts the usefulness of a debate on this question, which

[2] S Waddams, *Dimensions of Private Law: Categories and Concepts in Anglo-American Private Law* (Cambridge, Cambridge University Press, 2003).
[3] See chs 7 and 12.
[4] *Ibid.* ch 12.
[5] See ch 11.
[6] L Smith, 'Comments on the Paper of Robert Chambers' (presented at the Understanding Unjust Enrichment Symposium, January 2003).
[7] *Ibid.*
[8] L Smith, *Law of Tracing* (Oxford, Oxford University Press, 1997).

has divided the leading unjust enrichment scholars of the common law world, should we not entertain the possibility that both sides might be right?

It has been asserted that 'proprietary interests contingent on tracing... always arise from unjust enrichment,'[9] and, on the other hand, that the assertion of a property interest excludes unjust enrichment (because no concept other than property is necessary).[10] Both assertions are true in their own terms, but they each assume a sharp dichotomy between property and unjust enrichment that it has been in practice the very function of the law of tracing to transcend. Tracing permits the assertion of property-like rights in some circumstances against assets in the defendant's hands even though the claimant does not have a full legal property interest. One of the reasons for permitting such a claim has undoubtedly been to avoid unjust enrichment.[11] But a principal reason for recognizing the defendant's enrichment to be unjust has in turn been that the defendant has taken or received something that has been perceived to belong (though not, *ex hypothesi*, in a strictly legal sense) to the plaintiff.[12] Thus the proprietary overtones cannot be avoided and the concepts of property and unjust enrichment have been intertwined. It is in this light that suggestions are to be understood that a proprietary remedy is appropriate only where there is some kind of pre-existing link, connection, or nexus between the claim and the property.[13] It has been rightly pointed out that such concepts are 'malleable,'[14] but this is not to show that they have been irrelevant, nor, in the actual practice of the courts, uninfluential.

These suggestions have far-reaching implications for the classification of concepts, not only in respect of unjust enrichment, but throughout private law, and they cast doubt on many of the metaphors we are accustomed to use, such as mapping, and zoological classification. A place on a map cannot be in two continents simultaneously, nor (in conventional biology) can an animal be both a mammal and an insect, but the application of these ideas to legal concepts is by no means self-evident. Metaphors are useful,

[9] P Birks, 'Property and Unjust Enrichment: Categorical Truths' [1997] *New Zealand Law Review* 623, 661.

[10] RB Grantham and CEF Rickett, 'Tracing and Property Rights: The Categorical Truth' (2000) 63 *MLR* 905; *Foskett v McKeown* [2001] 1 AC 102 (HL).

[11] Thus R Goff and G Jones, *The Law of Restitution* (London, Sweet and Maxwell, 1966, and subsequent editions) and P Maddaugh and J McCamus, *The Law of Restitution* (Aurora, ON, Canada Law Book, 1990) have both included the subject in their respective treatises.

[12] Or as Smith (above n 8) 326, 332–33, 337 styles it: 'less than full ownership.'

[13] *Peter v Beblow* [1993] 1 SCR 980, (1993) 101 DLR (4th) 621 (SCC) 649–50. Peter Birks, to somewhat similar effect, insists on the need for the claim to have a 'proprietary base'; see P Birks, *An Introduction to the Law of Restitution* (Oxford, Oxford University Press, 1985) 378–85; P Birks, 'Establishing a Proprietary Base: *Re Goldcorp*' (1995) 3 *Restitution Law Review* 83.

[14] C Rotherham, 'Restitution and Property Rites: Reason and Ritual in the Law of Proprietary Remedies' (2000) 1 *Theoretical Inquiries in Law* 205, 226; C Rotherham, *Proprietary Remedies in Context* (Oxford, Hart Publishing, 2002) 330, 336, 338.

and indeed necessary, for the understanding of complex phenomena, but any metaphor, when pressed too far, may be misleading. Legal issues may involve, and have often involved, the simultaneous operation of several concepts, not so much as though the issues were separate districts on a map, but rather as a single book may be in several bibliographical classes at once (for example, history, law, economics, religion, philosophy, and politics).

I am not here casting doubt on the importance and independence of unjust enrichment as a concept: it is as important and as independent as the concepts of contract and wrongdoing. But a complex subject, like law, is not better understood by denying its complexity. When the actual history of Anglo-American law is examined it becomes apparent that the concepts just mentioned have, at the point of their operation, been mutually interdependent, and closely related also to concepts of property and public policy.

Index